D0209058

Riot, Rebellion, and Revolution

**Sponsored by the Joint Committee
on Latin American Studies of
the Social Science Research Council and
the American Council of Learned Societies**

CONTRIBUTORS

Ulises Beltrán
Raymond Th. J. Buve
John H. Coatsworth
Romana Falcón
John M. Hart
Evelyn Hu-DeHart
Friedrich Katz
William K. Meyers
Enrique Montalvo Ortega
Herbert J. Nickel
Leticia Reina
William B. Taylor
Hans Werner Tobler
John Tutino
Eric Van Young
Arturo Warman

RIOT, REBELLION, AND REVOLUTION

Rural Social Conflict in Mexico

Friedrich Katz, Editor

PRINCETON UNIVERSITY PRESS

Copyright © 1988 by Princeton University Press

Published by Princeton University Press, 41 William Street,
Princeton, New Jersey 08540
In the United Kingdom: Princeton University Press,
Oxford

All Rights Reserved

Library of Congress Cataloging-in-Publication Data

Riot, rebellion, and revolution.
Includes index.
1. Mexico—History. 2. Peasant uprisings—Mexico—History.
I. Katz, Friedrich.
F1228.9.R57 1988   972   88–15099
ISBN 0–691–07739–8   ISBN 0–691–02265–8 (pbk.)

Publication of this book has been aided by the Whitney Darrow
Fund of Princeton University Press

This book has been composed in Linotron Melior

Princeton University Press books are printed on acid-free paper,
and meet the guidelines for permanence and durability
of the Committee on Production Guidelines for Book Longevity
of the Council on Library Resources

Printed in the United States of America

DESIGNED BY LAURY A. EGAN

3   5   7   9   10   8   6   4   2

CONTENTS

PREFACE   ix

ONE · Introduction: Rural Revolts in Mexico
Friedrich Katz   3

PART I
Mexico: Unique Center of Rural Rebellion?

TWO · Patterns of Rural Rebellion in Latin America:
Mexico in Comparative Perspective
John H. Coatsworth   21

PART II
Pax Hispanica?

THREE · Rural Uprisings in Preconquest and Colonial Mexico
Friedrich Katz   65

FOUR · Agrarian Social Change and Peasant Rebellion
in Nineteenth-Century Mexico: The Example of Chalco
John Tutino   95

FIVE · Peasant Rebellion in the Northwest: The Yaqui
Indians of Sonora, 1740–1976
Evelyn Hu-DeHart   141

SIX · Moving Toward Revolt: Agrarian Origins of the
Hidalgo Rebellion in the Guadalajara Region
Eric Van Young   176

SEVEN · Banditry and Insurrection: Rural Unrest in Central
Jalisco, 1790–1816
William B. Taylor   205

PART III
From Indian Rebellions to Peasant Revolts

EIGHT · The 1840s Southwestern Mexico Peasants'
War: Conflict in a Transitional Society
John M. Hart   249

NINE · The Sierra Gorda Peasant Rebellion, 1847–50
Leticia Reina   269

TEN · Revolts and Peasant Mobilizations in Yucatán:
Indians, Peons, and Peasants from the Caste War to the Revolution
Enrique Montalvo Ortega   295

PART IV
Peasants and Peons in
the Mexican Revolution

ELEVEN · The Political Project of Zapatismo
Arturo Warman (Translated by Judith Brister)   321

TWELVE · "Neither Carranza nor Zapata!": The Rise and Fall of a
Peasant Movement that Tried to Challenge Both, Tlaxcala, 1910–19
Ramond Th. J. Buve   338

THIRTEEN · Agricultural Laborers in the Mexican Revolution
(1910–40): Some Hypotheses and Facts about Participation and Restraint in the Highlands of Puebla–Tlaxcala
Herbert J. Nickel   376

FOURTEEN · Charisma, Tradition, and Caciquismo: Revolution in
San Luis Potosí
Romana Falcón   417

FIFTEEN · Second Division of the North: Formation and
Fragmentation of the Laguna's Popular Movement, 1910–11
William K. Meyers   448

SIXTEEN · Peasants and the Shaping of the Revolutionary
State, 1910–40
Hans Werner Tobler   487

PART V
Nineteenth- and Twentieth-Century
Revolts in Perspective

SEVENTEEN · Rural Rebellions after 1810
Friedrich Katz   521

EIGHTEEN · Economic Fluctuations and Social Unrest
in Oaxaca, 1701–94
Ulises Beltrán   561

GLOSSARY OF SPANISH TERMS   573

NOTES ON CONTRIBUTORS   576

INDEX   579

PREFACE

This volume seeks to examine rural uprisings in Mexico from the sixteenth to the twentieth century, and to compare them in time and space. The work was made possible thanks to the generous help of the Social Science Research Council, which sponsored two conferences where scholars from several European countries, Mexico, and the United States met to present and compare their findings. At the first meeting, which took place in Ixtapa, Mexico, each participant presented a paper dealing with a rural uprising at a different time and place. At that meeting, common criteria were established and similarities and differences were delineated. Revised papers were presented at a second conference in New York City. The aim of these conferences was to produce a unified volume and not merely a collection of papers.

I would like to thank Enrique Florescano, who participated in our first meeting and made valuable comments on the papers presented there.

On behalf of all the participants I would like to express my gratitude to the Social Science Research Council, to its Joint Committee on Latin American Studies, to the collaborators of that committee, and to Reid Andrews, Brooke Larson, and Joan Dassin of the Council staff for their great help in organizing the conferences and completing this volume. I also would like to express my thanks to Robert Holden, Michael Ducey and Dawn Fogle Deaton of the University of Chicago for their contribution in putting together the final draft, to Susan Lundy for typing the several versions of the manuscript for this book, and to Linnéa Cameron for coordinating final details.

Friedrich Katz

Riot, Rebellion, and Revolution

CHAPTER ONE

Introduction: Rural Revolts

in Mexico

Friedrich Katz

In the aftermath of the Mexican Revolution of 1910–20 the revolutionary peasant became a subject not only of historical study, but also of literature, films, and paintings. With his sombrero, his machete, and his rifle he has marched or ridden through countless Hollywood or Mexican films, killing brutal overseers, hacienda owners, corrupt officials, and federal soldiers. Some of Mexico's greatest painters, such as Diego Rivera, have portrayed the peasant as one of the most important forces of Mexican history. But was this in fact the case? Or are we dealing with a legend forged only in the aftermath of the Revolution and applied to the Revolution itself and to earlier periods with the benefit of hindsight?

This was one of the main questions dealt with by a panel of historians specializing in agrarian revolts in Mexico from pre-Columbian times through to the twentieth century. They also asked whether—in both quantitative and qualitative terms—Mexico occupies a unique position in Latin America. Whatever the answer, one characteristic is unique to rural uprisings in Mexico: their close links with national revolutions. First, the conquest of Mexico was the one that was linked with a major popular uprising against the ruling pre-Hispanic elite; second, the independence movement, in contrast to its counterparts in South America constituted both a social revolution in which peasants played a major role, and a peasant uprising; and third, the 1910 Revolution seems to have had much wider rural support than most other social movements in Latin America in the twentieth century.

The phenomenon of rural uprisings is not new to Mexican historiography. A number of excellent studies (many of them written by contributors to this volume) have been produced on the subject, but they have tended to deal with limited periods of time and with a limited number of regions. The essays presented in this volume contain both profound analyses of rural uprisings as well as facts that up to now have been largely unknown. To a large extent, completely new primary sources have been utilized to describe rural uprisings in all periods to answer a common set of questions on Mexican history from the Aztec period to the 1910 Revolution.

The participants of the conference concentrated on the following issues:

(1) Who were the rebels? Among the heterogeneous social groups in the countryside, which tended most to revolt? Inhabitants of the free communal villages, hacienda residents, rancheros, or temporary laborers with no firm roots in the community? Were Indians or non-Indians more prone to revolt?

(2) What were the motives for revolt? How significant were the issues of land, water rights, and taxes? How important were issues of local autonomy and the appointment of local officials? Against whom were the revolts mainly directed: landowners, local officials, the clergy, or the state? What kind of alliances did rural revolutionaries enter into, and with whom? When and how did such movements become regional or national in scope?

(3) Was there any continuity in time and space among rural revolts?

(4) What were the long- and short-term effects of these uprisings on the peasants and on other segments of society? Did military defeat of peasant armies always lead to political, social, or economic disaster for the rural revolutionaries?

(5) Was Mexico an exception within Latin America with respect to both the number and the scope of its rural revolts?

In Chapter 3 I examine the hypothesis that rural uprisings were already endemic to large parts of Mexico throughout the period of Aztec rule, although their character was at times obscured by the fact that most of them were led by the traditional upper classes of the subject peoples, who suffered as much from Aztec domination as the peasants did. Nevertheless, there were also some very clear cases of peasant uprisings under peasant leadership. What emerged from this examination of pre-Hispanic patterns of revolt is a possible parallel between the Aztec period and the nineteenth and twentieth centuries. Throughout these times rural revolts seem to have been much more frequent and intense in Mexico than in other parts of

Latin America where a peasant class had developed. This seems to be particularly the case when revolts in central Mexico in Aztec times are compared with those in the other comparable, populous, and highly stratified society in pre-Columbian America: the Inca empire. There were very few revolts in Inca times and, unlike Hernán Cortés in Mexico, Francisco Pizarro in Peru was not considered a liberator by most of the Inca's subjects, nor did the coming of the Spaniards provoke a large-scale uprising similar to that in Mexico.

The pattern of rural uprisings in Mexico changed sharply (but not completely) from the sixteenth to the eighteenth century, i.e., during most of the colonial period. Rural violence was endemic to the frontier areas of New Spain, and Spanish rule in Mexico ended in the same way in which it had begun—in conjunction with a massive rural uprising.

Nevertheless, during the sixteenth and seventeenth (and to a lesser degree the eighteenth) centuries there seem to have been comparatively fewer rural revolts in the core areas of Mexico than at any earlier or later time in its history. This period was also an exception in yet another respect. From the sixteenth to the eighteenth centuries the Mexican countryside was far more peaceful than similar regions in other parts of Spain's huge American empire, and this comes out very clearly in John Coatsworth's essay (Chapter 2), which compares rural uprisings in Mexico to those in other parts of the continent. This chapter represents a first attempt to catalogue revolts according to regional and time patterns. For the colonial period Coatsworth concludes that the number, the scope, and intensity of rural revolts were far greater in Peru than they were in Mexico at this time. He attributes these differences to a variety of factors: the tradition of benign Inca rule; far more onerous taxes and labor services imposed by Spanish officials in Peru than in Mexico; the diversity of ethnic groups in Mexico with no common language or tradition to unite them, as in Peru; and the existence of a far stronger Indian nobility in Peru than in Mexico.

The reasons for rural passivity during the colonial period are the subject of the first part of John Tutino's essay in Chapter 4 on peasant uprisings in Chalco. Tutino argues that the success of Spanish colonial policy was due to its very real desire to maintain village communities as a counterweight to Spanish and Mexican landowners. The crown and large segments of the clergy allied to it not only feared the power of these landowners; they also wanted the tax revenues and the labor provided by the free villages. Spanish legislation attempted to protect communal landholdings and both the

courts and the clergy at times successfully prevented the expropriation of village lands. In the eyes of many peasants the crown thus
gained a large measure of legitimacy so that in general they preferred to resort to the courts rather than to revolt.

It is doubtful whether the efforts of the crown and clergy would
have been so successful but for the high Indian mortality in the early
colonial period. The reduction of the native Indian population from
something like twenty million to an estimated two million made it
relatively easy for landowners to expropriate the now uninhabited
village lands without encountering massive peasant resistance. In
addition, the great demographic catastrophe destroyed many communities' will to resist and the native leadership who might have
directed uprisings.

A good example of the tactical success of the colonial administration in controlling the Yaqui Indians of Sonora is presented by Evelyn Hu-DeHart in Chapter 5. In the nineteenth and twentieth centuries the Yaquis were considered the most hostile Mexican tribe,
yet they submitted passively to the Jesuits in the early colonial period, as did many other Indian groups in central Mexico. But they
were an exception among the inhabitants of the northern frontier
where, as I show in Chapter 3, many Indian groups mounted bloody
and frequently effective resistance against the Spaniards. This difference in attitude between the frontier and the core areas was due
to the fact that the northerners had always lived in a more or less
classless society and, unlike their counterparts in central Mexico,
had never worked for a ruling elite. As a result, Spanish domination
was much more objectionable in their eyes; in addition, many of
them led a nomadic existence so that it was much more difficult for
the Spaniards to subjugate them.

It took the Spaniards nearly two centuries—until the early eighteenth century—to dominate, exterminate, or marginalize Indians
such as the Tarahumara in Chihuahua who had offered the greatest
resistance. This subjugation, though, did not strengthen Spanish
rule significantly on the northern frontier. The exterminated or subjugated Indians were replaced by a far more dangerous foe: the
Apache who, with horses they had acquired from the Spaniards and
which had completely transformed their way of life, began swarm-
ing into Spanish-controlled areas to mount increasingly bloody
raids on Spanish settlements.

Rural instability on the northern Mexican frontier in the eighteenth century was matched by increasing restiveness in the core
areas of New Spain. This restiveness manifested itself at times by an

increasing number of lawsuits and demands by Indian villagers, at times even through the outbreaks of local revolts, and frequently by an increase in rural banditry.

Several authors deal with this unrest, which heralded the end of the Pax Hispanica. In Chapter 5, Evelyn Hu-DeHart describes how in 1740 the hitherto passive Yaquis rose against both the Jesuits and the Spanish colonial administration. They were only subdued with great difficulty by the Spanish military. An even bloodier uprising occurred at the other end of New Spain, in the Yucatán peninsula, with the messianic uprising of the Maya Indians under Jacinto Canek. In central Mexico, social unrest was less violent and less abrupt but nevertheless quite noticeable. Eric Van Young (Chapter 6) and William Taylor (Chapter 7) assess this unrest among village Indians around Mexico's second largest city, Guadalajara. Van Young examines one manifestation of Indian dissatisfaction: an increasing number of lawsuits and complaints, whereas Taylor deals with the more violent forms of restiveness in this area—the rise of banditry in the final years of Spanish colonial rule in this same area.

Both authors feel that there is no single explanation for increasing social unrest. But in the Guadalajara region a massive population increase may have been an important factor. By the eighteenth century the Indians of New Spain had developed immunity to some of the diseases introduced by the Spaniards, and their numbers were now increasing. But the lands that had been allotted to them by the crown when their numbers were low were insufficient to support the communities now, creating new social tensions. These tensions were exacerbated by the fact that not only the Indians but the mestizo and white populations of New Spain were also increasing, and these groups were beginning to encroach on Indian lands. This was one of the major factors, according to Evelyn Hu-DeHart, that triggered the Yaqui uprising of 1740, and Van Young shows how increasing settlements of non-Indians in Indian communities also exacerbated the Indians' resentment in the Guadalajara area.

The degree to which the colonial-era revolts were linked to economic fluctuations is discussed by Ulises Beltrán in Chapter 18. He applies quantitative methods to the study of eighteenth-century rural uprisings in the state of Oaxaca.

In the mid-eighteenth century, after nearly two centuries of decline, the Spanish monarchy attempted to revitalize the economy of Spain and to make it a great power again. Spain's economic demands on the colonies therefore increased, and these were translated into higher taxes and more forced labor from village communities.

As the crown's pressure on Indian communities increased, its mediating efforts and its perceived role as a protector of Indian rights began to decrease and its legitimacy in the eyes of its Indian subjects waned, as did that of the Catholic Church, which had played a similar role in the eyes of the Indians. All the chapters that deal with this late period of colonial rule show how this breakdown of the traditional role of the Catholic Church contributed to or even provoked rural uprisings. In Sonora, for example, part of the surplus that the Jesuits extracted from the Indians had always been held to provide for periods of hardship, but when a massive famine occurred in 1740 it was found the Jesuits had sent all the grain north to help establish missions in California, and there was none left to feed the Indians. Similarly, in Yucatán, the unfulfilled promises of Bishop Pérez to put an end to peonage precipitated an Indian uprising; in the Guadalajara region the conflict between communities and the church over the resources owned by religious *cofradías* (confraternities) led to conflicts; and all these difficulties were exacerbated by the effects of economic development. For example, in the Guadalajara region, hacendados began to impose restrictions on the amount of land they rented to Indians because they found it much more profitable to farm the lands themselves.

These factors are essential in providing an answer to one of the central questions raised by both Taylor and Van Young, that of why the Spanish colonial regime, which for nearly three centuries had been so successful in keeping the area peaceful, finally provoke the greatest rural revolt in nineteenth-century Latin America? Another equally important problem that both authors address is one that has long been obscured by popular legend and tradition, concerning the Hidalgo revolt of 1810. In countless *corridos*, murals, and storybooks the Hidalgo revolt has been depicted as a general uprising of nearly all Indian village communities in Mexico against Spanish rule. But this view has now been challenged by some historians and the issue of the extent of Indian village participation is particularly controversial. One of the main reasons for doubt was that the center of the revolt was the Bajío region northwest of Mexico City, which in many senses was atypical to the rest of Mexico. It had a relatively small Indian population and most of its inhabitants were mestizo or white. The number of free village communities was small.

The fact that such an atypical region constituted the core of the 1810 revolt, as well as the fact that more research has focused on the

Bajío in 1810 than on any other part of Mexico, have obscured the problem of the degree of participation of traditional village communities in Mexico's independence wars. One of the most important aspects of the essays of both Van Young and Taylor is that for the first time they examine a region in which Indian communities rebelled on a massive scale between 1810 and 1815. Both feel that the social, economic, and religious factors that transformed the Guadalajara communities in the late eighteenth century were crucial in explaining the outbreak of the 1810 revolt. Taylor discusses in detail the revolt itself, describing its course and a unique victory over the Spaniards by peasants who held out for nearly three years on an island on Lake Chapala.

One way to understand why people rebel is to compare those who do with others under partially similar circumstances who do not. Taylor compares villages that joined the revolt with others in the same area that remained peaceful, and with Indians in another part of Mexico, Oaxaca, who did not rebel at all.

The defeat of the popular insurrection led by Hidalgo and Morelos, and the assumption of power after independence in 1821 by the most conservative groups in Mexico, did not constitute the end, but rather the beginning of a series of rural uprisings in the nineteenth century that culminated in the national revolution of 1910. This sudden upsurge of rural violence occurred because there was a profound change in the character of the state compared with previous years. The colonial state had been strong, whereas until the late nineteenth century the Mexican state was weak and unstable. The colonial government had attempted to play off hacendados against Indian villages and to maintain the latter's integrity, but Mexican governments were unwilling to do this (their links to the hacendados were extremely strong). Even had they been willing to carry out such a policy, they would have been unable to do so since they had neither the strength nor the long-term support.

Armed struggles between elite groups had been rare during the colonial period, but such conflicts were characteristic of the nineteenth century, for a wide variety of reasons. Peasants with grievances against landlords felt that now the state had been decisively weakened the moment had come to settle their grievances by force. Similarly, landlords who knew the state would not and could not restrain them also felt that they could settle their conflicts with the peasants by force, seize their land, or violate their rights. On the other hand, some landlords, in their own disputes against the state, attempted to gain the armed support of the peasants living on their land. In fact, the several chapters that examine nineteenth-century uprisings show that all of these elements can be found, producing an enormous diversity. John Coatsworth argues that in the early nineteenth century the first cause was most common. "A far larger number of Indian uprisings were aggressive rather than defensive. . . . Post-independence revolts were more likely to involve land seizures carefully calculated to catch hacendados and the authorities unprepared to expel the invaders. Even in revolts precipitated by defensive reactions to intrusions, the villages often mounted offensives that went far beyond redressing their initial grievances."

The underlying cause of the Chalco revolts, according to John Tutino in Chapter 4, was very different from those described by John Coatsworth. The Chalco revolts of 1840–70 were triggered by landlords who began expropriating water rights that had traditionally belonged to or had been shared with the villagers. It was a straightforward struggle by villagers against landowners allied with the national government. The peasants' only allies were socialist intellectuals. In regions more distant from Mexico City a third case seems to have predominated in which temporary alliances developed between peasants and elites in attempts to resist control by the national government.

What emerges from these chapters is that the ideology of regional *caudillos* was not of crucial importance. Both liberals and conservatives attempted to mobilize peasants on their behalf when they fought a central government dominated by a rival group. In Chapter 8 John Hart describes the complexity of one of the most notable of these alliances, which was forged between rebellious peasants in the state of Guerrero and one of the state's wealthiest landowners and its liberal caudillo, Juan Alvarez. By the very nature of the forces involved—landlords and peasants—these alliances were risky, unstable, and contradictory. Hart describes the enormous difficulties Alvarez encountered when he attempted to prevent the peasants changing the character of the uprising from a defensive to an offensive one. But although Alvarez was eventually successful in controlling his peasant allies, the same cannot be said of other caudillos who attempted similar peasant mobilizations for their own ends.

Between 1840 and 1875, rival factions in the northern state of Sonora, liberals and conservatives, sought to utilize the Yaquis, considered to be among the finest fighting men in northern Mexico, in their factional conflicts. The Yaquis at first responded enthusiastically, and accepted the arms and other help provided. But, as Evelyn Hu-DeHart shows in the second part of Chapter 5, the Yaquis, imbued with a new sense of confidence, decided to disregard Mexican control and to use the newly acquired arms for their own ends, to regain the land they considered to be theirs. But this disastrous experience of the Sonoran elite was not heeded by their counterparts in southern Mexico. In Chapter 10, Enrique Montalvo Ortega describes how, in the state of Yucatán an elite faction armed the Maya Indians to gain their support in their conflict with a rival group. The results of this strategy were disastrous for the Yucatán oligarchy, in that they sparked the Caste War that almost led to the complete expulsion of all non-Indians from the peninsula. Although the rebellious Indians were unsuccessful in this endeavor, they did manage to set up an autonomous state in the southern part of Yucatán that retained its independence until 1902.

The extreme diversity of alliances formed by rural rebels was especially notable in the Sierra Gorda. In Chapter 9 Leticia Reina describes how in the 1840s rebellious peasants attempted to ally themselves with the invading Americans against the oligarchy of their region. The alliance then shifted to conservatives and at times to liberals. The issues that led to the various rebellions were as diverse as the allies and enemies of the rural rebels. In the Chalco region, water rights were the main point of dispute, in Guerrero it was land, and in the Sierra Gorda the main cause of conflict was access to timber on public and private land.

Most rural rebels suffered military defeat, but there were some notable exceptions. The rebellious village communities on Lake Chapala in the 1813–15 uprising were, according to Taylor, militarily successful and managed to maintain their autonomy. Neither the Yaquis in Sonora nor the Maya in Yucatán were ever decisively defeated in the nineteenth century. Even when peasants suffered military defeats, their uprisings did at times gain them some social, economic, and political advantages. Because of the rebelliousness of the Chalco peasants the Ley Lerdo, which required the sale of their communal landholdings, was not applied for many years.

When, for the first time since the colonial period, a strong Mexican state emerged under the presidency of Porfirio Díaz in the late nineteenth century, the number and the successes of peasant rebellions fell sharply, due mainly to the new-found strength of the Mexican government rather than to any kind of policy of compromise or conciliation on its part. On the contrary, unlike its colonial predecessors, the Díaz administration often encouraged or at least tolerated massive expropriations of peasants' land or curtailed the rights of large segments of the rural population. The government made no

effort to preserve even minimal control by villages over their lands
and rarely attempted to mediate in disputes between peasants and
landlords as their colonial predecessors had done. These policies
contributed in large measure to the outbreak of the national revolution in 1910 in which rural participation was decisive. But the term
"national" should nevertheless not be stretched too far. For a long
time, influenced by Frank Tannenbaum's largely excellent study
The Mexican Agrarian Revolution,[1] many researchers considered
the Mexican revolution a generalized rural uprising similar to the
uprising in Morelos and its surroundings under the leadership of
Emiliano Zapata. But as the various chapters of this volume show in
a convincing way, there was an enormous diversity of causes, patterns, and alliances of peasants during the 1910 Revolution, which
matched a similar diversity in the early nineteenth century.

The one characteristic of rural movements that is often stressed is
their great flexibility with regard to allies. Peasants would align
themselves with the most unlikely forces: revolutionary middle
classes, revolutionary hacendados, even nonrevolutionary hacendados, and the United States. They did not fit the rigid molds into
which social scientists have frequently attempted to place them.
This is the thrust of Arturo Warman's provocative Chapter 11, in
which he examines the figure of Emiliano Zapata as a national
leader. Warman disputes the contention that a regional leader like
Zapata could only have a regional perspective. He shows that Zapata
had formulated national policies on issues that did not directly affect the zone under his control, such as the problems of foreign capital and industrial labor. Were such programs only elaborated by the
few intellectuals in his movement for outside consumption? Were
they finally as meaningless for Zapatismo as were many of the programs elaborated by other leaders elsewhere in Mexico? Warman
says they were not, and examines how Zapata dealt with one of the
most complex problems facing all factions in the Mexican revolution that none had been able to resolve: the relationship between
civilian and military power. The Zapatistas were the only faction
that successfully limited the power of the military by establishing
clear-cut rules to ensure the supremacy of civilians over the military. In this sense Zapata was the only major military leader of the
Revolution to demand the subordination of the military to civilian

[1] Frank Tannenbaum, *The Mexican Agrarian Revolution* (Washington: Brookings
Institution, 1929).

society at a time when other political parties and political organizations were becoming dominated by the military.

A characteristic of all the chapters that focus on the Mexican revolution is that they not only pinpoint the type of alliances the peasants made with other segments of society, but they also attempt to assess the dominant partners in these alliances and to what degree the peasants managed to secure concessions, demands, and other advantages.

In the Tlaxcala region, a 1910 peasant uprising led by the Arenas brothers was similar in many respects to that of Zapata and was for a long time organically linked to it. After they were defeated by Carranza, the Arenas brothers decided that more could be gained from subordination and cooperation than from continuing what they considered a hopeless struggle. They made their peace with Carranza and in the process were branded traitors by Zapata (the leader of the movement, Domingo Arenas, was in fact later killed on Zapata's orders). As a condition for laying down their arms and subordinating themselves to Carranza, the Arenas brothers demanded that the government recognize all agrarian reforms they had carried out and allow them to continue with such reforms. This seems to have been the only case where a purely peasant movement joined Carranza. In Chapter 12, Raymond Buve studies the development of this unusual alliance for both the peasants and the government, and assesses whether they were correct in assuming that the alliance with Carranza would in fact preserve the agrarian reforms they had carried out.

For the Yaqui Indians of Sonora the Mexican revolution meant a return to the old and familiar pattern of fighting for outsiders in the hope of being rewarded for this by the recovery of their lands. The Yaquis, Evelyn Hu-DeHart observes, provided to diverse factions one of the most effective and tenacious fighting forces in the revolution. What they really gained in return is the subject of the concluding part of Chapter 5, which spans two centuries of Yaqui history.

In the state of San Luis Potosí revolutionary hacendados and peasants joined the Madero revolution against Porfirio Díaz, and then turned on each other. In Chapter 14 Romana Falcón describes the long and bloody confrontation that ensued, and how the peasant faction headed by the Cedillo brothers finally triumphed. The reality they created was not the egalitarian, communal society in the south, of which Emiliano Zapata had dreamed, but a hierarchical, militarized society that became more and more conservative. Such alliances between peasants and upper classes were often extremely tenuous and short lived.

William Meyers shows in Chapter 15 how a very different pattern emerged in one of Mexico's wealthiest agricultural regions, the Laguna area in the northern states of Coahuila and Durango. The Laguna, home of the wealthiest and most powerful revolutionary hacendados in Mexico, was to become the center of one of the most radical peasant movements. Meyers describes the nature of the movement and its utilization, repression, and cooptation by the "revolutionary hacendados."

In much of the popular literature, the Mexican revolution has been portrayed as a "peon revolution," implying that the resident hacienda workers spearheaded the uprisings against their masters. But all evidence to date shows that peons were not a primary force and at best played only a secondary role in revolutionary movements. Nevertheless, they did participate in revolutions under certain circumstances. In Chapter 13 Herbert J. Nickel and in Chapter 10 Enrique Montalvo Ortega examine peon involvement in two regions of Mexico: the Puebla–Tlaxcala area and Yucatán, respectively. The Puebla–Tlaxcala region was the scene of several rural uprisings, many of which were influenced by the Zapatista movement in Morelos. Until 1920, with very few exceptions, the hacienda peons studied by Nickel refused to participate in any of these uprisings and remained "loyal" to the hacendados. Their loyalty was only shaken by movements sponsored or endorsed by the governments that emerged after the revolution.

In 1914, after Carranza's General Pablo Gonzalez abolished debt peonage, some peons did leave the haciendas. Government-supported unions had some limited success in organizing hacienda peons, and in the 1930s some petitioned the government for hacienda lands. Nickel makes it abundantly clear that on the whole, there was nothing that could be called a peon revolt on the large estates he examined in the Puebla–Tlaxcala region. The only exception to this general phenomenon—the only time when a peon movement came to constitute a major political force during the Revolution—was in the state of Yucatán, but this was not the result of a spontaneous uprising. The peon movement only emerged when a revolutionary army led by Salvador Alvarado entered the state of Yucatán to put down a secessionist movement led by some of the state's wealthiest hacendados. At this juncture Carrancistas organized the peons as a counterforce to the hacendados. In Chapter 10 Enrique Montalvo Ortega argues that the peon movement soon freed itself from outside control and constituted a political force of its own, the Socialist party of the southeast.

In the aftermath of the most violent phase of the 1910 Revolution, the utilization of peasants by other social groups did not cease but was to a certain degree institutionalized by postrevolutionary governments. In Chapter 16 Hans Werner Tobler examines two ways in which this process worked. On the one hand the revolutionary army, largely made up of peasants, was transformed and professionalized to such a degree that in the 1920s it was frequently used as an instrument of repression against agrarian reform movements in the countryside. The government also attempted to utilize these agrarian movements against rebellious factions and conservative enemies as the nineteenth-century caudillos had done. Unlike their prerevolutionary predecessors, the twentieth-century postrevolutionary governments were ready to make much more substantial concessions, primarily land redistribution, to their peasant supporters.

What general conclusions emerge from these essays? It cannot be said that rural revolts in Mexico were centered on one particular region or were the work of just one particular social group. Village communities largely composed of Indians seemed to have been at the center of most local revolts both in the colonial period and in the nineteenth century. They also played a major role in regional revolts in the nineteenth and early twentieth centuries. In contrast, some of the main centers of national peasant revolts were those regions where village communities and Indians were considered unimportant. Those Indians who did participate tended to come from the most assimilated sections of the Indian population.

The causes of rural rebellion varied sharply over time and space. In pre-Columbian times, as well as during Spanish colonial rule, taxes, tribute, and issues of local autonomy and religion tended to provoke uprisings, whereas in the nineteenth and twentieth centuries land and water rights were more important issues.

The essays in this volume show both the constant factors and sharp discontinuities in the history of rural revolts in Mexico. Certain factors have continued to influence rural uprisings from pre-Columbian times to the present: climatic uncertainties and the periodic agricultural crises they produced; poor natural communications between distant regions; the constant attempts by peoples of the central valley of Mexico over the last two thousand years to dominate the rest of the country, and the resistance of the peripheral areas to these efforts to centralize power. On the other hand, there are enormous discontinuities, of which perhaps the sharpest were those between the colonial period and later periods of Mexican history. On the whole the central government was most successful in the sixteenth and seventeenth centuries in curbing rural unrest and dominating the country. Many of the chapters in this volume attempt to explain the degree to which demographic factors (such as the high rate of Indian mortality in the sixteenth and seventeenth centuries), and conscious efforts by the Spanish crown to prevent the accumulation of power by local oligarchies, were responsible for this situation.

These essays also analyze why the crown was unable to maintain its policies into the late eighteenth and early nineteenth centuries, and assesses and describes the extremely diverse alliances between peasants and other segments of society, ranging from traditional caudillos to intellectuals and the middle classes.

One of the most interesting conclusions that emerges is that on the whole, in spite of military defeat, rural revolutionaries at least in the short term tended to gain far more from their uprisings than has generally been assumed, even though other segments of society may have been the prime beneficiaries, such as the creoles (*criollos*) in 1820 and the new bourgeoisie after 1920.

The essays in this volume are far more than individual case studies; they depict peasants who are not abstract sociological or historical categories, but people of flesh and blood. The essays show how erroneous is the idea that all peasant uprisings in Mexican history were the work of primitive rustics carrying out a hopeless struggle with perspectives limited to their small villages. Such uprisings did occur, but in many others the peasants showed themselves to be shrewd tacticians, entering into the most diverse alliances and attempting to shape national politics and utilizing upper-class conflicts and rivalries.

Were Mexico's peasants unique in Latin America in terms of their proclivity to revolt? This was the case only in limited periods of Mexico's history: perhaps the five hundred years preceding the Spanish conquest of Mexico, the years 1810–20, and 1840–70. What made Mexico's peasants unique was not so much the number of uprisings as the level of their participation in national revolutions. The role of peasants during the conquest, the independence movement, and the 1910 revolution, which brought a new bourgeoisie and important segments of the middle class to power, is unique. The most important contributions of these essays to the history of peasant uprisings, perhaps not only in Mexico but also in Latin America in general, is their disclosure of the complex relationships of peasants to other classes of society, the role of ethnic factors and the village community, the peasants' links to hacendados and regional strongmen, the role of the church, the effects of the frontier, and the enormous importance of a variety of phenomena frequently subsumed under the name "modernization."

Historians frequently like to ask (more in private than public), "what would have happened if . . . ?" What kind of a society would have emerged if the peasants had not been defeated but had won? The answer these essays give to this question is, not unexpectedly, ambiguous. On the one hand, there is the vision of a new and different society created by the greatest peasant leader that Mexico produced, Emiliano Zapata. In Chapter 11 Warman clearly shows that this vision was by no means limited to just returning or granting of land to peasant communities, but was a project that went far deeper. Perhaps for the first time in Mexican history there was a concrete attempt to implement a system where the state and the bureaucracy would be controlled by a civilian government. However, there are contrary experiences of other societies where peasants did win, did implement far-reaching land reforms, and did produce societies in which a new ruling class emerged and began to dominate society using means similar to those of their predecessors in the prerevolutionary period. This was clearly the case in Yucatán once the Indian revolutionaries consolidated their control over the southern part of the peninsula and created a new ruling class. A new upper class also emerged in regions of Tlaxcala where agrarian revolutionaries had triumphed, as well as in San Luis Potosí after the leader of the greatest peasant uprising in the region, Saturnino Cedillo, assumed control.

These two tendencies are but a small sample of the wide variety that characterizes the causes, development, strategies, composition, allies, programs, and results of peasant revolts in Mexico; these essays certainly reflect that heterogeneity.

PART I

Mexico: Unique Center of Rural Rebellion?

CHAPTER TWO

Patterns of Rural Rebellion

in Latin America: Mexico in

Comparative Perspective

John H. Coatsworth

The incidence, magnitude, timing, causes, and effects of rural social unrest in Latin America have fascinated historians and social
scientists (as well as policy makers) for more than half a century.[1]
Work on Mexico, as this volume attests, has been especially prominent in the past decade. This continuously growing literature displays two notable characteristics. First, it consists largely of case
studies, often published as articles based on doctoral dissertations.
Second, it has begun to display the comparative sensibilities of the
not-so "new social history," although comparisons are usually limited to a single time period or region. The limited scope of most of
the work in this field has discouraged efforts to analyze patterns of
rural unrest across long time periods and large regions. This, in turn,
has made it difficult for historians to situate particular events and
processes in their general context, or to assess the experience of one
period or region against that of other places and times. Nonetheless,
case studies and comparative observations have accumulated to a
point where, taken together, they invite such an effort. The purpose
of this essay is thus to survey the literature on rural rebellions in
Latin America across approximately two centuries, from the end of

[1] The author wishes to thank the following scholars for generously taking time to
comment upon earlier drafts of this chapter: Friedrich Katz, John Monteiro, Scarlett
O'Phelan Godoy, Rebecca Scott, William B. Taylor, and John Tutino. The support of
the Social Sciences Divisional Research Fund of the University of Chicago is also
gratefully acknowledged.

the seventeenth to the turn of the twentieth, in order to suggest points of comparison between the experience of Mexico and that of the rest of the region.

It will first be useful to address a series of definitional issues. The purpose is not so much to elaborate a set of terms and isolate their meanings, as it is to introduce a number of theoretical and historiographical issues that stand out in the literature. The terms "peasant" and "peasant movement" are widely used to denote a particular rural social stratum and its purposeful self-organization. Peasants, however, have been so variously identified that a generally accepted definition has yet to be produced.[2] Usually the term refers to rural producers who possess (but do not necessarily own) the means of producing their own subsistence and a marketable surplus—that is, smallholders, squatters, members of corporate Indian villages, service tenants, cash renters, sharecroppers and the like. In this sense, the term excludes slaves, permanent resident workers on large estates (including debt peons), cowboys (*vaqueros, gauchos*), migrants and other wage laborers, and supervisory personnel. It also excludes the proprietors of large estates, artisans, intermediaries of various kinds, religious professionals, lawyers, police, and other social types often found in rural areas. This rough distinction serves well for some analytical purposes, but since many of these nonpeasant classes and strata have been recorded as active participants in rural social movements, focusing on peasants alone would impose too narrow a limit on any comparative discussion.

Rural social "movements" may be defined to include any collective behavior that has as its motive or unintended effect an alteration (or preservation under assault) in the material conditions, social organization or political position of the participants.[3] One advantage of so inclusive a focus is that it abstracts from particular, time-bound and circumstantial characterizations of collective action. For example, collective behavior that is viewed as illegal and rebellious at one period or in one area may represent normal, rou-

[2] See, for example, Henry A. Landsberger, "The Role of Peasant Movements and Revolts in Development," in *Rural Protests: Peasant Movements and Social Change*, ed. Landsberger (London: Macmillan, 1974), 1–8, for a discussion of the issues. For a recent debate, see Harry E. Vanden, "Marxism and the Peasantry in Latin America: Marginalization and Mobilization," *Latin American Perspectives* 9 no. 4 (1982): 38–60; Timothy F. Harding, "Critique of Vanden's Marxism and the Peasantry," *Latin American Perspectives* 9 no. 4 (1982): 99–106.

[3] Landsberger, "The Role of Peasant Movements," pp. 8–22; see also Richard K. Horner, "Agrarian Movements and Their Historical Conditions," *Peasant Studies* 8 no. 1 (1979): 1–16.

tine, and acceptable stratagems employed by contending litigants in disputes over land or water at another time or place. The term "movement" also abstracts from the problematical distinction between the daily struggle of rural people to survive and the development of collective purpose or volition. What appears, for example, as the peaceful acceptance of external authority by rural communities, or the routinely deferential attitude of tenants and peons on a large estate may, on second look, involve a series of collective as well as individual confrontations that serve constantly to shift the terms of social relations without ever reaching the point of overt, self-conscious, or extralegal group action. The neat distinction between rebellion and submission may mean more to distant authorities and later historians than to the participants themselves. Nonetheless, so inclusive a definition of subject matter requires the historian to abandon command of larger trends and patterns in order to master anthropological data of such intricacy that only the case study can be made manageable.

This chapter has a less conventional focus. The social strata examined include all rural people who are economically deprived (in contrast to those whom local standards define as better off) and politically subordinate (as opposed to those who have more effective and continuous access to political power). But the discussion is limited to include only illegal or extralegal collective action. Two assumptions inform this unusual combination of a broadly inclusive specification of the social types to be observed and a highly restricted focus on a narrow range of illegal behaviors. The first assumption is that patterns of rebellious behavior may be usefully examined across highly varied social and economic formations. The second is that illegal collective action constitutes an analytically fruitful object of separate study. The second assumption is well grounded in theoretical and historical work.[4] The first, however, challenges a long-standing historiographical tradition that implicitly draws a sharp distinction between rural social conflict in slave and nonslave societies.[5] This distinction serves well the analytical purposes that gave rise to it, since patterns of social conflict in slave societies differed in important ways from those in nonslave regions. Nonetheless, this essay includes comparisons between rural up-

[4] See Theda Skocpol, "What Makes Peasants Revolutionary?" in *Power and Protest in the Countryside: Studies of Rural Unrest in Asia, Europe, and Latin America*, ed. Robert P. Weller and Scott E. Guggenheim (Durham: Duke University Press, 1982), pp. 157–79.

[5] None of the work cited below treats both slave and nonslave revolts together.

heavals in these differing social formations because they serve to advance the analysis of rural rebellion in both.

More problematical on theoretical as well as empirical grounds is the exclusive focus on *rural* phenomena. Nearly all of the rural conflicts analyzed below had their urban counterparts. Slaves revolted in cities and towns as well as on the plantations; most of the large-scale slave insurrections of nineteenth-century Brazil, for example, erupted in urban areas rather than in the countryside. Patterns of resistance and rebellion now associated with uniquely rural settings were common in mining towns and administrative centers throughout the Spanish empire, and continued long after independence. The separation of town and country, a central feature of modern society, did not take definitive shape until late in the nineteenth century in most of Latin America. Patterns of urban revolt—like food riots, miners' protests, and tax revolts—all retained their ties (direct or indirect) to traditions of rural rebellion until well into the twentieth century. Excluding these conflicts forces the historian to omit treatment of important continuities in the development of social movements in premodern societies. In the case of Latin America, this omission arises largely from lacunae in research. With the exception of Brazilian slave insurrections in the nineteenth century, the history of precapitalist urban social struggles has yet to be written.[6]

The first two sections of this chapter review the main patterns of rural rebellion and their distributions in time and across subregions of Latin America. The third section discusses the issue of causation, that is, the economic, sociocultural, and political determinants of rural rebellion. The fourth section raises a number of general historiographical issues related to the role of rural social unrest in the transition to modern social and political systems, and summarizes

[6] See Chester L. Guthrie, "Riots in Seventeenth Century Mexico City: A Study of Social and Economic Conditions," in *Greater America: Essays in Honor of Herbert Eugene Bolton*, ed. Adele Ogden and Engel Sluiter (Berkeley: University of California Press, 1945), pp. 243–58; Alan Probert, "The Pachuca Papers: The Real del Monte Partido Riots, 1776," *Journal of the West* 12 no. 1 (1973): 85–125; Torcuato di Tella, "The Dangerous Classes in EarlyNineteenth-Century Mexico," *Journal of Latin American Studies* 5 (1973): 79–103. For an example of a twentieth-century urban riot that followed closely the pattern described by William B. Taylor in *Drinking, Homicide and Rebellion in Colonial Mexican Villages* (Stanford: Stanford University Press, 1979), chap. 4, for village uprisings in the eighteenth century, see Rodney Anderson's account of events in the mining town of Cuencame in 1909 in *Outcasts in Their Own Land: Mexican Industrial Workers, 1906–1911* (DeKalb: Northern Illinois University Press, 1976), p. 227.

the comparison of rural rebellions in Mexico with their counterparts in other regions of Latin America.

Patterns of Rural Rebellion

Any scheme of classification is open to challenge. What follows is a schematic checklist of the principal types or patterns of illegal collective action employed by Latin America's rural people that have come to the attention of historians. The checklist emerged inductively from a review of accounts of hundreds of conflicts (large and small) in the two centuries from 1700 to 1899.

REVOLTS INVOLVING MESOAMERICAN AND ANDEAN INDIAN VILLAGES

Three main types of illegal collective action have been associated with this type of rural socioeconomic organization: land invasions, village riots or uprisings, and "caste" wars. Of these, the first may have been the most common, and is clearly the least well documented. Often community affairs, land invasions ranged from surreptitious colonization of unused or abandoned estate lands to violent seizures accompanied by the burning of estate buildings, theft of livestock and other property, even the assassination of estate employees, foremen, and owners. In many cases, land invasions involved the recovery of lands putatively lost to estates many generations earlier, and in others, the loss was more recent. In Mexico, as elsewhere, land invasions usually involved single villages. There is some evidence to suggest that such events were less likely to be defined and treated as rebellious by colonial authorities than by post-independence regimes. Invasions of hacienda lands were not usually associated with village rebellions until after independence, though hacienda invasions of village lands were common and usually provoked prolonged litigation (and occasional resistance).[7]

The second pattern of rural rebellion associated with Indian village communities—the village riot or uprising—has only been systematically studied in the past decade. In Taylor's pathbreaking

[7] For recent examples, and a synthesis of historical work, see Eric Hobsbawm, "Peasant Land Occupations," *Past and Present* 64 (1974): 72–93. For historical examples, see Leticia Reina, *Las rebeliones de campesinos en México (1819–1906)* (Mexico: Siglo XXI, 1980), pp. 136, 143, 151–52, 157–60, 187–88, 231, 259, 277, 341, 427–28, 432; and Scarlett O'Phelan Godoy, "Tierras Comunales y Revuelta Social; Perú y Bolivia en el s. XVIII," *Allpanchis* 19 no. 22 (1983): 75–91.

work, eighteenth-century village uprisings in central Mexico and
Oaxaca are described as spontaneous affairs, usually confined to single communities, and most often provoked by the arbitrary acts of
public officials.[8] Similar phenomena have now been studied in Guatemala, Ecuador, Bolivia, and Peru, with simliar results.[9] Directly
economic provocations (new taxes, monopolies, forced sales) appear
to have been more commonly associated with the Andean village
uprisings than with those in Mexico and Guatemala where assaults
on village autonomy and "lifestyle" (imposition of new village officials, quarantines, boundary changes, prohibitions on fiestas) account for a large number of incidents. Though sometimes attributed
to the unique cultural insularity of indigenous communities in the
Americas, village tax revolts (and traditions of rioting against official
abuse) were common in other premodern societies, as Tilly has
shown for seventeenth-century France.[10]

Caste warfare may be defined as a regional uprising of Indian villagers directed at the expulsion or elimination of external (non-Indian) authority. In Mexico, these large-scale revolts were confined
to the northern and southern peripheries, while in the Andes the
more densely populated core provinces of the highlands witnessed
such events.[11]

[8] See Taylor, *Drinking, Homicide and Rebellion*, chap. 4.
[9] Severo Mártinez Pelaez, "Los motines de indios en el período colonial Guatemalteco," *Estudios Sociales Latinoamericanos* 2 no. 5 (1973): 201–28; also J. Daniel Contreras R., *Una rebelión indígena en el Partido de Totonicapan en 1820: El indio y la
independencia* (Guatemala: Imprenta Universitaria, 1951); Francisco de Solano, *Los
mayas del siglo* XVIII: *Pervivencia y transformación de la sociedad indígena guate-
malteca durante la administración borbónica* (Madrid: Ediciones Cultura Hispánica,
1974), 129, 145. On Ecuador, see Segundo Moreno Yañez, *Sublevaciones indígenas
en la Audiencia de Quito desde comienzos del siglo* XVIII *hasta finales de la Colonia*
(Bonn: Bonner Amerikanistische Studien, Bas 5, 1976). On the Viceroyalty of Peru,
see Scarlett O'Phelan Godoy, *Rebellions and Revolts in Eighteenth Century Peru and
Upper Peru*, Lateinamerikanische Forschungen 14 (Köln: Böhlau Verlag, 1985); by
the same author, "Tupac Amaru y las sublevaciones de siglo XVIII," in *Tupac Amaru
1780: Sociedad colonial y sublevaciones populares*, ed. Alberto Flores Galindo
(Lima: Retablo de Papel Ediciones, 1976), 67–81 and, by the same author, "El norte y
los movimientos anti-fiscales del siglo XVIII," *Historica* 1 no. 2 (1977):190–222. See
also Oscar Cornblitt, "Society and Mass Rebellion in Eighteenth-Century Peru and
Bolivia," in *Latin American Affairs*, St. Anthony's Papers, no. 22, ed. Raymond Carr
(London: Oxford University Press, 1970), pp. 9–44, and Jürgen Golte, *Repartos y rebeliones: Tupac Amaru y las contradicciones de la economía colonial* (Lima: Instituto de Estudios Peruanos, 1980).
[10] Charles Tilly, "Routine Conflicts and Peasant Rebellions in Seventeenth-Century
France," in *Power and Protest*, ed. Weller and Guggenheim, pp. 13–41.
[11] The classic work on Mexico is Nelson Reed, *Caste War in Yucatán* (Stanford:

UPRISINGS AGAINST HACIENDAS

Rural rebellions involving direct assaults on the haciendas (or fazendas in Brazil) were apparently quite rare in the colonial period, except where generalized revolts against Spanish authority (caste wars and nomad raids) put all European enterprises and institutions at risk. Disputes between Indian communities and neighboring haciendas seldom provoked caste wars. In both Mesoamerica and the Andes, the relatively independent colonial judiciary offered a measure of protection for the individual and corporate property rights of Indian villagers. After independence, political authority came to be linked more closely to local and regional elites, often dominated by hacendados and their allies, while the repressive apparatus of the state weakened. Rebellions associated with land seizures and the pillage of estates (even when ostensibly directed to other purposes) became common in Mexico by the 1840s and in the Andes by the 1890s.[12] In both regions, this change usually occurred in the context of large-scale, multiclass revolts linked to regional caudillos and national political movements.[13]

Far rarer were uprisings from within the haciendas. Save for a series of "coolie" revolts in Peru in the 1890s among Chinese laborers reduced to a status approximating that of slaves,[14] the large Spanish- and Luso-American estates were relatively immune from assaults by resident estate workers or peons. Protests and rebellions involving tenants, sharecroppers, cowboys, renters, and seasonal migrants were more common, but still relatively rare. These social strata did participate in rural violence, but usually in multiclass, regional revolts in which they seldom attacked the estates on which they lived.

MISSION REVOLTS AND NOMAD RAIDS

On the far-flung fringes of Spanish and Portuguese colonial settlement, the crown dispatched the clergy of the regular orders to establish missions to pacify the indigenous populations. These efforts met with varied success. Failures occurred when Indians who had

Stanford University Press, 1964). See also the essay by Enrique Montalvo, Chapter 10, this volume.

[12] See below, pp. 33–35.

[13] See below, pp. 35–39.

[14] See Wilfredo Kapsoli, "La crisis de la sociedad peruana en el contexto de la Guerra," in *Reflexiones en torno a la guerra de 1879*, ed. Jorge Basadre et al. (Lima: Francisco Campodonico F. and Centro de Investigación y Capitación, 1979), pp. 339ff.

settled peaceably in the missions rebelled either against the padres themselves or against the demands of private settlers who sought to exploit them as laborers on new estates and mining enterprises.[15] In addition to these "mission" revolts, frontier areas were often subject to predatory attacks from unpacified nomadic "tribes." In some areas, such as the Argentine pampas, Indian raiding formed part of a much larger pattern of institutionalized trading relations.[16]

REGIONAL, MULTICLASS, AND "PEASANT" REVOLTS

In the core areas of Spanish rule, the largest and most prolonged rural revolts involved formal and informal alliances between diverse social and ethnic strata. These revolts seldom included hacienda peons (except as retainers of the hacendados), but did involve tenants, sharecroppers, migrant laborers, and occasionally small farmers in addition to Indian villagers. The links between villagers and other rebellious strata varied considerably across time periods and regions. Often their protests were distinct and separate. After independence, Indian communities discovered ways to insert their protests into regional and even national politics through alliances with "popular" caudillos.[17] In Brazil, "peasant" movements with highly variable political linkages also developed.[18] In the slave

[15] For an account of what I have called a "mission revolt", see Evelyn Hu-DeHart, *Missionaries, Miners and Indians: Spanish Contact with the Yaqui Nation of Northwestern New Spain, 1533–1820* (Tucson: University of Arizona Press, 1981), chap. 2–3. See also Chapter 9, this volume.

[16] For nomad raiding, see the analysis of the pampa frontier case in Kristine Jones, *Conflict and Adaptation in the Argentine Pampas, 1750–1880* (unpublished dissertation, University of Chicago, 1984). For colonial Mexico, see José Luis Mirafuentes Galván, *Movimientos de resistencia y rebeliones de indígenas en el norte de México (1680–1821)* (Mexico: Archivo General de la Nación, 1975).

[17] Outstanding cases include Rafael Carrera in Guatemala; Juan Alvarez, Manuel Lozada and Miguel Negrete in Mexico; Andres Cáceres in Peru; and José Manuel Pando in Bolivia. On Carrera, see Ralph Lee Woodward, Jr., *Social Revolution in Guatemala: The Carrera Revolt* (New Orleans: Tulane University Press, 1971); on Alvarez, see Fernando Díaz y Díaz, *Caudillos y caciques: Antonio López de Santa Anna y Juan Alvarez* (Mexico: Colegio de México, 1972); on Negrete, see John M. Hart, "Miguel Negrete: La epopeya de un revolucionario," *Historia Mexicana* 24 no. 1 (1974): 70–93. On Lozada, see Jean Meyer, "El ocaso de Manuel Lozada," *Historia Mexicana* 18 no. 3 (1969): 535–68. On Cáceres, see Florencia E. Mallon, *The Defense of Community in Peru's Central Highlands: Peasant Struggle and Capitalist Transition, 1860–1940* (Princeton: Princeton University Press, 1983), chap. 3. On Pando, see Ramiro Condarco Morales, *Zaraté, el temible Willka: Historia de una rebelión indígena de 1899* (La Paz: n.p., 1965).

[18] See Manuel Correira de Andrade, "The Social and Ethnic Significance of the War

regions of Brazil and the Caribbean, however, the propensity of small producers to rebellious behavior appears to have been considerably less than elsewhere.

SLAVE-BASED REVOLTS

Three types of conflict are associated with slavery: plantation riots and uprisings, slave insurrections, and maroon warfare. Plantation uprisings tended to be provoked by arbitrary acts of superiors (usually owners and overseers), and to limit themselves to one or a few adjacent plantations. Plantation revolts, like Taylor's village riots, tended to be "reformist"—directed toward ending an abuse or improving some aspect of life without directly challenging the oppressive system itself.[19] Large-scale slave insurrections were far less common than plantation uprisings; like caste wars, the large-scale slave revolts usually sought the expulsion or extermination of the European elite. Maroon wars were linked to plantation uprisings as well as slave insurrections, but more often resulted from search-and-destroy operations mounted by the authorities against maroon settlements that constituted points of attraction for runaways or bases for "bandit" activities and raids on the plantations.[20]

These patterns of rural rebellion do not represent rigidly discrete types. The small-scale village and plantation revolts come closest to representing closed, separable events, but even in such cases the historian frequently confronts the potential for transformation. Caste wars and slave insurrections, revolutionary in their significance, could be sparked by small, apparently "reformist" rioting. The mechanisms of "contagion" presented themselves in two ways. At a single point in time, a small incident might touch off protests

---

of the Cabanos" in *Protest and Resistance in Angola and Brazil: Comparative Studies*, ed. Ronald H. Chilcote (Berkeley: University of California Press, 1972); Roderick J. Barman, "The Brazilian Peasantry Re-examined: The Implications of the Quebra-Quilo Revolt, 1874–75," *Hispanic American Historical Review* 57 no. 3 (1977): 401–24; and Bernard J. Seigel, "The Contestado Rebellion, 1912–16: A Case Study of Brazilian Messianism and Regional Dynamics," *Journal of Anthropological Research* 33 (1977): 202–13.

[19] For a typical case, which is remarkable only in that the rebelling slaves ran off, established a makeshift settlement and then proposed bargaining terms to the plantation and the authorities, see Stuart B. Schwartz, "Resistance and Accommodation in Eighteenth-Century Brazil: The Slaves' View of Slavery," *Hispanic American Historical Review* 57 no. 1 (1977): 69–81.

[20] For a convenient anthology of work on this subject, see *Maroon Societies*, ed. Richard Price (Garden City: Anchor Press, 1973).

against similar injustices in neighboring communities or plantations
and spread rapidly to encompass larger numbers of rebels and larger
goals as well.[21] Alternatively, an accumulation of small incidents
might prepare the ground for conspiracies with explicitly revolutionary goals.[22] Both dangers were recognized by ruling classes
throughout Latin America. Nonetheless, the large-scale upheavals
usually required special conditions that were not found in the circumstances that provoked small-scale uprisings.

The most complex rural rebellions were those involving diverse
strata of the rural population, each with its own needs and goals.
While even isolated indigenous communities developed complex
internal systems of status and property relations, the heterogeneity
of multiclass (and multiethnic) regional revolts like the Tupac
Amaru and Hidalgo movements poses difficult analytical problems
for the historian. These problems become most difficult after independence, when village communities throughout Mesoamerica and
the Andes appear as erstwhile participants in national (even international) political conflicts led by sectors and segments of national
elites, yet they frequently manage to insert their own objectives into
these struggles. Equally problematic are the large-scale "peasant" revolts of the Brazilian interior where precise data on the social
origins of the participants is usually lacking and where, in most
cases, the revolts are linked to (or exploited by) regional and national factions of the elite.

Where, When, and How Often
Rebellions Occurred

The incidence of rural rebellions in Latin America cannot be established with quantitative precision. Systematic study of these phenomena is still in its infancy. Sufficient data on several types of rebellion now exist, however, to make rough measurement and
generalization feasible. This section reports the results of a survey
of the secondary literature on six types of rural rebelliousness: Indian village rebellions, caste wars, plantation uprisings, slave insurrections, maroon wars, and regional or "peasant" revolts. The data

[21] This appears to have been what happened in Jamaica, when a small-scale rising
escalated into the "Baptists' War." See Michael Craton, *Testing the Chains* (Ithaca:
Cornell University Press, 1982), pp. 291–321.
[22] This was clearly the case in the Andes, where the accumulation of small-scale
village rebellions prepared the way for the Tupac Amaru revolt. See O'Phelan, "Tupac Amaru," pp. 67–71.

available for measuring the incidence of land invasions, mission revolts, and nomad raids proved insufficient for meaningful analysis.[23] Banditry proved impossible to measure not only because of the
lack of data for most regions and time periods, but also because of
the difficulties encountered by historians seeking to distinguish between "social" banditry and the more entrepreneurial variety.[24]

Table 2.1 summarizes the data on small-scale village riots and uprisings in Mesoamerica and the Andes between 1700 and 1820,
based chiefly on Taylor's work for Mexico,[25] Martínez Pelaez for
Guatemala,[26] O'Phelan Godoy and Golte for the Viceroyalty of
Peru,[27] and Moreno Yañez for the Audiencia of Quito in Ecuador.[28]
These sources record a total of 342 small-scale village uprisings. The
largest number took place in Mexico. Taylor reported a total of 142,
although this and other sources actually recorded some 137, after
larger-scale movements were eliminated. Excluded from the table
are most uprisings that included participants from more than five
villages or lasted more than one month. In Guatemala, community
uprisings totaled 42, in Ecuador there were 27, and in the Viceroyalty of Peru (today, Peru and Bolivia), there were 136. The Peruvian
data also exclude local revolts linked to the Tupac Amaru insurrec-

---

[23] All of these "types" of rebellious behavior occurred most frequently as small-
scale events. Mission revolts, however, often reached formidable proportions; the literature contains evidence of several such large-scale risings in northern Mexico in
the colonial era, while only one, the revolt in the Campa region, occurred in Peru.
See Hu-DeHart, Chapter 5, this volume, on the largest of the Mexican mission revolts.
On the Campa rebellion, see Jay Lehnertz, "Juan Santos, Primitive rebel on the campa
frontier (1742–52)," *Actas y Memorias*, xxxix *Congreso Internacional de America-
nistas* 4 (1962): 111–25; Mario Castro Arenas, *La rebelión de Juan Santos* (Lima: Milla
Batres, 1973); Stefano Varese, *La Sal de los Cerros: Notas etnográficos e históricos
sobre los campa de la selva del Perú* (Lima: Universidad Peruana de Ciencias y Tecnología, 1968), chap. 3.

[24] See Peter Singelmann, "Political Structure and Social Banditry in Northeast Bra-
zil," *Journal of Latin American Studies* 7 no. 1 (1975): 59–83; and Linda Lewin, "The
Oligarchical Limitations of Social Banditry in Brazil: The Case of the 'Good Thief'
Antonio Silvino," *Past and Present* 82 (1979): 116–46. On Mexico, see Paul J. Van-
derwood, *Disorder and Progress: Bandits, Police and Mexican Development* (Lincoln:
University of Nebraska Press, 1981), chap. 1.

[25] Taylor, *Drinking, Homicide and Rebellion*, chap. 4; see also Arturo Soberón
Mora, "Motín de los indios de Ayacuba, 1744," *Boletín del Archivo General de la
Nación* 7 no. 3 (1979): 24–37; Miraflores Galván, *Movimientos* 50; and Luis González
Obregón, *Rebeliones indígenas y precursores de la independencia mexicana en los
siglos* xvi, xvii y xviii (2d ed., Mexico: Ediciones Fuente Cultural, 1952).

[26] See note 9.
[27] See note 9.
[28] See note 9.

Table 2.1
Village Riots and Uprisings, 1700–1819

Years	Mexico	Guatemala	Viceroyalty of Peru	Ecuador	Totals
1700–09	4	2	1	2	9
1710–19	7	1	2	—	10
1720–29	6	2	6	—	14
1730–39	9	2	16	2	29
1740–49	9	4	7	—	20
1750–59	6	1	10	1	18
1760–69	17	2	25	4	48
1770–79	18	2	62	5	87
1780–89	19	7	Tupac Amaru	6	32
1790–99	12	4	4	2	22
1800–09	23	10	1	2	36
1810–19	7[a]	5	2	3	17
Totals	137	42	136	27	343

SOURCES: For Mexico see Taylor, *Drinking, Homicide and Rebellion*, ch. 4 and Appendix; see also Arturo Soberón Mora, "Motín de los indios de Ayacuba, 1744," *Boletín del Archivo General de la Nación* (1979): 24–37. For Guatemala and Ecuador, see sources cited in footnote 9. For Peru, the main source is O'Phelan, *Rebellions and Revolts*; the Appendix to this work briefly describes each rebellion. O'Phelan's data have been adjusted to eliminate large-scale conflicts as well as urban, miners', and obraje rebellions. For the period 1765–79, Golte (*Repartos y rebeliones*, 141–46) gives brief accounts of 38 revolts not covered by O'Phelan, and these have been added to the table.

[a] This decade includes the Hidalgo revolt in Mexico; village risings linked to this are excluded. Undercounting is likely.

tion in the 1780s, while the Mexican data exclude local revolts linked to the Hidalgo movement.

In all these regions, the number of village uprisings increased after mid-century. In Peru, Ecuador, and Mexico, the rise took place in the 1760s. In Mexico, the expulsion of the Jesuits in 1767 was linked to a number of the uprisings in that decade, perhaps as many as ten out of a total of seventeen, although the sources are not precise on this point. In Guatemala, where the numbers are small to begin with, there is no shift in the data until the 1780s. In Peru, unlike elsewhere, the number of village uprisings reached an early peak in the 1730s, but then declined through the 1750s. Like Mexico and Ecuador, village rebellions rose sharply in the 1760s, but unlike any other region, Peru experienced another quantum leap in the 1770s that culminated in the Tupac Amaru movements beginning in 1780 and continuing in regional revolts throughout the Andes until 1784. In Mexico, no such generalized upheaval took place until Hidalgo's Grito de Dolores in 1810. The number of local rebellions continued at a higher level than before 1760, but did not rise sharply in any decade before 1810 as it did in Peru during the ten years before Tupac Amaru. In Ecuador and Guatemala, large-scale regional and colony-wide revolts did not take place at all before independence.[29]

The pattern of village uprisings changed in both regions after independence. Table 2.2 summarizes the data for the independence period from 1820 to 1899, during which time Mexico again led all other regions in the number of these small-scale incidents. The historical literature contains reports of 102 village uprisings in this period in Mexico; in Peru and Bolivia the total is 61. Historical work on nineteenth-century Guatemala and Ecuador is much thinner, so the data showing small numbers of incidents in these countries after independence are certain to undergo revision in the future. For Mexico, the largest number of cases are reported in Reina's important work; for Peru, Ecuador, and Central America the sources are more diverse.[30] In any case, the independence period data again suggest

[29] The Viceroyalty of New Grenada, which included modern Ecuador and Colombia, experienced a major regional rebellion, the Comunero revolt, in 1781. The data reported above refer only to the Audiencia of Quito in modern Ecuador. In the Comunero regions of Colombia, local revolts among the predominantly European and mestizo population preceded the 1781 violence. Unlike the Viceroyalty of Peru, the indigenous population was small and played only a minor role in these events. See Anthony McFarlane, "Civil Disorders and Popular Protests in Late Colonial New Grenada," *Hispanic American Historical Review* 64 no. 1 (1984): 17–54. On the Comunero Revolt, see John L. Phelan, *The People and the King: The Comunero Revolution in Colombia, 1781* (Madison: University of Wisconsin Press, 1978).

[30] Reina, *Las rebeliones*. See also Reina, "Las luchas campesinas: 1820–1901," in *Las luchas populares en México en el siglo XIX*, ed. L. Reina et al. (Mexico: Cuadernos de la Casa Chata, Secretaría de Educación Pública, 1983), pp. 13–171; and Jean Meyer, *Problemas campesinos y revueltas agrarias (1821–1910)* (Mexico: Sep-Setentas, 1973). On Peru, see Peter Blanchard, "Indian Unrest in the Peruvian Sierra in the Late Nineteenth Century," *The Americas* 38 no. 4 (1982): 449–62; Wilfredo Kapsoli et al., *Los movimientos de campesinos en el Perú: 1879–1965* (Lima: Delva Editores, 1977); Mallon, *Defense of Community*; Michael Gonzales, "Neocolonialism and Indian Unrest in Southern Peru, 1867–1898" (paper presented to SSRC conference on "Resistance and Rebellion in the Andean World, Eighteenth and Nineteenth Centuries," University of Wisconsin, April, 1984); Rosalind C. Gow, "Land and Revolution: Indian Resistance to Latifundio Expansion and Modernization in the South-

Table 2.2
Village Riots and Uprisings, 1820–1899

Years	Mexico	Guatemala	Peru and Bolivia	Ecuador	Totals
1820–29	4	1	—	—	5
1830–39	4	—	1	1	6
1840–49	14	—	—	1	15
1850–59	30	—	—	1	31
1860–69	8	—	2	2	12
1870–79	20	1	2	1	24
1880–89	6	—	21	2	29
1890–99	16	1	35	4	56
Totals	102	3	61	12	178

SOURCES: See note 30; Michael Gonzales, *Plantation Agriculture and Social Control in Northern Peru, 1875–1933* (Austin: University of Texas Press, 1985); Woodward, *Social Revolution in Guatemala*; Contreras R., "Una rebelión en el partido de Totonicapan."

important differences in the timing of village uprisings between Mexico and the Andes.

In the Andes, the number of village uprisings dropped sharply after the Tupac Amaru insurrection and remained low for a century. In Mexico, by contrast, the decline following the suppression of the Hidalgo movement lasted for less than thirty years. From the 1840s

ern Andes, 1880–1968" (paper presented to SSRC conference on "Resistance and Rebellion," University of Wisconsin, April 1984); Emilo Vásquez, *La rebelión de Juan Bustamante* (Lima: Editorial Juan Mejía Baca, 1976); on Bolivia, see Condarco Morales, *Zaraté, el temible Willka*; Tristan Platt, "Andean Rebellion and the Rise of the Liberal Party: The Origins of the Anti-Constitutionalist Alliance during the Bolivian Revolution of 1899" (paper presented to SSRC conference on "Resistance and Rebellion," University of Wisconsin, April 1984). On Ecuador, see Oswaldo Albornoz P., *Las luchas indígenas en el Ecuador* (Guayaquil: Editorial Claridad, n.d.); Julio Castillo Jácome, *La provincia del Chimborazo en 1942* (Riobamba: Talleres Gráficos de la Editorial "Progreso," 1942); Rodolfo Maldonado y Basabe, *Monografía de la Provincia del Chimborazo* (Riobamba: Librería e Imprenta "Nacional," 1930). On Central America (El Salvador), see Julio Alberto Dominguez Sosa, *Ensayo histórico sobre las tribus nonualcos y su caudillo Anastasio Aquino* (San Salvador: Ministerio de Educación, 1964).

to the 1870s, Mexico experienced not only a resurgence of village revolts, but also an unprecedented upsurge in large-scale caste wars and regional rebellions. The data on Guatemala and Ecuador are too sparse to permit analysis, but what evidence there is indicates a period of relative calm similar to Peru and Bolivia. The data thus suggest that Mexico's experience in the middle decades of the nineteenth century resulted from circumstances it did not share with other regions. This impression is reinforced by the timing of the major nineteenth-century rural slave revolts that ended in the 1830s, while Mexico was still relatively peaceful (see below).

Nineteenth-century uprisings, unlike their colonial predecessors, seldom occurred in isolation from larger regional and national developments. Table 2.3 summarizes the data on large-scale nonslave revolts in rural Latin America, and includes village-based revolts as well as multiclass, regional insurrections, and "peasant" uprisings. Most of the large-scale village-based revolts were caste wars, the avowed purpose of which was to expel or exterminate European or white rulers. Some, however, were similar to small-scale village uprisings and sought merely to redress a recent wrong or to protest an abuse of authority. Aside from Tupac Amaru and the Hidalgo revolt, none of the large-scale colonial revolts, except the short-lived guerrilla struggle for independence in the Huánuco area of Peru, can be said to have involved cross-class alliances and none save these three were linked to external political figures or movements.[31] Including Tupac Amaru and Hidalgo, only eight of forty-nine large-scale nonslave rebellions occurred in the colonial period—five in Mexico, and three in Peru.

In the Mexican case, three of the large-scale colonial rebellions were caste wars, two of which occurred in the extreme south of the colony.[32] The third (and much smaller) rebellion took place on the

[31] On Tupac Amaru, see sources cited in note 9. On the Huánuco guerrillas, see Joëlle Chassin and Martine Dauzier, "La participation des indiens au mouvement d'indépendence; le soulèvement de Huánuco, Péru, en 1812," *Cahiers des Amériques Latines* 23 (1981): 7–45. Arguably, guerrilla or *montonero* units led by Indian kurakas between 1820 and 1824 might be added to this list, but see Heraclio Bonilla and Karen Spalding, "La independencia en el Perú: Las palabras y los hechos," in *La independencia en el Perú*, ed. Ella Dunbar Temple (Lima: Instituto de Estudios Peruanos, 1981), pp. 70–114.

[32] On the Tzeltal, see Robert Wasserstrom, "Indian Uprisings under Spanish Colonialism: Southern Mexico in 1712," in *Power and Protest*, ed. Weller and Guggenheim, pp. 42–56; Herbert Klein, "Peasant Communities in Revolt: The Tzeltal Republic of 1712," *Pacific Historical Review* 35 no. 3 (1966): 247–64; on the Canek caste war in Yucatán in 1761, see González Obregón, *Rebeliones indígenas*, pp. 469–74.

Table 2.3
Regional, "Peasant," and Caste Wars, 1700–1899

Year(s)	Country or colony	Region, state or province	Type[a]	Name given to even
1712–13	Mexico	Chiapas	Caste	Tzeltal revolt
1749–50	Peru	Huarochirí	Caste	
1756	Mexico	Actopan	Villages	
1761	Mexico	Yucatán	Caste	Canek's revolt
1769	Mexico	Tulancingo	Caste	Followers of "New Savior"
1780–84	Peru	Southern Peru	Regional	Tupac Amaru
1810–11	Mexico	Bajío	Regional	Hidalgo movement
1812	Peru	Huánuco	Regional	Independence revol
1825–33	Mexico	Sonora	Caste	Yaqui rebellion led Banderas
1832–40	Brazil	Northeast	Peasant	War of the Cabanos
1833	El Salvador	San Vicente	Caste	
1836–38	Mexico	Papantla	Regional	
1837	Guatemala		Regional	Rafael Carrera caudillo
1838–41	Brazil	Marianhao	Peasant	"Balaida"
1839	Ecuador	Chimborazo	Villages	
1842–43	Mexico	Guerrero	Regional	
1844	Mexico	Guerrero	Regional	
1845	Mexico	Oaxaca	Regional	
1845	Mexico	Puebla	Regional	
1847–99	Mexico	Yucatán	Caste	Maya "Caste War"
1847–49	Mexico	Sierra Gorda	Regional	
1847–48	Mexico	Veracruz	Regional	
1849–50	Mexico	Oaxaca	Villages	
1849	Mexico	Guerrero	Regional	
1852	Brazil	Pernambuco	Peasant	"Movimento dos Marimbondos"
1852	Brazil	Paraiba	Peasant	"Ronco de Abeha"
1855–73	Mexico	Nayarit	Regional	Lozada caudillo
1858	Brazil		Peasant	"Carne sem osso"
1861	Mexico	Hidalgo	Regional	
1865	Jamaica		Peasant	Morant Bay
1866–67	Peru	Huancané	Regional	Led by Juan Bustamante

Table 2.3 (*cont.*)

Year(s)	Country or colony	Region, state or province	Type[a]	Name given to event
1868	Mexico	Mexico	Regional	Led by Julio Lopez
1869–70	Mexico	Chiapas	Caste	
1871	Ecuador	Chimborazo	Villages	
1872–75	Argentina	Juyjuy	Peasant	
1874–75	Brazil	Northeast	Peasant	"Quebra-Quilo"
1876	Barbados		Peasant	"Federation riots"
1875–99	Mexico	Sonora	Caste	Yaqui rebellion
1877	Mexico	Sierra Gorda	Regional	
1877–83	Mexico	Huasteca	Regional	
1880	Brazil		Peasant	"Vintem"
1883–84	Peru	Huancayo	Regional	
1885	Peru	Ancash	Regional	Atusparia's revolt
1888–99	Peru	Huancayo	Regional	Comas federation
1889	Bolivia	Chayanta	Regional	
1897	Brazil	Canudos	Peasant	
1899	Bolivia		Regional	Zárate's revolt
1899	Bolivia	Chayanta	Regional	

SOURCES: On Mexico, see Reina, *Las rebeliones*; Meyer, *Revueltas agrarias*; Wasserstrom, "Indian Uprisings under Spanish Colonialism: Southern Mexico in 1712," in *Power and Protest*, ed. Weller and Guggenheim, 42–56; González Obregón, *Rebeliones indígenas*, 469–74; Taylor, *Drinking, Homicide and Rebellion*, 124, 146; Reed, *Caste War*; Hu-De-Hart, *Yaqui Resistance and Survival*, chap. 2. The Hidalgo movement is discussed in Hamill, Jr., *The Hidalgo Revolt*. On Peru and Bolivia, see notes 9, 30, 31; Spalding, *Huarochirí*, chap. 9; Stern, "The Age of Andean Insurrection"; Gonzales, *Plantation Agriculture and Social Control*; Condarco Morales, *Zaraté, el temible Willka*. For information on Tupac Amaru see note 9. On Ecuador, see Castillo Jácome, *La provincia de Chimborazo*, 141–42, 165–66. On Central America see Dominguez Sosa, *Ensayo histórico sobre las tribus nonualcos*; and Woodward, *Social Revolution in Guatemala*. The sources for Brazil may be found in note 18. On Argentina, see Duncan and Rutledge, *Land and Labor in Latin America*. For information on Jamaica, see Craton, *Testing the Chains*, 327–28; for Barbados, see Craton, *Testing the Chains*, 325, 329.

[a] Caste is used here to denote movements of indigenous peoples whose aim was to expel or exterminate white rulers.

Villages designates revolts that like small-scale village uprisings, were directed to the redress of a particular grievance.

Regional is used where diverse groups of rural poor, usually including indigenous villagers, linked their revolt to regional or national political movements and thus to other strata of the population.

Peasant is used where diverse strata of the rural poor revolted without direct links to regional or national political movements.

fringe of the central plateau in the modern state of Hidalgo.[33] The
two remaining revolts emphasize the pitfalls of combining in a single table every movement that attracted the adherence of more than
a few villages. One of the two was, of course, the Hidalgo revolt,
which was a major national event. The other was a regional uprising
of villages in the Actopán district of the modern state of Hidalgo,
which erupted in 1756 when government officials attempted to impose a forced labor draft to bring laborers from the area's villages to
the mines at Pachuca.[34] All three of the Peruvian revolts, on the
other hand, occurred in densely settled core areas of the viceroyalty.[35] The contrast between Peru and Mexico thus stands out
clearly. Mexican authorities could count on the relative absence of
large-scale social violence in the colony's core areas of settlement,
those of Peru had reason to be fearful.[36]

After independence, regional revolts followed the trend found in
the data on village uprisings. In Mexico, all eighteen large-scale revolts took place between 1825 and 1883, ten of them in the 1840s
and 1850s.[37] In South America, only three large-scale uprisings, two

[33] Taylor, Drinking, Homicide and Rebellion, pp. 124, 146, reports that in 1769 the
followers of a "new savior" in the Tulancingo area numbered "several thousands,"
who called for death to the Spaniards and the establishment of a new theocratic order
with Indian priests.

[34] Ibid., pp. 125, 140.

[35] On Tupac Amaru, see note 9. On Huarochirí, see Karen Spalding, Huarochirí, An
Andean Society Under Inca and Spanish Rule (Stanford: Stanford University Press,
1984), chap. 9; on the 1812 movement in the Huánuco region, see note 30.

[36] Two major conflicts do not appear in the data in Table 2.3. The revolt on the
Campa frontier, which spilled over into the sierra provinces on occasion, lasted from
1742 until sometime after 1752. Its leader, Juan Santos Atahualpa, developed a considerable following in the highlands, but except for the short-lived occupation of An-
damarca in 1752, failed to inspire a major uprising. This revolt is thus excluded from
the data as an arguable case of a mission uprising. For a discussion of the significance
of the Atahualpa revolt, see Steve J. Stern, "The Age of Andean Insurrection, 1742–
82: A Reappraisal" (paper presented to SSRC conference on "Resistance and Rebellion," University of Wisconsin, April 1984). Stern's essay also emphasizes the continuous threat of insurrection faced by the Peruvian authorities in this period.

[37] For sources on Mexico, see note 30 and Reed, Caste War; Jean Meyer, "El Reyno
de Lozada en Tepic (1856–1873)," Actes du XLIIᵉ Congrès International des Ameri-
canistes, vol. 3 (Paris: Societé des Americanistes, 1978), pp. 95–107; Evelyn Hu-
DeHart, Yaqui Resistance and Survival: The Struggle for Land and Autonomy, 1821–
1910 (Madison: University of Wisconsin Press, 1984), chap. 2; Marie-France Houdart-
Morizot, "Du Bon Usage des Mouvements Indiens: rebelles et rebellions de la Sierra
Gorda, Mexique (1847–1849)," Cahiers des Amériques Latines 23 (1981): 47–100; and
Chapters 4, 5, 8, and 9, this volume. On the Hidalgo movement, Hugh M. Hamill, Jr.,
The Hidalgo Revolt: Prelude to Mexican Independence (Gainesville: University of
Florida Press, 1966).

of them in Ecuador, occurred between 1820 and 1880.[38] It is possible, of course, that the absence of nineteenth-century village-based revolts, especially small-scale movements in Peru and Bolivia, is a product of research lacunae rather than real passivity. In the last two decades of the nineteenth century, in any case, both localized village uprisings and explosive regional movements engulfed large areas of the Andes.[39] In Mexico, however, the last two decades of the nineteenth-century were relatively peaceful. Except for the continuing war against the Yaquis in Sonora and the Mayas in the interior of Yucatán, no large-scale movement occurred in Mexico after the pacification of the Huasteca region of San Luis Potosí in 1883. Table 2.1 does show an increase in the number of smaller village uprisings in the 1890s, but eleven of the sixteen recorded in that decade occurred in Chihuahua, in the far north of the country.[40] It is possible that further research will produce evidence of more widespread localized unrest, concealed beneath the façade of Porfirian normalcy. For the present, however, historians tend to accept the view that the Díaz regime was relatively successful in maintaining rural peace until after the turn of the century.

The pattern of slave and maroon unrest in Latin America differs considerably from that of conflicts in the nonslave regions (see Table 2.4). Most of the revolts in slave regions were small-scale plantation uprisings involving from one to several adjacent slave estates. Unfortunately, documentation of these events has lagged behind research on the small-scale village riots and rebellions of Mesoamerica and the Andes. In the two centuries from 1700 to 1899, a total of 104 plantation risings have been well enough documented in the historical literature to be entered in the table. Most of those studied in detail were directed, like village riots, to secure limited goals. Others, however, involved mass escapes into maroon territory, and some formed part of larger plots that never materialized. The largest number, as the table shows, have been recorded for Brazil, but more than half of these (13 of 22) occurred in the 1880s, on the eve of emancipation (see Table 2.5).[41] The second largest number were re-

[38] Castillo Jácome, *La provincia de Chimborazo*, pp. 141–42, 165–66; Vásquez, *La rebelión de Juan Bustamante*.

[39] See sources cited in note 30.

[40] Reina, *Las rebeliones*, p. 359; Meyer, *Revueltas agrarias*, pp. 24–25; personal communication from Friedrich Katz, April 1984.

[41] See Donald Cleveland, "Slave Resistance and Abolitionism in Brazil: The Campista Case, 1879–88," *Luso-Brazilian Review* 13 (1976): 182–93; Eugene Genovese, *From Rebellion to Revolution: Afro-American Slave Revolts in the Making of the*

Table 2.4
Slave and Maroon Conflicts in Latin America, 1700–1889

Years	Maroon wars	Slave insurrections	Total	Plantation uprisings	Total all patterns
1700–09	—	—	—	2	2
1710–19	—	—	—	—	—
1720–29	1	1	2	4	6
1730–39	2	4	6	4	10
1740–49	—	1	1	5	6
1750–59	1	3	4	1	5
1760–69	3	3	6	8	14
1770–79	2	2	4	10	14
1780–89	1	—	1	1	2
1790–99	4	4	8	5	13
1800–09	1	—	1	4	5
1810–19	—	2	2	3	5
1820–29	—	2	2	14	16
1830–39	—	1	1	9	10
1840–49	—	—	—	11	11
1850–59	—	—	—	1	1
1860–69	—	—	—	4	4
1870–79	—	—	—	5	5
1880–89	—	—	—	13	13
Totals	15	23	38	104	142

SOURCES: Genovese, *From Rebellion to Revolution*: Toplin, "Upheaval, Violence," 639–55; Pescatello, ed., *The African in Latin America*. For Brazil, see Reis, "A elite baiana face os movimentos sociais," 341–84, and Cleveland, "Slave Resistance and Abolitionism in Brazil," 182–93. The best source for slave rebellions in the British West Indies is Craton, *Testing the Chains*. For the French Caribbean, see Debien, "Le Marronage aux Antilles Françaises au XVIIIème siècle," 3–44. On Venezuela, see Brito Figueroa, *Las insurrecciones de los esclaves negros en la sociedad colonial venezolano*; Arcaya, *Insurrección de los negros de la Serranía de Coro*; Cardot, *La rebelión de Andresote (Valles del Yaracuy), 1730–33*; and Lombardi, *The Decline and Abolition of Negro Slavery in Venezuela, 1820–1854*. On the Guianas, see Rodway, *Guiana: British, Dutch, and French*; de Groot, "The Boni Maroon War, 1765–1793, Surinam and French Guiana," 30–48; and Schuler, "Ethnic Slave Rebellions in the Caribbean and the Guianas," 374–85. On Cuba, see Corwin, *Spain and the Abolition of Slavery*; and Pérez de la Riva, *La habitación rural en Cuba*. On Puerto Rico, see Baralt, *Esclavos rebeldes*. On Peru, see Kapsoli, *Sublevaciones de esclavos en el Perú*; and Franco, "Maroons and Slave Rebellions in the Spanish Territories," in Price, *Maroon Societies*, 35–48. Information on Mexico is from Carroll, "Mandinga: The Evolution of a Mexican Runaway Slave Community," 488–505.

Table 2.5
Plantation Uprisings, 1700–1889

Years	Brazil	Puerto Rico	Guianas and Surinam	Cuba	Jamaica	Belize	Mexico	Tortola	Peru	Tobago	Antigua	Venezuela	Others[a]	Totals
1700–09	—	—	—	—	—	—	—	—	—	—	1	—	1	2
1710–19	—	—	—	—	—	—	—	—	—	—	—	—	—	0
1720–29	1	—	—	1	1	—	1	—	—	—	—	—	—	4
1730–39	—	—	2	—	2	—	—	—	—	—	—	—	—	4
1740–49	—	—	2	—	1	—	2	—	—	—	—	—	—	5
1750–59	—	—	1	—	—	—	—	—	—	—	—	—	—	1
1760–69	—	—	2	—	2	2	1	—	1	—	—	—	—	8
1770–79	—	—	3	—	—	1	—	—	—	3	—	—	3	10
1780–89	—	—	—	—	—	—	—	—	1	—	—	—	—	1
1790–99	—	—	—	1	—	—	—	1	—	—	—	1	2	5
1800–09	—	1	2	1	—	—	—	—	—	—	—	—	—	4
1810–19	1	1	—	1	—	—	—	—	—	—	—	—	—	3
1820–29	6	2	—	1	1	1	—	1	—	—	—	—	2	14
1830–39	—	3	1	1	—	—	—	2	—	—	1	1	—	9
1840–49	—	5	—	3	—	—	—	—	1	—	—	—	2	11
1850–59	—	1	—	—	—	—	—	—	—	—	—	—	—	1
1860–69	—	4	—	—	—	—	—	—	—	—	—	—	—	4
1870–79	1	4	—	—	—	—	—	—	—	—	—	—	—	5
1880–89	13	—	—	—	—	—	—	—	—	—	—	—	—	13
Totals	22	21	13	9	7	4	4	4	3	3	2	2	10	104

SOURCES: See sources listed on Table 2.4.

[a] Others include: Barbados, Dominica, Ecuador, Bahamas (Exuma), Guadaloupe, Martinique, St. Croix.

corded for Puerto Rico, all after 1810.[42] This pattern owes more to the diligence of research, apparently, than to the actual pattern of localized slave resistance. Local records proved rich in documentation in these two cases; when researchers penetrate such records for earlier periods (in the case of Brazil) and for other regions more systematically, historians will be able to improve on the primarily qualitative analysis that characterizes the field.[43]

Historical research has concentrated on the large-scale slave insurrections and maroon wars. Like plantation risings, maroon conflicts may also be under-reported in the literature. Many maroon communities lasted only a short time before succumbing to internal divisions or external attacks, whereas others survived, carrying out small raids for provisions, tools, and new recruits (especially women) for long periods of time without ever attracting the attention of high colonial or national officials. Countless others no doubt survived in secrecy, their very existence hidden from both the authorities and historians. Table 2.5, therefore, counts only the major conflicts in which maroons offered effective resistance over extended periods of time. Small-scale maroon conflicts, in which maroon villages were destroyed and dispersed by security forces or plantation militia were not counted as maroon "wars," even if the

---

Modern World (Baton Rouge: Louisiana University Press, 1979), p. 99; Robert Brent Toplin, "Upheaval, Violence, and the Abolition of Slavery in Brazil: The Case of São Paulo," *Hispanic American Historical Review*, 49 no. 4 (1969): 639–55; Ann M. Pescatello, "Preto Power, Brazilian Style," in *The African in Latin America*, ed. A. M. Pescatello (New York: Knopf, 1975), pp. 216–20; João José Reis, "A elite baiana face os movimentos sociais, Bahia: 1824–1840," *Revista de Historia* 54(1976): 341–84.

[42] Guillermo A. Baralt, *Esclavos rebeldes: conspiraciones y sublevaciones de esclavos en Puerto Rico (1795–1873)* (Rio Piedras: Ediciones Huracán, 1981).

[43] The best source for slave rebellion in the British West Indies is Craton, *Testing the Chains*; on Venezuela, see Federico Brito Figueroa, *Las insurrecciones de los esclaves negros en la sociedad colonial venezolano* (Caracas: Editorial Cantaclaro, 1961), and John V. Lombardi, "*The Decline and Abolition of Negro Slavery in Venezuela, 1820–1854* (Westport: Greenwood, 1971). On the Guianas, see James Rodway, *Guiana: British, Dutch, and French* (London: T. Fisher Unwin, 1912), and Monica Schuler, "Ethnic Slave Rebellions in the Caribbean and the Guianas," *Journal of Social History* 3 no. 4 (1970): 374–85. On Cuba, See Arthur F. Corwin, *Spain and the Abolition of Slavery in Cuba, 1817–1884* (Austin: University of Texas Press, 1967); Francisco Pérez de la Riva, *La habitación rural en Cuba* (Havana: Editorial LEX, 1952). On Peru, see Wilfredo Kapsoli, *Sublevaciones de esclavos en el Perú: Siglo* XVIII (Lima: Universidad Ricardo Palma, 1973); José L. Franco, "Maroons and Slave Rebellions in the Spanish Territories," in Price, *Maroon Societies*, pp. 35–48. On Mexico, see Patrick J. Carroll, "Mandinga: The Evolution of a Mexican Runaway Slave Community," *Comparative Studies in Society and History* 19 no. 4 (1977): 488–505.

communities involved offered some resistance. In St. Domingue, as
elsewhere in the Caribbean, these small-scale encounters appear to
have been more numerous in the early decades of the eighteenth
century, unlike the prolonged maroon wars that were more common
after mid-century.[44]

As Table 2.4 indicates, the recorded incidence of slave and maroon
violence was distributed more evenly over time than were rural rebellions in the nonslave regions. In part this was due to the sequen-
tial development of plantation economies. At any point in time over
the eighteenth and early nineteenth centuries, the historian encounters a diverse pattern, with some plantation societies still in their
infancy, others operating in full flower, and still others in decay.

Although the pattern shown in the table may reflect under-report-
ing in the case of plantation risings, this is not the case for major
maroon wars and large-scale slave insurrections. Here the table indicates a sharp difference between the eighteenth and the nineteenth centuries in the intensity of rural slave-based revolts. All but
one of 15 major maroon wars took place in the eighteenth century,
while 18 of 23 rural slave insurrections erupted before 1800. Major
slave revolts did occur in Brazil after 1800, but all save one were
primarily revolts of urban slaves and are thus excluded from the
table. Table 2.6 lists all the major maroon and slave conflicts by date
and location.

The most violent region to emerge from the data was the Caribbean coast of South America. Of 38 maroon wars and slave insurrections recorded between 1700 and 1832, half (19) occurred in the
Guianas, Surinam, and Venezuela.[45] The rest were spread more or
less evenly throughout the Caribbean islands and the mainland.
Only Jamaica (with four such explosions) and Grenada (with three)
experienced more than two major incidents. The total of 38 upheavals reflects, however, some double counting. In those cases (most
common in the Guianas and Surinam) where maroon wars provoked
a simultaneous slave insurrection, the table counts two events. Even

[44] See Gabriel Debien, "Le marronage aux Antilles Françaises au XVIIIe siècle," *Caribbean Studies* 6 no. 3 (1966): 3–44.
[45] See sources cited above and Silvia W. de Groot, "The Boni Maroon War, 1765–
1793, Surinam and French Guiana," *Boletín de Estudios Latinamericanos y del Caribe* 18 (1975): 30–48; Pedro M. Arcaya, *Insurrección de los negros de la Serranía de
Coro* (Caracas: Instituto Panamericano de Geografía e Historia, 1949); Carlos Felice
Cardot, *La rebelión de Andresote (Valles del Yaracuy), 1730–33* (Bogotá: Editorial
ABC, 1957).

Table 2.6
Maroon Wars and Slave Insurrection, 1700–1839

Years	Colony or country	State, region or province	Pattern	Comment
1726	Surinam	Seramica River area	Slave & Maroon	
1731–39	Jamaica		Maroon	First Maroon war
1731	Dutch Guiana	Berbice, Essequibo	Slave & Maroon	
1731–33	Venezuela	Yaracuy area	Slave	
1733–34	St. John		Slave	
1735	Mexico	Orizaba, Córdoba	Slave	
1747	Venezuela	Yare area	Slave	
1757–58	Surinam		Slave & Maroon	
1759	St. John		Slave	
1759	St. Croix		Slave	
1760	Jamaica		Slave	Tackey's rebellion
1763–64	Dutch Guiana	Berbice	Slave	Cuffey's rebellion
1765	Grenada		Slave & Maroon	
1765–93	Surinam and French Guiana		Maroon	Boni's war
1769–73	St. Vincent		Maroon	First Carib war
1771–74	Venezuela	Tuy area	Slave & Maroon	
1774–75	Dutch Guiana	Demerara	Slave & Maroon	
1785–90	Dominica		Maroon	First Maroon war
1791–1804	Haiti		Slave	
1795	Venezuela	Serranía de Coro	Slave	
1795	Dutch Guiana	Demerara	Slave & Maroon	
1795–96	St. Vincent		Maroon	Second Carib war
1795–96	Jamaica		Maroon	Second Maroon war
1795–97	Grenada		Slave & Maroon	Fedon's war
1796–97	St. Lucia		Maroon	Brigand's war
1809–14	Dominica		Maroon	Second Maroon war
1816	Barbados		Slave	Bussa's rebellion
1816	Brazil	Bahia	Slave	
1822	Surinam		Slave	
1823	British Guiana		Slave	
1831–32	Jamaica		Slave	Baptists' war

SOURCES: See sources listed in Table 2.4.

without double counting, however, the northern coast of South America stands out. Of 31 separate upheavals, 13 occurred in this region—seven of the 15 maroon wars and 12 of the 23 slave insurrections.

The temporal distribution of major slave and maroon outbreaks differed from that of conflicts in the nonslave regions. The concentration of slave and maroon conflicts in the eighteenth century (in contrast to the nineteenth century concentration of major nonslave upheavals) has already been mentioned. In addition, the pattern of events in the eighteenth century was different. Large-scale maroon and slave upheavals were concentrated disproportionately in four of the fourteen decades from 1700 to 1839. Major nonslave revolts were spread more evenly across this period until the 1830s. The two most important nonslave revolts occurred three decades apart (Tupac Amaru in 1780, Hidalgo in 1810). Slave and maroon revolts were concentrated disproportionately in the 1730s, the late 1750s and early 1760s, and in the 1790s. Of 38 such conflicts, 20 occurred in these years. Following independence, slave insurrections occurred regularly until the 1830s. In the nonslave regions the number of major rural conflicts fell off in the 1790s, just as slave and maroon revolts reached a peak, and (except for Hidalgo) did not revive until the 1830s in Mexico, and the 1880s in the Andes.

While the data are too sketchy to permit close analysis, there is little to suggest links between plantation uprisings and slave insurrections. Most of the small-scale events recorded in Table 2.4 (65 of 111) occurred after 1800, while all but five of the insurrections (18 of 23) took place before 1800. Nearly half of the plantation uprisings (50 of 111) took place in areas that never witnessed a major slave insurrection or maroon war. A few of the insurrections, however, began as localized plantation uprisings, gaining momentum as they spread from one place to the next. The links between maroon wars on the one hand, and plantation uprisings and slave insurrections on the other, are more difficult to measure. The links were closest in the Guianas, where most of the major slave insurrections and several of the smaller plantation uprisings involved maroons, either as precipitators or as allies. In the rest of the Americas, however, such links were rare. It was more common for maroon communities to attract runaways than to inspire revolts.[46]

In contrast to nonslave regions, then, major slave revolts and maroon wars were concentrated in the eighteenth century. Maroon

[46] See the essays by Debien and Franco in *Maroon Societies*, ed. Price.

wars were most common in the Guianas and Surinam, but rare elsewhere until the 1790s when international war precipitated major
maroon struggles, most of them encouraged by agents of the French
Republic in the British West Indies. Slave insurrections were most
numerous in the 1730s and 1790s. The last great maroon war, called
the Second Maroon War, in Dominica, ended in 1814, while major
slave insurrections continued until the "Baptist War" in Jamaica on
the eve of the British emancipation. Large-scale slave insurrections
ended just as Mexico's nineteenth-century regional and caste warfare was beginning, but a half century before major rural social violence revived in the Andes. Plantation revolts, like village uprisings,
were spread throughout the two centuries, ending in the late 1880s
with the last of the emancipations in Brazil and the Spanish islands.
Like village risings, however, plantation revolts seldom precipitated
large-scale movements. Large-scale slave and maroon violence disappeared from rural areas by the 1830s, while plantation risings
continued and both village uprisings and large-scale rebellions in
nonslave regions increased in number and intensity.

Causes of Rebellion

The historiography of causal agents and conditions is as diverse as
the rebelliousness it seeks to explain. One class of models places
rural rebellion, especially peasant revolt, in the context of systemic
changes in world or regional socioeconomic structures or modes of
production. The early development of commercial capitalism, the
expansion of the world market for agricultural products during the
industrial revolution and the major increase in international capital
flows in the age of imperialism have all been cited as having created
structural conditions that have led to rural revolt in the past four
centuries. Much of the historiography of rural discontent builds
upon one or another formulation of these general conditions. Advances in comparative analysis, often based on case studies that link
general, even worldwide, trends to particular instances of rebellious
behavior have contributed to a growing theoretical literature in recent years.[47]

[47] See, for example, Juan Martinéz-Alier, *Haciendas, Plantations and Collective
Farms: Agrarian Class Societies in Cuba and Peru* (London: Frank Cass, 1977); Ken-
neth Duncan and Ian Rutledge, ed., *Land and Labor in Latin America: Essays on the
Development of Agrarian Capitalism in the Nineteenth and Twentieth Centuries*
(London: Cambridge University Press, 1977); Jeffrey M. Paige, *Agrarian Revolution:
Social Movements and Export Economies in the Underdeveloped World* (New York:

Most historians thus cite economic variables in their lists of causal agents in rural social conflicts. Two different kinds of propositions are generally asserted, and often confused. The first cites general conditions or trends that may characterize entire regions over several decades (or even centuries). In a variety of otherwise contradictory models, long periods of economic growth (often identified with the development of capitalism) are widely believed to create more conflicts than long depressions or stagnation. Thus, for example, prosperous conditions involving higher world market prices for sugar and increased demand for slave imports are cited as factors that led to slave rebellions.[48] Similarly the expansion of haciendas at the expense of free villages is believed to have been associated with economic growth and (especially urban) population increase.[49] The commercialization of estates at the expense of traditional arrangements with tenants and sharecroppers,[50] or the penetration of private enterprise into frontier regions populated by missionized Indians,[51] are further examples of this general link between economic conditions and rural conflict. Even cases in which the state plays an obvious, even precipitating role, may be analyzed in this context by viewing public policy as deriving from economic trends, as in the case of Spain's Bourbon reforms.[52]

Demographic trends, usually linked to economic change, are also cited in this historical literature. Population advances in Spanish America during the eighteenth century, for example, increased pressure on the land and swelled the ranks of rebellious *forasteros* and migrants. McNeill has recently suggested that sharp and unprecedented increases in population growth rates in many parts of the globe, beginning in the mid-eighteenth century, help to account for an equally unprecedented wave of major peasant revolts that ex-

Free Press, 1975); Joel S. Migdal, *Peasants, Politics and Revolution: Pressures Toward Political and Social Change in the Third World* (Princeton: Princeton University Press, 1974).

[48] See Orlando Patterson, "Slavery and Slave Revolts: A Sociohistorical Analysis of the First Maroon War, 1665–1740," in *Maroon Societies*, ed. Price, pp. 281–89 and Baralt, *Esclavos rebeldes*, pp. 171–72. Baralt believes the Puerto Rican plantation uprisings were related to boom conditions in the 1810s and 1820s, and declining prices that forced planters to increase production rapidly in the 1840s.

[49] See John H. Coatsworth, "Railroads, Landholding and Agrarian Protest in the Early *Porfiriato*," *Hispanic American Historical Review* 54 no. 1 (1974): 48–71.

[50] For examples of this process, see David A. Brading, "La estructura de la producción agrícola en el Bajío de 1700 a 1850," *Historia Mexicana* 23 no. 2 (1973): 32–35.

[51] See Evelyn Hu-DeHart, Chapter 5, this volume.

[52] See below, p. 49.

ploded across Europe and Asia, as well as Latin America, in this
era.[53] In general, this kind of proposition refers to a global or contex-
tual variable. Long-term changes in economic (or demographic) conditions raise or reduce the probability of rural social and political
conflict.[54]

A second kind of model links short-term economic fluctuations to
rural conflict. Historians have plotted the incidence of rural conflict
against agricultural cycles of good and bad harvests or business
cycles that involve sharp alterations in the prices of major commercial export crops. Emphasis on short-term fluctuations, however,
does not necessarily reduce the importance of long-term trends. For
example, slave revolts and village rebellions may be more numerous
during periods of economic growth and may cluster in upswings of
short-term cycles within the larger trend. This may, in fact, have
been the case for village rebellions in eighteenth-century Mexico (as
Beltrán proposes in Chapter 18)[55] as well as for slave conspiracies
and rebellions in nineteenth-century Puerto Rico, as Baralt has suggested.[56] In Chapter 17, Katz employs a similar combination of
short- and long-term economic variables to compare the 1810 and
1910 revolutions in Mexico, both of which followed two or three
years of prolonged drought and an agricultural credit squeeze at the
end of a period of relative prosperity.[57]

The links between economic trends and public policy appear es-

[53] William McNeill, *The Great Frontier: Freedom and Hierarchy in Modern Times*
(Princeton: Princeton University Press, 1983), pp. 31–39. In Mexico, however, recent
research indicates that population growth slowed down after 1750. See Cecilia Rabel,
"La población novohispana a la luz de los regístros parroquiales: avances y perspec-
tivas de investigación" (unpublished paper, 1984).

[54] Migdal telescopes this kind of argument when he writes, "The relationship between the spread of capitalism from northwestern Europe to the far reaches of the
globe and the occurrence of peasant rebellion may be understood in the context of a
sudden and severe weakening of the social organizations that had exercised social
control among peasants," in Joel S. Migdal, "Capitalist Penetration in the Nineteenth
Century: Creating Conditions for New Patterns of Social Control," in *Power and Protest*, ed. Weller and Guggenheim, p. 58. For a more deterministic model of agrarian
revolt, see Gölte, *Rebelión y repartos*, cited above; for a critique of Golte's argument,
see Stern, "The Age of Andean Insurrection," and O'Phelan, *Rebellions and Revolts*,
chaps. 2–3.

[55] See Beltrán, Chapter 18, this volume.

[56] Baralt, *Esclavos rebeldes*, pp. 81–83.

[57] See Katz, Chapter 17, this volume. This model parallels earlier work that emphasized the psychological (or psychiatric) conditions for rebellious behavior. See, for
example, James C. Davies, "The J-Curve of Rising and Declining Satisfactions as a
Cause of Some Great Revolutions and a Contained Rebellion," in *Violence in America*, ed. T. R. Gurr and H. D. Graham (New York: Signet, 1969), pp. 671–709.

pecially important in comparing village uprisings in the Andes and Mesoamerica. The rapid increase in the number of such movements beginning in the 1760s in both areas coincided with the era of the Bourbon reforms when the Spanish state tightened administration of the colonies in order to make them more profitable to the crown. While precise estimates are not available for Peru, qualitative evidence suggests that Peru was the poorer of the two regions.[58] The surplus available to be extracted for the royal treasury was smaller and the pressures to increase exactions were thus felt more intensely. In Peru, nearly all of the village uprisings of the 1760s and 1770s were provoked by the predatory behavior of *corregidores* who collected the tribute, enforced new crown monopolies, and imposed the *repartimiento de mercancías*.[59] These same officials were responsible for recruiting forced labor for the *mita* where it continued to be practiced. In Mexico, by contrast, most of the revolts studied by Taylor arose from purely local grievances. Protests against new taxes, or abuses by tax collectors, were important in nearly half of the Mexican village uprisings, but other provocations played a more significant role than in Peru.[60] In addition, royal officials in Mexico could afford to be flexible in handling village uprisings because the treasury depended less on taxes extracted from the indigenous population (and more on mining and trade taxes) than in Peru.[61] In the Andes, local rebellions were uniformly repressed in those cases where information is available, and no changes in the system or its personnel were made until after the Tupac Amaru revolt.

During the nineteenth century, conflicts over land played a larger

[58] For estimates of Mexican GDP in the early nineteenth century, see John H. Coatsworth, "Obstacles to Economic Growth in Nineteenth Century Mexico," *American Historical Review* 83 no. 1 (1978): 80–100. The Viceroyalty of Peru produced less silver and gold in this period and the tax revenues of the colonial state were substantially smaller than those in Mexico. See John Fisher, *Government and Society in Colonial Peru: The Intendent System, 1784–1814* (London: Athlone, 1970); Herbert Klein and John J. TePaske, *The Royal Treasuries of the Spanish Empire in America*, vol. 2, *Peru* and vol. 2, *Upper Peru (Bolivia)* (Durham: Duke University Press, 1982). For a discussion, see Hans Jürgen Puhle and Nils Jacobsen, eds., "Introduction," in *The Economies of Mexico and Peru During the Late Colonial Period, 1760–1810* (Berlin: Colloquium Verlag, 1986): 1–25.

[59] See Golte, *Rebelión y repartos*; O'Phelan, "Tupac Amaru," and "El norte y los movimientos anti-fiscales."

[60] Taylor, *Drinking, Homicide and Rebellion*, pp. 134–43.

[61] On the Viceroyalty of Peru, see the fiscal data reported in Klein and TePaske, *The Royal Treasuries*, vols. 1 and 2. On Mexico, see John J. TePaske et al., *La real hacienda de Nueva España: La real caja de México* (Mexico: Instituto Nacional de Antropología e Historia, 1976).

role in rural conflicts in nonslave regions than in the colonial period, although taxation continued as an important cause of revolt in
both Mexico and the Andes. Of the 102 village uprisings in Mexico
after 1819, information on the precipitating causes is available in 54
cases. Complaints about taxation were important in only eight cases,
while disputes over land (protests against usurpations, violent land
seizures, and the like) were important in 40 cases.[62] In contrast, Taylor reported that land disputes precipitated only 30 of the 142 rebellions he catalogued for the eighteenth century. Disputes over the
collection of taxes and ecclesiastical fees and abusive official behavior accounted for the overwhelming majority of the riots and uprisings in central Mexico and Oaxaca in the colonial era.[63] Curiously,
the Mexican data do not clearly indicate the timing of the transition
from tax-based to land disputes, but in the Andes, Gonzales and
others have suggested that a clear demarkation can be found near
the turn of the twentieth century.[64] In Mexico, the change appears
to have been associated with independence, almost a century earlier. Land-based conflicts predominated in Mexico from the 1820s
and in every decade thereafter, predating the liberal land legislation
of the Juárez era. Although a number of states adopted legislation to
eliminate village and other corporate property rights, neither large-
nor small-scale revolts involved protests against these measures until the late 1860s and 1870s. Similar legislation in Peru and Bolivia
toward the end of the century may have been more closely linked to
both large- and small-scale uprisings in the 1880s and 1890s, but
most of these appear to have been precipitated by the imposition of
new taxes rather than by land problems until after the turn of the
century. In Mexico, the expropriation of village lands became extensive by the 1870s and continued throughout the Porfirian era. In
Peru and Bolivia, however, the process appears not to have begun
until late in the century and did not provoke widespread revolts until the twentieth century.[65]

[62] See Reina, *Las rebeliones.*

[63] Taylor, *Drinking, Homicide and Rebellion,* pp. 134–38.

[64] Gonzales, "Neocolonialism and Indian Unrest," p. 3; see also Karen Spalding,
"Class Structures in the Southern Peruvian Andes," in *Land and Power in Latin
America,* ed. Benjamin Orlove and Glynn Custred (New York: Holmes & Meier, 1981):
71–91, and Nils Jacobson, "Desarrollo económico y relaciones de clase en el sur andino (1780–1920): una replica a Karen Spalding," *Análisis* (1978): 18.

[65] On the expansion of the haciendas in late nineteenth-century Peru, see Alberto
Flores Galindo, *Arequipa y el sur andino: ensayo de historia regional (siglos XVIII–
XIX)* (Lima: Editorial Horizonte, 1977), chap. 2. See also Mallon, *Defense of Commu-*

Social determinants of rural conflict are also cited extensively in the literature. Rural rebellions took their shape from the social relations they disrupted, but some relationships were more unstable than others. This commonplace observation can be illustrated by comparing the hacienda with its slave-worked counterparts in Brazil and the Caribbean. As a general rule, haciendas seldom suffered from revolts by resident labor, while slave plantations often did. Even the comparison of debt peonage (relatively rare by the eighteenth century) with slavery does not alter the result. Individual debt peons fled, as did slaves. *Petit maronnage*, to use the slave term, is found in both instances. But peons rarely rebelled against their patrones as did slaves.

Irreducible differences in social relations obviously account for this contrast. Where rural labor was enslaved, revolt was endemic. Where laborers retained their freedom, no matter how circumscribed by social hierarchy, juridical distinctions of status, or economic necessity, patron–client relations (and mobility) worked to assuage tensions. Class rule in nonslave areas rested on the bedrock of an inherently stable social microcosm; in slave regions, rural order was never so secure. The internal strife of the slave plantations persisted even after emancipation; in Cuba, for example, freed slaves and plantation workers burned canefields and assaulted the *centrales* in diverse conflicts that lasted well into the twentieth century.[66] A similar contrast marks relations between the large estates and the free villages. Village rebellions and large-scale caste warfare had little impact on hacienda peons. More often than not, the hacendado could depend for protection (and local bullying) on his client-employees. In contrast, raiding by maroon villagers often sparked slave revolts. Indian villages did not constitute a threat to the social organization of the estates; maroon villages did.[67]

This contrast may be extended to a consideration of the small producers linked to the large estates, although the evidence on this point is not as good. In slave societies, free tenants, sharecroppers, and smallholders frequently "depended" in various ways on the large slave estates; in turn, they served in militias or private armies

---

nity, chaps. 2–4, on the central highlands, where a trend toward concentration of landholding in the 1860s and 1870s was aborted by the War of the Pacific.

[66] See Rebecca Scott, *Slave Emancipation in Cuba: The Transition to Free Labor, 1860–1899* (Princeton: Princeton University Press, 1985), Chap. 12, Lauren Derby, "Peasants, Politics and Plantations: A Revisionist Interpretation of Popular Resistance in Cuba, 1887–1917" (unpublished MA Thesis, University of Chicago, 1986).

[67] See maroon and village sources cited in notes 8, 9, 19, and 20.

that policed slaves, captured runaways, and defended against maroon attacks. In contrast, this stratum in nonslave regions constituted a less reliable ally of the estate owner and was more prone to
assert distinct aspirations, even if unlikely to become involved in
Indian village uprisings or caste war. This stratum may also have
been more prone to banditry and to involvement as foot soldiers and
supporters of regional caudillos (who were often, but not necessarily, their landlords or patrons).[68]

The influence of ethnic and cultural solidarity in these settings
also provides evidence for contrast, rather than parallel. This factor
is often linked to slave rebellions as well as Indian revolts. Public
authorities and great landowners in Latin America were almost always ethnically, culturally, and linguistically foreign to most rural
peoples. The extraordinary cohesiveness required for violent action
rested on mutual perceptions of these differences between ruler (or
owner) and the ruled. In slave regions the cultural unity of the subordinate population was often based, where it appeared, on a common, recent experience in Africa. The standard against which rulers
were judged and courage ignited was the experience of freedom in a
different society. The only parallel to this in nonslave areas was the
collective memory of mission Indians, sometimes reminded of their
past by confreres who had refused to settle down. The analog to the
African image of freedom in nonslave regions was the universal
peasant vision of a society free of the predations of outsiders. Both
visions proved difficult to realize in practice. Maroon communities
organized by escaped slaves were forced to adapt to an environment
different from Africa, a demographic imbalance that could not be
altered in the short run, and a need for strict military organization
to ward off (or carry out) attacks.[69] In the case of the Mesoamerican
and Andean Indians, cultural solidarity was enhanced by adapting
Christian religious symbols to new needs, or, as in the case of Peru,
by taking up the symbols of an idealized pre-Hispanic past. African
slaves did not usually need to innovate in this way. Solidarity and
subordination were not so inextricably mixed for them. For large-
scale revolts that could unite disparate (often feuding) Indian villages, syncretic or purified religious sanction was indispensable.
The potential for slave revolt could be raised merely by importing
larger numbers from the same region in Africa. Indian revolts were

[68] See Reina, Chapter 9, this volume.
[69] See Richard Price, "Introduction" to *Maroon Societies*, pp. 5–19.

inspired through a more complex transformation of beliefs and institutions that normally functioned to buttress order and stability.[70]

Recent work on rural movements has followed historiographical trends in European history by emphasizing the political determinants of rebellion in the countryside. In the formative period of slave colonies, for example, the weakness of administrative and military controls favored slave and maroon revolt. The rapid early development of slave plantations in the sugar colonies of the English, French, Dutch, and Danish empires exceeded the capacity of those states to provide police and protection in the late seventeenth and early eighteenth centuries. The ineffectiveness of campaigns against the maroons in Jamaica and elsewhere in the Caribbean in the early eighteenth century is a measure of this weakness. Early sugar plantations also displaced small farmers who provided the manpower for official and unofficial militias; in Brazil and the Spanish islands, slavery developed more gradually and without such displacement. The cohesiveness of the slave-owning class in these islands was substantially lower in this early stage of development, and the problem was exacerbated by widespread absenteeism, especially in the British islands. In the older colonies of Portugal and Spain, slave rebellions in the eighteenth century were rare.

In the era before the Bourbon reforms began in the 1760s, public administration in the Spanish mainland colonies was also relatively weak. Why did the Indians of the Andes and Mesoamerica fail to seize the opportunity afforded them in this period? The answer to this question has at least two parts. The first is that some Indians did. The revolts on the periphery of Spanish control in Peru and of Mexico in the first half of the 1700s may have been related to the ineffectiveness of administration and police and the incapacity of the state to maintain the relative isolation of the Indian republics from the private greed of creole interests. The second part of the answer relates to the relative calm of the core areas of Mesoamerica and the Andes. The weakness of the state in this period did not pro-

---

[70] This is not to diminish the role of religious ideology in slave revolts (Islam, for example, in the mainly urban revolts of Bahia in the nineteenth century). Nor do we intend the statement to suggest that slaves were less creative adapters and synthesizers of the diverse cultural traditions they brought with them and encountered in the New World. The point is that slavery often provoked revolts in which such innovations were absent or of minor significance. Indian caste wars, however, required an ideological expression that explained and justified the new world to be created. Slave insurrections, as Genovese has argued, fashioned their goals out of the desire for escape or (later) equality. See Genovese, *From Rebellion to Revolution*, pp. xviii–xx.

duce visible instability at the top. There were no major conflicts, certainly no violent clashes, among European and creole colonists or between them and Spanish authorities. Rather, the weakness of public adminstration was reflected in the delegation of public functions to corporate entities, and this worked to appease Indian discontents. Villages were corporate entities and the crown allowed them wide latitude for self-government. Moreover, the Spanish judiciary, despite its penetration by creole notables, maintained in most areas sufficient independence from local elites to encourage Indian communities to pursue their disputes over land with private or competing corporate interests through the courts.

In the second half of the eighteenth century this contrary dynamic worked in reverse. Centralization curbed slave revolts in the Caribbean while it provoked rebellion in the nonslave areas of the mainland. In the slave regions, maroon raids appear to have diminished along with slave revolts. Both were discouraged by more effective police and administration, except for the weakly governed Dutch colonies of Guiana and Surinam. The French and English islands were able to settle down until the French Revolution subverted effective government in Haiti, and the international warfare that began in 1796 undermined the stable regimes of the British islands. On the mainland, the Bourbon reforms had an opposite effect. Instead of stabilizing social conditions, they diminished stability by undermining corporate privileges and exemptions. Slaves paid no taxes as long as they were slaves; protests against the costs of centralization were left to the slave-owners. On the mainland, however, rising taxes together with administrative reforms that undermined the autonomy of indigenous villages sparked revolts from the southern Andes to northern Mexico. Even the sympathy of the Spanish judiciary seems to have waned; as early as the 1730s, as the Hernández data show for Morelos, in Mexico, legal decisions in land disputes between villages and haciendas began to shift markedly against the villages.[71]

The political determinants of rural revolt were modified by independence. Most slave areas (except Haiti and Brazil) remained colonies of the European powers. Slave and maroon conflicts continued, despite repression and the end of international war, but large-scale insurrections ended in the 1830s. In the nonslave regions, independence did not lead immediately to renewed rural rebellion. In

[71] Alicia Hernández Olive, "Haciendas y pueblos en el estado de Morelos, 1535–1810" (unpublished MA thesis, El Colegio de México, 1973).

the Andes, the disruptions of the independence wars were accompanied by a partial reversion to the conditions that made for relative peace before the Bourbon reforms. Weak governments were inefficient tax collectors. Economic depression removed the incentive to usurpation of village lands. The repartimiento de mercancías had been abolished in the wake of the Tupac Amaru revolt, while the *mita* had all but disappeared by independence as well. Independence regimes, despite their conservative and centralizing tendencies, avoided policies that might have unleashed old animosities. Village autonomy survived and may even have increased after independence. In Mexico, similar conditions prevailed, but unlike the Andes the social peace of the countryside proved short-lived. Large-scale rural revolts, frequently allied to warring factions of the elite, erupted over wide areas of the central plateau in the 1840s and 1850s. In Peru and Bolivia, political instability did not lead to rural rebellion on a large scale until the last two decades of the nineteenth century.

In both regions, despite differences in timing, the character of rural rebellion changed in important and similar ways. Beginning in Mexico in the 1840s, and in the Andes by the end of the century, rural revolts now usually involved direct assaults on the haciendas as well as civil authority. Weak governments exerted less fiscal pressure on rural communities but were equally unable to repress rebellious villagers when they turned from protests against taxes and official abuse to seizing (or retaking) lands from the haciendas. In Mexico, many of the revolts of this era were aggressive, rather than defensive. Bourbon village rebellions responded to intrusions; post-independence revolts were more likely to involve land seizures carefully calculated to catch hacendados and the authorities unprepared to expel the invaders. Even in revolts precipitated by defensive reaction to intrusions, the villages often reacted with offensives that went far beyond redressing the initial grievance. The weakness and fragmentation of political authority and the diversion of military resources to civil war and international conflicts facilitated the spread of rural revolt. Village rebellions in the nineteenth century often provoked or merged with larger regional movements. Contagion was facilitated by elite political conflicts. Post-independence rural revolts often involved alliances of convenience with non-Indian social and political interests, including mestizo townspeople, local caudillos, the Church, invading or defending armies. In Mexico, these rebellions apparently diminished during the Porfiriato, only to revive after 1910. In the rest of Latin America, similar patterns are visible, although the timing varied from place to place. The village uprisings that brought General Rafael Carrera to the presidency of Guatemala in 1837 and saved the Liberal party led by General José Manuel "Tata" Pando in Bolivia in 1899 are two outstanding examples.[72]

Throughout the Americas, the most consistently destabilizing phenomenon of all was international war.[73] Fighting among the European powers and, later, between the independent nations of the New World, played a significant role in provoking or providing opportunity for large-scale rural rebellions in both slave and nonslave regions. This was true for the slave islands of the Caribbean throughout the eighteenth century, but particularly in the 1790s. After independence, the cluster of major regional and village revolts in Mexico from the 1840s to the 1860s followed closely on the loss of Texas in the late 1830s, the war with the United States from 1846 to 1848, and the French occupation from 1862 to 1867. In Chapter 9, Reina describes one notable example of this.[74] In the Andes, the War of the Pacific, which lasted from 1879 to 1883, gave rise to widespread guerrilla warfare and regional revolts.[75] In some cases, rural revolts grew out of efforts to resist foreign invaders. In others, revolts were inspired indirectly as a result of intensified internal political conflicts that followed national humiliations.

The ideological and programmatic content of rural rebellions, about which much less is known, appears to have undergone at least two major transformations in these two centuries. Genovese has argued that the Haitian revolution crystallized slave discontents throughout the New World. "Henceforth," he argued, "slaves increasingly aimed not at secession from the dominant society but at joining it on equal terms."[76] Genovese describes this stance as "bourgeois democratic" in contrast to the "restorationist course" of earlier slave revolts in which rebels sought mainly to withdraw into

---

[72] See note 16.

[73] As Skocpol recently observed, "defeats in wars and international military interventions are the most likely ways for existing state power to be disrupted—opening the way either for autonomous peasant revolts, or for appeals by organized revolutionaries to peasant support in the countryside." In "What Makes Peasants Revolutionary?" in Power and Protest, ed. Weller and Guggenheim, p. 172.

[74] See Reina, Chapter 9, this volume.

[75] Blanchard, "Indian Unrest in the Peruvian Sierra," and Florencia Mallon, "Nationalist and Anti-State Coalitions in the War of the Pacific: Junín and Cajamarca, 1879–1900" (paper presented to SSRC conference on "Resistance and Rebellion," University of Wisconsin, April, 1984).

[76] Genovese, From Rebellion to Revolution, pp. xviii–xx.

maroon communities based on particularistic visions of social order brought with them from Africa. In the nonslave regions of the new world an equally fundamental transformation occurred in the nineteenth century. Beginning in Mexico in the 1840s, and later in the century in the Andes, indigenous villagers asserted claims not unlike those of Genovese's "bourgeois" slaves. But while slaves struggled to secure freedom from bondage, rural people in Mexico and the Andes fought for objectives that historians have not been able to identify as unambiguously modern. Nineteenth-century rural revolts in these areas involved claims to community lands and the collective self-government and autonomy of the colonial Indian village. Indians became peasants by asserting an image of the past.[77]

Conclusions: Mexico in Comparative Perspective

The history of rural rebellion in Mexico offers both striking similarities and significant contrasts to its counterparts in other regions of Latin America. While the unevenness of research across time periods and spatial boundaries is too great to remove many ambiguities in the data, it appears that Mexico's rural people asserted their rights and defended their interests with unparalleled combativeness in the two centuries from 1700 to 1900. No other region in the Americas presents the historian with so rich and diverse a historiography of rural struggle. The Mexican countryside probably witnessed more rebellions, large and small, in these two centuries than any other area in the Western hemisphere, slave or nonslave.[78]

In the colonial period, Mexico shared with other densely populated mainland colonies a large number of relatively small-scale village riots and uprisings. As in other areas, the number of these events increased after 1760. This common trend suggests that conditions common to all of the Spanish mainland colonies acted to heighten discontent and, specifically, to put increased pressure on the indigenous communities of Mesoamerica and the Andes. Economic and demographic trends affecting all of Spanish America

[77] As Womack put it, describing the rural folk of the Zapatista movement, they were "country people who did not want to move and therefore got into a Revolution." John Womack, Jr., *Zapata and the Mexican Revolution* (New York: Knopf, 1969), p. ix.

[78] This assertion is based, however, on the data presented in the tables above, where caution is advised because research lacunae may cause underrepresentation of some areas and time periods. Most noticeable is the lack of research on Andean village rebellions between the 1790s and the 1880s, on plantation revolts in Brazil and the Caribbean in most periods, and on small-scale rural movements during the Porfiriato in Mexico.

may have played a role. The centralization and fiscal zeal of the
Bourbon reformers clearly heightened tensions by weakening the
corporate autonomy of the villages, dispatching a larger number of
more intrusive officials, and intensifying fiscal extortions. In the Andes, however, the relative poverty of the region may have made it
more difficult for villagers to survive these pressures, while the dependence of the viceroyalty's treasury on tribute, income from the
repartimientos, and other taxes laid directly on the indigenous population simultaneously excluded the flexibility displayed by colonial officials in New Spain. Resistance was also promoted by the
relative linguistic and cultural unity of the indigenous population
and the survival of Indian kurakas, a stratum of indigenous leaders
that had all but disappeared in Mexico. Village protests were more
numerous in colonial Mexico than elsewhere, but they did not ag-
gregate into large-scale revolt or insurrection under indigenous leadership. While the Andes exploded in 1780 under Tupac Amaru and
his allies, Mexico remained relatively calm until the creole-led Hidalgo movement in 1810.

Unlike Tupac Amaru, the Hidalgo movement represented a sharp
break with the past in that Hidalgo demanded independence. The
Hidalgo revolt was the first great upheaval to hit the core area of
Mexico, in contrast to Tupac Amaru, for which there were several,
though smaller, precedents. More importantly, the Hidalgo movement demonstrated that creole leadership could link elite political
conflict to the resentments of the mass of the indigenous population
and thus overcome, through politics, the linguistic and cultural diversity that made large-scale mobilization in central Mexico otherwise impossible. Although three decades elapsed before the Texas
war and the U.S. invasion created conditions for new political mobilizations, the foundations had been laid. Mexico's Indian villagers
began to transform themselves into *campesinos* at the outset of their
nation's independent life. The very diversity that made widespread
rural revolt impossible in the colonial period facilitated the politicization of rural Mexico when the colonial state collapsed, because
politics represented the only viable means for aggregating rural community and class interests. From village revolts against abuses of
public authority, Mexico's rural rebels shifted to assaults on the
property rights of the new nation's economic elite. From spontaneous riots against intruders, Mexico's villagers leaped into calculated, large-scale rebellions that exploited the political and ideological fragmentation of the nation's rulers.[79]

[79] It is also worth noting that the proportion of mestizos and of Spanish-speaking

In the Andes, by contrast, the first steps in this direction were not made until the end of the century. The Tupac Amaru experience did not provide a guide to the insertion of rural discontent into the political conflicts that beset independent Peru and Bolivia, though Hispanized kurakas briefly played a significant role in mobilizing guerrilla units in support of the independence movement in Peru. As in Mexico, rural discontent seems to have diminished in the first years of independence. In Mexico, however, the lessons of Hidalgo were reinforced by mobilization for international wars, and for the intensified civil warfare they inspired. In the Andes, the process of trial and error by which indigenous communities learned to insert themselves into political strife took nearly a century after the repression that followed Tupac Amaru. International war did not crystallize this process until the 1880s.

Conflicts over land, which were common in Mexico by the 1840s, did not provoke revolt in the Andes until late in the century. At this point, on the eve of the Mexican Revolution, rural rebellion in the two regions developed new similarities. In Mexico, the economic growth that began in the restored republic (1867–76) and the repression of rural rebellions that became increasingly effective after the Porfirian coup, combined to provide both the incentives and the means to expropriate the lands of the free villages during the last two decades of the century. In Peru and Bolivia, too, this trend became widespread in some regions (often those first linked by rail to new markets, as in Mexico in the 1870s and 1880s) at the end of the nineteenth century and the first decade of the twentieth.[80] In Mexico, however, the political crisis of 1910–11 unleashed a whirlwind, for which a century of struggle had already prepared large numbers of rural people in central Mexico. Movements of comparable magnitude (though of smaller long-term political impact) did not take place until the 1950s in Bolivia and the 1960s in Peru.

Little has been written to acknowledge the effects of rural revolt on the transition to modern capitalist societies in nineteenth-century Latin America, nor has attention been focused on the relationship between rural social movements and the development of modern political systems. In the slave regions, historians debate whether

---

Indians in Mexico was higher than in Peru throughout this period. This, too, may help to explain the precocious politicization of rural conflict in Mexico.

[80] See Coatsworth, "Railroads, Landholding and Agrarian Protest"; Flores Galindo, *Arequipa y el sur andino*. See also Rory Miller, "Railways and Economic Development in Central Peru, 1890–1930," in *Social and Economic Change in Modern Peru*, ed. Rory Miller, Clifford T. Smith, and John Fisher (Liverpool: Centre for Latin American Studies, University of Liverpool, Monograph Series No. 6, n.d.), 27–52.

slave resistance played a more or less important role in hastening emancipation, but except for Cuba—where slaves participated in independence struggles and former slaves resisted the extension of plantation agriculture into Oriente province after the North American occupation—political histories are generally written without reference to rural conflict or rebellion.[81] One recent article that seeks to correct this deficiency in Peruvian historiography concludes by reaffirming it.[82] Mallon's recent work on peasant "nationalism" during the Chilean occupation of Peru in the 1880s, on the other hand, may inspire new efforts to explore the role of the country's indigenous majority in shaping the evolution of modern political institutions and ideologies.[83]

In Mexico, little attention has been paid to the decisive role of rural revolt in preventing the consolidation of conservative regimes in the independence era. Conservative attempts to impose centralist regimes and restore elements of colonial fiscal, regulatory, and paternalistic rule failed at least in part because rural rebellion impeded the consolidation of a strong central state. Mexico's liberal regimes also faced rural revolts. State governments, to whom political power and taxing authority devolved under liberal administrations, also failed to impose stability on the countryside. Rural unrest favored the liberal cause over the long term,[84] however, and rural support in the war against the French may have played a key role in turning the tide against Maximillian. In the Andes, where the countryside was relatively quiet, conservative regimes had an easier time of it. In both Peru and Bolivia, the equality of citizens proclaimed by Bolivar gave way to a return to the colonial system based on separate "republics" after independence.

In contrast to the historiography of other world regions, where landlord and peasant have *both* been assigned a crucial role in the development of modern political systems,[85] the Latin American lit-

---

[81] See Corwin, *Spain and the Abolition of Slavery*, chaps. 12–16; Louis A. Perez, Jr., " 'La Chambelona': Political Protest, Sugar, and Social Banditry in Cuba," *Inter-American Economic Affairs* 31 (1978): 3–28.

[82] Jean Piel, "The Place of the Peasantry in the National Life of Peru in the Nineteenth Century," *Past and Present* 46 (1970): 108–33.

[83] Mallon, "Nationalist and Anti-State Coalitions."

[84] This is because conservative programs for centralization of political authority and the restoration of an active, interventionist state depended more critically on social and political stability. Liberal schemes stressed the need to remove institutional obstacles to economic activity, an objective that could be served (if only in part) by the turbulence that prevented effective central government.

[85] See, for example, Barrington Moore, *Social Origins of Dictatorship and Democ-*

erature usually refers to landed elites and oligarchies as though their interests alone and unchallenged determined both the structure and the policies of modernizing regimes in the nineteenth century.[86] Nor have political scientists in their debates on the origins of contemporary authoritarianism yet managed to incorporate the historical confrontations of rural society among the conditions that foreclosed the development of democratic regimes in the region. The defeat of rural movements on the eve of Porfirian modernization, and their reemergence, again to be defeated, in the Mexican Revolution of 1910; the orderly, if not entirely peaceful emancipation of slaves in Brazil that ended the empire but left intact a reactionary alliance of landlords and commercial classes (both domestic and foreign); the successful repression of rural rebellions in the Andes in the early twentieth century—all contributed, in conditions of external dependence, to the vitality of authoritarian solutions to the problems of capitalist modernization.

Even here, however, Mexico's experience was somewhat different. Mexico's estates never did suffer from internal rebellion, as did slave plantations elsewhere, but the aggressiveness of village rebels and their ability to insert themselves into political conflicts threatened the haciendas from without as they had never been threatened during the colonial era. In the 1840s and 1850s, rural rebellions helped to push the estate system in many areas of Mexico to the point of collapse and disintegration.[87] The political consequences of this process were considerable. By weakening the estates, Mexico's rural rebels undermined the power of the country's fragmented landlord elite to the point where a more democratic evolution of the nation's political institutions became a real possibility. Indeed, Cosío Villegas, citing other causes, has argued that the restored republic of the late 1860s and 1870s represented the realization (if only short-lived) of just such an historic option.[88] While the Porfirian alliance of foreign capital and a restored landowning and commercial

---

racy: Lord and Peasant in the Making of the Modern World (Boston: Beacon Press, 1966).

[86] For an exception to this rule, see Leopoldo Allub, Orígenes del autoritarismo en América Latina (Mexico: Editorial Katún, 1983).

[87] See Brading,"La estructura," 197–237; Jan Bazant, "The Division of Some Mexican Haciendas During the Liberal Revolution, 1856–1862," Journal of Latin American Studies 3 no. 1 (1971): 25–37.

[88] Daniel Cosío Villegas, Historia moderna de México, la república restaurada, la vida política (Mexico: Editorial Hermes, 1955). See also Charles A. Hale, "The Liberal Impulse: Daniel Cosío Villegas and the Historia moderna de México," Hispanic American Historical Review 54 no. 3 (1974): 479–98.

bourgeoisie closed this route to the modern world, the Mexican Revolution opened new possibilities. Semo has contrasted Mexico's "revolutionary" transition to capitalism, with its violent upheavals in 1810, the 1850s to 1860s, and 1911–17, to the experience of other Latin American countries, suggesting that the mobilization of peasant participation in these conflicts had long-lasting effects on social, economic, and political development. Rural rebellion ultimately destroyed the country's landed oligarchy, opened the way to the agrarian reforms of the 1930s, and thus promoted industrial development at a more rapid pace than in other Latin American countries, where rural elites resisted policies that favored industry.[89] We may conclude, in any case, that the significance of rural rebellion in Mexican history (and in the historical evolution of other regions in Latin America), remains underestimated, though less so now than at any time in the past.

[89] Enrique Semo, "Las revoluciones en la historia de México," *Historia y Sociedad* 8 (1975): 49–61.

PART II

Pax Hispanica?

Rural Uprisings in Preconquest and Colonial Mexico

Friedrich Katz

Mexico's rural population has played a unique role in the history of Latin America. Mexico is the only country on the American continent where every major social transformation has been linked to rural upheavals. Some archaeologists believe that the falls of the great classic civilizations of Mesoamerica—those of the Mayan, Teotihuacan, and the Toltec empires—were closely linked to (although not exclusively caused by) rural uprisings.[1] No similar hypothesis has been formulated to explain the fall of societies in the Andean region, that other great cradle of Latin American civilization. Mexico's uniqueness was also apparent during the Spanish conquest; only in Mexico were the Spaniards able to precipitate and ride the crest of a social revolution in which the rural population rose up against the Aztecs, the rulers of much of what today constitutes Mexico. No similar large-scale revolts helped the Spaniards in their conquest of the Inca empire or of the Chibcha state of Colombia.

Between 1810 and 1820, in a series of major independence wars in which the Latin American countries gained their independence from Spain, Mexico again was the only country where these movements were linked to rural social upheavals. In 1910, Mexico was the first Latin American country to stage a major rural revolution.

What explains the unique role of peasants in Mexican history? Was this uniqueness limited to major turning points in Mexico's evolution or did it extend to the periods in between? Did the apparent

[1] See Enrique Nalda, "Mexico prehispánico: Orígen y formación de las clases sociales," in Mexico: Un pueblo en la historia, ed. Enrique Semo (Mexico, 1981), pp. 108–109, and J. Eric Thompson, The Rise and Fall of Maya Civilization (Norman, Okl., 1956), pp. 105–106.

stability of some periods of the pre-Columbian era, the years of Spanish rule, and the late nineteenth century, conceal a deeper continuity in which unknown or small-scale revolts, peasant uprisings, and continual struggles in rural areas continued to set Mexico apart from the rest of the continent? What were the consequences for the peasants who participated in these small-scale revolts and in major social revolutions?

There are two ways to answer these questions. One is what I would call the external way—a comparison of rural uprisings in Mexico with those that occurred in the rest of Latin America—as exemplified by John Coatsworth in Chapter 2, but here I concentrate on what could be called the internal way: a comparison of rural revolts within Mexico over time and space. This chapter deals primarily with the pre-Columbian and colonial periods. The salient features of later revolts that began with the struggle for independence are detailed first in order to provide a basis for comparison, but the focus here is on the period prior to 1810. In Chapter 17 I describe the period after 1810, and make some general conclusions about patterns of rural uprisings throughout Mexican history, even though with our current level of knowledge such a comparative approach can at best only provide hypotheses for further research.

In this essay I use the term "rural" instead of "peasant" revolt because rural is broader in scope and encompasses not only uprisings by village inhabitants but also those by hacienda peons as well as migratory workers and semi-rural, semi-industrial laborers. A clear definition of the term "rural revolt" presents a series of difficulties that are least pronounced for most of the colonial and Porfirian periods, when the state of Mexico was strong. With the exception of a few leaders who came from outside rural society such as urban intellectuals or priests, revolts in these two periods tended to be limited to the lower classes of rural society; the social, economic, political, and religious demands they formulated were clearly those of the lower classes. It is much more difficult to define rural uprisings for the period of Aztec rule and for most of the nineteenth century. During these times, when the central state was far weaker and less consolidated, regional chieftains, warlords, caudillos, and caciques—most of them wealthy landowners—revolted against the central government and frequently tended to make alliances with peasants and with peons on their estates. To what degree can these movements be termed rural uprisings?

The problem is even more complex with regard to the two great national revolutions that shook Mexico in 1810–20 and in 1910–20.

Large numbers of rural inhabitants of every kind joined revolutionary armies, often led by nonpeasants. To what degree, and under what circumstances, can these armies be labeled peasant armies, and when did they become something else? At what time did these peasants become professional soldiers or mercenaries? While there is no final answer to these questions, they cannot be ignored. I therefore include in this analysis every movement in which clearly identifiable organizations or entities representing the lower classes in Mexico's countryside participated: village communities, tribal organizations, and political organizations composed of and representing rural inhabitants. A second criterion was that the demands of the rebels had to have some bearing on the social, economic, political, or religious demands of the rural population. Such a definition can at times be misleading, but, I find it far more revealing than one that excludes movements in which peasants were aligned with or subordinated to other segments of society.

Historians dealing with pre-Columbian and colonial rural uprisings face two further problems. First, while numerous and well-preserved records exist for the colonial period, the same cannot be said for pre-Columbian times. Written records embrace at most two centuries before the conquest, were mostly written much later, were limited in scope, and were frequently influenced by Spanish concepts.[2] Earlier periods can only be documented archaeologically. Second, historians dealing with both pre-Columbian and colonial uprisings have to face the enormous ideological, political, and social impact of the 1910 revolution. While this impact has generated some excellent studies of nineteenth- and twentieth-century agrarian revolts, it has also at times led to a backward projection of these types of social movements, which were not necessarily the same as those in earlier periods. However, the main traits of nineteenth- and twentieth-century rural uprisings that have emerged from these studies have become extremely useful yardsticks for comparative study of rural revolutionary movements. The question now is whether the eight traits listed below are characteristic of "modern" Mexico, or whether they are so deeply embedded in Mexico's evolution that they can also be found in the colonial and pre-Columbian periods?

(1) *Frequency.* Between 1810 and 1920 (with the exception of a

---

[2] Fernando de Alva Ixtlilxóchitl, *Obras históricas* (Mexico, 1891–92). Diego Durán, *Historia de las Indias de Nueva España y tierra firme* (Mexico, 1867–80). Fernando Alvarado Tezozomoc, *Crónica Mexicana* (Mexico, 1945).

few years at the height of the Porfirian dictatorship) scarcely a year
passed without a rural uprising of some kind somewhere in Mexico.

(2) *Scope.* Two of these uprisings were national in scale. In contrast to the independence movements in South America headed by
Simon Bolivar and José de San Martin, the Mexican independence
movements in 1810 led and inspired by Miguel Hildalgo and José
María Morelos were major rural uprisings. In the 1910 revolution
peasant participation was probably greater than in any other social
revolution of twentieth-century Latin America, with the possible exceptions of Bolivia in the 1950s and Nicaragua in the 1970s. Even
peasant-based regional revolts such as the Caste War in Yucatán occurred only rarely in other Latin American countries.

(3) *Limited immediate impact on the rural population.* While rural revolts had profound consequences for Mexico's general evolution in the nineteenth and twentieth centuries, their immediate impact on the situation of peasants and other lower-class members of
rural society seems to have been limited in the short run. The armies
of Hidalgo and Morelos in the 1810 revolution, and of Emiliano Zapata and Francisco Villa in the 1910 revolution—all largely composed of peasants voicing strong agrarian demands—were defeated.
At the end of both revolutions the hacienda continued to be the
main form of land tenure in Mexico, and in the nineteenth century
the system was strengthened after independence. The 1910 revolution greatly weakened the hacienda, although this process only became really significant in 1934–40, a quarter century after the revolution began. Mexico's experience differed sharply from major
social revolutions elsewhere in Latin America, and in France, Russia, and Cuba, where the traditional large estates were partly or entirely destroyed within a few years after the outbreak of revolution.

(4) *Focus.* Both national and local revolts in the nineteenth and
early twentieth centuries often tended to question the legitimacy of
the existing social order and were frequently directed not only
against local officials but against the federal government as such.

(5) *Systems of alliances.* Rural revolts frequently overlapped uprisings by regional caciques against the central government, and in
many cases the two combined forces. Generally the caciques began
by assuming leadership, though they were not always able to retain
control of the movement once it became powerful.

(6) *Objectives.* Protests against land expropriations and demands
for land, water, and grazing rights tended to be the main objectives
of rural uprisings in the late nineteenth century and during the 1910

revolution, although protests against taxes and against limitations on local autonomy were also important.

(7) *Links with the frontier.* While the existence of a frontier was a characteristic of most countries on the American continent, Mexico was one of the few countries where a frontier did not contribute to the stabilization of the existing social order, but on the contrary constituted a major center of social revolution.

(8) *Limited influence on hacienda peons.* With some conspicuous exceptions, permanent hacienda residents, frequently referred to as peons, rarely revolted. The exceptions were the 1810 revolution and to a lesser extent the 1910 revolution, in which a significant number (but still a minority) of peons participated. Some peons rose up against their masters and the government, while others were mobilized by their own patrons, who at times armed them and led them into the revolution. It is frequently difficult to label such peons as "revolutionaries." They were primarily armed retainers fighting for their masters rather than men attempting to alter their social or economic situation. In a few exceptional, though significant cases during the 1910 revolution when revolutionary governments opposed the hacendados, it was the governments who encouraged the peons to defy their patrons.

These characteristics of nineteenth- and twentieth-century revolts were closely linked to a rapidly changing social and economic scene. In the early nineteenth century, control of the land had been vested in four groups or institutions: large landowners, the church, the state (which owned vacant public land), and the inhabitants of free villages, i.e., villages that owned communal land and enjoyed some administrative autonomy.

Apart from the hacendados and their administrators, the rural population was divided into three groups. First, the inhabitants of free villages enjoyed varying degrees of wealth and economic independence; some owned sufficient land to sustain themselves, while others were forced to labor part of the year on large estates, in mines, or urban factories. Second, hacienda residents' relations with the hacienda varied enormously; some were wealthy tenants or privileged retainers, while others were debt peons who lived like slaves. Third, a much smaller group of free but landless migrant laborers moved between large estates and jobs in towns and cities according to the season. By the end of the nineteenth century, the church, the state, and the free villages had lost most of their holdings to the large estates, yet the number of resident hacienda workers and of land-

less, seasonal laborers had increased substantially. A large proportion of the rural population still consisted of inhabitants of free villages, but their economic and social situations had changed
dramatically. Most of them had become economically dependent to
an unprecedented degree on neighboring large estates.[3]

In the following I attempt to relate these characteristics of nine-
teenth- and early twentieth-century rural movements and the land
tenure patterns of this period, to earlier periods of Mexican history.

Rural Uprisings in the Pre-Columbian Period

In terms of amounts of internal violence, the late fifteenth and early
sixteenth centuries were most similar to nineteenth-century Mexico
if we consider only the written records available. This was the time
when on the one hand the Aztecs attempted and largely succeeded
in conquering most of central Mexico and when on the other hand
there were constant rebellions by subject peoples and states unwilling to accept Aztec domination. It is not clear from Aztec sources
whether these revolts were mainly power struggles between rival
states and warlords, or whether they were similar to the nineteenth-
century mix of elite conflicts and rural movements with specific demands geared to the interests of the rural population. At first glance,
these revolts do not look like rural movements, but seem to have
been attempts by the traditional upper classes to regain power.

A revolt characteristic of the Aztec period occurred in Yanhuitlán
and Zozola in 1481. These states in the Mixtec region had been conquered by the Aztecs a short time before. When Aztec armies suffered a defeat at the hands of a rival state, Huexotzingo, the rulers of
both Yanhuitlán and Zozola thought that the time had come to
shake off Mexican rule. They were mistaken, and they paid a high
price for their mistake. The Aztecs sent a large punitive expedition
that destroyed Yanhuitlán and brought thousands of prisoners to
Tenochtitlán, where they were sacrificed to Huitzilopochtli, the Aztec war god. The inhabitants of Zozola, on hearing the fate of their
neighbors, preferred to destroy their capital city rather than to await
a similar Aztec reprisal. The people burned Zozola to the ground

[3] Andrés Molina Enrique, *Los grandes problemas nacionales* (Mexico, 1909); Frank
Tannenbaum, *The Mexican Agrarian Revolution* (Hamden, Conn., 1929), chap. 1.
While Tannenbaum's statistics have been the subject of much debate, recent schol-
arship has tended to confirm his view that a process of land consolidation had taken
place, particularly during the Porfirian era. See Alan Knight, *The Mexican Revolution*
(Cambridge, 1986), vol. 1, pp. 78–115.

and fled into the mountains together with the population of the surrounding countryside. The Aztecs were unable to find them and left Zozola without having achieved their aim.[4]

Another equally characteristic revolt took place in southern Mexico. An Aztec chronicle relates how the provinces of Tehuantepec, Xolotla, and others

decided to revolt against merchants from the Valley of Mexico coming to their cities every year to introduce delicacies and other worthless objects for which they received gold, jewels, feathers and other valuable products which they carried away with them. . . . They arrived heavily laden with worthless merchandise such as cheese which they made out of lake mud, foodstuffs which were made of worms, sacks of lake flies which they called aautli, potted ducks, and many other tidbits which the inhabitants of this province did not have. In addition, they also brought toys which they made themselves. In exchange they received cocoa, gold, feathers, and precious stones. When the inhabitants of these provinces became aware of what was happening, they determined to prevent this plundering of their cities for the benefit of the Mexican cities and provinces which only brought in tidbits and worthless objects.

After this resolve had been taken an army was raised, and surprise attacks were undertaken against the Mexicans, and the peoples of the other provinces travelling by these trade routes, in order to kill them.[5]

While there is no doubt that peasants participated to a very large degree in these revolts, Aztec chronicles do not furnish any proof that peasant demands or village communities played an important role in the outbreak of these revolts. The Aztec chronicles do not explain why Yanhuitlán and Zozola revolted. The indignation of the rulers of Tehuantepec at the practices of Aztec merchants does not necessarily reflect either peasant indignation nor peasant interests. Nevertheless, if one examines the social, political, and economic structures that the Aztecs imposed on their subject peoples, and if one considers the complaints that these people formulated as well as some very clear indications of what could be called a peasant class consciousness, the situation begins to look somewhat different.

[4] Fray Juan de Torquemada, *Monarquía Indian a México 1943–44*, vol. 1, p. 208.
[5] Durán, *Historia de las Indias*, vol. 1, p. 368.

In many respects the closest similarity to rural conditions in nine-
teenth- and early twentieth-century Mexico can be found in the late
pre-Hispanic period, in the century of Aztec rule that preceded the
Spanish conquest. Three of the four institutions or social classes
that owned large tracts of the land in the nineteenth-century were
also present in the Aztec period. The fifteenth-century equivalent of
the hacendados were Indian nobles both of the valley of Mexico and
of the peoples subjected by the Aztecs. Many of these nobles owned
large estates, whose products were sold in the huge markets in Tla-
telolco and in other cities. Unlike their successors, however, the Aztec nobles depended to a much greater degree upon the state. Estates
were granted to them not as private property but as land linked to
official bureaucratic positions, so that the loss of these offices also
meant loss of the land associated with them. Neither the position
nor the land was automatically inheritable, although in practice
very few nobles, unless they conspired against the ruler, were ever
demoted, and sons tended to inherit both the titles and the wealth
of their fathers.

Like the church of the nineteenth century, the Indian clergy (both
that of the Aztecs and of their subject peoples) owned vast tracts of
lands. As in later periods, village communities (known as *calpullis*
in central Mexico) also controlled a large share of the land. The one
institution that played a different role in the Aztec period than it
did in the nineteenth century was the state. The Aztec state was far
more powerful and active in economic terms than its successors in
the nineteenth and early twentieth centuries. It owned substantial
amounts of land that were either leased to officials or worked directly for the state. The state also controlled most of the income from
lands taken from subject peoples.[6]

The lower classes of rural society essentially comprised of members of village communities (*calpullis*) and landless serfs (*mayeques*), who worked on private and state-owned estates. In many
respects the mayeques were the equivalent of nineteenth-century
peons. Borah and Cook have estimated that in central Mexico outside Tenochtitlán there were 6,948,000 calpulli members and
3,474,000 mayeques.[7]

During Aztec rule there was a greater shift in ownership and con-

[6] Friedrich Katz, *Las relaciones socio-económicas de los Aztecas en los siglos* xv y
xvi (Mexico, 1966), pp. 28–29.

[7] Woodrow Borah and Sherburne F. Cook, "The Aboriginal Population of Central
Mexico on the Eve of the Spanish Conquest," *Ibero-Americana* 45 (1963): pp. 226–
58.

trol of resources than in preceding periods of history. The Aztecs did not replace the native aristocracy with their own nobility, but rather superimposed Aztec rule upon that of the traditional ruling class. The peasants of the conquered regions thus had to bear a double burden. The Aztecs expropriated large amounts of land and the subject people were forced to till land set aside not only for their own upper class, but for both the Aztec state and the nobility as well. At the same time, a multiplicity of other kinds of taxes and charges were imposed on them. They were forced to supply Aztec armies that passed through their territories with food and other goods and they were obliged to trade with Aztec merchants on conditions and at prices imposed by the latter.

The complaints against Aztec rule voiced by the rulers of conquered states contained very definite peasant demands. These were voiced very clearly by the ruler of the Totonac town of Cempoala when he spoke to Hernán Cortés of Aztec taxes. This ruler, called by the Spaniards the "fat cacique" (they could not pronounce his name), told the Spaniards (according to the conquistador Bernal Díaz del Castillo)

> that every year many of their sons and daughters were demanded of them for sacrifice, and others for service in the houses and plantations of their conquerors; and they made other complaints which were so numerous that I do not remember them all; but they said a multitude of tax gatherers carried off their wives and daughters if they were handsome and ravished them, and this they did throughout the land where the Totonac language was spoken, which contained over 30 towns.[8]

Not only were the conquered states voicing peasant demands, but the social organization of many of the states dominated by the Aztecs were such that the lower classes still had a strong input into policy making. According to one of the most reliable and best known Spanish chroniclers, Alonso de Zurita, who described the social organization of the Matlatzinca, a state subject to the Aztecs, the kings "treated their subjects and vassals so well that everyone wanted to be better than his predecessors for when one of them became a tyrant, there was a law that even if he was the supreme ruler, he would be deposed and replaced by another, and those who told

[8] Bernal Díaz del Castillo, *The Discovery and Conquest of Mexico* (New York, 1972), p. 90.

me this reported that they saw how one king was deposed since he ruled badly and did harm to his subjects."[9]

Even in those cases where upper-class rule was more firmly established, the price paid by the lower classes in case of an unsuccessful uprising was so high (they would all be sacrificed) that it would have been very foolish for the rulers to stage an uprising without the support of the lower classes.

While there are no documented instances of exclusively peasant or lower-class rebellions in Aztec times, there are at least two instances of rebelliousness, albeit not outright rebellions, both of which stemmed from the unwillingness of the lower classes to fight for the upper classes. These cases clearly demonstrate the existence of a kind of popular class consciousness in pre-Columbian Mexico.

The first such movement occurred in Tenochtitlán itself. In 1427, after the death of the ruler of Atzcapotzalco, whom the Aztecs had served until then, the Aztec nobility decided that the time had come to overthrow the rule of Atzcapotzalco and assume power for itself in the valley of Mexico. But the common people (at that time mostly peasants) did not want such a war, and protested. Finally, an agreement was reached between them, and the nobles declared to the peasants, "If we are not successful we shall surrender ourselves into your hands that you may eat our flesh and take vengeance upon us." In return the peasants declared, "We undertake if you are successful to serve you, to pay tribute money to you, to be your bondsmen, build your houses and serve you as veritable lords and to place at your disposal our sons, brothers and nieces and while you are waging war to bear your loads and your arms and to serve you everywhere, wherever you may go, and finally to sell you our possessions and persons for your service forever."[10] The Aztec nobles were successful and the result was a further subjection of the peasants, while the nobles acquired lands in newly conquered cities. "To the common people who had shown themselves in this battle to be cowardly and fearful and had sworn to serve the lords and victors, no land was given."[11] This story can be seen either as a real event or as an ideological construction in order to justify the privileges of the Aztec nobles, but either way it reveals the clear social differences in Tenochtitlán.

Perhaps the clearest expression of the profound antagonism between the lower classes and the aristocracy occurred in the town of

[9] Alonso de Zurita, *Breve y sumaria relación de los señores de la Nueva España* (Mexico, 1941), p. 199.

[10] Durán, *Historia de las Indias*, vol. 1, p. 75.

[11] Ibid., p. 97.

Cuetaxtla. Cuetaxtla's lower classes were so hostile to their own rulers that they sided with the Aztecs when the town's aristocracy attempted to put an end to the rule of Tenochtitlán. The common people felt that the rebellion was useless and that they would have to pay the price for it. They dissociated themselves from the nobility and asked the Aztecs to spare them, using words that were remarkably similar to those of peasant revolutionaries in many other parts of the world:

> Why do ye let our accursed overlords who are nothing but a pack of thieves and who have only brought death to us continue to live? Have we then not delivered unto you all the tribute which ye demanded? Was it our rulers perhaps who gave it to you? Is it not all the result of our sweat and toil? If we give blankets, do our rulers do the same? Is it they who weave the blankets? Is it not we and our women-folk? And if they give cocoa, gold, precious stones, feathers and fish and tribute, do they not come from us and do we not offer them to our Lord Moctezuma and to our Lords, the Mexicans . . . ? We desire that you should help us to acquire justice from our overlords. We desire that they be killed, annihilated and punished for they are responsible for our misery.

They also indicated that their overlords had treated them with the greatest possible ferocity, that they had tyrannized them and burdened them with excessive taxes and "that these lords had only one aim in life—to eat, drink and be merry, and they indulged in the most varied and dubious entertainments at the expense of the people."[12]

In this case, the Aztecs exhibited at least as strong a class consciousness as the peasants. The Aztec military commanders, who usually had no qualms when it came to killing, suddenly showed a striking restraint. "We have no right to kill anyone except in battle," the leader of the Aztec occupation forces in Cuetaxtla declared "First of all, Moctezuma must be asked for his counsel." And Moctezuma, who had previously wanted to have all the inhabitants of Cuetaxtla slaughtered, suddenly had doubts. In discussions with his deputy, Tlacallel, he wondered whether the execution of the nobles of Cuetaxtla would be wise. "Since they were nobles and created in the likeness of gods, would the gods not consider the execution of these nobles as a sacrilege?"[13] This attitude was quite similar to that

[12] Ibid., pp. 202f.
[13] Ibid.

of later Mexican governments, who were frequently far more lenient toward the caciques who headed rebellions than towards the peasants who followed them.

On the whole, although direct evidence is scarce, I believe that many of the revolts against Aztec rule resemble nineteenth-century alliances between peasants and regional caudillos directed against the federal government, centered in the same valley of Mexico as in pre-Hispanic times.

The Aztecs expropriated either community lands or labor on a large scale. Sometimes, they took away lands from local nobles or peasants in the same way as their nineteenth- and twentieth-century counterparts did. At other times, the Aztec state, while nominally leaving the land in possession of their original owners, would force them to work it for the Aztec state and deliver its produce to Tenochtitlán. Like most nineteenth-century governments, the Aztecs never gained legitimacy in the eyes of many of their subjects. Revolts were frequent and, as in the nineteenth century, revolts led by regional caciques overlapped with peasant movements. In the same way that the revolts of the nineteenth and early twentieth centuries finally culminated in the 1910 revolution, the frequent revolts against the Aztecs finally climaxed in a national revolt that coincided with the Spanish conquest.

According to a number of scholars, pre-Hispanic rural rebellions were not limited to the Aztec period. J. Eric Thompson suggests that peasant uprisings may have weakened the classic Maya civilization in the eighth, ninth, and tenth centuries,[14] and others believe that rural revolts may have had similar consequences for the civilization of Teotihuacan.[15] Revolts of previously subjugated frontier peoples probably contributed to the fall of Tula, but the existing archaeological evidence does not allow for any definitive conclusions. What is significant is that Mesoamerica (which encompassed southern and central Mexico as well as parts of Central America in the pre-Hispanic period) is the only region of Latin America where rural uprisings have even been suggested as a motive force in this period of history.

Rural Revolts during Spanish Rule

The one period that has seemed to constitute an exception with respect to the quantity, scope, and importance of rural uprisings was

[14] J. Eric Thompson, *The Rise and Fall of Maya Civilization* (Norman, Okla., 1966), pp. 105–106.
[15] Nalda, "Mexico Prehispánico," pp. 108–109.

the colonial era. While rural uprisings did occur, at times on a massive scale, they were concentrated mainly on the peripheries of New Spain. The central areas of the country were far more stable and quiet than they had been before or would ever be after the end of colonial rule.

Armed conflicts in colonial rural Mexico are of three types, each specific to a certain region. First, there were local rebellions aimed chiefly at eliminating particular grievances with the colonial administration, rather than seeking to overthrow the colonial system *in toto*. This type of unrest was concentrated in the central and southern core regions. Second, there were the movements of unconquered peoples of Mexico's northern frontier who resisted Spanish attempts to colonize them. Finally, there were large-scale uprisings against the colonial system by groups in the south who only superficially accepted Spanish norms and the Christian religion, and who sought to restore some elements of the traditional social, economic, and religious order.

The relatively local, limited-objective revolts that occurred in Mexico's core regions are discussed in William B. Taylor's *Drinking, Homicide and Rebellion*,[16] which focuses on social deviance and unrest among free villagers. What emerges from Taylor's survey of 142 insurrections is that they were small in scale, usually confined to particular village communities, and were only rarely led by outsiders. They tended to be spontaneous, sparked by local issues, and only occasionally did they involve disputes over land. They do not appear to have been linked to agricultural cycles or more general economic downturns. Taylor's study focused on the eighteenth century; work by other authors indicates that uprisings were far less frequent in the core regions of New Spain than they had been in the two previous centuries.[17]

What were the reasons for the 250 years of relative passivity in central Mexico, when uprisings were mainly limited to small outbreaks? Two observations must be addressed: the lack of armed resistance to the Spanish conquerors and the relative ease with which the Spaniards established their rule after the fall of Tenochtitlán; and the peasants' passive acceptance of Spanish rule.

The first question is somewhat easier to answer than the second.

---

[16] William B. Taylor, *Drinking, Homicide and Rebellion in Colonial Mexican Villages* (Stanford, 1979), pp. 113–52.

[17] In his impressive work, *The Aztecs under Spanish Rule: A History of the Indians of the Valley of Mexico, 1519–1810* (Stanford, 1964), Charles Gibson describes only two food riots by Indians in Mexico City, and mentions no rural revolts in the valley of Mexico.

Once the Aztec nobles surrendered to Cortés, the nobility of most central states, including the powerful Tarascan empire that had so successfully resisted the Aztecs, followed suit. This acceptance resulted from perceived military superiority of the Spaniards, as well as from assurances given to the nobles that they would be allowed to maintain their privileges, including much of their power and their land. In the first years after the conquest, this was no empty promise. Because of their relatively small numbers, the Spaniards needed allies to maintain their power. If the peasants had wanted to rise against the Spaniards, they would also have had to oppose their traditional leaders, many of whom in previous times had led rural revolts against the Aztecs, but who were now allied with the conquerors. There is no evidence that the peasants were inclined to rebel against the Spaniards, since the Spaniards were at first perceived as liberators from Aztec rule that many had considered extremely onerous. They were used to paying tribute to a ruling class, so Spanish demands for tribute were accepted. The Spaniards had won and thus their gods were considered superior, and conversion to Christianity became a mass phenomenon that was all the easier to accept because the church was ready to tolerate a large measure of religious syncretism. Colonial authorities, at least at first, declared that they would accept existing property structures; only those lands and properties belonging to the Aztec rulers would be confiscated by the Spaniards. The level of tribute would be similar to that of the Aztecs.[18]

It soon became clear that the Spanish *encomenderos* were not ready to accept the limitations on Indian services imposed by the crown, and the level of tribute became far more onerous than in Aztec times, as Spanish officials such as the Oidor Alonso de Zurita observed.[19] Nevertheless, the increasing Spanish excesses did not provoke widespread outbreaks of peasant discontent until the eighteenth and early nineteenth centuries.

Two kinds of conflicts were intimately linked to rural uprisings in the Aztec period and in the nineteenth and twentieth centuries—those in which elites fought each other using peasants, and those in which village communities clashed with other forces. Were these two kinds of conflicts present in the colonial era? Unlike other parts of the Spanish empire such as Peru, there were no significant armed

---

[18] Ibid., pp. 196, 264. See also Alonso de Zurita, *Breve y sumaria relación de los señores de la Nueva España* (Mexico, 1941), p. 154.

[19] Zurita, *Breve y sumaria*, p. 154.

conflicts among the elites in New Spain before Mexican independence. However, an analysis of the reasons for this "harmony" would go far beyond the scope of this essay.

The second type of conflict—between village communities and other social groups (landlords, the church, the state, local officials, etc.)—occurred frequently during the colonial period, and many villages lost land and traditional rights. The fact that these developments produced few and only locally significant armed confrontations was due to certain special characteristics of the Spanish administration and to certain unique effects of Spanish rule on indigenous society.

The colonial period may have been the only time in Mexican history before the 1910 revolution in which the state made a conscious effort to protect the village communities. These efforts, in which important segments of the church participated, reflected the common fears of both church and state of a too-strong and thus too-independent local Spanish nobility. Perhaps even more important was the fact that the free villages provided significant tax revenue both to the crown and to the church.[20] As a result, the Indians could seek, and at times receive, help from both the Spanish judicial system and the church. More important, perhaps, was the fact that the crown and the church, because of their efforts to control the hacendados and encomenderos, acquired legitimacy in many Indians' eyes. For a long time, this legitimacy constituted a powerful deterrent to any serious attack on the Spanish colonial system. Most rebellions were directed at local officials, and the Indians mostly remained firmly convinced that the crown, if it only knew, would redress their wrongs.

In the first century of Spanish rule the crown's efforts to maintain the integrity of village communities may have had a more radical consequence, in that they led to a kind of agrarian reform instituted by the Spanish authorities. During Aztec rule, between 30 and 50 percent of the rural population seems to have had no land of its own and lived outside traditional village communities. These landless peasants were slaves, serfs, or tenants working for the nobility or the state. Their numbers diminished in the first century of Spanish rule, and gradually many of them were settled by the Spaniards in villages and given rights of communal land ownership.[21]

The most important factor that inhibited any kind of massive In-

[20] Enrique Semo, "Conquista y colonia," in Semo, *Mexico*, pp. 213–31.

[21] Gibson, *Aztecs under Spanish Rule*, pp. 220–28.

dian uprising, however, was the unprecedented rise in Indian mortality; Borah and Cook have estimated that within a relatively short time, the Indian population fell from about twenty to fewer than two million.[22] While other estimates may be more conservative, it is clear that in the short run many potential rebels died. Those who survived were often demoralized and disorganized—since traditional social organizations frequently broke down. In contrast to the Aztec period, and to the nineteenth and twentieth centuries, the large-scale confiscation of communal village lands by the Spaniards could now take place "painlessly." Population pressure in late Aztec times had led to the cultivation of marginal land from which crop yields were variable, and frequently low. When the rural Indian population fell, the survivors concentrated on better land, thus increasing living standards, but the resultant acute labor shortage had two contradictory effects. On the one hand, the pressure increased on the survivors to work harder to produce more, while the labor shortage increased its value, and both the treatment of the rural population and living standards may well have improved.

In the long term, the Indian population recovered from the catastrophe and increased in the eighteenth century, to the extent that the land allotted to villages in the sixteenth and seventeenth centuries were often insufficient to support the now larger population. No additional lands were available to them because of the tremendous expansion of haciendas and of church holdings that had taken place in the meantime.[23] This new pressure on the land, though it constituted only one of many factors, helps to account for the increase in the number of rural uprisings, culminating in the independence wars at the beginning of the nineteenth century. Increasing rural unrest manifested itself in all Indian regions of Latin America. It was less pronounced in eighteenth-century Mexico than in Peru for instance, where the greatest Indian revolt in the history of the continent broke out in 1780–81. Two factors that may have prevented similar, mainly Indian uprisings from spreading and becoming regional or even national in scope, were (1) the cultural, linguistic, and tribal diversity of the Indian population, and (2) the rivalries among them. Nahuatl never occupied the dominant position in Mexico that Quechua did in Peru, and the nature of the Aztec empire was such that it could never have generated myths of a golden

[22] Borah and Cook, "The Aboriginal Population," pp. 226–58.

[23] Eric Van Young, *Hacienda and Market in Eighteenth Century Mexico: The Rural Economy of the Guadalajara Region* (Berkeley, 1981), pp. 249–50.

past like those that so inspired Peruvian revolutionaries when they thought of the Inca period.

Apart from the village inhabitants whose social movements Taylor has studied, two other groups in the countryside which have been the object of far less research: hacienda residents and what could be called marginals. During the colonial period there were two broad types of haciendas: those worked mainly by permanent residents, and those where such residents only formed a kind of skeleton crew. The first type of estate, which for a long time was erroneously thought to be predominant in Mexico, was really concentrated along the northern frontier.[24] In the rest of the country most of the work on haciendas during planting and harvesting was performed by temporary laborers from adjoining villages or by migrants.[25]

It has frequently been assumed that most peons were debt peons, and that debts were simply a means by which hacendados could tie peons to their estate. There is little doubt that such was the case at times, but at others the debt represented a sort of bonus offered by an hacendado to attract workers in a period of labor scarcity, and in the latter situation, such a debt was a privilege. The status of peons thus ranged from that of privileged retainers to that of near slaves. In central regions many peons may have been better off than the temporary laborers from adjoining villages.[26] They were guaranteed help from the haciendas in times of famine or other natural catastrophes, and subsidies or loans by the hacienda owners for ceremonial purposes such as marriages or baptisms, etc. At other times and in other regions, especially in the southeast, the peons were far worse off than the inhabitants of free villages who had retained substantial areas of fertile land. In both cases, it comes as no surprise that hacienda peons were less likely to revolt than the inhabitants of free villages. As far as the privileged retainers were concerned, the motives for this attitude are obvious; others were effectively isolated and controlled by the estate owners.

Nor is there any evidence that peons were more prone to revolt in northern Mexico. On estates on the frontier with nomadic Indians where most hacienda laborers were resident peons, they were not a privileged minority with respect to other sectors of the rural popu-

[24] François Chevalier, *Land and Society in Colonial Mexico* (Berkeley, 1966), pp. 149–84.

[25] Gibson, *Aztecs under Spanish Rule*, pp. 246–49.

[26] James D. Riley, "Crown Law and Rural Labor in New Spain: The Status of Gañanes during the Eighteenth Century," *Hispanic American Historical Review* 64 no. 2 (1984): 259–63.

lation. Nevertheless, the hacendado had another way of ensuring his control over them—they depended on the armed forces of the estate for protection against raiding Indians. Despite the savagery and frequency of Apache attacks, the Sanchez Navarros, who owned one of the largest estate complexes in northern Mexico, did not arm their peons,[27] but forced them to rely for protection on a special force created by the estate owners, and this obviously reduced their potential for revolt. On many haciendas in regions such as Zacatecas in the north, which were not threatened by Apaches, peon working conditions seem to have been better than in the center and south of the country, perhaps due to labor shortages, and to the need to attract laborers from elsewhere. Nevertheless, by the end of the eighteenth century a growing number of peons in northern Mexico seemed to have developed a new type of consciousness that is illustrated by the growing number of petitions they presented to the Spanish authorities. In these petitions they requested recognition as free villages and asked the government to grant them land of their own on the estates on which they were working.[28]

Another social group that also deserves attention is the so-called marginals—mestizos and Indians who left their villages in the eighteenth century, when as a result of the population increase many were not able to receive lands from their communities. Some abandoned the countryside altogether and settled in the cities, others wandered north. Some of them constituted a semi-urban proletariat that settled in the Bajío region in northern Mexico. These men worked part-time in the towns and part-time on large estates as temporary laborers.[29] Another group went farther north and received lands as colonists in military settlements on Mexico's sparsely populated frontier.

There is no evidence that these two marginal groups participated in the limited type of village insurrections that Taylor described. The miners and part-time laborers of the Bajío, though, did stage mass riots such as the one in 1767, which had much in common with the uprisings of 1810. These semi-industrial laborers were to

[27] Charles H. Harris III, *American Family Empire: The Latifundio of the Sanchez Navarro Family 1765–1867* (Austin, 1975), p. 196.

[28] François Chevalier, "Survivances seigneuriales et présages de la revolution agraire dans le nord du Mexique," *Revue Historique* (July 1959).

[29] Eric R. Wolf, "The Mexican Bajío in the Eighteenth Century," *Synoptic Studies of Mexican Culture*, No. 17 (New Orleans, 1957). See also John Tutino, *From Insurrection to Revolution in Mexico: Social Bases of Agrarian Violence, 1750–1940* (Princeton, 1986).

constitute one of the core elements of the national revolutions that engulfed Mexico in 1810 and 1910.[30] While the marginals of the Bajío rose in 1810, the military colonists of the north remained passive and even loyal to the Spanish crown. One century later, the northern frontiersmen would constitute the core of the revolt in Mexico's north,[31] while those in the Bajío remained largely passive.

So far we have been concerned with local rebellions that aimed to redress particular grievances and, as such, were confined mainly to the central region. The second type of rural unrest was the resistance movement, particularly in the north. Conflicts and struggles along the northern frontier were of different patterns, sizes, and time scales from those of central Mexico. In the course of extending and consolidating their territory, the Spaniards often encountered fierce resistance. The northern tribes had never been conquered, nor were they accustomed to paying tribute to a domestic ruling class. They had never known anything that could be compared to the nobility of Tenochtitlán. Their nomadic mode of existence better enabled them to withstand the Spanish onslaught and to renew their resistance even after an apparent defeat. Such was the case in the spectacular Chichimec wars between 1550 and 1600 that posed a serious threat to colonial control of New Spain.[32] The Spanish cause was not helped by the dearth of settlers willing to leave the well-populated and wealthy areas of central Mexico and lay effective claim to the newly conquered territories as had the settlers of North America.

Initial Spanish efforts to overcome northern Indian resistance were marked by exceptional brutality. Traditional forms of subjugation like the encomienda and repartimiento were supplemented by large-scale slavery, and many Indians were deported for sale in other parts of the country. In the course of the seventeenth century, however, recognizing the failure of these strategies, the Spaniards turned to a new one based on the missionaries. Jesuit and Franciscan scholars, priests, teachers, and administrators had been very successful in helping to establish Spanish rule in central Mexico. There they had been sent to prepare the ground for secular domination and for control of the Indians by the encomenderos. They learned the Indians' language, converted them to Christianity, taught them European methods of cultivation and crafts, and introduced new animals. They attempted to gain the loyalty and confi-

---

[30] See Wolf, "Mexican Bajío"; Tutino, *Insurrection to Revolution*; Meyers, Chapter 15, this volume.

[31] Friedrich Katz, *The Secret War in Mexico* (Chicago; 1981), chap. 1.

[32] See Philip W. Powell, *La guerra Chichimeca* (Mexico, 1977).

dence of the traditional village elites and appointed them to village positions. The Indians were not required to pay tribute but only to support the missionaries. After an initial period of at least ten years, once the "missionized" Indians were considered to have been pacified and to have learned the rudiments of Christianity and Spanish civilization, the missionaries in central Mexico, much against their wishes, were required to make way for the civil authorities and the regular clergy.[33]

Along Mexico's northern frontier, however, missionary strategy had to change and adapt to completely new circumstances. It was clear to the Jesuits, the Franciscans, and eventually to Spanish authorities, that northern missions would not be a temporary affair as they had been in the central region. The northern Indians would never submit to secular Spanish authority. Thus the missionaries would have to bring about far greater changes in the lifestyles of the northern Indians than those in central Mexico in order to consolidate their control. In central Mexico, where the sedentary Indians lived in large villages, the missionaries did not carry out transfers of population as radical as those in the north, although in the period of high mortality the remaining inhabitants of several decimated Indian villages might be concentrated in one community. The northern nomadic Indians lived in small groups, and the missionaries felt that they could control them better if they were congregated in large villages. After the Indians' conversion, the missionaries required them to live in missions under the supervision of Jesuit or Franciscan priests, who then attempted to change the Indians' subsistence pattern. Among Indians who had lived from hunting and gathering, agriculture was introduced, but even for the tribes that had practiced agriculture before, life changed drastically. New instruments such as the plow and new crops were promoted, and European livestock, such as cattle, horses, pigs, etc., was imported. Every family received a plot of land large enough to sustain itself, and was allowed to work this plot for a certain number of days (three days per week among the Yaqui Indians of Sonora). Unlike the Indians of central Mexico, the mission wards were not required to work for Spanish landowners or authorities, but they were required to labor on community land for a specified amount of time. The proceeds of these lands were used to support the missionaries, to maintain the Indian population in times of hunger and famine, and to finance the

[33] Edward H. Spicer, *Cycles of Conquest* (Tucson, 1974), p. 292.

church activities elsewhere in the country or even in different parts of the world.

In central Mexico both the missionaries and the Spanish crown had attempted to weaken and dismantle any Indian authority above the village level. In the north, where no such authority existed, the missionaries frequently established village and even tribal Indian authorities for the first time, through which the missionaries attempted to rule their wards.[34]

Sometimes the missionaries' approach resulted in a spectacular success, sometimes in total failure, but on balance it fared better than previous Spanish strategies of colonization in the north. Several factors can be identified as critical to missionary success. The first was the degree of mobility and dispersal of the Indians the missionaries sought to colonize. The more nomadic and scattered the Indians, the less successful were the missionaries; neither Jesuits nor Franciscans ever came close to missionizing the Apaches or Comanches, for example. Effective control depended on concentrating tribes at a limited number of sites. The second factor was the degree of social stratification and centralization within the communities or tribes: the greater this was, the more likely the missionaries were to find allies to help them exercise effective social control. A third factor was the missionaries' ability to protect their wards from the domination of secular Spanish authorities and from the influx of settlers. A fourth factor was the incidence of disease and epidemics: by congregating Indians from widely distant settlements into large villages the missionaries frequently contributed to the spread of diseases.[35] Finally, there were the economic consequences of the missionary efforts.

Missionary efforts among the Yaquis and the Tarahumara illustrate well the significance of these factors. The Yaquis lived in an area of northern Mexico that was penetrated by the Jesuits in the mid-seventeenth century. After brief fighting at the beginning of the century, the Yaqui leaders themselves called in the missionaries and for more than a century completely submitted to their control. They willingly accepted proposals by the Jesuits to concentrate their population, dispersed among several hundred so-called *rancherías*, into eight compact villages. They acceded to a new and complex system of tribal organization. The Jesuits implemented new methods of in-

[34] Ibid., pp. 290–92.

[35] Linda A. Newson, "Indian Population Patterns in Colonial Spanish America," *Latin American Research Review* 20 no. 3 (1985): 58–60.

tensive agriculture, and the Yaquis acquired domesticated animals. They rebelled only once during the colonial period, in 1740, but it was of limited duration and intensity. The missionaries in fact were allowed to leave the Yaqui territories alive, and returned once the revolt subsided.

The same cannot be said of missionary efforts among the Tarahumara, which led to some of the bloodiest Indian uprisings in Spanish colonial history—in 1646, 1650, 1684, and 1698. Many of the missionaries were killed, settlements were dismantled. After the last of these uprisings, most of the Tarahumaras simply melted away into the nearly inaccessible mountains of the Sierra Madre. Only a minority maintained links with the missionaries.

The first difference between the Yaqui and Tarahumara was in their patterns of settlement. Both had lived in widely dispersed rancherías before the coming of the missionaries, but Yaqui rancherías were relatively large and housed several families, often as many as several hundred people, whereas those of the Tarahumara rarely housed more than a single family. The concentration imposed by the Jesuits thus came as much more of a shock to the Tarahumara than to the Yaquis.[36]

Both tribes had relatively egalitarian forms of social organization and neither had had sustained exposure to any kind of central authority. But, unlike the Tarahumara, the Yaquis had at least known the rudiments of a centralized organization during periods of warfare with the neighboring Mayo Indians. Centralization again proved easier for the Yaquis to accept than for the Tarahumara.

Even more important were the economic benefits the missionaries provided, although here, environmental differences were of decisive importance. Along the banks of the Yaqui River, the missionaries organized a system of intensive agriculture far more productive than the one the Yaqui had before, and new crops and livestock appear to have significantly improved Yaqui living standards. Among the Tarahumara, improvements were much more modest, if there were any at all. Because so much of the region was mountainous, the possibilities for intensive agriculture were much smaller, and the introduction of crops and livestock by the Spaniards could not compensate the Indians for the loss of their traditional nomadic way of life.

Most importantly, however, only in the case of the Yaquis were the missionaries able to protect their wards against an onslaught of Spanish entrepreneurs. As soon as the Jesuits had congregated the

---

[36] Spicer, *Cycles of Conquest*, pp. 55–56.

Tarahumaras in large settlements, Spaniards forced many of them to work in the mines. The Jesuits attempted to resist these efforts, but they lacked the power to do so. The Yaquis were more fortunate than the Tarahumara, for no mines were discovered in their region until the early eighteenth century. As a result, the Yaqui settlements at first remained largely unaffected by the influx of Spanish settlers and colonists, and until the eighteenth century the Yaquis were not forced to work for them.[37] When the Spaniards finally settled the Yaqui region and attempted to impose the same kind of labor services on the northwestern Indians that they had imposed upon the Tarahumara, the Yaquis in fact revolted too.

By the eighteenth century many tribes, like the Conchos in Chihuahua, had been exterminated, or, like the Tarahumara, had retreated into the mountains of the Sierra Madre. Some, however, made peace with the Spaniards, largely because of the constant encroachment of Apaches and Comanches on sedentary Indians and Spaniards alike. The attacks tended on the one hand to prevent further northward advances by the Spaniards, and on the other to induce the Spaniards to make certain concessions to sedentary groups in an effort to forge a joint front against the attackers. In 1778, Teodoro de Croix, the Spanish intendante who administered the large frontier province of Nueva Vizcaya, set up a series of military colonies that would become a bulwark against Apache attacks, based on a kind of racial equality previously unknown in New Spain. Anyone willing to settle in these colonies, according to de Croix's decree, whether Indian or white, would receive land and help from the colonial administration.[38] In return he would have to remain for at least ten years in the settlement and be willing to fight the Apaches. Thus, the way was opened for many Indians to be given the full rights of Spaniards on the northern frontier and to be exempted from traditional labor services. The result of these measures was the creation of a new, free peasantry on the northern frontier composed of whites, mestizos, and Indians. These free peasants owed their land to the Spanish authorities and cooperated with the latter in fighting the Apaches. When in the 1780s, in a change in Spanish policy, the colonial administration literally bought off the Apaches by granting them large subsidies of food and cattle and thus pacified large seg-

[37] See Hu-DeHart, Chapter 5, this volume.
[38] Proclamation by the Caballero de Croix, November 15, 1778. This proclamation was reprinted in 1895 by the legal representative of the peasants of Namiquipa, Tomas Dozal y Hermosillo. This text can be found in Departamento Agrario, Sección de Terrenos Nacionales Chihuahua, Cruces 1.29(06)45.

ments of the frontier, the links between the free peasants of the
north and the colonial administration became even stronger. It is
thus not surprising that with some exceptions these peasants did not
participate in the independence wars against the Spaniards at the
beginning of the nineteenth century. On the contrary, many of them
fought in the Spanish army against the revolutionaries.

The third type of rural conflict on Mexico's southern periphery
during the colonial era, chiefly Indian upheavals in Chiapas and Yucatán, tended to challenge the colonial system as a whole, including
its religious basis, although they were fewer in number than either
in central or northern Mexico. Local riots with more limited aims
did not occur as frequently on Mexico's southern periphery as in its
central parts.

One reason for their reticence to resort to armed struggle was that
the Indians of the south had an alternative their counterparts in central Mexico did not have—they could retreat to remote jungle regions where the Spaniards exercised no control. The revolts that did
break out in the south caused considerably more apprehension
among the Spaniards than the limited riots of central Mexico. These
movements were larger in scope than those of the center, with tribal
and ethnic consciousness playing a far greater role. One of the most
dramatic instances of this type of rebellion was the Tzeltal rebellion
of 1712 in Chiapas. Religious dissent had begun to manifest itself
among the Tzeltal Indians in 1708, when they began to venerate a
hermit considered insane by the Spanish authorities. The priests removed the hermit to a monastery that year, but when he returned
only two years later, his influence grew even stronger. Hundreds of
Indians flocked to hear his sermons. This time both the clergy and
the civil authorities decided to deport him for good. The deportation
was in fact final because the hermit died (the reasons have never
been clarified) as he was leaving Chiapas. His death did not put an
end to religious dissidence, but on the contrary, a new and far
stronger millenarian movement emerged.

In 1712 a thirteen-year-old girl, María Candelaria, declared that
she had seen the virgin, who had spoken to her. The Indians of
María's village of Cancuc erected a shrine on the spot where according to the young girl the Virgin had first appeared to her. Hundreds,
then thousands, of Indians flocked to pray at the shrine and they
asked the church to recognize its legitimacy. The Dominican friars
of the most influential religious order in Chiapas, refused to accede
to these demands. They considered the shrine a sign of heresy and
attempted to destroy it, but when confronted by open threats of re-

bellion the friars withdrew. Their action nevertheless sparked the seeds of revolt. Under the leadership of one of the Tzeltal *caciques*, Sebastian Gómez, who later added the title "de la Gloria" to his name, a new cult of the Virgin challenged both the religious suprem- acy of the Catholic church and the secular authority of Spain. Gómez openly called for a war of extermination against the Span- iards. The elders of the Cancuc council proclaimed a new cult:

> now there was neither God nor king and they must only adore, believe in and obey the Virgin who had come down from heaven to the Pueblo of Cancuc ordering them expressly to kill all the priests and curates as well as all the Spaniards, mestizos, negroes and mulattoes in order that only Indians remain in these lands in freedom of conscience, without paying royal tributes nor ecclesiastical rights and extinguishing totally the Catholic religion and the dominion of the king.[39]

The rebellious Indians, who numbered more than 6,000 men at the height of the revolt, at first took the Spaniards by surprise, but their success was short-lived. After two months troops from Guate- mala and central Mexico arrived in Chiapas, crushed the uprising, and executed its leaders.[40]

In 1761 a revolt of smaller proportions than that of the Tzeltal occurred among the Maya Indians of Yucatán. Between 1,000 and 1,500 Maya Indians led by a wandering prophet called Jacinto Canek rose against the Spaniards in the town of Cisteil.[41] The revolt never extended beyond the confines of Cisteil and was put down by the Spaniards after a few weeks. Canek was captured and subjected to the most cruel punishment they knew: he was executed in public and dismembered before he died. The revolt is still a matter of much controversy, and even the name Canek has been given several inter- pretations. Some see it as his real name, others as a self-endowed royal itza surname, with which he had himself crowned king in the

[39] Fernando Jordán, *Crónica de un parts barbaro* (Chihuahua, Mexico, 1975), p. 215.

[40] Herbert S. Klein, "Peasant Communities in Revolt: The Tzeltal Republic of 1712," *Pacific Historical Review* (1966): 247–64. See also Henri Favre, *Changement et continuté chez les Mayas du Mexique* (Paris, 1971), p. 43; Robert Wasserstrom, *Class and Society in Central Chiapas* (Berkeley, 1983), chap. 4, pp. 69–106; Antonio García de León, *Resistencia y utopía* (Mexico, 1985), Vol. 1, pp. 78–87; Victoria R. Bricker, *The Indian Christ, The Indian King* (Austin, 1981), pp. 55–69.

[41] See Moisés Gonzalez Navarro, *Raza y tierra, la guerra de castas y el Henequen* (Mexico, 1970), pp. 34–37; Nancy M. Farriss, *Maya Society Under Colonial Rule: The Collective Enterprise of Survival* (Princeton, 1984), pp. 66–72.

church of Cisteil. According to the official report of the Spanish governor, Canek called on the Maya to revolt because of the corrupt behavior of the Catholic priests, the tyranny of the Spaniards, the forced labor, heavy taxes and the tributes, as well as the floggings and jailings imposed on the Indians. He promised that several thousand Englishmen who had occupied the region later known as British Honduras would come to their aid, and told the Indians, "many of you will die in battle, you should not fear eternal death, for by annointing you with this oil that I have, and saying at the moment of unction, 'God the Father, God the Son, God the Holy Spirit,' you will find the doors of paradise open."[42] The governor saw the Canek uprising as part of a more general plot in which many Indian servants and hacienda peons participated in order to expel the Spaniards from Yucatán.

Other historians believe that these accounts are enormously exaggerated. In their eyes, the plot was largely a fabrication of the Spanish governor that was intended to cover his own ineptitude. It had all started, according to one account, when during a drunken riot the Indians in Cisteil killed a Spanish merchant and intimidated a priest. The latter exaggerated these events out of all proportions and a punitive expedition was sent to Cisteil. The fourteen Spanish horsemen who entered the town in order to punish the alleged rebels were so drunk that they indiscriminately attacked civilians and were in turn killed by the incensed Indians. According to proponents of this story, the governor (in order to hide his own ineptness), invented the story of a planned Maya uprising against the Spaniards.[43] Whatever the origins of the rebellion, however, once it began it assumed far larger dimensions than similar riots in central Mexico, and unlike central Mexico, it immediately took on a religious and ethnic dimension. In this respect, it was similar to the rising of the Tzeltal Indians.

It is easier to describe the characteristics of these rebellions than to assess why they occurred when they did. One of the main reasons why southern rebellions tended to be both more Indian and more religious in character was that far fewer Spaniards had settled in the south than in central Mexico, since there were no mines in the south. Thus the clergy and Indian caciques exercised far greater control over the Indians than was the case in other parts of New

[42] Bricker, *The Indian Christ*, p. 74.
[43] Ibid., pp. 74–76.

Spain. Since the Indians in the south, unlike their counterparts on the northern frontier, had developed highly stratified societies whose lower classes were used to working for a ruling class, the priests demanded more from Indian labor than they did in northern Mexico, so that they aroused much more Indian hostility. In Yucatán, traditions of religious autonomy had also been strengthened by the fact that until the end of the seventeenth century, some Maya Indians in the remote Petén had managed to retain both their political independence and their religious identity. In Chiapas too, some Indians had managed to escape Spanish rule and to retain their culture, religion, and autonomy by fleeing into remote regions. Social and religious dissidence also tended to coincide in the south because there were fewer Spanish settlers. The church therefore assumed a more central role relative to secular authorities among the rural population than in many other parts of the country. As a result, economic and social conflicts soon led to confrontation with the church.

It is less easy to explain why the Tzeltal and Canek revolts occurred when they did. In both cases, some authors have assumed that the revolts were precipitated by the replacement of bishops with others who were less sympathetic and less responsive to Indian demands. Other authors feel that more long range forces were at work. In Chiapas, epidemics in the late seventeenth century decimated the population and thus reduced the number of taxpayers, with the result that the burden on the remaining Indian population increased.[44] In Yucatán, long-range economic tendencies may have constituted a basis for rebellion, but there is no clear evidence indicating that the town of Cisteil had suffered from such restrictions at the time of the rising. Spanish landowners, whose interests in the region had been limited before, set up larger sugar estates in the south of the peninsula in the eighteenth century and as a result, traditional access to land and water by village communities was restricted.[45] In central Mexico, these attacks on Indian lands had to a certain degree been "painless" because they occurred while the Indian population was low. This was not the case in eighteenth-century Yucatán, so the opposition to these measures was far greater. An additional factor that provoked Canek to revolt when he did was possible British encouragement. In 1761 Britain was at war with

[44] Wasserstrom, *Class and Society*, chap. 4.

[45] *Maya Society*, Farriss, pp. 366–75. Farriss, who has analyzed these long-term trends, does not state that there was a link between them and the Canek uprising.

Spain and, as already noted, smugglers in neighboring British Honduras supplied Canek with arms.

One significant difference between the rebellions of the south, the north, and the center was that those in the south had a far smaller chance of success than those elsewhere. The villagers in central Mexico who staged a rising or a riot to protest abuses by the colonial authorities may very well have been convinced, on the basis of other similar cases, that as long as they recognized the legitimacy of Spanish rule, the authorities might give in to their demands. On the whole they were right. In the majority of cases, as Taylor points out, reprisals were few and abuses were corrected.

In view of the weakness of Spanish rule in the north and the Indians' tradition of independence from colonial domination, the northern tribes who revolted believed that they had a good chance of succeeding. On the whole they were also right. The Tarahumara, whose revolts were the most significant on the northern frontier, were repeatedly defeated by the Spanish army. Nevertheless, the majority of them did succeed in eluding control by both the Spanish secular and missionary authorities and continued to lead a secluded and independent life in the Sierra Madre.

There was not a similar objective basis for the Chiapas rebels to hope for success in 1712. In Yucatán, Canek may have had somewhat more hope because of possible British involvement, but British promises, if they were made at all, were vague, and there was no precedent in the Maya region for success against the Spaniards. But even if there had been objective conditions for some kind of reconciliation with the colonial authorities, both the Tzeltal rebels and Canek put an end to them by creating a new religion and thus making the break with the Spaniards irrevocable. Religious expectations and calculations replaced expectations and calculations based on the correlation of forces. In Chiapas, the Tzeltal believed that the Virgin of Candelaria would lead them to victory, while in Yucatán Canek proclaimed that any Maya killed by the Spaniards in battle would be admitted to paradise.

Conclusion

In general, the Spanish colonial administration was far more successful until the end of the eighteenth century in conquering and ruling Mexico than the Aztecs had ever been. They extended their domain to Mexico's far north and far south, and faced far fewer challenges in central Mexico than had Tenochtitlán. The fact that the

Spaniards had better arms, more modern means of communication, horses, cattle, and a more diversified and more productive agricultural technology was not of decisive importance in this respect. In the nineteenth century, the Mexican state had similar advantages and yet the degree of control it exercised over most of Mexico was far weaker than that of their Aztec predecessors.

Several factors account for the weakening of potential Indian resistance against Spain. The most prominent was the massive mortality of the Indians in the sixteenth and seventeenth centuries; once the Indian population began to increase again in the eighteenth century, so did the number of revolts. Moreover, the Spaniards made serious efforts to indoctrinate the populations of their colonies, whereas the Aztecs never attempted to spread their religion throughout Mesoamerica. From the outset the Spaniards were determined to convert the population of Mexico to Catholicism, and they were enormously successful.

Unlike the Aztecs, the Spanish administration managed to gain legitimacy among the lower classes by providing them with some protection against the nobility and its own officials. At the same time, until the end of the eighteenth century the Spaniards never faced the kind of upper-class opposition that the Aztecs had faced from the nobility of their subject peoples. In Mexico, unlike Peru, a very large part of the indigenous nobility had either died during the epidemics and the conquest or been removed by the Spaniards and replaced by nobles of Spanish extraction. Thus, relations between Spain and the Mexican colonial upper class at first were not characterized by the kind of ethnic conflict that was a hallmark of Aztec relations with their subject rulers. In addition, until the latter part of the eighteenth century, the Spanish crown gave its nobles—in practice, thought not in theory—a great deal of political and economic leeway.

On the whole, the pattern of pre-Columbian revolts, especially in Aztec times, was much more like that of the nineteenth and early twentieth centuries than the social upheavals of the colonial period. Revolts against Aztec rule were frequent, large in scope, and peasants allied themselves with regional caciques. The revolts challenged the legitimacy of Aztec rule, and also opposed land expropriations and demands for tribute.

During most of the colonial period, until the late eighteenth century, there were relatively few revolts in the core areas of New Spain. They were extremely limited in scope and size, and rarely questioned the legitimacy of Spanish rule.

In the last years of the colonial period, Spain's relations with its Mexican colony deteriorated drastically as the policies of the crown produced an unprecedented degree of opposition, both within the lower classes and within important segments of its elite. An evolution that was in many respects similar had occurred in the last years of Aztec rule. Like the Aztecs on the eve of the Spanish conquest, the Spaniards in their last years attempted to increase revenues by putting greater financial pressure on their subjects, and attempted to assert their authority over their subjects by reducing their autonomy. Moctezuma attempted to impose his authority on neighboring Texcoco, which until then had been a largely autonomous ally of Tenochtitlán. The Bourbon reforms enacted by the Spanish crown in the late eighteenth century limited the autonomy of many provinces of New Spain. In the last years of their rule both the Spanish and Aztec authorities significantly increased taxes and antagonized large segments of Mexico's elite by limiting their upward mobility. Moctezuma decreed that warriors who had performed unusual feats in battle and who traditionally had been able to rise to upper class status would no longer be able to do so. The crown limited the access of Mexico's creoles to positions of power in New Spain. Both the rulers of Tenochtitlán and the rulers of Spain had been legitimized by religious support, but in the last years of their respective rules, this support was undercut: in precolonial Mexico by the appearance of a new religion in Texcoco, and in New Spain by increasing conflicts with parts of the church and the expulsion of the Jesuits. In both cases, demographic factors exacerbated the crises of the regimes, though not in identical ways. Population increases were probably linked to the famines that swept Mexico in late Aztec times. In New Spain, rural unrest was precipitated by increases in the Indian population for whom communal land was not available.

When these internal crises were combined with attacks from outside—Cortés' invasion of Mexico and Napoleon's invasion of Spain—the two empires collapsed under the weight of general uprisings in which the rural population played decisive roles.

CHAPTER FOUR

Agrarian Social Change and Peasant Rebellion in Nineteenth-Century Mexico: The Example of Chalco

John Tutino

Why do Mexican peasants rebel? Why do people who devote their lives to producing the necessities of survival choose one historical moment to risk death by challenging those who rule? Ultimately, peasants rarely win. They neither become the ruling elite, nor force existing elites to rule primarily in the peasants' interests. Yet, knowing that victory is all but impossible, Mexican peasants have repeatedly risen in rebellion. And since the exceptionally violent revolutionary decades of the early twentieth century, scholars have searched for explanations of peasant rebellions in Mexico.

Most recent analyses of Mexican agrarian history have focused on the colonial period. The agrarian radicals of the revolutionary era generally saw their task as the destruction of a cruel legacy of colonial rule. Modern scholars have followed that lead and produced numerous fine studies of colonial agrarian society.[1] Those analyses

[1] See, for example, Silvio Zavala, *La encomienda indiana* (Madrid: Centro de Estudios Historicos, 1935); Lesley Byrd Simpson, *The Encomienda in New Spain*, rev. ed. (Berkeley: University of California Press, 1966); François Chevalier, *La formación de los grandes latifundios en México*, trans. Antonio Alatorre (Mexico City: Problemas agrícolas e industriales de México, 1956); Charles Gibson, *The Aztecs Under Spanish Rule* (Stanford: Stanford University Press, 1964); William B. Taylor, *Landlord and Peasant in Colonial Oaxaca* (Stanford: Stanford University Press, 1972); Eric Van Young, *Hacienda and Market in Eighteenth-Century Mexico* (Berkeley: Univer-

have revealed a colonial society in which Spanish elites ruled Mexican peasants by various means and with varying levels of coercion. Inequality, often in the extreme, prevailed. Yet through the colonial era there was little peasant unrest in central Mexico, beyond brief, localized outbursts.[2] Two conclusions emerge: first, conquest, coercion, and inequality—even cruelty—cannot explain peasant rebellion in Mexico. The exploitation of peasants by elites is a distressingly constant feature of Mexican history; peasant rebellions have been much less common. Second, the relative stability of the colonial era indicates that the search for the historical origins of modern peasant rebellions should focus more on the nineteenth century. The decades from 1810 to 1930 appear rife with peasant violence, especially when compared with the colonial era. What changed during the nineteenth century to produce this striking increase in the level of violence between Mexican elites and peasants?

Study of the Chalco region, located just southeast of Mexico City, may help generate answers to this question. Chalco was a region of elite-owned and elite-operated estates (haciendas) that supplied maize and other products to Mexico City markets. Those estates shared the region with numerous peasant communities that included the majority of the local population. Haciendas and peasant communities disputed the region's limited land and water resources, yet they were linked together by labor relations essential to the survival of both: the haciendas needed seasonal peasant workers to plant and harvest crops; peasants needed that labor to supplement the meager produce of cultivating community lands. Such an agrarian structure was typical of conditions across the central highland valleys surrounding Mexico City. In addition, Chalco experienced periods of peasant unrest beginning in the late 1840s, as did numerous other central Mexican regions. Analysis of agrarian social change and peasant rebellion in Chalco may thus suggest explanations useful in understanding general developments in central highland Mexico.

This inquiry is possible due to the survival and accessibility of the archive of Mariano Riva Palacio. From the 1830s to 1870, he owned and operated several Chalco haciendas. He was also the dominant

<hr/>

sity of California Press, 1981); and Cheryl Martin, *Rural Society in Colonial Morelos* (Albuquerque: University of New Mexico Press, 1985).

[2] William B. Taylor, *Drinking, Homicide and Rebellion in Colonial Mexican Villages* (Stanford: Stanford University Press, 1979); and John Tutino, *Creole Mexico: Spanish Elites, Haciendas, and Indian Towns, 1750–1810*, unpublished Ph.D. dissertation, University of Texas at Austin, 1976.

political figure in the region. From that local base, Riva Palacio rose to become governor of the state of Mexico several times. He was also a leading figure in the convention that wrote the liberal Mexican constitution of 1857. Because of Riva Palacio's combined economic and political interests at Chalco, his archive covers nearly every aspect of life there during the middle decades of the nineteenth century. Although quantitative information on population and production is lacking, decades of letters from estate administrators, political allies and opponents, petitioners for favors, and disgruntled citizens produce a uniquely detailed portrait of a society undergoing difficult times of change.[3]

Riva Palacio's papers also include reports from local officials and estate managers worried about the peasant rebellion that erupted at Chalco in 1868. Those reports are complemented by recently published materials from the archive of the National Ministry of Defense.[4] It is thus possible to analyze the relations between agrarian social change and peasant rebellion at Chalco in good detail. Such analysis should suggest new perspectives on important, but neglected questions of nineteenth-century agrarian history.

The Colonial Legacy

Agrarian social developments in nineteenth-century central Mexico did not simply continue or intensify processes begun during the colonial period. The post-independence era brought new pressures to rural life, producing new adaptations within agrarian structures inherited from colonial times. An understanding of that earlier period cannot explain the problems of the nineteenth century. But such an understanding is an essential point of departure.

The conquest was the first event of Spanish–Indian relations in Mexico. A group of Spanish warrior-entrepreneurs used a combination of violence, diplomacy, treachery, and good luck (for themselves, since Old World diseases ravaged Indians with no immunity) to exploit divisions inherent in the Mexican political structure and to establish themselves as colonial rulers. The conquest subordinated Mexican lords and their states to Spaniards; it did not present

[3] The Riva Palacio papers are held in the Benson Latin American Collection Library of the University of Texas at Austin. They are served by a fine index: Jack Autrey Dabbs, *The Mariano Riva Palacio Archive*, 3 vols. (Mexico City: Editorial Jus, 1967–72).

[4] Leticia Reina, *Las rebeliones campesinas en México, 1819–1906* (Mexico City: Siglo XXI, 1980), pp. 64–82.

Spaniards with immediate opportunities to rule the mass of Mexican peasants. During the first decades after the conquest, Spaniards ruled and profited in Mexico primarily by turning to their own benefit a system of tribute extraction they inherited from the Aztecs and other pre-Hispanic rulers. Native lords continued to collect tributes in goods and periodic labor services from peasant dependants, who now passed most of the proceeds on to the conquering Spaniards. The grants to Spaniards of the rights to collect such tributes were called *encomiendas*, a Spanish label for an enduring Mexican means of rule.[5]

The encomienda system of early colonial rule thus left the land and control of most production in the hands of peasant families. It left the power to mediate between peasants and Spaniards in the hands of Mexican lords. It allowed Spaniards to prosper and rule with minimal disruption of the existing social structure. But, much to the regret of the conquerors and their heirs, this early colonial power structure could not survive. The Spanish crown feared colonial rule through encomiendas because such grants gave too much independent power to Spanish colonials. But the crown had little success curtailing the conquerors' power until the continuing depopulation caused by smallpox and other diseases drastically reduced the Mexican population. Encomiendas gave Spaniards a portion of peasant produce and labor, linking Spanish wealth directly to the Mexican population. By the mid-sixteenth century, the Mexican population was cut in half and colonial Spaniards were complaining of economic decline. The diseases that devastated Indian society created an economic crisis for the conquering Spaniards.

That weakening of the colonial elite gave the representatives of the crown an opportunity to establish state power. Beginning in the 1550s, administrators began to regulate encomienda tributes and to eliminate the periodic labor services. Simultaneously, they worked with churchmen to congregate the surviving peasants, then living sparsely scattered across the countryside, into compact villages. The

[5] This discussion of the colonial agrarian structure reflects my ongoing analysis for a work entitled "Peasants and Patriarchs: Agrarian Society in Central Mexico, 1500–1800." Here I cite only the most important and general works; Simpson, *The Encomienda*; Gibson, *Aztecs*; Peggy K. Liss, *Mexico Under Spain, 1521–1556* (Chicago: University of Chicago Press, 1975); and Pedro Carrasco, "La economía prehispánica de México," and Johanna Broda, "Las comunidades indígenas y las formas del extracción del excedente: época prehispánica y colonial," both in *Ensayos sobre el desarrollo económico de México y América Latina, 1500–1975*, ed. Enrique Florescano (Mexico City: Fondo de Cultura Económica, 1979), pp. 15–53, 54–92.

proclaimed goal of that resettlement was more effective justice under crown officials and more effective christianization under local
clergy. But few among the officials of church and state lamented the
consequent restructuring of rural landholdings. Relocated peasants
were to keep their traditional lands if these were nearby, or to receive new holdings adjacent to the village. By reducing scattered
peasant lands to compact holdings, the colonial authorities forced
the vacation of large, contiguous areas. These could be granted by
the state to worthy Spaniards—encomenderos, merchants, and officials (or their relatives). The congregation of peasant communities
began in the 1550s and continued into the early seventeenth century.[6] The granting of vacated lands to Spaniards accelerated in the
1570s and continued to about 1630.

Spanish elites could thus begin to organize commercial estate production to supply the mining towns of the north, and the expanding
colonial capital at Mexico City.[7] Meanwhile, the peasant population
continued to shrink, reaching a low point around the 1620s. The
result was the relatively easy creation of commercial estates, but a
severe shortage of potential workers. Chalco was one of many central highland regions that by the early 1600s had numerous estates
that looked to profit by selling maize and other products in Mexico
City, yet faced persistent difficulties in recruiting the surviving local
peasants to do the work. Before 1630, the state tried to require and
regulate the seasonal labor of Mexican peasants through the system
called *repartimiento*, but by the 1630s, the peasant villagers at
Chalco and elsewhere simply refused to provide the workers demanded.

By the mid-seventeenth century, then, the state had used its supervision of peasant congregations and of land grants to Spaniards
to create a rural social structure in which estates held much land,
while peasant communities retained holdings generally sufficient
for the subsistence of their reduced populations. But the state had
failed to control the pivotal relation between estates and peasant
communities—the provision of seasonal labor. Facing a problem
with varied regional and local complexities, the state stepped back
and allowed local bargaining between estates and peasant communities to organize labor relations. But the state retained a pivotal me-

[6] Peter Gerhard, "Congregaciones de indios en la Neuva España antes de 1570,"
Historia Mexicana 26 (1977): 347–95.
[7] See Richard Boyer, "Mexico in the Seventeenth Century: Transition of a Colonial
Society," *Hispanic American Historical Review* 57 no. 3 (1977): 455–78.

diating role, for its courts arbitrated disputes between landed elites and peasants.

Peasant community leaders, local notables who inherited their status from pre-Hispanic traditions, survived as pivotal mediators between their communities, the haciendas, and the colonial state. Lacking a bureaucracy capable of implementing the congregation of peasant communities, the state had worked through surviving notables. These were allowed to organize the congregations and given extensive land rights and exclusive political privileges in the new *repúblicas de indios*. Colonial peasant property rights were vested in those restructured communities, while peasant families cultivated individual plots they passed on through inheritance. Local notables thus retained under Spanish rule predominant powers within the peasant communities.

They used those powers to claim the pivotal roles of labor brokers controlling the supply of seasonal peasant workers to nearby estates. Estate operators could only plant, cultivate, and harvest crops with workers obtained via peasant community notables. Such brokerage further consolidated the notables' local power, and also reinforced the community as the primary institution of peasant life. Commercial estates and peasant communities remained interspersed across central Mexico, perhaps disputing local lands, but inextricably linked by labor relations essential to both and mediated by the local notables.

This rural structure in which state-sanctioned estates controlled by Spanish elites shared the countryside with state-sanctioned peasant communities led by local notables proved adaptable enough to survive the tripling of the peasant population during the last century of colonial rule. The colonial agrarian structure had been consolidated during a period of low population, favoring peasant interests. But as peasant numbers increased after 1650, the communities could gain few new lands. Peasants inevitably faced the shrinkage of holdings relative to a growing population as community lands became ever less sufficient to providing peasant subsistence. Meanwhile, nearby estates could bring surplus lands into cultivation to produce more food; peasants short of land would have little choice but to labor more at the estates to produce that additional food, and then use their wages to buy it.

Within such a rural structure, peasant population growth all but guaranteed expanded production and profits to estate operators. It also made the power of local notables increasingly crucial. Controlling much community land as well as labor relations with haciendas, the notables also profited from population pressures—though on an obviously reduced scale. Most peasants could only continue to subsist, and they would subsist less on the direct cultivation of their family holdings within communities, and more by working for wages and buying in local markets. The rural structure of colonial Mexico allowed for the progressive commercialization of peasant life, without abrupt social changes. Peasants would remain residents of their communities, subject to traditional notables, while becoming increasingly more dependent on the Spaniards' commercial economy.[8]

Thus able to cushion change, the colonial rural structure survived into the nineteenth century. Despite obvious and generally increasing inequalities, it revealed a remarkable stability, evidenced by the scarcity and brevity of violent tensions. The colonial power structure survived because it was a structure of symbiotic exploitation. Spaniards ruled and profited while peasants worked and served. But within the prevailing social structure, neither could function without the other. Spaniards could not profit without the cheap, seasonal labor provided by peasant communities. And as peasant population expanded, peasants could not subsist without the income from that labor.[9]

Should an estate operator seek a quick advantage by claiming a community's landholdings, he would quickly face the local notables, who could refuse workers for planting and harvesting crops. Equally important, the undermining of the landed base of the peasant communities was not in the estates' interests: they needed peasants to work only seasonally and thus community lands sustained their work force without cost to the estate during the rest of each year. When, despite such considerations, disputes between estates and communities periodically erupted, local notables quickly turned to the colonial courts for a resolution. The notables' repeated recourse to the Spanish state suggests that they perceived the colonial courts as effective mediators between the unequal interests of estates and their communities.

From the conquest, colonial officials had feared the independent power of colonial elites. And one effective means to limit elite power was to protect the countervailing landed power of the peasant communities. The colonial courts generally defended the rights of

[8] This interpretation of the colonial power structure summarizes the more detailed analysis in Tutino, *Creole Mexico*.

[9] The notion of symbiotic exploitation is developed in Tutino, *Creole Mexico*. A similar perspective appears in Angel Palerm, "Sobre la formación del sistema colonial: Apuntes para una discusión," in *Ensayos*, ed. Florescano, pp. 93–126.

peasant communities to at least subsistence landholdings and minimal local autonomy. The resulting agrarian structure incorporated
estates and communities that simultaneously confronted and complemented each other, with the balance maintained by the mediating state. Neither landed elites, community notables, nor state officials saw gain in disrupting that balance to the end of the colonial
era.

The perceptions of the peasant majority are less apparent. We
know that they rarely attempted overt rebellion. Did that indicate a
minimal satisfaction with the colonial situation? Were peasants
merely resigned to the impossibility of a better situation? Or were
they often angry, but convinced that protest and especially rebellion
could only lead to repression and worse conditions? The dearth of
studies of the internal structure of Mexican peasant communities
prevents any knowledgeable answer—and remains the primary gap
in our understanding of Mexican agrarian social history. One conclusion appears reasonable: the colonial agrarian structure obviously favored Spanish elites over Mexican peasants. But the same
structure and state were also clearly committed to the minimal survival of landed peasant communities. The mediating colonial state
accommodated conflicts between elites and peasants, sustaining the
elites' power to profit and the peasants' ability to subsist. The state's
success is perhaps best revealed in the fact that it maintained social
peace amidst obvious inequalities, without standing armed forces,
for over two centuries.

When the last half-century of colonial rule brought increasing
population growth, commercialization, and peasant dependence on
estate labor, tensions escalated. Both court disputes and local uprisings became increasingly numerous in central highland Mexico, but
even when violence erupted, court mediation eventually prevailed.
The structure of symbiotic exploitation proved able to absorb the
proliferating conflicts, preventing the development of any overt
challenges to the colonial agrarian structure.[10] Even when Father
Miguel Hidalgo and thousands of rebels entered the central highlands in 1810 calling for independence and social reforms, the structure held. Most peasants stayed at home, while notables placed notices in the Mexico City press proclaiming their communities'
loyalty to the colonial regime.[11] Ongoing disputes between estates

[10] See Taylor, *Drinking, Homicide, and Rebellion.*
[11] Lucas Alamán, *Historia de Méjico,* Vol. 1 (Mexico City: Editorial Jus, 1972), pp.
255-56.

and communities remained in the courts. As late as 1810, violent rebellion held little attraction for the peasant communities of central highland Mexico.

Independence: State Collapse and Elite Crisis

The power structure that maintained the stability of colonial agrarian society in central Mexico collapsed following independence in 1821. The successful proclamation of Mexican independence was led not by a reformer such as Hidalgo, but by Agustín Iturbide, a military officer known for his success in crushing rebel groups. Iturbide led a movement representing elites who aimed to claim national independence without disrupting the established Mexican social structure. But such a goal of attaining political autonomy without sacrificing existing economic power—obviously attractive to Mexican elites—proved impossibly contradictory.

The colonial state had been essential to the colonial social structure, mediating between landed elites and peasant communities. The elimination of the colonial state, however, did not lead to the creation of a national state that mediated with similar effect. From the perspective of the state, Mexican independence was primarily a process of dissolution. After 1821 Mexico had no judicial system capable of effectively mediating between elites and peasants. The new national governments were generally of brief duration and more interested in representing elite interests than in mediating between landlords and peasant communities. The political conflicts and wars of the post-independence decades primarily disputed which elites would control the new state. A state that was new, weak, disputed, and conceived by elites as an elite representative could not take over the mediating power of the colonial state.[12]

Meanwhile, Mexican elites faced a worsening economic crisis. During the colonial centuries, landed elites had accepted the mediation of the state in their relations with peasant communities in part because the operation of landed estates had remained generally profitable. After independence, profits became scarce, and bankruptcies and estate auctions became more numerous. Just as the state was unable to mediate effectively, Mexican landed elites faced economic

[12] See Michael Costeloe, *La primera república federal de México, 1824–1835* (Mexico City: Fondo de Cultura Económica, 1975); and Carlos San Juan Victoria and Salvador Velázquez Ramírez, "La formación del estado y las políticas económicas, 1821–1880," in *Mexico en el siglo XIX, 1821-1910*, ed. Ciro Cardoso (Mexico City: Editorial Nueva Imagen, 1980), pp. 66–76.

difficulties that led them to seek new ways to profit during the uncertain times that followed independence. From the 1820s, Mexican elites sought to alter agrarian social and economic relations, not from strength, but from weakness.[13]

To understand the roots of such actions—so prominent in the tensions at Chalco after independence—a brief inquiry into the economics of elite life before and after independence is illuminating. From the late sixteenth through the eighteenth centuries, Mexican elites profited through a continuing integration of commercial and landed activities. Wealth accumulated in commerce and mining was repeatedly invested in landed estates. Commerce and mining were most profitable, but also exceptionally risky. Successful traders and miners, aware of the risks, looked to the operation of commercial landed estates to preserve their wealth—and thus to preserve their families' positions in the colonial elite. The operation of haciendas did not, probably could not, create wealth for colonial elites; instead, a hacienda was held as an investment to produce consistently modest profits to sustain an elite family.

That regular investment of capital in the landed sector of the economy was crucial to successful estate operations. Mexican haciendas generally earned profits not by supplying urban markets regularly, but by holding crops from years of good harvests until periodic frost or drought created scarcities and high prices. Peak profits were then claimed—as long as the estate operator had sufficient capital to pay for estate operations while awaiting such high prices. Successful colonial estate operators profited because they financed their operations with family capital. And they maintained their family capital by generations of marriages with the heirs to commercial wealth. The continuous colonial fusion of commercial and landed wealth gave security and thus elite status to newly rich speculators, and provided the capital that allowed established landed families to maintain profitable hacienda operations.

But the social process of elite reinforcement broke down during the struggles for independence. The most prominent and successful merchants of late colonial Mexico were immigrants from Spain; facing insurrections proclaimed against Spain and native Spaniards, many merchants left Mexico and took their capital with them. And few Spaniards came to Mexico after 1810 looking to gain wealth in

---

[13] The remainder of this section summarizes and reinterprets my earlier essay, "Hacienda Social Relations in Mexico: The Chalco Region in the Era of Independence," *Hispanic American Historical Review* 55 no. 3 (1975): 496–528.

commerce. The traditional source of elite capital was thus sharply curtailed by Mexican independence. Yet the disruptions of independence simultaneously raised the landed elites' need for capital.

The wars of independence severely disrupted commerce and mining for a decade. The production of silver that had led the booming Mexican economy during the later eighteenth century all but collapsed. Many estates suffered from the depredations of civil war, while others deteriorated with the disruptions of production and exchange. After 1821, estate owners needed more capital to rebuild the commercial estate economy, but capital was becoming increasingly scarce.

The merchants who came to Mexico after independence to replace the departed Spaniards were largely British, European, or North American. They showed little interest in marrying into Mexican elite families. Flooded Mexican silver mines were simultaneously leased to British companies that had access to the technology of steam pumps, and the capital to bring them to Mexico. As a result, after independence, the capital of commerce and mining increasingly flowed out of Mexico, rather than into the coffers of Mexican elite families. Those who did join the landed elite after 1821 had generally risen through political and military success. They joined the elite, bringing much interest in the affairs of state, but little wealth. Such newcomers attempted to use landed estates to create wealth, rather than to sustain wealth already amassed. That contradicted the established economic role of haciendas and increased the demands for scarce capital among landed elites.

The banking institutions of the church had traditionally supplemented the capital of commerce in funding the landed elite in Mexico. But church economic affairs suffered equally from the disruptions and depredations of independence. Tithe collections fell, while debtors often defaulted on payments. Church lenders faced increasing demands for capital with shrinking supplies.[14] Predictably, estate owners in the 1820s began to lament that capital was scarce and too expensive. And many found no alternative but to turn to millers, bankers, and other urban grain dealers for the funds to finance estate operations. Those dealers were willing to provide financing, but generally through contracts that called for the delivery of the crops immediately after the harvest at a predetermined

---

[14] Asunción Lavrin, "Problems and policies in the administration of nunneries in Mexico, 1800–1835," *The Americas* 28 no. 1 (1971): 55–77; Michael Costeloe, *Church Wealth in Mexico* (London: Cambridge University Press, 1967).

price. Estate operators could no longer hold their crops for times of peak prices. Profits plummeted—or were shifted to the urban dealers—and bankruptcies followed with lamented frequency.

Independence did not challenge the property rights of the haciendas. No government aimed to change the prevailing agrarian structure. But the changes in the economic process of elite life caused by independence and reinforced by civil wars and trade disruptions, left landed elite families facing severe economic decline during the decades of new nationhood. Those families could not reverse the changes that had undermined their wealth—the changes were inevitable in the process of independence—and so they looked for other solutions. They turned to the new national state for help, and against local peasant communities, seeking new resources and more subservient workers. Mexican elites attempted to build a national state that would directly serve their interests. But they found limited success, in large part due to the weakness of the commercial economy and the consequent shortages in tax collections. And despite, or perhaps because of, their financial weakness, after independence landed elites also turned to challenging peasant communities— seeking lands, water, and more tractable workers. Again their success was minimal, and again they failed largely because of their own financial problems. But in both their attempts to control the national state and their attacks on peasant communities, landed elites escalated the tensions in Mexican society, setting the nation on a course toward increasing violence.

Independence also brought changes to the structure of peasant communities, the third major actor in the colonial agrarian power structure. Unfortunately, the internal organization of peasant communities for periods before or after independence has been little studied. We know that, after independence, legal distinctions based on racial and ethnic categories were abolished. The *repúblicas de indios* and their ruling local notables thus lost their exclusive legal privileges. We also know that the state of Mexico, including Chalco and other central highland regions, limited municipal status to towns with populations over four thousand. Many peasant communities thus lost the right to independent local councils and became dependent on nearby larger towns.[15]

The results produced by these legal changes are unknown. Did

[15] Peter Gerhard, "La evolución del pueblo mexicano, 1519–1975," *Historia Mexicana* 24 (1975): 576–77.

local notables carry on as always, ignoring changes legislated by weak, unstable regimes? Or did the end of the notables' privileged status open the communities to more political competition, perhaps leading to increased local instability? All that can be stated with confidence is that the peasant communities were not decisively weakened in the immediate aftermath of independence. Through the 1860s, those at Chalco and elsewhere repeatedly demonstrated an ability to act under local leaders to challenge the actions of landed elites and state officials. It appears that the peasant communities survived the difficulties of independence better than either the landed elites or the state.

With the state divided and weak, and landholders facing financial difficulties, while peasant communities remained relatively strong, conflict developed. After independence estate operators at Chalco saw local peasants as perverse obstacles to estate profitability. Wages had risen to a maximum of three reales daily, up from the colonial peak of two reales. And Chalco peasants successfully insisted on tending their own crops first, laboring at the estates only when time permitted. In the eyes of estate managers, such conditions were a major problem that continued through the 1840s. The administrator of the Axalco estate in 1841 could only write of "*indios desagradables*" who were obstacles to estate profits. He saw the Chalco peasants as perverse, for they would not work without regular weekly payment in cash. His estate was short of cash, and thus unable to complete needed work—while the few peasants available labored elsewhere. In 1844 the spring planting was delayed at the same estate due to the persisting labor shortage, while a nearby estate employed all available workers by paying wages above the prevailing rate. And in 1849, the harvest was delayed at Mariano Riva Palacio's Asunción estate because the peasants of Temamatla and other nearby communities would not labor until they finished harvesting their own crops.[16]

The Chalco peasants sustained such bargaining power because they remained cohesive under the leadership of local elites, while estate operators faced financial difficulties. The available demographic evidence suggests that the population growth characteristic of the eighteenth century subsided early in the nineteenth.[17] Limited

---

[16] Mariano Riva Palacio papers (hereafter MRP), 1171, 11 Oct. 1841; 1180, 24 Oct. 1841; 1447, 30 May 1844; 2447, 12 Nov. 1849; 3507, 28 Nov. 1849.

[17] Gloria Pedrero Nieto, "Un estudio regional: Chalco," in *Siete ensayos sobre la hacienda mexicana, 1780–1880*, ed. Enrique Semo (Mexico City: Instituto Nacional de Antropología e Historia, 1977), pp. 99–150.

population growth at Chalco and elsewhere in the central highlands would reduce the pressures of peasant numbers on community resources, thus lessening the pressures pushing peasants to labor at the estates.

After independence, disease continued periodically to strike the Mexican population. Cholera struck Chalco in 1833 and again in 1850, reducing the peasant population. In 1850, the manager at Asunción reported that eight estate residents were stricken and two had died. At the neighboring community of Zula, from which Asunción recruited many workers, fifty became ill and at least seven died. Similar results were reported from other estates and communities at Chalco and elsewhere in the central highlands. When such diseases struck, estates could not recruit enough workers to cultivate crops, allowing weeds to invade their fields and reducing yields.[18] The residents of Chalco lived with the grim paradox of peasant life: the suffering and death of epidemic disease reduced peasant numbers and thus helped to preserve their bargaining power against elites and their estates.

Into the mid-nineteenth century, Chalco elites faced severe economic difficulties, which they blamed in large part on intransigent local peasants: they were not sufficiently willing, docile, and cheap workers. Chalco peasants did not cause the economic problems of estate operators, but by sustaining tight community organization while the elites faced financial problems, the peasants were a painful thorn in the side of the landed elites. And since elites could not solve the problems that caused their difficulties, they turned against the peasants.

The Estate Offensive, 1849–56

The defeat of Mexico in the war against the United States forced Mexican elites to face the weakness of their economy and the near impotence of their national state. Following the disastrous conflict, those who presumed to rule Mexico wrote numerous tracts seeking the causes of national weakness.[19] The evidence from Chalco reveals that during the same period from 1849 to 1856, elites attempted substantial innovations in estate agriculture. They experimented with

[18] MRP, 3875, 24 Feb. 1850; 4281, 9 June 1850; 4284, 10 June 1850; 4332, 19 June 1580; 4394, 3 July 1850; 4398, 3 July 1850.

[19] Charles Hale, *Mexican Liberalism in the Age of Mora* (New Haven: Yale University Press, 1968); Moisés González Navarro, *Anatomía del poder en México, 1848–1853* (Mexico City: El Colegio de México, 1977).

new products and new techniques of production, looking for profits in a time of crisis.

The experiments proceeded along two fronts. One looked for more profitable means to produce the maize, wheat, and other products long cultivated at Chalco, and the other experimented with dairy farming on newly irrigated alfalfa pastures. Both developments looked to improve yields and generate new revenues; both led to heightened conflicts with Chalco peasant communities.

Experimentation with seed varieties had rarely concerned colonial estate agriculturalists. Each year they had simply planted seed from the previous harvest. But from the late 1840s, Chalco estates began to try planting wheat, maize, and vegetable seed or seedlings brought in from other regions reporting high yields.[20] The use of manure as fertilizer had also been unimportant to Mexican estate agriculture during the colonial years; a British visitor reported shortly after independence that Mexican agriculturalists seemed curiously uninterested in manuring. But during the early 1850s, manure became an obsession among Chalco estate administrators. They increased local flocks of sheep to obtain more waste and experimented with various mixtures with maize stalks to stretch their fertilizer supplies.[21] Simultaneously, Chalco estates began to experiment with new implements: imported plows that turned over deeper soil became common, and a few estates invested in new winnowing machines to separate grain from chaff (and to reduce labor requirements).[22] Together, these experiments in seed selection, the use of fertilizers, and the use of new implements revealed a willingness of Chalco elites to innovate—when faced with economic crisis.

In addition, beginning in the late 1840s at least six Chalco haciendas turned to dairying. They purchased herds of cows and developed alfalfa pastures, which in turn required irrigation and extensive manuring.[23] The attraction of dairying was that it could quickly help surmount shortages of operating capital. Milk was sold daily and thus generated regular income that could reduce reliance on scarce and expensive credit.[24]

[20] MRP, 5915c, 4 June 1856; 7079, 12 Oct. 1857.

[21] W. Bullock, *Six Months' Residence and Travels in Mexico* (1824; repr. Port Washington, N.Y.: Kennicat Press, 1971), p. 277; MRP, 5871, 10 Mar. 1856; 5915h, 13 July 1856; 5915k, 19 Aug. 1856; 5915n, 9 Sept. 1856.

[22] MRP, 5915i, 5 Aug. 1856; Jorge Basave Kunhardt, "Algunos aspectos de la técnica agrícola en las haciendas," in *Siete Ensayos*, ed. Semo, pp. 241–42.

[23] MRP, 5915L, 26 Aug. 1856; 8019A, n.d.; 7113, 27 Oct. 1857.

[24] MRP, 3254, 9 Oct. 1849; 3334, 23 Oct. 1849; 3446, 12 Nov. 1849; 3507, 28 Nov.

The expected gains were not always realized. By 1857 so many Chalco estates were producing milk that they had saturated the market. Much of the local milk production could not be sold.[25] Perhaps even more distressing to the innovators, the shift to dairying increased estate labor requirements. The planting and manuring of extensive alfalfa pastures increased the number of workers needed at a time when recruiting Chalco peasants remained difficult.[26]

All the innovations in Chalco estate agriculture produced one additional result: estate operators moved to gain increasing control of the region's water supplies. When the Asunción estate began dairying in 1849, it also built a new dam and related irrigation ditches. Similar construction followed at the Buenavista estate.[27] And at the hacienda called Zoquiapan, the turn to dairying led to the construction of an elaborate new irrigation system. A foreign engineer called Mr. Alan designed and directed the construction of a series of catch basins in the highlands above the estate along with canals to bring the newly controlled waters to estate fields.[28]

The Asunción and González estates even experimented with drilling artesian wells. Another foreigner named Bener contracted to search for underground water, but he was not familiar with the local water table, and Riva Palacio and other Chalco estate owners were not familiar with the high cost of such technical innovation. The results were a prolonged contract dispute and only partial success in finding new water supplies.[29]

Facing continued financial problems after independence, by the late 1840s Chalco's landed elites developed a willingness to innovate in search of profits. But their innovations only increased estate labor demands, thus worsening one of the problems, and the increased demand for water led to construction projects that created new conflicts with peasant communities.

The Peasant Counteroffensive, 1849–56

Chalco peasant communities did not passively accept the estates' moves to acquire increased control of local land and water re-

1849; 3540, 4 Dec. 1849; 3801, 30 Jan. 1850; 3912, 5 Mar. 1850; 4254, 5 June 1850; 4285, 10 June 1850; 7445, Feb.–Mar. 1862.

[25] MRP, 26 Aug. 1857.

[26] MRP, 20 Aug. 1849; 5915b, 20 May 1856; 5915c, 4 June 1856; 5915g, 6 July 1856.

[27] MRP, 3080, 31 July 1849; 3417, 6 Nov. 1849; 3546, 4 Dec. 1849; 3912, 5 Mar. 1850; 4254, 5 June 1850; 6446, 26 Apr. 1857.

[28] MRP, 5015, 6 Feb. 1851; 5177, 13 May 1851.

[29] MRP, 5683, 15 Mar. 1855; 5685, 27 Mar. 1855; 6556, 12 May 1856; 6627, 4 June 1857.

sources. Local leaders challenged estate actions in the courts, and when court rulings were not favorable, they led community members into the fields to obstruct estate projects directly. From 1849 on, Chalco was the scene of deepening conflicts between estates and peasant communities. Before examining those conflicts, however, it is helpful to place them in the context of a wider series of uncoordinated peasant protests that developed simultaneously across much of central and southern Mexico.

The caste war in Yucatán that pitted back-country Maya Indians against political elites, landed elites, and nearly the entire Hispanic population of the peninsula beginning in 1847 is well known. So are the simultaneous conflicts that brought violence to the Sierra Gorda and the isthmus of Tehuantepec. All those insurrections developed in peripheral regions while the rulers of Mexico and their armies were occupied against the foreign invader. The relationship between peasant violence and state weakness is rarely more clear.[30]

In the southern reaches of the state of Mexico (the modern state of Guerrero), peasant protests began in 1842 and continued for a decade. There, the political competition between Nicholas Bravo and Juan Alvarez presented peasant communities with a division in the power structure and a perceived opportunity to protest. Alvarez responded, primarily in regions near to Bravo's power base, by attempting to mediate between landholders and peasant communities. Like the colonial state, Alvarez would end the hostilities with a show of force, promise a fair examination of claims, and grant at least some concessions to the peasants. Such mediation earned Alvarez the animosity of most Mexican elites.[31]

In the central highland basins surrounding Mexico City, the late 1840s and early 1850s also produced an explosion of peasant discontent that sporadically became violent. The causes are not always clear. Many protesting peasants and irate landholders cited the well-known precedent of a legal victory gained by several communities in the valley of Toluca in a land dispute with the Condes de Santiago—one of Mexico's oldest landed elite families.[32] The importance of the knowledge of that victory and of the evident weakness of a state that had just lost a war is not known. But beginning in 1848 in

[30] See Nelson Reed, *The Caste War of Yucatán* (Stanford: Stanford University Press, 1964); Moisés González Navarro, *Raza y tierra* (Mexico City: El Colegio de México, 1970); John Tutino, "Rebelión indígena en Tehuantepec," *Cuadernos Políticos* 24 (1980): 89–101; and Reina, *Rebeliones*, pp. 233–34, 240–42, 291–302.

[31] Fernando Diaz Diaz, *Caudillos y Caciques* (Mexico City: El Colegio de México, 1972); pp. 96, 171–175; Reina, *Rebeliones*, pp. 85–120, 169.

[32] González Navarro, *Anatomía*, pp. 165–66.

the Mezquital north of Mexico City, around Otumba and San Juan Teotihuacan to the east, and near Xochimilco to the south, peasants threatened or used violence in disputes over land, water control, taxes, and the control of local office-holding.[33] Central Mexican peasants saw the postwar years as the time to protest a variety of encroachments on their resource control and general local autonomy.

The lowland basins around Cuernavaca and Cuautla, just south of Chalco, experienced relatively intense conflicts beginning in 1849. In that sugar-producing region, peasants rose several times to challenge the resources claimed by estates. At times, the protesters were supported by local merchants and even the local militia—which was quickly disarmed and disbanded. The region that would become the heartland of the agrarian revolution led by Emiliano Zapata in 1910 was already seething with peasant discontent by 1850.[34] But that discontent remained localized, sporadic, and without political organization or orientation.

From the vantage of prominent landholding politicians such as Andres Quintana Roo and Francisco Pimentel, the years after 1848 were most unsettling. They saw peasants threatening legitimate elite and state rule. They wrote of peasants ignoring the decisions of the courts, refusing to respect state-sanctioned titles to property, neglecting to pay rents, and working poorly when they worked for elites at all. Such writings reveal a developing siege mentality among Mexican landed elites, in that they saw insubordinate peasants attacking their rights to property and power.[35]

This era of peasant protest deserves a general detailed analysis. For the present, analysis of its development at Chalco may provide preliminary insights. Beginning in 1849 peasants there participated in several challenges to local estate property claims.

At least one conflict at Chalco began in response to news of the peasant victory in the valley of Toluca. In 1851 the leaders of the town of Amecameca reopened an old land dispute hoping for a more favorable resolution. There followed threats of violence and the controversy continued to 1855, but the outcome is unclear in the docu-

---

[33] MRP, 3986, 18 Mar. 1850; 4091, 29 Apr. 1850; Reina, *Rebeliones*, pp. 61, 63, 123.
[34] Reina, *Rebeliones*, pp. 157–70.
[35] González Navarro, *Anatomía*, pp. 162–65; Francisco Pimentel, *Memoria sobre las causas que han originado la situación actual de la raza indígena de México y medios de remediarla* (Mexico City: Imprenta de Andrade y Escalante, 1864), pp. 203–204.

ments.[36] But most of the peasant protest that proliferated at Chalco beginning in 1849 responded more directly to the recent estate offensive. As estate operators looked to improve production and eventually profits by building new irrigation works, they could not avoid encroachments on community resource controls. The communities, in turn, reacted with court challenges and with physical obstruction that at times led to violent confrontations. At Chalco it was the landed elites' decision to begin a new offensive against community resources, at a time of economic difficulty and evident state weakness, that provoked increasing conflict.

When Riva Palacio constructed the new dam to expand the irrigation system at Asunción in 1849, peasant lands in the jurisdictions of both Chalco and Temamatla were flooded. Peasants publicly threatened to destroy the dam and a local official wrote Riva Palacio suggesting compromise, because the peasants could not be controlled. When the project was completed, it was apparent that the newly harnessed waters would be useful for irrigating the lands held by peasants at Cuicingo. The estate claimed those lands and the peasants rioted in protest. Riva Palacio tried to blunt that discontent by using his political power to persuade the town of Temamatla to provide lands for the peasants he had dispossessed. Sufficient anger remained that one group of peasants built a makeshift dam blocking the river above Riva Palacio's new irrigation system. And local officials expressed reluctance to enforce the court order calling for the destruction of the peasants' dam, fearing an outbreak of violence. Again, the details of the final resolution are unknown, but in June 1850 the Asunción estate was cultivating irrigated fields at Cuicingo.[37]

Similar disputes erupted elsewhere at Chalco as estates seeking more water to irrigate more lands encroached on peasant access to that scarce but essential resource. The cultivation of irrigated pastures of alfalfa at Tomacoco in the mid-1850s led the estate to usurp irrigation waters formerly shared with peasants. The communities took their complaints to the courts, and won.[38]

The most intense, enduring, and violent dispute at Chalco in the mid-nineteenth century pitted the peasants of San Francisco Acuautla against the hacienda of Zoquiapan, which was owned by the Villaurrutía family, heirs of the colonial Marques de Castañiza. When

[36] MRP, 5484, 16 Oct. 1851; 5683, 15 Mar. 1855.
[37] MRP, 3046, 5 Mar. 1849; 3080, 31 July 1849; 3721, 13 July 1849; 3723, 14 Jan. 1850; 3912, 5 Mar. 1850; 4254, 5 June 1850.
[38] MRP, 7113, 27 Oct. 1857.

in 1849 the landowners decided to build an elaborate new irrigation system designed to capture water in the highlands above Chalco and channel it to estate fields, they provoked conflict with Acuautla. That community was situated in the uplands east of Chalco, and much of the new construction was on lands its residents customarily used. The peasants of Acuautla lost croplands, pastures, and woodlands to the estate's irrigation system.

Late in 1849 the community hired a Mexico City attorney named Luis María Aguilar to represent them in the courts. He visited Acuautla early in October. Surely to protect himself politically from the potential repercussions of representing a Chalco peasant community, Aguilar wrote of his visit to Riva Palacio. His letter reveals much about a nineteenth-century Mexican liberal's view of peasants.

Aguilar was horrified by his reception at the community, being greeted with fireworks and festival music. He saw in such attitudes only self-denigration, which he blamed on long influence of rural priests who in his view treated peasants as "beasts of burden." Aguilar saw the solution to the problem in the elimination of the distinction between *gente de razón* (people of reason) and Indians. Aguilar proclaimed that all people, even Indians, shared faculties of reason. And they thus could be assigned Spanish surnames, which would be useful in making contracts and taking censuses for militia recruitment and taxation.[39]

The peasants of Acuautla would have been pleased to know that their lawyer believed that they shared in human reason; his interest in taxation and militia recruitment they would find more distressing. They would surely have smiled at his presumption that their deferential greeting revealed self-denigration. When the lawyer failed in court, the peasants of Acuautla revealed abundant supplies of self-esteem and courage.

Early in 1850, the court ruled in the estate's favor. A small fraction of the disputed lands were allocated to Acuautla, while the estate gained the rest. The court ruling was to be implemented in a judicial survey in the disputed fields. The estate owner reported the resulting confrontation to Riva Palacio:

> During the morning there were no problems. And although the townspeople came en masse to claim that they were due twice the land allotted them, the judge told them that given the participation of their representative, they could have no role in the

[39] MRP, 3270, 11 Oct. 1857.

proceedings. All would be handled through the representative. The survey resumed and the Indians returned home.

But in the afternoon a community leader arrived and told the judge that if the survey continued, he could not control the consequences, given the volatility of the townspeople. The judge answered that he lacked the power to suspend the survey, for he was executing a court order. His answer was barely finished when the entire community appeared, advancing in close formation, armed with stones and sticks. The judge and his aides were unarmed and believed it prudent to retire to Chalco and suspend the proceedings.

The attack made the Indians the masters of the fields and left the authority that is supposed to instill respect in them in a sorry predicament. I believe that the judge will ask for assistance to complete the survey and impose respect with armed force—the only recourse remaining. As you are aware of the precedents to this event, and you know the people of Acuautla, excuse my repetition of another example of their insubordination, and of the losses they have imposed on the estate. But you will agree with the need to limit their continued impudence. Thus I implore you to take the steps necessary so that they will not do away with us all.[40]

Early in March 1850, fifteen armed men sent by the prefect of Texcoco stood guard and enforced the completion of the survey.[41] But the dispute did not end. The peasants of Acuautla returned to court and early in 1851 won a slightly more favorable ruling. They were allotted an additional two caballerías (about 210 acres) of land. Yet they remained angry—and perhaps encouraged by the court's shift to their favor. The implementation of the second resolution required thirty armed guards. The peasants attacked the proceedings again with sticks and stones, but could not prevent its completion. The commander of the guard concluded that the peasants of Acuautla "will never accept any resolution that is not to their liking."[42]

The dispute continued. Following the second survey, construction of the irrigation works resumed, but the peasants responded by obstructing workers and seizing tools and armed guards were again required to reclaim tools and allow the work to continue. In May 1851, the conflict came to a violent head. The peasants had been

[40] MRP, 3804, 31 Jan. 1850.
[41] MRP, 3902, 4 Mar. 1850.
[42] MRP, 4955, 10 Jan. 1851.

obstructing the work while continuing to gather wood and graze animals on disputed lands. The estate began to seize the peasants' livestock. Tensions heightened, leading the estate owner to use his influence to persuade the minister of defense, Mariano Arista, to send
troops to quell the continuing "Indian riot."[43]

The owner then went to his estate, a few days ahead of the troops.
As he arrived, two leaders from Acuautla were with the manager,
demanding the return of the livestock. When the manager refused, a
fight erupted in which he was wounded by several machete blows.
He later died. Other estate employees responded with firearms,
holding the peasants off until a larger militia force arrived near
nightfall and forced the peasants back to Acuautla. The next morning fifty members of the Chalco national guard—mostly armed estate
employees—went directly to Acuautla and captured one of the two
leaders and thirty-five other peasant protesters.

The brief armed conflict ended before the cavalry company arrived from Mexico City, yet the owner of Zoquiapan remained ap-
prehensive. The peasants of Acuautla had become increasingly bold
and were only subdued by the mobilization of the national guard—
a process that took time and disrupted estate operations across
Chalco. He wrote again to Riva Palacio demanding the quick and
severe punishment of the "rebels" and the creation of a substantial
police force to protect estate rights.[44]

Within two weeks of the violent confrontation, the peasants of
Acuautla again began to threaten the estate. The estate owner then
offered his final solution. He would pay the community for the
lands it claimed—if the residents would use the money to move to
another part of the state.[45] Did such an offer reveal a lack of confidence in estate land claims, despite court victories? Or did it reflect
doubt in the state's ability to enforce court rulings? It certainly revealed an ignorance of peasant values. Payment in cash and a forced
relocation were not likely to compensate for the loss of community
control of traditional holdings.

The dispute then disappears from the documents. But when a
more general peasant uprising broke out at Chalco in 1868, the peasants of Acuautla would lead their neighbors in attacking estate land
claims.

[43] MRP, 5015, 6 Feb. 1851; 5023, 8 Feb. 1851; 5172, 10 May 1851; 5178, 13 May
1851.
[44] MRP, 5177, 13 May 1851; 5178, 13 May 1851; 5023, 31 May 1851; 5207, 2 June
1851.
[45] MRP, 5189, 23 May 1851.

The Elites' Solution: Rural Police

With the collapse of the colonial mediating state, the worsening of the financial difficulties of landed elites, and the attempts by those elites to make the national state an agent of elite interest, tensions between elites and peasants escalated through the decades after independence, culminating in the conflicts that began in the late 1840s. Elites at Chalco and elsewhere provoked peasants not from strength, but in attempts to overcome their own weakness. Only a strong state could allow such attempts to succeed. And while most Mexican governments after independence worked primarily in the interest of the elites, few were enduring or strong. With the violence of the late 1840s, elites saw the strengthening of the state as the only solution. The rulers of numerous Mexican states turned to creating rural police forces.[46]

The state of Mexico legislated the creation of rural police in October in 1849. In December the subprefect at Chalco called a meeting of estate owners and operators to implement the legislation locally. The alliance of landed elites and the state could not have been more apparent.[47] By early 1850, a small force was established at Chalco, but well below the desired strength. Given the prevailing financial difficulties of estate operators, tax receipts were low and the authorities could not fund the desired police unit. Later in 1850, the force was armed with fifty rifles sent by the ministry of defense, and a second "proprietors' meeting" was called to seek funds for increased police personnel.[48] Meanwhile, a police reserve was created at Chalco by deputizing the "armed dependants" of major local landholders. Again, police were clearly seen as instruments of elite interests, yet the financial problems that plagued the elite kept the new police forces below full strength. Late in December 1851 another proprietors' meeting attempted to recruit funds to bring the Chalco unit up to its full complement.[49]

In June 1855 renewed local disturbances led the subprefect once more to try to strengthen the police force. He envisioned a more effective mounted patrol, but since his treasury could not sustain such a force he turned again to local estate owners, calling for contributions of horses or the money to purchase them. They liked his pro-

---

[46] González Navarro, *Anatomía*, pp. 123–24.

[47] MRP, 3575, 10 Dec. 1849.

[48] MRP, 3902, 4 Mar. 1850; 4452, 13 July 1850; 4718, 10 Oct. 1850; 4815, 29 Oct. 1850.

[49] MRP, 5207, 2 June 1851; 5543, 27 Dec. 1851.

posal, but many pleaded shortages of cash and did not fulfill their quotas. Early in 1856 the mounted patrol was only partially manned and supplied, and the subprefect was threatening fines against land-holders who did not contribute.

From the late 1840s, the state of Mexico accepted the landed elites' pleas for rural police to protect estates from peasant attack. But the continuing economic difficulties of estate operators made the money to sustain police forces scarce. The 4,800 peso annual expense of maintaining twenty mounted men at Chalco could not be extracted from Chalco elites on a regular basis.[50] The irony is clear. Chalco elites wanted an allied state with effective rural police to protect them against peasants increasingly ready to challenge land and water claims. But the problems of estate profitability, in part created and prolonged by peasant opposition, prevented the estab-lishment of an effective police force, and the problem worked to un-dermine the proposed solution.

The police at Chalco, and probably elsewhere in central Mexico, were thus of limited effect during their early years. But the clear shift of the landed elites and allied state rulers to reliance on police powers to resolve conflicts with peasants signified a pivotal change in agrarian social relations. Because post-independence governments were unwilling and unable to play the role of mediator between elites and peasants, conflict escalated. With no mediator, rulers could see no solution but the repression of peasants by force of arms. The message was apparent: the balance of violent power would increasingly determine agrarian social relations in Mexico.

The Liberals' Solution: Abolition of Community Landholding

The development of police forces was seen as a way to strengthen the state's ability to protect elites against the peasant counteroffen-sive of the mid-nineteenth century. But the liberal segment of the Mexican elite had more comprehensive plans that could simultane-ously undermine the ability of peasant communities to resist eco-nomic and political encroachments. The liberals proposed the abo-lition of community property rights. They would not deprive peasants of land; only of the community basis of landholding—the foundation of community solidarity. Indian peasants with small

[50] MRP, 5701, 15 June 1855; 5807, 2 Oct. 1855; 5869, 6 Mar. 1856; 5870, 8 Mar. 1856; 7255a, 10 Jan. 1859.

plots would be left to face estate operators or government officials alone, not as community groups with joint property rights.

There can be little doubt that the destruction of peasant community strength was a primary goal of the Lerdo Law of 1856, the centerpiece of the famed liberal reforms, named after treasury minister Miguel Lerdo de Tejada. The political discussions that followed the proclamation of the law, as well as subsequent scholarly debates, have focused on its application to church properties. The threat to peasant communities has appeared as an unintended result of the liberals' opposition to church wealth and of their belief in economic individualism, but close examination of long-developing liberal thinking and of nineteenth-century social conflicts indicates that the attack on peasant community landholding was fully intended and clearly aimed to free Mexican landholders from peasant opposition.

The ideology of Mexican liberalism evolved from the Spanish enlightenment, led by men such as Pedro Rodríguez de Campomanes and Gasper Melchor de Jovellanas—both of whom proposed the abolition of peasant community landholding—and the Spanish liberal constitution of 1813 called for the division of communal lands. The issue was debated in the constitutional conventions of the new Mexican nation and of several states in the 1820s. Although the early national constitutions refrained from attacking community property, that caution reflected fear of social disruption more than liberal interests.[51]

Yet by the late 1820s, twelve Mexican states had passed laws ending community landholding, including the central highland states of Mexico, Puebla, and Michoacan.[52] But new, weak, and politically divided state governments could not implement such radical changes in peasant land tenure. Then, in the late 1840s, when peasant protests mounted and for a time appeared to threaten elite rule, numerous states again legislated the abolition of community landholding. The close correlation between the development of peasant protests and the passage of laws against community landholding underlines the intent of that legislation.[53] But again in the late 1840s, state power was insufficient to implement such radical changes. With no effective bureaucracy and minimal police forces, state officials could only ask community officials to report on their

[51] Hale, *Mexican Liberalism*, pp. 225–31; Donald J. Fraser, "La política de desamortización en las comunidades indígenas, 1856–1872," *Historia Mexicana* 21 no. 4 (1972): 618–19.

[52] González Navarro, *Anatomía*, pp. 142–43; Fraser, "Política," pp. 622–23.

[53] González Navarro, *Anatomía*, p. 143; Fraser, "Política," pp. 625–26.

properties prior to dividing them. Local leaders could simply refuse
to comply, leaving the legislation an unenforceable announcement
of liberal opposition to peasant community property rights.[54] The
elite consensus in opposition to community property is suggested
by similar legislation, again unenforced, proposed by the last conservative regime of Santa Ana.[55]

The Lerdo law of June 25, 1856 thus culminated at a national level
policies long developing in Mexican political life. The liberals' law
decreed that all "rural and urban estates" held by civil and ecclesiastical corporations were to be "adjudicated in property to the rent-
ors." The law gave tenants or other occupants three months to
claim holdings, after which time they would be available to the public. The government would receive a 5 percent tax on each transac-
tion.[56] Following the proclamation of the law, numerous rulings
made it clear that the liberals had every intention of terminating
community proprietorship of peasant lands.[57]

The peasants quickly perceived that intention.[58] At Chalco, discontent led to secret organizations, which began protests. On August
19, 1856, the subprefect reported that in both Amecameca and San
Gregorio, "there are secret meetings of Indians, it appears to oppose
the implementation of the law of June 25 past, and to take by force
some lands of the haciendas."[59] Early in September, the manager of
the Asunción estate wrote Riva Palacio:

> Last night I was in Temamatla and was told the following in
> great secrecy: that don Francisco de Sales on several nights,
> when the citizens have retired so that no one could observe his
> activities, has brought together in his house people from
> Chalco, Zula, Cocotitlan, San Gregorio, Tlapala, Chimalpa, etc.,
> to discuss a war of castes; . . . that one of these nights at a des-
> ignated hour, they would attack the families de razón in the
> towns and at the haciendas.

[54] Margarita Menegus Bornemann, "Ocoyoacac: Una comunidad agraria en el siglo
XIX," Estudios Politícos 6 no. 18–19 (1979): 91.
[55] Fraser, "Política," p. 627; Antonio Huitron H., Bienes comunales en el estado de
México (Toluca: Gobierno del Estado de México, 1972), pp. 92–94.
[56] Miguel Lerdo de Tejada, Memoria de la Secretaría de Hacienda . . . México, 1857
(Mexico City, 1857), pp. 3–6.
[57] Ibid., pp. 4–5, 25, 70–71, 324–89; Fraser, "Politíca," pp. 632–34; T. G. Powell, El
liberalismo y el campesinado en el centro de México, 1850–1876 (Mexico City: Secretaría de Educación Publica, 1974), p. 140.
[58] See Powell, El liberalismo, pp. 83–84.
[59] MRP, 5915k, 19 Aug. 1856.

The plotting had begun nearly six weeks earlier, and the planned rising waited only for the purchase of arms. The manager asked Riva Palacio for rifles to protect the estate; he found the news so threatening that he chose to keep it from the estate employees, who would bear the brunt of any attack.[60]

The liberals' threat to abolish community landholding, the foundation of peasant solidarity and of local leaders' power, provoked discussions of rebellion. With the threat coming not from local estates but from the national government, peasant communities looked for strength in regional coordination, and they worked to arm themselves with more than sticks and stones, or their traditional machetes. The liberal assault on peasant communities clearly escalated the scale and intensity of peasant protest at Chalco.

But the violence threatened at Chalco never developed; the threat itself appears to have served the peasant interest. While a few properties that had been rented to support town governments at Chalco passed to the tenants in 1856, there was no general attempt to apply the Lerdo law to peasant subsistence lands there. The peasants did not claim their plots as private property; and few outsiders were willing to denounce peasant holdings after the three-month limit had passed. Chalco is rarely mentioned in the listing of properties alienated in the state of Mexico in the last six months of 1856.[61]

Peasant opposition and threats of violence were not limited to Chalco.[62] By October of 1856, Lerdo was aware that peasants were generally ignoring the reform law. He believed that they were being misled, but he also recognized that most peasants could not pay the costs of boundary surveys, titles, and the tax owed the government. He thus issued a revised implementation ruling, giving lands valued at less than 200 pesos automatically to their occupants—with no tax, no survey, and no title. He stated his goal as serving "public peace, the welfare of the most destitute classes, and the implementation and development of the rules dictated for the mobilization of property."[63]

The new ruling eliminated the need for active implementation of the Lerdo law as it applied to small peasant holdings of community lands. The liberals could simply announce the completion of the reform, and peasant communities could carry on locally as usual,

---

[60] MRP, 5915m, 2 Sept. 1856.

[61] Powell, *El liberalismo*, p. 76; Pedrero, "Chalco," p. 110; Lerdo, *Memoria, 1857*, pp. 324–89.

[62] Lerdo, *Memoria, 1857*, pp. 113–16; 156–61.

[63] Ibid., pp. 58–59.

effectively ignoring the new property law. Problems would have to develop in the future: peasants would continue to hold their plots, but the state would consider them private property and refuse to recognize community titles, and the peasants would have no titles to individual plots.

Lerdo's October ruling is also perhaps the clearest statement of the intent of the liberal move against community property. They did not want to make peasants landless, but they did want to force the "mobilization of property." To a liberal, such mobilization would favor economic expansion, but to peasants, immobile property had long served to protect a minimum subsistence base that cushioned their increasing involvement in the commercial economy. The mobilization of property and the accelerated commercialization of rural life would hasten the demise of peasant culture—and of peasant ability to stand against the expanding powers of the national state and the landed elites. Peasants at Chalco and elsewhere were not misled in their opposition to the Lerdo law.

What landed elites expected from the law is revealed in a letter to Riva Palacio from another Chalco landholder in April 1857. He complained that community lands there had not been divided, and pressed for rapid action. He stated that only the end of community property rights could eliminate future conflicts between communities and landholders.[64] The estate owner could write privately what laws and ideologies would not proclaim publicly: Peasant families with small, private holdings would still need to labor at estates, but could no longer sustain the community cohesion that had presented so many problems to landholders.

The Lerdo law was incorporated into the liberal constitution of 1857, which Mariano Riva Palacio and his son Vincente helped write, with little debate and by an overwhelming vote of 76 to 3.[65] The opposition provoked by that new charter focused overwhelmingly on the provisions undermining the economic power of the church. There was little political debate about the alienation of peasant community lands. The dearth of debate, however, should not be seen as suggesting that such provisions were unimportant to political leaders. Rather, it suggests that the alienation of community properties was one reform that reflected a political consensus. Few political leaders were ready to speak in defense of peasant community property. Liberal ideology of economic individualism com-

[64] MRP, 6421, 13 April 1857.
[65] Powell, *El liberalismo*, p. 82.

plemented nicely the desire of Mexican landed elites to weaken the peasant communities. The alienation of peasant community lands was a primary liberal policy aimed at strengthening the power of the state and alleviating economic problems facing landed elites by undermining the landed base of peasant community strength.[66]

Efforts by the separate Mexican states to eliminate community landholding earlier in the nineteenth century had failed. The liberal reformers of 1856 and 1857 had aimed to make those policies more effective by imposing them on a national level. The states had also tried to impose elite interests by creating rural police, also with little success. The liberal reformers of the 1850s also believed that rural police were essential in enforcing state power in rural Mexico, and began to create a national rural force.[67] The liberals turned opposition to community landholding and reliance on armed force to contain the inevitable peasant protests into national policies.

But the liberal rulers of the nation after 1856 also found great difficulties in implementing their land reforms and creating effective police. The opposition of conservative elites and their clerical allies to the anti-clerical portions of the reforms led to a decade of political warfare. And that gave the peasants of central Mexico a respite from the application of the reform laws—along with more evidence of the weakness of the divided national state.

Political Turmoil and More Elite Crisis, 1857–67

The alliance of conservatives and clerics in opposition to the liberal reformers produced a bloody civil war that began in 1857 and ended with another liberal victory in 1859. In the early 1860s, the conservatives, facing elimination from Mexican political life, made a last desperate attempt to retain power by allying with French troops and the puppet monarchy of Maximilian of Habsburg. Thus from 1857 until the fall of Maximilian's regime in 1867 there was again no single, effective state in Mexico. That was made clear to peasants by the resumption of political warfare and the emergence of endemic banditry, which no political force could contain or control. The implementation of the Lerdo law in peasant communities became impossible. And most Chalco peasants remained peaceful, apparently

---

[66] Ibid., pp. 87–89; Fraser, "Política," p. 627; MRP, 6350, 28 Mar. 1857; 6435, 18 Apr. 1857; 6458, 24 Apr. 1857.

[67] For the development of national rural police, see Paul Vanderwood, *Disorder and Progress: Bandits, Police, and Mexican Development* (Lincoln: University of Nebraska Press, 1981).

content to watch competing armies and brigands fight among themselves with deadly results.

Early in the civil war of 1857, Chalco elites saw the conflict as useful to local social control. A gathering of "the most honorable and wealthy citizens" compiled lists of the region's "most pernicious inhabitants" to be drafted into the liberal army.[68] But the civil war quickly proved beyond control. As battles approached Chalco, landholders, officials, estate managers, and town merchants fled the region for the safety of Mexico City.[69] The peasants were left to fend for themselves.

When the liberals reclaimed the national government early in 1859, banditry continued to plague Chalco and much of central Mexico. The principal response by the government then headed by Benito Juárez was to build up a national rural police force. Simultaneously, landholders at Chalco worked to re-establish local peace by strengthening local police. But once again economic difficulties made the funds to sustain effective police scarce.[70]

Early in 1862 the French invaded Mexico, beginning another year of political warfare, and again leaving the countryside to brigands. When the French gained a military victory in 1863, they too saw police as the only solution to rural unrest. They even followed the Mexican liberal precedent of organizing local police forces through meetings of major landholders—who were again asked to pay for police equipment and salaries.[71] Perhaps the only consensus among all parties to the political conflicts of 1857 through 1867 was the belief that police repression was the only answer to endemic rural unrest. The power of violence had claimed a central role in Mexican social relations—not only would control of the state be disputed on the battlefield, but social control would be a question of police ac-

[68] MRP, 6473, 27 Apr. 1857.

[69] MRP, 6718, 4 July 1857; 7007, 23 Sept. 1857; 7079, 12 Oct. 1857; 7098, 19 Oct. 1857; 7102, 21 Oct. 1857; 7108, 24 Oct. 1857; 7113, 27 Oct. 1857; 7175, 4 Jan. 1858; 7228, 2 Sept. 1858; 7232, 3 Nov. 1858; 7237, 12 Nov. 1858; 7241, 2 Dec. 1858; 7242, 3 Dec. 1858; 7243, 6 Dec. 1858; 7246, 18 Dec. 1858; 7248, 31 Dec. 1858; 7252, 8 Jan. 1859; 7253, 8 Jan. 1859; 7254, 9 Jan. 1859; 7255, 7256, 10 Jan. 1859.

[70] MRP, 7255a, 10 Jan. 1859; 7256, 10 Jan. 1859; 7260, 16 Jan. 1858; 7262, 21 Jan. 1859; 7265, 22 Jan. 1859; 7288, 16 May 1859; 7306, 22 Dec. 1859; 7307, Dec. 1859; 7402, 25 May 1861; 7419, 12 Aug. 1861; 7422, 3 Sept. 1861; 7441, 22 Jan. 1862; 7457, 21 Apr. 1862; see also Vanderwood, *Disorder and Progress.*

[71] MRP, 7526, 5 Feb. 1863; 7527, 7 Feb. 1863; 7538, 10 Feb. 1863; 7531, 25 Feb. 1863; 7533, 11 Mar. 1863; 7543, 25 Mar. 1863; 7555, 13 May 1863; 7558, 24 May 1863; 7559, 25 May 1863; 7597, 16 Aug. 1864; 7605, 2 Dec. 1864; 7613, 27 Jan. 1865; 7679, 6 July 1866.

tion. The mediating power of the colonial state, a state that ruled without police and with little overt conflict, was but a distant and vague memory by 1860.

While elites turned increasingly to violence as the principal means of social control, they faced deepening economic problems. In October 1857 the Tomacoco estate owner's debts had mounted to the point that he was forced to sell the property, but in such difficult times, no buyer appeared, leading him to offer to sell parcels of land to neighboring estate owners.[72] In June 1858, the Villaurrutía clan was forced by creditors to lease the Zoquiapan estate—with payments going directly to the creditors.[73] The peasants of Acuautla surely delighted in the problems of their recent foe.

While the economic disruptions of political turmoil reduced estate profits, the contending parties envisioned landed estates as major contributors to their treasuries. To sustain armies in the field and to attempt to build new regimes, liberals, conservatives, and Frenchmen levied taxes, special contributions, and forced loans on estates. During 1860, for example, the liberals levied two forced loans at Chalco that might cost an estate owner nearly 1000 pesos.[74] Many could not pay, or would not pay, whether demands came from political friends or foes. At least one Chalco property was embargoed by a liberal commander for nonpayment of 500 pesos in taxes.[75]

Two examples of elite family crises may illustrate the general problems of the decade of turmoil. Three young sisters named Garrido had inherited the Atoyac estate at Chalco in 1855. The property was then leased, but when the contract ended in 1859 the tenant refused to continue, citing lack of profit. Riva Palacio, guardian of the sisters' interests, sought a new tenant, but when he failed, he leased the estate to his own son. That only brought the financial problems into the guardian's family, forcing Riva Palacio to enter into a financial partnership with the estate administrator in 1860. No improvement followed. The surviving financial accounts revealed why. In 1855, 1859, 1861, 1862, and 1864 the estate expenses were increased by an average of 1000 pesos to pay special taxes, forced loans, and the costs of redeeming church mortgages. With such burdensome extra outlays in times of economic uncertainties, Riva Palacio saw no recourse but to sell the estate in 1864. Only one

[72] MRP, 7113, 27 Oct. 1857.

[73] MRP, 7212, 8 June 1858; 7217, 19 July 1858.

[74] MRP, 7331, 22 June 1860; 7336, 11 July 1860; 7352, 30 Nov. 1860.

[75] MRP, 7440, 21 Jan. 1862; 7712, 4 Jan. 1867; 7712A, 5 Jan. 1867; 7712B, 6 Jan. 1867.

buyer appeared, and obtained the estate for the reduced price of 40,000 pesos.[76]

Atilano Sánchez faced similar problems. During the decades since independence, he had served as chief notary of the Juzgado de Capellanías, the Mexico City Cathedral's mortgage bank. With favored access to capital, he invested in haciendas. During the 1830s he had owned the Moral estate at Chalco, and helped finance others in the region. In the late 1830s, he sold Moral and invested in the Buenavista property, near Apan, northeast of Mexico City. Hoping to increase the value of the estate, he spent over 10,000 pesos in improvements during the 1850s, but he had obtained the capital through loans that the economic and political disruptions of the times left him unable to repay. He tried to sell the property, valued at 125,000 pesos, but received no offer over 115,000 pesos. He held on, hoping that the French intervention would bring stability and profits. But disruptions continued and he lost 7,000 pesos yearly. He had to sell livestock and implements to pay operating expenses. Finally he sold the estate in 1866 to one Martínez de la Torre for 103,000 pesos. Sánchez considered the sale a theft forced by hard times. The once prominent banker and estate owner was left to live on the payments of 330 pesos monthly he received from the new owner, but Sánchez also owed 180 pesos monthly for past debts, and he lamented being reduced to living on but 150 pesos each month.[77] That was not poverty; most rural Mexicans earned less than half of 150 pesos each year. But Sánchez had lost his place in the landed elite.

While some landowners at Chalco and similar regions across central Mexico lost estates between 1857 and 1867, all faced severe financial problems. The continuing disputes over the composition and control of the Mexican state prevented the success of economic reforms and placed financial burdens on estate operators. The crisis of the Mexican elite continued, and perhaps deepened, during the decade of turmoil.

Agrarian Adaptation to Crisis: Sharecropping

Through the 1860s, estate profits at Chalco remained scarce. Landed elites continued to lament their inability to obtain workers on demand for low wages. Their response was to turn increasingly to

[76] MRP, 7313, 1 Mar. 1860; 8019A, n.d.
[77] MRP, 7682, 20 July 1866.

sharecropping. Share tenancies might relieve some of the estate operators' pressing problems. But sharecropping could also escalate conflicts between elites and peasants.

Sharecropping was rare in the Mexican central highlands during the late colonial and early national decades.[78] The first references to sharecropping at Chalco date from 1856, when the manager at Asunción noted that part of the estate's maize and all of its more labor intensive beans and chickpeas were being cultivated by sharecroppers. In 1858, the manager at Buenavista could avoid capture by political opponents by posing as a sharecropper.[79]

Why estates turned to sharecropping is apparent. The cash shortages that caused difficulties in labor recruitment were avoided by sharecropping. Tenants became responsible for performing labor. If the crop failed, as periodically happened in the central Mexican climate, the estate lost little, and the burden was shifted to the tenant. If the crop was good, the estate got half the harvest at almost no expense. Of course, the estate sacrificed much potential profit through sharecropping. But the financial difficulties of the mid-nineteenth century had already made profits rare. Estates at Chalco and elsewhere were thus willing to share some potential profits in exchange for shifting the risks of loss and the burdens of labor recruitment to the sharecroppers.

Chalco peasants accepted sharecropping for different reasons. Most remained dependent on income from nearby estates to supplement their subsistence production. If an estate ceased to offer seasonal labor and instead only offered sharecropping, many peasants had little choice but to accept. In addition, sharecroppers gained some control over production, and received for their efforts basic subsistence staples. The shift to sharecropping clearly reflected the economic weakness of Chalco estate operators, and was perhaps viewed as a modest gain by the local peasants.

An inventory of the Asunción estate completed in 1868 indicated that one-fourth of the estate's maize was being cultivated by sharecroppers. Those tenants had earlier planted nearly half the estate's crops, but having been allotted less fertile and unirrigated fields, they had suffered severe losses to drought. Meanwhile, all of the estate's beans and chickpeas remained in the care of sharecroppers. Indicative of the continuing cohesion of Chalco communities, the

[78] See Tutino, "Creole Mexico," and "Hacienda Social Relations."
[79] MRP, 5915a, 5 May 1856; 5915c, 4 June 1856; 5915d, 10 June 1856; 7175, 5 Jan. 1858.

sharecropping contracts at Asunción were not with individual peasants, but with communities and their leaders.[80]

There is little more detailed information about sharecropping at Chalco. But materials from the Jalpa estates, north of Mexico City in a region similar to Chalco, provides useful insights. In 1864, 58 percent of the maize at Jalpa was raised by sharecroppers, but by 1866, the percentage had risen to 72. The manager explained the shift to greater sharecropping by pointing to the tumultuous times that made laborers and the cash to pay them increasingly scarce.[81]

At Jalpa, sharecropping agreements were with individuals rather than communities. The details of the contracts are also known: the estate provided land, seed, a plow team, and irrigation water (if available), leaving the sharecropper responsible only for labor. The estate and tenant divided the harvest evenly, with the estate holding seed for the next planting from its half. For the few larger sharecroppers able to provide their own plow teams, the estate paid for half the cost of the harvest.[82] Such agreements were relatively favorable to the sharecroppers, and again underline the economic problems facing central Mexican estate operators.

Sharecropping was an adaptation of agrarian social relations resulting from declining estate economic power. Peasants perhaps enjoyed the increase in their direct control of cultivation. Yet sharecropping also brought the potential to increase conflicts between peasants and estate operators. Since the sixteenth century, when central Mexican peasants raised subsistence crops, they did so primarily on lands they held as members of communities. Their economic dependence on estates was largely restricted to seasonal labor. In that traditional division of peasant labor, periodic crop failures were easily viewed as events of an uncontrollable nature; peasants often collected wages for laboring at estates, even if the estate crop later failed. The development of sharecropping in the mid-nineteenth century introduced changes that would increase peasant resentment of estates in times of climatic crisis. For the first time, peasants were cultivating estate resources on their own account. With good harvests, the estate might appear a benefactor, but when crops failed, as they did at least once each decade in central Mexico,

[80] MRP, 7290, 1868.

[81] MRP, 7595, 23 May to 18 June 1864; 7595c, 21 June 1864; 7612, 8 Jan. 1865; 7615, 9 Feb. 1865; 7670, 28 May 1866; "Ynventario de los enseres y muebles de la Hacienda de Jalpa . . . Agosto de 1866," Papeles de los Condes de Regla, Washington State University Archives, Pullman, Washington.

[82] "Ynventario," p. 47.

the resulting hunger appeared less an act of nature and more an imposition of landlords who gave peasants only marginal lands without irrigation—while irrigated estates fields flourished nearby. And, of course, the labor of peasants on shared crops that failed was never remunerated. Thus sharecropping could make hunger appear more a social problem and less a climatic one. Peasants might therefore become more receptive to social solutions.

Peasant Rebellion at Chalco, 1868

In June 1867 liberal armies again occupied Mexico City, soon followed by President Benito Juárez, ending a decade of political warfare. For the rest of the century, political conflict was to be among liberals—and was generally less disruptive. But for Juárez and the liberals, occupying the national government was not equivalent to ruling Mexico. Establishing an effective national state that exercised power in urban and rural areas would remain a long and difficult process. Between 1867 and 1870, the Juárez regime faced endemic banditry, numerous scattered peasant uprisings, and multiple regional revolts. In the central highlands around the capital, several peasants uprisings erupted simultaneously late in 1869 and lasted into 1870. One of the first rebellions against the reestablished liberal regime occurred at Chalco in 1868.

When the liberals reclaimed national power, they remained convinced of the necessity of their reform laws, including the alienation of peasant community lands. And they remained firm believers that protest against their reforms was best met with police power.[83] But the implementation of the reforms and the creation of effective police required a unified and well-financed regime. After 1867, government unity began to improve, but the liberal state remained economically weak, reflecting the continued difficulties of the estate economy. Shortly before taking power in 1867, Juárez levied one more forced loan on estate operators and again faced the elites' combined reluctance and inability to pay.[84] The new liberal state was firmly in power, but poorly funded.

It was in that context that the peasant rebellion of 1868 developed at Chalco. The liberals were calling for the rapid implementation of the law to alienate peasant community lands at a time of continued difficulties in the estate economy. And perhaps the shift toward

[83] Powell, *El liberalismo*, pp. 131–32; Fraser, "Politica," p. 652.
[84] MRP, 7721, 28 Mar. 1867; 7723, 15 Apr. 1867.

sharecropping had also served to heighten tensions. Plotting began in the town of Acuautla before February 1868. Early discussions were held in the home of Viviano Amaya, the local leader believed responsible for the death of the manager of Zoquiapan over a decade earlier.[85] The continuity with earlier protests is clear, but a new element in 1868 was the presence of Julio López, formerly an estate employee near Texcoco, formerly a soldier in liberal armies, and formerly a student of the radical activist Plotino Rhodakanaty.[86] López provided organizational and ideological leadership that worked to unite the peasants of several communities into a single rebellion.

On February 2, 1868, López issued his first proclamation. He declared himself a true liberal and patriot, emphasizing his recent efforts for the liberal cause. Claiming no grievance against the liberal regime, he called for rebellion only against the owners of Chalco estates.[87] López was surely hoping to blunt the state reaction to his rebellion, yet he was simultaneously offering the liberals the opportunity to take a mediating role. The state could negotiate between landholders and peasants, rather than simply backing elite claims. A report written on February 4 to Riva Palacio spoke of a group of "terrorists" led by López and numbering sixty or seventy men. The rising was said to be supported by the peasants of the villages from Coatepec to Huexoculco in the highlands just east of the Chalco plain, but the core of the rebels were from Acuautla. The report concluded by noting a surprising lack of pillaging and violence.[88]

By February 18, the liberal regime had decided against mediation, and sent fifty troops to pursue the rebels.[89] On February 22, the manager of the Compañía estate reported that the active rebels remained a small band of leaders plus a few bandits. The *"gente de a pie"* (the common peasants who came on foot) had not joined in any numbers. That limited rebel numbers, but allowed a mobility frustrating to the troops.

On February 23, López looked to recruit more rebels by issuing another proclamation. He called for unity among peasant communities in an effort to regain lands usurped by elites. He argued that the custom of appealing abuses in the courts only produced unful-

[85] Reina, *Rebeliones*, pp. 81–82.

[86] John Hart, *Anarchism and the Mexican Working Class, 1860–1931* (Austin: University of Texas Press, 1978), pp. 19–20, 32.

[87] Reina, *Rebeliones*, p. 71.

[88] MRP, 7824, 4 Feb. 1868.

[89] Reina, *Rebeliones*, p. 66.

filled promises, while the peasants lost time and money.[90] The same day, López sent a message to the troops ordering them to leave the region or suffer dire consequences. He circulated in the towns and haciendas of Chalco notices offering lands to those who would join him in arms or provide sustenance, while threatening death to all in opposition. The manager at Compañía reported that estate dependants were feigning illness, or just leaving. He saw no defense but more troops.[91]

With troops patrolling Chalco, López found many sympathizers, but few willing to rise in arms. His mobile band was reduced to fewer than twenty men during the last week of February. Confident that the uprising was waning, the troops left Chalco. That made the first days of March uneasy ones for estate managers and others tied to Chalco landed elites. There were rumors that General Miguel Negrete directed the rebels, but no real evidence. With the troops gone, rebel numbers rose again, responding to the offers of estate land. The rebels continued to behave as model rebels, engaging in no vandalism, no random violence, which bothered estate managers because it meant that the rebels were being sustained well by the peasant communities.[92]

Early in March the government again sent troops under General Rafael Cuellar. On March 6, the leaders of Acuautla issued a proclamation stating their grievances and proposing solutions. They cited the reasons for their long conflict with Zoquiapan; they had repeatedly produced their titles in court, but "justice always favored the powerful." As recently as 1862, during the brief liberal government, four village leaders who took claims to court were summarily arrested and drafted into the liberal army. They were sure that if President Juárez knew of such facts, he would disapprove, and they proposed that he establish a special high court to review Chalco land titles. They insisted that the estates present their titles first, and that during the review, neither side should use disputed lands.[93] The peasants were again asking the state to take a mediating role.

López confirmed that position in his declaration of March 7. He then called himself "representative by unanimous vote" of the pueblos of Chalco. He emphasized that rebellion had become necessary only because local judges were acting as landlord agents. López's claims to elected leadership may have been genuine, for he had

[90] Ibid., p. 72.
[91] MRP, 7836, 24 Feb. 1868.
[92] MRP, 7840, 1 Mar. 1868; Hart, *Anarchism*, p. 34.
[93] Reina, *Rebeliones*, pp. 72–74.

called a meeting of two representatives of each Chalco community on March 4.[94]

Skirmishing between rebels and troops followed, with a few casualties on each side. On March 12, General Rafael Cuellar met with López and offered guarantees if the rebels would lay down their arms. López requested twelve hours to consider the proposal. Then, at the appointed hour, he marched toward Tlalmanalco with a force of 150 armed rebels. Cuellar's troops responded with fire and most of the peasants fled in retreat, firing randomly as they dispersed into the highlands.[95] Chalco peasants were apparently ready to support the rebels in many ways, but untrained in combat, they were reluctant to risk life in open confrontation with government troops. The guerrilla war would continue, and it would remain organized and well supported by local peasants, but no mass mobilization of armed Chalco peasants would occur.[96]

His weakness in the face of government troops was evident, and on March 14, López again emphasized that he had no quarrel with the state, only the landed elites. The government, however, recognized no such distinction. It did not want to mediate between peasants and landholders. With little room to maneuver, López and twenty-five of his rebels surrendered on March 19, received safe conduct passes, and returned home.[97]

In the wake of that surrender, the leaders of several Chalco communities sent to the government on March 22 their explanation for the local unrest. They blamed López and his rebel core for beginning the problems, but believed that their success in gaining supporters resulted from the "misery and misfortunes" caused by "the large number of ambitious landlords who possess the lands of the towns in which we were born, the community water supplies, and the woodlands and pastures that are ours." They went on to suggest that the landlords' greed had been facilitated for too long by "the tolerance and ignorance of our fathers and grandfathers," who exhausted themselves working through legal channels—which were also controlled by the landlords.

The community leaders insisted on their opposition to rebellion, but argued that the only means to avoid violence was for the government to conduct an impartial examination of land titles and then a

[94] Ibid., pp. 74–75.
[95] MRP, 7852, 13 Mar. 1868.
[96] Ibid.
[97] Reina, *Rebeliones*, pp. 66–67.

survey of Chalco properties. A mediating state was again the solution in the eyes of the community leaders.[98]

Chalco remained calm during April and May. Local officials and estate managers believed that the troops had completely frightened the peasants. One official toured the rebellious communities, reprimanding them. A few local merchants even began to denounce community lands under the provisions of the Lerdo law.[99] What landlords, officials, and merchants did not perceive was that the peasants had taken advantage of the government's offer of surrender to plant their crops. Among peasants, subsistence comes first.

When the planting was completed, the rebellion resumed. López rose again on May 29. The government in Mexico City was quickly deluged with pleas from estate owners, managers, and local officials at Chalco for troops.[100] Seeking additional support for this second rising, López turned his attention to the communities on the Chalco plain. The residents there lived surrounded by haciendas upon which most of them depended; they had not risen earlier. But this time the peasants of Zula, near Asunción, and San Gregorio Cuautzingo, next to Compañía, joined the rebels. And the managers of those estates received messages from López declaring that pastures and woodlands were community property, for which peasants would pay no rent.[101]

By June 4, 1868, the active rebel force again neared seventy men, including forty mounted. Officials and estate managers were sure the rebels were receiving support from most of the region's peasant communities. Many estate owners and managers saw sufficient threat to pack their valuables and evacuate the region.[102] On June 7, state and national governments again began to send troops to Chalco, but this time they took no chances. By June 13, there were 400 soldiers at Chalco, with another 150 on the way. From June 9–18, the government forces chased rebels who moved easily through the rugged volcanic highlands that separated Chalco from the Puebla basin in the east.

At first, the increase in government force apparently increased the number of rebels who fought with López; by June 12 he was said to be leading a hundred men. But the rebels were eventually sur-

[98] Ibid., pp. 75–76.
[99] MRP, 7855, 17 Mar. 1868; 7859, 19 Mar. 1868; 7872, 24 Apr. 1868; 7873, 25 Apr. 1868.
[100] Reina, *Rebeliones*, p. 67; MRP, 7886, 2 June 1868.
[101] MRP, 7887, 2 June 1868; 7888, 3 June 1868.
[102] MRP, 7889, 4 June 1868.

rounded in the highlands by far larger numbers of trained soldiers. In early skirmishes, the rebels would lose, leave behind a few casualties, but could then escape into the highlands. But on June 17, fifty insurgents were captured on the outskirts of Acuautla. López escaped again, but the main rebel force was crushed.[103]

The peasants of Acuautla quickly turned their attention to seeking lenient treatment. On June 26, residents of Acuautla, Coatepec, and San Pablo—all rebel communities—proclaimed themselves "peaceful and hardworking men" engaged in a judicial dispute with the Zoquiapan estate. They argued that they had been attacked by government troops. The government ignored their plea. Captured peasants who appeared to be rebel followers were forced into the army. Those believed to be local leaders were sentenced to exile in Yucatán.[104]

On July 7, Julio López was captured and, after quick consultation with the Minister of Defense, Ignacio Mejía, he was summarily executed. Two weeks later, the same fate befell his second in command, one Adelaido Amaro. There followed numerous appeals of sentences to armed service and to Yucatán, including one against a woman rebel, but most were eventually upheld by President Juárez. Early in October 1868, those banished to Yucatán sailed from Veracruz.[105]

Overwhelming armed force crushed the second outburst of peasant rebellion at Chalco in the summer of 1868. Peasants could not oppose such force. Simultaneously, the summer of 1868 proved one of extreme drought.[106] Chalco estate inventories reveal substantial crop losses concentrated on lands let to sharecroppers.[107] The coming of scarcity surely heightened peasant discontent, but crop failure also undermined the peasants' ability to sustain a rebellion. The combination of troops and drought turned most Chalco peasants to the most immediate concerns of family survival.

Taking no chances, the government left troops at Chalco to the end of the year. Early in 1869, the peasants of San Gregorio Cuautzingo rose to claim lands held by the Compañía estate. But their neighbors would not join, and they were easily defeated. It took

[103] MRP, 7892, 7 June 1868; 7893, 9 June 1868; 1896, 9 June 1868; 7898, 12 June 1868; 7899, 13 June 1868; 7900, 14 June 1868; 7901, 14 June 1868; 7904, 19 June 1868; Reina, Rebeliones, pp. 67–68.

[104] MRP, 7904, 19 June 1868; Reina, Rebeliones, pp. 77–78.

[105] Reina, Rebeliones, pp. 69–70, 80–81.

[106] Enrique Florescano, ed., Análisis histórico de las sequias en México (Mexico City: Comisión del Plan Nacional Hidráulico, 1980), pp. 106–107.

[107] MRP, 7290, 1868.

nearly six months, but the liberals fully defeated the first major peasant uprising to challenge their rule following the departure of the French. Refusing to mediate, the state won with armed force—and then turned once again to building a police force capable of preventing future disturbances.[108]

Not surprisingly, Chalco remained calm when in the fall of 1869 peasant rebellions developed in several neighboring regions of the central highlands. In the valleys of Morelos to the south, Puebla to the east, and the Mezquital to the north, peasants rose starting September of 1869 and attacked nearby haciendas. Those uprisings also produced ideological leaders such as Francisco Islas who proclaimed his "plan de comunismo" in the Mezquital.[109] Numerous skirmishes followed, but government troops won again by January 1870.

The uprisings of 1869 extended over an area far larger than had those at Chalco the previous year, suggesting that they tapped a more general discontent. Yet their goals were similar to those of the Chalco rebels. The main difference between them appears to be one of timing in the agricultural cycle so central to peasant life. We have seen how the drought of 1868 helped suppress the rising at Chalco. The peasants of Morelos, Puebla, and the Mezquital waited instead until the fall of 1869, when the first good harvest following a year of scarcity was maturing. The months of hunger had surely heightened peasant discontent; the availability of food made sustained rebellion possible.[110]

One can only speculate about the results had Chalco peasants waited to join their neighbors in 1869. The liberal regime would have faced far greater difficulties. Would it have responded by accepting the mediating power the peasant rebels kept offering? Or would Juárez and his allies simply have fought longer to eventually suppress the larger rebellion? As they occurred historically, the central Mexican peasant uprisings of the late 1860s remained regionally isolated from each other. Breaking out in two separate waves surely made it easier for the liberal rulers to crush them with force. The violent suppression of peasant protest was also a major step toward

[108] MRP, 7911, 7 July 1868; 7916, 27 July 1868; 7921, 4 Aug. 1868; 7935, 10 Sept. 1868; 7973, 3 Jan. 1869; 7990, 3 Feb. 1869; 7994, 16 Feb. 1869; 7996, 22 Feb. 1869.

[109] MRP, 8048, 5 Sept. 1869; 8065, 26 Sept. 1869; 8109, 12 Oct. 1869; 8111, 12 Oct. 1869; 8150, 17 Oct. 1869; 8154, 18 Oct. 1869; 8181, 24 Oct. 1869; 8347, 24 Dec. 1869; 8331, 21 Dec. 1869; Reina, *Rebeliones*, pp. 132–35.

[110] Similar timing occurred in the origins of the Hidalgo revolt of 1810.

the liberals' consolidation of a cohesive national state—perhaps their primary contribution to Mexican history.

The Results of Rebellion at Chalco

Viewed as a military conflict, the Chalco rebellion of 1868 resulted in defeat for the peasants. But considering the larger social consequences of the uprising suggests more mixed results. The military power of a state committed to sustaining the landed elite guaranteed that Chalco peasants would gain no additional lands. Nor would the state cease to represent elite interests. But the peasant rebels did succeed in inflicting severe economic losses on Chalco estate owners and operators. The willingness of the peasants to resort to violence generally slowed the attacks on community landholding by elites and the liberal state.

The one clear victory gained by Chalco peasants was the worsening of the financial difficulties that plagued the landed elite. During several years following the conflict, bankrupt estate owners had to offer their estates for sale. Many found no one willing or able to buy entire haciendas, and offered to sell their properties in parcels—and still found no buyers. Landholders unable to pay taxes saw the state that had fought to protect their claims take estates for auction, although few bidders could be found for Chalco properties in the early 1870s. The peasant rising of 1868 had prolonged and worsened the post-independence crisis of the landed elite.[111]

Most notable was the collapse of the Riva Palacio family's local economic power. With mounting debts and little income, the aging Mariano Riva Palacio sold the estates centered at Asunción before the end of 1870 to Felipe Berriozábal, a former administrator of the properties. With little capital, Berriozábal became proprietor of the Asunción haciendas by paying only 4,000 pesos while recognizing 78,000 pesos owed to Riva Palacio, plus another 38,000 pesos that Riva Palacio still owed the Garrido family. The new owner took on a huge debt along with all the risks of operating an estate at Chalco.

Early in 1871, he reported that his reduced profits were not sufficient to cover debts owed Riva Palacio and the Garridos, and he complained to Riva Palacio of his untenable position. Berriozábal hung on until 1873 when he defaulted on payments to Riva Palacio. The courts would have to auction the estate, but if bids were few

---

[111] MRP, 8150, 17 Oct. 1869; 8844, 19 Sept. 1870; 8979, 13 Dec. 1870; 9115, 14 Feb. 1871; 9195, 1 May 1871; 9540, 3 Oct. 1871; 9754, 1 Dec. 1871.

and too low to cover the outstanding debts—as Berriozábal expected—the properties would revert to Riva Palacio, who did not
want to regain such financial liabilities. Berriozábal pleaded for an
arrangement to prevent such an outcome.[112] That is the last reference to Chalco estates in the Riva Palacio papers. What happened to
Berriozábal is unclear, but by 1890, all of the Chalco properties once
held by Riva Palacio belonged to one Fermín Galarza. Galarza apparently belonged to a new generation of Chalco estate owners who
purchased properties cheaply beginning in the 1870s and then
found financial success under the peace imposed by Porfiro Díaz.[113]

Chalco peasants surely gained satisfaction from the economic demise of the Riva Palacio family, yet their principal victory was less
visible. A survey of Chalco landholdings completed in 1890 reveals
two major peasant victories. First, the estates surveyed had increased their landholdings little over the course of the nineteenth
century, and second, nearly every estate surveyed was bounded by
lands listed as belonging to peasant communities. Of course, the liberal legislation was still in force and such lands were legally held
by individual families, but the surveyors recognized the prevailing
reality of continuing community holdings.[114]

Chalco peasants could not defeat the Mexican state nor eliminate
landed elites. The peasants' victory was not in winning, but in de-
laying their own defeat. Mexican peasants have repeatedly revealed
a preference for remaining peasants—living in peasant communities, producing as much of their own subsistence as possible, while
entering the commercial economy but minimally.[115] The success of
peasants at Chalco and in other central highland regions was to
slow, though not halt, the attempts by landlords and liberals to undermine the landed foundation of peasant community life. Such
limited victories of delay were the most peasants could expect in
nineteenth-century Mexico.

Later in the century, under the rule of Porfirio Díaz, the Mexican
state would become stronger and landed elites richer, while peasant
population growth and a general commercialization of the economy
would again threaten peasant life. Even where peasant landholding
survived, more and more peasants became increasingly dependent

---

[112] MRP, 9007, 2 Jan. 1871; 9990, 19 Feb. 1873.

[113] Pedrero, "Chalco," pp. 127, 128, 132, 135.

[114] Ibid., pp. 106, 111, 127–50.

[115] See especially Arturo Warman, . . . Y venimos a contradecir: Los campesinos de
morelos y el estado nacional (Mexico City: La Casa Chata, 1976).

on the wages of labor to sustain their families.[116] Demographic, economic, and political developments of the later nineteenth century all pressed peasant life toward extinction. The 1868 victory of the rebels at Chalco was to delay that extinction at least another generation. To those who aimed to rule, such a victory was little; to peasants whose goal was merely to remain peasants, it meant nearly everything.

Conclusion: Peasant Violence and National Politics

The common assertion that Mexican independence brought little social change is not sustained by the evidence from Chalco and nearby central highland regions. The rulers of the emerging Mexican nation were never reformers who aimed to benefit Mexican peasants. But structural changes inherent in national independence set off a chain of developments that changed Mexican agrarian society substantially. Rural social relations shifted from stable, symbiotic exploitation to violent conflict. The mediating power of the colonial state was eliminated just as landed elites faced financial ruin. The result was a weak and often divided national state that sought to serve as representative for economically failing landed elites. Unable to surmount their national political and economic problems, in the late 1840s Chalco elites turned to solutions in agricultural innovation. But such solutions threatened the customary resource control of Chalco peasants. The peasants responded with court challenges, physical obstruction, and limited violence. The landed elites and the state responded to peasant opposition by trying to create a rural police force—with but limited success.

   Conflict between peasants and landed elites was escalating when the liberals claimed national power in 1856. The new rulers quickly tried to resolve that conflict by decreeing the abolition of peasant community landholding. Such reform aimed to undermine the strength of the peasant communities, while gaining landed elite support for the liberals, but they only succeeded in further alienating peasants. Anticlerical aspects of the liberal reforms quickly set off a civil war that was followed by a foreign intervention. The decade of political warfare until 1867 precluded any concerted attack on peasant community landholding, but when the liberals returned to power under Juárez, they turned again to their policies of alienating community lands and building rural police. Regions in which agrar-

[116] Menegus Bornemann, "Ocoyoacac," pp. 92–112.

ian conflict had produced sporadic violence in the late 1840s and early 1850s, erupted with substantial rebellions in 1868 and 1869.

Facing the experienced troops of the unified liberal state, the peasants lost militarily, but they gained limited successes in inflicting additional economic losses on landholders and by convincing both state and landed elites of the costs of any assault on peasant community lands. Through their rebellion, Chalco peasants claimed the possibility of living as peasants for a few decades more.

Through this agrarian social evolution, violence emerged as the primary aspect of relations between peasants and elites in central Mexico. The rule by accommodation characteristic of the colonial mediating state gave way in the mid-nineteenth century to rule by a national state committed to sustaining elite interests through violence when challenged by peasants.

Meanwhile, peasants at Chalco and elsewhere became increasingly receptive to politically oriented and ideologically committed leaders. Through the early 1850s, peasant protests and rebellions in central highland Mexico remained distinctly local in origin and outlook, but as the liberal national state directly joined landed elites in attacking peasant communities, peasants came to see their difficulties in a wider social and political context. Leaders like Julio López were just beginning to learn to organize peasant unrest for national political purposes in the late 1860s. But the shift toward ideological orientation and political organization is apparent.

The peasant risings of the late 1860s were larger and more sustained than those that preceded them in the central Mexican highlands. Compared to the conflicts that began in 1910, however, those of the mid-nineteenth century remained brief and regionally isolated. Yet peasant grievances changed little. Protests repeatedly focused on encroachments against community autonomy by landed elites, backed by national states. Perhaps the expansion of commercial activities made such grievances increasingly acute as the nineteenth century progressed, but the expansion of peasant violence also related directly to changing relations with national political life. Through the uprisings of the late 1860s, central Mexican peasants showed their awareness of national political developments by repeatedly pressing their claims whenever national elites were visibly weak or divided. But the peasants at Chalco and elsewhere would not become participants in national political conflicts. They clearly perceived the political wars of 1857 through 1867 as affairs of elites. By waiting until the resolution of those political conflicts to rebel, they faced a unified state. Perhaps the major lesson learned by peasants from the defeated uprisings of 1868 and 1869 was that they could not fight long against the armies of a unified state—even when that state and its elite allies faced severe economic difficulties.

By 1910, central Mexican peasants were ready to take their goals of land reform and their abilities to sustain violent rebellion into the heart of elite political conflicts. Deeply divided elites were willing to court peasant support, if only for their own political advantage. The result was an extended period of violent revolutionary conflict, which, again, the peasants could not win. They never claimed control of the national state, but they did force political leaders to compromise with peasant interests. The resulting authoritarian state did mediate between landed elites and peasants to entrench its own power. Peasant participation in the struggles of the early twentieth century inflicted severe defeat on landed elites—and claimed for many peasants the ability to survive as peasants for another generation. In a world of strengthening states and commercializing economies, that was the maximum victory possible for peasants. The destruction of peasant life in central Mexico was postponed until the middle of the twentieth century.

CHAPTER FIVE

Peasant Rebellion in the Northwest:

The Yaqui Indians of Sonora,

1740–1976

Evelyn Hu-DeHart

The Yaqui nation, in the northwestern state of Sonora, has stood out in Mexican history for its long and successful resistance to acculturation and assimilation into Mexican society. Ever since the Europeans "discovered" the Yaquis in 1533, they have insisted on their tribal identity above all else, and have waged numerous wars to prevent the loss of their communities, land, and distinct way of life in the fertile Yaqui River valley. They have steadfastly maintained some form of tribal organization and government for more than four centuries. Yaqui exile barrios exist outside the valley in large Sonoran and Arizonan towns. Because their identity as Yaquis is firmly rooted in the land, they have remained primarily an agricultural people, even though during long periods of their history in the nineteenth and twentieth centuries they were prevented from deriving all their subsistence from the soil in their contested homeland; in fact, many became temporary wage laborers in the haciendas, mines, and railroads of Sonora and Arizona.

Unlike some other frontier Indian communities, Yaqui participation in the larger economy, beginning as early as the mid-seventeenth century, did not result in their permanent assimilation. For even as they worked for wages, they struggled to preserve their own autonomous communities, physically, politically, and culturally separate from the rest of society. This dual characteristic of separatism on the one hand, and partial integration on the other is the source of Yaqui strength and the key to their survival. An agricultural, indigenous people, they did not lead an isolated subsistence living totally removed from the mainstream of first colonial, then Mexican, society; this makes them different from most of Mexico's Indian communities. For their cultural survival, however, they have had to pay a dear price—a stance of almost permanent rebelliousness from the mid-eighteenth century on.

This chapter explores Yaqui revolts and resistance through nearly four centuries. The discussion is divided into four parts: the colonial era (1533–1820); the nineteenth century from independence through the early Porfiriato (1821–87); the late Porfiriato through the Mexican revolution (1887–1920); and the post-revolutionary era (1920–1980s). Each period was highlighted by one or more serious revolts, and distinguished by a different form of resistance.

The Colonial Period and the Yaqui Revolt of 1740

New Spain's northwest frontier was a sparsely populated region.[1] Neglected by the Hapsburgs after some initial exploration and prospecting ventures because of its remoteness and the hostility of the Indian tribes (including the Yaquis), it became the core of the Jesuit empire in Mexico. Unchallenged by any serious secular competition for a century and a half, the Jesuits meticulously missionized all the native peoples up to the Pimería Alta (Arizona), socially and economically reorganizing each distinct linguistic/cultural group into neat mission centers in their original territories. Undisputed Jesuit hegemony on this frontier resulted in a *paz jesuita* that prevailed until the Bourbons came to power in the eighteenth century. To revitalize New Spain and create new sources of revenue for the imperial coffers, the Bourbons encouraged the frontier's economic development, centered around mining and necessarily predicated on access to the missionized indigenous population for labor. The Jesuits' resistance to this encroachment on their domain culminated in their expulsion from New Spain in 1767. With this major obstacle removed, Bourbon economic development of the northwest continued until destroyed by the independence movement, which found practically no adherents in any sector—Indians, whites, or mestizos—of this frontier society.

In the Jesuits' Mexican empire, the Yaqui mission was the show-

---

[1] The discussion in this section is based on my monograph: *Missions, Mines and Indians: History of Spanish Contact with the Yaqui Nation of Northwestern New Spain, 1533–1820* (Tuscon: University of Arizona Press, 1981). When necessary and of particular interest, I cite particular documents or sources.

case and cornerstone. With a population of 30,000, it was the largest indigenous nation of the northwest and culturally the most advanced, having progressed to a sedentary existence more dependent on agriculture than on gathering. Originally distributed among some eighty scattered *rancherías* or hamlets, each one politically and economically autonomous—uniting only for the purpose of territorial defense against invaders—these primitive cultivators were reorganized by two Jesuit missionaries in the beginning of the seventeenth century into one mission with eight tightly structured communities along the banks of the Yaqui River. This consolidation allowed for closer Jesuit supervision and a more rational system of production that quickly yielded a surplus. The reorganization also heightened the Yaquis' sense of cultural and political unity; significantly, their myth of creation begins with these eight mission pueblos.

Under Jesuit rule, then, the Yaqui mission became the most cohesive, productive, secure, stable, and docile of all Jesuit missions. In the pueblos, families cultivated food on assigned land for their own subsistence three days of the week. For another three days the men worked on the communal plots and ranches, producing the mission's surplus, which the Jesuits expropriated in its entirety, using it to found new missions, to trade with the few local settlers, and occasionally to alleviate food shortages in the Yaqui mission itself. Besides establishing the new work schedules, the Jesuits enhanced productivity by introducing new crops (wheat, cotton), new tools and technology (the plow and controlled irrigation), new crafts (weaving for women), as well as horses and cattle for the new ranching economy. For over a hundred years Yaquis acquiesced to these directed changes.

Then in 1740, the Yaquis, leading several neighboring tribes, mounted the most serious revolt within the missionary domain. The bitter conflict, which involved the small Spanish population in the region as well as Yaquis and Jesuits, was part of a wave of frontier rebellions that spelled the decline of Jesuit hegemony. We can better place this first Yaqui revolt in proper historical perspective if we summarize Yaqui history after the revolt for the remainder of the colony. After 1740 the Yaquis did not rise up again while Spain ruled. Unlike most other mission communities in the northwest, they did not disintegrate with the departure of their Jesuit protectors in 1767, but actually ensured their own survival by becoming an indispensable source of labor for the burgeoning mining economy. At the same time, they retained their ex-mission pueblos, which (as free villages) continued to exist much as they had under the Jesuits, with one notable exception: they no longer produced vast surplus. Of course, the Bourbon state could have demanded it—and indeed it attempted several times without success to collect tribute from the Yaquis for the first time ever—but settled instead for their labor in the mines, which the Yaquis willingly provided.[2] In 1740, why did the Yaqui rise up after having gone along with the Jesuits for over a century? Who participated and who led it?

Three interrelated conflicts on the frontier came to a head to produce the 1740 revolt. First, as their prospects for development brightened at the end of the seventeenth century, mine owners and hacendados intensified their demands for more Indian agricultural produce and especially the labor of the mission Indians. Second, local civil and military authorities, newly appointed by the Bourbons, more forcefully asserted their jurisdiction over temporal affairs in the missions—authority that Habsburg officials had implicitly surrendered to the Jesuits. Third, Yaquis themselves for the first time began to press for certain fundamental changes in the mission system, although, as we shall see, not for a definitive end to a system that had accorded them considerable protection and benefits.[3]

---

[2] During the entire Jesuit period, as long as the Yaquis remained under the mission system, they were not subject to taxation by the secular state. After 1767, the Bourbons tried to collect tribute from the Yaquis, but never with success, and eventually abandoned the effort.

[3] The *Pastells Collection* of Rome, which is on microfilm at the Knights of Columbus Vatican Film Library of St. Louis University (St. Louis, Missouri), has gathered together most of the documents pertaining to the 1740 Yaqui rebellion. The single most important document in Pastells is actually a compilation of copies of all the important documents on the case. In June 1744, the Viceroy Conde de Fuenclara submitted to the crown the final and definitive report on the rebellion. In addition to his own brief cover letter, he forwarded hundreds of pages of copied evidence from all parties involved, spanning a period of some ten years. Unless otherwise stated, all data concerning the 1740 revolt can be found in the letter of Viceroy Conde de Fuenclara to His Majesty, 25 June 1744, *Pastells* 32: 323–712 (hereafter *Fuenclara 1744*). The most important Jesuit document on the 1740 revolt was penned by Father Mateo Ansaldo: "El Pl Mateo Ansaldo Rector del Colegio de San Pedro y San Pablo de Méjico sobre la sublevación de los indios presente este escrito contra las injurias que el Huidobro pone en las autos que a los R. P. entregaron," 5 Dec. 1743, *Pastells* 18: 91–104. Appended to this document is an anonymous report entitled: "Hecho de la Raíz, Causas y Progresos, hasta su conclusión de la rebelión de los Indios Hiaquis, Maios y convezinos en la Gobernación de Sinaloa en el año de 1740, siendo Gobernador Vitalicio Don Manuel Bernal de Huidobro," *Pastells* 18: 72–90. A twentieth-century Jesuit historian, Gerardo Decorme, believes that this anonymous report was written by none other than the controversial Father Diego González of the Yaqui mission; see Gerardo Decorme, *La obra de los Jesuitas mexicanos durante la época colonial, 1572–1767*, Vol. 2: *Las misiones* (Mexico: Antigua Lib. Robredo de J. Porrúa e Hijos, 1941), p. 333.

The specific issue was the secularization of the missions. *Vecinos* (Spanish settlers) and the colonial authorities argued that the time was long overdue for the missions to be turned over to secular priests and for the Indians to be integrated into colonial society and serve its needs; after all, the original mission ideal allowed for ten, at most twenty, years for missionaries to pacify, civilize, and prepare frontier tribes for social integration. The Jesuits in turn argued that the peculiarities of the frontier and its Indian cultures required the indefinite postponement of secularization. In reality, of course, they deliberately perpetuated paternalistic rule over their Indian charges in order to justify a permanent role on the frontier. Caught in the middle of this ideological and political dispute were the Yaquis, who as it turned out did not simply remain passive victims, but reacted to influence the course of events. They seemed to prefer neither total integration into colonial society, nor continuous unquestioned loyalty to the mission.

Each of the three parties involved offered different explanations for the uprising. Significantly, all emphasized longstanding sources of conflict while minimizing the immediate causes of the 1740 rebellion—floods leading to famine and subsequent raiding of mission granaries, Spanish ranches, and *reales de minas* by Yaquis and other Indians seeking food.

In their official report on the revolt, the Jesuits accused local authorities, in particular Governor Manuel Bernal de Huidobro and alcalde mayor Miguel de Quiróz, of an attempted invasion of Indian land that caused the Indians "enormous pain" and plunged them into "desperation." It was the Spanish usurpation of Indian land that drove them to rebellion, the Jesuits concluded. In fact, there is not much evidence to support this contention. What must have worried the Jesuits more were plans announced by Huidobro, when appointed lifetime governor of the northwest in 1734, to reform the mission system. Although not implemented at the time, the proposals were a barely disguised scheme for the gradual secularization of the mission. The governor suggested granting Indians more economic autonomy, assessing a tribute payment from them, and having outsiders monitor Jesuit conduct inside the mission. These reforms would have effectively eroded Jesuit authority, which had hitherto been absolute.

Related to the same fear of an inexorable movement toward secularization was the increasingly frequent contact between Indians and Spaniards, through the mines and through the frontier militias, which included a large number of Indians legally recruited from the missions. From these limited experiences with the Spanish world outside the mission, a small but vocal group of Yaquis emerged, too acculturated and too susceptible to Spanish influence for Jesuit comfort. These *ladino* Yaquis began to break down the Indian isolation that the fathers had so carefully constructed and jealously safeguarded. Not surprisingly, the leaders of the 1740 revolt were precisely such ladino Yaquis. Not only were they not afraid to speak out, to express heretical ideas, but they too readily approached civil authorities with their complaints, thus sidestepping the missionaries who had traditionally counted on serving as the Indians' intermediaries and brokers in all their communication with the Spanish world. Such independent thinking and behavior undermined Jesuit authority and facilitated the move towards secularization. Unable to accept the fact that their own actions might have somehow alienated the Yaquis and driven them to seek redress outside the mission, the Jesuits blamed the governor and his subordinates for inciting the Indian uprising.

As for Governor Huidobro, rather than deny that he had tried to interfere in mission affairs, he argued that it was his duty to defend the "royal jurisdiction" and assert the crown's interest over that of the Jesuit order, which meant weakening the mission system. He and his fellow vecinos, mine owners, and landowners encountered open defiance from the missionaries when they tried to recruit the authorized number of workers from the missions under the *repartimiento* labor system. Without access to such labor, the mines could not function, the economy would not flourish, and the royal coffers would not be enriched. In 1736, a group of vecinos argued in a letter to the viceroy that because the Jesuits exploited the Yaquis to reap yearly profits of two to three thousand pesos, the Indians wanted freedom from Jesuit tutelage and wanted to pay tribute to the crown. Huidobro also maintained that the missions would prosper and progress if administered by clerics or friars "not given to acquiring so much power, or to controlling everything." Actually, Huidobro and the vecinos probably would not have pushed strenuously for secularization at this time had the order cooperated more with the fortnightly labor rotations for the mines. But when Jesuits counseled Yaquis to ignore the work orders, they encouraged disrespect for the crown, damaged its authority and credibility, and contributed directly to the outbreak of rebellion in 1740.

The third party to this conflict were the Yaquis. For the first time under Jesuit rule, an articulate and independent Yaqui leadership had appeared. Juan Ignacio Usacamea, better known as El Muni, was a militia captain and gobernador of Ráum pueblo; his collaborator Bernabé was gobernador of Huírivis. As early as March 1736, they discussed grievances with civil authorities that centered around abuses committed by certain resident Jesuits and their assistants, including not only handpicked Yaqui magistrates such as Captain General Gurrola, but outsiders (mestizos, mulattoes, and even other Indians) brought in by the missionaries. Several months later, to punish and isolate these dissidents, the priests called in Lt. Governor Manuel de Mena (then heading the local government in the governor's absence), who obligingly ordered the arrest of Muni, Bernabé, and several others accused of conspiracy to foment an uprising. Much to the alarm of Mena and the Jesuits, the arrest provoked an immediate outcry outside the jail of Pótam; some two thousand armed Yaquis demanded and got the release of Muni, Bernabé, and the others. The spontaneous demonstration underscored the wide base of support that Muni and Bernabé enjoyed.

Instead of taking this minor uprising as a cue to respond to the grievances, however, the Jesuits merely removed two controversial priests discredited by the incident and replaced them in November 1736 with the even tougher Father Nápoli. Bent on disciplining Muni and Bernabé once and for all, he removed them from their respective offices in Ráum and Huírivis, citing insubordination and insolence. Muni and Bernabé appealed to various local officials for justice, but none dared antagonize the powerful Jesuits except for Governor Huidobro, who, upon his return in July 1738, conducted a thorough investigation. From Father Nápoli he heard charges against Muni and Bernabé that they had appropriated all communal goods in their pueblos for themselves, leaving nothing for the priests, and that many Yaquis were already worshipping Muni on their knees as if he were a god. Their audacity, Nápoli said, can be characterized as "hombrearse"—presuming to act like civilized adults by calling themselves "señor," roving around with an armed retinue, and otherwise dressing like Spaniards with guns, swords, etc. From Muni and Bernabé, the governor heard complaints about the excessive work loads demanded of them, their wives, and children, especially for the production and transportation of goods and cattle for California. Their communal ranches were depleted of cattle because the priests had dispatched over six hundred head to California, and sold two hundred each to Los Alamos and the Villa de Sinaloa (both Spanish towns). Yet the Yaqui people did not see or enjoy the profits from the sale of their surplus. Huidobro's answer to these grievances was to dispatch Muni and Bernabé to Mexico

City to testify personally before the viceroy and Archbishop Vizar-
rón. The archbishop, who was not particularly fond of the Jesuits,
issued an invitation to the Yaquis to visit him.

The Jesuits regarded this move by Huidobro as hostile to their interests and an incitement to rebellion. Throughout 1738 and 1739,
and up to the actual outbreak in early 1740, they kept alerting local
authorities to signs of rebellion in the Yaqui pueblos, only to have
Huidobro and his subordinates dismiss them as "false alarms" not
worthy of attention. At this time the missionaries were inclined to
call any act of insubordination a sure sign of impending revolt. They
even began removing valuable ornaments from mission churches for
safekeeping in California, a move that the Yaquis later added to their
growing list of abuses. Meanwhile, when pressed for more Indians
to work in the mines, Father Nápoli simply insisted that he had no
Yaquis to spare for the vecinos.

While tensions built up in the Yaqui region, Muni and Bernabé
received their private audience with the viceroy in July 1739. The
petition they presented is one of the few original Yaqui documents
in existence. It was widely circulated in high official circles in Mexico City and among the Jesuit hierarchy as well. Contrary to the Jesuits' worst fears, the statement fell short of a passionate plea for secularization. On the other hand, it was definitely critical of certain
priests and, more importantly, of certain longstanding mission practices, criticisms firmly rooted in the daily interactions between Jesuits and Indians. Concerning specific grievances of recent origin, the
Yaquis urged the removal of Fathers Nápoli and González, as well
as the native officials and outsiders they had imposed on the Yaquis.
They also asked for compensation from Lt. Governor Mena for the
"damages" he had caused them with the unwarranted arrests at Pótam. Muni demanded the restitution of his land, which he claimed
Father González had taken from him as punishment for an alleged
offense. One request, which surely must have comforted the missionaries in their moment of despair over the statement in general,
was for an additional resident priest to supplement the one missionary left for the four pueblos of Huírivis, Ráum, Pótam, and Belém.

Other sections of the petition probably caused the Jesuits greater
concern. Muni and Bernabé asked the viceroy to allow their people
the right to carry their traditional arms, that is, bows and arrows;
that they not be forced to work in the mission without pay; that the
padres not take away their land and convert it to other uses; that
they be allowed to elect their own officials without missionary interference; that the Jesuit provincial protect the Indians from exces-

sive work loads in the pueblos, especially during their fiestas and for transporting provisions to California; that they be allowed to sell some of their produce to whomever they pleased; and that the padres not stop them from working in the mines. Finally, they requested the appointment of former alcalde mayor Quiróz as "protector of Indians." The Viceroy's response is not recorded.

To be sure, Jesuits had real cause for alarm, for these proposals struck at the very foundation of absolute Jesuit power within the mission and in regulating Yaqui interaction with the Spanish world outside. But just as the vecinos in the mid-eighteenth century would have settled for a loosening of Jesuit control over the mission population short of outright secularization, these ladino Yaquis seemed to argue for a similar relaxation of Jesuit rule, one less autocratic and less paternalistic. Nowhere in this lengthy statement did the Yaqui leaders ask that the mission be closed. Nor did they echo the vecinos' claim (made in the 1736 letter to the viceroy mentioned above) that they desired to pay tribute to the crown or the vecinos' other claim that they preferred secular priests to Jesuit fathers. It was during the absence of Muni and Bernabé that the uprising began, and by the time the two returned home the revolt had passed its most active and violent phase. Upon their return, they immediately agreed to help pacify the rebels, but the Jesuits nevertheless insisted on identifying Muni and Bernabé as the instigators because of the seditious ideas they espoused. It might seem that the actual revolt had little to do with Muni and Bernabé's grievances, since it was precipitated by floods and famine.

In late 1739 and early 1740, a totally unfamiliar sight appeared in the Yaqui area—that of hungry foraging Indians. Soon these desperate individuals began raiding mission granaries, where the mission surpluses were stored, and nearby Spanish ranches and haciendas for food. During this famine, the missionaries' handling of the problem departed drastically from the tradition their predecessors had established. Seldom if ever under Jesuit rule did Yaquis have to resort to gathering wild foods or to banditry for survival, for the missionaries had always managed to take adequate care of them by tapping the mission's supplies. During the famine of 1655, for example, while Jesuits in some of the less prosperous missions reported following their flock into the mountains in search of food, the priests assigned to the Yaquis doled out a prodigious amount of food from the communal granaries, some six thousand rations each day for four months.[4] In 1739, however, Nápoli and his colleagues decided

[4] "Apologético defensorio y puntual manifesto que los Padres de la Compañía de

they would send the surplus to California as usual, an incomprehensible decision that the Yaquis could only interpret as being motivated by vindictiveness. When Indians from nearby missions approached the prosperous Yaqui mission for relief, Nápoli turned them away empty-handed. When he finally agreed to sell a niggardly quantity of maize, he demanded an exorbitant price that few could afford.

Another possible explanation for Nápoli's unresponsiveness could be because the four pueblos directly under his care—the four lower pueblos that included Muni and Bernabé's Ráum and Huírivis—were less affected by the swelling of the river. The fact that he had been transferred from California to the Yaqui might also help explain why he placed the needs of his former charges above those of the Yaquis. Nevertheless, Father Nápoli's insensitivity forced many hungry people to raid and plunder, and confirmed the validity of Muni's and Bernabé's complaint that they lacked authority to dispose of the surplus.

The hardest hit of all the pueblos was Bácum, located on the upper Yaqui River. According to one witness, flood waters destroyed "all the cattle and crops. . . . and that because of this they [Yaquis] fled up a hill, that from there they began to plunder; that because Father Fentanes punished them, they became incensed and threw him out of the mission."[5] By February 1740, widespread plundering had generalized into the beginnings of a massive uprising. Vecinos in isolated locations abandoned their mines and homes for larger towns and haciendas. By April the Yaqui River was "all drums and arrows"; by the end of May, groups of Mayos, Fuerteños, Guaymeños, and Pimas Bajos had taken up arms and joined the raiding. From late May to the surrender in mid-October, except for the handful of prisoners held in the Yaqui region, the rebels had cleared an

Jesús, misioneros de las Provincias de Zinaloa y Zonora, ofrecen por noviembre de este año de 1657, al Rectísimo Tribunal y Senado Justísimo de la Razón, de la Equidad y de la Justicia, contra las antiguas, presentes y futuras calumnias, que les ha forjado la envidia, les fabrica la malevolencia y cada día les esta maquinando la iniquidad." *Archivo General de la Nación de México, Ramo de Historia* 316: 359–425; reproduced in large part in Pablo Herrera Carrillo, "Sinaloa a mediados del siglo XVII," *Congreso Mexicano de historia, memorias y revistas* (Mexico City, 1960), pp. 145–74.

[5] Testimony of the coyote Juan Frías, taken by Huidobro, in *Fuenclara 1744*, pp. 391–92. *Fuenclara 1744* contains several summaries of the significant events leading up to the outbreak of revolt in 1740. One of the best is the report of Auditor de Guerra Marquez de Altamira, Mexico, 12 June 1743; he concurred that the rebellion began with the raids, in turn precipitated by the difficult times of recent years.

area of over one hundred leagues from the Fuerte River in the south to the Pimería Alta in the north of all *yoris* (whites, Spaniards), vecinos, and missionaries alike. Most of them fled to Alamos or safer towns farther south. With all mining operations halted and all communication cut off, the rebels enjoyed *de facto* control of the region.

Governor Huidobro estimated the combined rebel strength at twelve to fourteen thousand, organized into strike units of as large as three to four hundred. Jesuits contested these figures as exaggerated, pointing out they were based on the false assumption that all Indians of the northwest had joined arms. Far from being a "race war" (*guerra de castas*) directed at annihilating all white people, as some frightened vecinos charged, the rebels aimed their violence primarily at Spanish property. They burned and pillaged the vecinos' homes, storehouses, mines, and chapels. They took slightly over one hundred prisoners, mostly women and children; but they killed surprisingly few. Only in one report of a rebel assault were as many as five deaths noted.[6]

Apart from raiding mission granaries for provisions, which they regarded as theirs anyway, the rebels generally spared mission properties. Indeed, many became irate when Father Nápoli stripped mission churches of valuable ornaments for shipment to California. Most of the violence took place outside the Indian pueblos, with the vecinos sustaining almost all the damages and losses to life and property. Not a single missionary was killed by rebels, although one elderly priest died from the terror and ordeal of flight from the Mayo.

Governor Huidobro's handling of the crisis provoked much controversy, at first with the missionaries, but as the revolt continued, with some vecinos as well. After the first attacks on Spanish property, he dispatched small contingents of ten to twelve presidial soldiers to pursue the raiders. When these retaliatory actions proved

[6] The report of five casualties was contained in anti-Huidobro testimonies gathered by his rival and successor, Agustín de Vildósola; see Vecinos of Alamos, testimonies, Alamos, 13 February 1743, *Pastells* 34: 385–438. In fleeing Ostimuri, these vecinos testified that they left behind five dead. In fleeing from Cedros, vecinos reported that the rebels killed "a few" and took seventy women and children prisoners. One of the many myths that have grown up around this revolt concern the high number of Spanish deaths. Also, it seems ironic that, more than anyone else, Jesuits sensationalized accounts of Yaqui brutality and violence. They claimed, for example, rebels raped white women—wives of prominent vecinos—then dragged them off naked to the Yaqui River along with innocent children. The reasons for these exaggerations are not clear, but they simply could have been the Jesuits' way of demonstrating what was bound to happen when they, the moral guardians, were removed from the Indian communities; in short, a not so subtle warning against secularization.

ineffective, he tried "*modos suaves*," or mild methods of pacification that offered reconciliation. Given his critical shortage of men
and provisions, the governor argued in his own defense that a full-
scale military campaign was simply out of the question. Consequently, when the rebellion proved uncontainable, Huidobro retreated southwards, eventually to the fortified town of Alamos. In
his wake followed most of the terrified vecinos and missionaries.
During his retreat and repeatedly at Alamos, the governor appealed
to the viceroy for reinforcements from Nueva Vizcaya and the northern presidios.

During this active, violent phase of the rebellion, the Indians appeared to have no clear-cut leadership. A number of chieftains,
mostly Yaquis, appeared, some short-lived, and none with the overall command of all rebel bands. Huidobro reported that the revolt
seemed to consist of a number of rebel bands of varying sizes, each
acting on its own. There did not appear to have been much overall
coordination or grand strategy.

In July and August, two groups reached the northernmost extension of the revolt, in Pima territory. There they encountered their
first formidable adversary in militia captain Agustín de Vildósola,
who repelled two massive attacks on the town of Tecoripa and inflicted large casualties on the rebels. These defeats marked the turning point and produced a much-needed hero around whom the demoralized vecinos and missionaries could rally. Together with other
crucial Spanish victories in the south, with the arrival in late August
of some reinforcements, and with the return of Bernabé that same
month, a Spanish victory seemed to be at hand. On September 7,
Huidobro dispatched Bernabé to the Yaqui area, where rebel chiefs
had already extended peace feelers. On October 13, Bernabé returned to Alamos with a large group of prominent Yaquis, bringing
in tow 103 Spanish prisoners. For days afterwards additional groups
of repentant Indians came to surrender.

When Huidobro finally emerged from his sanctuary in November,
it was not to conduct an active military campaign so much as to
consolidate the peace after the rebels' capitulation. In December
1740 and January 1741, accompanied by Bernabé and Muni, he
toured the Yaqui pueblos, took the census, confiscated and burned
weapons, and returned stolen property and cattle. He noted that
many Yaquis had already gone to the Sonora and Vizcaya mines to
work, while others were once again plying the supply boats to California, or tending to their fields and cattle. In short, it appeared that
most Yaquis had resumed their customary activities. The governor

also followed the viceroy's instructions in installing Muni as captain general of the Yaqui and Bernabé as *alferez* or captain, both with permission to bear arms. These appointments were apparently the only concrete concessions the Yaquis won from the viceroy.

The governor's own fate was not as felicitous. As a result of the many charges of cowardice and incompetence that vecinos and especially Jesuits had made against him, he was relieved of his office and summoned to Mexico City to defend himself. Captain Vildósola became the new governor, while entirely new groups of Jesuit missionaries arrived to take up posts along the Yaqui and Mayo Rivers.

At first the Jesuits enthusiastically supported Vildósola's appointment and applauded some of his early decisions, notably the capture of Muni and Bernabé in June 1741 together with the arrest of forty-three of their associates, including the rebel chieftain Calixto.[7] They were probably less comfortable with the garrisons posted in the Yaqui Valley and at other strategic locations in the rebel-torn area, because of the proximity of these soldiers to mission Indians, even if the purpose was to keep the peace. But most of all, the honeymoon was short-lived because Vildósola turned out to be just as committed to promoting secular interests as his ill-fated predecessor had been. As soon as he assumed office he visited the important reales and haciendas in the rebel area to encourage vecinos and mineros to return and revive their enterprises, promising them adequate armed protection. In mid-1742, when he reinspected the Yaqui pueblos, Vildósola exhorted the Indians to be loyal to the crown and work for the Spanish mines and haciendas.[8] Before long, Jesuits were denouncing Vildósola as vehemently as they had Huidobro. In sum, the tension between secular and Jesuit interests that had preceded the revolt remained unresolved, and even heightened with time.

Lasting six months, the 1740 revolt, headed by the Yaqui nation but joined by many others in the region, conformed to the characteristics of a classical, large-scale peasant rebellion. Grievances were deep-seated, rooted in the excessive expropriation of surplus, in this case by Jesuit missionaries rather than private landlords or the state. In addition, these mission Indians reacted to insensitive, abusive behavior by some of the priests, particularly their failure to relieve the

---

[7] Calixto himself testified that he rebelled because of the rumored deaths of Muni and Bernabé, and that Father Nápoli confirmed the reports; see *Fuenclara 1744*, p. 400.

[8] A number of letters from Vildósola to the viceroy covered these events: 7 May 1741, 11 July 1741, 1 Aug. 1741, *Pastells* 30: 364–72, 379–96, 406.

hungry with the mission's abundant surplus. No clear, overall command emerged during the revolt; rather, the uprising, which by one account involved well over ten thousand rebels, consisted of many localized bands, each with its chieftain.

The Muni and Bernabé protest movement that preceded the armed phase did not lead directly to violence, but indicated the growing alienation between Jesuits and Yaquis, and the growing attraction or "pull" of the mines as an alternative to the mission. After their surrender, those Yaquis who did not return to the fields opted for the mines. The presence of this alternative, and how the Yaquis took advantage of it, made the Yaqui situation unique. Because it was the "pull" of the mines as much as (if not more than) the "push" of the mission that determined Yaqui mobility, the Indians were neither losing their land nor were they forced to work for wages. In fact, in this sparsely populated, labor-scarce, and rapidly developing frontier, had not the Yaquis voluntarily accommodated the needs of the secular Spanish economy, then some form of coercion, including forcing them off the land, would probably have been necessary. Muni and Bernabé seemed aware of the need to strike a balance between defending their own communities and cooperating with the yori society and economy.

The Nineteenth Century:
Independence to Early Porfiriato

If the entire colonial period witnessed only one major Yaqui rebellion, the nineteenth century was marked by almost continuous Yaqui revolts that took a variety of forms. Some were autonomous Indian affairs, that is, led and fought by Yaquis, frequently with other Indian allies, especially the Mayos to the south. At other times, Yaquis allied with larger Mexican or even foreign political movements, such as various conservative factions and the French imperialists.

The many political factions vying for control of the state, operating first as federalists and centralists, later as liberals and conservatives, usually tried to enlist the military support of the Yaquis, appealing to them not so much in ideological terms, but through promises of land and autonomy. In fact, however, almost all Mexicans in Sonora wanted to integrate Yaquis politically into Mexican society, in anticipation of the high value of Yaqui land and labor.

While retaining much of the social and political structure forged during Jesuit days, Yaqui society underwent certain fundamental changes after the Jesuit expulsion and with Mexican independence.

Unlike most other mission communities in the northwest, the Yaqui villages did not disintegrate with the expulsion of their Jesuit protectors, partly because they had begun to assert their independence with the 1740 rebellion, and partly because of the accommodation they had made with the colonial economy. In the absence of good, consistent information for the post-Jesuit period, it is difficult to depict Yaqui society in the early nineteenth century, or to pinpoint the changes that took place.

Nevertheless, the available data allow us to draw the following inferences. The eight ex-mission pueblos became eight free villages, each retaining its individual identity while sharing a growing sense of their common "Yaqui-ness." One thing was certain: they no longer produced the vast surpluses that the missionaries had once directed and expropriated.[9] When possible, Yaquis complemented subsistence agriculture and ranching in the pueblos with wage labor outside. When independence abruptly ended the Bourbon mining revival, wage labor opportunities were drastically curtailed, and some Yaquis survived in part by raiding Mexican properties. Indeed, such raids soon became indistinguishable from Yaqui revolts.

Because the Yaquis did not produce a surplus, their social structure remained egalitarian and undifferentiated by class. No group of Yaquis emerged to take the place of the departing Jesuits. A military-type leadership developed instead. Starting with the 1740 rebellion, then during the late Bourbon period as the Yaquis defended themselves against marauding frontier Indians (mostly Seris and Pimas rather than Apaches, who did not penetrate Yaqui territory), and finally through the decades of almost continuous uprisings in the nineteenth century. Yaqui society became decidedly militaristic. Not surprisingly, the dominant leadership figure became the captain-general, an individual who attained his position through personal attributes and not inheritance. Serving under him were the Yaqui militias and corresponding officials whose positions were first created by José de Gálvez, Bourbon visitador-general and the minister of the Indies. Traditional elected positions, such as those of the village gobernadores, continued to exist, but they kept a low profile. It cannot be said, however, that the military elements constituted some kind of ruling class. Another consequence of the expulsion of the Jesuits was the continuous decline in the influence of

[9] The Bourbon state at first attempted to extract an agricultural surplus from the Yaquis in the form of tribute payment, but when the Yaquis resisted, the state settled instead for Yaqui surplus labor, which they willingly gave.

the church and church personnel. Only an occasional priest entered
the Yaqui pueblos and attempted to exert some influence on them,
usually with questionable results.

As the nineteenth century continued, there was growing factionalism among the Yaquis and their traditional allies, such as the
Mayos, between those who wanted to continue fighting, and those
who opted to end the wars. Divisions generally occurred along
pueblo rather than personal lines. In part, factionalism was due to
the desire of many Yaquis for peace; in part, it was stimulated by
deliberate Mexican efforts to divide and conquer. At the same time,
all Yaquis at all times stuck unwaveringly to their nonnegotiable
principle of autonomy, which meant exclusive Yaqui residence and
collective control of their traditional homeland on both sides of the
Yaqui River. Autonomy also meant a clear separation between their
own tribal government and the Mexican government. Yet this assertion of the principle of cultural and political separation never entailed total isolation and noninteraction with the larger Mexican society. On the contrary, as already emphasized, Yaquis worked
whenever possible in the outside economy and engaged in limited
trade with the outside world.

The Yaquis' reaction to a perceived outside threat to their autonomy and territorial integrity became quite predictable. They usually
retaliated quickly, before the situation had deteriorated beyond the
point of recovery. Their resistance took flexible and innovative
forms. They adapted quickly and as best they could to changing circumstances both within their own communities and in the larger
environment, as is illustrated below. Furthermore, the Yaquis realized that their resistance and occasional alliance with competing
political factions helped perpetuate chaos, division, and impotence
in the state government, an advantage for them because a weak government could not effectively implement the profound political reforms that would be required to integrate the Yaquis within Mexican
society.

The first Yaqui rebellion after Mexican independence was led by
Captain-General Juan Banderas and lasted from 1828 to 1833. He
was a charismatic leader, sufficiently ladino or hispanized to make
references to Father Hidalgo, the Virgin of Guadalupe, Moctezuma,
and the Aztec empire. He spoke publicly of uniting all the Indian
nations of the northwest into one Indian confederation, and in so
doing conjured up the specter of a regional "race war" to exterminate all whites.[10] Banderas was also a practical leader who success-

---

[10] Juan Banderas, proclamations, in *Archivo de la Defensa Nacional de México*

fully led his people in resisting political reforms inimical to their interests. A decree in 1828 gave the supervision of the Yaqui pueblos to the nearby Mexican town of Buenavista. A second one promoted white migration and the colonization of Yaqui land, with Yaquis themselves instructed to come forth to receive titles to individual plots. The government reminded the Yaquis that they were full citizens under the state and federal constitutions, meaning that they had to vote in statewide elections and agree to be drafted into the state militia. The positions of captain-general would have to be abolished, since there would be no need to maintain separate Yaqui militia forces.[11]

Banderas' rebellion consisted of ignoring these pronouncements. He continued to use the title of captain-general, and to govern the Yaqui pueblos "with no law but his own discretion." Land remained undivided and titles unclaimed. In 1831, the government relented on the issue of Yaquis electing their traditional village and tribal officials, and even gave in on the question of the captain-general. But when it contrived to use the elections in July to remove Banderas from the scene, he responded immediately. In August, Banderas held a plebescite in Bácum pueblo, reinvested himself as captain-general, and declared the elections null and void.[12] While Banderas' armed bands roamed the entire state and terrorized the countryside, even at the height of his power he never attempted to take any Mexican town. He did not discourage Yaquis from working in haciendas, and in fact used hacienda workers as his "spies," as he called them. At the same time, he encouraged the Yaquis to cul-

---

(hereafter ADN) 272: 63–64; 274; 215. These statements are not dated, but their contents clearly indicate that they were written in the period 1825–26.

[11] State of Occidente, decrees no. 41, 44, 88, 89, 92, Alamos, January, February, and September 1828, Instituto Nacional de Antropologia e Historia, Fondo de Micropeliculas, Sonora (hereafter INAH Son). Briefly after independence, the states of Sonora and Sinaloa were joined as one, named Occidente.

[12] "Síndicos y alcaldes del partido Yaqui," to governor, Cócorit, 28 May 1828; Father Herreros, letter, 27 July 1828; José Ma. Madrid to Herreros, 25 July 1828; Governor Iriarte to Alcalde of Echojoa, 17 July 1828; Governor Iriarte to Ayuntamiento of Buenavista, 26 July 1828; state of Sonora, decree no. 16, Hermosillo, 1 June 1831, all in INAH Son 23. Juan M. Riesgo and Antonio J. Valdes, "Descripción de las principales poblaciones de Sonora en 1827," Memoria Estadística del Estado de Occidente, 1828 (Guadalajara: Imprenta del C. L. Alatorres, 1828), INAH Son 2. Toledo to governor, 22 May 1831; Escalante, orders to commander of Buenavista, 28 Sept. 1831, INAH Son 14. Diego Tavares to governor, 31 Aug. 1831, Patronato de la Historia de Sonora, Mexico City (PHS) 1:119; Anastasio Flores and José Ignacio Valenzuela, testimonies to Tavares, 12 Sept. 1831, PHS 1: 115–16. (It seemed that local Mexican authorities relied on Yaqui informers for what was happening inside the Yaqui River, suggesting that Mexican authorities were hesitant about entering themselves).

tivate their own land and produce their own food.[13] His force of personality and leadership were so crucial to the rebellion that it effectively ended with his capture and execution in 1833.

For the next thirty years, the Yaquis contributed to the general instability of Sonora by allying with various Mexican political factions, particularly with groups opposed to those that threatened to destroy their autonomous communities and colonize their land. Thus, they fought most bitterly against the Juárez liberals, led locally by Sonora's last caudillo, Ignacio Pesqueira, to the point of even supporting the French imperialists, whom the conservatives had invited to Mexico.

Successive governments between the 1830s and 1850s attempted to revive the abortive 1828 decrees concerning division and colonization of Yaqui territory. In several well-documented cases, Yaquis vigorously opposed Mexican encroachment on their land. The protesters usually first appealed to the state government to stop the invasion and if that failed, they took matters into their own hands, killing or ousting sell-out Yaqui officials, while engaging in armed uprising.[14] By mid-century, however, if Mexican occupation of Yaqui land still had not reached critical proportions, Yaquis were certainly aware that yoris were closing in on their borders. According to the 1849 census, the state's population had grown to 137,000 from 80,000 just after independence. A number of haciendas, ranches, and mines encircled Yaqui country. Notably, the Villa de Salvación, formerly Buenavista, the town closest to the Yaqui pueblos on the northern end, had grown to 3,200, making it the largest town in the state after Hermosillo, Alamos, Horcasitas, and Ures. Actual Mexican colonization of Yaqui pueblos was still at a low

---

[13] Regidor of Santa Cruz to Almada (not dated, but contents indicate February 1832); Ayuntamiento of Buenavista, report to state congress, 25 April 1832; Almada to governor, 25 Feb. 1832; Escalante to state congress, 5 March 1832; Ayuntamiento of Buenavista to governor, 27 Feb. 1832; Ramon Morales to governor, 27 March 1832; José Ignacio Bustamante (Opata Indian), testimony to Ayuntamiento of Buenavista, 24 April 1832, all in *INAH Son* 15. Ester Otero to Banderas and Captain General Cuchacame, 7 April 1832, *PHS* 1: 146.

[14] José María Armenta, various reports to governor, Cócorit, 12 March, 31 March, 4 April 1842, *INAH Son* 15; Pedro de Aguayo, amplifying state decree No. 89, Ures, 17 May 1842, *INAH Son* 10; Urrea to Minister of Foreign Relation, 20 February 1843, *INAH Son* 15; State of Sonora Congress, resolution, Ures, 30 April 1852, in *El Sonorense*, 7 May 1852, *INAH Son* 11; governor to Manuel Iñigo and Company, Guaymas, 24 June 1843, *INAH Son* 10; Iñigo to governor, Guaymas, 22 June 1843, *INAH Son* 10; governor to prefect of Guaymas Ures, 11 March 1854, *INAH Son* 16.

level; probably due to its proximity to Salvación, Cócorit had 150 yori families; the other seven from zero to six yori families.

Also by mid-century, Yaquis were divided about evenly between those who lived in the pueblos and outside the territory. Many worked in the mines and haciendas of Hermosillo, Buenavista, and Alamos districts. Indian peons, who included Mayos and Opatas in addition to the large number of Yaquis, drew a monthly salary of five to eight pesos and weekly food rations of two *almudas* of corn. This was apparently insufficient to live on, for most of the peons went into debt for five to six months. The Yaquis, however, managed to escape from the "servitude" of debt peonage because, a contemporary observer noted, they could always flee to the "immense forests of the Yaquis," where it was impossible to find or apprehend them.[15]

When Pesqueira came to power in 1854, he was determined to pacify the Yaquis once and for all, and to colonize their land. To assert political control over the Yaqui communities, his government replaced the eight traditional gobernadores with a Mexican justice of the peace. The government also attempted to suppress the Yaqui military organization by eliminating the post of captain-general and other military ranks, disbanding the Yaqui militia companies, and destroying their firearms, gunpowder, and other incendiary materials. Finally, Pesqueira stationed a contingent of state national guardsmen, which included a few Yaquis, inside Yaqui territory. The governor's elaborate colonization scheme called for the repatriation and resettlement of Sonorans who had failed in the California gold rush. He hoped that such Mexicans would pacify the Yaquis by "civilizing" them. He also hoped that colonization would "increase the agricultural production of Sonora and give a strong push to the public and private wealth of the state." Furthermore, the plan included the construction of a large reservoir for irrigation.[16] By the

---

[15] José de Anguilar, report to congress, Ures, 20 March 1850, *INAH Son* 11. Another report merely stated: "It is supposed that there is population in the Río of some 30,000 indios," in "Noticias del Río Yaqui," *Sociedad Mexicana de Geografía e Estadística, Boletín*, época 1, 2 (1850): 69; José Agustín de Escudero, *Noticias estadísticas de Sonora y Sinaloa* (Mexico: Tipografía de Rafael, 1849), pp. 39, 86.

[16] Emigración para Sonora. Junta Promovadora de la Emigración Hispano-Americano sobre Sonora," Los Angeles, 20 Oct. 1858; Ignacio Pesqueira to federal government on the colonization of Yaqui, Hermosillo, 12 Oct. 1859, *Estrella de Occidente*, 21 Oct. 1859; Pesqueira on the formation of the "Compañía Esploradora de los terrenos del Río Yaqui," Hermosillo, 30 Aug. 1859, *Estrella de Occidente*, 9 Sept. 1859, all in *INAH Son* 4. Pesqueira on the Yaqui reservoir project, Hermosillo, 12 Oct. 1859,

time Pesqueira was overthrown in 1877 and the Porfiristas came to power, none of these plans had been realized.

During the last years of Pesqueira's regime and the early years of the Porfiriato, the Yaqui resistance took a new turn under a new leader, Cajeme. A Yaqui who had spent his adolescence outside the Yaqui communities and served with distinction in Pesqueira's liberal army, he returned to the Yaqui River, when the caudillo rewarded him with an appointment as Yaqui alcalde mayor in 1873, confident no doubt that Cajeme would tame the rebellious Yaqui spirit. Cajeme stunned the Mexicans and probably the Yaquis as well when he organized a new rebellion.[17]

Under Cajeme, Yaqui resistance to Mexicans took a new form, and Yaqui society underwent significant changes. First of all, most of the Yaquis returned to the river to rebuild their old communities. Using a combination of Yaqui traditions and what he had learned from the Mexicans, Cajeme disciplined his people to rely on their own resources, initiative and leadership, rather than to work for, pillage from, or ally with, outsiders. Not since Jesuit days were the Yaquis more tightly organized, more self-sufficient economically, more prepared militarily. Cajeme's goal was not to extend Yaqui hegemony beyond the confines of Yaqui territory, but to strengthen and preserve that autonomy that they had always claimed. Even as he sometimes courted Mayo support, he was reluctant to move or tarry long beyond the Yaqui River, rarely leading armed Yaquis beyond their own boundaries. He never attacked Mexican towns.

To achieve self-sufficiency and to produce revenues, Cajeme revived the old Jesuit practice of community plots, which each pueblo cultivated with rotations of workers. This was perhaps the first time since Jesuit rule that the Yaquis produced a significant surplus. Most of the surplus was stored, although some was traded. Trade was an important part of Cajeme's regime; it produced revenues, and it continued the Yaqui tradition of not isolating themselves entirely from the outside world, while claiming the right to autonomy. The in-

---

Estrella de Occidente, 21 Oct. 1859, *INAH Son* 16. Laureano Calvo Berber, *Nociones de la historia de Sonora* (Mexico: Libería de Manuel Porrúa, 1958), p. 208.

[17] José T. Otero, address to the first session of the seventh constitutional congress, *La Constitución*, 18 September 1879, *INAH Son* 7. Ramón Corral, "Biografia de José María Leyva Cajeme," *Obras Completas*, vol. 1. This biography, first published in 1886 and written by one of Sonora's leading Porfiristas, is perhaps the most authoritative and informative on Cajeme. Curiously, for the period covered by this biography, all documents in the state archives, which abound in documents for all other periods, are missing.

creased revenues also enabled Cajeme to build up a good stockpile of weapons.

Another of Cajeme's revivals was to renew the importance of the traditional village gobernadores by making them his chief administrative assistants, subordinating under them the captains of war. The religious office of temastian (or sacristan) created by the Jesuits, assumed new importance. The sacristans were put in charge of organizing Yaqui fiestas and ceremonies. Finally, Cajeme reactivated the Yaqui councils, an institution that predated the Jesuits.[18] Although indisputably the supreme leader, Cajeme also intended to revitalize traditional tribal government as part of an overall plan to strengthen the bases of Yaqui culture.

Not surprisingly, the anomaly of an Indian "state-within-a-state" was unacceptable to the Mexican government. When the Porfiristas came to power in Sonora in 1879, they launched a two-pronged attack: a military campaign to crush Cajeme's Yaqui "republic," and large-scale development of Yaqui territory. In the 1880s, the Apaches were finally pacified and the first Sonoran railroads were built while new mining laws and relaxed restrictions brought a mining boom. North Americans supplied most of the capital, the technology, and a market. Railroads and mines in turn stimulated greater commercial activities, expanded the internal market, and contributed to the growth of towns and the general population.

As could be expected, the development and colonization of the Yaqui River valley presented the greatest difficulty to the Díaz government. By contrast, the Mayo River valley succumbed much more smoothly to Mexican control, with several of the pueblos elevated to municipio or town status.[19] Perhaps for this reason, Cajeme never seriously contemplated dominating the Mayos, accepting their alli-

---

[18] General José Montijo, report, Estrella de occidente, 21 January 1876; report on Carlos Conant, Estrella de Occidente, 10 Oct. 1873, INAH Son 6. Corral, "Cajeme," pp. 155–57. State legislature to secretary of war, 12 Oct. 1881, in Francisco Paso y Troncoso, Las guerras con las tribus Yaqui y Mayo del estado de Sonora (Mexico: Tipografía del Departmento del Estado Mayor, 1905), pp. 70–71.

[19] Report on the railroads, La Constitución, 17 February 1881; report on mining, La Constitución, 30 June 1881; state of Sonora, decree no. 107, Hermosillo, 7 July 1881, La Constitución, 21 July 1881, INAH Son 7. Several documented cases illustrate how Pimas and Pápagos were unable to prevent the alienation of their community land. In early 1880, Pimas of Onavas complained to the state government that, contrary to the law, they had not been given even their due share of land. They accused the prefect of Ures of indiscriminately selling off their land to hacendados and speculators; see municipality of Onavas, petition to governor, Ures, 20 March 1880, PHS 2: 140.

ance when it was offered, but never actively courting it. He was even reluctant to send armed Yaqui reinforcements to aid Mayo rebels who attempted to regain their lost communities.

After a number of intense, brutal campaigns, the Mexican army crushed Cajeme in 1887.[20] His strategy of a defensive war based on a series of fortifications distributed throughout Yaqui territory failed because the Yaqui will to resist was an insufficient match for the large and much better equipped federal army. The defeat meant that the Yaquis would have to change their form of resistance once again.

In taking on Cajeme, the federal government assumed for the first time primary responsibility for Yaqui pacification. Once a local issue, Yaquis had become a national problem, an embarrassment to President Díaz's program of national social integration and an obstacle to his national development goals. The Díaz government also inherited the same dilemma that had plagued all previous governments: how to force Yaquis into permanent submission without having to exterminate them. As Mexico "took off" economically, more than ever before the Yaquis were needed as cheap labor. Díaz himself in the late 1880s vetoed both an all-out military solution as well as deportation.

The Late Porfiriato and the Mexican Revolution

General Marcos Carrillo's appeal to the Yaquis in 1891 embodied the Porfiriato's Yaqui policy as illustrated by the following:

> The Supreme Government of the Republic has never intended to despoil you of the land which belongs legitimately to you in the Río Yaqui. . . . This same government, in order to better secure your properties, has ordered that land be distributed to you. . . . Not now or ever had the government desired the extermination of your race, because we have not made war . . . with the idea of destroying you, but only to make you submit to the laws. . . . . I offer you all the guarantees of the law given to good citizens, as well as the land which you are capable of tilling with your plows. . . . Here among us, forming part of the great Mexican family, is your future and that of your sons.[21]

[20] Various reports in La Constitución: 19 Feb. 1886; 26 March 1886; 2 April 1886, 21 and 23 May 1886; 18 and 25 June 1886, 2, 6, and 9 July 1886, all in INAH Son 8. Corral, "Cajeme," pp. 167–91; General Angel Martínez to Secretary of War, reports, 6, 9, 12, and 13 May 1886, in Troncoso, Guerras, pp. 124–29, 148–49; President Diáz to General Martínez, Mexico, 18 November 1886, PHS 6: 139–40.

[21] General Carillo to Yaqui rebels, Torín, 15 Feb. 1891, PHS 7: 97–99.

In sum, the general exhorted the Yaquis to integrate themselves into the larger Mexican society, to be good citizens in the Mexican sense, and to claim only that amount of land they were capable of cultivating, with the implication, of course, that the rest of the land would be put to other uses by other people. If any Yaqui preferred not to settle down in a Yaqui pueblo with a private plot of land alongside other colonists, the government gave him the option of working as a wage laborer in one of the state's varied and growing enterprises. Sonoran Porfirista Ramón Corral expressed it best: "By forming a common mass with the rest of the population, contact with the white would extinguish little by little their racial hatred, civilize them and create certain necessities which they could not obtain otherwise except by means of work within the confines of society."[22]

With few exceptions, most Yaquis declined to remain in their homeland as colonists, thus choosing the alternative of working outside Yaqui territory. The mass exodus of Yaquis that followed Cajeme's defeat amounted to a self-imposed exile that would have been acceptable to the government as a final solution to the Yaqui problem had it entailed no other consequences. But in opting for wage labor, the Yaquis in no way meant to abandon their historical struggle. Rather, they simply adapted, once again, to a changing set of circumstances. So, while most Yaquis found employment in mines, railroads, haciendas, and in towns on both sides of the border, a hard core of *broncos* (guerrillas) retained their arms and rebellious spirit. Under their new leader Tetabiate, they transformed the raids and hit-and-run attacks that had characterized Yaqui rebellions into a form of guerrilla warfare. Crucial to the success of this form of resistance was the social base composed of the widely dispersed Yaqui working population, who provided the guerrillas with material and moral support. It took the Mexicans more than two decades—up to the eve of the revolution—to learn to cope with this new and infinitely more troublesome form of revolt. The Díaz government experimented with every possible means of repression before arriving at the inevitable—massive deportation. It was a policy that worked, but at considerable political and economic cost.

As before, when the form of resistance changed, Yaqui internal social structure also had to adapt. During the long period of guerrilla warfare, the Yaqui pueblos that had been reconstructed during Cajeme's regime once again disintegrated. Yaquis kept alive the ideal of the autonomous, all-Yaqui community by creating, whenever

[22] Ramón Corral, report to state legislature, Hermosillo, 1886, *INAH Son* 12.

enough of them had gathered—in towns such as Hermosillo and Guaymas, and across the U.S. border in Tucson, Arizona—pueblos-in-exile, where they elected the traditional gobernadores, held council meetings, celebrated their fiestas, and performed their ceremonies.

Repeatedly, government attempts to distinguish between the guerrillas and the pacíficos (the workers) failed, just as had efforts to control the flow of arms and ammunition to the rebel forces.[23] Moreover, because of the great value placed on Yaqui workers in the labor-scarce but burgeoning economy, the government quickly discovered that many employers of Yaquis were unenthusiastic about search-and-seize operations on their properties, and even obstructed them. They feared losing good and irreplaceable peons. In fact, some patrones blamed government persecution of the Yaquis for exacerbating an already unstable labor situation. The problem, as one general recognized, had become social as well as military: "The interests of the men of business, big and small, who need Yaqui workers, have become strongly amalgamated with the interests of the Yaquis who lend their labor to these interests, making themselves truly useful."[24] For the Yaquis, without these employers all over the state and across the border, they simply could not have sustained the guerrilla movement. Thus, between Yaquis and their patrones, there was a mutually dependent and mutually beneficial relationship.

In 1897, the governor, General Luis Torres, negotiated a peace settlement with chief Tetabiate and the guerrillas. Two years later the uneasy peace was broken by a new Yaqui revolt, because neither side was willing to yield any ground on their respective positions. As Torres stated to the Yaquis: "There is no lack of land to cultivate; you have all you need. But now, seeing that you are scarcely able to cultivate a tenth of what you possess, you should be satisfied in that you have more than you need to cover your necessities."[25] Indeed, after the Peace of Ortiz, some six thousand Yaquis returned to the river—a repatriation reminiscent of Cajeme's heyday and indicative of how much the Yaquis desired to go home. This brought the resi-

[23] Various reports in La Constitución: 9 Aug. 1889, 7 March 1890, 18 April 1890, INAH Son 8; Troncoso, Guerras, p. 108. Various reports on rebel raids in April–November 1889, PHS 6: 285–334. General Carrillo to Corral, Tórin, 15 June 1890, PHS 7: 53; state of Sonora, circulars, 14 and 18 June 1890, PHS 7: 44–45, 55–58.

[24] Luis Torres to secretary of war, 3 Oct. 1895, ADN 14669: 138–41.

[25] Colonel Manuel Gil, "Diary," in Fortunato Hernández, Las razas indígenas de Sonora y las guerras del Yaqui (Mexico: Casa Edit. J. de Elizalde, 1902), pp. 161–63; Troncoso, Guerras, pp. 233–34; ADN 14658: 21.

dent Yaqui total to over seven thousand, about double the size of the resident yori (non-Yaqui) population. Almost all the Yaquis resettled the deserted pueblos of Bácum and Vícam; a few moved into established mixed colonies such as Cócorit, where they were far outnumbered by the yoris.[26]

When the resettled and almost exclusively Yaqui pueblos of Bácum and Vícam took up arms again in 1899, they made their reasons clear to General Torres: "What we want is that the whites and soldiers leave. If they leave willingly, then we will have peace; if not, then we will declare war, because the peace we signed in Ortíz was under the condition that whites and soldiers leave, and this had not been complied with." The rebels began by attempting to assassinate Loreto Villa, a Yaqui who had been collaborating closely with Mexican authorities. Villa remained loyal to the government, while Tetabiate soon joined the rebels. This short-lived armed uprising, aimed at expelling all non-Yaqui colonists and soldiers, ended in the tragic massacre of Mazocoba in January 1900.[27] But, true to form, the Yaquis refused to give up. Instead, they reverted to guerrilla tactics, although in a different form.

With Tetabiate's death at Mazocoba, the renewed guerrilla movement did not replace him with another overall chief. Rather, it splintered into several, practically independent, guerrilla bands, each with its own chieftain. This time, the Díaz government adopted the only sure and permanent solution—deportation. It realized that only by drying up the social base of support, the vast pacífico population in the countryside, could the elusive, invisible guerrillas be destroyed. The deportation of Yaqui men, women and children to central and southern Mexico, with no exceptions, became policy in 1902–3. Between 1903 and 1907, Governor Rafael Izábal reported he had personally deported some two thousand Yaquis. In 1908, deportation reached its height.[28]

---

[26] Gil, "Diary," in Hernández, *Razas indígenas*, pp. 162–63; Angel García Peña, report on Yaqui, 26 May 1900, in Troncoso, *Guerras*, pp. 269–72.

[27] Gil, "Diary," in Hernández, *Razas indígenas*, pp. 168–71; official reports of the 1899 campaign, July–December 1899, in Troncoso, *Guerras*, pp. 240–60; Lorenzo Torres to Luis Torres, report, 21 Jan. 1900, in Troncoso, *Guerras*, pp. 284–88; various reports in *La Constitución*: 15, 24, and 26 Nov. 1899, 9 Dec. 1899, 2 Feb. 1900; *INAH Son 8*.

[28] No tabulation of the total number of Yaquis deported has ever been found. John Kenneth Turner, in *Barbarous Mexico* (Austin: University of Texas Press, 1968) estimates 15,000, based on the boastful claims of a deportation officer, but this appears to be exaggerated, since the total Yaqui population was only between 20,000 and 30,000.

In May, General Torrez made an appeal to the guerrillas: "For the last time we communicate to you that . . . if you do not turn in all arms and ammunition immediately, the war will return and deportation of Yaquis to Yucatán will continue. You should understand that you are the cause of the death of your people, and the government . . . is disposed to exterminate all of you if you continue to rebel."[29] Still the guerrillas held out.

The generalized deportation amounted to a war-without-quarter, the solution tantamount to "extermination," in General Torres' words. For the Yaquis, it was the deportation that came closest to breaking their indomitable spirit. For the government, deportation produced the desired result of drying up the guerrillas' base of support and hence incapacitating the guerrillas' ability to continue to fight. By January 1909, having nowhere to turn for moral or material help, and seeing the Arizona border strictly patrolled for the first time due to the recession in the United States, one faction of guerrillas, under chief Luis Bule, surrendered. Other factions continued to hold out.

Unlike their experience during periods of voluntary exile in Sonora and Arizona, Yaqui deportees in Yucatán and elsewhere in southern Mexico were unable to create communities-in-exile to keep alive their culture and identity. In the end, what reprieved them from probable cultural extinction was the 1910 Revolution. As soon as Yaqui deportees learned of the overthrow of Díaz, most returned to Sonora, where many joined the revolutionary ranks of northern generals such as Villa, Maytorena, and Obregón. Their decision to join a larger Mexican political movement was reminiscent of mid-nineteenth-century alliances. The motives for making such alliances were basically the same—to advance their own goals. As before, they bargained for the return and exclusive use of all the land in their contested homeland, as well as the integrity of their traditional pueblos. What the Yaquis did not realize at the beginning of the Revolution was that no revolutionary leader would accede to their demands for autonomy and separatism, which ran counter to the vision of a modern, integrated nation. Also, in the process of finding out what different revolutionary factions stood for, Yaquis ended up fighting each other. Moreover, one small guerrilla faction under Luis Espinosa, refused to surrender to General Torres in 1909

---

[29] For a detailed discussion of the scope and mechanism, as well as the political and economic consequences of deportation, see Evelyn Hu-DeHart, "Development and Rural Rebellion: Pacification of the Yaquis in the Late Porfiriato," *Hispanic American Historical Review* 54 (February 1974): 72–93.

and steadfastly refused to fight alongside any Mexicans during the Revolution. Espinosa's few Yaquis, then, played the important role of keeping unbroken the Yaqui tradition of resistance. Twice before 1920, Obregón or one of his generals conducted violent campaigns against these guerrillas, but failed to defeat them.

In 1920, President Adolfo de la Huerta, a native Sonoran, finally brought an end to the longstanding hostility between the Mexican state and the Yaqui rebels. He promised them repatriation and resettlement of their pueblos, as well as aid in reconstructing their homes. In some cases, this entailed evacuating and relocating non-Yaquis who had settled around old Yaqui villages, such as Bácum, Tórin, Pótam, and Cócorit. De la Huerta also agreed to negotiate with the traditional Yaqui officials of the eight pueblos as the acknowledged authority of all the Yaqui people. Under this policy, then, Yaquis were given a chance to resume their own way of life, although the trade-off was to accept the superiority of the Mexican state and the existence of non-Yaqui colonists among them.[30]

The Twentieth Century

If one is struck by the history of continuous rebellion in the nineteenth century, one is equally intrigued by the absence of any major armed revolt after 1920, save for a brief and minor uprising against Obregón in 1926. So, having pursued the question of why Yaquis rebelled, it is now time to reverse the question: why have they not mobilized since the Revolution?

The 1926 confrontation with President Obregón in Vícam station, deep in Yaqui territory, occurred when several Yaqui leaders questioned why certain reforms promised them in 1920 had not been implemented. They complained that too many yoris were living and exploiting land in their territory; that the government was not paying the Yaqui peacekeeping force regularly; and that they were disturbed by rumors of another military buildup near the Yaqui River. Obregón's response to an excited Yaqui crowd was to call in his troops, who proceeded to massacre a considerable number of Yaquis. Following this brutality, the government introduced 20,000 federal soldiers and several airplanes to bomb the Yaqui (many fled to the nearby Sierra de Bacatete; it took the army a year to flush them out). In 1927, most of them had descended from the sierra, only to

[30] Edward Spicer, *The Yaquis: A Cultural History* (Tucson: University of Arizona Press, 1980).

be promptly drafted into the federal army and sent out of the state. The military commander left a permanent detachment in the Yaqui Valley, an occupation force that included a Yaqui auxiliary dubbed the "tame batallion."[31]

For good reason, Yaquis have interpreted the 1926 uprising as the result of a planned provocation by Obregón, in order to justify another pacification campaign and renewed deportation of Yaquis out of the state, so that Mexicans could move in with even greater ease to exploit their land. They probably knew that Obregón had bought land in the valley south of the Yaqui River, the area targeted by the federal government for large-scale development. In 1926, President Plutarco Elías Calles, another Sonoran, and Obregón engineered the nationalization of the Richardson Company, a major landholder and pioneer land and water developer in the Yaqui Valley. That same year, the National Bank of Agricultural Credit was established to take over the entire network of small dams and canals. These canals channeled water from the river some thirty miles upstream from Cócorit to the valley for the benefit of the new landowners, including the Calles and Obregón families. Yaquis received no water at all from this project. Also in 1926, the town of Cajeme, later renamed Obregón when it became important, was established as the commercial center of the booming valley. So when the Yaquis confronted Obregón in 1926, they were fully aware of the federally sponsored and financed invasion of their land, and the expropriation of their water. The Obregón–Calles plans also spelled the end of the de la Huerta policies, which had included important concessions to Yaqui culture and interests.

When President Lázaro Cárdenas ousted the Sonoran clique from power in 1934, the Yaquis petitioned him repeatedly to redress their grievances. In late 1937, he responded by going beyond the de la Huerta program. He created the Yaqui *zona indígena* (reserve), which encompassed much, though not all, of the traditional Yaqui homeland. He then expropriated illegally large private landholdings in the valley and distributed this land to landless peasants in the form of *ejidos* (common lands). The Yaqui *zona* was conceived as one large *ejido*, and was unique in that no other indigenous people of Mexico was given such a concession.

In addition to the land reform, Cárdenas recognized the Yaquis'

[31] The incident is discussed in more detail in Claudio Dabdoub, *Historia de el valle del Yaqui* (Mexico: Librería de Manuel Porrúa, 1964), p. 222, and in Edward Spicer, "Pótam: A Yaqui Village in Sonora," *American Anthropologist* 56, no. 4 (August 1954): 34–35.

right to rebuild, on new sites, traditional Yaqui pueblos that had been irrevocably taken over by white colonists. He promised them water from the new dams the government planned to build, along with federal aid for education, sanitation, transportation, and communications. The populist president urged all Yaquis in Sonora, Mexico, and the United States to return to their homeland.[32]

For a decade after the Cárdenas reforms, the Yaquis quietly rebuilt their communities and engaged in traditional, or subsistence, farming. With a plot of good land and seasonal flood waters, a Yaqui with six hectares could raise enough food to feed his family for the entire year. He usually had his own mules and plow, the only implements he needed. He customarily planted corn, beans, melons, and some vegetables for family consumption, in addition to some wheat that he sold in order to acquire cash for ceremonial expenses. His only initial cash outlay for farming was for seeds, which he could also obtain on credit against the harvest. He counted on land and water being free, as had always been the case. Also consistent with the past, he paid no taxes to the government, state or federal. For a Yaqui, who gained status within his community not through material accumulation but strict observance of ceremonial duties, traditional subsistence farming provided the most flexible and stable kind of economic activity by which he could support his family and meet ceremonial demands.[33]

Although the Cárdenas concessions did not meet all the demands they had fought for, Yaquis were learning to live with them, and even to coexist with the yoris. Unfortunately for the Yaquis, conditions in the Yaqui River valley changed drastically after the Cárdenas era. His successors in the presidency, taking clear advantage of the store of good will and rural stability created by the agrarian reform, redirected the nation's priority toward rapid economic growth at all costs. This change in policy seriously affected the Yaquis' future.

[32] Some of the exchanges between Yaquis and President Cárdenas, and the actual Cárdenas land reform decrees, have been reproduced in Alfonso Fábila, Las tribus Yaquis de Sonora. Su cultura y anhelada autodeterminación (Mexico: Departmento de Asuntos Indígenas, 1940), pp. 295–313.

[33] Charles J. Erasmus, "Cultural Change in Northwest Mexico," in Contemporary Change in Traditional Societies, Vol. 3: Mexican and Peruvian Societies, ed. Julian H. Steward (Urbana: University of Illinois Press, 1967), pp. 33–34; Gilbert D. Bartell, Directed Culture Change Among the Sonoran Yaqui, Ph.D. Dissertation, University of Arizona, 1965, pp. 206–207; Cynthia Hewitt de Alcantara, Modernizing Mexican Agriculture: Socioeconomic Implications of Technological Change 1940–1970 (Geneva: United Nations Research Institute for Social Development), pp. 263–64.

The Angostura dam and the Obregón dam, completed in 1952, brought about more profound consequences for the Yaquis than all previous conflicts. These large irrigation systems represented the modern technology that has enabled the post-revolutionary Mexican state to force Yaquis to accept directed changes that a century of political and military pressures had failed to do. The irrigation works, state-sponsored and financed, formed the basis of the new commercial agricultural order built by private initiative on large estates, and which the post-Cárdenas regimes pushed at the expense of peasant ejidos and Indian communities. Developed by the "green revolution" experiments, the new technology was extremely costly and worked best on a large scale. It was not labor intensive, so for the first time Yaquis were no longer indispensable as cheap labor. Thus they lost their most valuable bargaining chip—the demand for their labor.

With the dams the federal government exerted total control over water, without which the semi-arid Yaqui Valley could not be made fertile. The Obregón dam diverted all water southward to the valley, thereby ending the traditional natural flooding of the river banks that had been so crucial to Yaqui subsistence agriculture. Henceforth, the Yaquis, along with other ejidatarios and private landowners, had to purchase their water from the federal Office of Water Resources (*Recursos Hidráulicos*). The government that had given the Yaqui people their own reserve of land, later took away the water that made the land productive.

After depriving the Yaquis of natural irrigation, the government had two choices: leave the Yaquis high and dry, literally, or help them gain access to water. In opting for the latter, the rural credit agency or *Banco Ejidal* extended credit to the capital-less Yaquis to buy water. But, because as a bank it was primarily interested in collecting on its loans with minimal losses, the bank insisted that its Yaqui creditors cultivate cash crops only and market them through the bank, for these crops were the only ones that could make the investment pay off. In choosing this path to help the Yaquis, the bank had also succeeded in forcefully integrating the Yaqui peasants into the Mexican economic system, one that is intensely competitive and individualistic, thus contradicting the basic Yaqui values of communal living and "conspicuous giving"—the sharing of surplus wealth rather than the private accumulation of surplus for individual advancement.[34]

---

[34] The term "conspicuous giving" was coined by Erasmus, presumably as a coun-

Attempting to safeguard Yaqui traditions through the profound changes of the 1950s were the eight pueblo governments. During peacetime, as had always been the case, each pueblo was theoretically autonomous; together they did not recognize a specific tribal chief. The pueblo governments consisted of a gobernador and five assistants, advised by a council of elders and served by a number of officers, including the recently created bilingual (Spanish–Yaqui) *secretario* to deal with the onslaught of new federal agencies that accompanied agrarian reform. The major responsibilities of these native magistrates were clearly defined: they decided who was a Yaqui, and who was therefore entitled to land within the zona (reserve); then they allocated land within the pueblos to Yaqui petitioners. They issued permits and assessed fees from outsiders who wished to exploit natural resources within the zona. They appointed native officeholders and negotiated as official representatives of the Yaqui people with Mexican government agents. Finally, they served as final arbitrators in civil disputes among Yaquis.[35] Although in form these pueblo governments have survived into the 1980s, like traditional agriculture, they too have been rendered weaker with the Yaquis' integration into the Mexican economic system. Even with the addition of the secretario, the gobernadores have found much of modern agriculture beyond the reach of their understanding.

The Banco Ejidal not only insisted that the Yaquis raise cash crops, but that they be organized collectively for production. The other ejidos in the Yaqui valley had been collectives at their inception, because it was Cárdenas' idea that by working the land as one large unit the *ejidatarios* would prove that "the advantages of large-scale operations in the irrigation districts need not be lost during an agrarian reform." The post-Cárdenas regimes, however, which favored private landowners over the ejidos, broke up these collectives just about the time that the Oberegón dam was built, because they were seen as a threat to the private and grossly misnamed "*pequeñas propiedades*."[36] Thus, it was ironic indeed that the Yaqui collectives, called credit societies, were formed at the time the col-

terpoint to the familiar term "conspicuous consumption" of more materially oriented cultures, see Erasmus, "Cultural Change."

[35] Thomas R. McGuire, *Politics, Economic Dependence, and Ethnicity in the Yaqui Valley, Sonora*, Ph.D. Dissertation, University of Arizona, 1979, p. 54.

[36] Hewitt, *Modernizing*, p. 181. See pp. 181–198 for an account of the collective ejidos in the Yaqui Valley. Chapters 1–4 of this excellent study examine the development of commercial agriculture in Sonora, with emphasis on the impact of the "green revolution."

lective ejidos in the valley were being dismantled. First of all, the banco did not consider the Yaqui collectives to constitute serious competition to the private landholders; and second, the new technology introduced by the banco could only work on large-scale cultivation.

There seemed little the Yaquis could do to resist the bank's program. By the end of the 1950s, 98 percent of all irrigated land in the zona had been put into commercial agriculture, and was thus under banco control. Besides extending credit for water to the Yaqui credit societies, the banco also lent them money for insecticides, pesticides, machinery, and outside skilled workers, such as tractor drivers. It was estimated that to plant one hectare of a cash crop required some 1,400 pesos, a sum clearly beyond the means of any Yaqui peasant.[37]

For the Yaquis, perhaps the most profound consequence of modern agriculture was the fact that it absorbed capital and technology heavily, but was not labor intensive, and required least of all the kind of unskilled manual work that Yaquis had traditionally performed. Thus, while in theory Yaqui credit society members could work on their own collectives for wages to be deducted from their share of year-end profits, in fact, they had very little work. The unskilled labor associated with seeding, cutting, and cleaning canals and irrigation ditches, weeding and harvesting, amounted to no more than one month's work out of the year. Few Yaquis were adequately trained for the better skilled jobs, such as tractor driving, which were usually contracted out to Mexicans and paid for out of the society's profits. After deductions to pay back the banco for the long list of loans and expenses, the Yaquis' share of the profits amounted to a meager sum. No wonder some embittered, demoralized Yaquis came to regard the banco as an exploitative new patrón, worse even than many prerevolutionary ones. The ironic conclusion is that modern agriculture has impoverished the Yaquis and rendered them powerless, in that they can no longer make such important decisions as what crops to plant.

Commercial agriculture has made Yaquis totally dependent on cash for survival, another profound change in their culture. Every basic necessity in life, from food to clothing, has to be bought in stores. Ironically, the Yaquis who in theory possess rich irrigated land cannot grow their own food. Since the 1960s, as Yaquis have increasingly opted to break up their credit societies for individual

[37] McGuire, "Politics," pp. 194–99.

plots, and yet find themselves with insufficient financial resources to farm by themselves, they have had two choices. They can rent out the plot to Mexican landowners, an illegal act widely practiced by other ejidatarios in the valley and apparently condoned by the government, and in some cases they can work for wages at the same time. Or, a lucky few may find a Mexican partner, usually a local shopkeeper, who would advance them money for seeds, water, and food for the family, tractor rental, and market their crops, against the future harvest.[38]

Another adjustment Yaquis have had to make to poverty is to depend more on yoris for financial aid in sponsoring their fiestas. Furthermore, since the late 1950s there has been a noticeable reduction in the length and number of ceremonies held in the pueblos. Not only was this a result of their loss of economic independence brought about by the banco's policies, but the banco actually tried to undermine Yaqui tradition deliberately. While it enlisted the help of the gobernadores in setting up the credit societies, the banco subsequently bypassed these native leaders in making decisions concerning the zona, arguing that Yaquis should learn, as have other Mexicans, to abide by Mexican law and customs, to honor Mexican contracts—in short, to abandon Yaqui communal laws and sanctions.[39]

Conclusion

For three centuries, the Yaquis have successfully resisted directed cultural change from secular states, and have successfully mobilized for action when they felt their territorial integrity and distinct way of life were threatened. At the same time, unlike some other Indian or peasant communities, they have never insulated themselves completely from the outside world. While they have persistently opposed yori settlement and colonization of Yaqui land, since the early Jesuit days they have also willingly worked for wages outside their communities. Armed resistance against invaders and developers inside the Yaqui valley, while participating in the economy outside the valley without concurrent integration into the yori social structure—this twin strategy ensured their survival as the Yaqui people into the twentieth century. So when they could no longer

[38] Hewitt, *Modernizing*, p. 277; Erasmus, "Cultural Change," pp. 75–77, McGuire, "Politics," pp. 202–10.

[39] Hewitt, *Modernizing*, pp. 271–73; Erasmus, "Cultural Change," pp. 30–31; McGuire, "Politics," pp. 213–14; Bartell, "Directed Change," p. 217.

halt the pace of colonization and development in their homeland, and when their labor was no longer indispensable to a modern agricultural economy, their cultural survival also became precarious.

The crucial turning point in Yaqui history occurred with the Cárdenas agrarian reforms of 1937. While granting social justice to the Yaqui people, they also laid the groundwork for their integration into the Mexican economic and social system. The principal agent of this directed change was the Banco Ejidal, which, through control of credit, forced the Yaquis to abandon their traditional agriculture in favor of modern agriculture, and to replace their independent subsistence farming with commercial or cash-crop cultivation. In the transition, the Yaqui free villagers lost all power over agricultural decisions. They have had to exchange their traditional economic independence and autonomy for external control, dependence, and poverty. Far from raising their standard of living, integration into Mexican society has left them worse off than just about any other group in the northwest, including other ejidatarios and the Mayos.

The most profound consequence of economic dependency has been the erosion of Yaqui identity, sense of community, and cultural cohesion. This phenomenon can best be measured by the declining commitment and observance of Yaqui traditions—the ceremonies and fiestas celebrated in the pueblos and wherever Yaquis congregated outside the Yaqui Valley. Historically, subsistence farming, "conspicuous giving," or the deemphasis of individual surplus production and accumulation, has maintained an egalitarian society, one with relatively equal distribution of wealth and without significant social differentiation. In the 1980s, the diminishing commitment to ceremonial observance first noted in the 1950s has continued; at the same time, the gap between rich and poor Yaquis— another recent phenomenon in their society—has also become more noticeable, though still not nearly as pronounced as in Mexican society as a whole. Moreover, there is some correlation between those Yaquis who are getting richer—and thereby becoming more successful by Mexican standards—and the declining commitment of Yaqui culture. That is, as more Yaquis work among Mexicans in the Mexican economy, the interest in accumulating wealth grows as the inclination to give conspicuously declines. This is especially noticeable among younger Yaquis, those most likely to work outside the zona. Also, those who have managed to acquire some wealth are less likely to return to the pueblos and to the pressures of conforming to traditional values.

In sum, the necessity to interact with Mexicans in a money economy has considerably weakened the traditional institutions of a distinct Yaqui culture along the Yaqui River. To be successful by Mexican standards means rejection of Yaqui tradition. Even with the
zona indígena guaranteed by Mexico's agrarian reform, even with
nominal political autonomy represented by the pueblo governments, the loss of economic independence will continue to impov-
erish and marginalize the Yaquis. The progressive cultural erosion
explains why Yaquis have not managed to mobilize successfully for
political action in the last half-century.

Since the agrarian reforms and irrigation projects of the thirties,
forties and fifties, the social situation in the Yaqui region has become much more complex. Vying for precious land and water are
fifteen thousand or so Yaquis living in or near the zona, thousands
of ejidatarios and landless peasants—many of them originally labor
migrants from central and southern Mexico—and the powerful
group of misnamed "pequeños proprietarios," who are in fact large
landowners and form the backbone of the valley's lucrative commercial agriculture. In the dramatic events of November 1976, when
outgoing President Luis Echeverría confiscated some 106,666 hectares of farm and grazing land for distribution to more than eight
thousand landless peasants, Yaqui pleas for recognition of their
rights were virtually ignored, while the well organized and well led
peasant invaders, the powerful landowners, and the Mexican state,
confronted each other.[40]

[40] The November 1976 land invasion is covered in the following U.S. newspaper
articles: New York Times, 20 Nov. 1976; 4 and 12 Dec. 1976; Los Angeles Times, 20
and 22 Nov. 1976; 1, 5, and 25 Dec. 1976 (these can be found in Information Services
on Latin America, vol. 15, nos. 5 and 6, 1976). The Echeverría government alleged
that some seventy families had in fact concentrated Yaqui Valley land in their hands.
This kind of practice—registering the maximum amount allowed by law in the names
of extended family members and sometimes even unrelated individuals—was a common way to circumvent the Mexican land laws designed to prevent the resurgence of
latifundia. The total holdings of some of these families exceeded one thousand hectares.

A recent published book also treats this confrontation in the context of President
Echeverría's politics. See Steven E. Sanderson, Agrarian Populism and the Mexican
State: The Struggle for Land in Sonora (Berkeley: University of California Press,
1981), pp. 186–202.

CHAPTER SIX

Moving Toward Revolt:

Agrarian Origins of the

Hidalgo Rebellion in

the Guadalajara Region

Eric Van Young

Whatever else it may have been, the rebellion proclaimed and led by Father Miguel Hidalgo in September 1810 was also a massive peasant revolt. Beginning at least with Lucas Alamán, observers and historians of the period 1810–21 have universally acknowledged the pre-eminent role of rural people in the armies and insurgent bands (*gavillas*) that fought the royalist forces for control of New Spain.[1]

[1] Lucas Alamán, *Historia de Méjico*, vol. 1 (México, 1968), pp. 244–46. Among modern writers see, for example, Hugh Hamill, *The Hidalgo Revolt: Prelude to Mexican Independence* (Gainesville, 1966), pp. 89ff; Eric R. Wolf, "El Bajío en el siglo XVIII. Un análisis de integración cultural," in *Los beneficiarios del desarrollo regional*, comp. David Barkin (México, 1972), pp. 63–95; Brian R. Hamnett, "The Economic and Social Dimensions of the Revolution of Independence in Mexico, 1800–1824," *Ibero-Amerikanisches Archiv* (New Series) 6, no. 1 (1980): 1–27; Torcuato S. Di Tella, "Las clases peligrosas en la independencia de México," in *El ocaso del órden colonial en la América Latina*, ed. Tulio Halperín-Donghi (Buenos Aires, 1975); John M. Tutino, "Agrarian Insurgency: Social Origins of the Hidalgo Movement" (1980, unpublished). In fact, statements about the social composition of the insurgent forces must be of a very tentative nature, since to date no systematic social history of the early phases of the movement has been published. Two stimulating preliminary efforts in that direction have been made by William Taylor (Chapter 7, this volume), and Tutino "Agrarian Insurgency." The terms "rural" and "peasant" are not used interchangeably in this essay; the distinction between them will emerge as the argument develops, rather than in a series of formal definitions at the outset. This chapter represents a preliminary step in the direction of a larger, more detailed study of the

Nor is this surprising, considering the overwhelmingly rural character of Mexico in the early nineteenth century. The strikingly rural nature of the movement may sometimes be forgotten, inasmuch as writers on the topic often address the political outcome of the wars of independence, which seemingly had little if anything to do with popular aspirations; or the emergence of so-called "caste war" elements, which pitted whites against nonwhites in open conflict. But when one takes a hard look at peasant participation in the wars of independence, a host of questions arise as to its background, extent, timing, motives, goals, and significance. It is the purpose of this essay to crack the simple façade of peasant rebellion by asking some of those questions with specific reference to one of the major focuses of rebellion—the Guadalajara region in west central Mexico in 1810–11. The major part of the chapter concerns the economic and social development of the Guadalajara region during the century before the Hidalgo movement, and attempts to describe the preconditions for rural revolt there. The answers to some of the questions asked relate, therefore, not so much to the nature and course of the rebellion itself as to its initiating conditions and the characteristic modes of popular protest likely to emerge from them.

Certainly large-scale violent action by rural people against constituted authority was not new or unusual in colonial Mexico, nor was it to disappear between 1810 and the outbreak of the revolution of 1910.[2] As rural uprisings, however, the Hidalgo rebellion of 1810–11 and the continuing insurgent military activity that followed it over the next ten years, had certain ostensibly unique features that distinguished them (particularly during their early phases) from uprisings before and after. First, the sustained character of the movement, at least from the organizational point of view, was unusual. While it is true that insurgent armies and guerrilla bands shared a certain evanescent quality, and while it is also true that the royalist government virtually succeeded in pacifying most of New Spain after 1816, it must be noted that the independence movement re-

social history of the Mexican independence movement from 1810 to 1816. The author would like to acknowledge support for the research from the Andrew W. Mellon Foundation and the Institute of Latin American Studies, University of Texas at Austin, for a faculty summer research grant, and from the Dora Bonham Fund of the Department of History, University of Texas at Austin.

[2] On the colonial period, see the path-breaking study of William B. Taylor, *Drinking, Homicide, and Rebellion in Colonial Mexican Villages* (Stanford, 1979); on the nineteenth century see Jean Meyer, *Problemas campesinos y revueltas agrarias (1821–1910)* (México, 1973); Leticia Reina, *Las rebeliones campesinas en México, 1819–1906* (México, 1980).

mained alive until 1821. To the extent that this was so, and to the extent that peasants and other rural dwellers continued actively involved in insurrectionary activity, one may speak of a certain degree of continuity in the rebellion as a peasant movement.

Second, the scale of the movement, both in terms of geography and numbers of people involved, distinguished it from other revolts up to the 1910 revolution. At its height, in its initial phase, the insurrectionary movement managed to field armies truly enormous for the time and place, composed largely of rural people. In late 1810, as Hidalgo's force marched on the viceregal capital, its ranks swelled to an estimated 80,000 men.[3] By January 1811, as the rebels prepared to face the royalist army at what was to be the climactic battle at the Puente de Calderón, near Guadalajara, the insurgent forces, by dint of new recruits added to the remnant of the original forces, numbered as high as 100,000 men, albeit badly organized and ill-equipped.[4] The size of these armies clearly dwarfed anything that might have been called a peasant rebellion during the colonial period, as did the forces subsequently involved in guerrilla activity during the liberation struggle in New Spain after 1811.

Third, the fact that the insurgent movement had obviously political goals, even though these may not have been clearly articulated by the leadership, distinguishes it from other movements of a predominantly peasant flavor. This political program, such as it was, became clearer as the rebellion reached its climax in early 1811, and may be summarized under the rubric of political independence from Spain. Finally, and related to the third point, is the fact that the theater or scope of the movement's political goals was considerably larger than previous rebellions against constituted authority. The ostensible goals of the movement, as its ideology began to crystallize under royalist military pressure and counterinsurgent propaganda, were not limited to a reformist critique of bad bureaucratic practices, but embraced a full-scale and frontal assault on the legitimacy

[3] Hamill, *The Hidalgo Revolt*, pp. 149–50.

[4] Archivo General de la Nación (México), Operaciones de Guerra (hereafter AGN-OG), 171: 88, Calleja to Venegas, 17 January 1811. This was Mariscal Félix Calleja's initial report to Viceroy Venegas concerning the engagement at Calderón, and although Calleja subsequently changed the numbers slightly in various versions, he remained quite consistent in his near-100,000 estimate. For the citation of other sources and a full discussion of the controversy surrounding the estimates, see Alma Rosa Bárcenas Díaz, *Puente de Calderón: Reconstrucción histórico-geográfico de una batalla (1811)* (tésis de licenciado en historia, UNAM, 1980), pp. 58–64. Hamill, *The Hidalgo Revolt*, pp. 197–98, cites 80,000 men as the size of the rebel force at Calderón.

of the colonial compact as a whole. This was no rebellion against a single tax (though the abolition of Indian and *casta* tribute figured importantly in Hidalgo's public pronouncements) or against a local magistrate who had overstepped the bounds of probity in his dealings with villagers, but a strike for political independence and the creation of a nation state.

These unique characteristics of the Hidalgo rebellion, especially as they touch upon political ideology and goals, have brought us rather a long way from what are thought to be some of the particular concerns of peasants in revolt—ownership of the land, the disposal of economic surpluses, the integrity of village communities, the balance of power in local country districts, etc. Indeed, a number of difficulties crop up when one attempts to take those characteristics as the *only* characteristics of the protracted and largely rural violence that rocked Mexico in 1810–21. In the first place, there is the problem of regional diversity within the movement, not only in terms of how warfare in the countryside was conducted from region to region within New Spain, but also in terms of which regions responded to the call to take up arms and which did not. The two major focuses of the first phase of the rebellion, the primary one of the Bajío, and the secondary one of the Guadalajara region, were very different insofar as their social and economic structures were concerned.[5] In particular, although both areas were undergoing change with the impact of developing commercial agriculture, in the Guadalajara region the landowning Indian villages were hit hardest by this trend, while in the Bajío the brunt of the change was borne by a more heterogeneous population of tenant farmers, sharecroppers, and resident hacienda laborers, most of them non-Indian. If the ethnic, social, and economic characteristics of the rural masses in these two pivotal regions were, in fact, different from each other, and if a greater part of the rural population in the Guadalajara region

[5] On the Guadalajara region, see Eric Van Young, *Hacienda and Market in Eighteenth-Century Mexico: The Rural Economy of the Guadalajara Region, 1675–1820* (Berkeley, 1981); *Rural Life in Eighteenth-Century Mexico: The Guadalajara Region, 1675–1820*, Ph.D. Thesis, Berkeley, 1978. On the Bajío, see, among others, Wolf, "El Bajío"; David A. Brading, *Haciendas and Ranchos in the Mexican Bajío: León, 1700–1860* (Cambridge, 1978); Tutino, "Agrarian Insurgency." A case could be made that the Guadalajara region was engulfed in the Hidalgo rebellion through a process of insurrectionary contagion from the Bajío, compounded by local reaction to brutal royalist counterinsurgency tactics. But the rebelliousness of parts of the Guadalajara region was so widespread and sustained that it seems reasonable to assume that some longer-term, "structural" conditions prevailed there as well, which predisposed major groups in the regional population to revolt.

can be described as classically "peasant," then it is reasonable to assume that rural people in these areas took up arms for different reasons. Any attempt to construct generalizations about "peasants in revolt" for the period 1810–21 must have its difficulties compounded when one adds to the situation the divergent characteristics of other areas such as the valley of Mexico, Michoacán, and Guerrero. To state that major peasant revolts broke out in areas of Mexico that were experiencing rapid social and economic change is to say a great deal and very little at one and the same time. The picture that emerges from such considerations is a crazy-quilt of regional diversity that belies any notion of a monolithic peasant movement in these years, *unless* one takes at face value the claims of insurgent proclamations and propaganda that the goals of the movement were entirely political, and rather simple at that. For various reasons this does not seem a credible explanation for the massive participation of rural people in armed violence. The political crisis of 1808 and after, and the ideology and slogans that were intended both to mobilize and justify popular protest, thus begin to look more like a proximate cause for rebellion than an ultimate cause.

This brings us to the role of ideology in the popular movements, and to the second difficulty with characterizing the peasant component in any meaningful way. At this point we know very little about peasant aspirations or about what rural people thought they were doing when they took up arms, particularly in 1810–16. Especially in its early phases, the movement was so short-lived and so nonprogrammatic that it is difficult to tell what the peasants thought they were doing. One possibility—that the rural masses took seriously the political situation and the slogans and program of the creole directorate of the rebellion—we have for the moment dismissed as unlikely. A second possibility—that the political crisis in New Spain and the "Grito" of Father Hidalgo simply provided excuses for bored and resentful peasants and rural laborers to embark on an orgy of pillage, rape, and murder—does not seem very credible either. This view accords the role of ideas in the peasant sector of the movement little or no importance at all, and sees Hidalgo and his creole lieutenants as having somehow "whipped up" popular sentiments and anger they could not then control: Padre Hidalgo riding the tiger. But most reasonably well socialized people, even when sharing the peculiar psychology of crowds, seem loath to challenge authority in any major way, and are certainly reluctant to murder people or destroy property. Contemporaries such as Lucas Alamán, who left a somewhat lurid account of the storming of the Alhóndiga in Guanajuato in 1810 and the ensuing carnage, were, one suspects, prepared to find such savage behavior among the "populacho" for their own reasons, and found it.[6] Still, a great deal of savagery was perpetrated by the insurgents upon their victims, even before the "blood and iron" policy of Calleja, Cruz, and other royalist commanders made it obvious to the rebels that they had nothing to lose. But the scale and nature of this violence suggest not some inherent barbarism on the part of peasants and other rural dwellers, not some irremediable superego lacunae, but a fundamental sense that something had gone wrong in the world, and that the external realities no longer conformed to the moral order of country people. I suggest that ideological considerations did, in fact, play a very important part in mobilizing peasants, but that these grew out of a moral substrate that was unlikely to have been touched directly by narrower political ideas or slogans.

The third difficulty in characterizing the Hidalgo revolt and subsequent insurgent activities as peasant rebellions consists in separating out elements of ethnic conflict from those of class conflict as motives for revolt. We know, certainly, that race and class were not perfectly congruent categories during the late colonial period.[7] Just as certainly, what we know to this point about the social composition of the insurgent forces suggests that they were remarkably heterogeneous (this would have varied, of course, according to time and place), spanning the socio-racial hierarchy from Indians at the bottom to members of the creole elite at the top. Yet the indications that race and racial antagonisms played a role in the mental structures of conflict are abundant enough. The issue of the abolition of tribute, certainly a badge of inferior social status grounded firmly in racial criteria, confirms this view, as does the evidence that the various massacres of European Spaniards (Guanajuato, Valladolid, Guadalajara, etc.) were carried out, at least in part, in response to the popular sentiments of Hidalgo's "dark armies."[8] Certainly royalist propaganda played skillfully on white fears of Indians on the rampage in undermining potential creole support for the movement.

Yet how are we to reconcile these contradictory lines of evidence? To put the question another way, was the popular component of the Hidalgo rebellion and the scattered outbreaks that followed it an In-

[6] Alamán, *Historia de Méjico*, vol. 1, pp. 278–81.

[7] See, for example, John K. Chance, *Race and Class in Colonial Oaxaca* (Stanford, 1978).

[8] On this point, see Hamill, *The Hidalgo Revolt*, p. 183.

dian movement or a peasant movement?[9] A clear and unequivocal answer to the question of whether the wars of independence were race wars or class wars may, in fact, not be possible, but such an answer would make an enormous difference in our interpretation of late colonial history, and of the nature of the independence period as symptomatic of the strains that wracked late colonial society.

I would suggest that for large areas of Mexico, and for major groups of people who actively participated in armed conflicts during the wars of independence, the categories of Indian and peasant did overlap in a meaningful way. Furthermore, the intensity of the conflict was due precisely to that congruence, and grew out of the circumstances of agrarian change that prevailed during the late colonial period. Under those circumstances, particularly in the Guadalajara region, the growth of commercial agriculture was at the root of increasing demands on the traditional rural economy in which the landholding Indian village still occupied a prominent place. A combination of population pressure in the countryside and a growing need for land in the commercial agricultural sector created what must have been perceived by Indian villagers as an attack on their status as independent peasants. What is more, since a substantial, though by no means total, control over the means of production within the peasant economy still resided in the communal village, the locus of the Indian peasant's economic life was the same as the locus of his personal and cultural identity. The process of proletarianization to which the Indian peasantry in parts of Mexico was subjected during the eighteenth century was therefore simultaneously a process of deculturation. Certainly the conjunction of "Indianness" and "peasantness" was not the only element involved in mobilizing rural people when the political pretexts could be furnished, but it was a vital element, especially in the Guadalajara region.[10]

We are then led directly to the question of why rural people joined the insurrection, whether in the initial phase of mass armed

[9] The formulation of this question depends, of course, on making the valid distinction between Indian and peasant (something that Latin Americanists sometimes forget to do), and on using the category peasant in an economic and perhaps a social sense, without any ethnic or racial baggage, as theoretically "pure."

[10] On the process of proletarianization in the Guadalajara region in the late eighteenth century, see Van Young, *Hacienda and Market*, pp. 343–57. On land conflicts and Indian village identity, see Eric Van Young, "Conflict and Solidarity in Indian Village Life: The Guadalajara Region in the Late Colonial Period," *Hispanic American Historical Review* 64 (February 1984): 55–79. For an interpretation of change in the Bajío region that takes into account similar elements, see Tutino, "Agrarian Insurgency."

confrontation, or in the later phases of guerrilla activity. If it is true that agrarian changes in the late colonial period created the precondition for a massive upheaval, and that those changes affected primarily land use and ownership, then one should be able to characterize the peasant component of the independence rebellions as land revolts, or at least to see in them important elements of this classic type of peasant demand. But on the whole, this does not seem to have been the case. It is true that the nonprogrammatic nature of the initial phase of the uprisings, under Hidalgo's leadership, might obscure such demands even if they were present. It is also true that Hidalgo and later leaders did address themselves occasionally to the land question, though seldom in a systematic way. Hidalgo's famous decree of December 5, 1810, which abrogated existing agreements leasing out communal Indian lands to non-Indians, and returning the effective exploitation of these lands to the communities that owned them, was at least a feeble attempt to come to grips with complicated problems of land hunger in the villages of central Mexico.[11] Furthermore, on the level of spontaneous popular expression—making policy with the barrel of a gun—seizures of non-Indian lands, particularly of haciendas, seem to have occurred with some frequency during 1810–21. In 1812, for example, an army of 4,000 "Indians" was said to have seized control of a major rural estate belonging to the Condesa de Regla in the Tulancingo area.[12] But seizure was not necessarily expropriation, and even less division and permanent ownership. On the whole, land does not seem to have been an explicitly important issue in peasant participation during these rebellions.

The absence of land as a major issue in policy formulations, public pronouncements, and ideological elaborations does not necessarily mean that it was not an issue in bringing peasants to arms.[13] How, then, to resolve this puzzle in which agrarian change is likely

[11] *Colección de acuerdos, órdenes y decretos sobre tierras, casas y solares de los indígenas. Bienes de sus comunidades, y fundos legales de los pueblos del estado de Jalisco* (Guadalajara, 1849–82), vol. 2, p. 5; see also Van Young, *Hacienda and Market*, p. 292.

[12] AGN-OG, vol. 17, exp. 1, 1812; for a similar incident in the area of Atotonilco el Grande, see Archivo General de la Nación (México), Infidencias (hereafter AGN, Infidencias), vol. 2, exp. 7, 1811. The rising and adherence en masse to the rebel cause by the Indian village of Teocaltiche, in the Altos of Jalisco, seems also to have been related to land shortage problems; see AGN, Infidencias, vol. 13, exp. 6, 1816.

[13] It is possible, for one thing, that as investigations into the social history of the rebellion progress this issue will become clear and more evidence will be unearthed pointing to the land question.

to have induced land hunger in a traditional peasant economy, but where violent protest shows little sign of land as a major issue? Did the land question during the wars of independence become transmuted somehow into other issues that were able to mobilize the rural masses to violent action under the banner of political protest? I would suggest that that is in fact what happened, though the reasons for it are not clear as yet. It is not necessary to accept a "knee-jerk" hypothesis concerning the relationship between agrarian conditions and violent protest, nor does it seem possible to do so in this case. One possibility that might explain the lack of a simple causal relationship is that on the whole the colonial courts did a fairly good job in the arena of conflict resolution over land ownership, and that peasants for the most part accepted the legitimacy of the landholding system and demonstrated some restraint in their demands, even while experiencing, in certain areas of the country, considerable population pressures on productive resources.

Furthermore, the land question as a motivation for rebellion can be preserved if one begins to think in terms of intervening variables instead of a simple knee-jerk formulation. Here the idea of the "compromise of community" as a motivation for peasant insurrection may be helpful, especially where class position, and ethnic and cultural identity were highly congruent. The historical resilience of the peasant community in Mexico suggests that the maintenance of village identity and autonomy are key factors in understanding the history of rural society there. When expressed in political terms, as during the wars of independence, this resilience could sometimes take on a flavor both xenophobic and reactionary vis-à-vis the encroachment of outsiders, including the state. Nor was the expression of such sentiments unknown during the initial phases of the independence movement, though how common it was is open to question. Two members of the Indian *cabildo* (town council) of Tlaxcala, for example, were accused of attempting to foment insurrection among the Indians in the region by preaching a return to complete political autonomy "as in the old days."[14] It has even been suggested by the anthropologist George Foster, among others, that the communal Indian village (and communal peasant villages in general) breeds a particular peasant cognitive formation that tends to see the social world—relationships within communities as well as between

---

[14] AGN, Infidencias, vol. 5, exp. 4, 1810. On the nature and significance of Indian village identity in Mexico, see Taylor, *Drinking, Homicide and Rebellion*, and Van Young, "Conflict and Solidarity."

them and outsiders—in very definite terms, with the village at its center and with the universe as a kind of zero–sum game.[15] The struggle to preserve village identity intact may then be seen to subsume the land question, inasmuch as the land question is inextricably related to a coherent cosmology with the communal village as its central entity. Whatever the case, it will be necessary to examine the role of popular ideology and symbolism in the light of some such formulation if we are to grasp the significance of peasant participation in the rebellions of the independence period.

In summary, three simple, preliminary hypotheses can be put forward to explain the independence movements of 1810–16. First, these were layered movements that encompassed different social groups and different goals, and they were not particularly well integrated. Second, much of the impetus for these protests was local in origin, and had more to do with social and economic conditions within Mexico than with fortuitous political events in the outside world, though these latter may have triggered them off. Third, the content of the protest movements, at least at the bottom, among the nonelite groups, was social rather than political, with their energy ultimately channeled toward political ends.

Although the Guadalajara region was one of the major early focuses of the rebellion, apparently with a strong peasant component, not much work has been done as yet on the social history of the movement there.[16] The importance of the city and the region in the last phase of the Hidalgo rebellion hinged on a number of factors. The city had already been captured by José Antonio Torres in November 1811, and thus ultimately provided an ideal place in which Hidalgo could regroup his nearly shattered army after the defeat at Aculco early in the month. Furthermore, with its audiencia, bureaucracy, and considerable wealth, the city was an obvious target for

[15] George M. Foster, "Peasant Society and the Image of Limited Good," in *Peasant Society: A Reader*, ed. Jack M. Potter, May N. Díaz, and George M. Foster (Boston, 1967), pp. 300–23. For a somewhat different view of many of the same questions, see Eric R. Wolf, "Closed Corporate Peasant Communities in Mesoamerica and Central Java," *Southwestern Journal of Anthropology* 13 (1957), pp. 1–18.

[16] Standard histories of the city of Guadalajara or the state of Jalisco are likely to devote considerable coverage to the independence era; see, for example, Luis Pérez Verdía, *Historia particular del estado de Jalisco* (Guadalajara, 1951); and José María Muriá, ed., *Historia de Jalisco* (Guadalajara, 1980–). More specialized studies that contain much information, but which do not stress the social composition or origins of the movement, include José Ramírez Flores, *El gobierno insurgente en Guadalajara, 1810–1811* (Guadalajara, 1969); Bárcenas Díaz, *Puente de Calderón*; and Luis Pérez Verdía, *Apuntes históricos sobre la Guerra de Independencia en Jalisco* (Guadalajara, 1886).

rebel military action, and provided a home for Hidalgo's short-lived insurgent government. Finally, Hidalgo and his supporters seem to have realized that a potentially large army could be raised in the region. It seems likely that factors of deeper significance and longer standing than Hidalgo's mere presence in the region, or his propagandistic efforts, account for his tumultuous welcome to the city and the enthusiasm with which locals flocked to his banner in late 1810 and early 1811. What were the local conditions that made the region so socially explosive?

Agrarian Change in the Guadalajara Region During the Eighteenth Century

During the Bourbon century Guadalajara and its hinterland were progressively integrated into a regional economy whose motor of development was the growth of the city itself. The city's increasing demand for meat, grain, and other food products, as well as for primary materials for industrial processing, spurred the commercialization of the agricultural economy in the surrounding area and expanded the boundaries of the regional cash economy to encompass groups and places that had been relatively isolated as late as 1700. The major elements of this system were already in place in the seventeenth century, or even in the sixteenth, but during the last decades of colonial rule the traditional economic equilibrium in the countryside shifted dramatically in favor of the large haciendas at the expense of the village Indian peasant population.

The city of Guadalajara grew from a dusty, sleepy town of about 5,000 in 1700 to a thriving city of some 40,000 by 1820.[17] Moreover, the growth of the city during that century was much more rapid than during the preceding century, and reached its peak in the period

[17] Jean-Pierre Berthe, "Introduction a l'histoire de Guadalajara et de sa région," in Centre National de la Recherche Scientifique, Villes et régions en Amérique Latine (Paris, 1970), p. 71; Archivo Histórico Municipal de Guadalajara (hereafter AHMG), caja 41, 1813; Ramón María Serrera Contreras, "Estado económico de la Intendencia de Guadalajara a principios del siglo XIX," in Instituto Nacional de Antropología e Historia, Lecturas históricas sobre Jalisco antes de la Independencia (Guadalajara, 1976), p. 202; Luis Páez Brotchie, Guadalajara, Jalisco, México; su crecimiento, división y nomenclatura durante la época colonial, 1542–1821 (Guadalajara, 1951), p. 185. The figure for 1820 is an estimate based on several divergent sources; for a discussion of those sources, and of the population trend of the city and its region during the colonial period, see Van Young, Hacienda and Market, pp. 28–39. For the general history of the city, see also Hélène Riviére D'Arc, Guadalajara y su región: influencias y dificultades de una meterópoli mexicana (México, 1973).

1793–1813, when the urban population increased by more than half. By 1793, Guadalajara was probably the fourth largest city in New Spain, behind Mexico City, Puebla, and Guanajuato.[18] The city swelled with a constant stream of immigrants from the countryside during the late colonial years and in the early decades after independence.[19] Underwriting this important urban growth was Guadalajara's role as the administrative capital of sprawling Nueva Galicia; as the commercial emporium for much of western and northwestern Mexico; as banker for the region; and as supplier of manufactured goods for a large and far-flung area. By the early nineteenth century Guadalajara had grown into a major textile-producing region, nearly rivaling Puebla in cotton production.[20] The overall regional population also grew rapidly during the eighteenth century, led by the recovery of Indian population from its nadir in about 1650, and later by the increase of mixed-blood groups.

Along with the movement of people, goods, credit, and political decisions in and out of the city came an ever-increasing flow of foodstuffs to support the urban population. Although continuous and accurate figures on meat consumption in Guadalajara are difficult to come by, it appears that beef consumption increased slightly after about 1750, despite rising prices, and that large numbers of sheep continued to be consumed.[21] The consumption of maize, the basic staple item in the diet of the urban poor and working people, approximately doubled, rising from about 45,000 fanegas per year at mid-century to some 80,000 per year in the early nineteenth century.[22] The consumption of wheat and flour in the city, interestingly enough, although it remained far behind maize in absolute importance, rose much more rapidly during the eighteenth century, increasing seven- to eightfold between 1750 and the outbreak of the wars of independence. The elaborate regulatory mechanisms estab-

---

[18] Alexander von Humboldt, *Ensayo político sobre el Reino de la Nueva España*, ed. Juan A. Ortega y Medina (México, 1966), p. 38; AHMG, caja 15, 1793.

[19] Sherburne F. Cook, "Las migraciones en la historia de la población mexicana: Datos modelo del occidente del centro de México," in *Historia y sociedad en el mundo de habla española; homenaje a José Miranda*, ed. Bernardo García Martínez (México, 1970), pp. 365–67.

[20] Serrera Contreras, "Estado económico," p. 203; Robert A. Potash, *El banco de Avío de México* (México, 1959), p. 18; Humboldt, *Ensayo político*, p. 451.

[21] On meat consumption patterns and marketing practices, as well as on the municipal meat monopoly (*abasto de carnes*) and its problems, see Van Young, *Hacienda and Market*, pp. 44–58.

[22] AHMG, various cajas. On the grain trade in late colonial Guadalajara, including both maize and wheat, see Van Young, *Hacienda and Market*, pp. 59–103.

lished by the municipal government for the grain and meat trades—
the *abasto de carnes* for meat, the *pósito* and *alhóndiga* for maize,
and various similar projects for wheat—functioned more or less effectively up to about 1770 or so in ensuring that supplies roughly
corresponded to demand, and also served as a means by which the
elite landowners of the region (who also played a dominant role in
city government) could control access to the largest regional market.
In the last decades of the century, however, as demand rapidly increased both in the city and among the growing rural population,
the older mechanisms began to show signs of strain, prices began to
climb, and the earlier wide margin between supply and demand
shrank. Consumption patterns in Guadalajara apparently began to
alter, making the city population largely consumers of grain rather
than meat. With the increasing demand, especially for grain, the
supply area, or "food-shed," of the city expanded to embrace an
ever-larger region in the late colonial period, with the Los Altos
area, in particular, becoming a major maize supplier.[23] If the regional agricultural economy, on the whole, managed to supply the
basic needs of Guadalajara, the terrible famine of 1785-86 nonetheless indicated that the city's lifeline was a slender thread that held
it from plunging into the Malthusian abyss.[24]

The increased demand of the regional urban population was met
primarily through an expansion of commercial estate agriculture.
Higher levels of production were achieved, however, not through
the technological improvements that had revolutionized European
agriculture during the seventeenth and eighteenth centuries, but
through a more intensive application of available technology and a
recombination of the major factors of production—land, labor, and
capital.[25] The new husbandry that so impressed contemporary ob-

[23] AHMG, various cajas, alhóndiga books.

[24] On the harvest failure and famine of 1785–1786 in the Guadalajara region, see
Van Young, *Hacienda and Market*, pp. 94–103. On New Spain as a whole, see En-
rique Florescano, *Precios del maíz y crisis agrícolas en México (1708–1810)* (México,
1969), pp. 159–63; Charles Gibson, *The Aztecs Under Spanish Rule: A History of the
Indians of the Valley of Mexico, 1519–1810* (Stanford, 1964), pp. 316–17; David A.
Brading and Celia Wu, "Population Growth and Crisis: León, 1720–1816," *Journal of
Latin American Studies* 5(1973): 32–36.

[25] On the general backwardness of agricultural technology in late colonial Mexico,
see Enrique Florescano, *Estructuras y problemas agrarios de México (1500–1821)*
(México, 1971), p. 128ff; and Humboldt, *Ensayo político*, p. 256. On technological
improvements in European agriculture, see B. H. Slicher Van Bath, *The Agrarian History of Western Europe, A.D. 500–1850* (London, 1963), and Jerome Blum, *The End
of the Old Order in Rural Europe* (Princeton, 1978).

servers in Europe was simply not applicable to the human and geographic conditions of late-colonial Mexico. But if technology did not change appreciably, the degree of exploitation of the traditional productive arrangements did, and the main beneficiary of these changes was the large hacienda. Underwritten by a strong market demand, abundant capital from the expanding mining, manufacturing, and commercial sectors of the regional economy, and a growing rural labor pool, estate agricultural production increased, bringing in its train a whole series of far-ranging changes in the economic and social arrangements of the countryside.

In terms of estate production, the major change that occurred during the eighteenth century was a shift away from the traditional, extensive livestock economy and towards a more labor-intensive cereal-producing regimen. Under the old system, the major outlets for the cattle and other livestock of the Guadalajara region lay outside western Mexico itself, in the more prosperous and populous areas of central and southern New Spain. Between 1700 and 1800 the annual level of cattle exports from New Galicia as a whole (an entity much larger than the Guadalajara region) dropped from about 20,000 head to about 10,000 head, and total livestock exports followed approximately the same downward trend, though they were subject to considerable fluctuation and cyclical variation.[26] Furthermore, an internal reorientation of the livestock industry occurred within New Galicia as a whole, leaving districts further away from the provincial capital with the lion's share of the remaining export trade, and drying up the trade in the areas nearest the city. This suggests that the urban market itself was absorbing livestock, particularly cattle, that had previously been sent to market outside the region, and perhaps also that land was increasingly being devoted to other economic uses, primarily cereal production.

A look at patterns of value and investment in estate agriculture during the eighteenth century tends to confirm the hypothesis of a shift in hacienda production away from livestock and toward cere-

[26] Archivo de Instrumentos Públicos de Guadalajara, Libros de Gobierno de la Audiencia de la Nueva Galicia (hereafter AIPG-LG), various years. For a detailed discussion of the decline in the long-distance livestock trade out of the Guadalajara region, see Van Young, *Hacienda and Market*, pp. 193–207; and for a different view of the secular trend in the regional economy—that livestock exports were increasing in importance at the end of the colonial period, rather than decreasing—see Ramón María Serrera Contreras, *Guadalajara ganadera: Estudio regional novohispano, 1760–1805* (Sevilla, 1977).

als for urban consumption.[27] Even by the middle of the eighteenth century, land was regarded in the Guadalajara region as being a relatively plentiful and inexpensive production factor in agriculture. During the early eighteenth century, prime agricultural land in the Guadalajara region was worth perhaps one-tenth of similar land in the Puebla–Tlaxcala region, and as late as the 1760s farmland near Mexico City was even more disproportionately valuable than land near the capital of New Galicia.[28] All this had changed by the end of the century. Property values in general, and the value of large rural estates in particular, increased substantially, and in some cases spectacularly, especially where the owner had access to large amounts of capital for investment purposes. Previously underdeveloped estates in favored but formerly marginal areas generally experienced the greatest relative increases in value during this period. The magnificent hacienda of El Cabezón–La Vega, in the Ameca valley west of Guadalajara, for example, increased 500 percent in value during the thirty years between 1763 and 1793, while it was owned and entailed by the wealthy ex-miner from Rosario, Manuel Calixto Cañedo.[29] Overall, the most spectacular growth in value in the region seems to have been the case of the Hacienda de Atequiza, near Lake Chapala, which increased in value by 800 percent between 1725 and 1821, but increases on the order of several hundred percent in a few decades were not at all uncommon.

The increase in the value of rural estates in the Guadalajara region was due more to active capital investment by landowners, in conjunction with a growing labor force, than to inflationary pressures or to the acquisition of new land.[30] Capital investment on late colo-

---

[27] David A. Brading describes much the same scenario for the Bajío in the eighteenth century in "Hacienda Profits and Tenant Farming in the Mexican Bajío" (unpublished, 1972); "La estructura de la producción agrícola en el Bajío de 1700 a 1850," *Historia Mexicana* 23 (1972): 197–237; *Haciendas and Ranchos*.

[28] Isabel González Sánchez, *Haciendas y ranchos de Tlaxcala en 1712* (México, 1969), table facing p. 80; Archivo de Instrumentos Públicos de Guadalajara, Protocolos de notarios públicos (hereafter AIPG, prot.), Manuel de Mena (the elder), 14: 78ᵛ–82ᵛ; Archivo de Instrumentos Públicos de Guadalajara, Ramo de Tierras y Aguas (hereafter AIPG, Tierras), leg. 33, exp. 38.

[29] On Cañedo's career and his properties, see Van Young, *Hacienda and Market*, pp. 161–64, 212–13, 311–12; see also Richard B. Lindley, *Haciendas and Economic Development: Guadalajara, Mexico, at Independence* (Austin, 1983); Jorge Palomino y Cañedo, *La casa y mayorazgo de Cañedo de Nueva Galicia* (México, 1947); Manuel Romero de Terreros, *Antiguas haciendas de México* (México, 1956); and Ricardo Lancaster-Jones, *Haciendas de Jalisco y aledaños, 1506–1821* (Guadalajara, 1974).

[30] Aside from privately accumulated capital based on mining, manufacturing, commercial, or even agricultural wealth itself, investment was possible using large sums

nial haciendas tended to take the form of buildings, storage facilities, fencing, and irrigation works, most of which were associated with the intensification of cereal production. Hacienda inventories and accounts of the period quite uniformly show a reduction in the number of livestock raised for sale, an increase in the number of work animals, an overall decrease in the size of livestock herds, and often an increase in the amount of tillage and fencing to protect farming lands.[31] To cite but one striking example of this process, the great grain-producing Hacienda de Huejotitán, located near Lake Chapala and owned for most of the eighteenth century by the Villaseñor family, underwent an almost complete reversal in the structure of its capital stock during the last decades of the century. In 1759, the value of the hacienda's livestock represented 61 percent of its total capital value, and irrigation, fencing, and tilled lands 21 percent. In 1808 the proportions had almost exactly reversed themselves, with livestock representing 22 percent of total capital value, and irrigation works, fencing, and tillage 55 percent.[32] The earlier emphasis on livestock production was due, of course, not only to the limited local demand for agricultural products, but also to the limited availability of labor—phenomena representing two sides of the same coin.

The increased labor demands that came with grain production were more easily met after the regional population, especially the village Indian population from which most estate laborers were drawn, had reached its nadir in the mid-seventeenth century and began to grow again. The great Jesuit Hacienda de Toluquilla, located in a fertile valley to the south of Guadalajara, was unable prof-

---

borrowed from the church. Conventional wisdom on this point is that money borrowed from ecclesiastical agencies was not turned to productive uses, but was used to underwrite the lifestyle and conspicuous consumption of landlords; see, for example, Florescano, *Estructuras y problemas agrarios*, pp. 162–78. But evidence from the Guadalajara region indicates that, on the contrary, church lending in agriculture did help to increase production in the late colonial period; see Van Young, *Hacienda and Market*, 182–91; and also for the Guadalajara region, see Linda Greenow, *Credit and Socioeconomic Change in Colonial Mexico: Loans and Mortages in Guadalajara, 1720–1820* (Boulder, 1983). On the question of church lending in Mexico, see Michael P. Costeloe, *Church Wealth in Mexico: A Study of the "Juzgado de Capellanías" in the Archbishopric of Mexico, 1800–1856* (Cambridge, 1967). For Spanish America, see Arnold J. Bauer, "The Church and Spanish American Agrarian Structure, 1765–1865," *The Americas* 28(1971): 78–98.

[31] See Van Young, *Hacienda and Market*, pp. 207–20.

[32] Biblioteca Pública del Estado (Guadalajara), Archivo del Juzgado General de Bienes de Difuntos (hereafter BPE-BD), leg. 106, exp. 3, 1759; leg. 180, no exped. no., 1808.

itably to produce grain for much of the seventeenth century because of a labor shortage. In mid-century, the hacienda administrator remarked that, "If it were not for the mules, cattle, and horses sold, the Colegio [owner of the estate] could not sustain itself, because the wheat farm requires intolerable work and is so expensive that you cannot believe how little profit it yields."[33] By the time the hacienda had come into the hands of the silver baron Francisco Javier Vizcarra, first Marqués de Pánuco, in the late eighteenth century, the major component of its income was from sales of grain, especially wheat.[34] Maize cultivation also grew enormously on rural estates, but in terms of the proportion of land devoted to tillage, wheat seems to have had the edge in its rate of expansion. Furthermore, wheat displaced maize on the most favored farming lands, and maize in turn probably displaced livestock grazing out toward more peripheral land of marginal quality. Finally, the structure of hacienda incomes followed patterns of investment and land use. Profits from cereal production represented an increasingly large proportion of income in estate agriculture, while the component represented by livestock sales tended to slip. On the whole, direct farming by landlords, using hired labor on what may be termed demesne farms, yielded a larger proportion of income on most large properties than did the renting out of hacienda lands or sharecropping.[35]

The ready availability of land and labor made the commercial agricultural expansion of the late eighteenth century possible. Insofar as land was concerned, the process at work during the century seems not to have been so much one of expropriation of unoccupied or peasant lands, as of the *mise en valeur* of land already within the orbit of estate agriculture. In fact, the great age of hacienda expansion was not the eighteenth century, but the seventeenth.[36] Most ha-

[33] Archivo General de la Nación (México), Jesuítas, vol. 1, exp. 12. A transcription of this and other documents relating to Toluquilla were generously lent to me by the late Professor Salvador Reynoso of Guadalajara.

[34] AHMG, caja 35, 1780; caja 11, exp. 2, 1786; AIPG, Tierras, leg. 33, exp. 18, 1809; Biblioteca Pública del Estado (Guadalajara), Archivo Judicial de la Audiencia de Nueva Galicia (hereafter BPE-AJA), 138:9:1489, 1796–1797.

[35] Van Young, *Hacienda and Market*, pp. 224–35. The situation on large estates in the Bajío offered something of a contrast, with sharecropping and renting much more important in the structure of hacienda income, and demesne production less; see Brading, *Haciendas and Ranchos*.

[36] For findings that parallel my own in this respect for other regions in Mexico, see François Chevalier, *La formation des grands domaines au Méxique: Terre et sociétè aux XVIe–XVIIe siécles* (Paris, 1952); Gibson, *The Aztecs*, p. 289; William B. Taylor,

ciendas seem to have been approximately the same size in 1700 as they were in 1800. It is true that small changes in extent of land-holdings took place during the century to round out parcels, to rationalize land use, and in some cases to raise money where land-owners were hard-pressed financially, but there is little evidence to indicate that large landowners gained significantly in terms of the amounts of land they owned by means of purchase, appropriation, or illegal seizure. This does not mean, however, that the development of commercial agriculture did not apply major pressures on the traditional landholding patterns in the countryside, both in terms of land use and effective control over resources. On the contrary, the putting of more and more land under the plow and the marginalization of livestock led to a situation in which land already held for some time under putatively legal titles was used in new ways—ways that clashed with older notions of prescriptive rights of usage both on the part of Indian peasants, and other landowners as well. The frequency and acrimoniousness of judicial and extrajudicial conflicts over land seems to have increased during the eighteenth century. Much of this conflict took the form of land suits between indigenous communities and haciendas, which sometimes dragged on in the colonial courts for years, but it was by no means limited to the struggle over resources between the peasant and commercial agricultural sectors of the rural economy. In terms of conflict over productive resources, the Guadalajara region during the late eighteenth century was a Hobbesian world in which neither racial nor class solidarity was likely to temper the war of all against all.

Very often at issue in these conflicts was not the ownership of prime farming lands, but the use of marginal lands that only decades before had been of little interest either to peasants or commercial farmers. But as the rural population of the region grew during the course of the eighteenth century, these marginal resources became increasingly important for the small-scale, interstitial economic activities that came to be of great importance in the peasant economy—such as wood-collecting, brick- and pottery-making, stone-quarrying, charcoal-burning, etc.—as well as additional farming land. On their side, hacendados needed the same lands for some of the same purposes, as well as for rough grazing for livestock and

Landlord and Peasant in Colonial Oaxaca (Stanford, 1972), pp. 280–81. But contrast the view of Florescano, *Estructuras y problemas agrarios*, p. 44, 140–48, 189–90, who strongly implies that major hacienda expansion continued throughout the eighteenth century, mostly by extralegal means. For a detailed treatment of hacienda size, expansion, and stability, see Van Young, *Hacienda and Market*, pp. 294–314.

general reserves. Large landowners and rancheros also fought among themselves for these resources. An important and graphic example of this type of conflict pitted the Hacienda de Cuisillos, to the west of Guadalajara, against several neighboring haciendas during the first half of the century. The masters of Cuisillos sought, among other things, to rationalize their farming and livestock operations by limiting common grazing rights to the stubble in the hacienda's fields, and they finally succeeded in extinguishing such traditional rights by the 1760s.[37] The right to freely collect wood, rather than grazing, was at issue in the suit between the hacendado and distilling magnate José Prudencio Cuervo and the Indian town of Tequila at the end of the century. With the simultaneous growth of the local distilling industry and Indian peasant population, the right to collect wood on the slopes of the Cerro de Tequila became a vitally important issue, and the parties to the dispute took it in deadly earnest, engaging in a court battle lasting five years. Eventually the conflict was resolved (at least temporarily) in an amicable fashion, but what is important is not so much the resolution but the forces that impelled conflict in the first place.[38] Conflicts over land ownership and use, often centering on much the same issues as in the cases cited abaove, were endemic between Indian pueblos as well, and occasionally were punctuated by violence.[39]

Although an aggressively expansionist commercial agriculture was responsible for much of the pressure on land resources during the late eighteenth century, pressures also came from within the peasant sector of the rural economy, primarily in the form of population growth. Indian pueblos that had been abandoned during the seventeenth century, or that had merged with other towns, began to revive during the eighteenth century and demanded the restitution of their ancient lands and titles.[40] New Indian towns and suburbs (*barrios*) grew up during the eighteenth century, and they, too, sought independent status and lands. Finally, already well-established peasant villages of long standing were constantly complaining during the last decades of the century that they had insufficient land to sustain their growing populations. The Indian pueblo of Ti-

[37] AIPG, Tierras, leg. 71, exp. 30, 1761; leg. 33, exp. 3, 1765; leg. 51, exp. 2, 1644–1805; leg. 25, exps. 13, 14, and 19, 1805–1816.

[38] AIPG, Tierras, leg. 40, exp. 22, 1799.

[39] For example, Jocotepec vs. San Cristóbal Zapotitlán—AIPG, Tierras, leg. 78, exps. 3–12, 1767.

[40] For example, the pueblo of San Nicolás, near Jalostotitlán in the Altos of Jalisco—AIPG, Tierras, leg. 27, exp. 12, 1802.

zapanito, for example, located just to the west of Lake Chapala, was perennially land-hungry during the eighteenth century. At mid-century, with a population of about a thousand people, the pueblo was already dangerously short of farming lands. By 1819, with its population almost doubled, Tizapanito still had the same land base and found itself in an "estado miserable" due to the lack of farming land.[41] Other Indian villages shared a similar fate, especially those in areas best suited to commercial agriculture, such as the northern margins of Lake Chapala, the valleys to the south and west of Guadalajara, and the Ameca–Cocula valley to the west.

One palpable effect of this population pressure on the Indian peasant economy of the region was that Indians withdrew to a great extent from the urban market as sellers of grain, particularly maize, and reentered the regional economy as sellers of labor and labor-intensive craft and agricultural products. Up to the 1780s it seems that there had been sufficient land under the control of Indian pueblos that Indian farmers could in any given year make an important contribution to the grain supply of the city. At mid-century the introduction of maize into the urban market by Indian producers represented a very respectable 25 percent of the total. By the 1780s this figure had dropped to about 5 percent, and after 1810 to about 1 percent.[42] The Indian slippage in land resources was not absolute, but relative, and under the conditions of the late eighteenth century Indian farmers were compelled to retain for their own consumption grain that they had formerly been free to market in the city. With a labor surplus in the peasant sector of the economy, collecting and craft activities, horticulture, and wage labor assumed major importance.

Thus, even if land had become an increasingly scarce resource in the late eighteenth century, labor as a production factor in commercial agriculture was not. In fact, the ready availability of a large, poorly paid labor force was one of the most important elements in the commercial agricultural prosperity of the late colonial period. As elsewhere in the Mexican core area, the elements in the sequence of labor systems—encomienda, repartimiento, and free wage labor with a strong admixture of debt peonage—overlapped and were intimately linked to the initial decline and the subsequent rapid recovery of the rural population. By the end of the eighteenth century,

[41] AIPG, Tierras, leg. 62, exps. 24 and 25; leg. 27, exp. 7.
[42] AHMG, various cajas; and see also Van Young, *Hacienda and Market*, pp. 236–69.

permanent resident peons on rural estates constituted the core of the region's rural labor force.

The elements associated with the classical system of hacienda labor elsewhere in Mexico were present—wages in the form of rations; *tiendas de raya*; a substantial component of debt in the wage structure; and exploitative labor conditions tempered to a degree by patriarchal social relations and the emotional benefits to be had from living in a surrogate community.[43] Wage levels were generally low, and as prices rose and nominal wages remained virtually stable throughout the century, real wages in agriculture tended to fall.[44] Nor, apparently, was debt on the part of laborers a major force in recruiting or keeping hacienda workers toward the end of the eighteenth century, since per capita debt levels tended to fall along with real wages. In the seventeenth and early eighteenth centuries, in a labor-scarce economy, advances in the form of cash, rations, and goods were considered indispensable in attracting laborers. One contemporary observer, commenting on the labor recruitment situation at about mid-century, stated: "It is just as incredible that laborers work without advance as to catch a star in your hand."[45] In the labor-abundant situation of the late eighteenth century, however, hacendados became increasingly casual about pursuing laborers who decamped owing debts. The most obvious reason for this was that the very function of debt—to ensure a steady and reliable supply of estate labor—had been assumed largely by rural population pressure. In addition, temporary wage labor, drawn for the most part from independent landholding villages with surplus manpower, helped to undercut the market position of wage laborers and became increasingly important.

It is difficult to speak with precision of a general fall in living standards among the mass of the rural population, both peasant and proletarian, during the late eighteenth century, but most of the admittedly fragmentary evidence points in that direction. For rural wage earners, especially those living permanently on haciendas, real wages seem to have fallen and with them per capita debt levels, an indication of a lessened bargaining power vis-à-vis employers. For the village-dwelling, largely Indian peasant population, low wages and insufficient land for family farming bespeak much the same conditions. In addition, the level of consumption of manufac-

---

[43] For a fuller discussion of all these points, see Van Young, *Hacienda and Market*, pp. 84–88.

[44] Van Young, *Hacienda and Market*, pp. 250–51.

[45] BPE-BD, leg. 94, exp. 7.

tured goods and certain luxury items seems to have remained stable in the countryside despite the increasing population, or to have dropped somewhat in certain towns. This situation is reflected in the royal sales tax (*alcabala*) figures for goods sold in provincial towns in the last decades of the century.[46]

The pressures brought to bear on peasant communities by the expansion of commercial agriculture on the one hand, and population growth on the other, were compounded during the eighteenth century by an increasing social and economic differentiation within village society. The tendency toward concentration of wealth within village society was an old one, though difficult to document with any precision.[47] Such concentration, especially of landed wealth, also characterized non-Indian towns.[48] The trend toward monetization of the rural economy, ever more apparent during the late colonial period, provided opportunities for the acquisition of wealth, even while the condition of the mass of rural dwellers seems to have worsened appreciably. Thus a contradiction arose between the increasing degree of social and economic inequality within village society, and the cosmological assumptions underlying the integration and continuity of that society.

The wealth of individual Indian families, whether commoners or elite group members, was based for the most part on the ownership of land acquired through private purchase. The viceregal authorities repeatedly attemped to outlaw, or at least regulate, such dealings, but apparently to little effect.[49] One example was that of Francisco Miguel, an Indian from the pueblo of Santa Cruz, in the district of Tlajomulco. By the time of his death in 1743, Miguel had built up a substantial personal estate almost entirely through his own labors (he had inherited little and his wife brought a very small dowry), including eighteen parcels of farmland (most of which he had purchased from other local Indians), several hundred head of livestock, agricultural tools, and two small houses.[50] Though probably larger than the average, Francisco Miguel's fortune was fairly representa-

[46] Biblioteca Pública del Estado (Guadalajara), Archivo Fiscal de la Audiencia de Nueva Galicia, various *libros de alcabalas*.

[47] On this tendency and its implications, see Van Young, "Conflict and Solidarity."

[48] For example, see the cadastral surveys of the important farming town of Cocula, to the west of Guadalajara, which indicate that the distribution of property became increasingly skewed between 1650 and 1800; AIPG, Tierras, leg. 51, exp. 1.

[49] AIPG, Tierras, leg. 41, exp. 20; *Colección de acuerdos sobre tierras*, vol. 2, pp. 287–89; Van Young, "Rural Life in Eighteenth-Century Mexico," pp. 584–85.

[50] AIPG, prot., Tlajomulco, vol. 2, 1743.

tive, in terms of its composition, of the kind of wealth Indians were likely to acquire. Exactly what proportion of the village population reached this level of wealth is impossible to determine, but at a guess it could hardly have exceeded 5–10 percent, including the powerholders within Indian society—the caciques, principales, and Indian alcaldes.

The wealth of Indian village elites was distinguished less by its nature than by the means of its acquisition, since in addition to acquiring property through the common mechanisms of inheritance, marriage, or purchase, the village notable could also use the power of his office, the prestige of his social position, and his connections with powerful outsiders. The outright expropriation of common land, the formation of a clientele within the village, and the manipulation of village resources for personal enrichment were common practices.[51] Village notables also worked in collusion with outsiders such as white officials, priests, and landowners. It is impossible to ascertain to what degree this kind of malfeasance on the part of Indian notables was generally recognized or protested against by the mass of village-dwelling peasants, but there is some evidence to indicate that it was explicitly acknowledged and caused considerable strain within village society.[52]

Under attack both from within and without, the communal landholding Indian village demonstrated a remarkable resilience in maintaining its social and economic identity throughout the colonial period and into the nineteenth century. A major factor in this resilience was the integrating function of conflict itself for the village community. It is by now a sociological commonplace that conflict between groups may have the effect of solidifying intragroup loyalties.[53] In the present case, conflict over land, whether in formal or informal, extralegal situations would have served the function of increasing intravillage solidarity. The pragmatic motives for this defense of village land resources, of course, are also obvious. Members of village society at all levels of the social hierarchy depended in some degree on traditional rights of prescriptive, common usage of

[51] AIPG, Tierras, leg. 14, exp. 7, 1800; leg. 27, exp. 4, 1789; leg. 40, exp. 11, 1798.

[52] AIPG, Tierras, leg. 27, exps. 4 and 5; leg. 78, exps. 3–12; AIPG, prot. Berroa, 22: 95ᵛ, Jocotepec, 1790s.

[53] See, for example, Lewis Coser, *The Functions of Social Conflict* (Glencoe, 1956) and Max Gluckman, *Custom and Conflict in Africa* (Oxford, 1966). Specifically for this aspect of agrarian relations in Mexico, see Eric R. Wolf, "Aspects of Group Relations in a Complex Society; Mexico," in *Peasants and Peasant Societies: Selected Readings*, ed. Teodor Shanin (Harmondsworth, 1971), pp. 50–68.

lands despite the widespread trend toward private ownership in the late colonial period. Judicial or extrajudicial struggle over land with nonvillagers also must have functioned to express and give vent to the endemic racial and social tensions that characterized rural life.[54]

But such conflicts over land with outsiders may also have served to deflect social tensions generated within village society by the increasing tendency toward social and economic differentiation. Collective anger and frustration within the village, especially provoked by elite behavior that could be construed as illegitimate, was directed toward outsiders instead of toward more proximate social objects. By this mechanism, behavior perceived as violating traditional norms and imperilling the traditional economic and social equilibrium within the village was projected onto outsiders; thus potentially destructive internal conflict was tempered, if not completely neutralized.[55] All members of the community reaped some benefits from this moral sleight of hand. The mass of the village-dwelling peasant population were able to stay within the economic environment of the village, which, although it might be imperfect, offered them at least the semblance of autonomy. On their side, the village elites were able to maintain their privileged access to the political and economic resources of the community, through which they often sought to improve their status in the world outside the village. Both groups thus used the continued existence of the village community for different ends: the mass of the peasants for social immobility, and the elites for social mobility.

The Guadalajara Region and the Rebellion: Linking Preconditions and Uprisings

The basic approach in the preceding pages has been to describe, for one of the major focuses of the 1810–11 and subsequent rebellions in New Spain, the "preconditions" for a massive popular uprising by rural people in favor of the vague political program of Miguel Hidalgo. These preconditions consisted in a number of changes—or perhaps "intensifications" would be a better term—that together acted as powerful solvents of the traditional social order in the countryside, particularly as regards peasants. They can be summa-

[54] See Van Young, *Hacienda and Market*, pp. 318–22; Eric Van Young, "Un homicidio colonial," *Boletín del Archivo Histórico de Jalisco* 3(1979): 2–4.

[55] This admittedly speculative construction of historical materials finds theoretical support in the ideas of George Foster, though the applicability of those ideas is not as general as Foster originally asserted; see Foster, "Peasant Society."

rized as population pressure within the peasant sector of the economy; falling living standards for large groups of rural dwellers, both peasants and laborers; an increasing proletarianization of rural people; widespread social strains and conflict, often focusing on the ownership and/or control of land; and the compromising of a traditional way of life and its symbol, the peasant village, from within the community itself. Yet if the description of preconditions is to have any meaning for the explanation of collective behavior in this case, and if, in relying on the idea of preconditions, we are not to fall into the *post hoc ergo propter hoc* fallacy, two requirements must be met. First, we must be able to prove that specific rural people living under such conditions were directly involved in that collective behavior in significantly large numbers, and that their participation was an expression of some perceived conditions or felt grievances. Second, we must be able to construct a credible explanatory scheme linking the specific nature of mass participation in violent protest to the nature and development of the movement itself.

The first requirement cannot be met at present, because we simply do not know enough about the social composition of the various rebellions and guerrilla foci to link them to the concrete preconditions described above, and that others have described for the Bajío region. In the nature of such movements, one would hardly expect explicit and homogeneous expressions from the rural insurgents concerning their motives for rebelling. The evidence I have seen suggests a wide range of circumstances for participation in the rebellion, most of which were decidedly nonideological. Nonetheless, military and criminal records of the time detail numerous instances of presumably underprivileged rural people, particularly Indian peasants, who participated in acts of rebellion, both in the Guadalajara region and elsewhere. For example, there are many straightforward cases of Indian peasants accused of membership in insurgent bands and of associated murders.[56] There also appear to be frequent cases in which large numbers of people in single villages conspired to rebel, actually rose up in arms together, or invaded and pillaged local haciendas, murdering the inhabitants.[57] Occasionally one catches glimpses of the motivations that pushed rural people into rebellion (or at least the perceptions of contemporary nonpeasant observers of those motives), or of the symbols that mobilized them. For example,

[56] Biblioteca Pública del Estado (Guadalajara), Criminal (hereafter BPE, Criminal), exp. 13, Autlán, 1813; exp. 16, Guadalajara, 1813. These documents were uncatalogued until recently.

[57] BPE, Criminal, exp. 82, Zacoalco, 1811; AGN, Infidencias, vol. 17, exps. 6–9, Chicontepec, 1810; vol. 2, exp. 7, Atotonilco el Grande, 1811.

several Indian peasant insurgents captured near Yurirapúndaro in 1810 claimed that they had been ordered to join Allende's forces by the caciques of their villages "by order of the King."[58] On the other hand, rebels in the Jocotepec area attempted to raise local Indians there in August 1811, with the story that Father Hidalgo was still alive and ready to lead a revived insurgency.[59] Occasionally, in commenting on rural rebellion, contemporary observers made intriguing but veiled statements that serve only to muddy the waters. Such was the case, for example, with the royalist officer who observed that the rebellious Indians of Tlaltenango had been ". . . llevados a los principios de la Insurección de las oscuras ideas que cubrían a muchos individuos (y en particular a los indios)."[60]

But for every case that seems to fall under the neat paradigm of preconditions→rebellion, one finds scores that do not fit into the pattern. For example, criminal activity seems to have been widespread during periods of rebellion, and was difficult to distinguish from ideologically based protest. Habitual criminals often joined insurgent bands, and rebels occasionally released thieves en masse from jails in captured towns.[61] Large numbers of insurgents, particularly rural people far from the inner councils of the movement, claimed, upon being captured, that they had been dragooned into the rebel forces upon threat of punishment or death.[62] So general was this excuse, particularly by those putative rebels captured after the battle of the Puente de Calderón in early 1811, that if they are to be believed, few people joined the insurgent forces voluntarily at all.[63] Some rural people accused of insurgency were simply swept up in the hysterical atmosphere that prevailed in large parts of the country in 1810 and 1811, and this fed on false accusations, idle gossip, presumably seditious statements, the peremptory seizure of people in the open countryside by the military.[64] Some people were

[58] AGN, Infidencias, vol. 5, exp. 8, 1810.

[59] BPE, Criminal, exp. 65, 1811.

[60] "Won over to the principles of the insurrection by the obscure ideas that covered many individuals (and in particular, the Indians)." BPE, Criminal, exp. 43, Tlaltenango, 1812.

[61] AGN-OG, vol. 15, exp. 10, Río Frío, 1810; BPE, Criminal, exp. 1, Juchipila, 1817; exp. 80, Apatzingán, 1815; exp. 31, Tepatitlán, 1812–1813. Defining political rebellion as crime, of course, is an age-old technique on the part of established authorities, allowing them to beg the question of a challenge to political legitimacy while simultaneously inflicting draconian punishments on captured rebels (bandits) who come within their reach.

[62] AGN, Infidencias, vol. 5, exp. 8, Yurirapúndaro, 1810.

[63] BPE, Criminal, exps, 7, 8, 41, 54, 63, 64, 67, 84, 94, 104, 119, 1811.

[64] BPE, Criminal, exp. 2, 1812, and various expedientes.

innocent bystanders, others just fools. Such was the case, for example, with the man captured as a spy by soldiers outside the city of
Guadalajara in 1811 for attempting to cross one of the local rivers
near the bridge of Huentitán. Ultimately, it turned out that he was
no spy at all, but had simply wagered his friends that he could cross
the river without being caught by the guards.[65] The point of all this,
of course, is not that participation by rural people in the insurgency
was random or without motivations rooted in social and economic
conditions, but rather that it was a complex human event about
which it is difficult to make convincing sociological generalizations.

As to the second requirement, we do not as yet have an entirely
credible explanatory or interpretive framework for the insurgent
movements that led eventually to independence in Mexico. At the
risk of oversimplifying, there appear to be two major schemes or
strains of thought that attempt to deal with this. The notion that
socioeconomic preconditions disposed certain rural areas of New
Spain to violent protest fits best (though by no means perfectly) into
the first of these schemes, that the struggle for independence, especially in its early phases, was a "class war" prompted by the economic and social oppression of the darker, laboring masses of the
country. This interpretation would see the insurgency, therefore, in
terms of a horizontal split, or splits, in the fabric of Mexican colonial
society.[66] But this theory cannot present a unified interpretation, of
course, in that it must account for the actions of at least two groups,
white elites and darker masses. In the case of the creole directorate
of the movement, this theory would see the rebellion as the attempt
of a middle class (or perhaps a "subelite") to seize political power
and social preeminence from the gachupín elite of high royal officials and their allies in commerce, the church, and elsewhere. As
applied to popular participation in the independence movement, especially on the part of rural people, this theory would view the taking up of arms as a kind of knee-jerk, reflex reaction to social and
economic oppression, rather like a Jacquerie in the classical European sense.

The alternative scheme of interpretation may be called the political protest theory, which sees the independence movement as a vertical split in the fabric of colonial society, between Spain and New
Spain, with the gachupín elite representing the proximate agents of
Spanish political domination.[67] This interpretation hinges on the

[65] BPE, Criminal, exp. 26, Guadalajara, 1811.

[66] Into this school of thought would fall very roughly, for example, the work of
Wolf, "El Bajío," and Di Tella, "Las clases peligrosas."

[67] Under this rubric would fall the work of Hamill, The Hidalgo Revolt, and much

idea that a colonial compact existed between New Spain and the mother country, in which the inefficiency or indifference of the Habsburgs and early Bourbons allowed the colony a large degree of political and economic autonomy while at the same time managing to extract at least some resources from it. An increasing strain was put on this fairly benign system, so the theory goes, by late Bourbon efforts to recolonize New Spain through a series of reforms that had the contradictory effect of stimulating economic prosperity at the same time that the creole elite was disenfranchized politically. The destruction of the legitimacy of the Spanish monarchy by political events in Europe and the United States in the period 1808–21 led to the final rupture of the compact and the breaking away of the disaffected colony through an armed movement that enjoyed wide support across much of Mexican society.

The problem with these two schemes is that they fail to answer a great many questions, especially insofar as the popular rural component of the independence movement is concerned. As to the class war scheme, the problem discussed at some length above, that of the degree of congruence between race and class in the colonial period, seems to give a simple interpretation along class lines a poor fit with the evidence. Did Indian peasants constitute a class, possibly a class of low "classness"? A second problem with this interpretation is that some oppressed areas did not take up arms in 1810, but remained calm, seemingly immune to revolutionary zeal, much as was to happen in 1910. Insofar as the creole directorate of the movement is concerned, it is by now almost a cliché based upon recent research in the social history of late colonial Mexico that creole and gachupín elites were so closely bound by ties of interest, kinship, and marriage as to be indistinguishable from each other.[68] The political protest explanation is even less useful when applied to the participation of the rural masses in the insurgency. There must have been grave limits to the value of political or ideological appeals in mobilizing rural people, particularly peasants. Thousands of these people, one imagines, must have lived a largely isolated, if still not completely insular, existence in the countryside, illiterate for the most part and removed from access to political power or preoccu-

---

of the traditional historiography on the period. In fact, of course, one rarely sees in the literature a pure representative of either the class war or political protest interpretations, but rather an emphasis on one aspect or the other.

[68] See, for example, David A. Brading, *Miners and Merchants in Bourbon Mexico, 1763–1810* (Cambridge, 1971); Doris Ladd, *The Mexican Nobility at Independence, 1780–1826* (Austin, 1976); John Kicza, *Colonial Entrepreneurs: Families and Business in Bourbon Mexico City* (Albuquerque, 1983); Lindley, *Kinship and Credit*.

pations with political matters. It is highly unlikely that such people cared about the colonial compact, or that considerations of monarchical legitimacy would have touched their lives, except insofar as kingship was the symbol of authority and of an understandable order in the world. Whether or not, for example, Godoy was the Queen's lover may have made some difference to the fate of Spain, but one suspects that it made no difference at all to a Mexican peasant of 1810.

Both the class war and the political protest theories may have a measure of validity, but neither of them goes far enough toward explaining the nature and causes of participation by rural people in the insurgency of 1810 and after. More convincing explanations will combine consideration of both secular trends in social and economic change, the effects of proximate causes for rebellion, possibly in the political sphere, and the mobilizing and radicalizing effects of rebellion itself, once under way, in touching off secondary movements. Research on these issues must also address the possible importance of intervening variables between protest, poverty and politics. Historians must also investigate the role of popular symbols and ideology in mobilizing mass rebellion. In this connection, for example, what was the role of priests in rural uprisings? Priests were certainly much in evidence in the wars of independence, not just at the top of insurgent leadership (Hidalgo, Morelos), but also at the lowest levels of political and military activity. One suspects that the reasons for this go beyond a defensive protest on the part of the church against the initiatives of late Bourbon regalist policy. Furthermore, what accounts for the apparent weakness and sparcity of popular ideological formulations in these movements?[69] Why is there so little in the way of a revolutionary eschatology or mythos, and no evidence of any millenarian elements among rural participants? These and other questions will only be answered when we have a social history of the popular insurgency of 1810 and the following years, and that history has still to be written.

---

[69] The one widely acknowledged exception to this seems to have been the use of the dark Virgin of Guadalupe as popular symbol and mascot of the insurgents, which often faced the white-skinned Virgin of los Remedios across revolutionary battlefields. The Virgin of Guadalupe was certainly an object of popular (especially peasant) veneration before the outbreak of the rebellion in 1810, but the choice of the Virgin as a device of the movement seems to have been made by Hidalgo. The degree to which she represented the popular world view, grievances, and aspiration has yet to be demonstrated.

CHAPTER SEVEN

Banditry and Insurrection:
Rural Unrest in Central Jalisco,
1790–1816

William B. Taylor

As the Introduction to this volume makes clear, we now know that peasant uprisings were endemic in eighteenth- and nineteenth-century Mexico. The vast majority, however, were local risings of single villages; during the colonial period few grew into regional insurrections or posed a threat to the state. This essay moves beyond my earlier work on these dramatic local events in Oaxaca and central Mexico to rural unrest of a different character in a different place: central Jalisco before and during the first war of independence (1810–16) when large-scale but still relatively short-lived armed insurrections overshadowed the local risings of the mature colony in several parts of the Mexican heartland. My purpose is to document the main forms of rural unrest in this region from 1790 to 1821 and to evaluate them in terms of social values and a changing economy, polity, and village society. In a modest way the purpose also is comparative: to understand why banditry and insurrection developed in central Jalisco in the early nineteenth century, while most of Oaxaca remained a zone of village revolts. Finally, to temper easy conclusions about rural insurrection in western Mexico, I consider two communities of central Jalisco that did not participate in the regional movements of 1810–11 and 1811–16.

The setting is a roughly rectangular area 70 miles long by 45 miles wide centered on Lake Chapala. It extends from Tala in the north-

The research for this essay was made possible by generous grants from the John Simon Guggenheim Memorial Foundation and the Social Science Research Council.

west corner, past Guadalajara to Tepatitlán in the northeast, to La
Barca in the southeast, and to Sayula in the southwest. Most of this
area lies within the basin of the Lerma and Santiago Rivers and includes a string of shallow lakes around Lake Chapala. It is within
the immediate orbit of Guadalajara, the major city of western Mexico
in the late eighteenth century. Within this area there were large private estates that were increasing their production of grains for the
expanding urban market in the late colonial period. It is also the
area of densest rural population in Nueva Galicia and the heartland
of settled Indian villages there at the time of the Spanish conquest.
In 1800 roughly half of the population was still classified as Indian
and some of the larger communities, as well as many smaller ones,
maintained the status of landholding Indian pueblos.

The Rise of Banditry, 1790–1821

Bandit gangs were not new to Nueva Galicia in the late colonial period, but there is evidence that banditry as a form of outlaw activity
and rural protest only became widespread there in the late 1780s,[1]
after the great famine and the epidemic of 1785–86. Intendant Jacobo Ugarte y Loyola, reporting on this rise of bandit activity, listed
41 ladrones famosos and suspected gang members being held in the
prisons of Nueva Galicia for highway robbery and cattle rustling as
of March 1795.[2] Trial records from the 1790s confirm that highway
robberies had become widespread.[3] Intendant José Fernández Abascal, who took office on February 10, 1800, understood highway robbery in New Galicia to be a serious, ongoing problem, but one that
did not threaten Spanish rule. He was not much impressed or encouraged by brief lulls in banditry. In a report of September 30,
1802, he commented, "when I entered this province it was free of
those feared gangs of robbers, but remnants of the old gangs and

[1] Archivo General de Indias (Sevilla), Audiencia de Guadalajara (hereafter AGI Guadalajara), legajo 120, 1753 campaign against salteadores de caminos, and various
mid-eighteenth-century criminal trials in the Archivo Judicial de la Audiencia de la
Nueva Galicia, Biblioteca del Estado de Jalisco, Guadalajara, fondos especiales (hereafter AJANG). For a more detailed account of banditry in New Galicia at the end of the
colonial period, see William B. Taylor, "Bandit Gangs in Late Colonial Times: Rural
Jalisco, Mexico, 1794–1821," Bibliotheca Americana 1, no. 2 (1982): 29–58.

[2] AGI Guadalajara, legajo 306.

[3] In addition to the districts already noted, one trial record in 1796 reported bands
of "mala gente" in the barrancas of Real de San Pedro Analco, AJANG Criminal, unnumbered legajo (label reads "1719–1787, legajo 1").

even some new ones always rear their heads."[4] The next year, with reports of *gavillas* (gangs) again on the loose, the government carried out executions of notorious *salteadores* (highway robbers) then in custody as an example to their fellows.

A new round of highway robberies and arrests occurred from 1805–07. Summary reports have not been located for this period, but twenty trials have been found (eleven for 1805, four for 1806, and five for 1807), from all over the province, but with the pockets of activity in central Jalisco from Zapotlán el Grande to Sayula, in the Lake Chapala districts of La Barca and Jocotepec, on the roads near Guadalajara, and in the Altos near Tepatitlán. It was at just this time that many delinquents and deserters from colonial militias were reported to be flocking to Guadalajara.[5]

From trial records and jail reports, the social background, organization and operations of bandit gangs can be roughly established. The usual salteador was in his late twenties or early thirties, from a poor socioeconomic background, illiterate, and likely to be classified racially as a Spaniard or an Indian. He had a prison record, possibly had escaped from jail shortly before arrest, and had traveled widely within the province. In most cases, he was not part of an organized, long-lived gang of robbers.[6]

Most salteadores shared a past of uprooted wandering. Many were without attachments to land or family, and most had traveled as landless laborers, militiamen, traders, or muleteers. Many others were fugitives and exiles—wanted for crimes of assault, robbery, and contraband trade, exiles from their towns for illicit sex, escapees from jail or deserters from the army. Others had recently been released from prison. Nearly all of the trial cases indicate that salteadores had previous criminal records or reputations as robbers. We do not know how many of the salteadores were recent escapees, but the prison records for Nueva Galicia in 1807 indicate that 18 percent of all men arrested during the first six months of that year had escaped by July 1. The stiff sentences meted out to these escapees in absentia gave them little choice but to remain on the run.

The salteadores do not appear to have been primarily rural or urban in their origins. In a sample of 136 salteadores, just over half (52

[4] AGI Guadalajara, legajo 306.

[5] AJANG Criminal, unnumbered legajo (label reads "1805–07–09").

[6] Women occasionally are listed among the members of gavillas. Agustín Marroquín had two women in his group, and two of the forty-one suspected bandits in jail in 1795 were women. These women were described as mistresses of gang members and it is not clear whether they bore arms or took part in the robberies.

percent) were from rural areas. There is little evidence that the salteadores of rural background were displaced peasants who had recently lost their lands. Since highway robberies took place in the
countryside, or at least outside towns and cities, a larger percentage
of rural bandits might be expected. Apparently this was not the case
although many of the city residents arrested as salteadores may, in
fact, have been recent migrants from the countryside—restless men
unable to find employment in the city. Urban employment and un-
deremployment may also have encouraged impatient men to "seek
their destiny" as robbers, as one man put it.[7]

One similarity in occupation connects nearly all of the salteadores—they occupied the lowest rungs of the economic ladder. All
but three of the 136 salteadores whose occupations are known were
from the poorest socioeconomic groups, whether urban or rural.
Rural salteadores were landless workers—day laborers, servants,
peons; urban salteadores were sweatshop employees, semiskilled
craftsmen, unskilled workers, or unemployed. As one salteador put
it, they were looking to "leave poverty behind."[8] Some were driven
to rob out of desperation, like the landless laborer with five small
children at home whose house had just been destroyed in an earth-
quake. Others, with less attachment to home and family, went on
the road simply looking for opportunity—"Let's see what God has
in store."[9]

Before independence, the gangs of salteadores were loosely organized. Usually there was a small core of two or three relatives or
compadres who inspired the formation of a larger gavilla to attack a
particular victim—a ranch or a rich traveler known to be on the
road—or simply to see what might come along.[10] But the larger
group was assembled on an impromptu basis, and most of the members did not know each other directly. They were often accepted
into the group on the recommendation of an acquaintance who
knew someone else in the gavilla. The larger groups were likely to

[7] AJANG Criminal, legajo 74 ("1806–1807").

[8] AJANG Criminal, legajo 141 ("1817 legajo 2").

[9] Ibid. Most members of gavillas of New Galicia do not fit Eric Hobsbawm's characterization of ordinary bandit gangs as members of a criminal caste, "criminals by
inheritance," or "from a subterranean world," *Bandidos* (Barcelona, 1976), p. 40.
Although it is unlikely that many of the gavilleros of New Galicia qualify as "social
bandits" in Hobsbawm's terms either, the social backgrounds of these pre-independ-
ence bandits generally fit the social profiles of "marginal men" posited by Hobsbawm
for social bandits: young, unattached men with criminal records, deserters, cowboys,
muleteers, contraband traders, and landless farmworkers, *Bandidos*, pp. 31f.

[10] AJANG Criminal, legajo 74 ("1806–1807").

be formed in prison, among unemployed men living in the same rooming house or neighborhood, or among casual acquaintances and drifters who met at illegal gambling events, fairs, or parties, or in taverns.[11] Occasionally the ranks of the gavillas were increased when the prisoners of small-town jails were freed, but few of the gavillas with as many as five members stayed together for more than one or two robberies. Membership was fluid and the salteadores were careful to avoid being seen together, often agreeing to meet clandestinely at the place of attack. Don Manuel Antonio de Santa María, Juez General de la Acordada, commented on this loose organization when he wrote on May 12, 1795, "they do not remain attached to just one gang but pass from one to another; some of those who have been partners in several robberies stick together while others of them find new companions for more robberies and misdeeds."[12]

There were some more tightly knit groups, especially in the Altos region and in several Indian pueblos where local men preyed upon traders traveling the nearby roads. Occasionally, too, more tightly connected gangs from other parts of Mexico entered Nueva Galicia. For example, Agustín Marroquín, a notorious criminal from Tulancingo, arrived in 1805 to attend the *feria* (festival) at San Juan de los Lagos and visit Guadalajara on his way north. He brought with him his mistress and at least five close friends and relatives.

Leadership is difficult to discern from the written record, partly because the gavillas were loosely organized and may not have required much leadership, but also because the probable leaders were rarely arrested and, when they were arrested, probably understated their role in order to avoid stiff sentences. Judging by who divided up the booty and who was said to have planned the robbery and carried firearms, the acknowledged leaders generally were those with the most experience, longest prison records, and greatest reputation as robbers. If a gavilla included a creole, he was likely to be the leader. In three instances, gavillas were led by "gentlemen robbers," one a creole *licenciado* (the holder of a licenciate degree, a title given to lawyers), the second a creole doctor, and the third a creole *ranchero* (ranch owner). In two cases, these creoles clearly were fugitives charged with serious crimes: the licenciado was a deserter from the royal army and the ranchero was accused of murder.

[11] The campaign against gang robbery in 1795 included new efforts to control gambling and drunkenness; AGI Guadalajara, legajo 306.
[12] AGI Guadalajara, legajo 306.

Gangs of thieves operating in the countryside of New Galicia were evenly divided between those who robbed the main roads, usually stripping their victims of all they possessed, leaving them naked, bound, and blindfolded in some desolate spot; and those who specialized in stealing livestock from ranches and towns. Stolen animals were easy to trace locally so cattle rustlers had to move the animals quickly to a distant town or slaughter them themselves. Cattle thieves sometimes also robbed travelers, but cattle rustling on a large scale was specialized work and required reliable middlemen. It was not an activity for the casual robber. Transient salteadores did not usually steal livestock other than the occasional horse or mule. Gangs of thieves also attacked isolated ranch houses and stores in small towns. Some gavillas prided themselves on not harming their victims, although the threat of physical harm was always present; others were less reluctant to injure and kill. In thirteen cases, the robbery victim was killed; in four others, women were raped as well as robbed.

Cattle rustlers typically operated from small towns and isolated ranchos. They needed a remote spot to hide the animals temporarily or slaughter them without attracting attention. Highway robbers also needed seclusion. They found it either in a remote rancho, in the mountains not far from a main road, or in the anonymity of the provincial capital of Guadalajara.

The coincidence of highway robbery and the growth of Guadalajara in the late colonial period is striking. Increased trade, industry, government, and other forms of wealth in Guadalajara after 1750 attracted a wide spectrum of migrants in search of new opportunities. A report of 1805 noted that the migration included many vagrants, deserters, and delinquents, a veritable "flood of malefactors."[13] According to Intendant Ugarte y Loyola in 1795, Guadalajara was a breeding ground for bands of robbers: "this city and its adjoining districts are populous; and the poor are very inclined to theft, perhaps because they lack crafts and industries in which to occupy themselves; and in their prosecution and punishment are born the roaming gangs, inspired by one or another especially disreputable leader."[14] Some highway robberies were committed without advance planning by groups of young rural men on their way to Gua-

---

[13] AJANG Criminal, legajo 91 ("1808"); legajo 127 ("1809"); caja 2, legajo 3, exp. 5 (criminal documents identified by *caja* numbers are filed in boxes in the main room of the *fondos especiales*; those with *legajo* numbers are tied in bundles and presently housed in a separate room with the Miscelánea collection).

[14] AGI Guadalajara, legajo 306.

dalajara in search of work. More often, gavillas were organized in the city and used it as their base. All roads in the province now led to Guadalajara, the capital and center of commerce. Guadalajara was the center of information about who was on the road and when important shipments would be made. It was also a good place for robbers to hide, meet accomplices, and fence their stolen goods.

In these bandit gangs from central Jalisco, it is difficult to draw a neat distinction between the social bandits Eric Hobsbawm has described in *Primitive Rebels* and *Bandits*, and the garden-variety robbers who plundered for personal gain. There is little evidence that common people in New Galicia before 1810 supported the highway robbers of their day. Salteadores occasionally gained the protection of local officials (there is the example of Don Juan Vigil, *subdelegado* of Real del Rosario, protecting the *ladrón de cuadrilla*, José Maria Peña[15]). On the other hand, there are many examples in the trials of peasant villagers and rural townspeople taking the initiative in arresting known bandits and warning royal officials of suspicious characters—arrests were often made simply on suspicion of wrongdoing and groups of well-armed strangers on good horses were suspected as a matter of course—and of the salteadores stealing from poor and rich alike and indiscriminately committing brutal acts of kidnapping, rape, and murder. There was little to admire in men like Domingo Elías, a notorious *ladrón de caminos reales* from Teocuitatlán, who raped young women of his town and roamed the roads robbing travelers and farms. He was the chief suspect in the murder of one of his partners in crime, since he was the last person to have seen him alive.[16] Most of the salteadores investigated or arrested before Independence were not even local men. They were more like Ignacio Carrillo, a 35-year-old loner born in Teocaltiche and residing in Guadalajara, who admitted to a string of at least fifteen highway robberies and murders in all directions from the capital between 1808 and 1813.

Perhaps in only a few cases from the Altos de Jalisco were social bandits an important part of the apparent boom in banditry in Nueva Galicia at the end of the eighteenth century. At the time, banditry by local men seems to have been more deeply rooted in the Altos, especially in the jurisdiction of Tepatitlán, than in other parts of the province. Reports of the subdelegado of Tepatitlán and his

[15] Ibid.
[16] AJANG Criminal, legajo 91 ("1808 legajo 48"). Elías was arrested on August 28, 1808.

lieutenants before independence speak of small bands of cattle rustlers and highway robbers "who live scattered in the hills and *barrancas*."[17] In 1807, Subdelegado don Luis de Quirós y Prado remarked on the difficulty of running to earth "the multitude of
bandits who presently infest that district and threaten travellers."

Royal officials knew the bandit captains of Tepatitlán only too
well, but they were rarely able to bring them to justice. Official reports from 1805–11 identify the notorious bandit leaders as don
Diego Vallejo of the Rancho del Carretero near the Reducción de las
Cañadas, Juan Pérez of Río del Salto, Pedro Cedillo of Rancho las
Tunas, Antonio Anastasio, Domingo de Huerta of Rancho del Ojo
del Agua, and don Juan Casillas who was related to the chaplain of
the Hacienda del Húmedo.[18] All were born and raised on ranchos or
haciendas in the region, in a way that dared royal officials to interfere with their activities. For example, Pérez and Cedillo lived in
veritable fortresses; they had built their houses "in the form of a
bastion with many lookouts all around which protect them better
and allow them to discharge the firearms they have stored up and
which they bear against those who try to attack them."[19]

The small gangs of bandits in the jurisdiction of Tepatitlán had
some of the characteristics of social bandits, but they were not
model Robin Hoods. Like social bandits, the gavillas of Tepatitlán
did not steal from their own people; they stole cattle from haciendas
and cofradias, primarily. They were men of the people—ranch
workers or local owners of small ranchos. Ranchero families in the
Altos had intermarried over many generations, and the bandits had
relatives throughout the region in nearly all walks of life. More important, these extended families seemed to support (if not openly
applaud) the actions of their wayward cousins, much as the villagers
of southern Spain and Sicily cheered the deeds and believed in the
goodness of their "noble robbers." Whether from fear or admiration,
Indian townspeople whose cofradía animals were occasionally
taken by bandits seemed to side with the bandoleros rather than
with the district officials. They lodged complaints against the subdelegados and lieutenants but rarely against the bandits. The small
groups of Tepatitlán bandits were hard to capture because local people hid them, refused to cooperate with the royal authorities against
them, and, most important, facilitated their crimes by buying and

[17] AJANG Criminal, legajo 6 ("1808 legajo 2").

[18] AJANG Criminal, caja 2 (Casillas); legajo 76 ("1807 legajo 1") (Pérez Cedillo); legajo 6 ("1808 legajo 2") (Anastasio and Huerta).

[19] AJANG Criminal, legajo 76 ("1807 legajo 1").

selling their stolen goods. It was probably true, as one subdelegado said, that the bandits of Tepatitlán had the local people "subjected to their arrogance."[20]

Judging by court records, the now chronic problem of bands of salteadores increased once the War of Independence broke out. After 1810 groups of mobile bandits began to operate more openly and with impunity over a wider field outside the district seats and centers of population. Often attached to a political cause, the gavillas of the independence period were reported to have increased in number and size throughout the province. There were several large gangs, but the gavillas up to 1821 generally were small in size. Of the 78 gavillas whose numbers are documented for 1790–1821, 50 had five or fewer members, and only seven gavillas before 1810 were reported with 20 or more members (40, 30, 30, 20, 20, 20, "over 20"). The size and number of gavillas with more than ten members increased in the decade of the war, 1811–21; the average size of 45 gavillas identified was over 13.5 members; the average for the previous decade (1800–10) was 5.6 for 33 gavillas. After 1810 there were at least 14 gangs reported to have ten or more members (200, 50, 40, 25, 20, 20, 20, 20, 20, 12, 10, 10, "over ten," and "many").

No part of the province was exempt. Bands of insurgents and bandits roamed Colima and other parts of the coast in 1811–12.[21] By 1814 the royalists were unconcerned about a major insurrection on the coast since local villagers were not joining up with the bands. As one official put it, "those Indians have been more willing to give their money and their horses to the rebels than to give themselves."[22] Also on the fringes of Nueva Galicia, purported bandits raided haciendas and ranchos, virtually destroyed the farm economy in some districts, and interrupted trade near Sierra de Pinos and along the Michoacán border south and east of Guadalajara throughout the independence period.[23]

In the Altos, bandit gangs spread and often merged with the insurgency. Pedro Moreno, with his base in the district of Lagos close to the Bajío, was the famous insurgent of the area, and ranches throughout the adjoining district of Villa Encarnación in 1815 and

---

[20] Ibid.

[21] AJANG Criminal, unnumbered legajo (label reads "1803").

[22] AJANG Criminal, caja 3, December 1814.

[23] AGI Guadalajara, 563, February 1815, bishop's report regarding the Michoacán border; Cathedral archive of the Archbishopric of Guadalajara (hereafter CAG), unnumbered box of manuscripts for the parish of Tlajomulco (Sierra de Pinos, April 1815).

1816 were said to be the hideouts of insurgents and runaways alike;[24] but there also seems to have been more organized violence than was realized in other parts of the Altos and the district of Cuquío closer to Guadalajara. Bands of creoles and Indians in the jurisdictions of Tepatitlán and Nochistlán operated under the direction of rebel priests Francisco Alvarez, "Ramos," and "Martínez" in 1810 and 1811.[25] Others from Yahualica fought under the bandit chief Jesús Barajas.[26] Jalostotitlán reportedly was occupied in 1810 by Ramón Gutiérrez and Marcos Díaz, who recruited local Indians into their bands.[27] Apparently there was even an important battle staged in the area before May 1811, "the Battle of Tepatitlán."[28] Many of those who fought in these early insurgent bands in the Altos were ranchers and ranch hands from rural Tepatitlán, Yahualica, and the Puesto del Húmedo, the area of much late colonial bandit activity.[29] All of these reputed insurgents were known salteadores and cattle rustlers before the war.[30] Some joined up when insurgent forces released them from jail.[31]

Central Jalisco closer to Guadalajara was also plagued by roaming bands of robbers with or without insurgent connections in 1810–21. All parts of the region were affected, from Zapopan to San Cristóbal de la Barranca, Ameca, Tequila, Cocula, San Martín de la Cal, Sayula, Teocuitatlán, Tlajomulco, Poncitlán, Tonalá, Tlaquepaque, Jocotepec, Zapotlán del Rey, and the outskirts of Guadalajara. Most were small gavillas of opportunists organized in Guadalajara, or roving groups of displaced Indians and mulattoes.[32] A few were long-standing ladrones famosos, but at least five gavillas still operating in 1816 were closely connected to the insurgency and were organized under rebel commanders: the Indian José Felipe—"caudillo de ga-

[24] AJANG Criminal, caja 3.

[25] AJANG Criminal, cajas 3 and 13.

[26] AJANG Criminal, caja 3.

[27] AJANG Criminal, legajo 105 ("1818").

[28] AJANG Criminal, caja 13.

[29] AJANG Criminal, cajas 2 and 14.

[30] Based on information before April 1812 on eight rebels in the jurisdiction of Tepatitlán in AJANG Criminal, caja 13; AJANG Criminal, caja 2, for a band of twelve to twenty men under Villarreal; AJANG Criminal, legajo 141 ("1817"), three creoles in the Tepatitlán jurisdiction, April 1817; legajo 105, two Indians in the Jalostotitlán district, May 1818; legajo 67 ("1818"), two creoles, puesto Tepame, July 1811; caja 5, eight creoles and mulattoes, Tepatitlán district, February 1812.

[31] AJANG Criminal, caja 13.

[32] For example, Indians in the jurisdiction of Zapopan in 1811, AJANG Criminal, caja 5. This trial record reports other similar bands operating in the area.

villa" near Sayula; "el cabecilla González" with 50 armed men near Toluquilla; and Vicente Cárdenas with 25 men, Juan Bernardino with 20, and "el cabecilla Monroy" with as many as 200 mounted men, all three operating on the south side of Lake Chapala.[33]

Although it is rarely possible to distinguish neatly among or within the gavillas of the independence period for political movements, social bandits, and common criminals, I suspect that after 1810 more of the gangs transcended ordinary criminal activity to avenge wrongs, if not to serve a studied political cause. The incessant royalist demands on rural people provided a new grievance if others were lacking. In Zapotlanejo in 1813, for instance, the royalist garrison extracted contributions and labor service from local people and tried to conscript men from ranchos in the area. Coercion led to desertions from the royal forces and growing local opposition to the crown's defenders.[34] As a result, the gavillas after 1810 probably received more aid and protection from rural people when they began to pillage the wealth of gachupines and some rich creoles during the first war of independence. Villagers who had a score to settle or were forced to choose one side of the war or another were more likely to see bandits in political terms, too.[35] But the written record does not allow us to say how many of the increasing acts of banditry, cattle rustling, and highway robbery after 1810 were politically motivated. Certainly some were simple robberies occurring within the favorable confusion of the war and the continuation of localized, individual protest of a few well-armed men holed up in abandoned ranchos, which was common enough in the Altos before 1810. Of the forty-one trials of members of bandit gangs in New Galicia studied for 1811–21, only seven were definitely linked to insurgent activity. Many of the other attacks seem like the activities of the small groups of bandits who preyed upon travelers before 1810. The social backgrounds of the bandits were the same—they were men of humble backgrounds with prison records—and many were drifters, deserters, escapees, or new arrivals in Guadalajara who had only recently met up with their partners in crime.[36] Even in cases where bandits seemed to merge with insurgent movements, trial witnesses observed that the bandits were no more than fellow travelers selling

---

[33] AJANG Criminal, caja 3.

[34] AJANG Criminal, caja 5, legajo 2, exp. 5.

[35] AJANG Criminal, caja 5.

[36] For example, the May 23, 1812 assault on the highway near Ameca by three armed men, AJANG Criminal, legajo 34 ("1820 legajo 7").

stolen cattle to the insurgents and perhaps joining them for an engagement or two.[37]

Indian Pueblos in the First War of Independence

The first war of independence, 1810–15, which is generally considered to have contained elements of a social revolution as well as an independence movement, found support in rural central Jalisco. The area that participated most actively was located south and west of Guadalajara, from Zacoalco to the rural communities near Lake Chapala.

It was through this area that José Antonio Torres and his troops marched and made war on their way to Guadalajara in October and November 1810. Torres was a mestizo hacienda overseer from near Irapuato (Guanajuato) who had joined the Hidalgo movement at its beginning in September 1810. He led the western thrust of the movement that aimed to capture Guadalajara. His approach took him through the northeast part of Michoacán to Zamora, over the hills past Mazamitla to Teocuitatlán and Sayula; then up to Guadalajara by way of Zacoalco.[38] Torres's forces grew along the way with Indian villagers and landless workers armed with clubs, lances, and slings. At Sayula he received representatives of Indian pueblos—Zacoalco prominent among them—who offered their support.[39] Zacoalco became the bloody battleground of Torres's conquest of central Jalisco. When news reached Guadalajara at the end of October that Torres occupied Zacoalco, the royalists armed "the flower of Guadalajara's youth" and marched there under the command of creole hacendado Tomás Ignacio Villaseñor, expecting the Indians to scatter at the sight of disciplined troops.[40] But the royalists underestimated their enemy, which one report based on eyewitness testimony described as mainly Indians from Zacoalco armed with sticks and slings and a small cavalry force of rancheros with lances and clubs.[41] The two sides met on the salt flats outside Zacoalco on the

---

[37] AJANG Criminal, caja 14, 1815–1817, jurisdiction of Cuquío.

[38] Luis Pérez Verdía, *Apuntes para la historia de la Independencia en Jalisco* (Guadalajara, 1953), p. 18. José Ramírez Flores, *El gobierno insurgente en Guadalajara, 1810–1811* (Guadalajara, 1980), p. 13.

[39] Ramírez Flores, *El gobierno insurgente*, p. 17.

[40] Pérez Verdía, *Apuntes*, p. 20; J. E. Hernández y Dávalos, *Colección de documentos para la historia de la Independencia de México de 1808 a 1821* (México, 1878) 2:202–203.

[41] Hernández y Dávalos, *Colección* 2:202.

morning of November 4, and the royalists were routed by a mass attack of the poorly armed insurgents relying on a barrage of stones and hand-to-hand combat.[42] According to eyewitnesses, 257 royalists were killed in this one engagement. The rustic character of the Torres forces at Zacoalco has been epitomized by the looting that took place after the battle. The Indian soldiers who found watches on their victims were said to have smashed them to bits when they heard the ticking, saying that these machines must have the devil inside.[43]

How many of the Torres forces at Zacoalco were local Indians is not known, but the sympathies of many Indians of Zacoalco are not in doubt. Many locals welcomed this chance to attack the gachupines and to strike out against their colonial enemies. Five Indian leaders of Zacoalco armed with firearms and spears were later accused of having forced local Spaniards and creoles to remain in town as hostages during the battle and thereafter threatening to put them out front as cannon fodder if Zacoalco were again attacked by the royalists.[44] On October 31, four days before the battle, a few local creoles and the *teniente de cura* were decreed by Torres to be Indians and thus were spared the vengeance that followed—a striking inversion of the judicial discretion that had permitted mestizos to pass as Spaniards under colonial law.[45] Witnesses said the Indians had nothing but insults for the Spaniards in Zacoalco, frequently calling them a "montón de pícaros" (a bunch of rogues). Peninsular merchants seem to have been singled out. According to Ramírez Flores, nine merchants from Sayula, one from Zacoalco, and one from Tapalpa were killed during the violence of Torres's march on Guadalajara.

After the battle, Zacoalco Indians supposedly pillaged haciendas on the way to Guadalajara. Up to 20,000 supporters, some of them local men, marched on the city with Torres (he arrived via Mexicalcingo on November 11 with his ragged forces in good order).[46] A few

---

[42] Pérez Verdía, *Apuntes*, p. 20, and AJANG Criminal, caja 9. Ramírez Flores, *El gobierno insurgente*, pp. 28–29 describes the battlesite.

[43] Pérez Verdía, *Apuntes*, p. 21.

[44] AJANG Criminal, legajo 39 ("1811 legajo 1"), March 23, 1811 trial.

[45] Ramírez Flores, *El gobierno insurgente*, pp. 24–25, describes this decree of "las calidades de indios," and on p. 38 lists the merchants killed.

[46] Pérez Verdía, *Apuntes*, pp. 22–24; Hernández y Dávalos, *Collección* 2:203. Indians of Cuquío under Col. Miguel Gómez Portugal and the *teniente de cura* of Tacotlán were reported to have joined Torres in Guadalajara in November 1810, marching south through Zapopan (Ramírez Flores, *El gobierno insurgente*, p. 52). Later, a contingent of Indian archers from Colotlán also joined the Torres forces before the Battle

weeks later some Zacoalco insurgents returned home with the head
of an executed gachupin. Others remained in Guadalajara and were
with Hidalgo (who arrived in Guadalajara on November 26 and
stayed until January 14, 1811) in the ill-fated battle of Calderón and
his flight north.

The extent to which active insurgency and social war spread from
Zacoalco to other towns and villages in the area is not altogether
clear. Supposedly the noise of the battle at Zacoalco attracted people
from nearby towns and many stayed to join the Torres forces.[47]
Some residents of San Antonio, Ajijic, San Juan, and Jocotepec, four
Indian towns on the northwest edge of Lake Chapala, accepted pardons on February 6, 1811, for their part in the insurrection and
therefore must have joined the Torres march on Guadalajara or had
used this time of confusion to attack local Spaniards.[48] Five Indian
farmers from Chapala were reported by the parish priest to have
joined Torres and returned only after the Battle of Calderón.[49] Other
lake villages harbored rebel leaders from the early months of the insurgency. The most notorious was Encarnación Rosas in Mezcala
who had defeated a royalist force at La Barca during November
1810.[50]

The two months of the Torres–Hidalgo occupation of Guadalajara
were something of a reign of terror in the area of Zacoalco and the
lake towns. Looting was common. The homes of the wealthy were
sacked and horses were robbed. The Indian captain Antonio Trinidad Vargas of San Pedro Tesistán, a new pueblo near Jocotepec, was
especially active in pillaging and anti-Spanish activity in the early
months of the insurrection.[51] Spaniards who passed through the
area during this time of trouble risked their lives. Indian villages
that aided Zacoalco in 1810 and 1811 picked up the slogan "Death
to the gachupines," and applied it. The Indians of Atemajac, for example, under the direction of their *gobernador* and *alcalde*, kept a
stockade on the outskirts of town and in early 1811 arrested and
robbed "uno de razón" (a non-Indian), a man from Colima who was

of Calderón in January 1811. Pérez Verdía, *Historia particular del estado de Jalisco*,
2d ed. (Guadalajara, 1951), 2:82.

[47] Hernández y Dávalos, *Collección* 2:203.
[48] AJANG Criminal, caja 5.
[49] AJANG Criminal, caja 1.
[50] Pérez Verdía, *Apuntes*, p. 103. Ramírez Flores, *El gobierno insurgente*, p. 26,
cites Indians of Cocula, Tizapanito, San Pedro Tesistán, and Atoyac answering
Torres's call to arms.
[51] AJANG Criminal, caja 5.

passing by. The gobernador ordered five local men to execute the man outside of town with his own lance and sword "because they said he was a gachupín."[52] At his trial in March 1811, the Indian gobernador offered little explanation for the execution beyond his drunkenness at the time and the claim that he acted on the orders of José Antonio Torres. The gobernador was also accused of sending ten armed men to participate in the revolution. This may be evidence of conscription of Indian soldiers by Torres, recalling the old repartimientos, the labor drafts in Indian communities that had been common in the area in the seventeenth and early eighteenth centuries.[53]

The battle of Zacoalco and Torres's occupation of Guadalajara did not witness a neat separation between Indian rebels on one hand and Spaniards on the other. Creoles were often caught in the middle and some, like the ranchero horsemen, supported the insurrection. Most creoles of Zacoalco were held hostage but a few took up arms for Torres.[54] Circumstances suddenly placed other creoles in political offices under the insurgent government. Don José Francisco Huerta, for example, was in Teocuitatlán with a royal commission at the time of Torres's entry. The Indians and non-Indians of the town elected him juez (magistrate) and he served, he claimed, without aiding the war effort.[55] While some creoles of rural central Jalisco supported the insurgency actively or tacitly, most did not; and well-to-do creoles in Guadalajara, for the most part, probably identified with the gachupin elite and royal government.[56] Indian nobles and villages seem to have been at the heart of the uprising during these months but, again, not all or even most Indians took part. Don Manuel Gutiérrez, an Indian noble and merchant of Zacoalco, later was able to prove with Spanish witnesses that he had remained

[52] AJANG Criminal, legajo 173 ("1811 legajo 2").

[53] Moisés González Navarro, *Repartimiento de indios en Nueva Galicia* (México, 1953). Another contemporary record reported the use by Torres of such a conscription from pueblos of central Jalisco during his stay in Guadalajara: AJANG Criminal, caja 12, legajo 124 records the cases of Pedro José Mandujano (an unmarried *indio peón* from San Martín de la Cal) and five Indian weavers of Tlajomulco who claimed to have been conscripted in this way.

[54] Examples are given in AJANG Criminal, legajo 39 ("1811 legajo 1").

[55] AJANG Criminal, caja 9.

[56] Richard B. Lindley, *Kinship and Credit in the Structure of Guadalajara's Oligarchy, 1800–1830*, Ph.D. dissertation, University of Texas at Austin, 1976. Lindley demonstrates the close ties and common interests of the city's peninsular and creole elites.

loyal to the crown and had been persecuted by the Torres partisans.[57] Undoubtedly there were others.

After the disastrous battle of Calderón on January 17, 1811, and the insurgents' flight from Guadalajara, rebel domination in the Zacoalco area also gave way. In the month after the battle, the Indian leaders and other insurgents of the Zacoalco area and San Pedro Tesistán attempted another uprising in Zacoalco, but it failed and they fled south to Zapotlán el Grande, plundering as they went.[58] In Zapotlán, Sayula, and six Indian pueblos, another short-lived revolt was staged that threatened the life of the subdelegado. By the end of March 1811, however, the royal government had recovered nominal control with a punitive expedition under Rosendo Porlier, who termed his adversaries, "those ridiculous Indian insurgents."[59] The streets of Zacoalco and other towns in the district were patrolled by royal forces under the command of the district lieutenant. The local Indian insurgents had fled their homes and their Indian and creole leaders from Zacoalco, Atemajac, Sayula, and San Pedro Tesistán were arrested, summarily tried, and executed by Porlier in Sayula or by the Junta de Seguridad in Guadalajara; their severed heads were displayed in the plazas of their home towns as a grim reminder of the fate that awaited captured rebels.[60]

Zacoalco's days at the center of the insurgency were over, but memory of the uprising remained and new plans for rebellion were hatched by erstwhile leaders. In May 1811, two Indians were arrested for forming a company of armed men to kill the parish priest, the *alguacil* (magistrate), other Spaniards, and members of an opposing Indian faction. To gain popular support they had appealed to the old peasant dream of local sovereignty, telling townspeople that they need not obey any royal judge.[61] With the return of the royalists, Zacoalco's Indians were sharply divided over political loyalties and their plans for the future. The local rebels were isolated now, without many followers who would risk their lives. The *peninsular* priest Manuel Arteaga returned to his post and in June

[57] AJANG Civil, caja 255, doc. 10-3427 (hereafter, citations to these documents appear in the form 255-10-3427).

[58] AJANG Criminal, legajo 39 ("1811 legajo 1"). Documentation on the punitive expedition of the royalists to Zacoalco and the south in February and March 1811 is contained in Hernández y Dávalos, *Collección* 3:233–28.

[59] Hernández y Dávalos, *Collección* 3:224.

[60] AJANG Criminal, legajo 173 ("1811 legajo 2"), legajo 39 ("1811 legajo 1"), Hernández y Dávalos, *Collección* 3:227–28.

[61] Their attack was planned for Good Friday, AJANG Criminal, caja 9, legajo 2, exp. 21.

1813 issued a broadside that gloated over the restoration of the Spanish monarchy and fulminated against the few remaining "enemies of peace" in town.[62] But as the new Indian gobernador in May 1811 knew, the developments of the late colonial period had spawned "a generation of rebels" in Zacoalco.[63]

The longest and most important resistance in central Jalisco occurred in the villages on Lake Chapala between October 1811 and November 1816. It began with royalist efforts to mop up the small bands that remained in a few villages from the time of Torres. The prime target was Encarnación Rosas, the Indian captain from Tlachichilco who had staged raids into Atotonilco, Mezcala, and Chapala, and was hiding in Mezcala with 60–70 poorly armed supporters.[64] Royalists troops attacked Mezcala in October 1811, but were routed by the Indians; 60 royalists were killed and their firearms taken. On November 1, over 200 royalist soldiers under the command of José Antonio Serrato attacked Rosas and about 100 followers at San Pedro Ixicán.[65] This time Rosas was driven out and the town was destroyed by fire in retaliation for aiding the rebels. This defeat may have been a turning point for the peasant rebels since local Indians were reported to be outraged by the destruction of the town and the resistance now gained hundreds of new adherents and another notable Indian leader, José Santa Anna.[66] In the following months royalist razings of other towns and villages, including Jocotepec and Tizapán, indiscrimate executions of suspected rebels, and the brutal occupation of Poncitlán by Father Alvarez, "el cura chicharronero" ("the chitlin priest," who gained his nickname by burning alive rebels and sympathizers), served more to stir up peasant opposition rather than to break village morale.[67]

Three days after the defeat at San Pedro, Rosas reappeared with 400 men to punish the royalists, again killing many and routing the rest.[68] In December 1811, intendant and military commander José de la Cruz ordered a major force from Guadalajara to attack Rosas and other rebels in the north shore villages. With the aid of Father Mar-

[62] AGI Mexico 1482. Hernández y Dávalos, *Collección* 3:226 speaks of Arteaga as an "europeo."
[63] AJANG Criminal, caja 9.
[64] Pérez Verdía, *Apuntes*, p. 103; AJANG Criminal, caja 1.
[65] Pérez Verdía, *Apuntes*, p. 103 says the Indians had only six *fusiles* and did not know how to operate firearms.
[66] Pérez Verdía, *Apuntes*, pp. 103–104.
[67] Ibid., p. 106; AJANG Criminal, caja 1.
[68] Pérez Vería, *Apuntes*, p. 104.

cos Castellanos, the vicar of Ocotlán, Rosas and Santa Anna and about 600 men from Mezcala, Tlachichilco, and San Pedro Ixicán took refuge on the Isla de Mezcala, a small island a mile or so offshore from the village of Mezcala. About 350 acres in size and 100 feet above water level, the island had been used as a royal prison and *presidio* in the eighteenth century and was already reasonably well fortified with a solid stone prison and ramparts. It had also been a sacred place to lakeshore villagers. Early in the colonial period, according to local belief, a solitary hermit priest led an exemplary life there. He was visited only by local Indians who brought him vegetables from time to time.[69] For a brief period in 1812 the island's official rebel chief was don Luis Macías, owner of the hacienda de los Reyes. He was followed by Josef Leonardo (Real Sargento), "un tal Vargas," and Comandante Morillo, but the enduring leaders were Castellanos and Santa Anna.[70]

Three unsuccessful royalist assaults on the island were made in 1812 and 1813. The third, on June 29, 1813, was the most ambitious, with four boats brought overland from San Blas, each with a 24-pound mortar, five other vessels, and 600 men.[71] Each time the royalists were turned back with heavy losses of men and equipment.[72] By then the island was a veritable bastion with new stone barricades and a rock wall. According to a rebel officer captured in February 1814, as many as 1,000 men resided there, equipped with 100 canoes, 300 muskets, and 14 cannons.[73] By July 1813 Cruz decided that he could not win a decisive battle and resolved to blockade the island and starve out the insurgents.[74] He garrisoned all boat launches around the lake, and waited. It was a long wait—forty months—during which time there were skirmishes on shore almost

[69] Fr. Antonio Tello, *Crónica de Xalisco* (Guadalajara, 1945) 4:79.

[70] Pérez Verdía mentions Macías only at the very beginning of the occupation of the island and does not comment on his fate (*Apuntes*, pp. 105–17). He is puzzled by the disappearance of Rosas from the record of this period after 1812. According to one of Rosas's officers who was captured in February 1814, Rosas died on the island early in the occupation (AJANG Criminal, caja 1). Pérez Verdía's statement that Padre Castellanos was the chief engineer and ordnance officer by 1812 seems at variance with contemporary testimony that Leonardo, Vargas, and Morillo were the commanders of the island through early 1814.

[71] Biblioteca del Estado de Jalisco (BEJ), fondos especiales, Colección Miscelánea, vol. 506, no. 21.

[72] Pérez Verdía, *Apuntes*, pp. 109–11; Hernández y Dávalos, *Collección* 3:864–65.

[73] AJANG Criminal, caja 1.

[74] Pérez Verdía, *Apuntes*, p. 112.

every day.[75] Santa Anna and other men stole ashore to attack Ocotlán, Ajijic, San Juan, and royalist detachments near Chapala and at the ranchería la Columba and the hacienda Tizapán,[76] and insurgent bands on land also made hit-and-run attacks on the royalist stations. The only important royalist victory against the rebels was on April 16, 1814, when the islanders who had earlier attacked Ajijic were forced ashore at Tuxcueca. Many escaped but each side was reported to have lost about 100 men.

Cruz offered an unconditional pardon to the island rebels in November 1814, but there were no takers. In 1816 he gave the Mezcala insurrection nearly undivided attention, assigning General José Narváez and 8,000 soldiers to maintain the blockade and patrol the lakeshore towns. Again, in October 1816, Cruz offered a general pardon, which was again refused, but on November 25, 1816, the rebels Santa Anna and Castellanos met with Cruz in Tlachichilco and signed a truce. In addition to the general pardon, Cruz agreed to rebuild all the destroyed towns, to provide the lakeshore villages with oxen, land, and seed, and to exempt them from the tribute tax. Castellanos was granted several chaplaincies and the parish of Ajijic. Santa Anna was named governor of the island.[77]

How did the rebels hold out so long on that barren, rocky little island? Pérez Verdía is silent on this question, but a contemporary investigation and scraps of trial evidence provide elements of an answer. The island rebels could not have held out without help from villages and bands of supporters on shore. Islanders sometimes raided coastal towns to provision their forces but in the early stages most of the supplies came from Tizapán on the other side of the lake (until the town was destroyed by the royalists in 1812). Several creoles from Tizapán were actively involved—don Javier Celis was accused of spying for the islanders, and the administrator of the hacienda Tizapán of supplying arms and food. Thereafter, supplies came from more distant supporters such as Captain José María Vargas near San Gabriel and Zacoalco. Bands of rebels and bandits from the south side of the lake seem to have been particularly important in harassing the royalist garrisons and transporting supplies. As many as 500 men served under "Chávez" of Cuyacapan, José María Gutiérrez, and Salvador Lázaro of Tuxcueca.[78] Groups of men were

[75] Ibid., p. 113.

[76] Ibid, pp. 115–17; AJANG Criminal, caja 2.

[77] Pérez Verdía, *Apuntes*, pp. 123, 127.

[78] AJANG Criminal, caja 1; some bands operated on the north shore of the lake, as well, especially Indians who raided Chapala in 1813; AJANG Criminal, caja 2.

sometimes sent off the island to bring in new recruits and to drop supplies for the island forces at isolated points on the lake shore. One of the captains on land with close connections to the island was Eusebio María Rodríguez, a 40-year-old Indian farmer and *obraje* worker from Santa Cruz. After serving with Rosas in the early land battles and joining the retreat to the island, Rodríguez returned to the coastal villages in early 1812 to lead a small gavilla near Tizapán. He served under Comandante José María Gutiérrez and his band of some 300 men armed with seven muskets, fifteen spears, plus machetes and slings. He communicated with the island by smoke signals to warn of impending attack and to mark the location of supply drops for the islanders.[79] Rodríguez was briefly in contact with Ignacio López Rayón and the Morelos movement at Uruapan in 1813. López Rayón appointed the commander of the island as the military governor of nine lake towns, but no other evidence has yet come to light that the Mezcala insurrection was aided or closely connected to the Morelos movement.

Toward the end, most of the forces on the island came from the seven north shore villages of San Pedro Ixicán, Santa Cruz, Santa María, San Sebastián, San Miguel, Jamay, and Mezcala, and the nearby town of Poncitlán.[80] Sustained support for a long-lived rebellion in many peasant villages is unusual and certainly the Isla de Mezcala rebellion is the prime example for Jalisco before 1821. Rebellions rarely sweep along everything in their path and support for the island rebels was not, of course, universal among the lake villages. Some villagers who took part in the Torres movement returned home in 1811 with pardons as model subjects of the crown, and it was not uncommon for recent recruits to leave the insurrection and appeal to their parish priests for pardon.[81]

The movement endured partly because of bands of roving supporters and suppliers on the south shore and broad support in north shore villages that had been destroyed by the royalists, and partly because of the well-defended, self-contained island base. In addi-

---

[79] AJANG Criminal, caja 1. Rodríguez was arrested in Februarya 1814, after recruiting young men from Chapala and Santa Cruz. He and three aides were summarily tried and executed.

[80] Pérez Verdía, *Apuntes*, p. 129, quotes Castellanos for San Pedro, Santa Cruz, Santa María, San Sebastián, and San Miguel. He also mentions Mezcala; and Jamay is documented in AJANG Civil, legajo 109. Smaller numbers of recruits also came from Chapala and Tlachichilco.

[81] AJANG Criminal, caja 1, *cura* of Chapala; caja 3, examples of bandit captains coming in for pardons in July 1816.

tion to a ready-made fortress, the islanders were able to produce their own ammunition—gunpowder from saltpeter supplied by Josef María Mireles of Tizapán, and cannonballs from native rock. The greatest enemies of the island rebels were chronic food shortages and disease, both of which struck hardest in 1816 during the months before the truce was signed.

It is remarkable that no manifestos were circulated to publicize the aims of the rebels (at least none is known to historians). Certainly they were outraged by the destruction of towns in 1811, but there was probably more to this insurrection than just revenge. The closest we can come to their goals with written documentation is the terms of the truce, which guaranteed the villagers land, seed, and oxen, and the reconstruction of their towns. Although they seem to have had little contact with the Morelos movement, their claim to a right to survive as landholding farmers drew them close to the political program outlined by Morelos.

The Conditions of Unrest
in Central Jalisco

The rise of banditry and the insurgency of the Independence period in central Jalisco followed substantial changes in the material conditions of the region in the eighteenth century. These changes, particularly population growth, commercial agriculture, and land pressure, recently have been richly documented and studied by Eric Van Young.[82] The Indian villages, which made up about half of the rural population in central Jalisco, grew dramatically in the eighteenth century, doubling, sometimes tripling and quadrupling their numbers with new mestizo and Spanish residents as well as by natural increase of the Indian group in the last century of Spanish rule. After 1780, their farmlands were no longer sufficient to allow more than a few communities to continue selling corn and wheat in Guadalajara. Most of the towns that still produced some grain for sale were located along the corridor of support for Torres as he marched to Guadalajara in November 1810: Zacoalco, Jocotepec, Tizapanito, Acatlán, and Tlajomulco. Most villages, however, no longer produced enough corn even for subsistence needs. Guadalajara grew dramatically from 1750 on, as an active center of trade, government, and some industry in a province that enjoyed new prosperity. The

[82] Eric Van Young, *Rural Life in Eighteenth-Century Mexico: The Guadalajara Region, 1675–1820*, Ph.D. Dissertation, University of California, Berkeley, 1978.

city's population growth rate often reached 10 percent annually and drew many migrants from rural districts close to the city. The growth of the city meant a growing demand there for food, especially grain, and this, in turn, promoted commercial agriculture, conversion of pasture to farmland, and capital investments in irrigation and storage facilities on the large estates within easy reach of the city. The principal beneficiaries of the new demand for farm products were the landlords. Some of the haciendas of central Jalisco dating from the seventeenth century were now consolidated into larger estates. They emphasized farming, increased their resident work force, disputed land rights along their borders, and claimed as *realengas* the neighboring lands occupied by Indian villagers without written title. Entails were created and ownership of these large estates became notably more stable after 1770. The rural economy was becoming increasingly monetized, land shortages and population growth in the villages created a buyer's market for agricultural labor, and many villagers were forced to leave home in search of employment. The result was more conflict within villages and between villages and haciendas after 1760. As Van Young observes, "the major arena of conflict was the court system"—the haciendas and villages engaged in costly legal disputes over boundaries and rental agreements that generally took the place of armed conflict. The haciendas usually won the support of the courts when there was reasonable doubt about the Indians' title.

All of these changes toward a cash economy—increased wage labor, and the disruption of subsistence strategies in rural villages that had already privatized most of their common lands and were less cohesive as communities and less attached to farming than the peasants of central and southern Mexico—affected families and individuals within communities in an unequal way.[83] Some families benefited by consolidating their landholdings, controlling the use of community property, or by setting up small businesses and workshops, but most faced declining resources and an uncertain future. The result of these changes, coupled with a long history of regular activities by villagers outside the local community, was growing in-

---

[83] Joel S. Migdal, *Peasants, Politics, and Revolution: Pressures toward Political and Social Change in the Third World* (Princeton, 1974), chap. 1, relates such changes to peasant insurrection and revolution. For Jocotepec in 1800 and Zacoalco in 1794 there is evidence that a few Indian leaders had succeeded in acquiring relatively large properties at the expense of other members of the community, some of whom were destitute; AJANG Civil 216-24-2746 and BEJ *fondos especiales*, Archivo Fiscal de la Real Audiencia de Nueva Galicia (AFRANG), vol. 570.

ternal tensions and weaker village institutions that perhaps were more vulnerable to sudden disruption from famine, disease, or political unrest. The pressure was only partly relieved by migration.

The area of peasant insurrections in central Jalisco went through this chain of developments. Zacoalco to Santa Ana Acatlán and the villages near Lake Chapala were in the middle of the hacienda grain belt that had developed to supply the Guadalajara market. The peasant village population increased substantially in the eighteenth century; great estates were consolidated and entailed; and virtually every land boundary in the vicinity shared by a hacienda and a village was contested in court cases during the second half of the century. Most of the pueblos lost these lengthy cases. Zacoalco was the biggest loser of all, in that it failed to gain a favorable verdict for any of the six sites it contested. Land shortages in this region were accentuated by long-term rentals of Indian lands to neighboring haciendas and some outright sales.[84] Hacendados near Lake Chapala gained the upper hand in district politics as well as in lands with uncertain titles. In 1798 the owner of the hacienda de los Cedros was appointed the *alcalde mayor*'s deputy for Chapala and its subject towns when it was decided that the administrative centers of Zacoalco and Sayula were too far away to provide efficient administration.[85]

The pueblos in this area were feeling the strains of land shortages, pressure from haciendas, and population growth; but it is also noteworthy that the pueblos of the Torres and Isla de Mezcala insurrections were among the most prosperous communities with an Indian majority. The rebels were not landless drifters or *jornaleros*, by and large. Most owned some farmland and livestock or they fished or made shoes, soap, and other items for sale. Perhaps they felt the pinch of the late eighteenth-century changes more acutely than other communities because they had more to lose.

Zacoalco's turbulent political history at the end of the colonial period would have made this community especially open to rebel-

---

[84] AJANG Civil legajo 174 (label reads "1806–1807"), Civil 1271-1-1360, AFRANG vol. 570 contain examples for Zacoalco ; AJANG Civil 178-14-2003 for Cajititlán in 1792. The written titles of many Indian villages of central Jalisco and the adjacent Provincia de Avalos date from this period of hacienda pressure after 1770; for example, Crescenciano Brambila, *El nuevo obispado de Autlán* (Colima, 1962), pp. 186–87. In most cases, it was too late to claim lands long used but never confirmed in writing, because the late eighteenth-century titles of pueblos generally were for the townsite of one square league and little more. During this same period, other villages complained that their titles were stolen or confiscated by royal authorities.

[85] AJANG Civil, 169-17-1877.

lion and insurrection. Zacoalco and its subject villages were at the center of protracted land suits with neighboring haciendas in the late eighteenth century. The smaller villages, confined to a one-square league area, were short of usable farmland, but the large *cabecera* of Zacoalco was judged to have more than it could use: the league, eight *sitios de ganado mayor*, and over seventeen *caballerías* of farmland.[86] The Indian community actually owned much more—another sixty caballerías and two square leagues—but these lands were rented out to non-Indians residing in Zacoalco or let out on shares.[87] Boundaries were in dispute continually from 1754 to 1806, despite final verdicts in 1777 and 1784 which conceded to the Indians very little of the land they claimed. The 1777 verdict touched off three decades of small-scale uprisings and boundary encroachments by the disgruntled Zacoalco Indians. The lieutenant in 1783 feared that the insolence of these Indians would lead to a serious threat to peace in the district.[88]

Zacoalco had something of a tradition of community revolt in defense of village rights that recalls the examples of Tlacochahuaya in the valley of Oaxaca and the district of Metepec in central Mexico. In 1756 the Indians of two Zacoalco barrios rose up against the priest and magistrate for requiring them to register in a new census.[89] More than anything, the Indians were resisting the hated one-real fee that the lieutenant demanded of all registrants. In the brief tumult, men shouted that they were not sheep and did not want to be counted, and two Indian women called the lieutenant a "teniente de mierda" to his face. In 1795 the Zacoalco Indians again took the law into their own hands when they were ordered to leave their dispersed hamlets and resettle in a compact group in the center of town.[90] The Indian unrest in this community was also fueled by corrupt royal officials and disputes among the growing number of creoles who settled in town in the years of prosperity after 1730. In 1746, the recently established Spanish *cofradía* (lay brotherhood) of Zacoalco divided into factions over who should be elected mayordomo. The result was several years of public invective and formal litigation. Beneath it all was a struggle for influence between the secular priest of Sayula and the Franciscans of Zacoalco.[91] The priest

---

[86] AJANG Criminal, legajo 104 ("1790–99, leg. 12").
[87] AJANG Civil, 127-1-1360.
[88] AJANG Civil, 155-4-1736.
[89] AJANG Civil, 59-9-753.
[90] AJANG Criminal, legajo 104 ("1790–99, leg. 12").
[91] CAG, cofradía documents box 1, complaint against d. Juan de Echagarai.

and magistrate of Zacoalco frequently were at each other's throat over their jurisdictions, privileges, and duties; and the Indian officials lodged formal complaints against the local lieutenant in 1769 and 1795 for accepting bribes, extorting contributions, and seizing private property.[92] The 1795 abuses were so blatant that the *peninsular* lieutenant, Gregorio Bringas, was convicted and sentenced to four years' presidio service.

Zacoalco, then, was a community with repeated stirrings of Indian unrest over land and abuse of royal authority by district officials. Unlike the central Mexico and Oaxaca villages that had similar complaints and used limited revolts to dramatize their dissatisfaction and express their solidarity as village members, Zacoalco in 1800 was a community in transition between two worlds. The landholding Indian farmers and ranchers had held onto old local ways and sentiments longer than many Indian villagers of central Jalisco; but Zacoalco was also a larger and more open town with a substantial non-Indian population. A census taken on the eve of the Independence wars in September 1810 listed 2,364 Indians and 2,033 Spaniards and castas in the town and vicinity of Zacoalco. The center of town was occupied mainly by non-Indians. In a region of large private estates, Zacoalco was a place where the Indian language, communal property, and attachment to farming were rapidly disappearing, and where wage and shop labor, cottage industries in shoes and soap, and other features of a cash economy were well established.

Differences between the rural unrest of central Jalisco and the parts of Oaxaca suggest some distinctive features of early nineteenth-century banditry and uprisings near Guadalajara. Oaxaca had numerous village rebellions in the eighteenth century, but little banditry and only modest peasant support for the revolution attempted in the first war of independence. In central Jalisco, by contrast, village revolts were less common, banditry was more widespread before 1810, and an important zone of landed villages took part in the early stages of the independence struggle. It might be argued that independence activity in Jalisco and Oaxaca cannot be compared because Oaxaca was isolated in the south while Jalisco was near the Bajío, the center of the Hidalgo insurrection from which a mass movement could more easily spread, as it did under José Antonio Torres. But the armed struggle and promise of rural revolution were brought to Oaxaca, too—under Morelos, whose forces swept down through the Mixteca to the valley of Oaxaca in 1812 and occupied

[92] AJANG Civil, 59-11-755 and 82-7-918; Criminal, legajo 121 ("1780–89, leg. 14").

Antequera (the city of Oaxaca) for a brief period. Except on the edges of the Mixteca, his arrival touched off little of the peasant fury that was seen in central Jalisco.

In Oaxaca, the numerous village revolts of the colonial period were staged by communities possessing substantial landholdings and strong community institutions and traditions. These villages suffered material distress from population growth, colonial tax and labor demands, and the commercialization of agriculture in the late colonial period. But it was not the kind of pervasive, dislocating threat to their way of life that might have weakened local attachments, promoted a concept of struggle between Indians and Spaniards, and united villagers in regional insurrections. The conditions for revolt in Oaxaca had more to do with single, inward-looking villages and small districts that experienced encroachments in the form of fees and taxes that broke the customary schedules, boundary disputes, unusual labor demands, abusive royal officials or the arrest of local notables. In most cases, these revolts were defensive responses to acts of royal officials that threatened to change existing relationships or they were the result of rivalries among Indian villages or factions over access to local power.

Despite the impressive level of violence in some of the Oaxaca uprisings, few were examples of complete breakdown in the system of accommodation between colonial rulers and village subjects. Only in the relationships between the village and the local alcalde mayor, lieutenant, priest, or tax collector can we speak of accommodation giving way to violent conflict. The door usually was open on the peasants' side for negotiation with higher authorities who were still accepted as legitimate but distant rulers. Oaxaca villagers did not see themselves as a deprived class that would unite against a common oppressor. For most, the enemies were neighboring villages as well as abusive local magistrates or priests, not the higher authorities who were ultimately responsible for the burden of taxes and service. This local political unity and militant myopia made the Oaxaca peasants good village rebels but poor revolutionaries.

The Jalisco "Indian" communities that contributed to banditry and the independence struggle held some land, but they were less tied to the land and their viewpoint was not so localized. As the lieutenant of Atotonilco el Alto said in 1789, "even though it is said that not all of them are Indians, they are at least the color of Indians."[93] Their communities had a less cohesive village structure and

[93] AJANG Civil, 117-4-1249.

a more proto-Mexican way of life. They were more inclined to appeal to outside authority over petty internal political matters, and their people were more accustomed to making their living away from home. Village lands had long ago been divided into private parcels, and *bienes de comunidad* (community property, especially land) outside the cofradías were relatively unimportant. Villagers rarely cooperated in common tasks or communal labor and seemed less attached to the village. Less good farmland was available and ranching was a more important economic activity than in Oaxaca. These weaker village ties were part of a more outward orientation and more movement outside the village in search of employment, trade, and adventure that would enable political movements in times of disruption to reach peasant families more directly than in Oaxaca.

It is striking that Morelos was successful in enlisting peasant support on his way to Antequera mainly in the part of the rural Mixteca that had become a zone of commercial production in recent years (cochineal in this case) somewhat like the changes of central Jalisco in the late eighteenth century. These pockets of Oaxaca villages may have been experiencing the differential impact of commercial farming on peasant families with marginal farmland (soils are thinner and more susceptible to erosion, and rainfall in the Mixteca is less dependable than in the central valleys of Oaxaca) and growing contacts outside the village for families and individuals. The Oaxaca peasants thought of themselves primarily as members of the village community ("the people of Mitla," etc.) rather than as members of a tribe or language group (such as Zapotecs or Mixtecs) or "Indians." Villagers of central Jalisco were more likely to identify themselves as Indians and to share this sense of identity with people from other rural communities. There were few bitter rivalries between villages in central Jalisco, partly because few villages shared borders. Nearly all were bounded by Spanish estates in the eighteenth century, and it was with these estates that problems of boundary markers and encroachment would usually arise. Together, these conditions made the central Jalisco villagers more open to the idea of an insurrection of Indians against Spanish rulers and landowners.

Ironically, these people of central Jalisco who thought of themselves as Indians were much less "Indian" or native American in an anthropological sense than the people of rural Oaxaca. The reason is that the very idea of "Indian" identity was a European invention that had grouped native Americans into a subordinate social and legal category. Those who dealt most often with the formal institu-

tions of Spanish rule, had lost their native languages, and were losing their fierce local community attachments and the illusion of village autonomy are precisely the ones who knew themselves as
Indians.

Several factors in addition to economic change are also linked to
the patterns of unrest and insurrection in central Jalisco, particularly changes in the Catholic Church, folk religion, and Bourbon politics, which weakened the traditional bonds between villages and
the state and set some villages against their parish priests.

The pueblos in this region that had joined the insurrection had
been missionized in the early colonial period by the Franciscans,
who were more than spiritual leaders; they were also promoters of
communal institutions with a religious content. The Franciscans inspired the establishment of the Indian hospitals and hospital chapels in the villages under their direction in the early seventeenth century, and organized lay brotherhoods dedicated to the Virgin Mary
of the Immaculate Conception, which then acquired land and livestock to support the hospitals. These Indian hospitals and their supporting Cofradías de la Limpia Concepción were of exceptional importance in central Jalisco, at least in comparison to those in other
parts of Oaxaca and central Mexico. As other community institutions declined—community lands were divided, sold, or rented to
outsiders, and the *arcas de comunidad* (community treasuries) typically were empty in the Indian pueblos of central Jalisco from the
mid-seventeenth century on—these hospitals and cofradías came to
be places and institutions that served as gathering points of community loyalty and community property. Ordinarily the hospital
and its chapel were kept in good repair and the cult of the Virgin
thrived with the support of cofradía ranches while the parish church
fell into ruins. Because of earthquakes and the care taken to maintain the hospital and its chapel (the usual communal labor service
in these communities in the eighteenth century was in support of
these brotherhoods and chapels), the chapel served as the parish
church for years at a time in some of these places. The chapel became the focal point of community sentiment, serving as the meeting place for clandestine gatherings and popular fiestas in the years
just before 1810.

The Hidalgo insurrection with the Virgin of Guadalupe as its em-
blem offered a natural bridge to rebellion for Indian pueblos of central Jalisco with their important local cults of the Virgin of the Immaculate Conception. The Indian fighters at the Battle of Zacoalco

were reported to have adorned their hats with her image.[94] Hidalgo, himself a rural parish priest in 1810, chose his patroness of independence wisely, for the Virgin of Guadalupe was more than an abstract dark-skinned symbol of Mexican nationalism. She was a representation of the Virgin of the Immaculate Conception—the patroness of Indian hospitals and their cofradías, an image rich in meaning for the idea that Indian villagers were chosen people, and arguably the most powerful religious symbol in the Mexican countryside.[95]

Pueblos in Zacoalco and the lake region also had something of a folk tradition of miraculous crosses which became regional cults and might have made it easier to bridge local interests and rivalries and promote regional insurrection in times of sudden disruption. One documented instance occurred in 1720 when an Indian *principal* (noble) of Jocotepec appeared with a tree limb in the shape of a cross with a faint, supposedly natural image of a man on it.[96] The

---

[94] Hernández y Dávalos, *Collección* 2:202.

[95] The powerful connection between the Virgin of the Immaculate Conception as community patroness, the Virgin of Guadalupe, and war between Indians and Spaniards is still remembered in pueblos of the Lake Chapala region today. It has been documented recently in the dialogue of the town of Mezcala's *danza de la conquista*, a re-enactment of the Spanish conquest of Mexico in 1519–1521, published by Francisco Talavera S., "Cuaderno de la danza de la conquista," *Revista Jalisco* no. 2 (1980):46–62. The people of Mezcala, whose patroness is the Virgin of the Immaculate Conception, perform the dance on December 12, the Day of the Virgin of Guadalupe. The dialogue between the Spanish soldiers and Indian chiefs—particularly between Cortés and the Indian king—is filled with militant allusions to the Virgin Mary. Cortés and his soldiers repeatedly invoke the protection of the Virgin and threaten war on the Indians in order to impose the worship of the "sacred Virgin Mary." At one point she is called the "mother of consummate power." Late in the danza she becomes specifically the Virgin of Guadalupe and is invoked by the Indian king for protection against the Spanish soldiers. Finally, this version of the danza de la conquista remembers her as the symbol of Mexico and its protectress in the War of Independence, a war that in Mezcala's collective memory is implicitly connected to the conquest as another war of Indians against Spaniards:

> Oh Mexican flag!
> Oh tricolored banner!
> Oh Virgin of Guadalupe!
> Your children know how to love you.
> I much prefer to die
> Than to see you shackled
> By the foreign hordes
> That try to conquer us.

[96] CAG, cofradía documents, box 1, 1721 "autos pertenecientes a la cofradía del Santo Cristo de la Espiración del pueblo de Jocotepec."

principal traveled to neighboring towns with his reputedly miraculous Christ to collect alms to build a special chapel for it outside
Jocotepec. His peregrinations apparently created quite a stir in the
Indian pueblos of the district, especially in Tlajomulco, San Agustín, and Santa Cruz, and there was a small boom in the sale of chips
from the cross as holy relics. Until the principal and his associates
were arrested and silenced, Indians from surrounding towns flocked
to his homemade chapel to see the miraculous artifact. In the words
of the parish priest of Jocotepec who leveled charges against the
false cult, "the common people are prone to novelties" in this region.

Two developments in the history of the Franciscans and Indian hospitals in the Lake Chapala area in the eighteenth century may have
helped prepare the way for insurrection. First, after 1750, most of
the Franciscan parishes were secularized; that is, the Franciscans
were removed and secular priests were substituted. The result was
less continuity in parish administration as the vicars and tenientes
de curas came and went every few years in the service of absentee
or infirm *propietarios* (landowning *párrocos* or beneficed parish
priests who enjoyed what amounted to tenure). Villagers had not
always revered and obeyed their Franciscan fathers, but the number
of complaints by and against the secular priests of these parishes of
central Jalisco in the late eighteenth century suggests that the unwritten covenant of loyalty and cooperation between párroco and
Indian parishioners could no longer be taken for granted. In some
cases, such as Ocotlán in the last years of the colonial period, the
solitary párroco identified only with the Spaniards who lived in the
vicinity and was alienated from his Indian parishioners, viewing
them as "idiots, vice-ridden, and drug addicts by profession."[97] This
estrangement had political implications, for the parish was, after all,
a crucial link between the colonial state and its village subjects. For
villagers who rarely saw royal officials and then only when taxes
were due, the parish priest and his vicars were the moral embodi-
ment of the colonial system. Questioning the priest was a step toward breaking with higher authorities.[98]

[97] AJANG Civil, 231-1-3008.
[98] The position of the church was declining in other ways as well; see Nelson Reed, *The Caste War of Yucatán* (Stanford, 1964), p. 199; William B. Taylor, *Drinking, Homicide and Rebellion in Colonial Mexican Villages* (Stanford, 1979), pp. 141–43; and Nancy M. Farriss, *Crown and Clergy in Colonial Mexico, 1750–1821: The Crisis of Ecclesiastical Privilege* (London, 1968).

The former Franciscan parishes may have been estranged from their new secular priests and the position of the parish priest was diminished in general here and elsewhere under the later Bourbons, but rural villages still wanted to have their own priest who could command their respect and mediate in the here and the hereafter. There were still opportunities for revered priests—like Marcos Castellanos—to direct the political activities of their parishioners once the war broke out, although for some it must have been increasingly difficult for royalist supporters in 1810–11 to maintain local credibility.

Second, the wealth of cofradías in land and livestock was a sore point in these villages in the late eighteenth century as the population grew and food and farmland became scarce. In a sense, "sheep were eating men," as they had in sixteenth-century Spain. The village cofradías owned hundreds of cattle and sheep and grazed them on their own ranches or on a designated portion of the village lands. The result, in any case, was pressure on already limited Indian farmlands. Were the cofradía holdings communal property (*bienes de comunidad*)? Village officials at the end of the colonial period often acted as if they were, selling cofradía animals to pay tribute and underwrite land litigation, slaughtering them for food in the famine of 1785–86, and cultivating areas of the cofradía ranches. The church disputed the Indians' use of the cofradía properties for mundane purposes, arguing in court that these were inalienable ecclesiastical properties that could be used only for religious purposes unless the bishop specifically permitted other uses. Litigation between villages and priests over the management and use of cofradía property in central Jalisco was acrimonious and without easy resolution in the late eighteenth century. Over the objections of the priests, some villages continued to use cofradía property without the bishop's sanction. By 1810 cofradía properties of many pueblos were much diminished, and the court cases over their disposition continued long after independence was achieved in 1821.[99]

Bourbon political reforms in New Galicia after 1750 also contributed to the climate of change and uncertainty that may have weakened the traditional institutions of justice and customary ways of resolving conflict within the colonial law. There was a trend toward

[99] This tension between village and parish priest and the special importance of Indian hospitals and cofradías is richly documented in the cathedral archive of Guadalajara. Ramón Serrera, *Guadalajara ganadera* (Sevilla, 1978), pp. 339–75, has drawn valuable information on the property of cofradías in New Galicia from the Archivo General de Indias.

militarizing political administration in the province, especially after
1790. Subdelegados and their lieutenants more often than before
were Spanish military officers who were inclined to use force rather
than persuasion. Hacendados in the late colonial period were arming their trusted workers in case of boundary scuffles or bandits. The
growth of an independent Acordada to control banditry after 1790
also extended new institutions of force in public life as did the mobilization of a small standing army and a new program for conscription of able-bodied non-Indians into enlarged militia units.

The provincial sentiment for which Guadalajara and Jalisco are
well known blossomed in the eighteenth century and sensitized a
broad spectrum of local people—from magistrates to bishops, merchants, artisans, and cowboys—to the arbitrary dictates and innovations of viceroys in Mexico City and bureaucrats in Spain. Areas
like central Jalisco may have been quite sensitive to the Bourbons'
unwitting violations of what John Phelan called the "unwritten constitution" of delicately balanced customary relationships between
sovereign and subject. If the old rules and laws could no longer be
counted upon, the judges and priests would start to look more like
venal intruders than defenders of justice to their village subjects.
Bourbon attacks on the traditional position of the church by secular-
izing parishes, requiring priests to minister only in Spanish, the
consolidación de vales (the 1804 law of consolidation, by which the
royal government called in the liens held by the church on real
property), and replacing curate schoolteachers with lay teachers in
new primary schools (part of a general move to enhance the power
of the crown) may actually have weakened the state's legitimacy in
the eyes of peasants by tampering with the local, customary expectations of the parish priest and threatening to remove him from the
center of community life. Other Bourbon innovations—particularly
new, higher taxes and extraordinary contributions—were viewed by
villagers as violations of custom as well as unscrupulous gouging by
royal representatives.

External events, finally, are inseparable from the uprisings and
sustained involvement of numbers of Indian townspeople from the
Zacoalco area and the lake towns in insurgency after September
1810. The march of the Torres forces through Zacoalco precipitated
the involvement there and, as we have seen, attracted some peasant
support in the lake towns as well. The Spaniards' "scorched-earth"
approach to mopping up insurgent activity around Lake Chapala
brought hundreds of people, perhaps whole towns, into the insurgency at Mezcala Island. The Spaniards' cruel repressions in various

pueblos drove lake villagers into the insurgent camp and helped lead them to guerrilla resistance that lasted nearly five years.

Two Exceptions

It is important to recognize that the rural unrest centered in the Za-coalco–Lake Chapala area did not engulf all parts of central Jalisco or all predominantly Indian communities in relatively prosperous circumstances. The period of insurgency did not sweep along all of the important Indian towns and former Franciscan parishes nearby that were experiencing similar population pressure, land shortages, commercialization of agriculture, secret *juntas*, and internal dissent. Contagion and epidemics were the metaphors that the royalists used to express their fears and plan their response to the insurgency, as if quarantine of the infected areas could be achieved and would halt the spread of sedition. But Tlajomulco and Tonalá, two of the largest and in several ways most open communities with Indian majorities in the area, had little to do with the independence cause and the war against gachupines and "city slickers."

In the late seventeenth century Tlajomulco was a prosperous farming district of nine Indian communities, one hacienda, six la-bores, and a population of 2,287.[100] Indians outnumbered Spaniards and castas by twelve to one. While the Indians did seasonal work on the rich Spanish farms and ranches nearby, they retained good farm-land of their own. Communal habits had not yet been submerged. There were well-maintained Indian hospitals and chapels in eight of the nine pueblos supported by propertied cofradías dedicated to Mary the Immaculate. Some cofradía lands still were worked in common for the benefit of the hospitals, and Indians continued to speak a local version of Náhuatl.[101]

Like the towns caught up in the insurrections after 1810, Tlajo-mulco was in the heart of the grain belt, surrounded by large estates producing for sale in Guadalajara. Tlajomulco remained a relatively prosperous place for Indians; but during the course of the eighteenth century, cofradías and communal lands were rented out to neigh-boring estates or to migrants from other towns in central Jalisco who came to live on the outskirts of town.[102] Pueblo cofradía herds held

---

[100] CAG, *relación* written by Fr. Francisco Barrena, OFM, in 1689.

[101] CAG, *cofradía* documents, box 2, 1769, "sobre las tierras de Moyutlán, Cañada del Platanar."

[102] Van Young, *Rural Life*, p. 575; AJANG Civil, 197-24-2404; CAG, *cofradía* documents, box 2, 1758, "sobre el rancho de Nuestra Señora de Guadalupe, 1767 bienes

steady until the 1760s, then began to decline in number, especially after the famine of 1785–86. As early as 1775, three of Tlajomulco's cofradías (not including the hospital cofradía) had only fifty head of cattle combined.[103] Cofradía activities including the hospitals declined along with their properties. The population of the district of Tlajomulco grew fourfold to 10,598 in 1821.[104] Non-Indians increased as a proportion of the total population to about 30 percent; and the Indian language fell into disuse. But demographic changes should not be overplayed. The population of Tlajomulco grew by only 27 percent between 1767 and 1813 (1,678 to 2,126) and the proportion of Indians there dropped only slightly, from 79 percent in 1767 to 76 percent in 1813.

Population growth in this district did mean that farmland, which had been abundant a century before, was now in short supply. Tlajomulco still produced some corn for sale as well as for local consumption, but more local men turned to crafts—Tlajomulco was a weaving center in the late colonial period with regular trade to Guadalajara nearby—or day labor on the prospering private estates. Others, including the municipal councils, took their grievances to court, complaining of boundary encroachments and damage to their fields by the cattle of the surrounding ranches, complaining of the rentals of their lands and claiming pueblo rather than church ownership of the cofradía properties.[105] So many disputes from Tlajomulco were reaching the royal courts in the last decades of colonial rule that Spanish landowners complained of the litigious nature of the Indians: "the character of the Tlajomulco Indians is disposed toward disputes."[106] Formal suits also were a manifestation of increasing tension within the community of Tlajomulco in the late colonial period. Disputes among local factions over the annual cabildo elections now found their way onto the audiencia's docket.[107] The subdelegado lamented that one party of these Indians was as bad as another—they were all irresponsible drunkards, he said—and had begun to have secret meetings in which they plotted revenge.[108]

---

de cofradías de la parroquia," 1776 "sobre que las cofradías de Tlaxomulco se unan en la del Santíssimo Sacramento," 1810 "liquidación de reales pertenecientes a los arriendos del sitio de Cacaluta."

[103] CAG, 1775–1776, "bienes de cofradías de la parroquia."

[104] CAG, 1821, "inventario de la parroquia de Tlajomulco."

[105] AJANG Civil, 197-24-2404.

[106] Van Young, *Rural Life*, p. 644.

[107] AJANG Civil, 223-20-2908 and 267-17-3656.

[108] AJANG Civil, 267-17-3656.

Coming on the eve of Torres's occupation of Guadalajara, the unrest in Tlajomulco sounds ominous, especially since Tlajomulco was near the line of Torres's march from Zacoalco into the city and had longstanding contacts with Jocotepec and the north shore villages. Yet there was surprisingly little partisan activity at Tlajomulco during the independence war. A few weavers from the town joined Torres at the battle of Calderón (later they claimed they were conscripted and went against their will), but apparently there was no mass support or emergence of important bands of insurgents in Tlajomulco in 1810–11.[109] After 1812, royal officials were fearful that the Isla de Mezcala movement would spread to Tlajomulco. A few rebel bands did operate in the mountains near Tlajomulco but again there was no mass movement in support of the insurgents. Several Indian men from San Juan in the jurisdiction of Tlajomulco briefly joined the lake shore people of San Luis in November 1814 after a captain from Mezcala Island raided the hacienda San Lucas nearby, but they deserted before an attack planned against Jocotepec was carried out. This incident, and the case of eleven men of San Lucas who were pardoned by the royalist general Félix María Calleja, are the only clear examples that have come to light of local Indians joining the insurgency.[110]

Royal officials and Spanish *vecinos* of Tlajomulco reported that the Indians professed loyalty to the crown although they were not much help in defending the district against insurgents. But on the whole, they were not active proponents of insurgency, either. The lieutenants and priests of Tlajomulco during the war still thought of the local people as "indios inquietos" (restless Indians) but even after 1810 the Indians were absorbed in their local affairs and continued to work out their many conflicts in the traditional way; that is, they continued to go to court with their disagreements over land rights, elections, illegal fees, and abusive Spanish officials. During one land suit in 1817 the people of Tlajomulco claimed that their titles and privileges went back to Nuño de Guzmán who rewarded them for their loyal service in the conquest.[111] This petition proceeded to recall the ancient chiefs of the community who had fought alongside Guzmán. Perhaps because they remembered their ancestors' part in the conquest and saw themselves as a community entitled to special privileges under Spanish law, they continued to pre-

---

[109] AJANG Criminal, caja 12.
[110] Ibid.
[111] AJANG Civil, legajo 92 ("1806–1828").

fer to operate within the colonial system of justice even when other ways of redressing grievances presented themselves in 1810. The closest Tlajomulco came to a *tumulto* during the Independence period was on October 3, 1815, when the Indian community staged a joyous mass demonstration in support of their parish priest who had just returned from Guadalajara with a judgment in his favor in a heated dispute with the subdelegado. The *cura*, Dr. José Francisco Dávila, opposed to the insurgency in spite of his own problems with district officials, was said to have enjoyed excellent relations with most of his Indian parishioners. He may have been particularly important in persuading the local Indians to stay out of the way.[112]

Tonalá remained the most self-consciously indigenous town in central Jalisco in the eighteenth century. It was also the most litigious of towns—the cabildo and individual Indians pursuing in the full formality of the courts disputes over non-Indians residing among them, abuse of authority by the priest and the subdelegado and his lieutenants, illegal gambling, the *cabecera* (district seat) vs. *sujetos* (subject communities) over political rights and autonomy, parish jurisdiction, land boundaries, internal disputes, and jealousies among local officials, and a string of real and imagined slights to personal honor by royal officials and prominent Indians.[113] Tonalá went through some of the stormiest residencias (judicial inquiries into the conduct of royal officials, in this case of the district magistrates and their lieutenants) on record in the late colonial period.

In some ways, the situation in Tonalá in the eighteenth century was similar to Tlajomulco. It was a district of good farmland and water sources close to Guadalajara, with a cluster of Indian pueblos (eleven in all) and private estates (three haciendas, six ranchos and one estancia). Tonalá experienced land shortages as a result of population growth, and it was one of the first districts to witness the expansion of commercial farming, thus putting new pressure on land and water and required labor drafts from the pueblos to work on local haciendas. As in Tlajomulco, Indians outnumbered Spaniards by five or six to one. Both cabeceras were seen by Spaniards as seedbeds of disrespect for royal representatives and potential centers of rebellion. Tonalá earned its reputation in a *tumulto* in 1791

[112] AJANG Civil, legajo 110 ("1800–1809").

[113] Especially the inventory of records added to the Tonalá archive for 1788–1796 in AJANG Civil, 200-13-2464.

and a long record of menacing crowds.[114] Both communities were troubled by litigious political factions.

In several important ways, however, the town of Tonalá was different from Tlajomulco. Non-Indians were kept at a greater distance; only five Spaniards (mainly shopkeepers) were reported living in town in 1792.[115] Its considerable wealth was based less on farmland than on the famous pottery ("the best the kingdom has to offer," said Dr. José Menéndez Valdez in 1792),[116] and was traded throughout the viceroyalty. Pottery alone was estimated to yield 30,000 pesos a year income for the potters and traders of Tonalá. As the admiring Menéndez Valdez commented, "with this industry it should have been the happiest [town] in the Intendancy." It was not, he claimed, because the Indians were addicted to drinking and gambling. Many Indians of Tonalá in the late colonial period were reported to own strings of mules and to be engaged in far-flung trade, as well as pottery manufacture.[117] Until the 1770s, the Indians of Tonalá enjoyed an abundance of farmland as well, in spite of boundary disputes with neighboring estates and even after giving up some of their excess lands to Salatitán in 1707 and having their boundaries remeasured in 1757.[118] Other pueblos in the district that lacked a lucrative craft were less fortunate and their problems eventually became Tonalá's. In 1775 the audiencia decided that Tonalá had excess lands beyond its league to the north and west totaling 28⅝ caballerías that should be assigned to Salatitán, a village that lacked decent fields.[119] By 1778 Tonalá was back in court claiming that some of its people did not have sufficient farmland and that much of the community land was "rocky and sterile."[120] Tonalá did not win its case,

[114] AJANG Civil, 171-14-1901.

[115] AGI Guadalajara, 250.

[116] Ibid.

[117] CAG, 1765 report by Fr. Cecilio Antonio Caio, OFM. Van Young, *Rural Life*, pp. 545–46 documents only four in the pueblo who sold to muleteers in 1739. The trade seems to have broadened considerably by the 1760s.

[118] CAG, unsorted parish papers, 1776 land dispute between Tonalá and Salatitán; Van Young, *Rural Life*, p. 577.

[119] Ibid.

[120] AJANG Civil, 83-1-1920. Even the 1775 assignment apparently did not offer Salatitán any margin of safety in food and production for sale. The priest of Salatitán in July 1790 said he had received no clerical fees from his parishioners since the epidemic and crop failure of 1785–86. He claimed that the Indians were still short of land and unable to feed him. An increasing number of them were forced to subsist by working on neighboring haciendas and tilling their small gardens. During the 1786 epidemic, 183 Indians had died while only 147 were added by birth and migration

and it is possible that this claim was inspired by a desire to recover some of what was lost in 1775 rather than that the people of Tonalá were facing a critical shortage. It is true that some Tonalá families no longer farmed, but these may have included potters and traders who chose not to do so.

Even with the Independence insurrection swirling around them, it seems to have been business as usual for the Indians of Tonalá. There was conflict, but it was not much different from the monotonous disputes and suits that had stamped this town for generations. And they were dealt with in the usual way—by reviling the subdelegado, an occasional short-lived village tumulto, and more litigation. The small mountain of law suits initiated by local men and women continued to grow from 1811–21.

In no other pueblo of central Jalisco were there such bitter and protracted suits with subdelegados and their lieutenants. The contested residencia of the subdelegado that began in 1809 dragged on through 1811. Claims were made against Indians for insulting the subdelegado and counterclaims were made against him for abuse of office.[121] Indian officials of Tonalá continued to be touchy about their dignity. In 1817 the Indians' *alcalde de segundo voto* charged the subdelegado's scribe with insulting him and warned the court that "if this crime is not punished as it should be, in the future no one will accept any community office."[122] The Indian cabildo in 1818 and 1819 pressed for an early residencia of Subdelegado Tomás Sandi and his lieutenant, Gervasio Acosta, charging that Acosta abused his authority, whipped Indians for no reason, and levied illegal contributions and fines. Sandi defended himself and his lieutenant with countercharges that the Indians were rebellious ingrates, drunkards, and "adictos a la insurrección."

Sandi's litany of complaints centered on the Indian alcalde, Toribio Covarrubias, whom he accused of leading a tumulto against the lieutenant on the day of Corpus Christi in 1818, for releasing his friends from jail, for flouting royal authority, disrespecting the King's representatives (specifically for shoving and insulting the lieutenant), and threatening to expel all non-Indians from Tonalá.[123] Toribio replied that these charges against him were lies and he produced the parish priest as his star character witness. The párroco

---

between 1785 and 1790. The population of Salatitán in 1790 stood at 463. CAG, box of Tlajomulco parish records.

[121] AJANG Criminal, legajo 80 ("1815–1833"), legajo 42 ("1813–1812 leg.3").

[122] AJANG Criminal, legajo 63 ("1818 leg. 4").

[123] AJANG Criminal, legajo 89 ("1818 leg. 2").

swore that Toribio was a good Christian, the most devout of all local Indians, a leader who donated his wealth and labor to the greater glory of God's works, and a stern and upstanding governor of his people who was vigilant in implementing a new plan to ensure public order in Tonalá.[124] The most serious of the charges on both sides seem to have been largely hyperbole, inspired by a spirit of revenge. In particular, the charges of sympathy with the insurgents were without foundation in the estimation of the audiencia's attorney. His recommendation that both sides be ordered to respect the law and royal authority made it clear that he was angered by the exaggerated sense of pride and vengeance that pervaded this series of political disputes in Tonalá. Thereafter, he seems to have routinely dismissed the suits and countersuits against the subdelegados and Indians of Tonalá for "outrages, insults, and disrespect" that continued to appear on the high court's docket.[125] Villager agitation and insolence to local officers of the crown were hallmarks of political life in Tonalá before and during the independence period, but it is striking that the grievances and dissatisfaction did not spill over into support for the insurgency that was taking place nearby in the Altos and near Lake Chapala. The people of Tonalá seemed immersed in their own local affairs and the stacks of formal complaints they took to the audiencia indicated a solid, albeit grudging, loyalty to this legal system and to the Spanish crown.

Despite the differences, Tonalá and Tlajomulco in 1810 had features in common that may explain their absence from the fighting between 1810 and 1816. They were populous and prosperous Indian districts that were less disturbed by the economic and political changes of the late eighteenth century. Each had substantial farmland, a lucrative craft, and relatively few designated non-Indians residing in their towns. Since both were located close to Guadalajara, they had ready access to and were regular users of the range of colonial courts from the alcalde mayor to the audiencia as an arena for settling local disputes. Finally, the people of both communities thought of themselves as indigenous—remembering with pride the pre-Hispanic ancestors of their towns and identifying themselves less than other villagers of central Jalisco as "Indians" in the colonial meaning of that word. Their political violence during the independence period looks much like the local village tumultos of Oa-

[124] Ibid.
[125] AJANG Criminal, legajo 54 ("1821 leg. 2").

xaca—as much a dramatic outburst to get the attention of the colonial
authorities as a declaration of village autonomy.

Conclusion

Unrest in the countryside of central Jalisco increased from 1790 to
1821, first in the form of banditry, then as insurrection in the first
war of independence. The independence war here was a limited insurrection. It centered in a number of formerly prosperous "Indian"
communities with important support from bandit gangs and a few
creoles but, except for the brief period under Torres, it was not a
general uprising for national independence or a social revolution.
For most of the communities caught up in the political explosion
after September 1810, it remained a local conflict and fed on local
grievances.

Central Jalisco and the towns that furnished important local support to the insurgency against Spaniards and Spanish rule after 1810
roughly fit the circumstances of peasant insurrection proposed by
Joel Migdal and others: freeholding peasant villagers near a rapidly
expanding urban center, in a rural setting where population growth,
commercial agriculture and recent expansion of a market economy
with capitalist features were taking place and which experienced a
sudden disruption of normal social patterns.[126] Together, these developments accentuated peasant land shortages and new social and
economic differentiation within the pueblos; contributed to the further weakening of community ties that had restrained mobility; required adjustments in traditional ways of living and finding a livelihood; and made peasants more open to new kinds of political
action.

The rise of banditry in the region after 1785 may have been an
early sign of the social effects of these economic changes in the
eighteenth century: new riches from trade and commerce and the
expanding market economy of Guadalajara, coupled with a rapidly
growing village population faced with increasing shortages of food
and opportunities for younger generations. This banditry seems to
have had less to do with the primitive social protest posited by Eric
Hobsbawm under similar conditions than it did with restless young
men facing uncertain futures as landless farmworkers or as villagers
being increasingly squeezed by population growth and land short-

[126] Migdal, *Peasants, Politics, and Revolution*, chap. 1; pp. 254–60; Enrique Semo,
ed., *Historia mexicana: Economía y lucha de clases* (México, 1978), pp. 189–99.

ages, who were looking for a quick and sure way into a share of the new wealth they saw moving along the roads to Guadalajara. Migration and banditry at this time would have mixed push and pull factors: people forced out of pueblos by population increases and land shortages on the one hand, and the expectation of employment and a better living in the burgeoning towns or on the road, on the other. After the political breakdown in September 1810 banditry grew and sometimes merged with political and social movements, but it was not at the heart of the insurrection. Large bandit gangs loosely connected to Independence movements and social banditry after 1810 were most evident in the jurisdiction of Tepatitlán in the Altos, where the rural society was composed largely of rancheros, large estate owners, and farmworkers, and where the main economic activities were ranching and trade. The insurrections centered on transitional "Indian" pueblos in the area south of Guadalajara.

Insurrection was not, however, simply a matter of more open, disintegrating Indian pueblos near large urban centers going on the warpath. Pueblos of central Jalisco had not reached such an acute economic crisis that it would explain neatly the turmoil of 1810–16. There was a core of village resentment, feelings of injustice, and revivalist identity shaped by Indian hospitals, the Virgin of the Immaculate Conception, the removal of the Franciscans from parish duties, the struggle over control of cofradía property, prolonged and costly land litigation that went against the Indians of the Zacoalco district, and changes in colonial rule in this region in the late eighteenth century that contributed to political unrest and a weakening of the bonds of loyalty to the colonial state and church.

Insurrections were rare and sporadic enough in central Jalisco that a straight materialist explanation is deeply distorted by the idiosyncrasies of particular places, people, and events. By no means all of the important pueblos with Indian majorities in central Jalisco that were undergoing the unsettling changes described here joined the War of Independence once the detonator—the forces of José Antonio Torres—had been applied. In fact, two of the largest Indian communities similar to Zacoalco played no important part in the war at all. In most others, including Zacoalco and some lakeshore towns, individuals and groups rather than whole communities took part— local support for Torres came largely from villagers before he reached Guadalajara, but it was not collective action by whole pueblos. Feelings of injustice seem to have been less centered in village identity than was true of Oaxaca. So the popular biological metaphors of contagion and cancer engulfing the communities in their

path have little descriptive value, though insurrections clearly included people from places where the violence did not begin. The
lakeshore towns, for example, were touched only lightly by the
Torres movement, with individuals rather than neighborhoods or
whole communities joining up. In 1811 the persistence of a few
rebel gangs in the lake area led to royalist efforts at scorched-earth
eradication; this in turn led to a new insurrection that might have
been avoided by a more temperate royal program of pacification.
There was still room for a revered local priest to keep his parishioners neutral if not royalist (as in Tlajomulco) or catalyze them into
action (judging by the parish priests who led local forces under Hidalgo and Morelos in the first war of independence).

   The making of peasant insurrection in central Jalisco took more
than resolve, outward orientation, economic dislocation, a sense of
injustice, weakened ties to the state, new taxes, sudden disruption,
and leadership. Arms were needed, as well as supplies, communications, and a safe place to regroup if the enemy was not quickly
defeated. The only village insurrection in central Jalisco that lasted
for more than a few months occurred in the Lake Chapala area. The
lakeshore villages were not leading rebels in the first months of the
war but, once drawn in by the harsh royalist repressions, they were
able to combine their efforts and hold off the enemy for years. The
lake setting would seem to have been very important to their success. Communications and shipments of supplies over water were
faster and easier than over land. Mezcala Island, the penal colony
that symbolized Spanish coercion to the villagers, was a defensible
base. It was already an island fortress; it was neutral, even sacred
ground to them. After seizing it from the penal authorities, they
could gather there without feeling that it was the ground of any one
village. It had an unobstructed view of the shoreline and surrounding hills that enabled the islanders to anticipate attack and contact
allies on land by smoke signals. As long as friends on shore sent
supplies, the islanders could hold out indefinitely against royalists
who tried and failed to take the island.

PART III

From Indian Rebellions
to Peasant Revolts

CHAPTER EIGHT

The 1840s Southwestern Mexico Peasants' War: Conflict in a Transitional Society

John M. Hart

> Men make their own history, but not out of whole cloth.
> They make it out of conditions not of their own choosing,
> but such as lies ready to hand. The traditions of all past
> generations weigh on the brain of the living.
>
> KARL MARX
> *The Eighteenth Brumaire of Louis Bonaparte*

Between 1842 and 1845 village-based peasant uprisings swept the southwestern region of Mexico, and in their course of upheaval and suppression laid bare the cultural, political, and economic contradictions of Mexican society.[1] The zone of unrest encompassed parts of the present-day states of Oaxaca, Guerrero, Puebla, Morelos, Mexico, Chiapas, and Michoacan. The growth of commercial export agriculture, competition among rival factions and among the elites, the many-faceted grievances of the campesinos, and the garrison-state nature of the national government all played prominent parts in the inception, growth, and ultimate suppression of the rebellion. During the rest of the nineteenth century the continuing northward movement in the development of commercial agriculture and export-ori-

---

[1] Peasant is defined in this study as one who has the power to determine the product of a relatively small parcel of land worked either individually or in common through village consensus. *Campesino* is a more general term applied to both agrarian workers and peasants. Middle peasants are the village elites and local property owners with higher status than those who till the land. Regional and provincial elites are those people whose economic power and high social standing caused them to aspire to rule in the periphery, in states geographically isolated from Mexico City and who were therefore accustomed through practice to semi-autonomous power.

ented industry caused repeated and similar waves of violence to sweep the affected areas of the nation until the generalized conflagration of 1910.

The four-year wave of unrest and its equally lengthy aftershocks, to 1849, was characterized by clearly identifiable conditions in the different regimes involved in the revolt and by universal social contradictions that transcended not only the enormous geographic zone involved, but the participatory population as well. This rebellion, like most others in central Mexico between 1810 and 1910, was "modern" in its economic causation, resulting from economic and social dislocations caused by the development of private estates and commercial land usage that deprived the villages. The rebels shared some of the most advanced aspirations and highest values of the liberal social order, including self-determination, free trade, and the abolition of head taxes and tithes. Yet, their rebellion was also rooted in a defense of the traditional, relatively autonomous free-village economy, polity, and way of life. It combined the self-defined, self-led peasant uprising with elite crises at both local and national levels. It became a conspiratorial anarchic reaction to outside intrusion that idealized the greater degree of economic and political autonomy of the past.

The uprisings began in the economic development zone between the northern border of Oaxaca and Acapulco, in which village economies were being overtaken by absentee-owned estate agriculture. The spark that ignited the uprisings was an elite crisis that paralyzed the state's repressive mechanisms and set in motion the alienated middle peasants, in this case the traditional leadership of the villages Nahuatl, Yope, and Tlapaneca. The elite crisis then triggered a much deeper struggle between besieged indigenous peasants who were striving to save their way of life, and intrusive, Europeanized Mexicans with their alien language, mores, and economy. In each of the far-flung areas where the greatest violence and turmoil took place (the Costa Chica, Tlapa, Puebla, the Balsas River basin of northern Guerrero and southern Michoacan, and along the isthmian road in Tehuantepec) commercial estate agriculture was most advanced. Significantly less violence occurred in the middle of the rebellious zone, along the Pacific coast of Oaxaca, where elements of village heirarchies had developed small-scale coffee raising.[2]

---

[2] For a description of the uprising see José María Tornel, Secretario de Guerra y Marina, *Memoria del Ministerio* (México, 1844), pp. 54–60; see also Leticia Reina, *Las rebeliones campesinas en México (1819–1906)* (Mexico: Siglo XXI, 1980), pp. 85–120, 157–64, 233–39, 245–46; Jean Meyer, *Probemas campesinas y revueltas agrarias*

Figure 8.1. Limits and focal points of unrest during the uprisings of the 1840s.

Rapid land tenure transformation in the region and the over-whelming shock resulting from the expansion of latifundia agriculture threatened the very survival of village entities. As they were progressively deprived of their economic base, the villagers did not have the alternative of escape to urban centers that was so prevalent in later campesino culture. Because the Mexican industrial revolution had not yet begun, and because campesino and Indian cultures were still distinct from the European influenced cities, large-scale urban migratory assimilation was out of the question.

In 1842 the municipio of Tecoanapa in the south of the present-day state of Guerrero and its surrounding pueblos and poblados faced the desperate problem of envelopment because of land seizures by the expansionist hacienda of San Marcos. For its owners, the hacienda was a highly profitable mixture of mining, timber, live-stock, and agricultural enterprises. It was representative of the growth and commercial-capitalist agriculture that transformed parts of central and southern Mexico in terms of land ownership and usage, external trade, culture, and class relationships at a time in the nineteenth century customarily described as "economically stagnant." The relationship between the expansion of capitalist agricultural activity, changing land tenure systems, and agrarian unrest in southern Mexico from Yucatán to Michoacan requires rejection of the "stagnation" theory for the southwest of the country.

The hacienda of San Marcos was the product of the early eighteenth-century entrepreneurial efforts of Jacinto del Castillo y Merlo and later Colonel Juan Eusebio Gallo of the Acapulco garrison. In the 1740s, Gallo consolidated a considerable portion of the core holdings of the estate and profitably produced cotton in the Nexpa River valley, marketed carnadas to the Manilla Noa, and sold cotton, cacao, salt, timber, cattle, sheep, fighting bulls, and a variety of other products to Acapulco, the burgeoning mines of Sultepec, and the growing urban markets of Cuernavaca and Mexico City. Gallo began a vast commercial export estate similar to his other operations near Guadalajara in Jalisco and Ciudad Victoria in Tamaulipas. His family was highly entrepreneurial. His brother, a high official in the Catedral Nacional, ran a similar network of truck farms around Mexico City. In 1765 his heirs sold San Marcos for $22,000 to Don Francisco Palacio y Castillo.[3]

(1821–1910) (Mexico, 1973), p. 10; and *Documentos y apuntes históricos del Estado de Guerrero*, Vol. 7 (Mexico, 1946), p. 295.

[3] Archivo General de la Nación (hereafter AGN), Ramo *Tierras*, vols. 1212–1213. Especially vol. 1212, fojas 1–667. For sale of estate, see vol. 1213, f. 43. For early

For the next twenty-five years the estate prospered, growing along with the dynamic eighteenth-century economy of New Spain. By 1778 the powerful owner, Don José Antonio Palacio del Castillo of Mexico City and his wife Doña Teresa Suarez del Rosal, controlled properties extending from the municipio of Cuajiniquilapa on the coast at the Oaxaca border, inland to Ometepec, deep into the present-day state of Guerrero to Nazintla, to the Omitlan River. In the north running toward the coast, the properties extended along the Papagayo River through ancient Cacahuatepec, to Chacalapa, and included scattered properties between the Omitlan River and Tixtla on the Chilpancingo–Chilapa road. A transformation in land tenure had changed peasant-owned subsistance properties to commercial export agricultural estates owned by capitalist outsiders.[4]

From the 1780s through the early years of the nineteenth century, however, the hacienda suffered great losses. First the estate's administrator Manual Garcia Herreros y Sanz defrauded the youthful heiress Maria Antonia Palacio del Castillo, finally convincing her to sell out in 1790 for only $122,928. Six years later young Maria Antonia's new Spanish merchant husband, Don Antonio Fernandez de la Muria sued in court. In 1799 after a struggle involving regidores of Mexico City the estate was restored to its former owners by the audiencia.[5] Between 1800 and 1810 the hacienda floundered, beset by drought, labor unrest at Sultepec, and loss of the galleon trade. Then the revolution came. The mines at Sultepec, which the hacienda had supplied with timber, beef, salt and agricultural produce, closed. Cattle drives to Mexico City were impossible. The estate managers fled and the properties fell into disuse. Local villages began to work nearby lands that historically they claimed, but to which the hacienda also held title.[6]

After independence, the estate, under new ownership and regaining its urban markets, began to reconsolidate, but it was greatly reduced in size. Its southern border ran from the ocean along the Copala River through Mexcaltepec, seventy kilometers north of its earlier boundary. In the interior, the villages in the region of Tecoanapa, Nazintla, and Tixtla had not suffered active administration from the San Marcos estate for almost twenty years.[7]

---

estate formation see *Tierras*, vol. 154, expediente 5, f. 170; vol. 462, exp. 1, f. 320; vol. 910, exp. 2, fs. 5–53; vol. 2735-1A, exp. 17, fs. 12-14; vol. 2763, exp. 26, f. 27; and vol. 3668, exp. 5; and AGN, *Mercedes*, vol. 5, f. 156.

[4] AGN, *Tierras*, vol. 1213, fs. 1–64.

[5] Ibid.

[6] Ibid.

[7] Archivo Histórico de la Secretaría de Reforma Agraria (hereafter AHSRA), San Mar-

De jure, the hacienda's lands still extended from the Papagayo to the Copala and inland to Nazintla with scattered holdings further north. In the late 1820s the owner began to consolidate his claims, moving against the cofradía and pueblo communes within the boundaries of the hacienda. Through a series of land seizures made possible by periodic and complicated state land tenure legislation enacted after 1824, the remaining free village peasants of the Tecoanapa region, like those throughout most of the southwestern region under study here, faced the choice of joining in the fate of many of their neighbors as resident laborers on the growing estates, working lands that they regarded as their own, or of emigrating.[8]

The villagers of southern Guerrero, the mulattoes and zambos (mixed bloods) of the coast, the mestizos of the valleys, and the indigenous population of the Sierra had revolted in 1832–33 because of the renewed land enclosure process and an increased head tax. On that occasion they joined the campesinos to the south as far as the isthmus of Tehuantepec in an attempt to throw off what they regarded as the foreign governments of Mexico City, Acapulco, and Chilpancingo, and in order to eliminate what constituted cultural intrusions and the expropriation of their productivity. As a village leader once put it to me, "Why should we campesinos, the food producers, feed the cities and not obtain enough in return to support ourselves?" That uprising was quelled through a mixture of armed force and mediation offered by the strong man of Acapulco, liberal General Juan Alvarez. By 1842 the hacienda of San Marcos had regained much of its former grandeur by reclaiming lost properties and using the land denunciation laws of 1828 to foreclose on ancient holdings claimed by villages throughout the region. By 1842 the estate covered over 200,000 hectares.[9]

It was then that an elite crisis, the concerns of which were beyond the peasants' political horizons, unleashed them into one of the most violent of the Mexican elite's most frightening concerns, the peasants' war. In 1841 the new, conservative, and oftentimes presi-

cos, Municipio San Marcos, ejidal, 23:1226 (723.6), 4 bundles; San Juan Colotlipa, Muni. Quechultenango, ejidal, 25: 1206 (723.6), 8 bundles; and Nazintla, Muni. Quechultenango, communal, 276.1/35, (723.6), 7 bundles; and Tecoanapa, Muni. Tecoanapa, ejidal, 23:13772 (723.6), 3 bundles.

[8] Ibid.; and Lamatzintla, Muni, Chilapa, ejidal, 23:10228 (723.6), 6 bundles.

[9] Ibid.; Noticias históricas sobre los pueblos de Ajuchitlán, Coyuca, Cutzmala, Coahuayutla, Petatlán. Tecpán, Atoyac (México: Vargas Rea, 1947), pp. 1–34; and Miguel Dominguez, La erección del Estado de Guerrero; Antecedentes históricos (México, 1949), pp. 20–47.

dent of Mexico, Antonio López de Santa Anna, accepted a plan to create a new state out of the territory of the department of Mexico that presently comprises the state of Guerrero. An assembly of "notables" agreed to the boundaries of the new department and the selection of Chilpancingo as its capital. The cacique of Chilpancingo, Nicholas Bravo, a conservative ally of the president, commander-in-chief of the army of the south, and future president himself, convened the assembly, and it was clear that politically and militarily he would dominate the new department.[10]

However, Alvarez and local liberal strongmen traditionally controlled much of the coastal region of the would-be new department, including the Acapulco area and the Costa Chica district to the immediate south, including Tecoanapa. Alvarez was a staunch rival and enemy of Santa Anna and Bravo. The reorganization of the department of Mexico threatened to place areas of the Costa Chica, then part of the department of Puebla with its remote administration, under the aegis of Bravo in nearby Chilpancingo. Under prevailing conditions Alvarez dominated the Pacific zones of the department of Puebla and had long held sway over territories as far away as Tlapa where he owned haciendas. The proposed changes placed all of those territories within the jurisdiction of Bravo, his hated rival. The liberals opposed the proposed placement of Tecoanapa, the Costa Chica and the Tlapa region to the northeast in the department of Puebla.[11] The reorganization would have undermined the liberals' already strong position vis-à-vis the conservatives in southwestern Mexico.

In February 1842, Santa Anna moved to strengthen his national political position and that of his conservative private landholder allies. He authorized hacendados to maintain cavalry units upon approval of the governors of the departments and imposed new head taxes of one real per capita per month on the villages.

In March the plan to incorporate the coastal region into the new department controlled by the conservative cacique of Chilpancingo was approved. In desperation, the liberal caudillo of the Costa Chica and his chieftain from Acapulco toured their territories calling upon the people to join them in protesting the redrawing of state boundaries, the new taxes, and state militias. They reminded the people of Tecoanapa of the liberals' long-time support of municipio political

---

[10] Dominguez, *Erección del Estado*, pp. 20–47; *Noticias históricas sobre los pueblos*, pp. 1–34; and Luis Guevara Ramírez, *Síntesis histórica del Estado de Guerrero* (México: Collección de Estudios Históricos Guerrerenses, 1959), pp. 70–113.

[11] Ibid.

rights and "agrarian justice." In a public speech Alvarez called upon the peasants of Tecoanapa to be prepared to fight if necessary to defend their traditional political rights and their land. It was clear from their behavior after the uprising began, that the liberal leadership in the area wanted peasant support in order to block Santa Anna, but they did not anticipate the widespread class-based social upheaval that was about to ensue.[12]

When the liberal politicians departed, a wave of fear swept across the towns near Tecoanapa. The men of the rancherías, poblados, and pueblos of the district met on a hillside outside the municipio and, in a panic, decided that they were about to lose everything. The neighboring hacienda of San Marcos, with its opulent, educated, and hated owner, Dr. Gutiérrez Martinez, fell victim to the peasants' attack. The house was burned, crops seized, old property markers replaced, and disputed lands were returned to the campesinos.[13]

To the alarm of the race-conscious local property owners and mayordomos, Afro-Mexican hacienda workers with grievances over land claims played a prominent part in the violence, which then spread to neighboring estates. The initial ambivalence of the hacienda tenants to the revolution soon became intense hostility comparable to that of the Tarascan participants in the Independencia who at first hesitated and then turned Michoacan into a bleeding ground. Many of the haciendas were owned by conservative absentee proprietors who lived in Mexico City or Acapulco. The local units of the army of the south were commanded by Alvarez, the liberal caudillo of Acapulco. He delayed for several days in his compliance with orders from Mexico City to quell the revolt. The government of the department of Puebla openly refused to comply with government orders to suppress the rising, because in the beginning the Puebla leaders incorrectly viewed the insurgency as one in support of the coastal region's petition to be incorporated to its jurisdictions.

At first the liberal coastal authorities appreciated neither the depth of violence nor the attack on commercial agriculture and private property that the uprising represented. But when the rebellion threatened estates owned by liberal allies of General Alvarez, they applied a brutal repression virtually annihilating Tecoanapa in or-

[12] Ibid.; *La Voz de Michoacan*, February 27, April 5, 6, 24, 28, May 1, 5, 22, 26, 1842.

[13] Tornel, *Memoria de Guerra*, pp. 54–55; Dominguez, *Erección del Estado*, pp. 22–30, 47; Guevara Ramirez, *Síntesis histórica*, pp. 70–113.

der to close off the contagion before it could spread. "Peace" was restored in the region by April 18, but the authorities were too late.[14]

Following the punishment of the rebels who had gone too far at Tecoanapa by liberal dragoons, campesino rebels scattered across the countryside, carrying what was becoming a scorched-earth type of revolution to much of a 60,000 square mile area. Within two weeks a mix of aroused village peasants and hacienda workers were committing acts of violence against landowners in an area ranging from northern Oaxaca to the valleys just south of Chilapa.[15]

Alvarez was accused by the authorities of inducing part of the violence at the town of Quechultenango by entering it with 2,000 campesinos and calling upon the citizens, as the peasants understood him, to seize their usurped lands. The villages, pueblos, and poblados in the municipio of Chilapa joined in alliance with those of Quechultenango seizing property, burning estates, driving out mayordomos and loyal estate employees, and reclaiming their lost lands by replacing land boundary markers that they claimed had originally been moved by the estate owners. The peasants rebelled under the leadership of José de Abarca, elected comisario of the defense committee of the pueblo of Ayahualulco. The Abarcas were one of the ex-cabecerra's leading families. Manuel Abarca was a general in the liberal forces of Juan Alvarez. Most landowners involved lived in Chilapa or Chilpancingo, but the largest properties were owned by the heirs to the estate of the Aztec emperor. In May the peasants south of Chilapa were temporarily suppressed by forces sent out by Nicolas Bravo, the conservative caudillo of Chilpancingo, but a desperate struggle reduced the great estate houses to rubble, fields were burned, machinery smashed, and hundreds left dead. Revolutionary campesino emmisaries had long since spread out over the countryside north to Zitlala, west to Tixtla, and east to Atlixtac—the eastern border of the Nahuatl-speaking zone with the Yope in that part of Guerrero. The ensuing violence between elites and peasants was even more extreme, constituting a war almost without quarter. By now, Alvarez was assisting the government in its attempts to parley with the rebels.[16]

---

[14] Tornel, *Memoria de Guerra*, pp. 54–55; Reina, *Rebeliones campesinas*, pp. 85–120; Dominguez, *Erección del Estado*, pp. 23–30; and Guevara Ramirez, *Síntesis histórica*, p. 71.

[15] Reina, *Rebeliones campesinas*, pp. 85–120, 157–64, 233–39, 245–46; Tornel, *Memoria de Guerra*, pp. 55–60; Dominguez, *Erección del Estado*, pp. 43–47; Guevara Ramirez, *Síntesis histórica*, pp. 70–113; *Noticias históricos*, pp. 7–34.

[16] Tornel, *Memoria de Guerra*, pp. 55–57; Reina, *Rebeliones campesinas*, pp. 85–

The lands involved are pitifully poor, but peasant resistance was extreme in the south of the Chilapa district because of the political crisis that had developed between the mountaintop pueblo of Ayahualulco and the municipio caciques of Chilapa. National political conflict that paralyzed the government's ability to quickly snuff out the revolt combined with local contradictions between old and emergent elite sectors linked to a new economy and independent nationhood to provoke peasants' war. Ayahualulco's experience of conflict with Chilapa, land loss, subjugation, and resistance, is common to the peasant population of the region, but its record of leadership is exceptional.[17]

In late pre-Columbian times Ayahualulco was a powerful Nahuatl-speaking cabecerra of a district that extended from the area of present-day Tixtla on the west, eastward to the Yope zone around Atlixtac. From north to south the pueblo controlled the area from Zitlala to Quechultenango. In 1480 it was the dominant force in a war that encompassed the area, and later, led a prolonged resistance to the Spanish intruders. Throughout the three centuries of Spanish rule the pueblo continued as a cabecerra and center of indigenous resistance, leading the peasants in periodic rebellions against the Spanish encomenderos and their caciques, and the Montezuma heirs, headquartered in Chilapa.[18]

Throughout the colonial era and the nineteenth century the leaders of Ayahualulco sought to defend the indigenous culture, to maintain the "Mexican" language, and to retain the land holdings of other pueblos in its district. For instance, unlike villages in other

---

120; interview with Ignacio Mendoza, comisario y presidente de varios trabajos en el pueblo, Ayahualulco, August 2, 1980.

[17] Interview, Mendoza; August 2, 1980; and AHSRA, Ayahualulco, Muni. Chilapa, ejidal, 21:702 (723.6), 6 bundles; Nazintla, Muni, Quechultenango, communal, 276.1/35, (723.6); San Juan, Colotlipa, Muni. Quechultenango; ejidal, 25:1206 (723.6), 6 bundles; Lamatzintla, Muni. Chilapa, ejidal 23:10228, (723.6), 6 bundles; Quechutenango, Muni. same, ejidal 23:1322 (783.6), 6 bundles; Tlanicuilulco, Muni. Quechultenango, ejidal 23:11880 (723.6), 2 bundles; Juxtlahuaca, Muni. Quechultenango, 23:9761 (723.6), 7 bundles; Xiloxuxican, Muni. Chilapa, ejidal 23:1291 (723.6), 5 bundles; Atzacualoya y Anexos, Muni. Chilapa, communal, 276.1/531 (723.6), 5 bundles; San Jeronimo Palantla, Muni. Chilapa, communal, 276.1/531 (723.6), 3 bundles; Acalco, Muni. Chilapa, ejidal 23:1292 3 bundles; San Angel, Muni. Chilapa, ejidal 23:1293 (723.6), 6 bundles; Vista Hermosa, Muni. Chilapa, ejidal 23:1376 (723.6), 5 bundles; and Acatlan, Muni. Chilapa, communal 267.1/107 (723.6), 8 bundles.

[18] Interview, Mendosa, August 2, 1980; and AHSRA, Ayahualulco, Muni. Chilapa, ejidal 21:702 (723.6), 6 bundles; Lamatzintla, Muni. Chilapa, ejidal 23:10228 (723.6), 6 bundles; Colotlipa, Muni. Quechultenango, ejidal 25:1206 (723.6), 8 bundles; and Nazintla, Muni. Quechultenango, communal, 276.1/35 (723.6), 7 bundles.

parts of Mexico, they avoided the adoption of Christian names. The defense of indigenous values brought Ayahualulco into repeated confrontations with the Augustinian order that had built a monastery at Payanatzing and owned properties extending to Apantanizingo and constituted much of Ayahualulco's pre-Columbian territory. The mayordomos of the Montezumas, headquartered in Chilapa, used armed force and legal artifice to gain ever-larger holdings, and also engaged in violent encounters with Ayahualulcans. During the independence struggle Ayahualulco and the people of the valley materially supported and participated in the insurrectionist army of the south.[19]

After 1821 an alliance between the heirs of Montezuma and Nicolas Bravo of Chilpancingo resulted in the district cabecerra finally being moved from communal Ayahualulco to the smaller, less prosperous, but predominantly mestizo and private-enterprise, Chilapa. After the loss of its de jure status as district cabecerra, Ayahualulco progressively lost its economic and demographic strength, but persisted in its role of "mata de la indigena," leading the neighboring pueblos in a desperate resistance against outside intruders.[20]

From the time of the independence wars through the 1840s, the fighting in Guerrero consisted largely of local units and engagements. The peasant insurgents frequently seized and redistributed estate properties when the national or regional discipline lapsed. The peasants south of Chilapa fought for control over the means of production and for their way of life. More than one hundred pueblos, rancherías, and other poblados in Guerrero alone, with histories of land tenure, political, and cultural disputes similar to those of Ayahualulco, participated in the 1842 uprising.[21]

Between 1828 and 1831 the first land laws were applied to the valleys south of Chilapa, and a handful of entreprenuers in Mexico City, Chilapa, and Chilpancingo, including the heirs of Moctezuma, benefited from the property redistribution: "Casi todos los estados comenzaron la repartición de las tierras de las comunidades antes de la Reforma." During the ensuing land seizures the valley below Ayahualulco was patrolled by armed men directed by the Montezuma mayordomo "El Gigante" Martín Salmeron. The peasants bar-

[19] Ibid.

[20] Ibid. Mata de la Indigena—homeland of the indigenous.

[21] Interview, Mendoza, August 2, 1980; Tornel, *Memoria de Guerra*, pp. 55–56; and Reina, *Rebeliones campesinas*, pp. 85–120. The independence revolution in Guerrero is discussed at length in the author's forthcoming study *A Social History of the Mexican Peasant Wars, 1810–1910*.

gained as best they could, but they lost heavily; some pueblos were reduced to a minimal one-half square kilometer plot immediately adjacent to the populated zone, while others on poorer sites fared even worse than this. Without proper documentation even their populated zones were condemned. Those settlements with a thinned-out linear hillside dispersal were especially vulnerable and several simply disintegrated.[22]

The people of Ayahualulco lost their bottom lands as a result of the 1830s disputes, but resisted being converted into day laborers on commercial estates by striking a bargain with the owners of a nearby mountaintop, the Montezuma family. In return for clearing the upper reaches of the mountain and giving the timber to the owners, Ayahualulco was entitled to purchase the cleared land at a reasonable price. In 1833 an armed dispute broke out between the pueblo and the Montezumas over the amount and cost of the land to be ceded. The fighting intensified and merged with the general peasants' uprising that swept Guerrero that year. Army intervention in the district resulted in possession of the land remaining with the Montezumas. Ayahualulco retained pueblo status but became what it had sought to avoid, a village of tenant farmers. In the thirteen years since national independence it had lost cabacerra status, much of its population, and virtually all of its land.[23]

In 1842 a new generation of Ayahualulcans remembered the humiliations of 1832, received the revolutionary emmisaries from Tecoanapa, and fought again as they would do in several later nineteenth-century peasant uprisings before joining Zapata in 1910, and still later, Genaro Vaquez, Lucio Cabanas, and unrest as recent as 1978.

In 1842 the pueblo still identified with certain calpulli and the "Mexican" language indicating a conscious link with its pre-Columbian elite lineage. It has served for over five hundred years, as a rallying point for the people of the district in defense of indigenous

[22] For discussion of state land laws see Meyer, *Problemas campesinas*, pp. 116–19. In Jalisco they are dated 1825, 1828, 1830, 1831, 1832, 1833–41, etc.; Interview, Mendoza, August 2, 1980; Dominguez, *Erección del Estado*, 20–23, 27–28; *Noticias históricas* pp. 12–34; Reina, *Rebeliones campesinas*, pp. 85–88; and AHSRA, Ayahualulco, Muni. Chilapa, ejidal, 21:702 (723.6), 6 bundles; and Nazintla, Muni. Quechultenango, communal, 276.1/35 (723.6), 7 bundles.

[23] Interview, Mendoza, August 2, 1980; AHSRA, Ayahualulco, Muni. Chilapa, ejidal, 21:702 (723.6), 6 bundles; and Nazintla, Muni. Quechultenango, communal, 276.1/35 (723.6), 7 bundles.

culture, village polity, and the peasant economy against outside transgressors and commercial agriculture.[24]

While Bravo's cavalry from Chilpancingo reestablished law and order for the elite around Ayahualulco and as far away as the devastated hacienda of Nanzintla twenty-five kilometers to the south, armed peasant contingents had already left the region carrying the uprising in all directions. They moved north beyond the municipio district of Zitlala toward Sultepec and Cuernavaca. Soon the Yope pueblos around Atlixtac became involved, including San Feliciano de Petatlán, which had lost lands originally granted by the crown in 1537 and confirmed by the Audiencia on June 19, 1774. The rebellion rapidly spread further on into areas south and north of Tlapa, across the district of Huamuxtitlán, finally invading the department of Puebla. The local law enforcers fled from the countryside and sought refuge in Tlapa, which the insurgents duly surrounded and beseiged, while another force headed west following the Balsas River basin toward Michoacan.[25]

However, it was the contingent that left the valley below Ayahualulco and struck out toward Tlapa that posed the gravest threat to the government. In 1843, despite defeat by forces at Hueycaltenango, the rebels worked their influence on the Yopes who seized and redistributed lands, burned haciendas, and confiscated crops. The revolt soon spread into the Tlapa district, and enveloped the town and its many "Españoles."[26]

The area, populated by Tepaneca, Nahua, and Mixtec peoples, was an agricultural zone containing several new tobacco, sugar, "experimental" cotton estates and *trapiches* (cotton mills), as well as some livestock haciendas. It was undergoing a rapid shift from traditional peasant and village properties to industrial and commercially oriented holdings. General Alvarez owned several commercial properties, including the hacienda La Providencia. The zone of transformation extended to Matamoros in the present state of Puebla, and east into the Tlaxiaco area of Oaxaca. The uprising spread without any apparent limiting influences based on ethnic barriers. The pueblos Oztocingo, Ocotequila, Potuicha, Patlicha, Zapotitlán Tablas, Cuautololo, Copantoyac, and Tlalquitzalapa all had primitive property grants, and in 1758, during the first serious encroachments, the land titles were authenticated. Between 1818 and

[24] Ibid.

[25] Tornel, *Memoria de Guerra*, pp. 56–59; *Documentos históricos*, vol. 7, p. 295; AHSRA, Petatlan, Muni. Atlixtac, communal, 276.1/720, 7 bundles.

[26] Tornel, *Memoria de Guerra*, pp. 56–59; *Documentos históricos*, vol. 7, p. 295.

1828 the procedure was repeated: "Con fecha 5 de febrero de 1827
. . . el Juez de Primera Intancia procedió . . . [al] deslinde y amojo-
namiento de las tierras de dichos naturales." In 1830 and 1835 the
Tlapa pueblos rebelled, and in 1843 the fighting reached its zenith.
For about two weeks several thousand poorly armed and disorganized peasants could not take Tlapa, but the federal army was unable
to break through and lift the seige until May 10. Meanwhile, an army
moving southwest from Puebla to help relieve Tlapa was inter-
cepted in southeastern Puebla by the campesino insurgents and suffered heavy losses.[27]

The fighting in the Tlapa–Tlaxiaco area continued intermittently
until 1849. The 1843 uprising was not suppressed by an alliance of
the forces of Bravo and Alvarez until 1844, but it exploded a few
months later when the government announced new taxes on all
heads of families. Alvarez, charged by the government to restore order in the area, mixed advocacy that the head tax be abolished, land
returned to the villages, and a new tobacco tax repealed, with
repression of those who continued to rebel.[28]

The rebellion spread from Tlapa northward into Huamuxtitlán,
Cualác, and into the districts around Chiautla, Acatlan, and Izucar
in southwest Puebla. The area, ethnically composed of Mixtec
and mestizo peoples, had undergone a remarkable land consolidation during the last half of the eighteenth century that provoked a
large-scale Indian uprising in 1780. The expansion of commercial
agriculture continued until the independence wars, and by the
1840s almost all of the Tlapa district was contained within seven
landed estates. Some of the estate produce was oriented toward a
new copper mine, while other production was sent to Puebla and
Mexico City. The campesino response, besides participation in the
1780, 1810–21, 1830, and 1835 uprisings, included a pervasive social banditry featuring claims to the legendary tradition of "robbing
from the rich in order to give to the poor."[29]

        [27] Tornel, *Memoria de Guerra*, p. 57; *El Siglo* xix (Mexico), no. 139, February 23,
1842; Juzgado de Letras de Tlapa, April 24, 1843, Packet 3, Archivo Judicial, Puebla;
Documentos históricos, vol. 7, p. 295; and AHSRA, Tlapa, Muni. Tlapa, ejidal,
23:10203 (723.6), 8 bundles; Tlaquilzingo, Muni. Tlapa, ejidal, 23:18593 (723.6), 4
bundles; Copantoyac, Muni. Copantoyac, communal, 276.1/2346, 1 bundle. The data
on the pueblos mentioned are located primarily in the Copantoyac bundle. Trapiches
in the Tlaxiaco area dated from 1715. AHSRA, Tlaxiaco, Muni. Tlaxiaco, communal,
276.1/1149 (723.7), 11 bundles. For the quote on the moving of mojoneras, see San
Miguel Chiepetlan, Muni. Tlapa, communal, 276.1/2241 (723.7), 2 bundles.
        [28] Ibid.
        [29] Ibid.; Reina Cruz Valdes, "Levantamientos populares en Tlapa en los años 1842–

By 1843 land disputes in the Tlapa, Tlaxiaco, and Izucar area following the consolidation of commercial agriculture, were complemented by desperate efforts to preserve Indian cultural life and campesino demands for redress of "raquíticos" salaries. The rebels, although still pre-ideological, promulgated several plans to protest taxes, and demanded municipal autonomy, return of lands, and higher salaries on the estates. Pueblos with deep grievances included Ahuatepec, Acatzingo, Xalpatlahuac, and Tlaquilzingo (the latter had lost properties to the estate La Mesa Ahuacatitla). The fighting in Tlapa, present-day southern Puebla, and northwestern Oaxaca, continued intermittently until 1849.[30]

The northern zone of rebellion extended from southern Morelos around Tlaquiltenango, Xochicalco, and Miacatlán, westward to the districts of Ocuilán, Sultepec, Texcaltitlán, and Tlataya in the state of Mexico. Further west the rebellion spread from the Cutzmalá and Zirandero area in the Balsas basin of Guerrero northward to Aguililla in Michoacan. The Michoacan–Guerrero area was the site of many new tropical and citrus fruit orchards which left the campesinos with nowhere to plant: "porque los latifundistas no nos dan un plano de tierra para saciar nuestras necesidades." In 1833 the pueblo of El Carmen, located in the midst of the Michoacan–Guerrero border conflict, reported that its disputed lands had been held for "over one century by a private party." These towns rebelled first in 1843–44 and, after a new head tax was announced, again in 1845.[31]

Sultepec's pueblos long interspersed legal and armed resistance

---

1849" (unpublished paper, Seminarios de Investigación, Puebla, 1978). Interview with Licenciado Eric M. A. Jasso Herrera, Consejero Agrario, Secretaría de Reforma Agraria, Oaxaca, August 7–8, 1980. The major estate in Huamuxtlán municipio was San Narciso. In neighboring Cualác municipio a Mercedes grant was successfully defended in 1758 and 1767 but lost before 1835. AHSRA, Cualác, Muni. Cualác, ejidal and communal, 25:23198, 2 bundles. The large estates in the Tlaxiaco area were the haciendas La Concepción and San José. For socioeconomic conditions see AHSRA, Tlaxiaco, Muni. Tlaxiaco, communal, 276.1/1149 (723.7), 11 bundles; San Agustín Tlacotepec (for San Bartolo and other centers of unrest), Muni. same, communal 276.1/544 (723.7), 14 bundles; and Santiago Juxtlahuaca, Muni. same, communal, 276.1/10002, 14 bundles. The caciques of the latter pueblo lost their documents during the 1811 revolution.

[30] Ibid.

[31] AHSRA, San Lucas, Muni. San Lucas, ejidal, 25:2811 (723.5), 5 bundles; El Carmen, Muni. Huetamo de Nunez, ejidal, 23:13202 (723.5), 2 bundles, Huetamo de Nunez, Muni. same, ejidal, 23:2810 (723.5), 2 bundles; Tornel, Memoria de Guerra, p. 58; Reina, Rebeliones campesinas, pp. 85–120; and Meyer, Problemas campesinas, p. 10.

to timber, water, and other resource seizures by neighboring mine owners and the landed estates that comprised the mining industry's infrastructure. In 1829 Texcaltitlán "expresó agravios" against the expanding hacienda La Gavia and the ex conde de Regla: "Que la hacienda no les permite sembrar las tierras que sembraron el año pasado (1828)." The land had been in the pueblo's hands since the granting of twelve sitios de ganado mayor in 1592. Unrest, ranging from violent industrial strikes that included sabotage and murders beginning in the 1770s, was a constant. The eastern pueblos in Sultepec's district resisted land takeovers by the expanding hacienda Puente del Ixtla. In southwestern Morelos sugar production burgeoned amid complaints by immigrant Oaxacan campesinos that they had not been given lands promised them in return for settling on haciendas some twenty years earlier. Long-time pueblos claimed usurpation of their properties. Rebellion by the rancherías and pueblos in and around the haciendas Puente del Ixtla and Temixco was extremely short-lived because of the authorities' rapid access to the area via the Mexico–Acapulco road.[32]

Along the Pacific coast of Oaxaca centuries-old local disputes set the district towns of Jicayán and Pochutla, with their entrepreneurial caciques, against their communal sujetos. After independence, the local political and economic elites emerged with sizable and highly profitable coffee fincas at the expense of the communal lands claimed by the sujetos in their districts. In 1842–43 the campesinos in the communal pueblos near Jicayán and Pochutla, whose former lands were now planted under coffee, joined the revolt that spread southward from Tecoanapa. In the municipio de Azoyú the conflict derived from local cacique's efforts to utilize lands for coffee production: ". . . en el año pasado de 1833, por queja que promovió el

[32] Ibid. AHSRA, Sultepec, Muni. same, ejidal, 25:13996 (725.27), 4 bundles; Zacualpan, Muni. same, communal, 276.1 (2738), 1 bundle; Santiago Texcaltitlán, Muni. Texcaltitlán, ejidal, 25 and 23:2489 (725.2), 5 bundles; Almoloya de Alquisiras, Muni. same, ejidal, 24:11032 (725.2), 2 bundles; Xochitepec, Muni. same, ejidal, 23:3001 (724.10), 6 bundles; and Santa Rosa Treinta (Los Treinta), Muni. Tlaltízapan, ejidal, 23:2988 (724.10), 5 bundles. The SRA determined that this village had lost all of its land prior to 1856. Also see AGN, Junta Protectora de las Clases Menesterosas, Tomo 4, f. 147–49, June 2, 1866, San Bartolome Atlacholoya. ". . . este pueblo se halla despojada de sus tierras y aguas en gran parte desde algunos años a esta fecha por las haciendas de Trienta Pesos, Chiconcuac y del Puente . . . citaremos un decreto del año de 1846 . . . los de la hacienda de Chiconcuac con un tieoteo matando tres hombres"; and, f. 151, Alpuyeca and Xochitepec: "desde por principios del siglo décimo sexto. . . . les ha traido muchos males sufriendo sus pueblos. . . . muchos despojos. . . . sin poderles resistir por la carencia de los títulos."

pueblo de Huehuetán y su cacica, doña Ambrosia de Vargas, contra el común. . . . de Azoyú . . . sucediendose las desgracias y los horrores de la guerra hasta la fecha 1835 . . ." But new disputes broke out in 1841 related to the "Ley de 8 febrero 1832." A process of land consolidation was underway recreating the holdings of the hacienda de Copala, pitting the ambitious mestiza cacique against Indian communes. Ambrosia de Vargas' holdings extended from Azoyú territory to those of San Nicolás Cuajiniquilapa, forty kilometers away. Violence became the norm in the region. Land disputes have continued since independence between Azoyú and San Nicolás Cuajiniquilapa; between 1919 and 1925 the Secretaría de Reforma Agraria reported 134 campesino deaths at the hands of the estate's vaqueros.[33]

The most important southern rebellion centered on the Pacific side of the isthmus of Tehuantepec in Oaxaca southeastward into northern Chiapas.[34] There, Esteban Marueo, owner and operator of the enormous La Marquesana hacienda complex, marketed coffee, cotton, cacao, tobacco, and other commercial crops. The estate originally was part of the Marquesado del Valle. During the uprisings of the early 1830s, Tlalixtac defended its pueblo rights with petitions in 1832 and 1835. Tomaltepec appealed to the supreme court in 1823.

The beginnings of the estate originated from a sitio de ganado mayor issued in 1584. In 1707 Ixtepec fought with "transgressors" from the hacienda over lands, but it was already surrounded by estates and the lands of other pueblos. In 1828, 1829, 1834, and 1835 Tomaltepec pleaded for the return of despoiled lands: "nuestro pueblo desde tiempo immemorial . . . hemos . . . posesión de un sitio de ganado menor y un merced." Violence erupted in 1811, 1813, and 1830. Marueo exploited differences between the pueblos to gain lands in 1821–32, aided by enabling legislation passed in 1828. The pueblos fought back, but were defeated.

On May 23 and 24, 1842 the Juéz in nearby Juchitán "celebrated" new mojonera positions between the hacienda and the Zapotec pueblos of Tlalixtac, Ixtepec, Ixtaltepec, and Chihuitán, among others. By then the estate occupied at least 61 kilometers of the trans-isthmian road, and extended over one hundred kilometers

---

[33] Tornel, *Memoria de Guerra*, p. 55; Reina, *Rebeliones campesinas*, pp. 85–120, 233–34; and AHSRA, Sala Estatal, Chilpancingo, Guerrero, Azoyú, Muni. Azoyú, ejidal, 23:10139 (723.6), 9 bundles.

[34] Reina, *Rebeliones campesinas*, pp. 233–34; Meyer, *Problemas campesinas*, pp. 10–11.

south into the state of Chipas, and had completely enveloped the cabecerra of Santa Maria Chimalapa and others. Some settlements had already been reduced to de facto ranchería status, yet continued to claim pueblo rights. Between 1842 and 1844 a full-scale war broke out that ended with the total defeat of the pueblos by the Mexican army. Marueo further extended his holdings, reducing many of the rebellious pueblos' landholdings even further. By 1862 most had been reduced to their residential territories and a small adjacent field.[35]

Only the macroeconomic market forces of the international coffee economy seemed to have an effect on this hacendado family. In 1904 Julian Marueo sold 21,964 hectares to a consortium of "small holders" despite the protests of the residual, but still resisting commune of Almoloya.

In 1980 the power of the owner of this estate was great enough to have delayed land redistribution during the last two presidential terms through court actions, despite the orders of national presidents that "dotación" take place. The owners are high-ranking members of Mexican society. Their names and further hacienda and town records are not available at this time through government agencies.[36]

Conclusion

The growth of commercial agriculture via the expansion of great estates and political rivalries between regional elites and the national government led to the 1840s southwestern peasants' war. The rebellious regional elites, led by the liberal caudillo of Acapulco, Juan Alvarez, called upon and received the support of village leaders over a wide area of southern and south-central Guerrero, because of local economic and political contradictions that spilled over into adjacent areas. The government's inability to rule was rooted in elite division and a highly restricted level of political participation.

As a result of elite divisiveness, local military superiority was lost and the peasants were only defeated after troops brought in from far removed areas of the nation caused heavy casualties and extreme

[35] AHSRA, Sala Estatal, Oaxaca, Ixtaltepec, Muni. same, communal, 276.1/776, 5 bundles; Almoloya, Muni. El Barrio de la Soledad, communal, 276.1/1959, 2 bundles; Santo Domingo Chihuitán, Muni. same, communal, 276.1/298, 5 bundles; Ixtepec, Muni. same, communal, 276.1/298 (723.7), 2 bundles; Santiago Ixtáltepec, Muni. Ixtáltepec, communal, 276.1/215, 1 bundle; Santo Domingo Tomáltepec, communal and ejidal, 276.1/216, 8 bundles; and San Pedro Pochutla, Muni. Putla de Guerrero, communal, 276.1/2328, 9 bundles.

[36] Interview with Jasso Herrera, August 7–8, 1980.

privation after many years of fighting. The crucial role of elite paralysis is seen in the fact that progress toward a restoration of order was only made after President Antonio Lopez de Santa Anna obtained the cooperation of the caudillo of Acapulco. That aid was obtained because of peasant threats to his holdings and those of his allies and the political concessions made by Nicolas Bravo of Chilpancingo and the national government.

Forces that worked against successful peasant revolutions appear once again as universals. The limited horizons of the uprisings led to fragmented and uncoordinated violence. The great fear associated with the redrawing of state lines led to the pursuit of only limited, locally realizable goals. Peasant demobilizations immediately followed the conciliation of individual village versus hacienda disputes. Promises regarding contested political jurisdictions and minor wage adjustments satisfied other rebel contingents. Sometimes the promise of arbitration caused disarmament. Poor communications, geography and ethnocultural differences isolated areas, so that word of rebellion often reached towns beyond the sierra Guerrero only after peace had been restored at its point of origin. Shortages of arms and supplies, combined with the need for planting and harvesting, mandated short, interrupted campaigns to create a pattern of seemingly recurrent rebellion. An example of the sporadic nature of the peasant's war was Ayahualulco's belated and naive realization that promises of land had been broken by the hacendados.

Government repression worked its usual wonders in bringing the rebellion to a close. But the government's efforts were inhibited by the military prowess and dissident–liberal alliances of Alvarez. He required diplomatic treatment from Santa Anna and Bravo in order to forestall civil war. Alvarez still only entered the struggle decisively when his properties and those of his allies were threatened by the peasants. He consolidated his military position against the national regime even further during the 1847 American invasion.

Mexico's defeat in the war with the U.S. served as another classic precipitator of revolution. With a weakened national government, Alvarez's improved position in the coastal periphery now became strategic. In 1853 he launched the successful Ayutla revolution that toppled the national regime. Ayutla, the former Tlapaneca cabecerra in the Costa Chica, was in the heart of the 1842 Tecoanapa rebellion zone. By offering the village the scenario of decentralized government offered by federalism and the civil liberties of liberalism, Alvarez gained a solid following.[37]

[37] For discussion of Alvarez and his relationship with peasant communities see

In 1842–45 a sense of deprivation and desperation pervaded the rural population in the south. They had fought long and hard during the independence struggle to realize a new, more just order. But an era of landowner rule followed ten years of war and marauding armies. The domestic economy lagged for years while commercial estates committed to export agriculture recouped losses incurred during the village risings of the independence wars. Political reorganizations were carried out to the detriment of indigenous cabecerras and to the advantage of Europeanized elites connected to Mexico City. Then the land grabbing began, aided by legislation from the state governments, and the villages sought allies wherever they could find them.

Provincial elites in Mexico developed over an extended period of time into semi-autonomous political groups. Repeatedly, throughout the nineteenth century, they resisted the attempts by the authorities of Mexico City to impose the centralized power. Local elite dissent was an important element in the upheavals in the Bajío and southwest in the 1810s, again in the southwest and Yucatán in the 1830s and 1840s, in the west and near north in the 1850s and 1870s, and in the far north after 1900. The pattern of resistance paralleled the movement northward from Tehuantepec–Yucatán of externally controlled commercial agriculture, livestock, and mineral production during the nineteenth century. The new outside capitalists and increasingly intrusive national governments frequently displaced the local elites from political and economic power while depriving the campesinos of what they regarded as their land.

When Alvarez, the peasant villagers' principal ally in the provincial elite, warned the people of Tecoanapa or Ayahualulco that they were about to lose their patrimony, they rebelled. Alvarez was a hacendado, but he was their hacendado, a sometimes defender of traditional village rights. In areas such as Sultepec, southern Morelos, coastal Oaxaca, the isthmus of Tehuantepec and the Balsas River basin where regional elite support was lacking, peasant defeat was definitive. Entire villages, including pre-Columbian sites such as Xochicalco were dispersed, leaving the survivors of the southwest demoralized and intimidated.

Meyer, *Problemas campesinas*, pp. 59–61, 120–24; Miguel Mejía Fernandez, *Política agraria en México en el siglo* XIX (México, 1979), pp. 130–34; and Reina, *Rebeliones campesinas*, pp. 90–92.

CHAPTER NINE

The Sierra Gorda
Peasant Rebellion, 1847–50

Leticia Reina[1]

The Sierra Gorda rebellion of 1847–50 was quite different from other movements in the center and south of Mexico. It was set in a little-known region overlapping the states of Guanajuato, Querétaro, and San Luis Potosí. The historiography of the region is limited, partial, and fragmented. Although histories of the three states do exist, they scarcely mention the Sierra Gorda; neither do they consider the Sierra Gorda a region with a defined ecology and history of its own. Thus it is necessary to describe some aspects of the regional process to introduce the study of the peasant movement that arose here.

Natural Resources and Rebellions

Today the Sierra Gorda is an underpopulated, arid, and peaceful region, but in the past, its mountains offered abundant natural riches that attracted large numbers of people and stimulated considerable economic activity; the area became the scene of great conflict. Its forests contained a wide variety of trees: red and black evergreen oak, brush oak, oak, huayamel pine, canil cedar, quirámboro, red ebony tree, coral wood, Havana cedar, walnut, muleberry, brazilwood, and many others. The waterfalls and rivers permitted the growth of fruit trees appropriate to the many climatic zones of the

[1] My thanks to the Instituto Nacional de Antropología e Historia for the support it has given me as an investigator of the Institute. I wish to thank the Consejo Nacional de Ciencia y Tecnología for the financial assistance that made it possible to consult regional archives. I also wish to express my gratitude to Dr. Friedrich Katz for the careful reading he has given the article. Thanks must also go to my sister Patricia for her patience in correcting and typing the manuscript.

plains and valleys. At the same time, the soil was fertile, allowing the development of an abundant and varied agriculture. In the mountains, silver, gold, tin, and other minerals such as cinnabar, silver, copper, lead, and red ochre were found.[2]

During the nineteenth century, the rough terrain and the natural wealth of the mountains also provided a stage for individuals opposed to the established order. It became the hideaway for bandits, army deserters, caciques in rebellion against the government, as well as socialists challenging the political system. The struggles that unfolded there for and against the state always had the peasant movements as a backdrop.

In the late preclassical period, about 800 to 200 B.C., the inhabitants of the Sierra Gorda mined the region's minerals. From artifacts dating from this period, we can infer that the inhabitants were semi-nomads who alternated between agriculture and mining according to the season. The latter acquired importance because mining permitted commerce with the Olmecs who, in turn, traded the cinnabar of the Sierra Gorda as far away as Tabasco.

The great variety and specialization of the mining utensils found in the region seem to have been associated with ceremonial centers. Many mine entrances served as cemeteries, and in tombs, beside the remains, offerings of cinnabar and natural mercury have been found. Cinnabar, because of its red color, may have been related to blood and therefore to life, and was kept in receptacles, or be used for body decoration. The symbolic importance of mercury, a heavy, liquid mineral "whose surface can form the most perfect and ephemeral mirrors,"[3] is unknown.

All mining activities and the growth of towns that thrived in the area appear to have ceased by the tenth century A.D. Exact reasons are not known, but may have resulted from the constant invasions by semi-nomadic Chichimec groups, who forced these communities to abandon their fertile land to seek refuge among the "civilized peoples" of Mesoamerica. According to historiographers of the colo-

[2] The geographical descriptions of the region are taken from García Cubas, *Diccionario geográfico, histórico y biográfico de los Estados Unidos Mexicanos* (México: Antigua Imprenta de Murguía, 1889).

[3] Adolfo Langenscheidt and Carlos Tan Lay, "La minería prehispánica en la Sierra Gorda," in *Problemas del desarrollo histórico de Querétaro 1531–1981*. The authors state, "we hypothesize that the exploitation of mines in the Sierra Gorda was carried out, first by the Olmecs by the fourth century B.C. and later by the peoples culturally affiliated with Teotihuacan and Central Veracruz, possibly receiving some influence from Toltec and Huasteca affiliated peoples at a later date."

nial period, they migrated south where they found societies that conquered and dominated them with ease.

The invading Chichimec groups may have repopulated the Sierra Gorda, sustaining themselves as hunters and gatherers, and by the early sixteenth century they too were exploiting the minerals.

The Conquest

With the assistance of the Indian Conín, baptized don Fernando de Tapia, the Spanish conquerors advanced north to the site of the city of Querétaro. This indigenous cacique achieved the surrender of several Otomí towns by means of an alliance between the caciques of Tula and Tepeji, who in turn were supported by Tarascan and Hauchichile armies. Soon after the conquest, Augustinian missionaries arrived to carry out their evangelical work, and in the seventeenth century the Spaniards took over the mines and began systematic exploitation. At the same time, they founded *alcaldías* (mayoralties) such as Cademeyta, Tolimán, and Escanela.

In the early sixteenth century the Pame and Jonas Indians were dedicated to mining, mainly for ritual reasons. The destinations of their excess output are unknown, but it is possible that some was traded and that some was destined as tribute for the Aztecs.[4] They also practiced agriculture, around which they had developed a series of rituals. Agricultural products were complemented by the many fruits that grew in the various climatic zones of the region.

The inhabitants of the region were semi-nomadic; social cohesion was thus maintained not by the possession and distribution of land, but rather in the sense that they belonged to a territory in which they moved freely, shifting the places where they sold their labor.

The peoples of the Sierra Gorda strongly resisted Spanish domination, but the majority of the Chichimec tribes were exterminated. Only the Pame and Jonas Indians surrendered, and the Jonases continued their struggle during the eighteenth and nineteenth centuries for the right to exploit the forests, if not the land. In the early eighteenth century, it was thought that the region had been pacified, but a historian has noted that in 1704, "the great Indian rebellion started

---

[4] Rafael Roa Torres, *Historia del mineral de San Joaquín Ranas* (Querétaro: Imprenta del Estado de Querétaro, 1979); Francisco Pimentel, *Obras completas* (México: Tipográfico Económico, 1903) vol. 2, p. 415. Pimentel affirms that the "Pames formerly adored Monctezuma, to whom they had been subject for many years; they venerated him like a deity." From this reference one may infer that tribute was paid to the Aztecs.

and all those establishments [the mines and *alcaldías*] were swept away . . . and every day barbarity gained ground at the expense of civilization."[5]

A series of military campaigns failed to put down the rebellion, but finally the rebels of the Sierra Gorda were defeated by José Escandón, colonel of the regiment of Querétaro and the first count of the Sierra Gorda. The necessity for military repression made the failure of the Augustinian missions imminent, and they were replaced by the Franciscans. The viceroy, Juan Francisco Güemes (reigned 1746–55), ordered the founding of sixty missions in the Sierra, three to the Colegio de Pachuca and fifty-seven to the Colegio de San Fernando de México. Fray Junípero Serra, the Spanish Franciscan later known as the "apostle of California," was named president of the latter missions. Serra stayed in the region for just twelve years (1750–62), after which time he continued his mission in Baja California.

Serra and Escandón worked together to introduce important changes in the methods of conquest and colonization, and founded the missions of San Francisco de Tilaco, Nuestra Señora de la Luz de Tancoyal, San Miguel de Landa, Nuestra Señora de Agua de Comcá, and Santiago Jalpan; the latter came to be their center of operations.[6] The originality of their method lay in establishing productive *congregaciones* around the churches, organized for eventual self-sufficiency; they were to be the basis of future towns. He accomplished much; it was said "that his converts were satisfied and came to have five thousand *fanegas* of maize [375,000 kilos] in their warehouses and they had erected five churches."[7]

The northwest of the Sierra Gorda, which today includes northeast Guanajuato and southern San Luis Potosí, was pacified by Colonel Juan Antonio del Castillo y Llata, count of the Sierra Gorda, who founded the mission of la Purísima Concepción. Although he helped financially in the remodeling of several churches and in the construction of the Capuchín monastery in Salvatierra, his main interest lay in exploiting the mineral wealth of Xichú, Arteaga, Río Blanco, and Pinal.[8]

---

[5] Fernando Díaz Ramírez, *Historia del Estado de Querétaro* (Querétaro: Ediciones de Querétaro, 1979) vol. 1.

[6] Possibly, Jalpan is what was called the government of the Sierra Gorda in 1740. Guadalupe Ramírez Alvarez, *Cien años atrás: sitio de Querétaro y triunfo de la república* (Querétaro, 1967).

[7] Díaz Ramírez, *Historia. . . .* vol. 1.

[8] When Colonel Juan Antonio del Castillo y Llata (born in Spain in 1764, died in

With the development of mining, haciendas were founded and the Indians' complaints began. Their land was confiscated, they were forced into different lifestyles, and they were prevented from practicing their traditional customs, such as cutting firewood and timber, burning charcoal, cutting wild lettuce, scraping maguey plants (whose sap was used for medicinal purposes), as well as cutting prickly pears and other wild fruits. They also complained that the haciendas did not permit their cattle to graze on uncultivated monte lands. The Spaniards also took the Indians to their haciendas as prisoners, where they were whipped and their cattle confiscated, the latter to be returned only after ransoms had been paid, and "various priests charged parish fees without providing the corresponding services."[9]

During the colonial period missions and military outposts were founded on the pretext of pacifying the Indians and providing a buffer against barbarian attacks, but the real reason was the area's mineral wealth. The San Juan Nepomuceno mine alone, in the mineral of El Doctor in the Cadereyta district, reportedly generated more than 18 million pesos in viceregal revenues through the quinto.[10] In the mid-nineteenth century, the governent of Guanajuato state requested that a penetentiary be established[11] so that mercury deposits could be exploited using prison labor. During the colonial era the exploitation of this ore, necessary for the mining of precious minerals, had been prohibited. The existence of these minerals in the Sierra Gorda left a characteristic mark on the popular struggles in the region, between two economically powerful groups—the creoles and the peninsulares. The first group wanted to exploit the mercury but ultimately they had to submit to the will of the metropolis, which prohibited the manufacture of all that Spain could produce, such as mercury, wine and wool, products that today have become

Mexico in 1817) arrived in Mexico he began working with his brother, Francisco, as a merchant. Years later, he established himself in the Sierra Gorda to exploit the mines as part of a plan of conquest and devastation. A local historian (possibly a descendant) wrote, "He was misunderstood by the Indians, who mistreated him and stoned him." See Manuel M. de la Llata, Personajes de la historia Queretana, in manuscript, undated.

[9] Moisés González Navarro, Anatomía del poder político en México (1848–1853) (México: El Colegio de México, 1977). p. 39.

[10] Arturo Domínguez Paulín, Querétaro en la conquista de las Californias (México, 1966), pp. 75–76.

[11] Expediente instruido sobre el establecimiento de un presidio en Arteaga, para el laborío de minas de Azogue Protectado por el gobiermo del estado de Guanajuato (Guanajuato: Tipografía de Oriarte, 1848).

important in the state of Querétaro. The crown decreed that it alone had the right to produce mercury and to sell it at high prices in its colonies.

The mines of the Sierra Gorda maintained high production levels of gold, silver, marble, and jadeite, but not of mercury, lead, iron, or cinnabar. Nevertheless, the occasional cyclical crises in Spain permitted their temporary exploitation, such as during the war between Spain and England. Fernando VII, perhaps pressed by circumstances, decreed that mercury could be "freely traded, exempt from all taxes even of the *quinto* or the part which the miner should contribute."[12] Even so, Mexican mercury could not compete in the market with the mercury produced in Almadén, Spain.

In independent Mexico, the struggle for mercury production continued, not with the metropolis but with the commercial monopolies that wanted to guarantee for themselves the sale of Spanish mercury in the former colonies. In 1844 the Junta de Fomento de Minería of Mexico opened the Guadalupe and Victoria mercury mines, but eight months later they were abandoned for lack of funds.[13]

Economic and Demographic Characteristics

The Sierra Gorda is a mountain chain that includes a wide range of climates, from cold mountain peaks 3,500 meters above sea level to hot valleys and plains. This climatic diversity permitted the development of agriculture and cattle ranching, primarily as support services for the mining industry, as were forests, waterfalls, and rivers. Because of its stategic position the region also saw the rise of artisan production and trade using the natural corridor leading to Tampico, along which the region's merchants attempted to establish new routes avoiding traditional roads through Puebla and Veracruz. Such routes allowed them to escape the fiscal burdens of the commercial monopolies. Mining in the Sierra Gorda apparently produced no labor conflict or movements related directly to the extraction of ore.[14] From 1847 to 1857 (years of rebellion in the Sierra Gorda), the output of precious metals from Guanajuato and Querétaro increased, which may explain the miners' lack of involvement in the rebellion.

[12] Ibid., p. 35.

[13] Ibid.; and García Cubas, *Diccionario*, vol. 3–4, p. 172.

[14] No study has yet been done specifically about the miners, but to date no complaints, demands, or protests by them have been found.

The exploitation of timber for use in the mines, in tanning and construction, as well as for domestic uses such as cooking and heating, constituted a primary sector of the region's economy. The 1847 census of the mineral of Santa Anna reveals that out of thirteen occupations, four were dependent on forest products: charcoal producers, tanners, and firewood and lumber dealers; together these made up two-thirds of the total population.[15]

In 1824 charcoal, firewood, and lumber producers complained that the hacendados, "owners of part of the Sierra," exacted payments for the cutting of firewood and for charcoal production, and asked that certain documents executed in 1742 be sought, because they extended permission to cut freely the wood necessary to "supply the mines and maintain the cattle." Demands for the free exploitation of the forests were constant during the first half of the nineteenth century, and the unity and the struggle of the serranos revolved around it. But unlike peasant movements elsewhere, this one did not involve the restitution of land. In the 1824 manuscript, the petitioners accepted the fact that in 1742 they were forbidden to cultivate land unless they did so "by special agreement with the owners of the Sierra." This required those who did not work in the mines or on haciendas to become tenant farmers.[16]

While the indigenous communities of central and southern Mexico also fought for their forests, in the Sierra Gorda the struggle to defend forest exploitation was a primary concern, since to the serranos the forest was the source of their livelihoods. As the nineteenth century approached, there were still remnants of traditional pre-Hispanic communities, such as the Jonas and Pame Indians, who before restictions were placed upon planting, lived by exploiting and selling forest products, and the income helped pay the rental on the land they cultivated. Such was the origin of the tenant farmers of the Sierra who were often the dynamic sectors of the peasant rebellions. Ranchos were the most common settlements in late nineteenth-century records, followed by minerals, haciendas,

[15] Archivo histórico de Guanajuato de la Universidad de Guanajuato (hereafter AHG-UG), *Padrón de todos los hombres vecinos del mineral de Santa Ana, con los ranchos pertenecientes a su jurisdicción*, 1847. The breakdown is as follows: two cobblers, 61 laborers (*operarios*), two masons, two blacksmiths, nine muleteers, 119 charcoal makers, and ten lumber dealers. The census records a total of 357 inhabitants, 225 of whom made their living from forest products.

[16] AHG-UG, legajo Sierra de Guanajuato, documento manuscrito de los Leñadores, Carboneros, y Madereros enviado al gobierno del estado de Guanajuato, Firmado en 1824.

congregaciones, and pueblos. Pueblos were few in number, and even nonexistent in some municipalities because before the arrival of the Spaniards, the indigenous population had not settled in agricultural towns as in the rest of Mesoamerica. Population statistics for the Sierra Gorda in the 1840's have not yet been reconstructed, but it is possible that there were roughly equal numbers of tenant farmers and peons, since there were more ranchos than pueblos, the ranchos were widely dispersed and must have had few residents. The contrary was the case with the haciendas, which supported large numbers of peons, who were tied to the mines.

Away from the heart of the Sierra Gorda (Xichú in Guanajuato and Jalpan in Querétaro were mountainous areas in which there were two rebellions in the nineteenth century) toward the south the settlement type changed. Population density increased because of the large number of haciendas, although Indian tribes such as the Nahuas and the Otomís were able to subsist on their communal land. Agricultural and cattle production supported the mines and supplied artisan centers and factories of the cities of Guanajuato and Querétaro.[17] In the north of the Sierra Gorda, on the other hand, the population density was relatively low, since there were few haciendas, and more Indian communities were able to survive.

The Sierra Gorda Rebellion

In 1844 the peasants of Río Grande, Xichú, rose up against the authorities, protesting the military draft (leva) and the direct taxes that had been imposed to finance the war with the United States. The war exposed the contradictions among the different groups in power. Military coups were common, army units deserted; and rejected army commanders became military dissidents. This political situation precipitated the peasant rebellion of 1847–50 in the Sierra Gorda.

The war also encouraged, beginning in 1846, an uninterrupted arms trade throughout the cordillera. The North Americans who occupied Tampico sold cheap arms to the serranos, who rebelled in ever greater numbers because the invasion began to affect agricul-

---

[17] The Cadereyta region had high grain yields for the period. Curiously, agricultural production during the 1880s was greater than that of today; it is now considered an arid zone where yields do not even reach subsistence levels. García Cubas, *Diccionario*, and *Problemas del desarrollo histórico de Querétaro 1531–1981* (Querétaro, 1981).

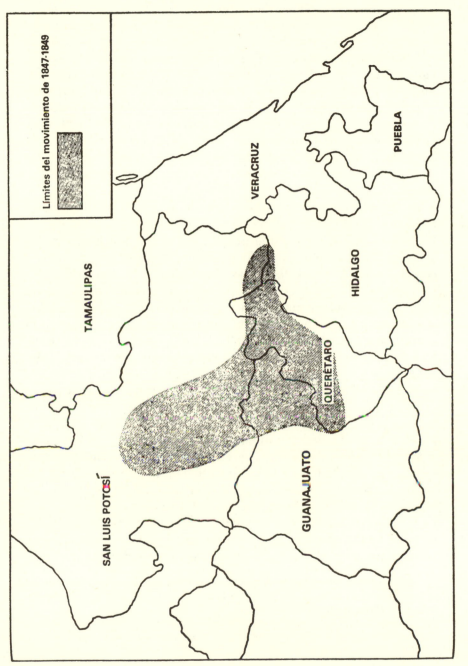

Figure 9.1. The Sierra Gorda rebellion. Limits of the movement in 1847–1849. Source: Leticia Reina, *Las rebeliones campesinas en México, 1819–1906* (Mexico: Siglo xxi Editores, 1980), p. 299.

tural production.[18] To sustain the war, the states of Querétaro, Puebla, and Mexico decreed the occupation of mortmain property, meaning that the government was authorized to sell the lands of the corporations, including the Indians' communal lands. The law of January 1847 authorized the government of Querétaro to dispose of up to 15 million pesos' worth of such properties.[19] The *Otomí* communities reacted by gathering in the state capital to protest, and in "considerable masses" they attacked government guards with fists, clubs, stones, and some firearms. But after three hours they were dispersed fairly easily, since both the governor and the *comandante general* of Querétaro were prepared, having anticipated the Indians' reaction.[20]

The central government asked the state of Querétaro to convince the Otomís of the justice of the law, because at the time the state had to raise money to finance the troops fighting the North Americans and that the only way to obtain the money was through the sale of communal land to private parties. Additionally, the army had neither men nor the resources to suppress the outbreaks. The dominant groups in Querétaro agreed that the people should be persuaded that the congress had issued the law "out of the pressing obligation of the nation to carry out a war with the United States to save the priceless asset of independence."[21] The strategy was unsuccessful, and among the Indians in the affected communities violence broke out everywhere. According to the state, the law was not understood.

The protests of the Otomís, Nahuas, and Totonacos of the Huasteca Veracruzana were echoed by an opposition political group that knew how to channel the Indian uprisings that were becoming so common in the Sierra Gorda. Tomás Mejía, an officer from Querétaro who some months before had helped defend Monterrey against the North Americans and sixteen years later would fight to defend the empire of Maximilian, joined the cause. Mejía provided another outlet for struggle for the discontented Indians and for a group of officers and civil authorities of a wide region who disagreed politically with the national government, which was now confined to the north

---

[18] Archivo Histórico del Estado de San Luis Potosí (hereafter AHESLP), Sección: Secretaría General de Gobierno. Ramo: Poder Legislativo, Decreto del Congreso del Estado, 6 de febrero de 1848.

[19] Archivo Histórico de la Secretaría de la Defensa Nacional (hereafter AHSDN), Exp. XI/481.3/2337. Cartas del Comandante General de Querétaro. Enero de 1847.

[20] Ibid.

[21] Ibid.

of Querétaro, and part of the states of San Luis Potosí, Hidalgo, and Puebla.[22]

On June 4, 1848, the organization of the movement began in the Real de San José de los Amoles, Jalpan, in the state of Querétaro. Representatives of the dissident army group gathered, along with *alcaldes* and prosecutors (*síndicos procuradores*) representing the regional civil authorities. Together with the peasants they signed a pledge that consolidated them as a group: "Motivated by the prudent considerations required by the interests of the people . . . for this cause I have proposed to invite the honorable gentlemen to proclaim a deliverance that can save us from the state of oppression caused by the onerous taxes of all kinds that have been rigorously demanded of us." Taking as their slogan, "Liberty and War on the Invader," they withdrew their recognition of the government, demanded war without pause against the U.S. invaders while on Mexican soil, punishment and expropriation for those who opposed the plan, and for all taxes to be rescinded.[23] This plan thus made possible a class alliance against the central government. Although Tomás Mejía and other signatories—who included peasants—did not commit themselves in writing with regard to the agrarian problem, it is probable that they did so orally as they traveled through the Sierra Gorda region. Otherwise, the support they found among the Indian pueblos of San Luis Potosí, Sierra de Hidalgo, and Puebla could not be explained.

On July 13 the Indian pueblos of the state of Hidalgo joined the rebellion in spite of the army's efforts to prevent it. In other neighboring areas the same phenomenon occurred, so that the movement extended as far as Huachinango in Puebla, to Tamazunchale in San Luis Potosí, and Huejutla in Hidalgo.[24] In fact the social base for the opposition group was made up fundamentally of Indians—the Otomí, Nahua, and Totonaca communities that struggled to recover their lands—forced the movement beyond Mejía's objectives. Without being aware of it, these Indians were defending the national territory by defending their own lands, just as Melchor Ocampo had proposed or as had occurred in Veracruz, Morelos, and Guerrero.

On August 13, 1848, President José Joaquín Herrera extended a

[22] AHSDN, Exp. XI/481.3/2830

[23] AHSDN, Exp. XI/481.3/2827. The act is reproduced in full in Leticia Reina, *Las rebeliones campesinas en México (1819–1906)* (México: Siglo XXI, 1980), pp. 292–93.

[24] Ibid.

pardon to the rebel Indians,[25] thus pacifying tribal areas. Mejía also requested a pardon and a guarantee that he would retain his position. President Herrera authorized the governor of Querétaro to settle the case and the latter passed it on to the military authorities, since it dealt with an army officer. The pardon was granted and Mejía reappeared in 1849 in the Sierra Gorda to repress the movement led by Eleuterio Quiróz.

Quiróz, leader of the serranos, was well aware of the injustices of the system. His rebelliousness brought him in conflict with authority and circumstances radicalized him to the point where be became the leader of the oppressed. As a muleteer on the hacienda of Tapanco, in San Luis Potosí, Quiróz had confronted and had been punished by the hacendado. He escaped, went into hiding in Arteaga, and was soon recruited into the army. While the unit fought the U.S. invaders, Quiróz deserted and fled to the mountains of Xichú. Don Miguel Chaire, an hacendado and auxiliary commander of the *mineral* of Xichú—who later pronounced himself in favor of the Americans—protected Quiróz and employed him as a laborer on one of his *fincas*.

In Xichú, in August 1847, Francisco Chaire, the son of don Miguel, deserted from the national guard. The San Luis Potosí authorities asked the *alcalde* of Xichú to apprehend the deserter and send him to San Luis to be punished. Don Miguel, overwhelmed by the duties on his embargoed properties (because of the slump in the tobacco business) and the loss of prestige, gathered a band of men to liberate his son. Among them was Quiróz, who had been attacking *alcaldes* in the area and robbing merchants.

The sixty men in Chaire's group were auxiliary soldiers and peons who worked for him on his properties. They took other men from jail, and armed them with guns stolen from the army. They declared themselves supporters of the Americans, and invited the peoples of the Sierra to rise up behind the Americans. Their declining fortunes made them confront the national system and create alliances with foreign troops and the "indios" who, as the press commented, "had always been scorned because of their color and customs."[26]

The Chaires, having nothing to lose after the embargo of their properties, offered the peons, soldiers, and ex-prisoners who joined them "the free use of the vacant lands and the wood of the Sierra,

[25] "Informe del General José Joaquín Herrera, Presidente de México en 1848," in *Los presidentes de México ante la nación, 1821–1966* (México: Editado por la Cámara de Diputados, 1966), p. 359.

[26] AHSDN, Exp. XI/481.3/2855.

and to all the masses the division of the haciendas, exemption from all types of taxes, the abolition of the military draft, the end of parish fees and the expropriation of all the followers of the government." With such promises they gathered a social force to rise up in favor of the Americans. A journalist wrote: "That was the day of disgrace for Xichú and the beginning of so many tragic days which hundreds of the families of the states of Guanajuato, San Luis Potosí, and Querétaro have bitterly mourned."[27]

The government of Guanajuato immediately offered to pardon the inhabitants of the Sierra in order to pacify them. The Chaire family took advantage of it, while Quiróz could do nothing since he was a deserter. There may have been others in the same situation, since a band of men quickly formed under Alvarado. Alvarado soon quit, however, leaving Quiróz in charge of the group, which he used to defend himself from the authorities who were pursuing him. For some serranos he represented the alternative of vengeance.

Just as some groups in power came out in favor of the North Americans, others took the opposite direction. In order to sustain the war against the United States, some hacendados in San Luis Potosí sent grain to maintain the troops, while others, such as Pablo Verástegui, owner of the hacienda of San Diego and other fincas in the Río Verde district, in the midst of development and expansion, organized the territory against the United States. Verástegui "offered his person and part of his wealth. To those who enlisted, the rent of their house and animals would be forgiven for the duration of the war, and to their families would be given each week two almudes of corn and a cuarterón of beans; to he who brought a horse, saddle, and arms, would be paid the value of whatever of these things were lost in service; to the family of the crippled or wounded in action, would be assigned a pension fixed in accord with the circumstances; and to all who distinguised themselves by their bravery and heroic action would be given a lifetime compensation in oxen and tierra de sembradura, in order to assure him the relief he deserved."[28] This signified the voluntary incorporation of peasants in the defense of the country.

On June 7, 1847, on the recommendation of the governor and ha-

[27] Hemeroteca Nacional (hereafter HN), El Siglo XIX, "Remitido," May 12, 1849. The biographical data on Quiróz and his participation in the pronunciamento of the Chaire family are taken from this periodical.

[28] AHESLP, Sección Secretaría General de Gobierno, Ramo: Gobernación, Cartas del mes de noviembre de 1847; Primo Feliciano Velázquez, Historias de San Luis Potosí (Mexico: Sociedad Mexicana de Estadísticas, 1946, 4 vols.).

cendado Ramón Adame, the state legislature of San Luis Potosí sent a letter to the government requesting that the national cause not be abandoned. It also "protested against any peace treaty that did not assure the independence, territorial integrity, and the honor of the nation and its arms," and warned that if any power or authority of the nation signed a peace treaty, the act would be rejected and both the signatories and the foreigners would be attacked.[29]

Meanwhile, his desertion obliged Quiróz to maintain an open and constant struggle against all forms of authority. It was said that Quiróz was an ignorant and rude man, but crafty and audacious in his resentment of the authorities; every day he became more obliged to seek forms of defense. His alternative was collective defense and soon he fortified himself with the help of the people of his native Sierra. Nevertheless, just before the peace treaties were signed, Quiróz sent an emissary to Mexico, offering his services against the North Americans, but the proposition was rejected by the government, perhaps because his strength was considered insignificant. From this moment, Quiróz became leader of a group of bandits who in December 1847 embarked on a series of crimes against the elite class of the region, beginning with the assassinations of Col. Villa and the alcaldes of Arteaga, Palmillos, Nogalito, and others. The bandits forced the hacendado Fernando Pérez to witness the rape of his daughters, and they cut off the arms of the hacendado Alejo Urías before killing him. These were the product of hatred, injustice, and oppression.

No force could stop the group, since it had moved into the heart of the Sierra (Xichú in Guanajuato and Jalpan in Querétaro), which offered the greatest safety due to its ruggedness.

The Popular Movement

What was at first a group of social bandits soon became a social movement. Quiróz and his men found sympathy and support among the people who were oppressed by heavy taxes, parish fees, tobacco monopolies, and the military draft. As peon and hacienda laborer, Quiróz knew well the living conditions of the hacienda peons and tenant farmers of the ranchos, with whom he identified and to whom he offered freedom from overtime work, regulated rents, the elimination of the system of dividing land for profit, and land reform. The first to join Quiróz were the tenant farmers of the ha-

[29] Ibid., p. 224.

cienda of Albercas, who were displeased with José González Cosío, native of Querétaro. He had imposed systems of control that became more onerous every day. Other workers from ranchos and haciendas followed them.

The remaining federal forces in San Luis de la Paz, Guanajuato, and the national guard in San Luis Potosí, which operated in Río Verde, could defend only the most important cities, and observe the rebels' movements in the rest of the region and report on them.[30] During the period of intervention, the contradictions within the regional and/or national power groups were sharpened in such a way that they began a series of coups d'etat, with different presidents, and military *pronunciamientos* in which different factions of the dominant classes assisted one or the other in the midst of the international conflict. On September 14, 1847, the government of Mexico moved to the state of Querétaro because Mexico City was taken by U.S. troops.[31] Faced with the climax of the nationwide peasant movement, derived from the internal contradictions and the effects of the international conflict, the government's only alternative was to accelerate the peace treaties before losing its property and power.

With the celebrations of the treaties of Guadalupe Hidalgo, various factions of the group in power declared themselves against them. Government officials protested and military officers took up arms, some in the Sierra Gorda; for example, the governor of San Luis Potosí disavowed the government for having signed a treaty "without requiring the previous withdrawal of the occupying forces." For this reason on February 6, 1848, the duties of the governor and his deputy were suspended and Julián de los Reyes was named provisional governor.[32]

Another instance of a *pronunciamiento* was that of General Mariano Paredes y Arrillaga, who had been president in 1846. After a period of exile he returned to offer his services against the U.S. invaders; the government not only refused to accept the offer, but tried to prevent him from returning abroad.[33] Paredes denounced the trea-

---

[30] AHESLP, Sección: Secretaría de Gobierno, Ramo: Guerra, Cartas del Inspector General de Guardia Nacional de San Luis Potosí, de los meses de enero, febrero, marzo, abril, mayo, junio y julio describiendo todos los movimientos y ataques de los serranos.

[31] Fernando Díaz Reyes Retana, *Vida militar y política del Sr. Gral. de division don Leonardo Márquiz Araujo* (Querétaro, 1978), p. 21; and HN, *El Siglo* XIX, "Remitido," May 12, 1849.

[32] AHESLP, Sección: Secretaría General de Gobierno, Ramo: Poder Legislativo, Decreto del Congreso del Estado, 6 de febrero de 1848.

[33] Díaz Reyes Retana, *Vida.*

ties, and the rebels in the mountains initiated talks to join his movement. On October 15, 1848, a proclamation appeared in Xichú that
was signed by the "Most excellent General in Chief of the First Section of the Regenerating Army of Liberty and Constitutional Independence, Don Mariano Paredes y Arrillaga, or by he who seconds
his voice, General Don Eleuterio Quiróz." The proclamation contained twelve articles that proposed opposition to the treaties, maintenance of the Catholic religion, opposition to the sale of territory,
confiscation of the property of those who supported such a sale, defense of the federal system, opposition to forcing the dispossessed
to lend their resources, respect for those who may do so, execution
of those who allowed themselves to be bribed, respect for the authorities whom they elected, respect for private property, and the
banning of communication between leaders.[34]

The plan amounted to an alliance between a group of dissident
officers and the rebels who were fighting to keep their freedom, but
the alliance did not last long because the plan only represented the
interests of a fraction of the dominant class. It not only demanded
respect for private property, but it failed to incorporate any of the
demands for which the peons, day-laborers, and tenants had risen
in arms. The alliance fell apart because the social movement exceeded the interests of its leaders, and especially because Paredes
withdrew from the leadership, realizing that it was impossible to
militarily control such "rabble." They attacked the haciendas of
Saucedo and Noria de Alday, going as far as Chichimequillas, Buenavista, and Jofre. In the midst of the repression, some of Paredes'
officers went to Guanajuato where one group supported Father Ja-
rauta and others the serranos.[35]

Eleuterio Quiróz knew how to handle guns, knew the terrain, and
had full control over the people who followed him. He reorganized
his men to form a guerrilla basis for resistance. General Anastasio
Bustamante ordered Captain Tomás Mejía to put down the peasants
in the Sierra Gorda. A year before, Mejía had formed and headed the
uprising in the area bordering the Sierra.[36]

[34] AHESLP, Sección: Secretaría General de Gobierno, Ramo: Guerra, Proclama del
General Mario Paredes y Arrillaga y Eleuterio Quiróz, firmado en Xichú el 15 de oc-
tubre de 1848. The proclamation can also be found in Nereo Rodríguez Barragán, *El
canónigo Mauricio Zavala, apostol del agrarismo en el valle del maíz* (San Luis Potosí: Sociedad Potosina de Estudios Históricos, 1972), pp. 18–19.

[35] Ibid., p. 20. HN, *El Monitor Republicano*, January 17, 22, 1849. HN, *El Siglo* xix,
Mexico, February 17, 18, 19, 22, 1849; this periodical contains news of various uprisings in different communities.

[36] AHSDN, Exp. XI/481.3/2855. HN, *El Monitor Republicano*, January 5, 1849, *El
Siglo* xix, February 26, 1849.

Federal troops could not control the rebellion because they had to divide their resources: some against the *campesinos–serranos*, and others against the pronunciamiento of General Leonardo Márquez, who set troops under his command against the constitutional government.[37] He signed a declaration on February 11, 1849, in favor of Santa Anna and against José Joaquín Herrera (the sixth president during this period) who was carrying out a series of liberal reforms.[38] State employees in San Luis Potosí complained because for some time much of their salaries had been sent to the forces suppressing the rebel movements. Hence, because it lacked sufficient funds, the state asked the military authorities to withdraw the troops from the Sierra. Then the authorities of the department of Río Verde turned in desperation to the hacendados, merchants, and manufacturers for help in maintaining an active regiment to protect the area, since it was known that Quiróz and his people were heading there.[39]

Meanwhile, the peasants continued to advance and defeated federal forces at the hacienda of Jabalí, clearing the way to Ciudad Fernández. Army chiefs such as Valentín Cruz argued that the defeat was due to the troops' lack of precaution and vigilance rather than to the peasants' numerical superiority.[40] The peasants' victory was largely due to the guerrillas' tactics in mountainous areas. Military leaders had some reason to fault their own troops, since the peasants skillfully utilized surprise attacks, hitting the army when it was disorganized, and then dispersing into the mountains.[41]

In this way the rebels advanced until they took the city of Río Verde, an occupation that worried the authorities a great deal: "Río Verde is one of the principal towns of the state, surrounded by well populated haciendas and sedition could increase greatly." This observation was correct, since despite the fact that the state legislature of Guanajuato had granted a general amnesty to the rebels as a political measure to establish peace, the rebels not only did not take advantage of the amnesty but took Río Verde and San Luis Potosí, where the huasteca peasants of the area joined them.[42]

On March 14, 1849, Quiróz proclaimed the "Political and Eminently Social Plan of the Regenerating Army of the Sierra Gorda,"[43]

---

[37] HN, *El Monitor Republicano*, January 5, 1849. *El Siglo* XIX, February 26, 1849.

[38] *Boletín de la Secretaría de Gobernación* (Mexico, 1952), pp. 438–39.

[39] HN, *El Siglo* XIX, March 6, 1849.

[40] HN, *El Siglo* XIX, March 19, 1849.

[41] AHSDN, Exp. XI/481.3/2855 from a series of military documents from March, 1849.

[42] HN, *El Siglo* XIX, "Xichú," March 10, 22, 1849.

[43] HN, "Plan político y eminentement social," *El Siglo* XIX, March 30, 1849. Gastón

which signified the alliance of the peasants and a regional power group. On the one hand, it wanted to resolve the peasant problem by transforming the haciendas of more than 1,500 peons into pueblos, cutting the tenants' rents, dividing uncultivated land, and abolishing rents on communal properties. The plan aimed at abolishing unpaid work required by landowners, and the direct or indirect payment of parochial fees, but it demanded the reinstatement of the governor and vice-governor of San Luis Potosí who had been dismissed for denouncing the peace treaties. These people represented a local power group among which there were former political authorities who had acted with some of the state's hacendados.

Among the ousted politicians was Manuel Verástegui, nephew of Pablo Verástegui, who contributed resources and men from his hacienda to back the war against the U.S. He had been removed from his post as provincial prefect of Río Verde, and met Quiróz through his family and through Valentín Camargo, the leader's secretary. Verástegui became an intellectual leader of the movement, he helped write the plan, and incorporated a series of political demands that involved peasants in sharing power. Perhaps the peasants envisioned the break-up of the big haciendas by means of the conflicts that Manuel Verástegui had with his uncle Pablo, who owned several large haciendas.

The plan backed the line of the liberals who then controlled the national government and were represented by President Herrera, but the movement had no chance of achieving its objectives, since by basing itself on popular forces and by attacking the existing forms of property, it actually condemned itself. In effect, the state governments of Querétaro, Guanajuato, and San Luis Potosí formed a coalition to pacify the Sierra Gorda. In addition to the combined action of the national guard, General Bustamante ordered the federal army into the Sierra Gorda, instructing the men to cover all the points where peasant uprisings had occurred.[44]

A few days after the proclamation of the "Plan of the Regenerating Army" (*Plan del ejército regenerador*), the peasants continued to attack haciendas and to take towns, including Santa María del Río. They had intended to reach San Luis Potosí, but now, outside home territory and their natural zone of refuge, they began to suffer a series of defeats. Months before the movement had started to weaken,

García Cantú, El socialismo en México, siglo XIX (Mexico: Editorial Era, 1969), pp. 55, 66. Reina, *Rebeliones*, pp. 300–302.

[44] AHSDN, Exp. XI/481.3/2855.

the government had begun a series of measures to suppress the Sierra Gorda rebellion, since there was a strong possibility that the Indian towns in Huasteca would join it.

Pacification Measures

The government resorted to various means of controlling the political and social movements of the Sierra Gorda. The repressive forces included national guard troops from Guanajuato, Querétaro, San Luis Potosí, Zacatecas, and Jalisco, who were coordinated by the federal army. Amnesty was an effective method used to subjugate certain opposition groups, but not all the rebels took advantage of it, either because they preferred to go fighting to achieve their objectives, or because as army deserters they were ineligible; this situation radicalized the movement and swelled its ranks. In April 1849, as a pacifying measure, the military leaders ordered the suspension of alcabala payments in Tierra Blanca and Xichú. The measure was approved by the state of Guanajuato, but it could not be carried out because it was subject to approval by the congress.[45]

A debate ensued in the national press over the Sierra Gorda situation. It was argued that the movement had not been controlled because the local authorities had given it too little importance at first. It was also claimed that the situation had been used for their own personal ends by local power groups who, "wanting to be on good terms" with the national government, had played down the increasing importance of the movement.

The press also made proposals to solve the problems that provoked the rebellion. In spite of the fact that the poverty of the tenants, peons, and day-laborers was caused by an exploitative system the press argued that the system of land tenure had given rise to the movement and that the land should therefore be divided while indemnifying the property owners.

As the situation became uncontrollable, government feared another caste war. On April 11, 1849, a document entitled "Bases for the pacification of the Sierra was published,"[46] in which "the supreme government of the union" proposed as a first measure that special laws be enacted to remedy "the afflictions of the people of the countryside . . . , thus attacking the root cause of their com-

[45] HN El Siglo XIX, "Alcabala," April 27, 1849. El Monitor Republicano, April 28, 1849.

[46] AHSDN, Exp. XI/481.3/3092. "Bases para la pacificación de la Sierra Gorda elaborados por el Supremo Goberno de la unión," April 11, 1849.

plaints." Other measures including the granting of amnesty (regardless of whether the rebels were army deserters) and the nomination
of Quiróz as commander of the national guard of Xichú.

Apparently, Quiróz had also been negotiating with the federal
army, which published another document entitled "Top Secret [*Su-
mamente reservado*]: Secret stipulations for the pacification of the
Sierra Gorda."[47] Quiróz was promised 10,000 pesos so that he could
"establish himself by buying lands . . . without the necessity of the
salary that he requests," and 5,000 pesos were given to each of the
"leaders who are influential and considered necessary." The document also recognized that the Verásteguis had not been compensated for the damage done by the rebels. Finally, it noted that an
effort would be made to "distribute the existing communal lands."

It is interesting to note that what in the first document appears
fundamental—"to remedy the afflictions of the people of the countryside"—in the second was mentioned last and with scant possibility of being resolved within the terms stated. In fact, there were no
community lands in the Sierra Gorda,[48] since this region had been
populated by semi-nomadic Indian groups. These documents were
sent to the Sierra to be discussed by important hacendados and the
federal army region's representative. The accord reached on May 15,
1849, involved the delivery of 3,000 pesos to Quiróz for distribution
among his forces, and 6,000 pesos to be distributed among those
who gave up their arms.[49] The accords for resolving the conflict
gradually broke down and the money issued to buy off the leaders
of the rebellion steadily diminished as it sifted down the ranks. It is

[47] AHSDN, Exp. XI/481.3/3092. Document produced by the Secretaría de Guerra y
Marina, unsigned, and dated April 11, 1849.

[48] In 1848, the state of Querétaro consisted of 36,333 *caballerías* of land distributed
as follows: 124 haciendas and 398 ranchos had 14,062 caballerías; *fundos* of towns,
205 caballerías; land held in common, 820 caballerías; land occupied by roads, rivers
streams, 6,850 caballerías; national lands totalled 14,396 caballerías. Taken from *Notas estadísticas del departamento de Querétaro* (México: Imprenta de José Mariano
Lara, 1848). Therefore, the percentage of community land was minimal and it is probable that it was concentrated around the Otomí communities in the south of the state.

[49] AHSDN, XI/481.3/3092, Secretaría de la División Bustamante, "Artículos Adicio-
nales, Reservados al Convenio de la Paz," signed in the hacienda del Noria de Charcas
by José González de Cosío—hacendado of the Sierra of Guanajuato who had conflicts
with his peons. He was possibly a relative of Francisco González de Cosío, governor
of Querétaro in 1882. The *Plan de Quiróz* was written by Luis Robles y Verástegui, a
politician from the family of hacendados. These articles were ratified by Anastasio
Bustamante, the general in charge of the organization of the different forces involved
in the pacification of the sierra. He had been given 15,000 pesos "for the expenses
which this occasioned." 11 April 1849.

not known whether the agreements were not implemented or whether the rebels did not accept the proposals, but the region was not at peace.

As the rebels moved away from the Sierra, the movement gathered more adherents although it became more vulnerable militarily without the protection of the rough terrain of its home territory, and was defeated in the attempt to take San Luis Potosí. With some dead, others in jail, and still others pardoned, Quiróz was arrested on October 3 and two months later he was executed.[50] Before the final defeat, however, some control measures had been taken, such as the banning of meetings, alcoholic beverages, and arms, and the use of prison labor on public works projects.[51] At the same time, the deportation of prisoners began, as had occurred with the Yaquis, the Maya, and the Chamulas. After Quiróz was shot in December, the captives were deported to Durango, Chihuahua, Tamaulipas, and Coahuila,[52] thus uprooting them from familiar surroundings and people, and preventing their rescue by relatives—as had often happened in the past—so that the movement could not reorganize.

The masses were controlled, but concessions had to be made to the oligarchy for the peace to be effective. In December, the government of Guanajuato decreed the establishment of a new department in the Sierra Gorda, and the pueblo of Xichú was renamed Villa Victoria, which "could have a town council as long as in the government's judgment there was an adequate number of competent people to carry out council functions."[53] Just before the decree was issued, the liberal government of President Herrera made concessions to the army. Federal army representatives were awarded large bonuses for the work they had done, and the state national guard forces were favored with the creation of three military colonies that included the concession of four *sitios de ganado mayor*. While preventive measures were being taken by the army, the population was "being made to feel the power of the law."[54]

Unlike the Otomí and Nahua pueblos on the borders of the Sierra

[50] González Navarro, *Anatomía*, p. 41.

[51] AHESLP, Sección: Secretaría General de Gobierno, Ramo: Guerra, Cartas del Inspector General de la Guardia Nacional, signed in April 1849. HN, *El Siglo* XIX, "San Luis Potosí," April 17, 1849.

[52] AHSDN, Exp. XI/481.3/3092, partes militares sobre deportados, December, 1849. González Navarro, *Anatomía*, p. 42.

[53] Ibid.

[54] AHSDN, Exp. XI/481.3/4780, decreto para establecer colonias militares. *Los presidentes* . . . , p. 382.

Gorda who had fought to defend their communal lands, possession of land was not a traditional demand of Pames and Jonases tenant farmers. Instead, they were motivated by the need for access to the forests, as expressed in the proclamations of 1847 that demanded improved living conditions and the relaxation of the system of repression and control. Even so, in the course of the struggle their demands changed according to the alliances they formed. Toward the end of the rebellion both the leader of the movement and the state decided that the main cause of poverty in the Sierra was the concentration of land in a few hands. Thus Quiróz asked in the *Plan Regenerador* that the haciendas of more than 1,500 peons be reclassified as pueblos, while the press and the Junta Directiva del Ramo de Colonización promoted the redistribution of land among the peasants:

> The division of land to invite new settlers, while offering them liberal concessions, would invite mockery if at the same time the indigenous people were treated as strangers in their own land and did not receive the consideration of the government. The ancient population ought to be cared for so it will multiply and prosper: and their prosperity cannot be expected without easy and abundant means of feeding themselves, which for the inhabitants of the countryside is not possible without productive land to work.[55]

The plan also dealt with concessions to power groups when open opposition was declared, and argued that the same should be done with the peasants: "Why would not one proceed thus with a numerous class which by its very existence deserves great consideration?"

The government of the republic took up the suggestions and resolved that with the creation of the military colonies, army deserters as well as the peasants (who throughout the Sierra had been only peons or tenants ever since the colonial period) would benefit. In addition, the Guanajuato state government was authorized to buy land from private parties to grant to the "settlers vacant lands of the Sierra" and with these to form *poblaciones*.[56]

[55] In the national press the uprisings were treated as those of unjustly oppressed farmers and the division of land was even proposed to solve the conflict. There were also journals, such as the official newspaper of San Luis Potosí, that called the rebels evildoers, bandits and criminals. The program of the Junta Directiva del Ramo de Colonización is taken from Francisco González Cosío, *Historia de la tenencia y explotación de campo desde la epoca precortesiana hasta las leyes del 6 de Enero de 1915* (México: Talleres Gráficos de la Nación, 1957), pp. 151–59.

[56] González Navarro, *Análisis*, pp. 42–43.

Other measures followed. Concessions were made to the hacendados, rancheros, and landowners, and rural and urban property owners were exempted from taxes for two years if they could prove that they had "suffered at the hands of the rebels of the Sierra Gorda, to the detriment of their interests, which makes them deserving of this favor." Likewise, the obligation to pay "the tax on luxury goods, taxes on profitable occupations, patent rights, and any other tax or direct contribution corresponding to the State" for a similar length of time was lifted for those "inhabitants of the towns which were invaded."[57]

These concessions to the regional oligarchy helped achieve relative stability in the region. In the state of Guanajuato, friction continued between the executive and legislative powers over the question of the kind of land tenure system that ought to prevail. The executive was torn between the need to divide the land on the one hand, and recognition of the impossibility of creating *poblaciones* and factories in the Sierra, on the other. Basically, what was at stake was the implementation of an old plan—the creation of a *presidio* and the encouragement of capital investment in the mining industry, although this time, "only silver could be mined and not cinnabar,"[58] as had always been desired.

With regard to the forests, various decrees were issued but all of them continued to protect property owners. Thus the peasants found no economic alternative that would ease their burdens. Oppression and hatred were reflected in a considerable increase in the social phenomenon known as banditry,[59] coinciding with the specter of anarchism and communism that began to appear in the Sierra Gorda around the 1850s.[60]

Summary and Conclusions

The social organization of the indigenous groups that inhabited the Sierra Gorda at the time of the conquest, as well as the type of colonization, imprinted specific characteristics on the peasant struggles of the eighteenth and early nineteenth centuries. The population subjugated by the army and the missionaries comprised a number of ethnic groups who wandered within the mountains. The nature of the terrain, the climate, and the diverse local economy required the

---

[57] HN, *El Universal*, "San Luis Potosí," October 5, 1850.
[58] *Informe de Gobierno de Arellano Lorenzo* (Guanajuato, 1851), pp. 21–25.
[59] Ibid.
[60] AHSDN, Exp. XI/481.3/3092, partes militares.

mobility of these groups, and in turn resulted in the absence of a legal system to control ownership of the land.

Since the region was lightly populated, colonization was achieved with the support of Otomí and Nahua groups that were expelled from their original communities in order to settle them in the sierra and acculturate the Pames and Jonases Indians. The semi-nomadic way of life of these groups was incompatible with permanent settlements, especially with respect to the possession of community lands. This situation encouraged an apparently simple dual system of land tenure: private property (mines, haciendas, and ranchos), and the *tierras baldías* or vacant public lands whose forests the Indians were allowed to freely exploit. During the eighteenth and early nineteenth centuries the amount of private property began to increase at the expense of the communal forests, and soon the Indians had to pay for the use of strips of land to grow crops to complement their foraging. The expansion of private property, leading to the loss of the Indians' rights to exploit the region's natural resources, was the basic cause of the serrano struggles up to the mid-nineteenth century.

The exploitation of the forests was fundamental in both household and regional economies. Wood for mining, construction and tanning was provided by free workers called *carboneros, madereros,* and *leñadores* who, in turn, needed to sell wood in order to pay rent on the lands they sowed, as well as for firewood for domestic use. The large numbers of peasant woodcutters were tenants; this was a dynamic group that always struggled for the free exploitation of the forests. They were the protagonists of the rebellion, although much later they were joined by peons, army deserters, and bandits fleeing from "justice."

Peasants were often used by regional power groups as tactical instruments to assist their own struggles against the structures that impeded their own economic or political purposes at the national level. Until the end of the nineteenth century, the Sierra Gorda was the setting of an important power conflict between colony and metropolis in that the crown impeded mine owners' exploitation of the abundant minerals of the Sierra. In independent Mexico, the mineowners' struggles continued for the same reason, but now against monopoly groups who for commercial reasons arranged to import a number of goods that could now be produced in Mexico.

In the 1840s the national political crisis was exacerbated by the intervention of the United States. The regional–national power struggle was expressed in the Sierra Gorda around the international conflict, which emphasized local social contradictions. Participating regional power groups most active in this way were the hacendados and the military, who also held public offices. Of the hacendados, some declared in favor of the United States and others against, but both were supported by their own hacienda peons, who were armed and convinced of the need to fight on the basis of promises to improve their working conditions.

Most of the military group denounced the central power and in some cases against the peace treaties signed by the Mexican and U.S. governments. The time and place of their pronouncement were decisive to the support they could muster. The Indian communities bordering the Sierra Gorda joined some military leaders under the promise that the latter would defend the communal lands they were about to lose; other military leaders drew support from discontented rural workers in the Sierra: the Pames and Jonases, *carboneros* and/ or tenants, peons, army deserters, and bandits, all of whom were being directly or indirectly exploited.

The war with the U.S. provoked an economic crisis in the countryside not only because of the looting and devastation, but also because the war distracted the peasants from the cultivation of their land and forced them to defend it. Curiously enough, a crisis did not occur in the mining industry, which actually registered an increase in activity in those years. Poor harvests worsened the peasants' living conditions, already hurt by tax increases. The economic crisis and the regional and national power struggles encouraged rural uprisings throughout the Sierra. Totally removed from the struggle for power, but motivated by the hope of improving their living conditions, the peasants created temporary alliances with various oligarchies (military leaders, hacendados), thus the social support for different competing power groups.

The aims of these peasants' alliances were to achieve their own objectives, and for this reason the alliances proved to be ephemeral. The dynamic of the peasant uprisings, when they achieved temporary autonomy, in terms of class objectives as well as leadership, always exceeded the demands of the hacendados and military leaders, often transforming them into uncontrollable rebellions. The peasants' leader Quiróz had personally suffered the injustices of the system, and upon falling into "illegality" had become a bandit. His actions went no farther than the attempt to take justice into his own hands; little by little, circumstances radicalized him and he became the leader of a popular movement.

In its final phases the peasant movement comprised (free workers with a long tradition of struggle), sharecroppers, day laborers, and hacienda peons. The primary demands of the rural rebels were to achieve better living and working conditions, but when Quiróz joined forces with someone with other class interests who wished to capitalize on the movement, the demand to convert haciendas with more than 1,500 peons into pueblos was incorporated. The attempt to tie the movement to political interests that were at odds with those of the peasants was a failure. The movement prospered as long as it moved within its own territory, fought on its own terms, and could seek protection in the mountains, but once the peasants left the Sierra and tried to attack towns for political reasons, they were defeated, their leader died, and with him the movement itself.

During the movement's final stage, the government instituted various measures to pacify the region, some directed toward the popular classes, and others to the groups in power. Once the war with the United States was over, the federal government had to make concessions to the region's elites in order to consolidate support. The military leaders received the largest benefits, in the form of lands on which they could settle. Taxes on hacendados were reduced, although for a while they were threatened with the reduction of their properties as well (though compensation would be paid) in order to divide them among the peasants. The mine owners had still not obtained permission to extract minerals and they had to content themselves with investing more money in silver mining.

Although the peasants did see their taxes reduced, their living conditions did not improve. With the formation of military colonies, regulations on forest exploitation were tightened, provoking changes in the occupational structure. Moreover, in spite of the pressure on the government to distribute land to the peasants— which had been the fundamental cause of poverty and the rebellion—the property owners of the region together with the political authorities always found ways to avoid carrying out such a measure.

Finally, the peasants were pacified by the coalition of forces of the power groups in various states, but the causes of the rebellion remained latent and would manifest themselves later in times of political crisis.

The partial efforts to redistribute land began to create changes in the land tenure system. Pueblos started to form and in them new forms of social organization that led the peasants to hope for a piece of land and to fight—some years later—to obtain it.

CHAPTER TEN

Revolts and Peasant Mobilizations in Yucatán: Indians, Peons, and Peasants from the Caste War to the Revolution

Enrique Montalvo Ortega

One of the most important peasant rebellions in Latin America occurred in the state of Yucatán in the nineteenth century, and has come to be known as the "Caste War." Later, as a result of the Mexican Revolution a social movement began in Yucatán in which agricultural workers actively participated with the aim of establishing a socialist society through a party with solid popular roots and a broad peasant base. Both movements demonstrated, in their times, the capacity to confront and transform the prevailing oppressive conditions, and in both cases there can be seen a strong spirit of rebellion against such conditions and those who created them.

In the half century that separated these movements, the social and economic structure of the region changed substantially; not only did the forms of production change but a new economy developed based on henequen cultivation, to the detriment of maize and other crops grown for local consumption. It was a period of economic boom for the ruling oligarchy, and led to reorganization and a strengthening of their political dominance.

The two forms of organization and mobilization developed from extremely different structures and social relations. A comparative analysis can illustrate as much about the extent of these same

changes as about the manner in which certain kinds of agricultural
workers (hacienda peons, free peasants, etc.) can manifest under certain circumstances their capacity to rebel or to conform with prevalent social norms. In addition, such a comparison permits a glimpse
of some of the ways in which the racial or ethnic element became
intertwined with class, resulting in certain political or ideological
transformations. But first it is necessary to review the historical
processes that gave rise to the structures and social groups in the
region.

The name of the nineteenth-century rebellion, the "Caste War,"
defines it as a racial or interethnic clash, and thus ignores a complex
of equally important factors. We therefore need to begin with precise
definitions of the terms "Indian" and "peasant."

The Indian as Historical Product
and his Regional Delimitation in Yucatán

The conquest of America by the Spaniards produced a new social
category: the Indians (indios). This, without doubt, was a colonial
creation intended to convert the region's inhabitants into "a type of
worker with beliefs and customs adequate to control and exploit
him systematically and in a secure form; a docile worker, with his
capacity for violence inhibited beneath the weight of religious vigilance and pacifying beliefs; a more productive worker, but not for
his own well-being, rather for the enrichment of diverse masters
who controlled perfectly the channeling of surplus labor."[1] Although this was the predominant and generalized intention of the
colonizers, it was not completely attained as the continuous rebellions in the colony demonstrate. At the same time, some areas remained outside the colonizers' control, giving rise to the existence
of free or relatively free zones in which, to a large measure, the indigenous peoples maintained their own forms of reproduction. The
majority of natives were transformed into indios and as such into
serfs in the service of the Spanish colony and its local agents, while
others remained at the margin. The former were exploited in a wide
variety of ways, ranging from slavery (employed at various times in
most parts of Mesoamerica) to encomienda, repartimiento, etc.
Other groups managed to retain their previous forms of production,
usually subsistence agriculture, although on occasion they were
forced to perform certain services, particularly in areas bordering

---

[1] Severo Martínez Peláez, Racismo y análisis histórico en la definición del indio
guatemalteco, Editado del Instituto de Investigaciones Económicas y Sociales de la
Universidad de San Carlos, Guatemala, p. 93.

the dominated zones. Free zones and colonized zones; free peasants and encomienda Indians; servants and peons; this was the reality of colonialism in Mesoamerica. Strictly speaking, only those living in the colonized zones can be considered Indians, with all of the connotations we have given the term. The others should be called "*naturales*," or, because of their predominant form of social and economic reproduction, "*campesinos*" or peasants. However, in normal usage all inhabitants of America are referred to with the generic name of indios, perhaps based on the idea that those who had not submitted to the dominant power would eventually do so.

The distinction between peasants and Indians is fundamental for an understanding of the social process that took place in Yucatán in the nineteenth century and the first three decades of the twentieth century, as well as for understanding the life of agricultural workers. The colonial matrix produced a profound differentiation (revealed in various levels of social and economic life) between free peasants who lived in the east of the peninsula, and those Indians who, whether or not they retained their peasant way of life, were subjugated to colonial authority through tribute, repartimiento (forced purchase of goods), or as slaves or encomienda workers. Such subjugation was basically supported by ideological-religious domination and military force.

At independence in 1821, Yucatán was already divided into two socially and economically distinct regions: the southeast, populated by free peasants among whom the colonial bonds had not been able to expand with sufficient force, and the west, in which the natives had already been subdued and in which there was already in motion a tendency toward new forms of exploitation, such as debt peonage on the new maize and livestock haciendas.[2] These two types of workers were distinguished by their lack of subjugation to the dominant classes, and by the type of work and the manner in which it developed. Independence stirred all parts of society, facilitating the development of new economic sectors, while inhibiting others. At the same time the contradictions within the ruling classes became more acute as they tried to adjust to the changing circumstances.

The Caste War and its Antecedents

After independence the complex of transformations, the development of new economic contradictions and the sharpening of preex-

[2] See Robert Patch, "La formación de estancias y haciendas en Yucatán durante la Colonia," *Revista de la Universidad de Yucatán*, 18 (July–Sept. 1976): 95–132.

isting ones, were manifested in the uprising initiated in 1847 that was to become the Caste War. This war lasted, in its various phases, with intervals and transformations in its magnitude and character, until the 1910 revolution. In its intensity and duration the Caste War demonstrated the capacity of peasant resistance to the efforts to repress and destroy that form of life and production by the dominant sectors of a new hacienda economy based on commercial cash crops.

INDEPENDENCE AND THE EXPLOITATION
OF INDIGENOUS PEOPLES

To comprehend the character of this uprising it is necessary to examine the nature of exploitation among agricultural workers, as well as the political movements that arose. This exploitation was based on the encomienda, tribute and contributions to the clergy, repartimientos, and labor servitude often based on indebtedness. Although independence activated the whole of Yucatecan society, it did not eliminate discrimination against the indigenous people, nor did it grant citizenship with equal rights. On the contrary, independence accentuated exploitation by favoring the expansionist and commercial tendencies in the hacienda economy over the peasant-centered forms of production. A nineteenth-century Yucatecan historian pointed out, in a decidedly romantic tone, that

> Independence should have imitated the conduct of the Spanish liberals who removed the unjust burdens which weighed down the Indians, and placed in their stead means for educating them, so that in the not too distant future, all of the races of the country could be equal. But bastard interests opposed this kind of thinking, . . . while tribute was abolished by Iturbide, obventions were left in existence, as well as obligatory personal work, humiliations by the authorities—civil and ecclesiastic—and other abuses sanctioned by custom. The Indian citizen continued to see the descendant of the conqueror as the author of his misery.[3]

[3] Eligio Ancona, *Historia de Yucatán*, Vol. 4, *La guerra social* (Mérida: Imprenta de M. Heredia Arguelles, 1880), p. 10. Moises González Navarro tends to confirm this hypothesis: "The ample legislation on agricultural work shows that the social structure of the colony was maintained intact in spite of independence from Spain and the formal equality of liberalism." *Raza y tierra* (Mexico City: El Colegio de México, 1970), p. 61.

This does not mean, however, that there were no changes in the economic structure of Yucatán. There is no doubt that independence
made the class contradictions more intense. The laws of the 1812
Cortés of Cádiz had obligated the church to cease collecting tribute
from the indigenous people. Nonetheless, the church mounted such
pressure that the government, claiming ignorance of the Spanish
constitution of Cádiz, reinstated the tributes. It was not until 1822
that tribute was abolished and replaced by a personal contribution
of 12 reales to be paid by everyone (Indian and non-Indian) except
those who could not work, soldiers, Franciscans, and slaves. In this
same year the indigenous republics were reinstated to facilitate
more efficient collection of the contributions from the natives.

Landowners had pressed for the suppression of the tribute, because they had to pay it for the Indians working on their haciendas,
and a political group known as the "Sanjuanistas," under the banner
of the defense of Indian rights, collaborated in the erosion of clerical
power. As a result of these conditions and the modification of relations in the colony, the clergy saw its power base substantially
weakened. This did not result in the compensatory advance in the
rights of Indians, for while some forms of exploitation disappeared,
other new forms, such as debt peonage, appeared, which also led to
the loss of Indian lands. The alienation of the cofradía lands was
decreed on January 22, 1821, and the appropriation of uncultivated
lands, on April 3, 1841.[4] Moreover, no sooner had these new forms
of exploitation been created than the Indians were used as combatants in the internal conflicts among the elites, specifically to settle
differences over the issue of federalism between power groups in
Mérida and Campeche, and between those in Yucatán and the cen-

---

[4] Recent studies on the role of the indigenous community have shown how this
association (*cofradía*) constituted itself in a form of community defense when faced
with businessmen and landowners eager to appropriate lands. Paradoxically, a form
of property that had served to enrich the clergy had also helped Indians to conserve
community lands, but at the cost of making the land property of the association and
of contributing part of the output for the celebration of religious festivals. Such an
institution also functioned as a mechanism for redistribution among members of the
community. In the case of Yucatán this was not possible due to the alienation of the
cofradía lands. In addition, the alienation of uncultivated lands began a multitude of
confiscation of indigenous lands, and the frequent appropriation of water rights by
the landowners was used to control the workforce by obligating them to work on their
lands. See Margarita Loera, *La economía campesina indígena durante la colonia, el
caso Calimaya y Tepemaxalco* (Mexico City: Instituto Nacional de Antropología e
Historia), mimeo.

tral government.[5] In 1842 those who had defended the state with arms were offered, "in addition to their *prest* [pay], a square league" of uncultivated land. Those who had given distinguished service were offered "a portion of uncultivated lands in proportion to their services and military rank."[6] In 1843 it was decreed that those who had defended Yucatán with their own arms were exempt from civil and religious contributions; but the majority of these promises were never kept.

Independence did not put an end to the exploitation of the indigenous people. The ruling elites took it upon themselves to reaffirm the indigenous peoples' position as an exploited class, as had been the case since the Spaniards arrived. New forms of exploitation of the Indians were devised, and accentuated to an ever greater degree their subordinate position. With the disappearance from the scene of the political power of the crown, which had been charged with establishing the limits of Indian exploitation (always set by the Indians' own rebellions), the elites hurled themselves against all that appeared to thwart their interests, first against the clergy to avoid paying the tribute of their workers, and later to accumulate land and appropriate water rights. These two efforts were strongly tied to the transformation of the regional economy and the growth of new types of production, such as the cultivation of sugar cane, whose expansion into the areas of free peasants was of primary importance in provoking the Caste War.

Rebellion and Confrontations

In its most intense form the Caste War lasted about seven years (1847–54), although it continued in the form of guerrilla resistance until 1901. Throughout this time, the confrontation led to repeated

[5] In the revolution of 1840, S. Santiago Iman, its principal caudillo, called Indians into his forces: he offered to exonerate them from tribute if they contributed to his undertaking, and for the first time they were given arms to fight against white troops defending the government . . . the chain of wars and uprisings in the peninsula that, since 1840, occurred without intermission, obligated the contending groups to call on the indigenous element frequently, flattering them with unrealizable promises and making them daily more aware of their own importance. . . . When Mexican forces invaded the peninsula during the dictatorship of Santa Anna, Governor Barbachano issued several decrees calling the Indians to arms . . . new internal convulsions returned to disturb the peninsula in 1846, again giving the occasion for the Indians to brandish arms in defense of principles they didn't understand . . ." Ancona, *Historia de Yucatán*, pp. 11–13.

[6] González Navarro, *Raza y tierra*, p. 71.

and extraordinary forms of violence, and on occasion, both sides held as an objective the total extermination of the enemy. Among the Maya leaders there were three tendencies. There was that of Cecilio Chi, who

> was undoubtedly one of the most bloodthirsty of all. . . . His program consisted of exterminating all individuals who were not pure members of the indigenous race, to make the Mayas absolute masters of the country of their elders. Manuel Antonio Ay believed that it was not necessary to spill so much blood in order to achieve the same objective and believed that the Indians could defeat their enemies and expel them from the peninsula. The aspirations of Jacinto Pat were less ignoble because although he wanted his race to rule, it was not with the objective of exterminating or expatriating the whites, but rather of substituting Mayas in the government of the country.[7]

The Indian leaders conspired to initiate the rebellion, but they were discovered, and cacique Ay, who was found carrying a letter from Cecilio Chi, was executed on July 26, 1847.[8] The execution took place in an extremely tense atmosphere and was followed by new acts of violence:[9] "At dawn on July 30, while the inhabitants of Tepich appeared given over to sleep, the Indians suddenly threw themselves over the houses of all those neighbors who did not belong to their race and in accord with the orders of their bloodthirsty chief [Chi], assassinated without pity whites, mestizos, mulattoes, pardoning only some women to satisfy their lust. . . . Only one individual escaped the massacre."[10] There then followed an open war between the indigenous people and the whites: continuous confron-

---

[7] Ancona, *Historia de Yucatán*, p. 19.

[8] The letter, aimed at arranging a meeting between the two leaders, was reproduced by Ancona with its original spelling, Ancona, *Historia de Yucatán*, p. 21.

[9] "A great number of Indians from the immediate area gathered to attend it [the execution], and D. Eulogio Rosado saw the necessity of placing an armed guard across the entire front of the garrison, for fear that this multitude, excited by the spectacle of the execution, would decide to commit some disorder or disturbance. The body of the executed criminal was taken to Chichimilá where it was placed for public view for 24 hours so that it could be seen by all the members of the population, who were keenly excited from the moment that they received notice of the sentence of death. This excitement caused such alarm among the few white families of Chichimilá that all, including the justice of the peace D. Antonio Rajon, left for Valladolid, protected by the guard which had conducted the mortal remains of the cacique. These were the first preludes of the formidable struggle in which the peninsula would become engulfed." Ibid., p. 23.

[10] Ibid., p. 26.

tations, assaults on, *poblaciones* (villages), and executions of Indians, many of whom were innocent.

The periodicals and chronicles of the time are replete with bloody accounts of the opponents' savage cruelty. It is, however, important to emphasize the repression directed against the village caciques, most of whom were pursued and imprisoned in Campeche. The chief Tixpehual was tortured, strung up by his ears and beaten. He declared that in Tixkokob the blood of beaten Indians formed a lake.[11]

The majority of Maya chiefs were "leading Indians and past governors who made their lives in common, like all the rest, who continued as agriculturalists, on their own or with voluntary workers who were paid the prevailing wages. They molest no one nor demand any unpaid service. They are respected by others Indians."[12] Likewise, in the mid-nineteenth century, "one could not find evidence of an acute class struggle taking place within the Indian estate. The caciques easily loaned money to all, paid their workers well, in silver or in specie, guided by the maxim, 'This is sweat of my brothers and it is not just for them to eat dear.' In fact, caciques and macehuales lived in the same way—almost without any difference. For all these reasons, the chiefs were respected by their subordinates."[13] Such social relations between leaders and followers had important effects on Maya internal organization and on their actions during the Caste War.

The war continued and unexpected advances were made by the rebels, who at the end of May 1848 occupied four-fifths of the Yucatán peninsula. The Spaniards sought refuge in Mérida, Campeche, and other towns along the Camino Real. Given the gravity of the situation and the threat of rebel attacks, the governor arranged to flee to Campeche and the bishop to Havana. It was decided to evacuate Mérida, but a lack of paper made the printing and circulation of the decree impossible.[14]

But the Maya halted their attack when they were only six leagues

[11] See Ancona, *Historia de Yucatán*, Vol. IV, p. 31; Serapio Baqueiro, *Ensayo histórico sobre las revoluciones de Yucatán desde el año de 1840 hasta 1904* (Mérida: Imprenta Manuel Heredia, 1878, 1879), pp. 255–56; González Navarro, *Raza y Tierra*, pp. 79, 80.

[12] Bartolomé del Granado y Abeza, cited by José Luis Dominguez, *Las luchas campesinas en Yaxcaba* (Tesis de Licenciatura en Anthropología, Universidad de Yucatán), p. 76.

[13] González Navarro, *Raza y tierra*, p. 76.

[14] Ibid., p. 86.

from Mérida and one league from Campeche, and then they began to retreat. This is baffling considering they were on the verge of victory; various hypotheses have been offered for their retreat. According to González Navarro—who agrees with Reed on this point—the Maya did not make their final attack "because the war was initiated and propelled by the Mayas of the frontier, the Huits, who had only recently ceased to belong to this category. The western Maya, on the other hand, had long been accustomed to peonage, united with the whites in the struggle against their own race, because, as Stephens had observed, they had transferred their loyalty from their people to the haciendas, something that did not occur among the eastern Maya. In effect, the advance of the rebels was maintained by incorporating the Indians in conquered areas but this failed in Tunkas, Izamal, Ticul, etc. In Ticul the people on orders from the cacique abandoned the town along with government troops as the rebels approached."[15]

A second hypothesis is that the cycle of maize cultivation determined the retreat; given that the attacking army was composed of peasants, planting was essential for their survival, so they decided to return to their lands to plant the corn before the rains. A third, much simpler reason why the Mayas did not attack Mérida could be because it did not interest them. The character of territorial defense that defined the struggle created as a central objective the attainment of sovereignty over a definite area, rather than the conquest of other areas or the extermination of the whites.

But whatever the reason for the rebel retreat, what is certain is that the Yucatán economy was left in a state of chaos. No tribute had been collected and it was impossible to re-establish it, since those involved in the rebellion numbered around 60,000 and only 18,000 remained loyal.[16] Divisions soon began to appear among the rebels. On December 13, 1848, Cecilio Chi was assassinated by his secretary and wife's lover. Florentino Chan, Ay's successor in the east, and Venancio Pec, chief of a group from the south, withdrew their recognition of Jacinto Pat on September 13, 1849, and "ordered his death because he had established whipping as punishment and a weekly work service, that is, the same things that had led us to rise up against the whites: 'this is not what we desire; liberty is what we want.' In the future there would be no contributions, no whippings, no land purchased for cultivation, nor would the troops collect war

[15] Ibid., p. 87.
[16] Ibid., p. 90.

booty. Finally Pec assassinated Jacinto Pat five leagues from Bacalar. With Pat's death, rebel authority fragmented and for the moment the remaining chiefs were Chan in the North and Pec in the South. The result was that the Indians lost initiative in military actions and their defenses were weakened."[17]

Soon there were factions within the rebels with their own political and military objectives: "By the end of 1853 the Indian population was divided into three principal groups: in the South, independent but peaceful; in the East, independent but rebellious; and the rest, the majority, dependent and faithful."[18] By 1849, a strategy of isolating the rebels in the eastern regions of the state was defining itself.[19] After the defeats of 1855 a sector of the whites, "simply decided that the rebellion, the so-called Caste War, had ended. . . . There had been no victory and years of fighting were left. But after 1855 it was considered as something else: not a rebellion, nor a Caste War, but rather a conflict between two sovereign powers, Mexico and Chan Santa Cruz. Of all the rebellions of the indigenous peoples, from the *araguacos* who hurled arrows against Columbus' sailors, this was the only successful one. And if they couldn't stop it, Yucatecan pride decreed that it should be ignored."[20]

With this the rebels fell back and formed a kind of religious community in Chan Santa Cruz, created the so-called *cruzob* (cult of the talking cross). From that point on, they adopted guerrilla tactics, in that they defended their own territory while organizing sporadic attacks on enemy regions. This pattern survived for the rest of the nineteenth century, until federal and local forces dealt the final blow to Chan Santa Cruz in 1901. "For those of the *cruzob* it had been a disaster. Their numbers had been greatly reduced by dropouts, epidemics and now by hunger, separated from their arms and

[17] Ibid., pp. 91, 92.

[18] Ibid., p. 100.

[19] "In February of 1849 there had already appeared an article in *El Fenix*, the periodical of Campeche, in which it was proposed that the rebels be left to rot out there in the wilderness, that they could never be civilized and that the *ladinos* should turn their attentions to the west. This idea extended itself and gained adherents because the military effort continued to paralyze the State. Colonel Rosado, after what he had seen at the beginning of the spring of 1852, communicated that the war had ended and that all efforts should be applied to restoration and reconstruction. The greater part of the Mayas who had first taken up arms were now subdued, including many thousands of eastern Huit tribesmen and their families, who had settled in new villages of 60 or 70 huts, each with its *ladino* overseer and church." Nelson Reed, *The Caste War of Yucatán* (Stanford: Stanford University Press, 1964), p. 149.

[20] Ibid., pp. 157, 158.

British munitions, unable to resist the *dzul* power, they retreated desperately and raging before the advance."[21]

According to Reina, because Yucatán had lost most of its labor force because of the war with the Indians, in 1851 the government decided to make the rebels surrender rather than to exterminate them. The need for labor was fundamental for the area, as expressed by Sierra O'Reilly and above all in the presidential instructions sent to the new commander then commissioned to the Yucatán. "The government expects that paying the troops with regularity, you need not rush to despoil the Indians of their provisions, pursuing them and forcing them to seek refuge in the outlying lands. You should see that the state concedes an amnesty, so that, knowing that it will give them quarter and that their fields won't be pillaged, they will return to live in society. To this end, . . . see that the troops take nothing from the Indians, and you could commission some priests and other clergy that they may induce them to return to civilized life."[22] But despite the president's intentions the facts demonstrate that this restraint was not exercised, at least in the short term. The negotiations of the priest Canuto Vela, the representative of the whites and mediator in the conflict, encountered continuous obstacles because the army had very little respect for the accords and continually violated them.

The presence of the ruling classes in the life of the Maya, their actions, and efforts to intervene, created and exacerbated a complex of tensions that were unleashed during the Caste War. An analysis of this conflict would thus provide an anatomy of Yucatecan society of the period, the discovery of the mechanisms of exploitation used

---

[21] According to Reed, "The villages through which Bravo's advance troops passed (Tabi, Nohpop, Sabache and the same Chan Santa Cruz) were evacuated and the refugees fled to the north or the south, to return and flee when the patrols arrived, and many of them sought the protection of the English Crown. Felipe May, who appeared to be the general of the stronghold, was a final victim of the party of war and was assassinated in April by his military subordinates. The surviving generals, Pat and Ek, led only small bands and had no central authority; they were demoralized and desperate. Against the single-shot arms that were held by the mouth, one could employ machete, if willing to accept high losses, but against repeating rifles it was suicide. They could not fight but didn't want to yield and hid in the most inaccessible places, in the swamps, without leaving tracks which would lead to where they had settled; they killed the roosters so that their song wouldn't lead to their discovery. Cornered and desperate, but still dangerous, they prayed to God and his refugee Cross." Ibid., p. 237.

[22] Cited in Leticia Reina, *Las rebeliones campesinas en México, 1819–1906* (Mexico City: Siglo XXI Editores, 1980), p. 378.

by criollo society over the natives, and the many forms of Indian resistance to that aggression.

During the struggle, the rebels stressed their demands. The treaty of Tzucacab in April 1848 provided for the abolition of personal tribute and set the payment for baptism at three reales and for marriage, ten reales. The treaty also established that the use of uncultivated areas (*montes*), the village community lands (*ejidas*), and land in the outlying zones (*baldios*) would be rent free, and could not be alienated. Lands registered and measured, but whose deed is not recognized by the government to return the value received for payment of these lands.[23] The Indians also demanded the return of 2,500 arms that the government had confiscated, and demanded that "the debts of all [indebted servants] be dissolved."[24]

The treaty, signed by the representative of Governor Barbachano, the priest Canuto Vela, and Jacinto Pat and his close associates on behalf of the rebels, was not accepted by other Indian leaders mainly because it named Barbachano and Pat governors-for-life of their respective groups. The other leaders, while hoping to achieve the same objectives, also rejected the treaty's failure to respect the idea of a separate territory for the rebels. This concept of Maya independence can be found in the official communication sent to the governor of Yucatán by John Francourt, superintendent of Belize, informing him of a meeting with two indigenous leaders commanded by Venancio Pac in November 1849. He reported their claim that "no arrangement will ever be satisfactory that does not assure us an independent government: they desire to be left a party of the country; indicating a line from Bacalor north to the Gulf of Mexico, and to be left free of the payment of tributes to the government of the State."[25] The Maya appeared disposed to reduce their territorial claims, but would emigrate to another region, like British Honduras, before they would accept the government of the whites. Shortly afterwards, in January 1850, Venancio Pec, together with other Indians, met with the ecclesiastical commission of Valladolid, and asked, as a condition for peace, that they not have to give up their arms, "that they be left this piece of land in which to live, because we cannot live among Spaniards," and asked also for indigenous control of the villages. Regarding the ownership and use of land, they emphasized, "it is not necessary that I ask for any land for my village; in this

---

[23] Ancona, *Historia de Yucatán*, Vol. IV, Appendix, p. xi.
[24] Ibid., p. xii.
[25] Reina, *Rebeliones campesinas*, p. 371.

paper signed by the government, it is written that each one know his village; if anyone has bought lands these are for his cornfields, whether he be Spaniard of Indian, since though he come among us, we are in mutual love. . . . All of the lands of the King that are in the North or the East, are not in the hands of the Indian to sell, nor the Spaniard; they remain for the poor to make their cornfields. This is known by the old map."[26]

The central problem of the rebel demands was land ownership and use, and the collection of tribute. Pat, the leader closest to the whites, who had also had various meetings with Governor Barbachano, wanted to achieve these demands by peaceful means, whereas other indigenous groups wanted to achieve them by establishing a separate autonomous territory, a kind of indigenous republic at the margin of Spanish domination.

The majority of rebels arose in zones where colonial control—economic, military, and religious (the latter based on the number of parish churches and priests installed there)—had been weakest. It was the inhabitants of the areas most recently exploited by the regional ruling groups that made up the rebel armies. The closer these armies had come to Mérida and Campeche, the more hostile were the Indians.

Although the precise social composition of the rebel groups is unknown, it can be assumed that most of them came from those who lived off the *milpa*, and that in recent times had experienced attempts to impose tributes. They had also fled from areas where labor was needed for new crops such as sugar cane. Many Indians had been deprived of their land, crops, or water, by means of laws applied to uncultivated areas with the aim of imposing on them the need to work for the new agricultural estates.

Certainly many factors influenced the exploitation that resulted in the Caste War, including the divisions among the ruling classes that led to the use of the Indians as soldiers. This occurred most often through contact established by Spanish military leaders with the Indian caciques in regions where conflicts developed, and through the renewed efforts to overexploit the tribute system and to impose new forms of forced labor on those who had not previously experienced such forms of subjugation. In such circumstances the rebellion acquired the form of a resistance struggle, in which the way of life, racial identity, and the relation with the land, production, and re-

[26] Letter of Florentino Chan and Venancio Pec to the ecclesiastical commission of Valladolid, 1850, in Ancona, *Historia de Yucatán*, Vol. IV, Appendix, pp. xxi, xxii.

production of their conditions of life, were manifested through the land. The strength and vividness of this ethnic experience could not be expressed in a territory under white control, especially when the whites needed the Maya to work on their haciendas, plantations, and in their nascent industries. For the Maya a sovereign territory was indispensable for the continuation of their way of life—both simple, peasants, as well as those who maintained ancient ethnic traditions. A series of myths and magic rituals such as the speaking cross responded to this longing for a Maya nation or kingdom.

The scant development of socioeconomic differentiation within the rebel groups permitted a strong identification between chiefs and followers when faced with a common enemy. The possibility of a rebellion with independent demands resided to a great degree in the fact that the fundamental relations linked to the forms of reproduction of material life escaped control by the ruling class. The central nuclei of the rebels lived in villages beyond the material and spiritual control of the whites. Strong forms of communal life were maintained at the margin of relations like peonage or debt servitude that limited the struggle for individual liberation. As a result the liberation from the evils they had begun to suffer as a consequence of white domination could only be accomplished by the removal of the "invaders." The desire to live within their own culture and productive system and to live it freely through the autonomous control of a territory, was what gave the Caste War its extraordinary force. The case of the Maya was, as Womack has said of the peasants of Morelos, one of those "who didn't want to change and, therefore, made a revolution."[27]

Changes in the Late Nineteenth Century

Many fundamental conditions of the Caste War were undergoing changes even after the danger of a rebel victory and invasion of western Yucatán were acknowledged. A new and prosperous economy based on henequen cultivation was emerging, and this was to give shape to a system of domination that lasted until the Mexican revolution of 1910.

The uprising curbed the expansion of the Yucatecan economy, destroyed a significant portion of existing productive forces, and restored native control in certain areas. As a result the dominant

[27] John Womack, *Zapata y la revolución Mexicana* (Mexico: Editores Siglo XXI, 1969), p. xi.

groups were obliged to abandon the most fertile lands in the south and to reorganize agricultural production, restricting it to the western zone close to Mérida, the capital. Diverse factors (credit, international market demands, technical feasibility, environmental conditions) combined to encourage the production of henequen, to the point of creating a single-crop agricultural system. Yucatecan exports of henequen grew from 13.7% in 1845 (representing 2.3% of total production) to 96.8% in 1902.[28] At the same time, imports of maize and other foodstuffs increased as their cultivation was abandoned. It is clear that the Caste War produced a reorganization of control over the previously subjugated natives in the western regions. This was clearly expressed in the growth and consolidation of the henequen hacienda as the increasingly dominant production unit in the Yucatán.

The subjugation of the rapidly growing workforce was achieved through the hacienda and the system of peonage. Between 1885 and 1900 the number of hacienda peons increased from 26,553 to 80,216. The expansion of henequen haciendas compressed the process of political and economic organization that had been taking place since 1850. The dominant sectors, given the impossibility of expanding into other regions, or other crops, such as sugar cane, incorporated the previously free Indians into the system of peonage.

In the nineteenth century an attempt was made to extend the frontiers of "colonized" territories, but this was violently halted by the Caste War. Expansion continued in the second half of the century only the form of the henequen plantation, whose growth in the west led to its becoming the center of the absorption and "peonization" of the free producers of the region. The hacienda was the first step in the process of integrating the Yucatán into the world economy, and later it was subjected to imperialist forms of domination through the commercial production of henequen. The henequen economy produced an extraordinary boom that peaked at the end of the nineteenth century, as was evidenced by the formation of banks, construction of railroads, telegraph and telephone lines, etc. The boom was based on the exploitation of growing numbers of peons incorporated into the haciendas. At the beginning of the imperialist operations, in order to reduce the export price of henequen, the general tendency was to increase the peons' productivity by establish-

[28] For a detailed study of the process of transformation of the Yucatecan economy in this period, see my article, "La hacienda henequenera, la transicion al capitalismo y la penetracion imperialista en Yucatán, 1850–1914," *Revista Mexican de ciencias políticas y sociales*, 91 (1978).

ing slave-like conditions, or slavery of the modern type, which increased the extraction of absolute surplus value.[29]

The Mexican Revolution in Yucatán

When the Mexican revolution began, internal order was based more on the hacendados' coercion of and direct control over the peons than on the peons' loyalty to the hacienda. The necessity to intensify production had substituted more rigid forms of discipline for the older form of paternalism. The basis for rebellion, or at least reasons for fleeing the haciendas, was evident. The rebellion in Valladolid in June 1910 illustrated the atmosphere of political life in the peninsula. According to one of its leaders, Miguel Ruz, the participation of hacienda peons, as well as peasants and village Indians, was significant. He emphasized that

> the abundant participation, apparently spontaneous and immediate, on the part of the hacienda Indians of the villages and the countryside, according to the tenor of the notices received from the areas of success, began at the struggles initiation and lasted to its completion. . . . On the fourth day [of July] in the morning I went, as an official of the military authority in the villages, ordering that they present themselves with arms and the forces under their command, which act was verified by all those who could at that moment assemble; the rest did not delay in voluntarily presenting themselves. These same Indians invited those of the adjacent rancherías and haciendas without it being required.
>
> On their arrival, they were told in a few words the object of the revolution and were offered on the achievement of our triumph, the cessation of forced labor and tribute and were promised guarantees according to the respective articles of our Constitution.[30]

Peons were mobilized on several haciendas such as Kuiche, Sahcatzin, Hihmas, and Tzama; at Ichmul, they entrenched themselves

[29] Cf. Enrique Montalvo, *Imperialismo y henequén, estudio de las clases sociales en Yucatán entre 1900 y 1919*, Universidad Iberoamericana, 1976,

[30] Reproduced in Carlos Menendez, "La primera chispa de la Revolución Mexicana," *La revista de Yucatán*, 1919, p. 145. Another fact that throws light on the participation of peons in this revolt is that the majority of the 168 rebels captured after the defeat of the movement were, "poor indigenous *finca* workers from the countryside." Ibid., p. 161.

in order to confront government forces, and on various haciendas in Espita they rebelled.[31] Much of the mobilization was not, however, the result of peon dissatisfaction, but rather was organized by progressive hacendados who were displeased with the alliances established between, on the one hand, the Díaz minister of development, Olegario Nolina, his son-in-law, and a group of large Yucatecan hacendados, and on the other, the American company International Harvester, which since 1902 had initiated efforts to reduce henequen prices, offering in exchange privileges to this group of hacendados.

The conflicts among the hacendados had a great effect on peon mobilization and also enabled the peons to develop an awareness of their situation. In Yucatán the confrontation between *Porfiristas* and anti-reelectionists revealed the conflicts between sectors or strata of the oligarchy and also between hacienda workers. Criticizing the activities of the anti-reelectionist Delio Moreno Cantón, a Porfirista claimed, "Those agitators promised the abolition of taxes, the pardoning of all debts of field workers, and other absurdities that appealed to the ignorant illiterates."[32] But the internal conflicts among hacendados were not sufficient to destroy the hacienda system, which was solidly organized and defended by all the hacendados to whom it was the key to their livelihoods. It was not until 1915 that the hacienda peons were liberated, and then it was thanks to the intervention of General Salvador Alvarado, sent by the constitutionalist government as commander of the southeast.

An enormous transformation in conditions of the field workers took place soon after the arrival of Alvarado. His government, in order to achieve peon liberation created a group of political agents, or propagandists. Regional leaders were contracted by this government to teach the constitution to the workers, inform them of their rights, help them to defend them, and, in general, to politicize and organize them according to the liberal program that they were attempting to introduce. With the aid of the propagandists, recruited from among professors, political leaders, dissatisfied young people mostly of urban origin, the agricultural workers began to organize themselves against the hacendados, demanding, among other things, that workers had a right to work where they wanted to, to be paid a salary for their work, that limits be placed on the length of the working day, that there be one day of rest per week, etc. Such demands were

[31] Cf. Ibid., pp. 27, 99.
[32] Alfonso López, *El verdadero Yucatán*, author's edition, n.d., p. 233.

closely tied to a new reformist, procapitalist, and anti-imperialist program supported by Alvarado's government in alliance with urban and rural workers and some progressive hacendados.

The role of peons was fundamental in the submission of the hacendados to the modernizing policies of the new government, and their potential for action was thus channeled into modernizing society as a whole. Although this modernization was leading to the transformation of peons into salaried workers, it constituted a change from their previous lack of liberty. To some extent this does explain the Indians' identification with the new movement. The peons of Yucatán became new political participants, marking the beginning of a radical transformation in their form of exploitation (they became salaried workers) and the beginning of their participation in a corporative and modernizing global project.

Within a few years the rural working conditions in the Yucatán had changed completely. In the henequen zone the precapitalist subsistence economy had disappeared and salaried work imposed. Given liberation and the advantages of agrarian reform, many peons abandoned the haciendas and dedicated themselves to producing for their own consumption.

Although old rebels such as refugees in Quintana Roo, did not participate in the revolutionary mobilizations, they did enter into negotiations with the government, which returned Santa Cruz and 20,000 hectares to them, and exempted them from taxation.[33] Although many continued a subsistence economy, others began to work for the *chicle* companies in the region. In fact, after Quintana Roo was separated from Yucatán in the early twentieth century the rebels had little to do with Yucatán.

Under Alvarado's government the organization of political parties began in Yucatán. The Socialist Workers' Party (Partido Socialista Obrero) was founded at this time, and was the predecessor of the Socialist Party of the Southeast (Partido Socialista del Sureste, PSSE), which later included important and numerous sectors of rural workers.

Immediately after the 1910 revolution the mobilizations seem to have lost their peasant character, given that the central factor was to impose salaried work, but within a short time the movement recovered it. In the struggle led by the PSSE, the participation of field

[33] Compare Miguel A. Bartolome and Alicia Barabas, *La resistencia maya Mexico* (Mexico City: Instituto Nacional de Antropología e Historia), p. 1977.

workers was extended to all the regions of Yucatán and was incorporated into a strongly anticapitalist political program.[34]

The PSSE did not try to struggle alone against the hacendados to reinstate precapitalist conditions, nor, as in the Caste War, to constitute a territory separate from the whites; rather, they aspired to reorganize all of society by means of a "country-to-city mobilization," as the socialist leader Carrillo Puerto liked to say. Besides organizing centers like the so-called resistance leagues, they tried to create a power base in society that was capable of transforming the relationships of production and the class structure.

The PSSE's first aim was achieved by helping restore the peasant's traditional (Maya) communal forms of production and organization, such as placing primary importance on maize and other subsistence crops, as opposed to the export-based cash crops imposed by the hacendados. To accomplish this, land was redistributed among the peasants, the principal supporters of the socialist government.

The expropriation of land by the hacendados, which had been interrupted by the Caste War, continued during the henequen boom and resulted in a deterioration of the ejidos. The reconstruction of these lands and the inclusion of multiple forms of communalism were some of the elements that explain the political success of the PSSE.

From 1918 to 1923 the agricultural workers reformulated, on a new basis and in different conditions, some of the central elements of the program advocated by the Maya rebels during the Caste War. They attempted to break the dependency on international trade that henequen entailed, to create conditions that encouraged self-sufficiency, and that, consequently, would create regional economic autonomy. Until the end of the 1920s the conflict was waged between socialists and liberals. The majority of peasants and rural workers allied with the PSSE, which represented their interests; landowners, business interests and a small number of peasants who remained loyal to the haciendas, formed the liberal contingent.

From the Caste War to the Mexican Revolution: The Peasant Revolts in a Historical Perspective

From the Caste War to the socialist movement of the 1920s, the peasant struggles in Yucatán were diverse and heterogeneous in charac-

[34] See Francisco Paoli and Enrique Montalvo, *El socialismo olvidado de Yucatán* (Mexico City: Editores Siglo XXI, 1977).

ter. Fundamentally the Caste War constituted the rebellion of a regionally, culturally, economically, and politically limited group that
defined itself in relation to a complex interweaving of historical and
social elements. The rebels mobilized against the expansion of the
dominant classes with the aim of constituting an antonomous territory under their own control. However, the struggle developed into
a frontier war, and the mobilization (rebellion) expressed resistance
to foreign penetration. The ethnic element—considered a central
one by many researchers and perhaps by the participants themselves—was not only the ideological form in which the material
conditions of existence were lived but also expressed a territorial or
national experience.

At the center of this rebellion were the free peasants who identified with their territory and who felt the significance of a national
experience. The peons, in spite of their similar ethnic or racial
origins, did not identify with territory, but with the hacienda as the
productive unit that provided a means of subsistence and, in times
of crisis or scarcity, a paternalistic relationship on which they believed they could rely. To the extent that the peons constituted political subjects whose basis of experience was their dependency
(and not autonomy), they were not incorporated into the struggle. In
fact, when promised better living conditions, many of them defended the hacienda system.

In this analysis I have demonstrated that this conflict had a predominantly territorial as well as ethnic dimension. At the outbreak
of the revolution, the rebels were isolated and almost defeated, and
the problem of territory posed half a century earlier had disappeared. At this point the problem that came to the forefront was the
difference between hacendados' and peons' living standards. Paternalism increasingly yielded to despotism and the survival of haciendas themselves was in crisis due to the violent decline in henequen
prices in 1903. The struggle was therefore transformed from one
based on the contradictions between two opposing forms of social
organization (expressed as the demand for the establishment of an
autonomous region during the Caste War), to one based on contradictions of system of exploitation (although many peons continued
to seek to regain their autonomy). However, the contradiction between common lands and hacienda lands (which had been expanding) was the basis of the confrontation between village peasants and
peons of the adjacent haciendas.

The potential subjects of the rebellion were, then, the peasants and peons of the henequen zone. A peon rebellion was difficult because of the social conditions and the organization and territorial control of the haciendas; the peons were isolated, their mobility was restricted, and even when they were able to escape, survival was difficult. Their dissatisfaction was manifested in isolated outbreaks, but these were put down with relative ease. Peon participation occurred only as a function of conflicts among hacendados (Porfiristas and anti-reelectionists).

The liberation of peons from the oppression of the haciendas was achieved by Alvarado's revolutionary government. Many of the peons preferred their autonomy to remaining on haciendas as salaried workers, as was demonstrated by the scarcity of labor following the liberation and the continuous complaints of the hacendados on the subject.

At this point we can analyze the degree to which the political and economic elites took part in or influenced the rebellions. Political confrontations within the elites during the Caste War were fundamental to the later struggle. Those peasants who were recruited and armed to settle the elites' differences were given military training, along with an awareness of their own potential. At the same time, free Maya peasants were organizing themselves and were planning to expand their territory.

In the case of the Mexican revolution the Constitutionalist army was the key factor. Although the disputes among the hacendados and the consequent struggles against Porfirismo demanded peon involvement in the disputes, this did not reach intense levels because the conditions of exploitation and oppression were not sufficient to incite rebellion; but a change in the situation came from above.

Although Alvarado's government achieved considerable success in its political objectives, the movement of agricultural workers, once liberated from the peonage and the domination of the old oligarchy, demonstrated an initiative and a capacity to present problems and demands that, in their radicalism, went beyond the political program of the constitutionalist government. A native movement thus developed that tried to capture the peasant dimension that grew out of the agricultural workers' demands.

Alvarado was expelled from the party he had founded, and a new ruling group of regional and, to a significant degree, peasant origin took control of the PSSE. The basic political nuclei in terms of organization and participation were the resistance leagues that extended throughout the state.

The PSSE in the beginning and later the state government (when the PSSE came to power) modified their political strategies in the countryside; they no longer only negotiated for improved hacienda working conditions, but rather to regain the peons' independence from the haciendas and hacendados. This strategy required the formulation of a totally different development program, founded on the production of crops for domestic consumption and strengthening the peasantry, rather than the production of export crops such as henequen.

The leadership of the PSSE changed from being urban to one that was primarily rural, as noted by one of the founders of the party: "During the presidency of Carrillo Puerto doctrines began to develop that were more socialist and agrarian and more in tune with the political styles of the time."[35] Marte R. Gómez has pointed out that in 1921 the pro-agrarian politics of the Yucatán government were an exception in the national context.[36]

The peasant mobilization led by the PSSE was not allowed to remain at the margins of the national context. The Delahuertists assassinated its principal leaders and Obregonists liquidated their most radical wing in order to integrate the Yucatán peasant movement as a base of support for the national state that was being formed. The ejido collectives formed under Cárdenas demonstrated this tendency, and the results can be seen today in the existence of an army of impoverished wage workers who are dependent on patrons.

It would seem that the outcomes of regional peasant movements and rebellions in Mexico have ultimately depended on the directions and correlations of forces at the national level. The Caste War of the mid-1800s was ended with strong military aid from the national government, and the peons of the henequen plantations were able to liberate themselves because the revolution imposed its rule in Yucatán. The PSSE movement could not ignore the dominant tendencies in the Mexican state, and ended up integrating itself within the Partido Nacional Revolucionario (PNR) and softening its radical character.

The recurring element we can identify in these movements has been the struggle to maintain the peasant mode of life; this aim preoccupied the rebels of the nineteenth century, and was the principal mobilizing factor of the peasants of the PSSE. But while it is

[35] Ramón Espadas, *Fundación del Partido Socialista Obrero* (Mérida: 1972), p. 15.
[36] See *Historia de la Comisión Nacional Agraria* (Mexico, CIAS-SAG, 1975).

true that peasant autonomy became an explosive and revolutionary force, in the medium and long term it was also a major weakness in that it confronted head on the integrating tendencies of a state in formation (in the nineteenth century) or in the process of consolidation (after the revolution), as well as the expansive tendencies of the world economy.

PART IV

Peasants and Peons in
the Mexican Revolution

CHAPTER ELEVEN

The Political Project

of Zapatismo

Arturo Warman
Translated by Judith Brister

> Revolutions will come and revolutions will go and I'll
> keep on with mine . . .
>> (Attributed to Emiliano Zapata)

In recent years, as our knowledge of Mexican peasant movements has advanced, analyses that stress their limitations, deficiencies, and hopelessness have become common. Exaggerating a little, I would say that while we study the other classes of society from the perspective of their potential to transform society, we study the peasant from the perspective of his limitations. A bourgeois pronouncement in 1780 is vision of the future, while Zapatismo is the relic of the past, as are the Indian rebellions of colonial times and the peasants' demands today. The defeats of other social movements are explained by the brutal disproportion of their numbers in relation to enemy forces, while those of the peasants are due to their intrinsic weakness.

In a rather unclear yet persistent manner, the idea—now almost dogma—has developed that peasant groups, or more precisely, the peasant class, cannot generate a global project for the transformation of complex societies. The origins of this prejudice can be traced with precision to nineteenth-century evolutionary models, although antecedents can be found. In those cases, the peasant was considered the remnant of a previous evolutionary stage, with no historic destiny possible but that of extinction. Urbanization and industrialization in Western nations was taken for granted and projected as universal and total. The assumption that the peasant—a survivor of the past—was destined to disappear influenced and still influences

analyses of peasants and their behavior. Emiliano Zapata's movement was called barbaric by his urban and conservative contemporaries, and his troops were described as "tribes and hordes." Paradoxically, they were also called "socialists and communists." It
seems absurd that today, using another language yet sometimes the
same, we persist in this approach. In this essay I attempt to demonstrate, in a preliminary and incomplete fashion, that Zapatismo generated a radical class-based and coherent political plan for the global
transformation of a complex society.

Zapatismo as a Subject

The revolutionary movement of the south of Mexico headed by
Emiliano Zapata between 1910 and 1919 was remarkable in many
ways. His radical intransigence on the issue of land distribution,
which exerted so much influence on the later development of the
country, is well known. It may be said that the ideological influence
of Zapatismo surpassed its military capacity and extended more
widely and profoundly than did its direct action. This fact serves as
a point of departure for stressing the need to acquire a thorough understanding of the origin, formation, and transformation of the ideology of Zapatismo.

It is today possible, and even somewhat unnecessary, to show that
the political proposition of the revolution of the south, which was
built around the agrarian issue, was not limited to that problem, but
rather explicitly encompassed multiple aspects of economic, social,
and political reality. Zapata made proposals regarding individual
guarantees, municipal liberties, state and national government, and
labor relations, as well as agrarian reform. Together with explicit
programs, the political action of Zapatismo implicitly proposed
methods required for the implementation of changes. Zapatista ideology above all expressed itself as a revolutionary practice, giving
its proclamations new political and analytic dimensions. The accomplishments of Zapatismo in the transformation of society exceeded its statements.

The formal programmatic proposals, together with the concrete
political practices of Zapatismo, comprised a complex yet coherent
project for the radical transformation of the state and entire society,
but it was neither systematized nor formalized in an ordered set of
legislative proposals. The formulation of a revolutionary plan for the
transformation of society does not begin with such a document;
rather, such a plan emerges from a complex and contradictory social

process. Zapatismo did not triumph. Formal comparisons between its plan and the formal proposals of the victors cannot be used to maintain that Zapatismo lacked a program or that its program was simply defensive. While the Zapatista plan was not systematized, it is increasingly clear that its elements were present. To retrieve and to order them is not the task of the combatants but of historians.

Zapatismo was notable for the abundant documentation it produced. This, in contrast to other peasant movements, is a result of the magnitude, duration, and the complexity of the movement. It also has to do with the fact that Zapatismo was the peasant movement that came closest to seizing power, and that it governed a territory for prolonged periods. The Army of the South created an administrative apparatus in its headquarters that recruited and used a small group of "urban intellectuals"—the secretaries, as John Womack calls them—who played an important role in publicizing and documenting the movement. Although many of the documents were destroyed, dispersed, or lost after its military defeat, those that remain are sufficiently rich and numerous to provide a good understanding of the ideological development of the movement. In addition to the documents, a series of participants' testimonies, the result of later fieldwork, enrich and complement the original documents and permit (albeit with limitations) the study of the ideology of the armed and civilian bases of the movement.

On the other hand, it is worth remembering that much ink has been spent attacking Zapatismo. Few movements were so fiercely opposed in the military as well as the ideological spheres, a situation that also generated a wealth of documentation. The incomprehension, terror and indignation provoked by the uprising generated authoritative information for the understanding of the political achievements of the Zapatista proposals. As almost always occurs in the case of peasant movements, documentation drawn up by the movement's political and military opponents surpasses that produced by the rebels in quantity and availability, and this resource has not really been exploited for the purpose of elucidating the class antagonisms generated by Zapatismo. More frequently, Zapatismo is compared, implicitly or explicitly, to the Bolshevik revolution in order to stress its limitations or deficiencies, but it is almost never contrasted with the concrete postulates of its enemies.

It is interesting to note that the documentation generated by Zapatismo is today more abundant, and more easily available, than it was twenty years ago. Scattered archives have been brought together and made public, and new documents are constantly being pub-

lished. The argument that the documentation for the study of Zapatismo is poor and restricted is today difficult to support. Zapatismo
increasingly has become an object of historical research. The abundant historiography with respect to Zapatismo is obviously irregular
and heterogeneous, but if forced to categorize, we could distinguish
two great moments in its development. In a first period, the principal objective of historians has been to locate Zapatismo in a national
context in order to establish it as a founding and integral current of
the triumphant "Mexican Revolution." The second moment was inaugurated by the publication of Womack's exceptional book, which
was preceded by the work of Sotelo Inclán. In the first, the external
relations of the movement are stressed in an attempt to legitimize it,
while in the second the purpose is to explain it.

Yet we still lack a clear idea of the ideological plan of Zapatismo,
of its model for transforming society. Even Womack's work, which
seems the most complete and penetrating in the sphere of ideology,
does not completely fill the vacuum. Unfortunately, the ingenious
statement in Womack's preface, that is ". . . a book about country
people who did not want to move and therefore got into a revolution," has been frequently misunderstood and misused to demonstrate a conservative and retrograde aspect of Zapatismo.

The Public Proposals

The pubic proposals of Zapatismo for social reform are contained in
plans, manifestoes, laws, and decrees. Although we do not have a
complete set of these documents at our disposal, those that have
been published can give us an idea of the evolution and scope of the
propositions of Zapatismo. It should be pointed out that they were
directed to the Mexican nation, and were thus largely propaganda,
but through them an attempt was made to explain positions taken,
to attack prejudices, refute lies and calumnies, and to win or maintain allies. Their function was not to establish the line of action, nor
did they constitute simple declarations of intent that might not be
carried out, like the agrarian proposals of the plan de San Luis Potosí of Francisco I. Madero. They were meant to justify completed
actions and to propose them as models for the whole nation. They
were not documents to govern the exercise of political power, but
rather propaganda for the broadening and deepening of processes
that had been initiated in practice. The public documents were the
consequence of revolutionary experience.

This constitutes a clear difference from other revolutionary programs that were sometimes more coherent in their formalization and even more radical, such as that of the Partido Liberal, which never became a revolutionary movement. The documents can also be distinguished from others that only made promises or declared intentions in order to gain support for the seizure of power, but which corresponded neither to the experience and objectives of the armed movements, nor to their social bases. In the public documents of Zapatismo, and in spite of their exalted and grandiloquent language, there is almost no demagoguery but rather propaganda in the strictest sense.

The plan de Ayala, the first Zapatista document, was promulgated in 1911, almost a year after the armed uprising and as a result of the failure of the negotiations for the immediate implementation of the agrarian promises of the plan de San Luis. Various authors and survivors have said that Zapata justified the drawing up of the document as an indignant response to the accusation that the rebels of the south lacked a banner or program, that they were simply a band of cattle thieves. The document was discussed by Zapata's military leaders until consensus was reached, a practice that would be followed with other important documents. The clarity and intransigence of their demand had already been expressed as concrete political action before the formulation of the plan. Its purpose was largely, although not exclusively, propaganda.

The same time lapse between revolutionary action and its public expression is seen in the legislative proposals. The Zapatista Ley Agraria was passed on October 28, 1915, almost six months after the successful distribution of land among 100 villages in the pueblo of Morelos, and almost four years after the first agrarian actions ordered by the Army of the South. Again the contrast can be made with formally similar documents, such as the Ley Agraria of January 6, 1915, issued by General Venustiano Carranza. Its objective was to regulate future action, which in practice would be repressed and confined to a symbolic level and subordinated to the pragmatic exercise and consolidation of governmental power.

Very few of the Zapatista laws could be applied after their passage, although there were precedents in their implementation, since the peasant army had lost control over the territory and the institutions of government. As Womack pointed out, the laws were propagandistic, directed toward extending Zapatista ideology and toward political agitation.

The writing of Zapatista documents appeared to be the responsibility of a few radical intellectuals who joined the movement who

fulfilled the function of a secretariat, especially in regard to foreign
relations. They were responsible for the rhetoric (more exalted than
but not very different from all the proclamations of the period), the
line of argument, and perhaps the introduction of some specific concepts. But the general content—the political line—was always subject to the approval of the military leaders. Thus the public documents accorded with Zapatista ideology, although they did not
always express them exactly.

There is a debate as to the extent to which the Zapatista ideology
can be attributed to these urban intellectuals, but I believe this is a
false problem arising from an elitist and personalistic view of history that is unable to distinguish the division of labor in social processes, the revolutions among them. The importance of intellectuals
should lie in a collective, mass process, which generates a model
and a proposal for change in society.

The public proposals of Zapatismo were not static and they
changed throughout the struggle. Nevertheless, those changes occurred after the formulation of a basic political plan that remained
unaltered from the time it was put forward in the plan de Ayala. The
changes were in the direction of making the essential proposals
more precise, or broadening them to include unanticipated problems or issues, or adjusting them to political situations. This process
of perfecting and adjusting sometimes resulted in greater radicali-
zation, or intransigence, yet the fundamental coherence and continuity of the public declarations regarding essential proposals, despite some contradictions, enable me to summarize some of the
main Zapatista propositions. This summary should not be considered a description, but rather an abstraction for expository purposes,
and it will obviously neither be complete nor detailed, but rather
schematic.

The agrarian problem was seen as the main issue in the reorganization of society, and the agrarian community was seen as the basic
social unit. Zapatismo proposed changing the agrarian structure by
giving back the historical landed property of the communities,
which would be given complete autonomy to define and establish
the forms whereby production would be organized in accordance
with their resources and traditions. In addition to the return of land,
there would be a system of individual, nontransferrable grants of
land whose utilization could be organized along cooperative lines.
To satisfy the demand for land, all land that exceeded the bounds of
the small, strictly defined holding would be expropriated. The limits of small property were rigorously defined and were exceeded by
those established in article 27 of the 1917 constitution, which the

Zapatista proclamations anticipated. The indemnification system was established for affected properties in accordance with the cadastral survey of 1914. In addition, it was stipulated that the assets of the enemies of the revolution should be confiscated, and was defined so broadly that in practice it included all the large landowners and a large proportion of the propertied class. Capital as well as rural property would be confiscated, and the money used to repay the agrarian debt resulting from the indemnification of private property.

This radical but still conventional proposal acquired a new dimension when the procedure for its implementation, as contained in the plan de Ayala, was added: the immediate takeover of lands by armed force was the first step of the agrarian reform. It would be up to the property owners to initiate the reclamation procedure and to demonstrate the legitimacy of their titles to the land before revolutionary courts. In this way the proposal became a revolutionary one which attempted to immediately transform the agrarian structure of the country.

The agrarian community, democratically organized, was conceived of not only as the corporate proprietor of the land, but also as the basic political unit. The result was the Zapatista stress on the free municipality, autonomous and with its own resources, as the central political entity. The state and federal governments were seen as units of service, of coordination, and as such would be given a small material base that would be located in the municipalities. The establishment of a parliamentary system by direct and universal vote was proposed. Again, conventional radicalism acquired another dimension when it was stipulated that state governors and the president would be named by councils of revolutionary leaders.

With respect to labor relations, the right to organize, to strike, and to boycott were recognized, as was the need for a general reform of labor legislation. The need for laws to attain the equality of women and to humanize divorce was recognized; so was the urgency of reforming the judiciary and strengthening its autonomy. Legislation providing a share for the nation of the gross income of the foreign companies that exploited natural resources would also be required. These and other political and social reforms were not spelled out in detail, but were left to be implemented after the triumph of the revolution.

Internal Documentation

The internal documentation generated by Zapata and his generals, is scattered and incomplete, but nevertheless abundant. Here we consider in detail the memoranda, general orders issued by Zapata, and some of his generals' letters referring to the application of the reforms.

In the memoranda there is no rhetoric—the language is clear and the organization strict. They were not propaganda but work tools, responding to concrete problems of struggle and government. The ideological expression is not basically conceptual but concrete, referring to immediate situations and problems. They constituted the bridge between the desired model and possible action, and through them an attempt was made to preserve and deepen the revolution in acts of war, in provisioning, in government. Although it can be assumed that many of these memoranda were written by "secretaries," that issue is secondary because by means of these memoranda the military and ideological leadership of Zapatismo expressed itself.

The letters and personal communications contain orders, scoldings, petitions, appointments, expressions of appreciation, etc., from all types of authors. Some were written with formality and care; others hurriedly. They are a rich but incomplete source and are thus more a suggestion than a sample of ideological processes, but perhaps this is because I have done little work with them.

In some memoranda an almost obsessive preoccupation with regulating the rebel army's relations with the civilian population is noticeable. This as a concrete expression of the political ideological program of the movement. They do not just stress the need for rigorous discipline and respectful behavior, but require an active relationship between the army and the civilian authorities for the implementation of the agrarian and political aspects of the revolutionary program. Military Zapatists never intended to eliminate the civilian authorities, even during the most difficult periods of the armed struggle, but rather to reconstruct them through the democratic process in the towns. The civilian authorities did not perceive themselves as foreign to the revolutionary movement, but rather as its essential components. The old authorities who had been imposed from outside were replaced by revolutionary groups freely elected by the communities. Zapatismo did not just demand respect for the revolutionary authorities, but subordinated the army to them in matters of government.

The relationship between the civilian population and the army of the south was not abstract, but on the contrary, was based on class identity. The memoranda in which priorities were set with regard to the confiscation of cattle is a case in point: first the cattle of the large landowners were confiscated, then those of the rich, and only in cases of extreme necessity those of poor peasants. In order to guarantee the future means of production it was absolutely prohibited to kill cattle. The term "capitalist" was linked to landowners, proprietors, and merchants when reference was made to war taxes. The concept of the "enemy of the cause" did not have just one political or partisan meaning for Zapatismo, but was an objective social definition.

In its relations with civilians, Zapatismo went much further than any other armed movement of its time in founding and attempting to organize a political party. The Zapatista party was to have been responsible, through local cells, for promoting, deepening, and monitoring social transformation. The Centro de Consulta para la Propaganda y la Unificacíon Revolucionaria and its local associations, established in 1916, tried to return to the villages their main role as the driving force of the revolutionary struggle, even at the expense of the army. In 1917 laws were passed to complement that effort, in an attempt to give the revolutionary authorities even broader autonomy with regard to military leaders. This call for the organization of the masses along party lines, so they would resume the vanguard position in the revolutionary movement, took place in a devastated territory. Not just the modern enclaves of the landowners, but traditional communities as well were ruined and isolated. The former protagonists of the struggle had disappeared, and therefore it should be a party that controlled the founding of a new society. Zapatismo, in its effort to create this civilian mass party, reacted in the most "modern" fashion to the consequences of the disappearance of the old society. The new society required other organisms, such as the party, to implement the revolutionary model.

The internal documents' emphasis on the relationship between the army and the villages (a more suitable term than civilians) also sheds light on the character of the army and its leadership. The Army of the South was not a professional army, but a popular, voluntary militia. Military needs called for permanent, full-time troops but the latter did not become professionalized once the carrying of arms became a livelihood. Perhaps the best illustration of the character of the militia is given in the memoranda sent out to improve the discipline of the troops, in which an attempt was made to regulate the soldiers' freedom to choose the leaders under which they wanted to serve, stipulating that they should request permission to change their units. Even more extraordinary was the stipulation that desertion would be punished with the immediate and summary disarming of the guilty party instead of execution. Occasionally soldiers and officers received "help" ("ayuda")—and with more propriety the terms "auxilio" or "socorro" are also used—from their direct superior or general headquarters. Soldiers' pay and almost all military financing came from the war taxes imposed on landowners and other rich individuals. Each soldier received one peso in "auyda," and officers two pesos after a two- or three-week campaign (one peso was the equivalent of two days' wages on the haciendas until 1913). Thus, many combatants were peons by day, and soldiers by night and on Sundays. After 1914, when the haciendas were definitely abandoned, resources were even scarcer. The Army of the South was not only an army of the poor, but it was also quite poor itself.

The top military leaders had privileges that the rest of the troops did not and without doubt there were abuses, as the correspondence reveals. But perhaps because opportunities were absent or because control was effective, the Zapatista leaders did not convert their privileges into permanent wealth, into capital. Furthermore, in times of defeat, the leaders shared the poverty and hunger of their troops. The distance between leaders and troops never became a class gulf, mainly because of Zapata's own fanatical intolerance of misconduct in his army's relations with the people, the real source of the army's wealth.

The Zapatist army never had an outside source of military supplies or food. The enemy was its main supplier. The first government of the Convención denied arms to Zapata, and Villa could not make good his offers of the Xochimilco pact. The ideological convergence of the great peasant armies never materialized as a political-military alliance. Zapatismo was always militarily isolated and self-sustaining. The army was always fed by the villages. The memoranda establish the mechanisms for the equitable sharing of this responsibility and the avoidance of abuses. The duration of the struggle and the surprising resilience of the Army of the South, even after the tragic year of 1918, firmly established an unbreakable link between the troops and the villages. The Zapatista army was able to dissolve into the villages from which it had emerged.

Under these circumstances, military units had a high degree of autonomy with respect to the general headquarters or other army corps. The notable cohesion among top Zapatista leaders, despite conflicts that persisted even after Zapata's death, was not the result of economic-military dependence or of an authoritarian structure. Zapatista ideology was a central element in its cohesiveness as both an armed force and as a political movement.

The Army of the South was an "armed league" of the villages of
Morelos, as Womack called it, an objective result of its origin, its
formation, and the conditions under which it struggled. Zapatismo
never attempted to change this character; on the contrary, it assumed this character as part of its ideology, of its model for a future
society. It tried to make armed power a part of the villages' sovereignty. On different occasions, the memoranda stressed the need
and even the obligation of the villages to arm themselves as the exercise of a basic right. The vision of a popular army rooted in the
villages through the peasant workers, organized freely and democratically, was an integral part of the Zapatista ideology. It is possible to speak of an antimilitarism in Zapatismo, an opposition that
extended to all the privileged professional castes, which were seen
as the usurpers of the power of the villages.

The idea of popular sovereignty is formulated more clearly in the
internal documents than in the public documents, which refer to it
in ways quite similar to those of other movements that participated
in the Mexican Revolution. For Zapatismo, popular sovereignty did
not mean formal and representative democracy in which sovereignty is exercised electorally, but it meant a direct democracy, permanently located in the social units that controlled the land, had
the autonomy to organize production, and exercised political-military functions. In this view, the idea of a village or agrarian community is not that of a geographical locality but rather that of a social class unit that adopts an organization.

Revolutionary Action or Practice

The connection between the public and internal statements and the
revolutionary action of Zapatismo is not well known. Nonetheless,
an hypothesis can be advanced that again contrasts with what we
know about other contemporary movements. This hypothesis is that
concrete political action went beyond the public statements and
should be considered an integral part of the ideology of the revolution of the south. In the revolutionary practice of Zapatismo, especially during 1915 when it governed the state of Morelos, the model
of society it sought to build was delineated with all the complexities
and contradictions implied by the initial steps from theory to practice.

The centerpiece of the ideological project was the agrarian issue.
All the private hacienda land in the state of Morelos was expropriated. From a legalistic point of view, the Zapatistas merely confis-

cated the assets of the enemies of the revolution as called for by the plan de Ayala; they never considered taking only one-third of the land, the measure stipulated by the Ley Agraria del Consejo Ejecutivo in order to preserve some small private plots. The landowners, as opponents of Zapatismo, had abandoned their properties, and the latter were completely redistributed to the pueblos under a new concept of agrarian property. Yet the project was never expressed in these terms. The revolutionary process, the armed struggle, made it quite natural to treat all the lands of the haciendas as territory conquered by the revolution, won from the enemy by force of arms.

The villages were the only beneficiaries of the agrarian redistribution. As far as is known, not even the individual land grants announced in the plan de Ayala were proposed. The struggle had also changed the definition of village and of agrarian community such that it was extended to include veteran fighters who were not even "comuneros" by origin. At the same time the definition was narrowed to exclude those who had taken positions against Zapatismo. It can be said that all of the inhabitants of the rural area and many of those who lived in semi-abandoned cities had been incorporated into the villages or had run away; there was no room left for neutrality.

The prolonged war had a severe effect on the composition of the towns, erasing or reducing socioeconomic differences among the inhabitants of the towns. Many wealthy people left and others ceased to be rich when they lost their cattle, grain reserves, or their savings. The rigid but limited wage stratification imposed by the sugar cane plantations collapsed when sugar production was suspended. The people who stayed in Morelos became greatly impoverished, but their incomes were also equalized, and they acquired similar interests in the short run. Again, this was the objective result of the war and of the struggle, but Zapatismo assumed it ideologically and in practice conceived and treated the agrarian community as a class unit, as the expression of the peasant workers, and acted accordingly.

The land was given to the villages, which had complete control over its use and administration. The general headquarters promoted the cultivation of sugar cane, which it considered the only way to obtain cash for arms. But almost all the towns resisted, even after personal visits from Emiliano Zapata to convince them; the comuneros' experience had taught them that the cultivation of sugar cane benefited only the mill owners. The villages' decision was respected, however, and led to the practical reformulation of the role of agro-industry or, in broader terms, of the relation between the countryside and capital. The sugar mills were separated from the cultivated lands, and the lands were given to the towns. The mills remained under the administration of top military leaders; today we would say that they were nationalized. The sugar mills were conceived of as units of service for agricultural producers, because they ground, processed, and sold the cane for the peasants, charging just enough to cover costs. In modern terms, the accumulation and reproduction of capital were transferred from the processing and marketing sector of the sugar industry to the primary producing sector; from the industrial, commercial, and financial processes to the peasants.

This conception of the accumulation model was carried forward with the founding of an agricultural bank that provided seeds and tools to the towns at no interest. It was thought that the bank should become a multiple-service financial institution, giving technical support to and administering the mills and other industrial installations without making a profit. Under this model, the state government would also provide funding for services to the autonomous communities. These services included not only traditional ones, such as sanitation and security, but also capital improvements and primary education, which were to be administered by the autonomous municipalities.

The communities and their governments, generally elected on the basis of their revolutionary positions, maintained their access to the general Zapatist headquarters and the latter frequently mediated disputes between the state government and individual military leaders, and among villages. The capacity to resolve those conflicts was grounded in the headquarter's respect for the autonomy of the communities, reciprocated by the enormous respect the communities had for General Zapata; in his mediation he often favored the towns over the military leaders. In this way the communities were recognized as the center of the revolution.

The idea of revolution in Zapatismo also deserves attention. For Emiliano Zapata there was a clear distinction between the seizure of government and the seizure of power; a transcript of a conversation between Zapata and Villa in Xochimilco illustrates the point. The government was conceived of as an instrument of oppression because of its centralism, its control by a professional caste separated from the people, and its repressive and expropriatory nature; it was a straightjacket for the revolution. The problem of the revolution was not the capture of government but its dissolution, in order to proceed toward a transformation of the state. The revolution was a process and not an act of taking control.

The revolutionary process was to develop the base of society and not the top. The change in daily existence, established and defended by armed force, was to precede the transformation of the state. Only in this way would it be irreversible. First the land, military power, and political autonomy should be given to the pueblos as the basic units of society to remake the state as a collective unit of service. The power of the old regime was to be dissolved and divided up at the base of society, to make way for a new state organization. The new state would emerge from the communities, confederating them without overpowering them.

In modern terms, which sometimes confuse more than they clarify, the change at the base of society involved the relocation and redistribution of the social surplus, which was to remain under the control of the primary producers. A new accumulation model was proposed that would move away from the points of concentration to the dispersed base of the civilian society. It was there that capital would be accumulated and reproduced; there that power was to be located, not in the centralized apparatus of capitalism. This was to be popular power in the strictest sense, without mediations.

The configuration of Zapatismo as a class-oriented political project exercised a decisive influence on its polity of alliances. Poverty and the geographical isolation, which signified military weakness, were recognized as severe limitations that could only be overcome through political-military alliances with other movements. For Zapatismo, the alliance became an obligatory condition of survival, developing a revolution from the bases of society. Thus, an alliance had to avoid becoming a mere truce, which the peasantry could not make use of to resupply and strengthen themselves, as their enemies could. Alliances had to be based on the unconditional acceptance of the plan of Ayala. The takeover of the land called for in the document would guarantee continuity and the grounding of the revolutionary movement in the peasant base, which alone signified survival to the revolution of the south.

Within these limits, which for many seemed triumphal and haughty, Zapatismo sought alliances desperately and urgently. In doing so, it committed errors and several times had to retreat from its unilateral, non-pact declarations in which it recognized one leader of the revolution. In spite of its increasing political and ideological influence, the movement of the south never attained an effective alliance with other armed groups. Only Zapatismo managed to formulate a political project or to construct a popular movement. The other grassroots peasant movements, such as Villismo, also failed to develop fully and did not achieve an alliance based on a common project. Zapatismo stood alone as a peasant class movement with a program for the reconstruction of society. As such it was defeated.

Bibliographic Note

Although the objective and the style of this essay make it difficult and complicated to point out connections between what is stated and asumed in the text and the sources used, it is necessary to indicate the larger connections. I start with what I call the public documents that were used:

1. Plan Político Social of 18 March, 1911.
2. Reformas al Plan de Ayala of 30 May, 1913.
3. Ratificación del Plan de Ayala of 19 June, 1914.
4. Plan de Milpa Alta, 6 August, 1919.
5. Pacto de Xochimilco, 4 December, 1914.
6. Programa de Reformas Políticos y Sociales de la Revolución aprobado por la Soberana Convención Revolucionaria, 18 April, 1916.

All the above documents were consulted in I *Planes políticos y otros documentos*, with a prologue by Manuel Gonzalez Ramirez, in the collection *Fuentes para la historia de la revolución mexicana* (México: Fondo de Cultura Económica, 1954).

7. Manifesto al Pueblo y a los Revolucionarios Mexicanos, 18 February, 1919.

Consulted in *Documentos inéditos sobre Emiliano Zapata y el cuartel general: seleccionados del archivo de Genevevo de la O, que conserva el Archivo General de la Nación* (México: Archivo General de la Nación, 1979).

8. Plan de Ayala, 25 November, 1911.
9. Ley Agraria, 28 October, 1915.

These documents were consulted in John Womack Jr., *Zapata y la revolución mexicana* (México: Siglo XXI, 1969). This book also provided extracts and summaries of laws and other public documents of Zapatismo.

Rosalind Rosoff and Anita Guilar's *Así firmaron el plan de Ayala*

(México: Sep-setentas, 1976), No. 241, provides interesting survivors' testimonies.

The work of Laura Espejel, Alicia Olivera de Bonfil, and Salvador Rueda, "El programa politico zapatista" (manuscript, Direccíon de Estudios Históricos, Instituto Nacional de Antropología e Historia [DEH-INAH], 1981), provides fragments and summaries of novel public documents, as well as very lively ideas. Unfortunately it could not be used, since I obtained a copy only when this essay was almost completed. For the same reason, I did not use it in the discussion of the historiography of Zapatista ideology, where it should naturally have been included.

Some of the above documents, as well as a large number of those I call internal documents in the text, were consulted in Gildardo Magaña, *Emiliano Zapata y el agrarismo en México*, 5 tomos (el 4 y 5 continuados por Carlos Perez Guerrero), (México: Editiorial Ruta, 1953).

The volume *Documentos inéditos* provided a large number of internal documents, and helped to update the results of a previous and almost forgotten venture into the Archivo de Zapata located at the Universidad Nacional Autonoma de México. Womack's book was, again, an important source of internal documents; only in this book is the formation of the Zapatist party discussed at any length.

With regard to revolutionary practice, the information is based mainly on fieldwork of the seminario de sociedades campesinas, of the now defunct Centro de Investigaciones Superiores del Instituto Nacional de Antropología e Historia (INAH), which took place between 1972 an 1974. To a certain extent, the results of that important collective work were synthesized in my book, *Y venimos a contradecir; Los campesinos de Morelos y el estado nacional* (México: Ediciones de la Casa Chata, 1976), No. 2. In addition, Womack's book was used as well as tapes from the Archivo de la Palabra at the INAH.

Finally, I would like to mention some sources that were consulted again to try to determine, analytically speaking, where the problem of Zapatist ideology is located. I begin, of course, with Womack, who in my opinion provides the most profound and rich analysis, the most penetrating and well written, although with a certain degree of understatement, which probably enhances the text. Jesus Sotelo Inclán's *Raíz y razón de Zapata* (México: Comisión Federal de Electricidad, 1970), was important in providing a description of the nature of the leadership of (calpuleque) Zapata. Robert P. Millon's *Zapata: the Ideology of a Peasant Revolutionary* (New York: International Publishers, 1969), is important as an attempt at codifying. Gerrit Huizer's "Emiliano Zapata and the Mexican Guerrillas in the Mexican Revolution," in *Agrarian Problems and Peasant Movements in Latin America*, ed. Rodolfo Stavenhagen (Garden City, N.Y.: Anchor Books, 1970), also constitutes an effort at systemization.

CHAPTER TWELVE

"Neither Carranza nor Zapata!":

The Rise and Fall of a Peasant

Movement that Tried to Challenge

Both, Tlaxcala, 1910–19

Raymond Th. J. Buve

Considerable attention has been given in recent years to Domingo Arenas' radical peasant movement, which controlled the southwestern region of the Mexican state of Tlaxcala between 1914 and 1918.[1] This interest can be attributed to the general progress in regional studies of the Mexican Revolution and the improved access to new archival resources. Moreover, there has been a new and critical interest in the study of peasant movements, reflecting the appearance of what Carr called revisionist scholarship, tending "to downplay the 'popular' character of the first decade of the revolutionary period."[2]

Even before 1910 the Tlaxcalan Revolutionary Movement (TRM)[3]

---

[1] Javier Garciadiego Dantan, "El movimiento arenista en la revolución Mexicana," paper, Chicago, 1980; Juan Felipe Leal, "Economía y movimientos sociales en los llanos de Apam, 1910–1940," Cap. 2 mss; Beatriz Cano Sánchez, INAH, is working on a biography of Arenas.

[2] Of special importance is the Tlaxcala state archive (AGET), from which was used the Fondo Revolución-Régimen Obregonista (FRRO), Legajos (legs), Justicia y Gobierno (JyG), Hacienda y Guerra (HyG), and Fomento (Fom). Barry Carr, "Recent regional Studies of the Mexican Revolution," *Latin American Research Review* 15 (1980):3–14.

[3] The term Tlaxcala Revolutionary Movement (TRM) is not used here in the sense of a unified movement or one formal organization—a situation that only existed for a

responded strongly to the issues of land and labor. To Madero's embarrassment the TRM, which was far too radical for his political
taste, won the governorship of the state in 1911, a success that generated an important process of peasant-worker mobilization and an
equally strong process of countermobilization among the distressed
local elites. In January 1913, the local elites finally succeeded in
bringing down the Maderista governor with federal help, and a period of violent repression began.

In 1913 and 1914 the Tlaxcalan Maderistas succeeded in organizing local guerilla units, but stayed out the mainstreams of the Zapatist and Constitutionalist movements. In mid-1914, after nearly
three years of fierce and violent political and military struggle
against local elites, the Tlaxcalan revolutionaries were about to
square acounts with their enemies, especially the landlords, but the
Constitutionalist movement of Venustiano Carranza thwarted them.
In November 1914, Domingo Arenas and a majority of the Tlaxcalan
revolutionary leaders rebelled against Carranza and sided with
Emiliano Zapata. Barely two years later, in December 1916, Arenas
decided to rejoin Carranza, and most of his officers and men followed him in the establishment of a virtually independent domain
and the dispossession of landowners, large and small.

Why did the Arenas movement follow such a radicalizing and independent course? In the first part of this essay we try to find the
answer in the interrelation of national level political developments
and specific characteristics of regional societal development in
Tlaxcala and nearby Puebla. In my view this combination resulted
in a fairly revengeful and radical peasant movement that consistently tried to achieve autonomy to implement its objectives.

In the second section I analyze the rise and fall of the Arenista
movement (1914–19). It took two years for Arenas to achieve the
autonomy and peace he longed for; only by rejoining Carranza in
December 1916 did he obtain the de facto autonomy he needed to
implement his ideals. At that historical moment, however, the consolidation of Carranza's power in central Mexico was only a matter
of time. In other words, Arenas' autonomy was probably doomed the
moment he finally achieved it, and we may assume his sudden
death only accelerated the process. However, the extension of Constitutionalist authority in Arenas' territory provoked tenacious resistance by the peasants, their local leaders, and Arenista chiefs.

---

short period—but is used for the combined parties, factions, and bands that emerged
between 1910 and 1918.

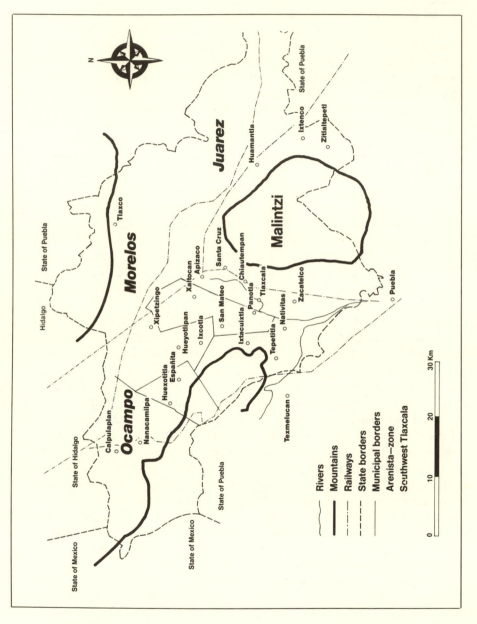

Figure 12.1. The State of Tlaxcala.

This brings us to the analysis of local Arenista interest groups: what happened to the rural properties after Arenas took control? Were lands divided among the peasants or exploited by Arenista leaders? It seems to have been a combination of peasants' and leaders' interests that produced the tenacious resistance on haciendas and in villages against the Constitutionalist attempts to eliminate hitherto protective Arenista military power and to "normalize" the land tenure situation, that is, to return lands to the owners. However, even the Tlaxcalan Constitutionalists were convinced of the necessity to step up Carrancista land reform if they ever wanted to pacify and control the local peasant population. Competitive agrarianism became, therefore, the central theme of the 1917–18 electoral campaign for governor and deputies: how to safeguard peasant interests in maintaining their Arenista land grants? Carranza, however, refused to heed the *agrarista* (peasant militia) initiatives of both his Tlaxcalan political friends and enemies, and as a consequence, it took the Tlaxcalan Constitutionalists several years to end "una guerra continua contra las autoridades."[4] The political pacification of Tlaxcala was only completed during the 1920s by the military and land reform policies of the Sonorenses.

The Tlaxcalan Revolutionary Movement up to the Arenas Rebellion (1914)

THE ORIGINS OF THE TLAXCALAN REVOLUTIONARY MOVEMENT

The agrarian structure of the central and southern parts of the state, which was the basis of the TRM and the "patria chica" of most of its leaders, was dominated by an indigenous landholding community. Between 1870 and 1910 capitalist economic modernization (railways, textiles, and commercial agriculture) seriously affected the status of local peasants and artisans. Continuous attempts to alienate existing natural resources (land, forests, water), to claim their labor and to interfere with community affairs made central and southern Tlaxcala in the last decade of the Porfiriato into a hotbed of social and political protest, intimately linked to the urban social movements of nearby Puebla and Orizaba.

Within this framework of restiveness and simmering protest, the revolutionary leadership originated. Many of these leaders, like Juan

[4] Archivo Secretaria de Reforma Agraria, Mexico (ASRA) exp. 4943 DT 131–34.

Cuamatzi, Máximo Rojas, and Anastasio Meneses, were smallholders, textile workers, or peddlers and had little formal education. Domingo and Cirillo Arenas herded the family flock and, like Antonio
Hidalgo, were factory workers. They all participated in the many
labor conflicts that struck the Puebla–Tlaxcala industries. During
the 1906–7 textile strike Tlaxcalan peasant workers developed close
contacts with convinced Magonistas in Puebla and Orizaba and later
they participated in the popular and fairly radical opposition movement to the Díaz régime headed by Aquiles Serdán in Puebla. Because of the internal rivalries among Puebla Maderistas, and the political apathy and conservatism of the local middle class, Aquiles
Serdán, an artisan with socialist leanings, succeeded not only in becoming the leader of the Maderista movement in Puebla, he also became widely accepted as such in Tlaxcala, among village peasants,
artisans, workers, tax-burdened small rancheros and urban "low-status intellectuals" (Cockcroft) like teachers and students, in several
cases educated at the Methodist College in Puebla. Serdán's revolt
ended in failure on November 20, 1910, and it provoked severe
repression in Puebla and Tlaxcala. The Tlaxcala guerilla units were
no match for the government. Cuamatzi was caught and shot; Hidalgo, Rojas, and the others went into hiding or joined Maderista
guerillas outside Tlaxcala.[5]

MOBILIZATION AND COUNTERMOBILIZATION: MADERISTAS VERSUS LIGUISTAS

After the fall of Díaz, however, Tlaxcala witnessed a fairly unique
process of political mobilization and corresponding polarization.
The Tlaxcalan revolutionaries succeeded in building a large village-
based political party. The Anti-Reelectionist party (ARP) launched
peasant worker Antonio Hidalgo as their candidate for governor
who had to complete the term of the removed Porfirista governor,
won the elections, and had them confirmed by the still Porfirista
state legislature. Moreover, the ARP had campaigned on the basis of

[5] Juan Felipe Leal and Margarita Menegus, "Los trabajadores de las haciendas de
Mazaquinahuac y El Rosario, Tlaxcala, en los albores de la revolución agraria 1910–
14," *Historia mexicana* 122 (1981): 233–78; Raymond Buve, "Peasant Movements,
Caudillos and Land Reform during the Revolution (1910–1917) in Tlaxcala, Mexico,"
Boletín de estudios Latinoamericanos y del Caribe 18 (1975): 112–52; John D. Cock-
croft, *Intellectual Precursors of the Mexican Revolution* (Austin, 1968), p. 4; Gilberto
Fabila et al., *Tlaxcala, tenencia y aprovechamiento de la tierra* (Mexico, 1955); David
G. LaFrance, "Madero, Serdán y el movimiento revolucionario," *Historia Mexicana*
115 (1980): 472–512.

a fairly radical program that sought the return of stolen lands to communities, the abolition of the land tax for smallholders, the foundation of agricultural colonies for landless peasants on large haciendas, better labor conditions for workers, the transfer of the hated rural police, the *cuerpo rural*, to another state and, last but not least, the punishment of Porfirista officials guilty of repression and murder. This rather surprising victory resulted not only from serious conflicts among the Tlaxcalan elites, but also from the ARP success in obtaining the support of the small Tlaxcala middle class for its essentially anti-elite program. Moreover, it seems that the urban network of friends, especially teachers and students from Puebla, had an important role in organizing the Tlaxcalan party. After the party reached state-level power and obtained federal recognition from President Madero, the influence of this urban network intensified. It played a crucial role in guiding the government of the barely literate Governor Antonio Hidalgo, provided part of his government officials, acted as spokesman of the party, shaped its quite radical image.[6]

The frightening prospect of a radical state government, which actually promoted peasant and labor movements, finally prompted the Tlaxcalan elites to join forces in the Liga de Agricultores (1912) to adopt statewide uniform labor policies, to reinforce the military in Tlaxcala, and to attempt to sabotage, and to remove a state government inimical to their interests. Hidalgo began to lose the support of his partisans among bureaucrats and deputies as a consequence of Liga pressure and sabotage, and the growing radicalism of anti-reelectionists, disillusioned by the failure of Hidalgo's agrarian policies and the slow progress in labor reforms. Already by early 1912 several ARP members rebelled, among them Domingo Arenas and Porfirio Bonilla, future leaders of the Arenista movement. Neutralizing the remaining ARP partisans among the state deputies by force and fraud, and with the help of federal aid to suppress a threatening popular mass mobilization by ARP leaders, the Liga was finally able

[6] Crisanto Cuellar Abaroa, *La revolución en el estado de Tlaxcala*, INERM (México, 1975) 1:93–101; Ez. M. Gracia, *Los Tlaxcaltecas en la etapa revolucionaria 1910–1917* (Tlaxcala, 1961), pp. 22–29; LaFrance, "Madero, Serdán," p. 503; Colección de folletos revolucionarios, Tlaxcala (CFR/TLAX): Al Pueblo Tlaxcalteca! Programa de gobierno del Edo de Tlaxcala discutido y aprobado por la Convención local del Partido Liberal Antireel . . . , Sept. 5, 1911; González Galindo, *El bien público*, órgano del Club Luz del Centenario, Puebla, no. 13, Sept. 11, 1910; no. 14, Sept. 18, 1910; Buve, "Peasant Movements," pp. 130–31; S. Rossains Rumbia, 1962 mss. The most important teachers were José Rumbia, secretary of Antonio Hidalgo, Porfirio del Castillo, secretary of Máximo Rojas, and Andrés Angulo, secretary of Domingo Arenas.

to bring down the Maderista government of Tlaxcala in the beginning of 1913.[7]

After being ousted from power and severely repressed by the Liga and the Huertista state government installed after Victoriano Huerta took power in Mexico City, the Tlaxcalan revolutionaries resorted to guerilla warfare. However, the various Tlaxcalan guerilla units were never able to match the strength, unity, and autonomy of the Zapata movement. They remained highly dependent on outside help, especially from revolutionary chiefs in the Sierra Norte de Puebla and Zapatists in the region of Volcanes. Only toward the end of 1913 did the Puebla friends succeed in bringing most of the Tlaxcalan revolutionary chiefs together in adherence to Carranza's plan de Guadalupe, but Máximo Rojas a veteran of the 1910 revolution was only accepted as military commander after long deliberations.[8] Moreover, the Tlaxcalan revolutionaries were unable to eliminate Huertista control of major plazas, towns, and the strategic rail connections that crossed Tlaxcala between the federal capital and Vera Cruz. Even by mid-1914, a number of the larger haciendas were still in operation.[9] In short, unlike the Zapata movement, the Tlaxcalan revolutionaries lacked a strong, unanimously accepted leadership and had never been able to create sufficient political autonomy to realize their major goals. In this rather delicate situation of control and command, the Tlaxcalan revolutionary units were incorporated into the Constitutionalist movement. In September 1914 General Pablo González appointed Rojas provisional governor, but none of the other chiefs obtained the rank of general, and the Tlaxcalan revolutionary units (called the Brigade Xicohténcatl) were placed under

[7] The Liga was the successor of the earlier Convención de Agricultores y Industriales de Tlaxcala, which broke down due to internal conflicts. See La Antigua República, época 7, Feb 2 and 23, 1908; La Nueva República, época 1, no. 48 Dec. 28, 1912; Buve, "Peasant Movements," pp. 131–32; Garciadiego mss 13–19; Leal and Menegus, "Los trabajadores"; Porfirio del Castillo, Puebla y Tlaxcala en los días de la revolución (México, 1953); pp. 119–20; S. Rossains Rumbia, mss 1962; interviews with Ing. Ez. M. Gracia, agrarista leader and local historian, Oct. 1968, and Mrs. Angulo, Feb. 1981.

[8] AGET/FRRO, leg JyG 1913, exp. 35, 63, 65; leg 261 HyG Jan. 1918 f.357; leg 268 Fom July 1918 f.42; Garciadiego mss: 20; Cuellar, La Revolución 1: 145–65.

[9] Buve, "Peasant Movements," pp. 136–38; Leal and Menegus, "Los trabajadores," pp. 24ff, give information on two northern haciendas. The haciendas around Huamantla and Calpulalpam also survived this period, but the situation in the south was much more serious: the Kennedys stayed with difficulty in control of hda Atoyac (AGET/FRRO leg JyG Dec. 1917 exp. 38) but Carvajal abandoned hda Mixco (HyG 1916 exp. 84).

the command of reliable Constitutionalist generals of the División de Oriente in Puebla.

Pablo González' attitude provoked intense personal frustration among Rojas' immediate commanding officers, Domingo Arenas among them.[10] However, there was more reason for conflict. Rojas' provisional government confiscated most of the rural and urban properties of Huertista officials and especially of the hated Liga leaders. Rojas appointed *interventores* and installed small garrisons on the confiscated haciendas to secure their production for the provisional government.[11] In addition to these official punitive acts against the so-called "Enemies of the Revolution," Tlaxcala witnessed, however, a large number of autonomous acts of land distribution by revolutionary chiefs, revenge, and probably also plain *bandolerismo*.[12] This happened, of course, in many parts of Mexico where a revolutionary government took power after Huerta's defeat. In the case of Tlaxcala, however, the specific political experiences and frustrations of local revolutionary rank and file may well have fostered a relatively strong and revengeful radicalism, which in the end clashed with more moderate Constitutionalist views and policies.

Personal ambitions, a zeal for autonomy, and social revenge finally provoked a major schism among the Tlaxcalan revolutionaries. On November 12, 1914, not only the majority of the brigade followed Arenas in his declaration for Zapata, but the same can be said of many of the village leaders, workers and peasants, in central and south Tlaxcala. In its initial popular explosion the rebellion re-

[10] Del Castillo, *Puebla y Tlaxcala*, p. 155; Buve, "Peasant Movements," p. 139; AGET/FRRO leg HyG Oct. 1914 exp. 99 tels. and corresp. Rojas and Srio de Gob. Del Castillo to Generals Pablo González, Antonio A. Medina and Gilberto Camacho.

[11] *Intervensions:* AGET/FRRO leg Junta Interventora 1914–15; HyG Mar. 1916 exp. 37, 39, 52. *Attacks:* HyG April 1917 f.152; JyG May 1917 f.118; HyG Aug. 1917 exp. 15, HyG Oct. 1917 f.36; Junta Interventora 1914–15 exp. 16. *Revenge:* AGET/FRRO leg 261 HyG Jan. 1918, f.357; leg 268 Fom July 1918 f.41; leg JyG Oct. 1917, exp. 42; HyG April 1917 exp. 152, etc.

[12] Complaints from municipalities of Calpulalpam, Hueyotlipan, Xaltocan, and hdas Mixco, San Nicolas el Grande, eg. AGET/FRRO leg HyG Oct. 1914 exp. 88, 99; Memo. de Drusina HyG May 1916 f.29; leg JyG Aug. 1917 exp. 183; May 1917 exp. 118; HyG May 1916 exp. 29; Aug 1917 exp. 15; Oct. 1917 f.36; leg Junta Interventora 1914–15 exp. 16; Cuellar, *La Revolución*, p. 199. *On land distribution:* Ez. M. Gracia, "La tenencia de tierra en Tlaxcala," mss (TTT), pp. 52–53; "Síntesis historica tlaxcalteca," mss (SHT), pp. 239–41; Del Castillo, *Puebla y Tlaxcala*, pp. 216–17. *Rancheros:* local reports and petitions in AGET/FRRO leg HyG Mar. 1916 exp. 34; Aug. 1917 exp. 37; 239 HyG Mar. 1918 f.31, 33, 46; 241 HyG May 1918 f.277, 286, 386, 396, 404, 429; 243 HyG July 1918 f.388 etc.

flected deep-seated, traditional beliefs about land and autonomy, as well as revenge on rural and urban owners and entrepreneurs.[13] Rojas remained with Carranza, but he only kept the loyalty of a few officers, mostly fellow villagers, officials of his own provisional government and his friends in the leadership of the recently founded Tlaxcalan Constitutionalist party, the successor of the extinct ARP. For a new Constitutionalist brigade, the Leales de Tlaxcala, Rojas had to start from scratch, recruiting among Puebla friends and soldiers from his own village and its surroundings.[14]

The Rise and Fall of Arenista Power (1914–19)

ROJISTAS AND ARENISTAS IN TLAXCALAN POLITICS (1914–1917)

From November 1914 onward, the Rojas' and the Arenas' factions of the TRM were involved in a continuous struggle for control of the state of Tlaxcala. As minor chiefs, however, the political options available to them were increasingly dependent on the changing balance of power between the Constitutionalists on the one hand, and Zapatistas and Villistas on the other. The vengeful agrarian radicalism of Tlaxcalan revolutionary leaders and their attempts to gain or retain local autonomy sooner or later had to clash with the progressive consolidation of Constitutionalist power in central Mexico and Carranza's firm intention to return as soon as possible to constitutional government and procedures.

Just after he rebelled, Arenas controlled most of Tlaxcala and parts of Puebla, but within a year Constitutionalist military successes had seriously reduced Arenista military power to the Sierra

[13] Del Castillo, *Puebla y Tlaxcala*, pp. 155–60, 171–77; Cuellar, *La Revolution* 1: 209; Gracia, *Las Tlaxcaltecas*, p. 56; Buve, "Peasant Movements," p. 140; Garciadiego mss; National Archives, Washington, Decimal File 1910–1929 (NAW/DF) 812.00: 13692, 13831, 13880, 13977, 14073, 14285. Consular reports Vera Cruz and Puebla to Secretary of State, Washington, D.C.

[14] AGET/FRRO leg JyG April 1915 exp. 17; Acta declaración dd. Nov. 7, 1914 signed by civil servants and military men in leg HyG 1914 exp. s/n. Acta elección Mesa Directiva Gran Partido Liberal del Estado, San Damian Texoloc, Aug. 6, 1914 and Acta Constitución Ejercito Constitucionalista Tlaxcalteca, San Damian Texoloc, Aug. 3, 1914, in Coll. Ant. Hidalgo Sandoval, Apizaco; Del Castillo, *Puebla y Tlaxcala*, pp. 169–80; Candelario Reyes mss, pp. 22–25 in Coll. Candelario Reyes, now held by the state government of Tlaxcala. Reyes worked between 1917 and 1921 in Tlaxcala as an official of the Federal Agrarian Commission.

Nevada and the Volcanes.[15] However, on December 1, 1916, Arenas signed an Act of Unification with Carranza. His military forces were to be incorporated as the División Arenas in the Constitutionalist army and Arenas' assignment as Constitutionalist commander involved the control and defense of the military district along the interoceanic railway. This assignment, with headquarters in Texmelucan, brought the Atoyac basin in Puebla and part of Tlaxcala under his control.[16]

Why did Arenas, generally considered to be a genuine agrarista, leave Zapata? Apart from the deteriorating Zapatista military control and Arenas' continuous quarrels with neighboring Zapatista chiefs, it has been suggested that the issue of land distribution may have played a crucial role. In Arenas' view, the agrarista ideal not only implied immediate and direct restitution of hacienda lands to villages, but also the foundation of agricultural colonies of resident workers on the haciendas. To realize his ideal, Arenas was, according to Garciadiego, prepared to "gamble on two horses". He left the Zapata movement because of the rather dim prospects for implementing his agrarian ideals in Puebla and Tlaxcala. He joined Carranza only to maximize his chances for land reform. However, given the limited scope of the 1915 Carranza land reform decree—it only envisaged small donations of land to village communities and it prohibited autonomous actions of peasants to occupy hacienda lands— Arenas needed de facto autonomy from Constitutionalist authorities and, at the same time, avoidance of hostilities with Zapata. He succeeded in both for at least nine months. There is no doubt that Arenas, by joining Carranza, as Womack aptly points out, "secured peace and autonomy for his territory and through the villages there he was more revered than ever."[17]

---

[15] Xaltocan, Panotla, and Nativitas, within 5–10 miles of the capital were municipalities where arenista chiefs like Adolfo Bonilla distributed land, punished enemies, and even imprisoned civil officers of the constitutionalist government. See also AGET/FRRO legs HyG Jan 1916 exp. 48; Feb. 1916 exp. 19, 66; Mar. 1916 exp. 19, 27; June 1916 exp. 17; July 1916 exp. 14. El Regional, Bisemanal Constitucionalista, Tlaxcala, no. 1, Dec. 1914. El Republicano, Organo del Gran Partido Liberal del Edo, nos. 1, 2, 5, and 7, Sept.–Dec. 1915; Gracia, Los Tlaxcaltecas, pp. 63–64; informes Rojas Oct. 1915, cited in Cuellar, La Revolución, 2: 24–29; Del Castillo, Puebla y Tlaxcala, pp. 179–181, 201–203; Buve, "Peasant Movements," p. 141; Garciadiego mss, pp. 26–28. Interviews with Ez. M. Gracia, Oct. 1967.

[16] Buve, "Peasant Movements," p. 142.

[17] Garciadiego mss, pp. 26–33, especially Arenas' relations with Everardo González and Fortino Ayaquica; Decreto de 6 de Enero de 1915, in Manuel Fabila, Cinco siglos de legislación agraria en Mexico (Mexico, 1940), pp. 270–74; Gracia Los Tlaxcalte-

Which parties on the Constitutionalist side were interested in bringing Arenas back and which ones were opposed? At first sight one is tempted to assume that federal and state Constitutionalist authorities, confronted with the persistent problem of pacification and control in Puebla and Tlaxcala, might have wanted Arenas back. This indeed seems to hold for some of the federal commanders like General Cesáreo Castro and Puebla state authorities, but not for those of Tlaxcala. Constitutionalist state authorities in Tlaxcala, and especially the military commander Rojas and his friends, seem to have persistently opposed every effort to bring Arenas back into Constitutionalist ranks. When reunification was finally agreed upon, the Tlaxcalan authorities were left out of negotiations and kept uninformed.[18] It is, indeed, hardly believable that they would have relished the prospect of sharing office and power with returning Arenistas. Even more, Arenas' return to the Constitutionalist camp, at a time when Carranza made it clear that he wanted to return to constitutional government, implied that the Rojistas had to reckon with the still quite popular Arenas and his friends as serious contenders in state-level elections.[19]

However, in 1917 things turned out somewhat different. Unlike Rojas, Arenas' major concern was not the organization of a political party and an electoral campaign, but the consolidation of his de facto autonomy. On the very day of the unification with Carranza, Arenas and his officers started the distribution of lands, confiscated tax revenues and imposed their own tax collectors and views on the administration of justice in the southwestern half of Tlaxcala and the valley of Texmelucan. Commander Rojas and the civilian Constitutionalist governor of Tlaxcala, Antonio M. Machorro, were unable to check Arenas.[20] Machorro desribed the situation: "Lo que

---

cas, pp. 30, 63; Reyes mss, pp. 27–28; Del Castillo, *Puebla y Tlaxcala*, pp. 227–38; John Womack, *Zapata and the Mexican Revolution* (New York, 1969), p. 283.

[18] AGET/FRRO leg HyG 1916 Arenas exp. 21 and 84 correspondence between Gob. Machorro of Tlaxcala, Gen. Cesareo Castro, Puebla, and Srio de Gobernación, Mexico. Garciadiego mss, pp. 30; Cuellar, *La Revolución* 2: 95–103.

[19] Buve, "Peasant Movements," pp. 147–49 can now be corroborated by the collection of local periodicals in the Biblioteca Andrés Angulo, INAH, Tlaxcala: e.g., *El Constitucional*, Semanario político, órgano del Partido Liberal Constitucionalista de Tlaxcala, la época, nos. 4 and 7 (Aug.–Sept. 1917); the Arenista *La Libertad*, bisemanal político y de información, nos. 1–9 (Jan.–Mar. 1918) edited in Texmelucan. See also *Universal*, Aug. 20, 1917, *El Democrata*, Feb. 25, 1918, and *Excelsior*, Mar. 11, 1918, on the political struggle in Tlaxcala; AGET/FRRO leg JyG June 1917 exp. 4.

[20] AGET/FRRO legs HyG 1916, HyG, and Fom 1917 contain many complaints of local authorities, landowners, rancheros, and sometimes villagers; legs JyG Mar., April,

Domingo Arenas no logró por medio de las armas, lo está llevando a cabor pacificamente bajo capa de rendición."[21]

By mid-1917, however, the Zapata movement was confined to Morelos and was struggling for survival. Arenas' military services, or perhaps better his neutrality, seemed therefore somewhat less essential to the federal government. Although it seems unlikely that Arenas seriously considered rejoining Zapata, he apparently did go on with his policy of "gambling on two horses," probably with the aim of securing a safe frontier with Zapata and enlarging his own following with Zapatist defectors. Arenas had several interviews with Zapata's emissaries and was killed in the last one at the end of August 1917.[22]

After Arenas' death, Carranza sought to eliminate Arenista power. He appointed a strong non-Tlaxcalan general, Luís M. Hernández, as governor of Tlaxcala. Hernández had played an important role in the unification arrangements of 1916 and knew the Tlaxcalan revolutionary chiefs. His main task was to extend the provisional government's authority in the south and west of Tlaxcala and to prepare for the constitutionally required elections of state governor and deputies.[23] The first point is discussed in detail below; the second point needs some clarification in advance.

At the moment of Arenas' death, the Arenistas were far behind Rojas in terms of political organization and the preparation of an electoral campaign. Rojas and several of his friends had already been launched by their party, the Partido Liberal Constitucionalista (PLC), as candidates for governor and deputies, and dozens of party

---

June, July 1917 demonstrate the problem of bandolerismo and the powerlessness of the provisional government; Garciadiego mss, p. 36; leg JyG May 1917 exp. 138 example of correspondence between Arenas and Gob. Rios Zertuche (DRZ); tels. Gob. Tlax., Pdte CNA and owners to Sria de Guerra, Mex. in Expediente General Domingo Arenas (EGDA), copies in Coll. Ez.M. Gracia, Chiautempan; Tes. Gral. Luís Machorro to Gob. Edo Feb. 15, 1917, in AGET/FRRO leg HyG 1916, Arenas exp. 84. Luís Machorro's view is supported by letters of the Recaudador de Rentas (R de R) and the Interventor de Fincas (IdF), Calpulalpam. See HyG Feb. 1916 exp. 25; May 1916 exp. 41; July 1916 exp. 14; Del Castillo, *Puebla y Tlaxcala*, pp. 156–58; Cuellar, *La Revolución* 2: 89–91, 96–99, 115–16; Garciadiego mss, pp. 34–38.

[21] Gob. A. Machorro to Srio de Edo y del Despacho de Gob, Mexico, Jan. 8, 1917, in AGET/FRRO leg HyG 1916 Arenas exp. 66.

[22] Cuellar, *La Revolución* 2: 122–26; Garciadiego mss, pp. 38, 44–45; tels and letters in EDGA copies in Coll. Gracia, Chiau.

[23] Informe Gob. Luís M. Hernández (LMH) to Srio de Gob. Feb. 26, 1918 in AGET/FRRO leg HyG 1916 Arenas exp. 84; correspondence between Gov. LMH, Gen. Margarito de la Puente, military commander of Tlaxcala, and Gen. Cesareo Castro. AGET/FRRO leg 238 HyG Feb. 1918 f.173, 175, 176, 277. Cuellar, *La Revolución* 2:134–40.

clubs had been founded.[24] Arenas did engage in discussions in the press on hot issues like his land grants to villages and landless laborers, but, as far as we know, when he died he still had not been proposed as candidate for governor, or he had not yet accepted such a candidacy. In a way, his sudden death resolved the problem. A group of Arenista politicians, mainly low-status intellectuals, recognized the inevitability of their adaptations to the political rules set by Carranza. They immediately started an electoral campaign, launched Anastasio Meneses (a trusted senior officer of Arenas) as candidate for governor, and founded dozens of clubs of the Arenista Partido Liberal (PL). Within a few weeks the Arenistas were virtually ex aequo with the Rojistas in terms of political strength.[25] Arenas' impressive accomplishments in land distribution gave his followers a solid popular base and set the trend for the electoral campaign: competitive agrarianism. While Governor Hernández slowly extended his authority in Arenista territory, Rojista and Arenista candidates for office vied with each other in their attempts to safeguard the Arenista land grants.

RURAL PROPERTY AND THE EMERGENCE OF LOCAL ARENISTA INTEREST GROUPS

In order to analyze this phenomenon of competitive agrarianism in Tlaxcala in 1917–18 we first provide some insight into the way Arenista chiefs controlled, distributed, and exploited rural properties. Arenas' unification with Carranza in Decmeber 1916 strengthened the former's military control in the south and west of Tlaxcala, where, only a few rural owners escaped confiscation or at least partial division of their properties. Exact figures will probably never

[24] AGET/FRRO PLCT File leg JyG Feb 1917 exp. 79, 80, 82; on May 27, 1917 the first issue of party newsletter La Patria de Xicohténcatl came from the government printing press; El Constitucional, cit. nos. 4, Aug. 26, 1917, no. 7, Sept. 23, 1917; El Universal, Aug. 20, 1917; Excelsior, Mar. 11, 1918; El Democrata, Feb. 25, 1918. Interviews with Ez. M. Gracia.

[25] El Ciudadano, Seminario dedicado a la explotación de las riquezas del país, No. 6, Aug. 20, 1917, No. 15, Nov. 4, 1917, No. 22, Jan. 23, 1918. Arenista oriented paper edited in Mexico City; Cauterio, el periódico de los revolucionarios, No. 76, Aug. 4, 1917, No. 78, Aug. 8, 1917, 2a época no. 9, Oct. 20, 1917; La Libertad, cit. Nos. 1–9 (Jan.–Mar. 1918). Machorro assured Cesareo Castro in spring 1917 that there was only one party in Tlaxcala! AGET/FRRO leg JyG Feb. 1917 exp. 15. Interviews with Ez. M. Gracia, Oct. 1967, Mrs. Angulo, Feb. 1981. Among the fifteen candidates for deputy on the PLT list for the 1918 elections we find at least seven teachers, students, and lawyers, a few junior officers of ranchero origin and several peasant workers (La Libertad, Nos. 1–7, Jan.–Mar. 1918).

become available, but on the basis of the evidence we may safely assume that none of the larger owners escaped this fate. The smaller owners and many peasants also had a hard time, losing their animals and implements, and sometimes being evicted. Even in municipalities within a few miles of the capital, Arenas was able to distribute lands, appoint agrarista committees to supervise the distribution and, if need be, the armed defense of these lands, and to jail uncooperative local authorities.[26]

This brings us to some important questions regarding the agrarian initiatives of Arenas and his senior officers. Exactly what happened to the rural properties, and which social groups among the peasantry got the most out of the land distribution, are difficult questions to answer. As soon as we leave the level of broad generalizations we have to tackle an impressive variety in local situations, in which a whole series of factors must be considered. First, there seems not to have been an established specific Arenista policy of land distribution, but a vague goal that many of Arenas' chiefs tried to carry out as they saw fit. Moreover, we have to take into account the personal greed of local commanders and the fact that the general deficiency of army services and transport made it imperative to have a basis for provisions, even after unification. Constitutionalist commanders faced the same problems.[27]

I propose, therefore, to analyze Arenista handling of rural properties along two dimensions: the exploitation and the distribution of properties. If we accept the relative autonomy of local chiefs in handling rural properties we may assume that the outcome in each case depended on the following variables: the characteristics of the local

[26] This view cannot be based on one solid document, but on a large number of letters and reports: government correspondence, see notes 20, 21; petitions from owners to the governor, the state (CLA) or Federal Agrarian Commission (CNA) (e.g., Ant. Izquierdo, owner San Diego Recoba, Huey. to Gob. Edo, Oct. 23, 1917 in AGET/FRRO leg HyG Oct. 1917 exp. 45; Fco Tellez Corona, Pozuelos, Calp. to Gob. Edo in HyG Jan. 1918 exp. 3); reports of CLA commissioners on properties, villages, Arenista colonies, or acts of land distribution (e.g., informe vocal David C. Manjárrez to CLA Jan. 31, 1918, in leg 261 Fom Jan. 1918; JyG June 1917 exp. 62); letters of municipal presidents or Arenista agrarian committees (JLA's) sometimes including land grant documents (e.g., Actas posesión Ixtacuixtla, Españita, and Santiago Michac in leg 268 Fom July 1918 f.248; 269 Fom Aug. 1918 f.36 and JyG Aug. 1917 exp. 112). Finally, letters of Arenista chiefs defending their acts of land distribution (e.g., Domingo Arenas, JyG Aug. 1917 exp. 112; transcr. of Arenas corresp. with Gen. Cesareo Castro HyG 1916 Arenas exp. 84; Felipe González, HyG May 1917 exp. 54; Adolfo Bonilla, JyG May 1917 exp. 109, etc.).

[27] Juan Felipe Leal, "Inflación y revolución: El caso de los trabajadores de Mazaquiahuac y el Rosario", Tlaxcala, paper, pp. 1–3; Garciadiego mss, pp. 35–41.

system of land tenure and production, the location of peasant communities, their leadership and relations with the nearby Arenista chieftain; the capacity of this chieftain to control the area, the maintenance requirements of his unit, and the possibilities there for profitable exploitation of maguey fields (pulque) or forests (charcoal, timber), etc. Last but not least, we have to deal with the status of the properties when they fell into Arenista hands. Were they abandoned, confiscated by the Rojas' government of 1914, or still being exploited? In the last case we have to take into account the capacity and willingness of local administrators or owners to deal with revolutionary chieftains and to make the best of it.

If the exploitation was indirect it generally consisted at least in the requisition of a part of the production by the Arenista chiefs and their forces, and mostly for their own benefit. Depending on the collaboration of a still resident administrator, or caretaker, this could take the form of robbery or forced deliveries. These types could be found all over Arenista territory. Direct exploitation supervised by Arenista chiefs seems to have been more frequent where Arenista military power remained strong and unchallenged; since some of the haciendas in these areas were a considerable distance from local peasant communities, direct exploitation by Arenista chiefs must have implied a considerable dependence on resident labor. Sometimes even local administrators and staff stayed or continued to work in cooperation with the occupying forces. Constitutionalist Governor Del Castillo (1915–16) complained therefore in a 1915 report that "los propietarios tienen sus empleados y explotan las fincas garantizadas por el Zapatismo." But in spite of Del Castillo's complaint, production must have been low for the time being, because many haciendas had been sacked and burned following Arenas' rebellion.[28]

A clear case of exploitation of properties for the benefit of local chieftains was that of Trinidad Telpalo around Nanacamilpa, a ranchero community in the foothills of the Sierra Nevada, in west

[28] Bernard Q. Nietschmann, *The Hacienda and Revolutionary Change in the Agricultural Occupance of the Llanos de Apam*, M.A. Thesis, Wisconsin, 1968, pp. 45–46; Leal, "Inflacion," pp. 1–7; Garciadiego mss, p. 38; hda *Mixco* HyG 1916 Arenas exp. 84; *Ixtafiayuca*, AGET/FRRO leg JyG Junta Interventora 1914–15 exp. 34; *Mazapa*, HyG Sep. 1916; Elucidating letters from owners Mariano Muñoz (San Ant. Techolote, La Compañia), Juan S. Rivas of the Sucs. Torres Adalid (S. Bartolomé del Monte), repr. Piedad Iturbe (S. Nicolas el Grande) and Fca Campero vda. de Pasquel (Zacacalco), all in legs 237 to 249 HyG 1918.

Tlaxcala. During the Porfiriato a large local hacienda had been divided in lots to be occupied by colonists. Most of the settlers had less than forty hectares, suited mainly to hazardous dry farming, small-scale pulque production, and some sheep farming. The surrounding monte was, however, especially suited to the production of timber, firewood, and charcoal, and it had been sold and divided among several larger owners who sometimes held properties elsewhere. The construction of the interoceanic railroad to Puebla and Mexico City connected this area to the urban market. Telpalo and his forces occupied Nanacamilpa and the monte in 1914 and gradually started to take over exploitation of the woods. Unification offered Telpalo and his officers not only recognition as local commanders of the Tlaxcala division of the railroad, but also the freedom to exploit the natural resources and a relatively undisturbed link with the urban market. Telpalo immediately saw his chances, confiscated all the products of the nearby haciendas and started wholesale woodcutting in the monte. Some local rancheros succeeded in becoming his friends, participated in this venture, and managed to obtain confiscated properties of "enemies of the revolution" as land grants. Those who did not belong to Telpalo's clique suffered from heavy faenas and forced deliveries imposed by Telpalo's men.

Sometimes sharecropping arrangements seemed to have been continued or even imposed as the Arenista forces simply substituted for former owners. Hacienda Axolotepec, for instance, had since 1909 been parcelled out and sold to *fraccionistas*, small owners-to-be who paid annual installments to the hacendado. When Felipe González and his forces took over the area of Espanita, the fraccionistas became their sharecroppers, and in the case of hacienda Ameca he required the same of the owner's sharecroppers. These sharecropping obligations figure among the complaints of villagers after Arenista control started to crumble in the municipality of Espanita.

Telpalo and González were not the only Arenista commanders who controlled and exploited haciendas mostly for their own benefit and that of a small group of associates, especially the leading village agraristas, those peasants who had an important role in the distribution of land and the exploitation of haciendas, and were prepared to defend their recently acquired interests. When Governor Hernández finally succeeded in bringing the bigger part of Arenista territory under his control, he found out that General Adolfo Bonilla and his local lieutenant, Pedro Susano, had controlled six haciendas in the

municipality of Hueyotlipan, while General Antonio Mora controlled the haciendas around the town of Calpulalpam.[29]

DISTRIBUTION OF PROPERTIES

Our second dimension refers to distribution primarily of properties
among local peasants. Here we can distinguish between two main
types: land grants to village communities and to colonies of landless
hacienda laborers. Especially in the west Tlaxcala municipalities of
Calpulalpam, Españita, and Hueyotlipan we find both types of land
grants, even within the limits of one hacienda.[30] Did the Arenista
distributions actually give land to peasants or only confirm an already de facto situation of occupation?

Although Arenas rebelled at the end of 1914, it seems that many
official acts of Arenista land distribution did not start before unification, that is, two years later. This may be due to the adverse conditions created by the state of war and Arenas' deficient military
control of the area. It does not imply, however, that the land stayed
under the control of the owners or administrators. Even if we take
into account the deliberate distortions in reports of owners and
agraristas,[31] it seems that many properties had been abandoned, especially in south and west Tlaxcala. If this was the case, villagers,
resident sharecroppers, or rural laborers could occupy lands, although they sometimes had to deliver part of their output to a local

[29] Gob. Machorro al Srio de Edo y Desp de Gob. Jan. 8, 1917, in AGET/FRRO leg HyG
1916 Arenas exp. 84; see also exp. 34; *Nanacamilpa*: HyG April 1917; Hoyo y suce-
sores, 272 Fom Oct 1918 f.333; Duran Huerta, 242 HyG June 1918 f 590; Jauregui de
Dandini, 241 HyG May 1918 f.131; 259 Fom Jan. 1918 f 122. Especially elucidating is
a letter of the Italian Ambassador S. Cambiagio to Aguirre Berlanga, Mar. 17, 1917,
trascr. to Gob. Tlax in HyG, April 1917. *Españita*: HyG May 1916 exp. 29; HyG Jan.
1918 exp. 3; 272 Fom Oct 1918 f.26; Viveros, hda Ameca, to Gob. May 25, 1918. HyG
May 1918 exp. 117. Cuellar, *La Revolución* 2:136–38. Gob. LMH's informe gives an
account of haciendas in west Tlaxcala exploited by Bonilla, Mora, González and Telpalo.

[30] Well documented cases are the hdas of Ameca, Miltepec and rcho Cuauhtepec
anexo of hda San Nicolas el Grande in Españita; hda Ixtafiayuca and rcho Cuesillos
in Calp. See Viveros (Ameco) corresp. in AGET/FRRO leg 272 Fom Oct 1918 f.2, 14, 19,
27, 37, 39, 41, 44, 67, 75, 76; Fom Jan. 1919 exp. 141, 142; Cuauhtepec leg 267 Fom
June 1918 f.435, 437–38, 441–42; *Ixtafiayuca-Cuesillos* leg Hyg 1916 Arenas exp. 84.

[31] In order to claim tax exemptions owners had an interest in proving that war and
bandolerismo forced them to cease exploitation and abandon their properties. Sometimes these reports were verified by the visitador de haciendas, who had to ensure
the requests were justified (see AGET/FRRO legs HyG 1917, 1918 on tax exemptions).
Agraristas were eager to prove that they had already been in actual possession of the
lands for many years and certainly before unification (see legs Fom 1917, 1918).

chieftain. Examples are the earlier mentioned sharecroppers and laborers of hacienda Ameca, and the fraccionistas of Axolotepec, Españita. We also know that chiefs like Bonilla immediately expropriated and redistributed property of alleged enemies of the revolution or village caciques. It is therefore likely that a certain amount of land already came into the hands of peasants in 1915 and 1916, although we may assume that conditions of war made occupation and exploitation hazardous.[32] Unification with Carranza in 1916 meant more peace and security, and it is clear from many reports that Arenistas started full-scale land distribution and exploitation in December 1916. But the unification treaty did not include any explicit stipulations regarding agrarian matters. It only alludes to "amplias garantias en sus vidas, familias e intereses" for the Arenista chieftains.[33] Since land distribution was one of Arenas' major goals, he must have considered this one of his interests. Until Arenas' death, Carranza's attitude was a prudent one. He insisted on proper constitutionalist procedures but avoided a confrontation with Arenas on the issue of his land grants. Arenas took advantage of the situation and started a campaign to protect his land grants in the future by having them confirmed by the Carrancista agrarian authorities. Arenas not only gave land to villagers and confirmed de facto occupations but also urged the villagers and colonists to start the Constitutionalist procedures as soon as possible. Arenista officers exhorted the Constitutionalist agrarian authorities in Tlaxcala to cooperate and speed up procedures. Here it seems important to stress that the commissioners of the Tlaxcalan Local Agrarian Commission (CLA) were virtually Arenista in their strong agrarian convictions.[34] In our view, many Arenista deeds that confirm land grants have to be interpreted within the framework of intended legalization following Carrancista procedures. Especially important for Arenistas seems to have been Carranza's September 19, 1916, decree on provisional possessions. It withdrew the authority of governors and military commanders to give villages provisional possession of the lands

---

[32] *Axolotepec* AGET/FRRO leg 267 Fom June 1918 f.447, 480–93; *Bonilla* leg HyG 1914 cit.

[33] See an alleged letter of Arenas to Fco Villa, Mar. 1917. It may be a fake, but there is an explicit reference to Carranza's recognition of Arenista land distribution. In EGDA copies Coll. Gracia; unification treaty cited in Cuellar, *La Revolución* 2:88–91.

[34] Cuellar, *La Revolución* 2:101-102; corresp. between DRZ and Arenas JyG May 1917 exp. 138; Folletos, see ASRA legs 5003, 4873, 4986. On David C. Manjárrez and Max. Ortega, Tlax CLA commissioners, see their commissions AGET/FRRO leg 261 Fom Jan. 1918 f.305, and reports, e.g., on Coll. Guadalupe leg 261 Fom Jan. 1918 f.309–10, *Españita* leg 269 Fom Aug. 1918 f.361–62; interviews Ez. M. Gracia, Oct. 1967.

they had asked for, pending the final decision of Carranza himself. From then on, village committees who were about to enter their petitions for land would have to wait for the final decision of Carranza before actually gaining possession of the land. This may be the reason why virtually all of the Arenista deeds found until now have been dated before September 19, 1916! Moreover, even villages that could not show documents tried to stay within the time limit of Carranza's decree in order to keep their de facto possessions of hacienda lands.[35] One clear example is the case of the villages Atoyatenco, Nopalucan, Tecuescomac, and Tepetitla situated around the large irrigated hacienda Atoyac of the Kennedy family near Tepetitla. According to their claims, they all should have obtained land from the hacienda between February and September 1916, but from the owner's correspondence with state and federal authorities we can deduce that the Kennedys did not cease exploitation before 1917. In spite of sacking and the loss of animals and implements, part of the hacienda was cultivated by sharecroppers from the villages. Another part had already been occupied by Atoyatenco and Tepetitla peasants, but the large confiscation began at the beginning of 1917 when Arenas ordered its repartition.[36] It is clear, therefore, that several Arenista deeds and claims of the peasants must have been deliberately antedated.

After Arenas' death, however, Carranza insisted on proper procedures. He refused to recognize the Arenista deeds handed out by Arenas or his officers without interference from the Constitutionalist bureaucracy. According to the Constitutionalist legislation village communities in Arenista territory were qualifed to present petitions for land to the state governor and start the required procedures, but before Carranza's final decision on their petitions the peasants were not allowed to occupy the lands they had requested. This implied that many peasants in Arenista territory were obliged to return the already occupied lands to the owner and ac-

[35] For the text of this decree, esp. art 2 transitorio see Manuel Fabila, *Cinco siglos,* pp. 296–97; elucidating are Governor Rojas' remarks on the subject in the margin of a petition of Españita village committee. He wants to know from Carranza "si las posesiones dadas a los pueblos por autoridades pasadas, que se fundaron en lo dispuesto en circular fecha 19 de septiembre de 1916 deben respetarse aun cuando no tengan documentos escrito esos pueblos. . . ." in leg 267 Fom June 1918 f.448.

[36] ASRA 5003; Archivo Delegación SRA, Tlaxcala (ADT) 144 d: 25; AGET/FRRO leg JyG Aug. 1917 exp. 112; leg HyG 1916 Arenas exp. 84; originals and copies corresp. Kennedys to U.S. Amb. Charles B. Parker, Gov. Machorro, a.o., Const. authorities; on Kennedy's negotiations with Arenas see Marciano Rojas to S.G. de Gob. Tlax dd. April 19, 1917, all in leg HyG 1916 Arenas exp. 84.

cept a sharecropping arrangement or be hired as rural laborers while awaiting Carranza's final decision.

As a consequence of this, a second Carrancista degree played an even more important role in the Arenista strategy for maintaining possession while trying to have it confirmed by Constitutionalist authorities. This was the circular issued by the National Agrarian Commission (CNA) on October 31, 1917, which stipulated that those peasants who cultivated hacienda lands, the possession of which was legally covered by Carranza's decree of September 1916, or lands turned over to them for cultivation by Constitutionalist authorities because of abandonment, were authorized to keep the crops.[37]

Especially the latter stipulation is important because it could help peasants who had simply invaded properties. Its promulgation came at a crucial moment for the Tlaxcalan agraristas because after Arenas' death, the owners tried to recover their properties and claimed their share of the standing crops. Once more villages and colonists clinged en masse to an item of Constitutionalist legislation, using it to keep the lands they had occupied and the standing crops. Stubbornly pretending that they were protected by Arenista deeds before September 19, 1916, or that the lands had been abandoned by the owners and had been turned over to them for cultivation by the municipal authorities, they refused to deliver the owner's share of the crops and stayed on the land. Moreover, it seems that the Tlaxcalan Constitutionalist authorities preferred a prudent, if not hands-off, attitude in this delicate issue of the posesiones provisionales.[38]

How many villages and resident groups of sharecroppers or rural laborers actually received land from Arenas or were confirmed in their possessions? Since we know that the Arenista attempts to obtain Constitutionalist recognition of their land grants started immediately after unification, we mainly have to look for data in the sources for 1917 and 1918. Governor Hernández claimed in May 1918 that the CLA in Tlaxcala had received 98 petitions presented by villages since 1915. About 60 must have been submitted in 1917, 45 of which referred to villages and colonies in southwest Tlaxcala. In

---

[37] Fabila, Cinco siglos, p. 334.

[38] AGET/FRRO leg 272 Fom Oct. 1918 f.146; 269 Fom Aug. 1918 f.355–56, f.361–62. Examples Michac 261 HyG Jan. 1918 f.206, Atoyatenco f.179; Xochitecatitla 260 Fom Feb. 1918 f.41; Tepetitla 262 HyG April 1918 f 188; Ixtacuixtla 268 Fom July 1918 f.257; Expañita 267 Fom June 1918 f.435; Huexotitla 252, f.149. See also n. 34 on Manjárrez, Ortega, and Sánchez Mejorada; and n. 35 on Rojas.

their petitions or corresponding letters many village agraristas pretended to claim Arenista land grants by Arenas himself or one of his officers, but it may well prove impossible to find sufficient reliable evidence. We have found copies or originals of Arenista land grant acts for 11 out of 37 petitioning villages in 1917, distributed over all the southwestern municipalities. But even if we find more of them, we are still not on solid ground because some of the alleged copies may be forgeries and even the original documents do not say much about when the peasants actually got the land. Owners, CLA commissioners, and officials like the visitador de hacienda and the interventor de fincas make it clear, however, that many peasants did have hacienda lands in their possession.[39] As far as the colonies are concerned, the Tlaxcalan CLA registered and initiated at least eight petitions from colonies, but if we take into account further reports of officials and complaints of owners there may have been much more.[40]

Why did the remaining colonies not enter petitions as the villages did? Several factors may have been involved. After Carranza made it finally clear in August 1918 that all Arenista possessions had to be returned to their owners and that petitioners had to be eligible for donations of land following the existing legislation, the Tlaxcalan CLA seems to have refused further petitions from colonies, because they did not have the required legal status of a pueblo. Moreover, from 1918 on, several colonies started to disintegrate as a consequence of the pressure of owners or even neighboring villages. The Llano Chico colony on the rancho Cuesillos was abandoned be-

[39] Informe presentada ante el XXV Congreso del Edo L. y S. de Tlaxcala por el Gob. prov. Gral. LMH, May 31, 1918, in P.O. del Estado, V, 1: 5 June 1918, compared with Melquiades Contreras' Relacion de poblados con posesión definitiva desde el año de 1915 a 1940, mss in ADT. Copies of originals referring to land grants for Ixtacuixtla and Tecuescomac, Ixt., Santorum and Calpulalpam, Calp., Expañita and Huexotitla, Esp., Xipetzingo and Ixcotla, Huey., Tepetitla, Lard., Atoyatenco and Michac, Nat. all in ASRA files or AGET/FRRO legs Fom 1917 and 1918.

[40] Registered: Felipe Hidalgo (hda El Corte) and Guadelupe (Mazapa), Calp.; Llibres de Tlaxcala (Cuauhtepec), Guadalupe and Reforma (Ameca), Juarez (Axolotepec) and Portezuelo (Ixtafiayuca), Esp. Division Arenas, Ixtacuixtla. See informe CLA March 1918 in AGET/FRRO leg 264 Fom April 1918 f.248–50, 269; CLA exp. Portezuelo, Esp., Felipe Hidalgo and Guadalupe, Calp. Reforma, Esp. all in legs Fom 1918. Interventor de Fincas, Calp. reports at the end of 1916 of El Progreso on Ixtafiayuca, and Llano Chico on rancho Cuesillos, both in Calp. leg HyG 1916 Arenas exp. 84. Letter Gob. Machorro to Min. de Gob. Mex. dd. Jan. 8, 1917. The visitador de haciendas reported to Gob. DRZ the founding of a colony in Atotonilco on rcho Ameyal, Ixtacuixtla, bordering Españita leg HyG Aug. 1917 exp. 23, 259, Fom Jan. 1918 f 81–82. See also no. 37.

cause the village of Calpulalpam considered the rancho an integral part of its village land. The colony of Llibres in the municipality of Españita succumbed to the threats of former landowners and the villagers of Pipillolla.[41]

Did the Arenista land grants and efforts to get the federal government to ratify them bring any tangible results for the peasants of southwest Tlaxcala? By May 1918, just before Rojas took over the governorship, at least forty-five villages and colonies in southwest Tlaxcala had entered petitions for land while they were struggling to keep the land donated or confirmed by Arenas. As far as the reception of petitions and the initiation of procedures is concerned, the Tlaxcalan Governors Rios Zertuche and Hernández seem to have gone along with Arenas' intentions. They approved most of the village petitions but were not authorized to give the villagers possession of lands, let alone to guarantee the Arenista possessions. Carranza, however, hesitated to confirm the governor's decisions. The colonists were even worse off. In spite of the sometimes glowing and sympathetic reports of CLA commissioners, their petitions had to be dismissed because of the lack of legal requirements.[42] In short, the Constitutionalist bureaucracy kept more than forty petitioning committees of villagers and colonists waiting for its decision while, as noted above, the area under Arenista protection slowly crumbled and the state government gradually implemented its policy to "normalize" land tenure.

"Una Nueva Casta de Caciques?"

Before going into this normalization policy we will attempt to make a rough, provisional analysis of local structures of Arenista interests (1917–18) that were to be affected by the normalization policy as it was executed by Governor Hernández .

With unification and the Arenista efforts to get the federal government to ratify their land grants, local agrarista committees appeared in many villages of the southwest. Were they elected by the community, appointed, or self-imposed? The minutes of several meetings do refer to assemblies[43] but, as we will see, these *juntas agrarias* sometimes developed into powerful economic interest groups under

---

[41] Carranza to Gob. Rojas AGET/FRRO leg 269 Fom Aug 1918 f.359; *Llibres*: leg 267 Fom June 1918 f. 435–42. The colonists of Llano Chico may have decided to incorporate into the agrarian census of Calpulalpam since they came from that village.

[42] Informe LMH May 1918 cit.; Relación de poblados cit.; informe CLA Mar. 1918 cit.

[43] E.g., AGET/FRRO leg 264 Fom April 1918 f.201–202.

some local chieftain, often linked to a regional Arenista commander. Whether the whole community profited from the increase in wealth is still open to question. Moreover, this type of development was definitely not limited to Arenista territory—we can find it too in Constitutionalist Tlaxcala, but to a much lesser degree. Governor Hernández makes this clear in his observation about agrarista committees in central Tlaxcala: "una nueva casta de caciques, más odiosos por sus procedimientos que el antiguo latifundista."[44]

Can we provide a provisional sketch of the various groups involved in local Arenista interest structures, their participation in the exploitation of natural resources, the hierarchy involved? On the basis of the available documentation on Arenista interest groups in the municipalities of Calpulalpam, Españita, Hueyotlipan, and Xaltocan we propose the following. In 1917 many juntas agrarias seem to have had a territorial base in an Arenista land grant or confirmation of an earlier occupation. This land, near to the villages, seems to have been cultivated by villagers. On top of this, the juntas often seem to have exploited a large range of mostly abandoned properties, which had not been included in the original land grant or were included only partially. This latter type of exploitation was often done in more or less joint ventures with neighboring villages, former laborers, and sharecroppers who had stayed on the hacienda and now cultivated on their own, sometimes organized in Arenista agricultural colonies. Together they exploited most, if not all, the properties of the area. Exploitation of these properties by the juntas had, moreover, a predatory character and concentrated on premature exhaustion of maguey fields, wholesale cutting down of the woods, and stripping the buildings and shacks of virtually everything that could be moved, used, or sold. One of the best documented cases is that of the powerful interests of the juntas agrarias of three villages in the municipality of Hueyotlipan. Under the umbrella of Arenista General Adolfo Bonilla and his local lieutenants Felipe González and Pedro Susano, the juntas of Xipetzingo, Ixcotla, and Hueyotlipan controlled many thousands of hectares up to the middle of 1918.

The junta of Xipetzingo claimed it had received the haciendas of Santiago Tlalpam and part of Cuamancingo with its *tinacales* (bodegas where the maguey juice is fermented into pulque) and implements as a grant from Arenas in February 1916. It also exploited the maguey fields, woods, and pastures of the abandoned haciendas of

[44] Informe LMH May 1918 cit.

La Blanca, San Sebastián, San Manuel and San Miguel la Presa. This was done together with the neighboring villages of Huiloapan and Ascensión. The junta of Ixcotla occupied Teozopilco and Las Tortolas after Bonilla had sacked and burned both properties. It exploited the maguey and wood resources, the limestone quarry, cultivated some maize, joined the villages of Huiloapan, San Mateo and Xipetzingo in exploiting La Blanca and the village of Hueyotlipan in exploiting the resources of hacienda Santa Cruz. More important was the junta of Hueyotlipan under the leadership of Pedro and Nicolas Susano, agrarista leaders and local Arenista officers, friends of Bonilla. They invaded the hacienda Tepalca and killed the administrator, then took over the hacienda of Santa Cruz, its *anexo* Tepepa and joined the villages of San Mateo and Ixcotla in the exploitation of La Blanca. Finally, the junta acquired the large haciendas of Recoba, San Antonio, and San Lorenzo Techalote after the forces of Bonilla had to leave Tlaxcala.[45]

Who was able to profit from this unprecedented local control over resources? It will perhaps never be possible to come to a thorough regional analysis, but in several cases owners and authorities maintained a continuous, detailed correspondence. Miguel Viveros, a merchant and Porfirista official, fought three years to get back his large haciendas, Ameca and Tepalca. His property amounted to nearly 4,300 hectares in the municipalities of Hueyotlipan and Españita. On the basis of his letters, those of his enemies, the juntas in Españita and Hueyotlipan, and the reports of David C. Manjárrez, a commissioner of the Tlaxcalan CLA who inspected the Viveros' haciendas, we are able to provisionally reconstruct the local tenure situation on two haciendas controlled by the local Arenista interest groups. On both haciendas, the land next to the villages was cultivated by village agraristas and was considered an Arenista land grant. Around the hacienda buildings we find groups of more or less independent cultivators, former resident laborers, and sharecroppers. On Ameca they had founded two Arenista colonies under the protection of Felipe González, but on Tepalca they managed on their own. We do have a detailed description of one of these colonies, Guadalupe, visited in 1917 by CLA commissioner David C. Manjárrez, a staunch supporter of the agraristas. Guadalupe consisted of

---

[45] *Tepalco*: AGET/FRRO leg 259 Fom Jan. 1918 f.111; 272 Fom Oct. 1918 f.2, 14, 67; *La Blanca*: leg 274 Fom Dec. 1918 f.82, 104; *Sta Cruz*: leg HyG Jan. 1918 exp. 11, leg 274 Fom Dec. 1918 f.104–105; *San Manuel*: leg 259 Fom Jan. 1918 f.74; *Xipetzingo*: leg 259 Fom Jan. 1918 f.74, leg 260 Fom Feb. 1918 f.152; *Tepepa*: leg 269 Fom Aug. 1918 f.298–305; Cuellar, *La Revolución* 2: 137; Relación de poblados cit.

thirty-nine rural laborers and their families who had constructed
new huts and gardens on longitudinal plots of 25 by 200 meters,
separated by rows of maguey. Next to these individual plots the colony intended to cultivate communally a tract of arable land with
maize, barley, and wheat; the 1917 results were rather disappointing, but a school was already under construction and the colony
even had a primitive water supply system that connected houses to
a nearby well.[46]

Several anexos or subunits of the haciendas had been occupied
with the support of Arenista forces by invading "entrepreneurs"
who forced the tenants or sharecroppers to deliver the landlords'
share of crop and the pulque production. In some cases these invasions probably had to do with the settling of old scores with the
landlord.[47] What was left of the haciendas seemed more or less free
for the type of predatory exploitation earlier referred to. Although
in the case of Ameca and Tepalca the administrators had been
chased away or killed, this was not always the case. The administrator of Santa Cruz managed to stay, collaborated with the junta of
Hueyotlipan in the exploitation of the hacienda and was even allowed to sell part of the crops.[48]

The documentation on Viveros' haciendas in Hueyotlipan also
gives us some clues to a possible hierarchical order in a local structure of Arenista interests. The base consisted of village agraristas
cultivating the Arenista land grant, colonists, groups of former laborers who worked independently, and squads of tlachiqueros (ex-
tractors of maguey juice) and woodcutters. At the intermediate level
we find village junta leaders, invading "entrepreneurs," surely
friends of Arenista chiefs, and a collaborating administrator. At the
top were the junta of Hueyotlipan and the Susano brothers. Apart
from a probably decisive voice in the partition of plots, they totally
controlled pulque production and its commercialization and may
have had big stakes in wood production and other commercial interests. Moreover, for the Susano brothers economic power coincided with recognized political power because after unification Nicolás Susano was elected municipal president of Hueyotlipan,

    [46] Viveros corresp., see AGET/FRRO leg HyG Feb. 1918; 241 HyG May 1918 f.117; 259
Fom Jan. 1918 f. 111, 116; 272 Fom Oct. 1918 f.2, 14, 17, 27, 35, 37, 39, 41, 44, and
67; Manjárrez, vocal CLA informe on Guadalupe AGET/FRO leg 261 Fom Jan. 1918
f.308–10; also 279, 306, 307; 272 Fom Nov. 1918 f. 75, 76.
    [47] Salvador Lira case, see AGET/FRRO leg 259 Fom Jan. 1918 f.116. Other examples:
Tellez Corona case, see leg HyG Jan. 1918 exp. 13; leg HyG 1916 Arenas exp. 84.
    [48] AGET/FRRO leg HyG Jan. 1918 exp. 11.

while his brother Pedro saw to it that they remained on good terms with the commander of the Constitutionalist military post on the nearby hacienda of Cuamancingo, situated next to the Mexican railway.[49]

Structures like that of Hueyotlipan can also be found in the neighboring municipalities of Xaltocan, Españita, and Calpulalpam so we may provisionally assume the existence of several interconnected local interest structures varying in scope, but altogether encompassing the heartland of Arenista control in southwest Tlaxcala in 1917. All of them had at least one thing in common: their claims and the resources they controlled could never have been maintained within the narrow limits of Carrancista land reform legislation and depended for the time being on Arenista military protection. When Governor Hernández decided to give Hueyotlipan about 1,500 hectares from the surrounding haciendas, it was less than one fifth of what the junta and the Susano brothers controlled in 1917 and it would still take several years before another president, Alvaro Obregón, would make a final decision.[50]

The Demise of Arenista Military Power and Interest Groups (1917–18)

We now can imagine what was at stake when the new governor, Hernández, tried to implement his normalization policy with the support of the recently appointed military commander of Tlaxcala, the stern General Margarito de la Puente. Hernández' policy consisted of three elements. First was the liquidation of Arenista military power. With the authorization of the federal government, Hernández tried to have the Arenista and Rojista forces withdrawn from Tlaxcala and replaced by non-Tlaxcalan troops to be used for garrisoning Arenista villages. In spite of Arenista resistance to federal orders for abandoning Tlaxcalan territory, Governor Hernández succeeded in gradually extending his control over the southwest. Between January 1918 and Hernández' departure in June, Arenista

[49] Mpal elections on Sept. 3, 1916 and Dec. 2, 1917. Nic. Susano elected twice. H. was the only municipality in southwest Tlaxcala where the elected candidate in 1916, i.e., before unification, actually became municipal president. The other municipal elections did not take place or were annulled because of the election of "enemigos de la causa constitucionalista." Cuellar, *La Revolución* 2: 80–81. Why was Susano elected? Two years later he was arrested by Rojas as a notorious Arenista, but he may have been still in hiding during the difficult guerilla years of Arenas' domain!

[50] Hueyotlipan file in AGET/FRRO leg Fom April 1918 exp. 4; JyG Mar. 1917 exp. 96; May 1917 exp. 109, Aug. 1917 exp. 83, 84.

chiefs and officers lost most of their military strongholds in the municipalities of Xaltocan, Hueyotlipan, and Espanita. Arenista troops also had to leave the municipality of Calpulalpam but Telpalo came back and stayed in Nanacamilpa until his troops were forcibly disarmed in June 1918.[51]

Second, Hernández sought to return landed properties to those owners who had not been affected by final presidential decisions on petitions for land and he wanted to secure the resumption of production under fair labor and sharecropping arrangements. In doing this he merely continued earlier policies of the Tlaxcalan constitutionalist government, which had not hesitated to step in as a contracting party in sharecropping arrangements, because it wanted to ensure adequate food production on abandoned properties in Tlaxcala.[52] Between December 1917 and March 1918 Hernández and other officials attended a series of assemblies in Arenista villages where properties were returned to the representatives of the owners. Local agraristas had to bring back stolen animals or implements but were at the same time urged to appoint agrarian representatives for the village and present a petition for land to the governor.[53] In doing this Hernández carefully kept in line with Carranza's refusal to recognize Arenista land grants or de facto possessions. Village communities were qualified to apply for land, but they had to return the (in Carranza's view) illegally occupied lands.

This brings us to Hernández' third objective: rapid, large-scale implementation of Carranza's land reform decree of 1915. The governor adhered to the Carrancista view that peasants had to conform to

[51] Cuellar, *La Revolución* 2: 131–38; letter Gob. LMH to Sria de Guerra, Mex. dd. Dec. 8, 1917 in Expediente General Cirilo Arenas (EGCA) copies Coll. Gracia, Chiau. It seems that part of the material he used is in AGET/FRRO leg HyG 1916 Arenas exp. 84. Informe LMH May 1918 cit; Vecinos Xalt., Huey., and Ixt. to Srio de Gobernación, Mex. dd. Jan. 24, 1918, in Cuellar, 2: 133; see corresp. between LMH and Gen. M. de la Puente AGET/FRRO leg 237 HyG Feb. 1918 f.169–76, 277; 242 HyG June 1918 f.590.

[52] All legs Fom 1918 between 259 (Jan.) and 274 (Dec.), e.g., AGET/FRRO leg 270 Fom Sept. 1918 f.396; 259 Fom Jan. 1918 f.306–18; ;260 Fom Feb. 1918 f.249–50; 261 Fom Mar. 1918 f.179, 182, 188, 215, 221. AGET/FRRO circulars 16 and 18 of the State Govt leg JyG April 1917 exp. 94; sharecropping decree Gov. DRZ leg 270 Fom Sept. 1918 f.396; On LMH's campaign leg 259 Fom Jan. 1918 f.306–18. Informe LMH May 1918 cit. in Cuellar, *La Revolución* 2: 153–63.

[53] Gov. LMHs and Major Figueroa's campaigns took place between December 1917 and March 1918. LMH went to Calpulpam, Santorum, Españita and Hueyotlipan. Figueroa had an escort of twenty soldiers and was ordered to return all the properties still exploited by the local Arenista juntas in Ixtacuixtla. AGET/FRRO leg 259 Fom Jan. 1918 f.73–74, 96, 99, 104, 114, 324, 329, 335; 261 HyG Jan. 1918 f.143; 270 Fom Sept. 1918 f.27–37; 243 HyG July 1918 f.933; 259 Fom Jan. 1918 f.104.

the traditional labor and sharecropping arrangements until a final decision on their petitions had been made by the president. On the other hand, he did his utmost to accelerate the decision-making process at the state level. When he left Tlaxcala in June 1918 most of his petitions had been decided upon and sent to Mexico City.[54]

The implementation of Hernández' normalization policy provoked a bitter struggle between local agrarista interests still supported by Arenista chiefs, albeit now only those from Texmelucan, and owners, administrators and others who had not been able to profit from Arenista control. The struggle is documented by the numerous complaints of owners and those who considered themselves victims of Arenista extortion. But also the Arenista village juntas complained en masse to the federal government about the (in their view) unjustified return of hacienda lands to the owners. Hernández, however, assumed that behind this protest were the disinherited Arenista chiefs.[55]

Let us give an example in order to elucidate this simultaneous process of Constitutionalist consolidation, the return of properties, and the promotion of land reform. In the Nativitas area, halfway between the capital of Tlaxcala and the Arenista headquarters in the town of Texmelucan, agraristas had occupied at least a part of the haciendas of Santa Marta, Aculco, Mixco, Santa Elena, San Antonio, Segura Michac, Santa Agueda, and Atoyac, although the tenure situations were definitely not the same on all properties. Mixco had been abandoned by its owners before Arenas' unification with Carranza, but the administrator of Atoyac stayed on, negotiated with Arenas' officers and tried to fight Arenas' decision to give the haciendas to the neighboring villages of Tepetitla, Atoyatenco, Tecuescomac, and Nopalucan. He had only slight success. The haciendas Santa Elena and Segura Michac met the same fate and were given as a land grant to Santiago Michac, although there still remained a group of loyal sharecroppers, as in the case of Atoyac. It seems, however, that the already deficient control of the owners deteriorated significantly during the first half of 1917, since agraristas now refused all sharecropping arrangements and loyal sharecroppers lost

[54] AGET/FRRO leg Fom Feb 1918 f.219; 261 HyG Jan. 1918 f.305; 273 Fom Nov. 1918 f.18. Cuellar, *La Revolución*, 2: 161–62.

[55] See AGET legs Fom 1918 259 (Jan.) to 274 (Dec.); 261 HyG Jan. 1918; Cuellar, *La Revolución* 2: 133, 135–38; also tels. Junta Agraria Calp. to Arenista chiefs Texmelucan, Dec. 1917 and letter Gob. LMH to Sria de Guerra dd. 8.12.1917 in EGCA copies Coll. Gracia.

lands to agraristas when a local junta started to divide the lands among its partisans.[56]

The normalization campaign of Governor Hernández in the Nativitas area started with the return of Atoyac to the Kennedy family in September 1917, and the distribution of the circular of October 1917, issued by the CNA, among the landlords and villagers. The villagers, especially the agraristas, clung to the clauses that stipulated that the standing crops on recognized provisional possessions, and on abandoned properties cultivated by peasants who had been authorized by municipal authorities, were to remain in the hands of the cultivators. The owners, however, stressed the only exception to this rule: ". . . salvo en los casos en que existen contratos de aparcería que hayan sido celebrados entre los cultivadores y los que se dicen propietarios de las tierras."[57] The owners claimed that they had concluded sharecropping arrangements with the peasants (which was partly true), and considered themselves entitled to a fixed share of the crop. The agraristas denied this and both parties looked for government support. Governor Hernández indeed intervened on behalf of the owners but at the same time quickly approved the local peasants' petitions for land. In February 1918, personal visits of the governor to the area and his firm land reform policy had apparently resulted in a incipient normalization of tenure and production. Except for the village of Tepetitla, nearest to Texmelucan, the other villages for the time being seemed to have agreed to sharecropping arrangements,[58] probably hoping for early presidential decisions after the governor had already approved seven petitions within two months. Moreover, three villages in the area did actually receive a land grant from President Carranza between November 1917 and January 1918.[59] As far as the still rebellious village of Tepetitla was concerned, Hernández contemplated forcing the agraristas of the "foco del Arenismo" out of the hacienda

[56] Carvajal properties (Mixco, Aculco, Sta Marta) leg 261 HyG Jan. 1918 f.86, 91, 94, 96, 172, 181, 266; Kennedy (Atoyac) leg 267 Fom June 1918 f.121, 122, 130, 132, 137, 145, 157, 198, 202, 206, 218, 231, 262; leg 237 HyG Jan. 1918; vda de Caso (San Antonio) ASRA 4943, vda de Rejon (Sta Elena) ASRA 4973 and Pacheca de Díaz Barriga (Segura Michac) ASRA 4986.

[57] Circular CNA Oct. 31, 1917, in Fabila, Cinco siglos, p. 334.

[58] Reports LMH to Srio A. de F. dd. Feb. 20 and 23, 1918, in AGET/FRRO leg 260 Feb. 1918 f.249, 250; leg 267 Fom June 1918 f.174–79.

[59] Decisions of LMH: Atoyatenco, El Milagro, Nopalucan, Xiloxochitla and Teacalco in Nov. 1917, Xochitecatitla and Santiago Michac in Jan. 1918. Presidential decisions on Tecuescomac, Tepectepec, and La Concordia. See Fichero, D.G. de Estad., Program. y Catastro, ASRA, Mexico.

lands and replacing them with loyal sharecroppers. It did not come to that because of the 1918 elections for governor and deputies. Arenista and Rojista deputies-to-be vied with each other for the favor of the Tepetitla agraristas. After Rojas won, several juntas in the area immeditely asked him to annul the sharecropping arrangements and guarantee the agraristas their possessions until the presidential decision. Provisional possession was to be a major issue in Tlaxcalan politics and it continued to provoke serious conflicts between owners and sharecroppers on the one hand, and agraristas on the other.[60]

However, the Nativitas example is not an isolated one. On the basis of the available documents (letters of municipal presidents, of owners and administrators, of juntas agrarias and of CLA commissioners) we may safely assume that tenacious resistance to Governor Hernández' normalization policy was widespread in all the municipalities of southwest Tlaxcala. The village agraristas immediately entered the required petitions for land, but in their view the only thing the governor and Carranza had to do was to confirm their Arenista land grants. They solidly refused to return the land and share the crops with the owners.[61] In this, the local agraristas definitely did not stand alone; they often received strong support from the clearly agrarista-oriented staff of the Tlaxcalan CLA, and in several municipalities (such as Calpulalpam, Hueyotlipan, and Tepetitla) they were backed by the municipal presidents.[62] Moreover, Arenista chiefs like Trinidad Telpalo and Felipe González deliberately stiffened the resistance of "their" agraristas. Telpalo simply ignored the order to stay out of Nanacamilpa and went on to protect his own interests and those of his friends. González obeyed and went to Texmelucan, but backed up his agraristas from there. When the returning owners, now supported by Governor Hernández, required the return of the tinacales, one third of the crop, and the return of the plots of hacienda Axolotepec to the fraccionistas (the smallholders who had bought these plots before the revolution) González advised his agraristas to keep a record of those who collaborated with the

[60] AGET/FRRO leg 260 Feb. 1918 f.33, 250; 267 Fom June 1918 f.362; 270 Fom Sept. 1918 f.401; See La Libertad Jan.–Mar. 1918 cit. points, e.g., the foundation of colonias agricolas, land grants to rancherías, etc.

[61] Aparceria problems AGET/FRRO leg HyG May 1916 exp. 29; 264 Fom April 1918 f.20; govt. orders leg 261 HyG Jan. 1918 f.120, 170; 267 Fom June 1918 f.441–42; 243 HyG July 1918 f.933; 259 Fom Jan. 1918 f.114–16.

[62] AGET/FRRO leg 272 Fom Oct. 1918 f.146, 149–51; 273 Fom Nov. 1918 f.147; 267 Fom June 1918 f.480; 259 Fom Jun 1918 f.111. For 1918–19 see also the detailed Viveros correspondence mentioned in no. 46.

government in order to punish them afterwards. This was done by way of small punitive assaults organized by González from Texmelucan. On González insistence, those agraristas on Axolotepec who had already turned over the plots to the fraccionistas came back and forced the fraccionistas once more to leave.[63] No wonder that up to 1919 many owners confessed in numerous complaints that they were simply unable to resume control and exploitation of their properties.[64]

Arenista Defeat and the Survival of Agrarismo (1918–19)

In the electoral campaign of 1918, many agraristas—especially the more prominent and perhaps privileged—perceived their situation as "caso delicadisimo por causa Gobernador" or "asunto gravíssimo por posesión de tierras."[65] For agrarista interests the obvious choice seemed to be the Arenista candidate Anastasio Meneses, but the choice was not always so obvious, since Arenista military protection proved less effective during the latter months of the campaign, and Carranza adamantly refused to exempt Arenista petitions from legal requirements and procedures. This section will consider the extent of Meneses' popular support, the effectiveness of Arenista military protection, the relations of Arenista chiefs to the Tlaxcalan Liberal party, and the possibility that the elections were rigged.

Meneses outstripped Rojas in popular support. Meneses' program gave more attention to land reform, including donations to smaller villages and colonies not yet recognized by Carranza law, as well as the creation of small properties. Activists from two clubs of the Arenista Liberal party in Calpulalpam visited colonies and villages all over western Tlaxcala and explained Meneses' program to the hundreds of agraristas who were waiting for the government to decide on their still unrecognized possessions.[66] In Nativitas activists from Rojas' Constitutionalist party and the Arenista Liberal party competed with each other in assisting village agrarian committees.

[63] AGET/FRRO 259 Fom Jan. 1918 f.104; HyG May 1916 exp. 29; La Libertad cit. no. 9. AGET/FRRO leg Fom April 1918 f.248–50.

[64] AGET/FRRO leg 274 Fom Dec. 1918 f.48, 104; 272 Fom Oct. 1918 f.67; see also Buve, "Movilización campesina y reforma agraria en los valles de Nativitas (1917–1923)," in El Trabajo y los trabajadores en la historia de Mexico, ed. E. C. Frost, W. C. Meyer, and J. Z. Vásquez (México, 1979).

[65] Tels. in copies ECGA Coll. Gracia, Chiau.

[66] Interviews with Ez. M. Gracia, Oct. 1967 and Mrs. Angulo, Feb. 1981; La Libertad, Excelsior, and El Democrata cit.

This provoked serious conflicts at the village level when agrarista leaders began to fear that their local opponents might find support in the other party.

The Arenistas' military capability in Tlaxcala seemed at the end of 1917 to have shrunk so much that the Arenistas were avoiding a military showdown with Governor Hernández. Bonilla, González, and other Arenista chiefs had been ordered to leave the state. Although they continued to defend the interests of their local agraristas, the transfer had, no doubt, affected their capacity to do so. The agraristas of Calpulalpam, for example, virtually cried out for help against Governor Hernández in their telegrams to Arenista headquarters in Texmelucan. Arenista leadership, however, seemed unable to protect them and the rebellious agrarista leaders of Calpulalpam went to jail.[67]

It is possible that the declining capacity for protection, divergent interests, and mounting irritation may have induced local agrarista leaders to look for support elsewhere. Some of them actually followed Arenas' own example of December 1916 and sided with his political opponent, Rojas. Moreover, Rojas badly needed Arenista defectors since he could not win the elections without at least a few Arenista districts. Rojas' Constitutionalist party tried to convince agraristas to change loyalties. An illustrative example is the case of the electoral district of Calpulalpam: with its junta in jail and its land officially returned to the former owners, the agraristas of Calpulalpam urgently requested the intervention of General Macario M. Hernández, a distinguished federal Constitutionalist commander but also a Tlaxcalteca and erstwhile pupil of a schoolteacher Isabel H. Gracia, a prominent member of the junta. General Hernández— not to be confused with Governor Luis M. Hernández—offered to intervene in exchange for Calpulalpam's support of Rojas. Shortly after his election, Rojas gave Calpulalpam a land grant of more than 8,000 hectares, considerably more than the original Arenista grant! But since Rojas had no authority to give possession, the agraristas had to wait for a presidential decision. Rojas frequently intervened but he was unable to convince the CNA and Carranza. In 1920 Calpuplalpam finally obtained about 1,000 hectares and was given possession by Rojas in person.[68]

In Nanacamilpa colony, within the same electoral district, the

[67] Tels. in copies EGCA Coll. Gracia, Chiau.; Interviews with Ez. M. Gracia, Oct. 1967.
[68] ASRA 4974 DL 2, 10, 20, 25–38, 39, 115, 137–69, 262–64, 348–52, 360–67, DT 156, 185, 192, 294–95.

junta had been founded in March 1917 and had started to distribute the surrounding lands among the original ranchero settlers and a number of newcomers, friends of Arenista chief Telpalo, who had settled in Nanacamilpa colony. Those who were considered "enemies of the revolution" were excluded, and as a consequence, a number of the original settlers, accused of loyalty to the old regime, lost their mostly small properties. In August 1917, even before Arenas' death, a number of Nanacamilpa rancheros, some of them junta members who had received lands from Arenas or Telpalo, established contacts with Rojas in the hope of obtaining tax exemptions and the confirmation of their possessions. Nanacamilpa needed recognition as a pueblo in order to submit a petition for land. Rojas, in the midst of his election campaign, promised help and after his election as governor, his majority in the state congress, with the now Rojista deputy for the district of Calpulalpam, soon approved pueblo status for Nanacamilpa. The dispossessed rancheros were apparently unable to get back their properties while Rojas was governor.[69]

Election day in May 1918 was preceded by violence and intimidation from both sides. The verification of the results by committees consisting of members of both parties took about ten weeks and was characterized by quarrels and complaints. Governor Hernández finally forced them to decide and Rojas came to power.[70]

As governor, Rojas was immediately confronted with a difficult, if not disastrous, situation. The state's finances were in complete disarray, mainly as a result of a still serious lack of tax revenues. In southwest Tlaxcala, in particular, many property owners still refused to pay taxes, alleging they did not control their properties or receive part of the crop. Moreover, public safety in rural areas was still a problem and was aggravated by Cirilo Arenas' rebellion of May 1918. Arenas finally rebelled against Carranza when the latter's intention to disarm and liquidate the División Arenas became increasingly obvious.[71] Rojas also faced "independent" bandoleros, deteriorating discipline among De la Puente's troops, armed agraristas who refused to be dislodged from occupied lands and, finally, conflicts between villages. The demarcation of *ejidos* (hacienda lands donated by Carranza to a village community) quite often provoked serious conflicts, especially when it implied that local share-

---

[69] P.O. del Estado, V, dd. Nov. 27, 1918; AGET/FRRO leg 272 Fom Oct. 1918 f.333, 335, 339, 343, 345; HyG Aug. 1917 exp. 35.

[70] Cuellar, *La Revolución* 2: 141–53.

[71] AGET/FRRO leg 242 HyG June 1918 f.659, 837; Garciadiego mss, pp. 50–51.

croppers or rural laborers were to lose their plots and jobs when "their" hacienda lands were donated to a neighboring village. The same was true for arrangements between villages over the maintenance of the irrigation systems of expropriated hacienda lands or the joint cultivation of haciendas still abandoned by their owners.[72] Rojas tried to cope with the situation by a campaign to disarm ex-Arenista soldiers and agraristas, by calling upon rebels to surrender and by increasing garrisons and military posts on haciendas and in villages.[73] The situation was especially serious in the southwest where rebels and bandoleros were robbing haciendas barely recovered from the earlier damage caused by the revolution. Muleteers, *tlachiqueros*, and woodcutters once more fled to the villages, and the agraristas' steadfast refusal to conclude sharecropping contracts was reinforced by the general situation of chaos and uncertainty.[74]

Did this imply that the agraristas supported Cirilo Arenas? Rojas' major problem was that he was in fact powerless to do much about the land issue. Most petitions had been submitted and decided upon by his predecessors, and President Carranza proved slow to make final decisions, in spite of Rojas' efforts to intervene. In the meantime, the agraristas should have complied with the Constitutionalist legal requirements to clear the lands or to accept a sharecropping contract. But as a former companion and paisano of Domingo Arenas, Rojas did not seem to be in a position to take a firm stand and use force in dislodging agraristas who refused sharecropping arrangements. On the other hand, as Garciadiego suggests, many villages whose petitions for land were already in the hands of the federal government may have hesitated to support Arenas, out of fear of jeopardizing their claims. The few villages that had already received land had even less reason for joining Arenas.[75] It seems certain, however, that Cirilo Arenas' rebellion gave the agraristas more leverage, at least for the time being, because the government had other priorities. It was not before 1921 that Rafael Apango, Rojas' successor, finally was able to bring an end to what his secretary of government called "una continua guerra contra las autoridades."[76]

---

[72] AGET/FRRO leg 241 HyG May 1918 f.419; 242 HyG June 1918 f.22.

[73] AGET/FRRO leg 242 HyG June 1918 f.278; 243 HyG July 1918 f.477 to 517; P.O. del Edo V, July 24, 1918.

[74] Especially AGET/FRRO leg 242 HyG June 1918, dozens of complaints.

[75] Garciadiego mss, pp. 50–51. Interviews with Candelario Reyes, Mar. 1967, Oct. 1977.

[76] ASRA 4943 DT 131–34.

By that time Arenismo as a political movement had largely lost its significance, mainly as a result of the "wrong" choice in the 1920 struggle between Carranza and the Sonorenses, since a majority of the Liberal party under the former Arenista military chief Antonio Mora had backed the loser. In 1918, however, the party was still strong. It held seven out of fifteen seats in the state congress and had flourishing clubs in virtually all the villages of the southwest.[77] It still remained attractive to agrarista-oriented members of the government party and it managed to keep afloat during Cirilo Arenas' rebellion. The chiefs and the politicians by now seemed to have gone their separate ways. Already in 1917 and 1918 Liberal party leader Andres Angulo and the party's newspaper *La Libertad* had voiced their irritation over the misconduct of Trinidad Telpalo and Felipe González, who regularly indulged in punitive assaults and robbery. In 1919 the Liberal party did not hesitate in denouncing Arenas' rebellion; by spring 1919 the rebellion had been effectively suppressed and Cirilo was caught, tried and, executed.[78]

Conclusion

This case study highlights the remarkable differences in the revolutionary process at the regional level, not only in the development of regional movements with different characteristics in terms of their economic basis, goals, leadership, and organization, but also the various patterns of alignment to the larger national-level revolutionary movements. Thanks to the studies of Womack, Warman, and others, we are slowly grasping the internal differentiation of the Zapata movement. Althought almost every historian would acknowledge the hybrid character of the Maderist and Constitutionalist movements, regional or local-level differences within these larger movements are still unclear. Yet we go on using the "blanket" terms Maderismo and Constitutionalismo. Let us take the example of the Tlaxcala revolutionary movement to illustrate the problem. Can we define this movement as Maderist, Constitutionalist, or Zapatist because the majority of the Tlaxcalan revolutionaries happened to join one of these larger movements at a certain historical moment? Or was the movement basically Maderist because it secured the governorship of Tlaxcala in 1911?

[77] Documents Convención (PLT) 1919 in Bibl. Andrés Angulo, INAH, Tlaxcala; Interviews with Ez. M. Gracia, Oct. 1967, idem Candelario Reyes, Mar. 1967, Oct. 1977.
[78] *La Libertad*, cit. no. 9, *Excelsior* Mar. 11, 1918 and *El Democrata* Feb. 25, 1918. Informe Gob. Rojas 1º de abril de 1919.

As we have seen, the Tlaxcalan revolutionary movement was a village-based peasant movement that had strong links to the urban industrial world and was heavily influenced, if not guided, by urban workers and intellectuals. These characteristics are not unique among peasant-based movements. The Tlaxcala case is unique because of the strong relations the Tlaxcalan revolutionaries had with one of the most radical groups in the Maderista movement, the PLM-inspired group around Aquiles Serdán in Puebla. The swift and wholesale mobilization of the Tlaxcalan revolutionaries for the Maderist cause resulted from their ideological affinity to the Maderista radicals in Puebla. After Serdán died in combat, his surviving friends continued to be influential in Tlaxcala and they even played an important role in having the Tlaxcalan revolutionaries recognize the plan de Guadalupe (1913).

Yet Serdán and his friends, the Tlaxcalan revolutionaries among them, were ideological strangers to the national Maderist leadership and the Madero government. The unexpected victory (1911) at the polls of the Tlaxcalan Maderist party, with its quite radical program of government was embarrassing, not only to the Tlaxcalan elites but also to the Madero government in Mexico. The Tlaxcalan Maderistas' victory probably owes more to local intra-elite conflicts than to the loyal support of the national Maderist leadership. Nevertheless, formal recognition of the Maderistas' victory by the state congress gave the revolutionaries a year-long experience in government, recognized as such by President Madero. The one-year government of peasant worker Antonio Hidalgo (1912) and his radical intellectual mentors provoked a unique process of political mobilization and countermobilization which ended in complete polarization of Tlaxcalan politics. The development of the TRM between 1910 and 1913 was, therefore, quite different from that of the Zapata movement. The same can be said of the war against Huerta (1913–14).

The Tlaxcalan revolutionaries were never able to reach a level of autonomous control over the state for more than short periods. The movement never had a strong and dominating leadership like that of the Zapata movement. Moreover, the strategic location of the state, and the vital rail connections to Mexico City, Puebla, and Vera Cruz, virtually forced the federal government, and every revolutionary movement with national ambitions, to try to control Tlaxcala. Even Arenas' zone of control (1915–17) was no exception to this rule; his control was never strong enough for him to implement his agrarian goals. Even his realignment with Carranza in December 1916 only gave him nine months of the autonomy he so desperately

wanted. He gained it, not so much because of his own military
strength, as because of external factors of a military-strategic nature.

In my view, therefore, the majority of the Tlaxcalan revolutionaries were as much Maderist in 1911 as they were Constitutionalist
and Zapatist in 1914. In other words, it was a regional movement
that differed significantly from the larger ones into which it became
incorporated, without losing its identity. Formal adherence to the
plan de Luis Potosí, the plan de Guadalupe, and the plan de Ayala
concealed differences of opinion regarding the goals and priorities
of the revolution, and the autonomy of its regional leadership. When
Madero's government did not heed the social revolutionary ambitions of Tlaxcalan leaders, and, later, the Constitutionalist leadership tried to impose itself on the Tlaxcalan revolutionaries, these
resulted in mutual distrust, conflict, and even rebellion. Zapata
proved unable to create the political conditions Arenas needed to
realize his ideals. Arenas rebelled and was able to gain considerable
de facto autonomy as a Constitutionalist commander. This situation
of autonomy not only enabled him to promote land distribution, but
the nearly total control over natural resources also facilitated the
emergence of interrelated networks of local Arenista interests:
chiefs, local agrarista leaders, and peasants had interests at stake,
although they undoubtedly varied in magnitude.

As Carranza consolidated his power in central Mexico, the Arenista military protection crumbled and Carranza was able to force
the Tlaxcalan revolutionary power politics into a civilian framework under his control. Goals and strategies of minor chiefs like Rojas and the Arenista leaders were increasingly limited by Constitutionalist power and policies. Rojas wanted state-level power but
remained a subordinate military commander, deliberately kept out
of the provisional government (1915–16) and the Constitutionalist
deal with Arenas. Arenista goals, which were incompatible with increasingly more effective Constitutionalist attempts to thwart autonomista tendencies among governors and regional commanders, were
seriously threatened by the normalization policy after Arenas'
death. Because chiefs, agrarista leaders and peasants had at least
one basic common interest—control over natural resources—land
became the main issue in the electoral contest of 1917–18. In south
and west Tlaxcala, the party that could guarantee the Arenista land
grants and possessions would enjoy solid mass support. In federal
Constitutionalist eyes it was of course out of the question that the
Arenistas could win, distrusted as they were because of their Zapatista careers and their display of autonomista tendencies, especially
in agrarian and fiscal matters, after they joined Carranza. But even

Rojas did prosper in the electoral contest; he was accepted as the constitutionalist candidate for governor, but probably seen as *el mal menor*. He badly needed federal support, especially quick decision making on the many land petitions, in order to wrest peasant support from the Arenistas. Carranza's refusal to do so cerrtainly impaired Rojas' capacity to control southwest Tlaxcala.

It is interesting to note that the interests of Arenista military chiefs diverged increasingly from those of their peasants and emerging Arenista politicians. Peasants feared the loss of their Arenista possessions but many of them were liable to land grants according to the Carrancista legislation. Once they obtained ejidos, they had reasons to remain loyal to the government. It would be far more difficult for Arenista chiefs to retain their considerable interests in the exploitation of haciendas, especially after their expulsion from the state of Tlaxcala. Their resistance and rebellious attitude provoked tensions with Arenista politicians who recognized the need to adapt to the new rules of the game set by a consolidating federal government.

Finally, the political process in Tlaxcala during 1917–18 gives us a fine example of Constitutionalist consolidation policy and the dilemmas at the regional level. In order to install a constitutional government under Constitutionalist control, the federal government had to liquidate Arenista military power, which until now had been able to protect the considerable interests of chiefs and their agrarista following in the distribution and exploitation of land. The transfer of military commanders and their troops was one thing; political pacification of their agrarista peasants was quite another. Tlaxcala's provisional Constitutionalist governors, and especially General Hernández, adopted a policy reminiscent of Sonorense land reform policies two years later. Although the governors kept to Carranza's 1915 land reform decree, they tried to give it a broad interpretation and did their utmost to accelerate land reform. They were hindered by federal sluggishness and Carranza's hesitation in taking final decisions on land distribution.

Had the land reform policies of the Constitutionalist governors not been thwarted by the federal government and Carranza, they might have contributed considerably to the pacification of the peasant population of southwest Tlaxcala and the demise of the Arenista movement. Now the demise was brought about by force and fraud in 1918 and by repression in 1920, justified by the alliance of part of the Arenista leadership with Carranza. Finally, Presidents De la Huerta and Obregón completed pacification by land reform policy, started in 1917 by the Constitutionalist governors of Tlaxcala.

CHAPTER THIRTEEN

Agricultural Laborers in
the Mexican Revolution (1910–40):
Some Hypotheses and Facts about
Participation and Restraint in
the Highlands of Puebla–Tlaxcala

Herbert J. Nickel[1]

Recent studies have established the extent of regional variations in development and socioeconomic conditions of Mexico's rural population.[2] Accordingly, a uniform contribution or reaction of peasants or rural workers to the Revolution of 1910–40 can hardly be expected. Nevertheless, there is still a lack of empirical data on the

[1] Research for this article was conducted with the assistance of the Deutsche Forschungsgemeinschaft (Bonn, Federal Republic of Germany) and the Social Science Research Council (New York). Translation assistance was provided by Martha Tyzenhouse and Rhonda Cobham-Sander.

[2] See Jan Bazant, "Peones arrendatarios y aparceros en México, 1851–1853," *Historia Mexicana* 90 (1973): 330–57; "Peones, arrendatarios y aparceros: 1868–1904," *Historia Mexicana* 93 (1974): 94–121; *Cinco haciendas mexicanas: Tres siglos de vida rural en San Luis Potosí (1600–1910)*, (Mexico City: El Colegio de México, 1975); Friedrich Katz, "Labor Conditions on Haciendas in Porfirian Mexico: Some Trends and Tendencies," *Hispanic American Historical Review* 54, no. 1 (1974): 1–47; Friedrich Katz, "Pancho Villa, Peasant Movements and Agrarian Reform in Northern Mexico," in *Caudillo and Peasant in the Mexican Revolution*, ed. D.A. Brading (London: Cambridge University Press, 1980), pp. 59–75; Raymond Buve, "Peasant Movements, Caudillos and Land Reform during the Revolution (1910–1917) in Tlaxcala, Mexico," *Boletín de Estudios Latinoamericanos y del Caribe* 18 (1975): 112–52; "Agricultores, dominación política y estructura agraria en la revolución mexicana: El caso de Tlax-

development of rural communities. Although most communities were kept under the control of the hacienda system toward the end of the Porfiriato, this control was not, as has often been assumed, so rigid or uniform as to deprive the dependent communities totally of their resources or their identity. Many residents retained the capacity to cause the latifundios serious difficulties and were eventually able to participate in fundamentally transforming the agrarian structure.

The participation of the various members of rural communities in the Revolution differed widely, not only in terms of intensity, but also with respect to the timing of their involvement. This variation is probably related to a number of factors: the substantial socioeconomic differentiation within the rural population, brought about by the unequal distribution of natural and human resources; incipient industrialization; and, in particular, the partial modernization of agriculture during the Porfiriato. This essay focuses on the diverse development of social relations and economic opportunities among the dependants of the large estates: at least nine such groups can be distinguished:

1. permanent hacienda employees who lived on the estates (*peones acasillados*);
2. permanent hacienda employees who lived in their own communities (*peones permanentes no acasillados*);
3. seasonal workers (*semaneros*);
4. sharecroppers (*aparceros, medieros*);
5. small-claim tenants;
6. "free" *minifundistas*, who were to some degree dependent on the haciendas for water and woodcutting rights;
7. deprived *campesinos*, who lost land as a result of liberal reforms, or who were illegally forced off their land;

cala," in *Haciendas in Central Mexico from the Late Colonial Times to the Revolution*, ed. Raymond Buve (Amsterdam: Centre for Latin American Research and Documentation, 1984), pp. 199–271; Arturo Warman, . . . *Y venimos a contradecir. Los campesinos de Morelos y el estado nacional* (Mexico City: Centro de Investigaciones Superiores del INAH, 1976); Hectór Aguilar Camín, *La frontera nómada. Sonora y la revolución mexicana* (Mexico City: Siglo xxi, 1977); Herbert J. Nickel, *Soziale Morphologie der mexikanischen Hacienda*, Wiesbaden: Franz Steiner, 1978); Herbert J. Nickel, "The Food Supply of Hacienda Labourers in Puebla–Tlaxcala During the Porfiriato: A First Approximation, in Buve, ed., *Haciendas*, pp. 113–59; Ian Jacobs, *Ranchero revolt: The Mexican Revolution in Guerrero* (Austin: University of Texas Press, 1982); Hans-Günther Mertens, *Wirtschaftliche und soziale Strukturen zentralmexikanischer Weizenhaciendas aus dem Tal von Atlixco* (1890–1912) (Wiesbaden: Franz Steiner, 1983).

8. muleteers (*arrieros*), who lost their means of livelihood after the introduction of the railroads; and
9. the new middle-class rancheros and sharecroppers who considered their privileges infringed upon by the government's favoritism toward large industrialists and foreigners.

Regional differences in development did not favor a unified agrarian movement. Instead, the differences were accentuated by numerous heterogeneous conflicts, by changes in traditional structures, or by conservation of such structures. Even within relatively small areas a remarkable degree of differentiation in the intensity of and motivation for the rural involvement can be observed.

From my investigation into the history of the Puebla–Tlaxcala highlands, it appears that the readiness of rural workers to take collective action against the existing system was less significant the farther the estates were located from towns, industrial sites, or transportation routes. Thus, it seems safe to assume that a distance-related (location-dependent) regional component was involved, if only as an intervening variable. Spontaneous action in the early years of the Revolution was, in any case, a relatively rare occurrence at the "periphery." Generally, the peones acasillados and also a large portion of the semaneros were mobilized only gradually by direct intervention "from without" (or "from above"), or, indirectly, by demonstration effects.

The analysis presented here attempts to explain why the peones acasillados of the haciendas hesitated to take part in the Revolution, or why, when they did take part, only to a limited extent. In this context I wish to draw attention to the internal differentiation of rural laborers according to their specific socioeconomic conditions, their respective chances to perceive the national or regional political and economic situation, or to communicate with and ally themselves to other "classes" or to the "*intelectualidad armada.*"[3] In addition, this essay deals with the differential development of living conditions and with the perception of deprivation among rural laborers as preconditions for their participating in or refraining from revolutionary activities. Finally, three case studies from the Puebla–Tlaxcala highlands are presented in order to demonstrate their empirical analogies.

[3] Eric R. Wolf, *Las luchas campesinas del siglo* xx (Mexico City; Siglo xxi, 1980), p. 402.

Some Hypotheses Concerning
Revolutionary Participation

The claim that agrarian revolutions are the direct result of the exploitation and impoverishment of peasants and rural workers has been convincingly challenged by various authors. Moore, for instance, has drawn attention to the case of India where even the most miserable conditions have not led to a peasant revolution.[4] In the case of Mexico, however, the working and living conditions in haciendas and ranchos, debt peonage, the decline of real wages, abuses of the *tienda de raya* (company store), the use of physical force in the treatment of laborers, as well as the landgrabbing hacendados and rancheros, and the complete subjugation of Indian villages are still widely held responsible for the participation of rural workers and peasants in the Revolution. This assessment of labor relations and of village decline has been challenged by empirical studies. The shift from attributing the origin of revolutions or peasant revolts from material need to the awareness of intolerable deprivation, or, in the words of Davies, to the perception of "an intolerable gap between what people want and what they get," has given rise to a series of perspectives that must be taken into consideration.[5]

Davies' social-psychological interpretation is reinforced by similar arguments from Feierabend and Feierabend, with references to Lerner, Deutsch, and others,[6] and focuses on intolerable discrepancies between expected and actual need satisfaction. Davies concentrates on a limited number of general preconditions that may lead to political instability, aggression, and revolution, but other variables may also be considered, such as the development of a general social crisis, or a simultaneous weakness of the leadership[7] that disallows stabilization of the system through reforms and the repression of revolutionary movements.[8]

[4] See Barrington Moore, *Soziale Ursprünge von Diktatur und Demokratie* (Frankfurt: Suhrkamp, 1969).

[5] James C. Davies, "Toward a Theory of Revolution," *American Sociological Review* 27, no. 1 (1962): 6.

[6] Ivor K. Feierabend and Rosalind L. Feierabend, "Aggressive Behaviors within Polities, 1948–1962: A Cross-National Study," in *When Men Revolt—and Why*, ed. James C. Davies (New York: Free Press, 1971), pp. 230ff. For a critique of this interpretation see, e.g., Volker Rittberger, "Über sozialwissenschaftliche Theorien der Revolution: Kritik und Versuch eines Neuansatzes," *Politische Vierteljahresschrift* (1971): 507f.

[7] John Dunn, *Moderne Revolutionen. Analysen eines politischen Phänomens* (Stuttgart: Philipp Reclam, Jr., 1974), p. 23.

[8] See Rittberger, "Über sozialwissenschaftliche Theorien," p. 510.

For movements of peasants and rural workers to rise above the status of rather ephemeral "rebellions" it is not only necessary that a profound "systemic frustration"[9] develop; the legitimacy of the government must also be disputed or the patron–client relationship devalued. An association with a new political elite prepared to take action against the old regime may also be required. Such a group, although it may have benefited from economic growth, may feel the slowness or absence of change with regard to the distribution of social prestige and political control to be unjust and intolerable.[10] It seems reasonable to assume that corresponding preconditions for mobilization were present at the outbreak of the Mexican Revolution, but it is unlikely that they would have manifested themselves to the same extent in all regions of the country and among all groups of peasants, sharecroppers, tenants, and other laborers who depended on the haciendas.

The emergence of a considerable conflict potential has to be traced back at least to the social and economic development of the late nineteenth century. After 1880, the Mexican economy was expanding, agriculture and transporation, had been partially modernized, economic opportunities were improving, and the traditional patron–client relations were changing. The expansion of production and favorable marketing opportunities encouraged several hacendados to accumulate more fields, and to raise the rent on leased land. They also increased their share of the harvest from the *aparcería*, gave notice of usage right terminations, and monetarized the relationship with their rural workers.

Accordingly, the absolute or relative income opportunities of those affected worsened in the decade before the Revolution. The situation was exacerbated by such factors as failed harvests, credit problems, and an international economic slump in 1906–7 that halted the development boom of the late nineteenth century. Modern means of transportation left a large number of muleteers unemployed; rancheros and tenants of the emerging rural middle class became frustrated with taxation levels as well with the thinly disguised privileges granted to foreigners and to business magnates and politicians.

Some social sectors had to face considerable losses of income and social standing, but not only those in rural areas. In Chihuahua, for example, where the income situation across the border offered fig-

---

[9] Feierabend and Feierabend, "Aggressive Behaviors," p. 230.
[10] Rittberger, "Über sozialwissenschaftliche Theorien," p. 510.

ures for compensation, a grave economic crisis was caused by extremely poor harvests caused by drought and frost, combined with mine closures and migration restrictions into the U.S. between 1907–10.

The conditions of industrial workers described by Wasserman must have affected the rural population as well, at least those segments that had lost access to subsistance farming. His statement about the building revolutionary potential fits well into the expectation-frustration model of Davies and others:

> The conditions from 1907 through 1910 were devastating to the working class because of the unprecedented prosperity of the preceding five years. What had a year earlier been a region of labor scarcity, increasing wages, upward mobility, and rising expectations was then a region of unemployment and starvation. Having experienced or seen a better life these workers were not content to suffer. Many joined rebel groups during 1910.
>
> Thus, there was in 1909–1910 a potential for revolution among some sectors of the working class, mostly among mining labor, in Chihuahua. Divorced from the land and traditional values, accustomed to and expecting a better life, these laborers formed what can be labelled the *déclassé* poor, who had their lot improved just enough in the inequitable system to want more. They needed among other things, leadership to become a revolutionary force. This was provided by the middle class, some of whom had previously been members of the working class.[11]

In view of the regional and internal differences within the Mexican peasantry and rural laborers, a similar build-up of revolutionary potential was not to be expected. Correspondingly, the underlying hypotheses of this contribution concentrate on differential behavior and restraint, particularly among hacienda dependants. This analysis is directed toward their economic situation and the preconditions for developing frustration and eventually a "revolutionary consciousness." The general background conditions of the Revolution and the activities of campesinos will be considered only marginally.[12]

[11] Mark Wasserman, *Oligarchy and Foreign Enterprise in Porfirian Mexico, 1876–1911*, Ph.D. Dissertation, University of Chicago 1975, pp. 287f.

[12] The term "*Revolution*" (capitalized) refers to events between 1910 and 1940 that are usually deemed (and perceived as) revolutionary. Whether or not this designation

It is obviously no easy task to determine empirically the level of satisfaction (over time) or the reasons for frustration among groups of hacienda dependants; their material situation is not sufficiently understood. Conventional assumptions about real incomes, the use of extraeconomic force, or living expenses can only be revised and broadened by laborious reconstructions and examinations of business accounts and correspondence.[13] Even more difficult seems to be the task of determining the "expected need satisfaction" or "need satisfaction gaps." The present effort must therefore be seen as exploratory, at best it may lead only to close approximations, because the available data are scattered and difficult, sometimes even impossible to access.[14] Nevertheless, a few indicators have been isolated: demands that had been denied, such as for allotments of rented land (*pegujales*), higher wages, cheaper food rations, or extended credit; or impoved compensation for crops produced, etc.

The expectations of rural laborers were probably formed by comparing their working and living standards with those of reference groups that might have benefited or suffered from hacienda modernization, or might have experienced temporary unemployment or the risks of making a living out of tiny plots of marginal land.

Hypotheses on the Participation of Rural Laborers

So far, the data suggest that rural laborers most fully integrated into the hacienda system were less likely to participate in revolutionary activities, or were only willing to do so at a later stage. This was particularly true of the peones acasillados who had unlimited work contracts, lived in workmen's settlements [*calpanerías*] on the estates, and enjoyed special social relations with their patrons.

At the same time, findings indicate that a second group, consisting of tenants, sharecroppers, seasonal or casual workers, campesinos,

---

is analytically adequate will not be discussed here, but generally, specific significances and/or deviating assessments are emphasized by quotation marks.

[13] See, for example, Marco Bellingeri, "L'economia del latifondo in Messico. L'hacienda San Antonio Tochatlaco dal 1880 al 1920," *Annali della Fondazione Luigi Einaudi* 10 (1976): 287–428; Herbert J. Nickel, "Zur Immobilität und Schuldknechtschaft mexikanischer Landarbeiter vor 1915," *Saeculum* 3 (1976): 289–328; Nickel, "The Food Supply"; Harry E. Cross, "Living Standards in Rural Nineteenth Century Mexico: Zacatecas, 1820–80," *Journal of Latin American Studies* 10, no. 1 (1978): 1–19; and Mertens, *Weizenhaciendas*.

[14] There is a significant lack of data with respect to Porfirian haciendas of the Mexican periphery such as Yucatán or Sonora.

and other members of rural communities with longstanding traditions of conflict with neighboring haciendas or the experience of being economically degraded by the expansion of estates, could be mobilized earlier, and showed more inclination to participate actively in the Revolution.

Finally, a third group or "marginal mass" may be isolated, which contained former muleteers, artisans, traders, unemployed and casual workers whose transition from the agricultural to the industrial and service sector had failed. They were prepared to join revolutionary groups and jumped at the chance of windfall profits from their activities. Such elements were characteristically concentrated in the larger villages and in cities where the revolutionary elite was primarily located, and where communication was relatively easy.

Between these extreme types there were transitional groups whose attitudes and composition depended on their different socioeconomic conditions and exposure to changes of communication and cohesion. It is worth noting that the example set by revolutionary groups—their successes in winning land, rights of usufruct, and ultimately gaining political support, as well as attempts at mobilization from without (from caudillos, military personnel, trade unionists, the new political and administrative elite)—led to the rise of a "revolutionary" spirit among previously passive groups. The resulting activities, particularly in the case of the rural latecomers, may have been adapted to administrative formalities of system-conforming bargaining within the framework of new legal statutes. Thus the ensuing participation may rather be seen as an activity already embraced by the "institutionalized Revolution."

Finally, location (center or periphery) played a part not only in differentiating the social and economic output of the system but also in structuring the perception of social and economic demands. In central locations, for instance, the turnover of the goods of daily life progressed faster and more comprehensively. Thus, an economic recession and the ensuing inflation could bring about an immediate decline in real incomes and could increase the risk of starvation. By contrast, at the periphery, with its tradition of subsistence agriculture and protective social relations, such changes percolated through the system relatively slowly. It may be assumed, accordingly, that in "central" places economic growth increased social and economic demands more swiftly than at the "periphery," and that during a recession expectations were likely to run faster into contradiction with declining opportunities.

The differential development of activities and restraints of two

groups within the rural population also warrants some comment.
The campesinos who were, or conceived themselves to be, victims
of hacienda modernization, and the tenants and sharcroppers who
also had taken losses during this process, and may have been forced
to enter service as farmhands, at least temporarily, on the large estates.

Since the main concern of this essay is with the hacienda workers,
small-scale tenants and sharecroppers whose socioeconomic status
was reduced by the termination or disadvantageous revision of their
contracts, and independent campesinos who may have lost land or
rights of usufruct, have been taken together as one type, designated
"deprived campesinos." Seasonal workers (semaneros) and sharecroppers (aparceros) of haciendas and ranchos, including estate laborers who lived in neighboring villages (peones no acasillados)
have been defined as a second type.[15] A third type comprising resident hacienda workers (peones acasillados), has also been isolated.

Deprived Campesinos

In rural areas the general economic growth at the beginning of the
Porfiriato had primarily benefited the small-claim tenants and sharecroppers, just as it most likely benefited the independent farmers in
the central area. But once the Porfiriato got underway, growing marketing opportunities, the economic yields from newly accessible
distant markets, and an extended receptivity of the market in general, offered better returns than the leasing of land. Hacendados increased the rents on leased land, and gave notice to tenants or
changed tenancies to sharecropper status. Sharecropping agreements were changed in favor of the haciendas, or the estates extended their own production by means of wage laborers.[16]

[15] Some haciendas distinguished between semaneros temporales and operarios
contratados de año. The second category may be identical with those semaneros who
worked almost all the year on the same estate. Sometimes cuadrillas (work teams)
were hired just for the harvest, and formal agreements were made before the authorities of the municipality. See correspondence and document collection of the owner
of the hacienda Ozumba, May 13, 1853; October 31, 1901; March 24, 1909; September
5, 1914.

[16] John Womack Jr., Zapata and the Mexican Revolution, (Harmondsworth: Penguin, 1972), p. 76; Bazant, Cinco haciendas, pp. 164ff; Edith B. Couturier, La hacienda de Hueyapan, 1550–1936 (Mexico City: Secretaría de Educación Pública,
1976), pp. 158ff; Warman, Y venimos, pp. 74ff, 84ff. On the deprivation of the descendants of military colonists at the northern Mexican frontier in Chihuahua, see
Katz, "Labor Conditions," pp. 60f. With respect to Yucatecan plantations, see Allen

The Ley Lerdo offered a further possibility for expanding production areas at the expense of the campesinos of Indian communities who held communal ownership of land and water. In addition, easily manipulated laws arranging the transfer of public lands (terrenos baldíos) into private ownership placed communities at a disadvantage.[17] For groups of campesinos who had lost either leased or owned land or shares in production areas, the reduction of "need satisfaction" was exacerbated by the economic slump after 1900. They also lost opportunities for production in the longer term because of being cut off from participation in the general economic upswing. These campesinos were among the main victims of the partial modernization of the hacienda economy, particularly toward the end of the Porfiriato.

At the same time, farmers who had achieved middle class status had every reason to feel frustrated, given the increasing influence of foreign investors whose encroachment on land inhibited their own expansion.

For the socially and economically degraded campesinos or arrieros at the turn of the century, there were scarcely any attractive opportunities for income and status outside of agriculture, especially after the economic slump. Many of them continued to direct their occupational aspirations toward the agricultural sector and toward social positions in the rural community. Others managed to get by as daily wage earners, aparceros and the like, until the Revolution, when they tried their chances at a violent return to the previous modes of ownership and autonomy, or sought attractive positions in the ranks of the new elite that emerged from the agrarian revolution.

Not all campesinos, however, were disadvantaged by the modernization of agriculture or of the haciendas. The Porfiriato was also characterized by an increase in the already significant number of middle-class rancheros and relatively well-off campesinos and sharecroppers. Ultimately, the privatization after the Ley Lerdo benefited both large landowners and an as yet indeterminate number of small farmers.

If, as Buve reported, there were well-to-do Tlaxcalan "agricultores acomodados, proprietarios y grandes aparceros" who sometimes

Wells, Henequén and Yucatán: An Analysis in Regional Economic Development, 1876–1915, Ph.D. Dissertation, State University of New York at Stony Brook, 1979, pp. 260ff.

[17] Nickel, Soziale Morphologie, pp. 86ff.

employed their own peons[18] and "peasant smallholders" who protested in 1905 against the imposition of taxes,[19] then various
grounds for "systemic frustration" may have existed, and led to the
moblization of relatively heterogeneous groups. At the same time
the existence of such a privileged section provided one reference
group against which the deprived campesinos could have measured
their social demands and their expected loss of opportunities.

SÉMANEROS, APARCEROS, AND
PEONES NO ACASILLADOS

The semaneros (aparceros and peones no acasillados) can be assigned to a middle position. On the one hand, the semaneros, who
were employed on haciendas in the "central" areas under contract
for a few weeks or throughout the year as occasional or permanent
workers, participated to a certain extent in the general economic upswing. At least during the peak period of demand they were able to
sell their labor for a higher fee than could peones acasillados. Moreover, some of them may have had supplementary incomes, as private minifundistas,[20] small-claim tenants, craftsmen, or casual industrial workers. On the other hand, their opportunities for making
a living during a recession were considerably restricted. Once the
haciendas tried to reduce the number of their semaneros, the latter
were no longer able to bargain for wages higher than those usually
paid to peones acasillados. They were probably also the first to be
affected by the use of machinery on the estates toward the end of the
Porfiriato.

As the haciendas were modernized, temporary workers were increasingly left with the status of an "agricultural reserve army."[21]
Further, as wage earners, they were affected by the depreciation of
real wages in the course of the overall price increases during the
Porfiriato, since hacendados, at least in the Puebla–Tlaxcala high-

---

[18] Raymond Buve, "Movilización campesina y reforma agraria en los valles de Nativitas, Tlaxcala (1917–1923): Estudio de un caso de lucha por recuperar tierras ha-
bida durante la revolución armada," in El trabajo y los trabajadores en la historia de
México, ed. Elsa C. Frost, Michael C. Meyer, and Josefina Z. Vázquéz (Mexico City: El
Colegio de México and University of Arizona Press, 1979), p. 536.

[19] Buve, "Peasant Movements," p. 126.

[20] See, for example, Mertens' references to the category of Dorfarbeiter (village
workers) who, besides being hacienda laborers, worked their own land in their villages (cf. Mertens, Weizenhaciendas, pp. 261ff).

[21] Compare the unemployment among rural laborers in the area of modern sugar
plantations in Morelos referred to by Warman, Y venimos, pp. 72, 89.

lands, often reduced the remuneration to semaneros exclusively to a sum of money.[22]

Among the aparceros, it is possible to differentiate between those who had lost their status in the course of hacienda modernization, and the sharecroppers, who probably originated from the system of the *terrazgueros* (tenant farmers) and who were thus closely connected to the semaneros (de año). Unfortunately, comprehensive data on aparceros' income and working conditions are not available. Where they were able to market their produce, going beyond the subsistence level and exceeding their rate of duty (the harvest share delivered to the hacienda), they must have benefited from economic development. Ultimately, they were also influenced by the recession, but these effects were mitigated by subsistence production. The available information does not, for the most part, reveal the background of the aparceros or the scope of their income opportunities.[23] But even where they had not previously been tenants or "free" campesinos, the modernization of leasing agreements may have led to such losses as the abrogation of traditional rights to wood, pasture, and water usage.

The permanent hacienda peons who did not live on the estates (the peones permanentes no acasillados) probably deserve to be considered as a group in their own right.[24] In order to simplify the typology they have consolidated here into one group together with the semaneros and aparceros. We may assume that they occupied a socioeconomic position between the "deprived campesinos" and the "peones acasillados" of large estates. The peones no acasillados appeared above all in regions with small estates and in areas with a high density of settlements, with haciendas and ranchos close to rural communities. Some of these peons may have been able to secure supplementary incomes in their rural communities. There, they would certainly have obtained further information about the social or economic situation elsewhere in the country; they may have heard, for example, about the strikes in the textile mills.

The wage rates of the peones no acasillados were probably higher than those of the peones acasillados, but their economic expectations must have been closer to those of the semaneros. Like them,

---

[22] Nickel, *Soziale Morphologie*, p. 348.

[23] See, for example, Buve, "Movilización campesina," p. 535. Some documents found in the archive of the hacienda Ozumba do not permit any substantial conclusions to be drawn.

[24] Especially since they might have had an additional income as smallholders or small-scale tenants.

they were able to make use of opportunities for additional income in their communities. Because they normally possessed fewer privileges (or fringe benefits) than the peones acasillados, it can be assumed that they were more dependent on market prices and thus experienced a definite reduction in real incomes.

PEONES ACASILLADOS OF THE HACIENDAS

The general economic growth and the partial modernization of the hacienda also affected the peones acasillados. In general, it may be assumed that their living standards improved slightly during the Porfiriato in comparison to the situation during the first half of the nineteenth century. They were given wage increases (at least in the "central" regions), improved accommodation, and somewhat more liberal credit opportunities. Furthermore, there was less manipulation of contractual debt claims requiring them to remain on the haciendas. It is worth noting, however, that some authors do not share this assessment, but rather emphasize a deterioration of income conditions.[25]

The peones acasillados were largely spared the depreciation of real incomes because many hacendados provided them with the traditional "subsistence insurance."[26] They received rations of basic foodstuffs, primarily maize, at reasonable prices or as partial payment in kind; alternatively, they were allowed to produce maize for themselves on allocated land and were thus less dependent on the market; in addition, the decline in real wages could be balanced in part by increased credit opportunities. Thus, for the peones acasillados in general, there was no important or lasting improvement in actual need satisfaction, but by the same token there was no dramatic reduction in economic opportunities just before the outbreak of the Revolution.

Their aspirations, as far as these can be ascertained from the available information,[27] were directed first and foremost toward relatively modest wage increases, more generous credit allowances. re-

[25] Bellingeri, "L'economia del latifondo," p. 414. He indicates a declining real income among peons of a pulque-producing hacienda of the state of Hidalgo between 1898 and 1910.

[26] James C. Scott, *The Moral Economy of the Peasant: Rebellion and Subsistence in Southeast Asia* (New Haven: Yale University Press, 1976), p. 65.

[27] In particular, the correspondence between hacienda employees and proprietors or their representatives, as well as records of the *juezes menores* (lower judges) from rural communities, are sources of information about demands and complaints of rural laborers.

duced workloads, better accommodation, allocations of land with better soil, larger reductions in the price of hacienda produce, and improved medical care. The lack of schools, for example (at least in the "periphery"), seems to have been scarcely mentioned.

Regional Differentiation

The varied regional engagement of "rural" groups was a striking characteristic of the Mexican agrarian revolution. In view of the different economic, social, and political conditions in areas like northern Mexico, the central highlands or Yucatán, this is not surprising. If one compares the revolutionary groups of these regions, those from the north seem to have been the most heterogeneous. In addition to members of deprived Yaqui and Mayo communities of Sonora, and the descendants of military colonists who had lost their land to haciendas, they included large numbers of casual workers who floated between jobs in factories, mines and farms, who sometimes crossed the border to the U.S. looking for employment opportunities. Unemployed lumberjacks, railroad workers, sharecroppers, cowboys, and peons from ranchos and haciendas must also be included.

This heterogeneity of revolutionary groups was associated with a lack of supraregional political aims, with specific local interests, and with their frequent lapses into banditry. In the central highlands the agrarian revolutionary component was much stronger. In some areas where Zapatistas or Arenistas dominated or influenced events, this component may have temporarily determined developments. Nevertheless, even in small highland areas the composition of the revolutionary elites and their followers varied considerably. Because this article deals particularly with the role of the rural laborers in the Revolution, this variation does not appreciably affect our analysis.

Empirical data from the central Mexican highlands, indicate the peones acasillados' obvious reluctance to participate, as well as a conspicuous variation in the distribution of regional participation. This distribution can be related to two variables: socioeconomic status, and location at the center or periphery. Location is considered to intervene in the determination of economic conditions and in the perception of exploitation and adverse economic opportunity.

When one considers the three groups (1) deprived campesinos, (2) semaneros, aparceros, and peones no acasillados, and (3) peones acasillados, the following hypotheses can be derived.

The stronger the representation in a given area of members of group 1 (deprived campesinos) and the smaller the presence of members of group 3 (peones acasillados), the greater is the perception of a "need satisfaction gap," and a corresponding revolutionary potential might be expected. In central areas the readiness to initiate or to participate in action was considerably greater than at the periphery (in this context central refers to the distance from larger cities, particularly to Mexico City, to main transport routes, and to factories). The relation of status groups and their central or peripheral locations can be arranged in a matrix:

	Position of region/locality	
Group	Central	Peripheral
(1) Deprived campesinos		
(2) Semaneros, aparceros, and peones no acasillados		
(3) Peones acasillados		

Correspondingly, the stronger group 1 predominated in a central region and the smaller the presence of members of group 3 was, the higher must have been the potential for revolt or revolution. The converse would apply for a "peripheral" location of group 3. The least revolutionary engagement was to be expected at the periphery, in areas with large haciendas mainly employing peones acasillados where the number of semaneros, aparceros, and peones no acasillados were insignificant, and where conflicts between haciendas and neighboring communities were rare.

The group of semaneros, aparceros, and peones no acasillados could be mobilized according to their socioeconomic status and their degree of centrality. For example, a high degree of centrality characterized those casual workers, sharecroppers, and campesinos who worked in agriculture as well as industry; Katz, Wasserman, Meyers, and Buve have analyzed their revolutionary engagement in Chihuahua and in Tlaxcala.[28]

[28] Katz, "Pancho Villa," p. 62; Wasserman, "Oligarchy and Foreign Enterprise," pp. 238ff; William K. Meyers, *The Second Division del Norte: Formation and Fragmen-*

A prerequisite for the transformation of a revolutionary potential into activity, and for the immediate mobilization of the rural population, would seem to be the strong representation of deprived campesinos, "peasant workers,"[29] and eventually seasonal workers or peones no acasillados who no longer enjoyed acceptable patron–client relations. Furthermore, this group would have to maintain contact with a middle class capable of articulating demands and endowed with political ambitions and leadership. This was the case in central areas.

At the periphery, particularly on haciendas whose workers consisted mainly of peones acasillados, it required a "mobilization from above" or, as Tobler commented, an "institutionalized revolution,"[30] before the peons would enter into disputes, and even then they tended to proceed formally on legal grounds.

The semaneros, aparceros, and peons from the communities without traditions of conflict and in peripheral locations became mobilized earlier, but likewise mostly "from above"; that is, through military governors, the Carranza decree of January 6, 1915, through regional caudillos, and finally through the example set by the actions of successful agrarista groups.

At this point it seems appropriate to note that the wider "rural population" that took part in the agrarian revolution in one way or another, might have included craftsmen, arrieros, factory workers, domestic servants, and the unemployed of the communities. We have almost no specific details of their participation in the conflicts within the agrarian revolution or in the agrarian reform. This is also true for some hacienda employees (meseros) who were engaged as craftsmen, foremen, muleteers, forest workers, etc. These groups are neglected here because of lack of information, not because they are considered insignificant.

Analogies with the Puebla–Tlaxcala Highlands

In the Puebla–Tlaxcala highlands the distribution of haciendas, ranchos, mills, factories, cities, and villages is remarkably varied. The

---

tation of the Laguna's Popular Movement 1910–1911," Paper for the Symposium on Comparative Peasant Revolts in Mexico (New York, 1982), pp. 10ff; Buve, "Peasant Movements," p. 128.

[29] See Buve, "Peasant Movements," p. 128. Katz designates the equivalent category in Chihuahua as "semi-agricultural and semi-industrial labourers"; "Pancho Villa," p. 62.

[30] Hans Werner Tobler, "Conclusion: Peasant Mobilisation and the Revolution," in Caudillo and Peasant, ed. Brading p. 254.

triangle Huejotzingo–Texmelucan, Apizaco, and Puebla contains a relatively high density of communities and estates (see Figure 13.1). This might account for the fact that around Huejotzingo–Texmelucan, for example, the estates were scarcely equipped with extensive calpanerías, and, therefore, the long-term workers also lived in the communities. The area's proximity to Puebla, Tlaxcala, Apizaco, Huejotzingo–Texmelucan, and Atlixco; its location on important national transportation routes; and the concentration of textile mills and factories, allow it to be classified as a relatively central region.

The extent of expropriation or, rather, privatization of common land after the Ley Lerdo is still unclear. Buve refers to it in Tlaxcala and also to the protests of peasants who had been beneficiaries of the privatization and refused to pay taxes.[31] The privatization of baldíos, however, was insignificant in the Puebla–Tlaxcala highlands.[32]

In collating population movements between 1877 and 1921 one can discern a continuous concentration of people in this triangle.[33] A determining factor in the rural mobilization "from below" was primarily the contact with the industrial sector: the experience with protest and strikes since the turn of the century. Buve formulates this very convincingly for western Tlaxcala: "intensified peasant protest went together with participation in urban movements, which . . . provided these peasants with knowledge of leadership and organization, relations with the urban world and ideological elements to be used in the forthcoming Mexican Revolution."[34] These preconditions led minifundistas, aparceros, semaneros, and probably also the nonresident laborers on the estates of the central highlands, to participate in the Revolution from the beginning, or at least very early on.

By contrast, in the northeast highlands, the density of communities and estates was much lower. After expansion the haciendas were considerably larger and could definitely be regarded as latifundios.[35] They predominately employed peones acasillados, as well as varying numbers of semaneros. At least in the area of Huamantla–Chalchicomula, conditions of sharecroppers and small-claim tenants toward the end of the Porfiriato probably no longer played a particularly important role.

A certain transitional form seems to be recognizable, however,

[31] Buve, "Peasant Movements," p. 126.
[32] See Anuario Estadístico for 1893 and 1907.
[33] See Nickel, Soziale Morphologie, pp. 199f.
[34] Buve, "Peasant Moveents," p. 124.
[35] See maps in Nickel, Soziale Morphologie, pp. 204f, 251.

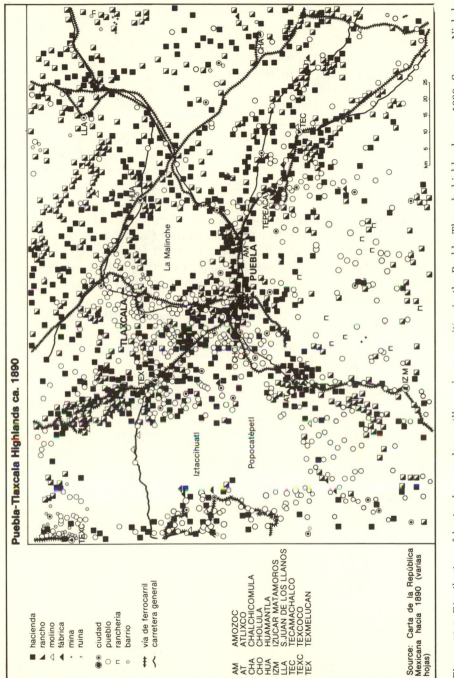

Puebla–Tlaxcala Highlands ca. 1890

Legend:

- ■ hacienda
- ▲ rancho
- △ molino
- ◀ fábrica
- + mina
- r ruina
- ◉ ciudad
- ○ pueblo
- ⊓ ranchería
- ○ barrio
- ┿┿┿ vía de ferrocarril
- ∕ carretera general

AM AMOZOC
AT ATLIXCO
CHA CHALCHICOMULA
CHO CHOLULA
HUA HUAMANTLA
IZM IZUCAR MATAMOROS
LLA S.JUAN DE LOS LLANOS
TEC TECAMACHALCO
TEXC TEXCOCO
TEX TEXMELUCAN

Source: Carta de la República
Mexicana hacia 1890 (varias
hojas)

Figure 13.1. Distribution of haciendas, ranchos, mills, and communities in the Puebla–Tlaxcala highlands, ca. 1890. Source: Nickel, *Soziale Morphologie*, p. 206.

among particular groups of semaneros who were not only recruited for one or several weeks during peak demand. With them a year's contract was settled at the beginning of the agricultural year, in which they agreed to work upon request in return for a daily wage, for a special price on maize rations, and possibly for a plot of land to be available if required. However, these recruiting practices, which probably stemmed from the terrazguero system, seem to have been gradually discontinued in favor of ad hoc recruitments toward the end of the Porfiriato. Generally, the large estates employed one or two cuádrillas from the same community on long-term contracts, and supplemented them in times of peak need by shorter-term arrangement with laborers, including some from other villages (see Figure 13.2).

Not only did the hacienda system in the northeast highlands turn out to dominate access to natural resources (land, water, forest); it also reduced the direct control over land left to rural communities down to their fundos legales. In some cases, these areas were encircled by the territories of individual haciendas, such as Tlachichuca, San José Chiapa, or Mazapiltepec.

Without the scope of the available information, it is impossible to

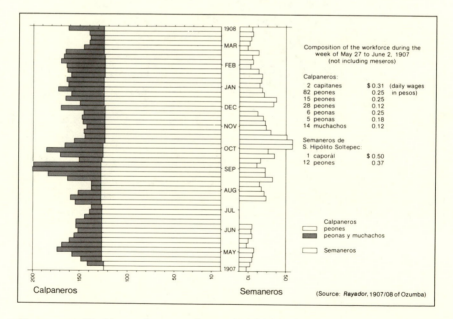

Figure 13.2. Weekly employment of agricultural laborers at Ozumba, from April 1, 1907, to March 28, 1908. Source: Nickel, *Soziale Morphologie*, p. 349.

determine whether or not these or other communities leased additional areas, such as rancho or hacienda land. Probably some communities or their residents occupied considerably more land than the often quoted proportions of land ownership may suggest.[36]

In the eastern highlands, which is given particular consideration here, there was certainly no substantial number of deprived campesinos resulting from losses of land to haciendas during the Porfiriato. With the exception of some small towns like Tepeaca, Chalchicomula, and Huamantla, the entire eastern region can be characterized as a "peripheral" area. In contrast to the "central" triangle, many haciendas had quite large calpanerías, since settlements were relatively widely dispersed (cf. Figure 13.1).

Given the status of the predominantly employed peones acasillados, the lack of collectives of deprived campesinos (suffering the consequences of expropriation in the late nineteenth century), and the distance to urban and industrial centers, a significant revolutionary potential was not developed, at least not on the haciendas. Thus, the steady workers participated in hardly any revolutionary activities. This restraint may have been due to the conservation of traditional labor relations; wages had always been low; and paternalistic privileges assured stable income conditions, even in times of crisis. The tiendas de raya also contributed (in spite of their bad reputation among hacienda critics) to the stablization of real wages, as generous préstamos may also have done.

As far as one can assess from hacienda correspondence, requests raised with the administrator or hacendado were usually related to better-quality maize rations or of allotted fields; for higher advances and/or credits; for more favorable piecework arrangements; or the observance of religious holidays. These were made in each case without calling the hacienda system into question.

The haciendas of the area, again in contrast to the central triangle, were affected by the Revolution in that they suffered raids, requisitions of livestock, grain, forage, and weapons, were pressed for contributions (préstamos forzados), lost payroll money to bandits and their transport lines were broken or made unsafe. The calpaneros also suffered through these assaults. The "revolutionary demands" of the semaneros threatened the hacienda system, apparently, to a lesser degree.

Where traditional conflicts between communities and neighbor-

---

[36] See for example, George M. McBride, The Land Systems of Mexico (New York: American Geographical Society, 1923), p. 154.

ing haciendas existed, these were revived in the early years of the Revolution.

At first invasions of hacienda land, and the "illegal" use of the montes by community residents were kept within limits in the peripheral region. The obvious successes of the Zapatistas, Carranza's restitution decree, the first land redistributions, and the agrarista agents, then encouraged the community residents to apply for allocations of land and to occupy fields. Land expropriations and reallocation were gradually formalized through reform laws and administrative procedures; to define these processes as revolutionary thus appears questionable. This terminology may be reserved for cases when villagers, former semaneros or aparceros invaded hacienda land without waiting for legal authorization; when they occupied fields that had not been allocated to them or that had been taken from them; and when they forcibly took possession of fields before the former owner had gathered the harvest due to him, or before the conclusion of expropriation proceedings.

The mobilization "from without" that largely characterized the periphery was found, in particular, among the peones acasillados. The Revolution took hold of the calpanerías last, and it did so for the most part through the administrative channels of the "institutionalized revolution" around 1930. At first, though, it has looked as if the military or the military governor of Puebla wanted to impose structural changes on the hacienda system. Peonage was abolished in this way in September 1914 by a decree of the constitutionalist northwest army.[37] A legal minimum wage was introduced, and the maximum length of the working day was set at eight hours. Initially, the military controlled revolutionary reforms (such as the abolition of peonage and the introduction of new labor laws), and eventually it took over the role of protecting the hacendados. In this way the military was also able to solve the problems of provisioning the troops quite elegantly. Until then this had been done, to the annoyance of hacendados and administrators, through thinly disguised extortion.

Toward the end of the 1920s the nervousness of the peones acasillados grew, as it became evident that in the course of expropriation the haciendas had ceded considerable areas of land to the communities. It must have also become clear to many agricultural laborers and lesser hacienda employees that jobs were being lost because of the increasing use of machinery. As their comprehension of the sit-

[37] *Periodico Oficial* (Estado de Puebla), 23 (1914): 260; 24 (1914): 264.

uation increased, their inclination to become campesinos and to strive for the establishment of an ejidal settlement on the grounds of the hacienda strengthened. By the early 1930s it had become unmistakably clear that in the near future no land for expropriation would be left to the peones acasillados, so that social and economic aspirations and demands regarding land and independent settlements arose. With the Código Agrario of 1934 the basis was established for removing this potential for conflict in a system-conforming way.

The following sketches of the situation of three estates, should illustrate the attempt at differentiation in more detail. Admittedly it has not as yet been possible to carry out a more systematic investigation of the problems presented here, so that the empirical findings are incomplete. The problem of insufficient data is compounded by the difficulty of gaining access to the available documents. During my visits in Puebla and Tlaxcala in the 1970s, government departments, community administrations, and landowners were so preoccupied with invasions of property that they understandably felt scientific curiosity to be intrusive. Hopefully, access to the documents of the former Departamento de Asuntos Agrarios y Colonización (DAAC) will be possible some day without much restriction.[38]

THE CASE OF RESURRECCIÓN–MANZANILLA

Since the seventeenth century there has been a tradition of land conflicts between the community of Resurrección, adjacent to the city of Puebla, and the former hacienda San Diego Manzanilla. From time to time the community has leased the rancho San Mateo, which lies above the estate and was, in colonial times, owned by the city of Puebla. In addition, the people of Resurrección burned charcoal for the market in Puebla, went into service as semaneros, or found other employment opportunities in the urban labor market nearby.[39]

Whereas the conflict with the estate in the colonial period was primarily over usage of wood and water from *jagüeyes*—a usage claimed by Resurrección and contested by Manzanilla—was reduced, residents of the community acted against the hacienda as early as the first years of the Revolution. Not only did they abruptly take up cutting wood in the forests (1912) but also made their wishes for restitution felt very early. As DAAC documents from

[38] The archive of the Departamento de Asuntos Agrarios y Colonización (herafter DAAC) later became the archive of the Secretaría de la Reforma Agraria. In 1982 it was in the process of being decentralized and, once again, not accessible.

[39] Nickel, *Soziale Morphologie*, pp. 163ff, 274ff.

1912 and 1914 show, this was pursued with great vehemence; more than once, residents of the community were executed in the atrium of the church of Resurrección.[40]

At that time a military unit stationed in Manzanilla was at the hacendado's disposal, and in 1915 the military commander at Puebla strictly forbade the community to invade the mountain areas of the hacienda, to take advantage of maguey plants, to drive cattle onto estate pastures, or to commit *actos atentatorios*.[41] The conflicts culminated in incidents of land occupation after the publication of the Ley Carranza on January 6, 1915. A letter of the governor of Puebla on February 26, 1915, reveals that land surveys on the grounds of the estate had already begun.

The petition for the restitution of former community land was rejected on March 29, 1917, as unfounded, however. There proved to be, in fact, no legal basis for the people of Resurrección's assertion that the owner of Manzanilla in the past had usurped community land. The documents in the National Archives suggest that the community of Resurrección was once an illegal establishment on the lands of the estate, and that there had been problems of demarcations between the hacienda and the community of Resurrección.

To strengthen its claims the community submitted a map from the year 1787, but it showed no usurpation of land by the estate. Since the accompanying documents very clearly establish that the residents of Resurrección contested only the right of access to a jagüey on the hacienda and the right to use wood (in the montes) for their personal use, it can be assumed that they probably knew that they lacked the necessary legal basis.[42]

In the case of Manzanilla, a hacienda that displays no large *calpanería*, it can be assumed that it had a "central" position as well as the community of Resurrección and that predominantly nonresident laborers were engaged. Aside from that, there was a perception of deprivation in neighboring Resurrección, evidently based on usage rights disputed as early as the colonial period, which could easily have been refused during the Porfiriato.

That the people of Resurrección were successful with their activities relatively late—the owner was able to hold off final expropriations favoring Resurrección until 1929—can be attributed to the military's special regard for the owner, whose father had been a general.

[40] Archive of the DAAC, Exp. 23.3531.(724.8), fol. 23.
[41] Ibid., fol. 11.
[42] Ibid., fols. 1ff, Nickel, *Soziale Morphologie*, pp. 163ff.

Another factor was that the community of Resurrección was in the position to acquire areas of the neighboring estates, including the rancho San Mateo,[43] resulting in a more difficult proof of need for land.

This also indicates that the "revolutionary" potential and corresponding activities are not predominantly tied to an especially severe material deprivation, but rather to their perception. The experience of conflict, the direct proximity to the state capital (Resurrección belonged to the municipio of Puebla), and the corresponding contacts and ideological support from Puebla allowed the people of Resurrección to become permanent agraristas, who up until very recently have repeatedly invaded the remaining landholdings (ranchos and fractions) of Manzanilla.

THE CASE OF OZUMBA

The hacienda Ozumba, which lies between San Juan de los Llanos and Chalchicomula, produced cereals, raised pigs, and had access to extensive pastures. The soil, however, over the 6,790 hectares was usable only to a very limited extent because of its high saltpeter content.[44] The hacienda lay within the jurisdiction of the municipio of San José Chiapa, a small community whose *fundo legal* came into being in 1820 on the grounds of the hacienda Tlaxcantla.[45]

There was no tradition among the residents of neighboring communities for demanding land or usage rights from Ozumba or the rancho Minillas. The last land conflicts, between the Jesuits, then owners of Ozumba, and private landowners, were definitely settled about 1750.[46] Before the outbreak of the Revolution, the hacienda's workforce consisted predominantly of meseros, peones acasillados, semaneros (see Figure 13.2), and occasional teams of bricklayers or sheepshearers.

Peones Acasillados and Semaneros
at Ozumba before the Revolution

The wages of the peones grandes, with the exception of both capitanes, were traditionally 25 (or 18) centavos per day, but the owners permitted, until the abolition of peonage, the peons' debts to grow,

[43] Nickel, *Soziale Morphologie*, pp. 167, 282.

[44] As for the situation, extension, and possible use of the hacienda, see Nickel, *Soziale Morphologie*, pp. 291ff.

[45] See map in Nickel, *Soziale Morphologie*, p. 171.

[46] Ibid., pp. 300ff.

and thus many peons were able to stabilize their real incomes. Aside from these permanently employed *jornaleros*, the hacienda employed additional *calpanería* residents when required; these *semaneros de la casa* were usually women and children, as well as some older laborers.

One can thus assume that the income situation of the peons (including the *préstamos*) employed during the Porfiriato was slightly improved, since the workers' debts were recalled only when they left the estate. From about 1890 they were cancelled at least in the case of debtor's death, and aside from that, about 1849 and 1897 considerable testamentary remissions of debt were ordered.[47]

Aside from the daily wage, adult peons received an allotment of land, préstamos, weekly maize rations at reasonable prices (Figure 13.3), as well as some pocket money (*chiltomin*). In addition, the clothing and fabrics given out at the hacienda at Easter were reasonably priced and available to workers on credit. Further, the hacendado usually contributed to the festivities honoring the patron saint.

Within this group there certainly appeared to be no discrepancy between supply and expectations at the outbreak of the Revolution. The often assumed shrinkage of real wages during the Porfiriato scarcely touched most peones acasillados, and this was the case in Ozumba or the region of Puebla–Tlaxcala. In the critical years 1906–9, the hacienda allowed a considerable number of peones acasillados a more generous margin of debt and thus stabilized the basis of subsistence for these employees.[48]

The third group of resident salaried employees, the *meseros*, in-

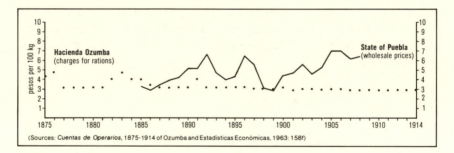

(Sources: *Cuentas de Operarios*, 1875-1914 of Ozumba and Estadísticas Económicas, 1963: 158f)

Figure 13.3. Development of the price of maize in the state of Puebla, compared with the price paid by peones acasillados at Ozumba.

[47] Ibid., pp. 315f, 350f.

[48] Herbert J. Nickel, "Peonaje e inmovilidad de los trabajadores agrícolas en México," *Anuario de Estudios Americanos* 36 (1979): 318ff, 339ff.

cluded craftsmen, shepherds, cowboys, foremen, drivers, etc., in addition to administrative personnel. They were relatively mobile, rarely indebted, and often received, in addition to their monthly wages, weekly spending money, and payment in kind without charge. In the lowest category, this was a weekly maize ration only.[49] During the Revolution, they seemed to be particularly loyal to the owner, and they were the first to whom he entrusted the defense of his interests. I have found no indication that the lower-paid meseros at Ozumba at this time were particularly involved in political activities. In the following I thus refer again to the peones de la casa.

The semaneros of Ozumba came mostly from the communities of San Hipólito Soltepec and San José Chiapa, but occasionally also from del Carmen, Ixtenco and other areas. A phase of steady income growth cannot be assumed, at least not from the wages received at Ozumba. Rather, it can be assumed that the semaneros were affected by the economic slump toward the end of the Porfiriato; as residents of free communities they were more dependent on the market and market prices, and thus may have suffered a decline in real wages. Also, in times of crisis haciendas often attempted to reduce the number of semaneros and to pay lower wages. One must consider, however, that at least some semaneros may have had additional sources of income. They may have served as semaneros only during the season, or may have been engaged in other activities, and thus were susceptible to periodic fluctuations in real incomes. But without complementary data on their economic situations within the communities it is difficult to substantiate this assumption.[50]

Finally, there are some indications that semaneros who were employed for longer periods received allotments of land with the obligation to work on call. Some cuadrillas of semaneros refused to accept the land and demanded instead higher wages, less expensive maize, and cash advances.[51] Before the outbreak of the Revolution

[49] See account books (cuentas de operarios) of the haciendas Ozumba and Rinconada and the income distribution schemes in both haciendas. See also Nickel, Soziale Morphologie, pp. 229, 344.

[50] At the same time, the data collected by the Comisiones Nacionales Agrarias should be considered. Statements recorded during the agency's enquiries, however, should be cross-checked, if possible.

[51] Letter from the owner to the administrator, March 24, 1909. The stock of letters and other documents received by the administrator is hereafter cited as OzAdC. See letter from the administrator to the owner of Ozumba from April 15, 1903. The stock of letters and other documents received by the estate owner's office in Puebla (here-

there were in the region of Ozumba no serious conflicts with peons, semaneros or neighboring communities threatening hacienda operations. There were merely a few indications of disputes over work standards or the behavior of hacienda staff.[52] In the following, I describe reactions of these two groups to the Revolution.

Ozumba during the Revolution

On November 22, 1910, the owner of Ozumba informed his administrator that he had heard of the suppression of a large group of ladrones who had attempted to seize the government of Tlaxcala but had failed. He would try to reach an agreement with some of the hacendados of the area to determine if they wanted to turn to the government for protection against these elements.[53]

In May 1911 the administrator of Ozumba was informed that there were rumors in Puebla of "revolutionaries" in the area of the estates, and that he should report daily to Puebla about this. Only five days later, these "revolutionaries" came to the hacienda. They took six cavalry rifles and two horses with them in exchange for a note of receipt and conducted themselves, according to the administrator, not too badly.

When shortly thereafter five other "revolutionaries" appeared, the administrator was able to respond to their demands for horses, weapons, and money by presenting their predecessors' receipt. And, when he had credibly assured them that there was no payroll money on the hacienda, they disappeared.[54] Raids of this kind, although not always so peaceful, were from then on everyday occurrences.

One can assume that Ozumba's administrator would have reported to the city in minute detail if there had been any noticeable sympathy for the "revolutionaries" among the peones acasillados, semaneros, or staff of the hacienda.

As early as January 1911, the administrator had been warned to be especially cautious in dealing with hacienda staff, as there had been word of strikes nearby at the hacienda San Francisco Aljibes and in the area of Apizaco. The owner gave orders to allow no agitators to enter the hacienda.[55] Because of the earlier events in Tlaxcala, the administrator soon received the instruction to employ no

---

after OzPrC) were consulted in the private collections of the inheritors of Roberto Sesma in Puebla.

[52] Nickel, *Soziale Morphologie*, pp. 356ff.

[53] OzAdC, owner to administrator; November 22, 1910.

[54] OzPrC, administrator to owner, May 17, 1911.

[55] OzAdC, owner to administrator, January 8, 1912.

more than the necessary number of workers for the maize harvest, even if the threshing had to remain undone for the time being, as the workers striking in Tlaxcala had been hired for the maize harvest.

On two occasions peons joined the "revolutionaries." In May 1911 a "battalion of revolutionaries" came to the hacienda that, according to information from the administrator, again was rather well-behaved and demanded only accommodation in the machero, barley and straw for the horses, and a *tercio* of maize for use in the calpanería to make tortillas. During the night and the next morning the group attacked two passenger trains passing through the area; from one they reportedly captured four bags of money, and from the other only 100 pesos.

After all, four peons from Ozumba had joined this group during the night; according to the administrator they were drunk. The next day "three of them, however, saw their mistake and went back to their quarters." It is interesting that the one peon who joined these "Maderistas" was the son of the highest-paid laborer on the estate, who could be assured of relatively generous préstamos. The son was described by the administrator as capricious, but, after three days he returned to the hacienda and was accused by the administrator of having taken part in robberies and for having stolen a coat from an employee of the hacienda Santiago.[56]

In a second case another peon joined the "Maderistas," but in this instance the administrator's main concern was to secure the debts he owed to the estate.[57] In March 1912 the hacienda was plagued by Zapatistas for the first time. They seized 21 zarapes, four Winchester guns, a rifle de salón, and a mailbag.[58]

When the discussion in the correspondence concerns Zapatistas it is always from the viewpoint of feared raids, requisitions, or encroachments, but never out of concern for the initiating of conflicts with the agricultural laborers or because of their possible solidarity with those in nearby rural communities. On several occasions the administrator was directed to treat the Zapatistas as well as possible on their visits to the hacienda, and to avoid any dispute.[59] Because a major problem proved to be the protection of the payroll, he avoided to some extent paying wages on the hacienda or kept the

[56] OzPrC, administrator to owner, May 22, 25, 28, 1911.

[57] Ibid., June 5, 1911.

[58] Account books of Ozumba, *Borrador*, March 29, 1912, p. 25; OzPrC, administrator to owner, April 1, 1912.

[59] OzAdC, owner to administrator, February 9, 1912; March 28, 1912; October 13, 1912.

details of payment secret (for example, effecting payments on Sundays in San Marcos).[60]

In September 1912 the administrator heard a rumor that an agitator, supposedly an individual from Apizaco was on his way to incite the hacienda workers. He was directed to arrest the man to give him a good beating, and to prevent his and other strangers' entry to the hacienda.[61] During 1913 efforts were therefore made to form an hacienda militia, but this was apparently never realized. The administrators of the area had some misgivings about such a militia because they feared it would reduce the workforce.

Finally, in March 1914, the administrator of Ozumba noted for the first time a "certain movement" among the peons. The occasion was evidently an angry exchange of words between the capitán and the mayordomo concerning a demand for revision of piecework conditions, but the administrator did not have to intervene.[62]

In conclusion, it can be said that in Ozumba neither the peones acasillados nor the semaneros revealed any inclination toward "revolutionary" activities. For the peones acasillados there was also no immediate demonstration of the "agrarian revolution," by passing Zapatistas, for example. At most, they were visited by regular and irregular troops, rebel commandos, and ordinary bandoleros on the hacienda or in the vicinity.

The Situation after the Decree of
Pablo González to Abolish Peonage

On September 3, 1914, the military governor of Puebla abolished peonage, and ordered regulation of working hours and a minimum wage. Only ten days later, a military unit came to the hacienda, ordered a meeting of the peons, and asked them about working conditions. The workers were urged to report immediately future grievances to the military command in San Marcos. The administrator reported no unusual occurrences in this connection.[63]

It is noteworthy that in December 1914 the administrator complained that some muchachos had disappeared and were reportedly working in Puebla. Eighteen adult employees were missing, evidently only temporarily, since some of them returned to work at

---

[60] Ibid., March 27, 1912.

[61] Ibid., September 7, 1912.

[62] OzPrC, administrator to owner, March 14, 1914.

[63] OzPrC, administrator to the owner's representative, September 14, 1914; and OzAdC, owner's representative to the administrator, September 18, 1914.

Ozumba in January and the full complement of employees was restored.[64]

In February 1915, about four weeks after Carranza's decree of restitution, an account appeared in the correspondence that "a very strong movement among the Indios on the question of land ownership" existed, "especially since the government has begun to distribute land."[65]

In the same year, the community of San José Chiapa was preliminarily allocated 272 hectares from Ozumba, lost the area again on appeal, and later (1928) finally received 426 hectares from the estate. These were the first serious long-term threats to the hacienda, including in particular the decree of the military governor of Puebla, Cesáreo Castro on May 12, 1916 that campesinos without land could apply for grants of up to six hectares, to be taken from neighboring haciendas and ranchos.[66]

In the spring of 1919 inhabitants of the community San Hipólito Soltepec probably stole several plows from Ozumba, including a heavy one that had to be abandoned. In June residents of this community attacked the estate. According to the administrator, the armed invaders entered the hacienda at night, during which the peones acasillados recognized some semaneros who had been employed by Ozumba. The administrator reported that after a gunfight the calpanería was invaded; there were lootings, attempted rapes, and beatings, and the blacksmith's house was completely stripped.[67] A month later the administrator demanded weapons in order "to repel assaults with the help of our own people."[68]

Here one must add that for the administrator, and more so for hacienda workers the political affiliations of the armed visitors were often unclear, and it is unlikely that they brought any sort of political message. Probably the peons found the visitors to be just as menacing as did the administrative staff and the owner.

The conflicts between the peones acasillados and the hacienda administration until early 1920 were not "revolutionary" in nature;

[64] Letters from the administrator to the estate owner (Roberto Sesma) in Habana, December 13, 1914; January 14, 1915. The stock of letters sent abroad, in particular to Europe, is hereafter cited as OzEuC.

[65] OzEuC, representative to owner in Habana, Febraury 10, 1915.

[66] Decree of the military governor of the state of Puebla, Cesáreo Castro, directed to the community administrations from May 12, 1916 (OzPrC).

[67] OzPrC, administrator to the representative, March 16, 1919; June 13, 1919.

[68] Ibid., July 8, 1919 ("hay que prevenirse para repeler algun atentado con nuestras personas ya que no tenemos auxilio . . .").

rather, they were disputes over wages, privileges (*pegujal*, maize prices, holidays), and piecework conditions. Their levels of expectation must therefore have been still moderate. There is no suggestion of a fundamental questioning among the hacienda peons nor of illegal practices. Above all, no formation of solidarity between the peones acasillados and the semaneros of Chiapa or Soltepec can be discerned.

Residents of Soltepec occupied a large portion of Ozumba's agricultural fields in the 1920s, and in 1931 were finally awarded 1,154 hectares. In contrast to the often expressed assumption that the hacendados had been able to select the transferred lands, this was not the case at Ozumba; rather, the ejidatarios of Soltepec carried out their wishes to the particular displeasure of the former owner.

Because the Soltepec ejidatarios who forcibly defended the land that was provisionally awarded to them but legally disputed, one could say only of *them* that they had "revolutionarily" damaged the structure of the hacienda Ozumba. Otherwise in the course of the Revolution the estate was hardly touched by raids, forced contributions, and massive theft, aside from the lost claims on indebted laborers.[69]

Until about 1924 there were repeated raids, occasionally with exchanges of gunfire (mostly rather theatrical and without injury), thefts of livestock, and other unpleasantnesses of that kind. Later, the owner successfully strove for the stationing of a military unit on the hacienda, after which the raids ceased. The troops were still stationed there in 1932.

In the early 1920s, however, the relationship between the peones acasillados and the hacienda management became precarious. Up until then it had been relatively easy for the estate to keep potential agitators (*mitoteros*) away or to dismiss them. Such orders had been issued to the administrator as early as 1912.[70]

Eight years later the trade union movement showed its effect on Ozumba. In November 1920 the authorized representative of the estate seemed rather uneasy when he reported to the hacendado:

Tenemos agravante bastante serio; los famosos sindicalistas han principiado á tratar de ganarse á los pueblos y á las haciendas y ya empezaron á establecerles por San Hipólito y las haciendas colindantes y á la vez han enviado agentes por San Juan, San Andres y por otros rumbos y por las primeras ya consiguieron

[69] Nickel, *Soziale Morphologie*, p. 374.
[70] OzAdC, owner to administrator, December 25, 1911; January 8, 1912.

la primera huelga y en San Cristobal, San Luis y las otras colindantes ya los peones se declararon en huelga exijiendo un jor-
nal de dos pesos por ocho horas de trabajo y aun en Ozumba
mismo ya empiezan conque si no se les rebabja el tiempo se
declararan en huelga y cosas por el estilo.[71]

In 1921 a strike occurred because of what appeared to the workers
to be too fast a work pace. A letter by the administrator indicates the
altered work situation, about which he complained "one finds oneself" in a time in which one may not use criticism of any sort and
less pressure than before to move the peons to fulfill their duties.[72]
They, for their part, tried to make it clear to the administrator that
the old times were gone: "ya no es el tiempo de antes entonces qué
libertades nos dió Carranza?" ("Now, times have changed, but what
kind of liberties did Carranza give us?").[73] By August 1926 the
strike had ended. The administrator even spoke about a case of "re-
beldía" among the peons and asked the military for assistance in
keeping the peace.[74]

Up until 1930 the hacienda administration was, however, at least
in the position to fence the calpaneros off from union representatives,
although the estates had received orders in late 1921 to nominate peons for the formation of a trade union.[75] The administrator was instructed not to employ semaneros who had provoked strikes in the past.

The military unit turned out to be useful after all, not only in protecting the estate from raids, but it also helped to ensure "law and
order" within the hacienda. For example, the unit helped the
administration to end a work stoppage, and to get rid of an annoying

[71] "We have a rather serious problem: the famous trade unionists (syndicalists)
have begun to try to win the *pueblos* and the haciendas and they have already begun
to establish themselves around San Hipolito and the adjacent haciendas and at the
same time they have sent agents to San Juan, San Andres and other areas. In the first
areas they have already brought about [achieved] their first strike, and in San Cristobal, San Luis, and the other adjacent haciendas, the peons have already declared
themselves on strike, demanding a two peso wage for eight hours of work. Even in
Ozumba itself, they have already stated their position—if the number of work hours
is not reduced, they will declare a strike and similar actions." OzEuC, representative
to owner in San Antonio, Texas, November 5, 1912.

[72] OzPrC, administrator to owner, September 15, 1921 ("por que estamos en días de
no poder hacerles ya ninguna reprención y menos obligarlos a cumplir"; Manuel Bre-
tón to Roberto Sesma).

[73] OzPrC, administrator to owner, October 21, 1920.

[74] OzPrC, August 2, 4, 5, 21, 1926; OzAdC, August 3, 7, 1926.

[75] OzAdC, owner to administrator, December 20, 1921 ("sindicato de trabajadores").

worker who made himself noticeable because of his pro-union tendencies.[76]

Even after 1930 the peons were not able to develop an efficient
organization, but they found an ally in the community administration of San José Chiapa through their conflicts with the hacienda.
Before 1910 village representatives had received occasional complaints from workers, the more so as there was a *juez menor*, but
later the community intervened actively on behalf of the calpaneros,
and apparently attempted to enforce against the hacienda their
claims of authority, which had been so often denied in the past.
After 1930 the owner had to face the fact that peones acasillados
tried to found their own community on the estate, in order to become eligile for ejido grants of land.

Nevertheless, until October 1931 the calpaneros had been prepared to send their wives into the *servicio de tezquiz* (i.e., to prepare
tortillas for the estate's administrators) in the *casa principal*. Now
they refused this service and demanded to be free of the obligation.
When the owner made it understood that there was a connection
between the maize rations and the servicio de tezquiz, the calpaneros explained that they were prepared to pay for the maize but refused to perform services. This finally completed the monetarization
of labor conditions on the estate.[77]

At least one group of calpaneros applied to the governor of Puebla
in December 1931 for an allocation of land on which to establish a
core settlement with the required production areas. The group argued that "sixty-nine fathers of families as well as single adults until
now have lived in slavery and poverty because the wages are paltry
and the cultivation of fields takes place under unfavorable conditions of sharecropping."[78]

In another letter of the same day, written in the name of 265 calpanería residents, they demanded the return of lands "which once
had belonged to their ancestors and which had been usurped by latifundistas under the protection of dictatorial governments."[79] The

[76] Ibid., August 3, 1926; January 13, 14, 1928.

[77] OzPrC, administrator to owner, October 24, 1931 ("contestaron que ellos pagan
su maíz, y que ahora no están dispuestos a cumplir lo que sus abuelos trataron").

[78] Archive of the DAAC, Exp. 23:12983.(724.8), p. 1 ("Que en este lugar existen se-
senta y nueve individuos jéfes dé familia y numerosos solteros mayores de dieciseis
años, los que han llevado hasta el presente una vida de esclavitud y de miseria, de-
bido a los exiguos salarios y a las condiciones de aparcería").

[79] Ibid., p. 2 ("las tierras que fueron de los antepasados de los solicitantes, usurpa-
dos por los latifundistas al amparo de gobiernos dictatoriales").

details cited by the petitioners, who ranged in age from one to seventy-five years, concerning sharecropping and usurpation of land were incorrect, and lead one to believe that an externally formulated text had probably been taken over and used as their own.

One year later calpaneros attempted to establish a settlement of their own at one of the two railway stations belonging to the hacienda, but still without success. Finally, numerous calpaneros from Ozumba turned to the president of Mexico. In a telegram they asked him to intervene against further endowment of land to the community of San Hipólito Soltepec (for the extension of its ejido) because in this way they would lose not only the production areas granted to them by the hacienda, but also their means of employment:

> Nosotros calpaneros hacienda Ozumba suplicamos usted ayúdenos poderosa influencia motivo a que pueblo San Hipólito Soltepec dotado ampliamente, indebidamente quiere cambiar ejidos otros terrenos, lo cual perjudica nuestras personas pues en terrenos quieren quitar injustamente tenemos solares sostiniemiento nuestras familias y cambiando ejidos los perderemos y perderemos nuestro trabajo pues hacienda no podría seguir dándolo motivo a que sobraría gente.
>
> Esperamos ayuda clase necesitada campesina somos nosotros. Muy respetuosamente.[80]

Apparently some of the peones acasillados oriented themselves toward the newly developing ejido communities and directed their expectations toward similar opportunities. The remaining employees counted more on paternalistic help from within the traditional system and yet feared, not without reason, that the continuing expropriations would destroy the basis of existence for rural laborers.

Possibly the peons also wavered in their objectives and expectations. Their efforts to obtain land and their own ejidal settlements came to an end only after the legal requirements were modified in 1934, with the establishment of a *colonía agrícola* (San José

---

[80] "We the workers of Ozumba hacienda respectfully request that you help us [with your] powerful influence because San Hipolito Soltepec pueblo, already well endowed, wrongly (illegally) wishes to exchange *ejidos* for other lands, which would harm our people—the fact is that on the land which they wish to unjustly take, we have plots [*solares*] which sustain our families and changing for *ejidos* we will lose them and we will lose our jobs because the hacienda would not justify a surplus of people. We await your help, the needy peasant [*campesina*] class that we are. Very respectfully." OzPrC, *Carta nocturna*, San Marcos, March 10, 1933, dirigida al C. Presidente de la República, Palacio Nacional, Mexico City. Punctuation in the *carta* retained.

Ozumba) and an endowment of 1,076 hectares. These efforts progressed in full accordance with legal statutes, and the hacienda Ozumba was thereby liquidated as a latifundio. In that process the peones acasillados had not participated in a way that could be called "revolutionary." And even the semaneros of the communities such as San José Chiapa and San Hipólito Soltepec, who earlier attempted to obtain land from the state—and eventually succeeded— did not participate in the Revolution before it became institutionalized.

THE CASE OF RINCONADA

The hacienda Rinconada belonged to the municipio Soltepec and to the district of Chalchicomula. It was about a third smaller than Ozumba, but in contrast it had extensive montes. The estate was crossed by the F. C. Mexicano railway line (Veracruz to Mexico City) and was equipped with a railway station. Agricultural production concentrated on cereal crops and raising of pigs and sheep; in addition the montes were used as pasture land and as a source of timber, firewood, and charcoal for sale. During the Porfiriato the owners' family occupied two other adjacent estates, La Higuera and El Pozo, whose general managers were subordinate to the administrator of Rinconada.

The partially available documents of the administrator's correspondence and the accounting office indicate that the working conditions in Rinconada at the turn of the century did not differ significantly from those at Ozumba, although the latter had in many areas more modern equipment. Both haciendas predominantly employed peones acasillados and additional semaneros. The records of both estates for this time document neither tenants nor aparceros. Because I found no indication that the reactions of the peones acasillados or semaneros in the early years of the Revolution differed considerably from those at Ozumba, I confine myself to the presentation of some complementary information.

The Situation before the Revolution

In the colonial period Rinconada was a part of a *mayorazgo*. According to the administrator of the hacienda Ozumba (which until 1767 had belonged to the Jesuits), in the seventeenth and eighteenth centuries the owners of Rinconada engaged in fierce land conflicts with the neighboring communities of Santa Margarita Mazapiltepec and San Hipólito Soltepec, and eventually prevailed such that both communities retained only their fundos legales.[81] The fundo legal of Mazapiltepec was actually enclosed on three sides by the hacienda.[82]

Because the montes belonged to the estate, a classic field of conflict was established. Similar to the case of Resurrección—Manzanilla, the communities claimed usage rights on the montes for their own needs. While the hacienda defined the concept of domestic use restrictively, the community residents interpreted it more broadly. Thus in 1909, for example, there was a written dispute over the community's right to collect firewood and to set up lime ovens in the montes for the restoration of a church steeple.[83] In view of this background, it is not surprising that the seizures on the hacienda during the Revolution began in the montes and that they were initiated by the neighboring communities.

The working conditions leave no particular characteristics behind in the account books. The usual wages were paid, the usual advances and credits were granted, and the workers were provided with inexpensive maize and the customary "privileges."

The repeated offer from the Soltepec mayor's office to send an offender into forced labor at Rinconada "en calidad de corrección á su mal manejo hasta que esta Presidencia lo pida"[84] appears striking to me, but a *compadrazgo* (ritual kinship) relationship probably existed between the writer (the *presidente?*) and the hacendado.

The Early Years of the Revolution

In May 1911 problems began to emerge. The presidencia of El Seco organized a militia for the protection of the "sociedad contra los desordenes interiores y toda suerte de abusos que se cometan; así como también y principalmente, contra los actos vandálicos de propios y extraños," and requested a mounted and armed member of the hacienda to report for service. At the same time the commu-

[81] Archivo de Jesuítas, Universidad Autónoma de Puebla (Mexico), Letter of Miguel de San Martín administrator of Ozumba, to Antonio de Paredes, the padre rector of the Colegio Espíritu Santo (?) at Puebla, October 22, 1757, p. 8; *Carpetón* 180, hacienda Rinconada, sobre tierras, 1757.

[82] See map in Nickel, *Soziale morphologie*, p. 380.

[83] Letter from the municipal authorities of Mazapiltepec to the administrator of the hacienda Rinconada, November 5, 8, 1909. The stock of letters and other documents received by the administrator of Rinconada is hereafter cited RiAdC. They were consulted at Rinconada.

[84] RiAdC, letter from the municipal authorities of Soltepec to the administrator of Rinconada, March 23, 1909.

nity offered to help the estate in case of need.[85] Some months later the mayor (?) of Soltepec reported to his padrino that there were some agitators (*mitoteros*) in his community. He was disconcerted by the order of the state government to announce a general proclamation against illegal invasions of land, and asked for advice.[86] In March 1912 some Zapatistas in the montes as well as the transport of the payroll money and Easter advances, however, still presented more problems for the administrator.[87] A short time later the hacienda feared indeed an invasion of the montes and the changing of boundary markers by Villanueva residents.[88] After all, the administrator had orders, in the event of a visit to the estate by Zapatistas, not to resist but rather to offer them something ("y darles algo de lo que pidan"), and in no way to threaten the lives of the employees and laborers.[89] The correspondence suggests that in 1912 the community of Mazapiltepec proposed to solve border disputes of its own accord.[90]

On January 1, 1914, the administrator was requested by the owner to report what he knew about the Revolution in the vicinity of Rinconada, so I assume that up until then no unusual occurrences had taken place. Two months later the hacendado rather indignantly asked for the name of that "general" who with his men had been harassing the estate, and defense measures were discussed.[91] The tensions with Mazapiltepec continued. The administrator was directed to send some peons into the montes to collect firewood in order to demonstrate the estate's rights of possession. Hostilities were to be avoided, however, as long as the "pre-constitutional period" lasted.[92]

Changes Brought about by Military Decrees

No indications of unrest or discord in the calpanería were reported in the detailed correspondence up to the September 1914 decree of Pablo González concerning the working conditions in the ha-

[85] RiAdC, letter from the municipal authorities of El Seco to Bernardino Tamariz Oropeza at Rinconada, May 23, 1911.

[86] RiAdC, letter from the municipal authorities of Soltepec (signed by Antonio Lopez) to Manuel Tamariz Oropeza at Rinconada, September 21, 1911.

[87] RiAdC, owners to administrator, March 27, 1912.

[88] Ibid., June 1, 1912.

[89] Ibid., February 16, 1912.

[90] Ibid., August 7, 1915; the letter refers to August 1912.

[91] Ibid., January 1, 1914; March 21, 1914.

[92] Ibid., October 21, 1914.

cienda, so it must be assumed that in Rinconada, too, the estate workers showed no revolutionary impulses. Annoyance, however, provoked the hacienda management's tactic of depreciating the ordered wage payments (now at 0.80 pesos instead of 0.25) by the removal of "privileges" (that is, by charging for what had until then been free services, such as accommodations, firewood, etc.), and by increasing the price of maize rations from four to nine pesos per carga.[93] However, these reductions were gradually retracted, especially because inflation also considerably reduced the cost of labor. Thus in April 1916 the estate waived the payment of rent for the *pegujales*.[94]

In 1915 a letter to the administrator indicated the owner's concern that the peons might leave the hacienda, so an improvement of the wages and of payments-in-kind was suggested as a solution.[95] Until the end of 1919 the correspondence indicates no particular difficulties with the peones acasillados.

Carranza's restitution decree and the 1917 constitution changed the agrarian structure more decisively than had the decree on working conditions by Pablo González. Whereas in the years before 1915 the community of Mazapiltepec (and eventually Villanueva) had just intensified a traditional land conflict with Rinconada, the Carranza decree and later the constitution mobilized the residents of this and other neighboring communities (including Villanueva, el Seco, and Soltepec) to invade the estate's montes. The owners of the hacienda Rinconada reacted from then on with bureaucratic maneuvers rather than arms against the illegal occupants, and attempted to stop or retard the measures of the Comisión Agraria through appeals.

The instructions to the administrator from Puebla were that, although living in an era of anarchy, one should only offer resistance if it seemed prudent.[96] The resigned assessment of the situation is reflected in the complaint: "La plaga Carrancista es tan mala como la Zapatista, pero no hay que dejarse y veremos que resulta" ("The Carrancista plague is as bad as the Zapatista one, but without it what would happen?").[97]

[93] Ibid., September 5, 9, 1914.
[94] Ibid., April 18, 1916. This favor was granted on condition that the laborers stayed until the end of harvesting.
[95] Ibid., July 19, 1917.
[96] Ibid., October 21, 1915.
[97] Ibid., June 8, 1917.

The Situation Since 1917

During the illegal use of the montes and the visits from land surveyors of the Comisión Agraria, the owners of Rinconada were annoyed by a military unit that was transferred there, since the losses from the soldiers' unpaid bills were apparently quite high. The owners found the behavior of the uninvited guests to be so insufferable that the administrator received the order: "No dándoles leña, ni maíz ni piezas, ni colchones ni camas, tendrrían (sic)—como debe ser—que ir a otras partes y'dejarnos en paz" ("Don't give them wood, nor maize, nor bits, nor mattresses, nor beds, they will have to—as is should be—go elsewhere and leave us in peace").[98] As a few weeks later another unit of thirty-two soldiers was quartered at Rinconada, renewed attempts were made to transfer them to another estate.[99]

Whereas in 1919 the communities of Mazapiltepec and Villanueva were formally granted land from Rinconada, the estate's agricultural laborers still appear to have been content with system-conforming concessions granted by the hacienda. The benefiting communities complained in 1920 about estate "caporales" and "trabajadores," who had threatened ejidatarios and laid waste to the fields.[100] Understandably, it is today almost impossible to determine whether the Rinconada personnel reacted to the encroachment of the ejidatarios or out of annoyance over the expropriations. The Rinconada dependants, however, were not incited to react by the owners, who at all times acted rather cautiously and with resignation, set their hopes rather on the judicial system and on military protection. In view of the land losses, the administrator was directed to employ the smallest possible workforce and not to hire "un solo semanero mientras no veamos el desenlace (sic) de las tierras" ("a single semanero until we see the settlement").[101]

In November 1920, the hacienda was confronted with the disturbing demand to allow a union to be established within the estate. One month before, the estate had already dealt with the possibility of a strike and had prepared itself; the owners instructed the administrator to offer wage increases, but only after an agreement with sur-

[98] Ibid., October 20, 1917.
[99] Ibid., November 26, 1917; December 13, 15, 1917.
[100] RiAdC, letters from municipal authorities of Mazapiltepec (May 26, 1920) and Villanueva (September 30, 1920) to the administrator.
[101] RiAdC, owners to administrator, April 1, 1920; and April 15, 1921 ("para las pocas tierras que tiene actualmente la hacienda, es mucha la cuadrilla y hay que ver la manera de que no resulten onerosos los trabajadores").

rounding estates had been made. Above all, they pleaded for a solution to the problem in a "peaceful and reasonable manner," that is to say, above all without trade unions.[102]

On the El Pozo estate belonging to the hacienda, there was still no labor organization in July 1938, and in the owner's view most peones acasillados had no intention of organizing themselves. The administrator was nevertheless advised to watch that outsiders did not engineer petitions for such an organization to be set up.[103]

More than through the trade-union movement, the hacienda was beset by constant invasions, further expropriations, and renewed community land claims, together with attempts to establish an agrarian colony on the estate grounds.[104] Finally, the estate workers expressed their apprehension that the communities would take all the land for themselves and do away with their jobs.[105] Despite numerous invasions in the 1940s and early 1950s by "*agraristas*" from Mazapiltepec, Soltepec, and Xicotenco, the estate was apparently still able to guard most peones acasillados against "revolutionary elements" and to prevent "disturbios y contrariedades innecesarias" ("unnecessary disturbances and obstacles")[106]

While the "*indios bandidos de Soltepec*," as well as the ejidatarios and invaders from neighboring communities, took possession of hacienda lands, mostly within the framework of the reform laws, the estate preserved traditional social relations for a remarkably long time. Even forty years after the outbreak of the Revolution the estate owners succeeded in driving away a "mitotero," whom they held responsible for a work stoppage. They expressed their concern over the laborers' incessant requests for credit (and their indebtedness). Even in 1950 the remuneration offered by the former hacienda to the peons still looked rather prerevolutionary:

> Deben entender los peones que sí después de todas las granjerías que tienen en ésa, como son: casa, solar, almud, agua, milpero que le cuide sus milpas, burrero que les cuide sus burras, maíz a un peso cuartilla, cuando está a nueve pesos en el mer-

[102] Ibid., October 30, 1920; November 3, 5, 1920 ("deseando nosotros por nuestra parte, que esto se resolviera de una manera pacífica y por la razón").

[103] Ibid., July 20, 1938.

[104] Ibid., December 22, 1937. In the same letter the owners complain about the delay in the explusion by the military of those who planned to found the colony.

[105] Ibid., January 19, 1937 ("de que los trabajadores están inquietos por lo que les dicen los de los pueblos, esto es, que van a tomar todas las tierras de la hacienda y se van a quedar ellos sin donde trabajar").

[106] Ibid., March 22, 1945.

cado, préstamos siempre que le necesitan y a veces aunque no lo necesiten, leña etc., etc., aun así no están contentes, nadie les obliga a prestar allá sus servicios pues que ninguno está forzado, si no están conformes con el órden que debe haber en todo el negocio, pueden buscar trabajo en donde mejor les acomode, la cuestión es, que los que prestan allá sus servicios, cumplan debidamente."[107]

The Revolution had, at least, not reached the calpanería.

[107] "The peons must understand that if after all the advantages that they have here such as a house, a *solar*, an *almud*, a *milpero* to look after their milpas, a *burrero* to care for their burros, a *cuartilla* of maize at one peso when it costs nine in the market, loans whenever they need them and sometimes when they don't, fire wood, etc, etc, even with all this they are not content, no one is forcing them to lend their services there; no one is forced. If they do not agree with the order which there must be in any business, they should look for work where it is more their taste; the issue is then that those who work there must fulfill their duties as they should." Ibid., October 11, 1951.

CHAPTER FOURTEEN

Charisma, Tradition, and Caciquismo: Revolution in San Luis Potosí

Romana Falcón

Virtually since it began, the Mexican Revolution has been considered a popular and agrarian movement, both with regard to the social origin of the bulk of its participants and with respect to the deep-rooted problems that led to the overthrow of a government and a regime. This original characterization of the revolution seems to be confirmed by the systematic and organized movement of the rural communities of Morelos to recover their land, and by the subsequent movements that emerged in several states of the republic (such as Yucatán, Veracruz, and Michoacán), where political and military organization of the peasantry brought about important reforms and changes in the structure of rural property.

The classic interpretation is nevertheless one that, despite the fact that the violent revolutionary phase ended more than sixty-five years ago, continues to provoke serious controversies. In recent years, some of the standard notions regarding the Mexican Revolution have been subjected to a thorough revision, to the extent that both its origins and its course are presently undergoing a general reinterpretation. This shift has reached the point where doubts have even been raised about whether "revolution" is indeed an appropriate term.[1]

---

[1] Ramón Eduardo Ruiz, *The Great Rebellion, México 1905–1924* (New York: Norton, 1980); Jorge Vera Estañol, *La revolución Mexicana: Orígenes y resultados* (México: Porrúa, 1957); Gilbert Joseph, *Revolution from Without: Yucatán, Mexico and the United States, 1880–1924.* (London: Cambridge University Press, 1982); Raymond Buve, "Peasant Movements, Caudillos and Land Reform during the Revolution (1910–1917) in Tlaxcala, Mexico," *Boletín de Estudios Latinoamericanos y del Caribe* 18 (1975): 112–52.

Today it is clear that the Mexican Revolution was not a single, generalized movement, but rather a mosaic of local uprisings, each with its own roots and objectives. The spectrum of variation in these local movements was much wider than had previously been suspected. The social origins of their participants, both followers and leaders, the causes of the insurrections, the objectives proclaimed by each, the changes actually accomplished—all of these varied greatly. At one extreme, to deal only with the familiar names, is the movement led by Francisco I. Madero, scion of one of the more powerful landholding families in Mexico, which was concerned primarily with democratizing the political life of the country and renewing the cadres of government. At the other is the agrarian movement of Morelos, led by Emiliano Zapata. Between these two lies a wide range of state regional uprisings that together made up the revolution.

To sum up, it may be said that the principal challenge in analyzing the Mexican Revolution is to achieve a profound understanding of its heterogeneity, so that in time we may construct a global vision that takes into account the complexity of that historical process and allows a more precise understanding of its origins, evolution, and achievements.

It is important to notice that today the "revisionist" view is being revised, giving new strength to the basic ideas of the "classic" interpretation, and therefore to the importance of the role played by the peasantry. Knight, who has undertaken the task of reconstructing a new general interpretation of the 1910 movement, maintains that

> it was the popular movement, deriving from the countryside and significantly, though not exclusively, impelled by agrarian resentments, which was at the heart of the revolution. . . . Such an interpretation may seem platitudinous, but it challenges views which, from different perspectives but with growing vigour, deny that the revolution represented a genuine mass movement, embodying definite popular grievances (notably of an agrarian kind), and which prefer to posit a revolution initiated, controlled and consummated by "bourgeois" leadership, capable of mobilising (and demobilising) a dependent, duped populace.[2]

[2] Alan Knight, "Peasant and Caudillo in Revolutionary Mexico, 1910–1917," in *Caudillo and Peasant in the Mexican Revolution*, ed. D. A. Brading (London: Cambridge University Press, 1980), p. 19. James Cockroft, *Mexico: Class Formation, Capital Accumulation, and the State* (New York: Monthly Review Press, 1983). Cockroft maintains a similar view: "The driving social force of the revolutionary upheaval of

But beyond the position that one assumes in this controversy—and to a degree that depends on each case study, since one can point to sharply contrasting conclusions—there is no doubt that the task of understanding why and how the rural population participated in the revolution is of the greatest significance. Such comprehension would clearly benefit monographic research and general considerations about this historical event. At least in the northern state of San Luis Potosí—which will serve as the basis for this discussion—it was the impact of the agrarian world that, in large part, left its social stamp on the revolution, and which obliged it to be more profound and complex than a mere political struggle among old and new elites.

In order to understand the motives and the ways in which the peasants participated in the 1910 movement, and to comprehend why a significant sector of the rural population took no part in it, one can assume several theoretical approaches. One of the possibilities, is the application of the Max Weber's political sociology and most particularly his typology of domination.[3] These categories allow us to distinguish among various forms of domination, according to the predominant type of legitimacy, be it "traditional," "charismatic," or "rational," although in no concrete case do these manifest themselves in an exclusive or pure form. From this point of view, one can study the popular and mainly rural mobilization during the revolution, contrasting its different forms of authority and power relationships. Accordingly, peasant action in San Luis Potosí, which at first glance might appear to be homogeneous, can be seen to have

1911–1916 was the rural peasantry and proletariat. To the dispossessed peasant small ranchero, Indian comunero, or rural proletarian, the enemy—the landlord-capitalist—was still very much in evidence. To these people the solution was simple: take back the land and water, seize the mills, provide for self, family, and community rather than for the boss. And this is what thousands of jornaleros and peasants did. . . . The most active revolutionaries among the peasantry were the landless wage-labor workers and jornaleros, rather than the sharecroppers, tenant farmers, or allotment-holding farmers" (p. 100). A parallel interpretation is found in Gustavo Esteva, La batalla en el México rural (México: Siglo XXI, 1982), p. 16. For a more "popular" view of Carranza, see Richmond Douglas, Venustiano Carranza's Nationalist Struggle 1893–1920 (University of Nebraska Press, 1983). In his recent work on the Porfiriato and the revolution up to 1940, Hans Werner Tobler concludes, in contrast with Ruiz, that the 1910 movement should indeed be considered a revolution: Die mexikanische Revolution (Frankfurt: Suhrkamp, 1984).

[3] Max Weber, Economía y sociedad: Esbozo de sociología comprensiva (México: FCE, Sección de Obras de Sociología, 1969), pp. 170–204, 704–889. Knight has used this focus to examine the revolutionary coalitions of Carranzistas and Villistas; see Knight, "Peasant and Caudillo," in Brading, ed.

been composed of various movements, each spurred into action by different forms of political legitimacy. Certainly class considerations bear a significant weight in the differentiation of these revolutionary groups, but it would be unproductive to limit the analysis to this variable, since distinctions between the various participants would remain, to a large extent, unexplained. Although the social bases are similar, noteworthy differences exist among their objectives and strategies, their political style, and their forms of internal organization. The variations among these groups are largely determined by their contrasting views of the world and political cultures. An approach that takes such class relations into account and at the same time emphasizes the components of culture and political ideology, may provide an explanation of the diversity of objectives, forms of recruitment, and bonds between the peasants and their leaders.

In a somewhat schematic manner, we may distinguish various forms of political authority around which the actions of San Luis Potosí peasants converged during the revolution. They do not imply a chronological order, nor are they exclusive, since they occasionally coexisted, at times in complementary manner, while at others in opposition. During the armed struggle (1910–20) two such forms were intertwined. The first was characterized by the traditional dominant role of large and middle landowners who, through their inherited legitimacy, together with the good salaries they could offer, recruited some of their workers and the peasants in their home towns. Mostly, these leaders were able to impose their conservative and merely political outlook over the revolutionary process in the state. But this was not the only kind of mobilization. At the same time, there was one of a more popular nature, where the leaders clearly identified with the strong discontent felt in their rural areas. This kind of revolutionaries showed little interest in what was happening beyond their zones of operation, and maintained the loyalty of their followers by establishing warm and strong personal relationships with each of them, as well as by distributing the spoils of war.

Between 1920 and 1925 when, at least in relative terms, peace was finally restored in San Luis, there was an upsurge of political activity among the peasantry. A new type of radical leadership put out a more institutional and impersonal call for the political organization of the peasantry throughout the state; this type of mobilization would eventually culminate in an important agrarian reform.

During the following decade, the fate of all San Luis Potosí became largely dependent on one of the revolutionary leaders, Saturnino Cedillo, who was more closely identified with the peasants.—

The basis of his strong cacicazgo were the private militias he was able to build with those long time followers over whom he had established his authority during the years as guerrillas. In the 1920s, because of the greater stability in their lives, and the abundant resources Cedillo was able to offer them, the power relationships among them began to change. The close personal bond was maintained, but it no longer sprang from the allegiances formed during military campaigns. It now acquired more traditional and paternalistic forms not entirely different from those which, for centuries, had linked peasants to landowners.

One fundamental point remains to be made: this work is not intended to provide a history of the revolution in San Luis Potosí. Rather, it is an attempt to emphasize and contrast the most noteworthy characteristics of the forms of peasant participation in the revolutionary movement in the state.[4]

Traditional and Popular Rebellions: Alliances and Antagonisms (1910–20)

Although life was arduous for the peasants of San Luis Potosí during the Porfiriato, the 1910 revolution did not originate with a peasant protest against Díaz' agrarian policy. On the contrary, to a large extent, it was organized by the beneficiaries of the old regime.

During the Porfiriato some government policies ran counter to the interests of certain privileged and middle classes, who formed opposition fronts frequently headed by rancheros. Numerous power struggles broke out between factions of local elites. Since these landowners had traditionally enjoyed their workers loyalty, they were able to hold their positions as leaders and benefited from the various uprisings that then took place. Throughout the revolution, a strong and independent peasant movement both in the formulation of its demands and in the designation of its leadership was prevented largely by the persistence of the traditional form of authority that had been exercised by rancheros and hacendados for many years, and even for centuries.

Among those small-scale, frequently prosperous rural proprietors who upheld this kind of traditional rule, the group of rancheros organized around the Santos family acquired special importance. Since 1829, the Santos had exercized authority as caciques (political

---

[4] A detailed analysis of this case study can be seen in Romana Falcón, *Revolución y caciquismo: San Luis Potosí 1910–1938* (México: El Colegio de México, 1984).

bosses) in a section of the Huasteca, the fertile region in southeastern San Luis Potosí. Through thick and thin they managed to maintain a degree of regional preeminence during the Porfiriato, the revolution, and even up to the 1970s. Although they had become an
important regional economic force and retained local political control prior to, and at beginning of the Diaz regime, the Santos suffered
several setbacks. An important one occurred when the Porfirian governors decided to divide all San Luis Potosí communal lands among
private owners, a measure that had been basically conceived as a
means of destroying indigenous peasant rebellions in the Huasteca.
At the same time, it was intended to force many Huasteco landowners (such as the Santos) who possessed land in the form of undivided joint properties (condueñazgos) to put an end to their "feudal" tradition and to accept a new era of progress and modernization.
This policy ended by creating antagonisms between the Huastecan
proprietors and the governors. More important still, during the Porfiriato the Santos lost their local hegemony to a rival faction, also
headed by rancheros. The Santos' political problems were exacerbated after they led an unsuccessful local revolt during the 1880s,
an uprising related to an agrarian rebellion among the Huastecan
Indians. When the Santos lost control over the municipal government, it became more difficult for them to continue increasing their
landholdings, because it was through this channel that they had
seized ejidal lands and some municipal properties. Furthermore, as
authorities they had been able to force local Indian peasants to perform forced labor for the municipality (or on the caciques's own
property) in lieu of paying taxes.[5]

It is here that we find the roots of many of the vertical mobilizations that characterized the revolution in San Luis Potosí. The traditional domination suffered by the Huastecan Indians had obliged
them to offer free labor to their local authorities, who were usually
well known landowners. Both the peasants who lived in communities and those who were permanently employed on the haciendas
(peones acasillados) were required, for example, to deliver messages, to repair public buildings and roads, to work in the houses of
the authorities, and most important of all, to provide military service and help maintain the troops. No payment was given for any of
these services. For this reason, during the nineteenth century, the

[5] Enrique Márquez, La casa de los señores santos: Un cacicazgo en la huasteca
potosina, 1897–1910, MA Thesis, El Colegio de México, 1979, pp. 14ff; Romana Falcón, "¿Los orígenes populares de la revolución en 1910? El caso de San Luis Potosí,"
Historia Mexicana 29, no. 2 (19): 208ff.

government was able to count on "submissive Indians" to help put down several of their brothers' revolts. The paternalistic relationships between *condueños* and Indians was a symbiosis that had come to seem vital for the survival of both groups:

A *condueño* sets up his house wherever he likes, and gets a group of Indians to settle nearby on his land. The Indians, in return for the privilege of building houses and opening their garden plots or small canefields, are obliged to clear, plant and harvest a corn or beanfield for the owner without pay. He who has the most Indians is the richest, and as in the *encomienda* days refers to them as "my Indians." . . . When [the rains] water the land, the Indians go out to sow it with their digging sticks. When the time comes, they harvest the crop, carry it on their backs to their Lord's house, and there shuck and store it.[6]

The ties between the Santos family and the Indians of Tampamolón were intense and complex. Although Pedro Antonio Santos was accused by Indians in 1879 of having "dealt them blows, of striking them with the flat side of a sword, and of kicking them," some insurgent Indians joined his forces when the clan revolted during the following months. In 1910, when Pedro Antonio de los Santos' son went to the Huasteca to form an armed band of Madero supporters, he found most of his recuits among the workers of his farm and of those of relatives and friends.[7]

This case was not unique. During the revolution, other large landowners and rancheros were able to count on the support of the Huastecan Indians. Among the most important leaders of the anti-Porfirian uprising in this region were Pedro Montoya, the Terrazas brothers, and the Lárragas, all of whom belonged to a class of privileged rancheros. Like the Santos, they initiated their operations with their own hacienda peons, to whom they were able to speak in their own Indian language. During the armed struggle, the Lárragas recruited approximately four thousand "pure Indians" armed with arrows, rifles, pickaxes, and machetes who, according to one revolutionary, "came racing down, gesticulating and shrieking like

[6] Quoted in Márquez "La casa," pp. 7 (of notes), 9–17, 42–47. On the services the Indians were obliged to perform, see Nefi Fernández and Ma. Clementina Estéban, "La revolución en Tampamolón Corona y sus alrededores," in *Mi pueblo durante la revolución* (México: INAH, Museo de Culturas Populares, Colección Divulgación, 1985), p. 9.

[7] Márquez, "La casa," pp. 9–17, 42–47, 56, 66.

savages.''[8] From beginning it was clear that these Huastecan leaders
had ample resources at their disposal, and a limited view of the
overall objectives of the armed struggle. The good wages and weapons they were able to provide to their followers diminished the
problems of recruitment. The Lárragas, for example, who paid their
forces with their own money, at the outset of the movement would
allow neither robberies nor "forced loans" in the areas under their
control. From the beginning, these families were most concerned
that the revolt not lead to attacks on influential persons and their
property, or go beyond purely political disputes.[9]

Another outstanding leader, Isauro Verástegui, belonged to one of
the oldest and most prosperous families of San Luis, although he
was most likely of its poorest branch. The Verásteguis enjoyed a tradition of leadership, and one family member had been an ideologue
of the Sierra Gorda rebellion which, in 1848, demanded reforms in
favor of tenant farmers.

As in other parts of the country, by 1913 more Huastecan rancheros joined the revolution, like José Rodríguez Cabo, owner of "El
Limón," and Salomón Morales, the strongman of Huehuetlan, who
rose to infamy on the eve of the revolution because of the atrocities
he commited with his Indian workers, and after killing another hacendado "because he had abducted several of his Indians."[10]

The influence of the small and medium landowners in determining the direction and results of certain popular mobilizations during
the revolution has until recently been largely ignored. In several
areas of Mexico peasants became involved because of their strong
vertical ties with the local petty bourgeoisie. These narrow and complex bonds of traditional and paternalistic authority united diverse
social groups, regardless of their class interests.

The region of the Huastecas of San Luis Potosí, Hidalgo, Tamaulipas and Veracruz is one of the most interesting cases to illustrate this
point. For example, in the affluent community of Pisaflores in the
Huasteca hidalgüense bordering the Santos' domain, two rival fac-

[8] El Legionario, August, October, November 1955; June, 1953.

[9] For a more detailed account see Falcón, "Los orígenes," pp. 215ff.

[10] El Estandarte (May 2–9, 1911); Hilario Meníndez, La huasteca y su evolución
social (México, 1955), pp. 16ff. Eutiquio Mendoza, Gotitas de placer y chubascos de
Amargura: Memorias de la revolución mexicana en las huastecas (México: El Granito
de Oro, 1960), p. 16ff. Jan Bazant, Cinco haciendas mexicanas: Tres siglos de vida
rural en San Luis Potosí 1600–1900 (México: El Colegio de México, 1975), pp. 68ff.
Ciro de la Garza, La revolución mexicana en el estado de Tamaulipas (México, Librería de Manuel Porrúa, 1973), Vol. 1, p. 182. For the case of Morales, see Márquez,
"La Casa," p. 58; Fernández and Esteban, "La revolución," p. 11.

tions led by rancheros dominated the political and military life of the zone during the Porfiriato, the revolution, and in subsequent decades.[11] In the neighboring Huasteca veracruzana the rural middle class also participated in revolutionary leadership, although it should be noted that at least in one case, Adalberto Tejeda actively promoted a radical agrarian movement from the beginning of the armed struggle.[12]

Not only in the Huasteca but also in the arid plateau of central and northern San Luis Potosí landowners occupied a center stage in the revolutionary process. It was here that, from the very beginning, serious clashes developed between the more political and traditional revolution led by rancheros and hacendados and the various popular and agrarian movements that also came into existence. This trend of intrarevolutionary warfare was promoted at the highest level. Madero himself refused to recognize Nicolás Torres as leader of the anti-Porfirian struggle in the northeast, Torres being one of the few revolutionaries who had emerged from the lower peasant classes. Lack of discipline and violent attacks against property, and particularly against farm employees, characterized the band of followers of this poor and illiterate former peon. At the same time, their actions, unlike those of the ranchero and hacendado groups, were of an intensely generous nature: upon seizing a farm, they would distribute corn and other goods among the peasants. Madero delegated the leadership of this region to three prominent hacendados, one of them a son-in-law of the Díaz-Gutiérrez family who, during the Porfiriato, controlled San Luis for more than two decades. From that time on, it was clear that some of the wealthier leaders would use all means available to oppose those most closely identified with the peasants in their zones of operation. For this reason, neither the landowners whose properties were affected, nor the guardians of the old regime, undertook the assassination of Torres; this task was completed by the Maderista leaders themselves.

Once Díaz had fallen, many of the traditional authorities, caciques

[11] Frans Schryer, *The Rancheros of Pisaflores: The History of a Peasant Bourgeoisie in Twentieth Century Mexico* (Toronto: University of Toronto Press, 1980). See also the case of Guerrero, Ian Jacobs, *Ranchero Revolt: The Mexican Revolution in Guerrero* (Austin: University of Texas Press, 1982).

[12] See Romana Falcón, *La semilla en el Surco: Adalberto Tejeda y el radicalismo en Veracruz 1883–1960* (México: El Colegio de México, 1986). Another important case is that of Manuel Pelaez: see, Heather Fowler Salamini, *Caciquismo and the Mexican Revolution: The Case of Manuel Pelaez*, Paper presented at the Sixth Conference of Mexican and United States Historians, Chicago, 1981.

and leaders of the Porfiriato were able to restrict popular action imposing their own interests and vision of the world upon much of the revolutionary process. Particularly during the Maderista phase, they managed to block political representation of the workers. More important still, just as the Porfirian rurales had done before, the Maderista authorities violently repressed uprisings staged by miners, hacienda laborers, city slum dwellers, etc. Even though many peasants had participated in the anti-Porfirian movement, local leaders were able—at least at the beginning—to limit the struggle basically to a merely political one, and power was again confined to the traditional elite.[13]

Until now we have dealt only with one type of revolutionary movement, i.e., that led by landowners with narrow and mainly political objectives. But, as in all of Mexico, the revolution was a very complex phenomenon. In very early times in the rural areas of San Luis Potosí began a more popular and socially oriented kind of rebellion aimed, somewhat erratically, at destroying important segments of the status quo. This agrarian restlessness would eventually leave a profound imprint on San Luis, pushing the revolution beyond the limits of a conflict among elites. It was most intense in those regions with a tradition of agrarian struggle, particularly in the southeast: the Huasteca and its surroundings. Its roots were old and profound. Since the mid-nineteenth century, social unrest had repeatedly exploded there, because of the Indian communities' refusal to accept the expropriation of their lands. In 1849, the Huastecan Indians attempted what was called "the first communist experiment in the country," and seven years later they demanded the "death of private property" and the communal division of land.[14] The most important of the Huastecan rebellions began in 1879 when, under the banner of "agrarian law and the municipal government," Indians occupied Tamazunchale in order to recover land taken by the rancheros and hacendados.[15] This agrarian legacy influenced the revolts of 1882, 1883, and 1905 in the Valle del Maíz, neighboring the

[13] For a more detailed version of this event see Falcón, "Los orígenes," pp. 222–26, 229–37; Falcón Revolución, Ch. 1, 2.

[14] Varas Rea, ed. Rebelión y plan de los indios huastecos de Tantoyeca, 1856 (México: Biblioteca de Historiadores Mexicanos, 1956); James Cockroft, Precursores intelectuales de la revolución mexicana (México: Siglo XXI, 1971), pp. 52ff; Gastón García Cantú, El socialismo en México (Mexico City: Editores Era, 1969), pp. 230ff.

[15] Márquez, "La casa,"; Primo Feliciano Velázquez, Historia de San Luis Potosí (México, Sociedad Mexicana de Geografía y Estadística, 1946), Vol. 4, pp. 74ff; Joaquín Meade, Historia de valles: Monografía de la huasteca potosina (San Luis Potosí: Sociedad Potosina de Estudios Históricos, 1970), pp. 129ff.

Huasteca. During subsequent years, several "subversives" continued pillaging the southeast.[16]

In August 1910, when Madero was about to make his call to arms, some Huastecan Indians rebelled once again in an attempt to recover their communal land. What probably would have constituted the state's most combative and revolutionary group, with the most intense tradition of agrarian struggle, was suppressed by the government.[17] This event would have profound consequences, paving the way for the pre-eminence of landed revolutionaries and their clients.

Once the cracks had appeared in the old structure, tensions poured forth. In the beginning, the most persistent and spontaneous demands of local communities were of a political rather than a social nature, a search for local autonomy and the "settling of accounts" with caciques and authorities notorious for their abuses of power and their illegal stay of office. But these demands did not lead to others that might have contributed to a genuine change in political leadership, of different social origins and objectives. To begin with, swords in hand, the Maderista urban and rural police firmly put down most popular riots. This violent response, together with the notorious continuity between the old and new regimes that permitted leading Porfiristas to retain important positions throughout the political and military structure, accounts for the fact that these popular demands only resulted in the election of new authorities from among the "more distinguished young men of society." *Presidencias municipales* and *jefaturas políticas* (political chieftainships) were usually given to members of the traditional elite as well as representatives of the middle sector.[18]

As the government's authority eroded, social tensions began to surface. Between 1911 and 1913 in particular, the peasants of San Luis protested and rebelled, less in demand for land, than for higher wages, better pay for their products, shorter work days, and im-

[16] Velázquez, *Historia*, pp. 77ff.; Moisés González Navarro, *El porfiriato: La vida social*, in *Historia Moderna de México*, ed. Daniel Cosío Villegas (México: Hermes, 1957), pp. 243ff.; Meade *Historia*, p. 160.

[17] It is important to note that this Indian uprising of August 1910 also had strong links with "some decent, educated people," i.e., anti-reelectionist leaders and rancheros. *El Estandarte*, August 7, 9, 10, 12, 14, 30; September 2, 3; November 14, 1910; *El Legionario*, October 1955; the newspaper *Diario del Hogar* erroneously considered that the revolt was not of an anti-reelectionist origin; see Charles Cumberland, *Mexican Revolution: Genesis under Madero* (Austin, University of Texas Press, 2d ed., 1974), p. 117.

[18] Falcón, *Revolución*, pp. 58–62.

proved living conditions. The repressions exercised by landowners
and new Maderista authorities only served to spread violence. For
example, in late 1911, laborers of the hacienda El Pardo, led by the
local judge and priest, denounced the nonpayment of several days'
wages. When the hacendado and his employees replied with rifle
fire from inside the hacienda buildings, killing several people, the
peasants armed themselves with whatever they could and beat the
farm manager to near death. Another peon tried to hang the owner,
who managed to shoot his attacker. As on other occasions, Maderista soldiers (in this case of Pedro Antonio de los Santos) imposed
order and meted out exemplary punishment: the execution of their
leaders.[19]

The peasants of San Luis Potosí rebelled for land only in very localized zones, particularly the southwestern region engulfing the
Huasteca and Valle del Maíz. Some of these villages struggled for
the restitution of their land in a very consistent manner. A case in
point was the 1911 uprising of the Indians of Huichamon and those
of San Miguelito. Another outstanding example was Villa de Reyes,
a village near the capital city, that from the Porfiriato and throughout the revolution demanded the restitution of its land.[20] But not
even in the Huasteca, with its long tradition of agrarian unrest was
this the only or the most frequent cause of agitation. The Huastecan
Indians had more immediate abuses to complain about, in themselves more than sufficient to provoke rebellion: difficult working
conditions in the haciendas, excessive taxes, officials who forced
them to work for nothing because "they were Indians," and in general the fact that the Spanish-speaking population continued to
"abuse them like animals, rather than treating them like rational human beings."[21]

A multitude of small popular peasant bands sprang up, often of
short-lived existence, but they frequently enjoyed rural support.
Their leaders did not, for the most part, concern themselves with
drawing up traditional grandiloquent plans and pronouncements;
they simply identified themselves with the general rural discontent,
demanded certain rights for peasants, and sought to dispense justice. In contrast to the rebellions headed by rancheros and hacen-

[19] El Estandarte, June 20, 22, 1911.

[20] Ibid., August 20; October 8, November 10, 28; December 18, 22, 1911; January
24, 1912; National Archives, Washington, D.C. (hereafter NAW), Record Group (RG)
59; 812.00/5140 Bonney to the State Department, September 26, 1912.

[21] Archivo General de la Nación (AGN), Fondo Trabajo (Labor Fund) (FT), Caja (C)
11, Expediente (E) 6, foja (f) 6; residents of Tancanhuitz to Madero, January 24, 1913.

dados, the leadership of this "popular" kind of revolution derived less from traditional authority and the good salaries paid to soldiers, than from their identification with popular demands, their strong personal relationships with their men, their military abilities, and their success in obtaining booty to be divided up among their followers. Usually, these bands confined their zones of operation to very small regions, and would only respond to incidents in other parts of the country, when the participants themselves were directly affected. Although the actions of these small groups seemed to have only short-term effects, they left a profound mark. In a cumulative way, they undermined the legitimacy of the great propietors and the hierarchy of rural society.

The examples are many, particularly in the early days. In 1912, an old revolutionary warned Madero that, as long as an end was not put to the "unjust acts" committed on the haciendas no one would be capable of restraining the peasants of San Luis Potosí from swelling rebel ranks.[22] In the north of the state, Lázaro Gómez gained renown by respecting private property, while having the hacienda administrators most notorious for mistreating their peons taken out and shot. That same year, Elías Frotuna stunned the village of Santa María del Río by stating that he intended to distribute large landholdings, while other leaders, such as Isabel Robles, distributed corn among the peasants.[23] After 1912, several other revolutionaries included agrarian distribution among their fundamental objectives. In June, Alberto Carrera Torres, a former anti-Porfirian leader from Tula, Tamaulipas (an area near the Valle del Maíz) proposed to return the ejidos to the villages, as well as to distribute land to the landless. The military and ideological importance of this teacher and law student was to be decisive in the development of the revolution in San Luis.[24]

Then another band of revolutionaries of relatively humble origin appeared, whose roots could be found in the problems of the poor peasants: the Cedillo brothers (Cleofas, Magdaleno, and Saturnino)

[22] Ibid., c11, e6, f6: Ugalde to Cepeda, February 1912; NAW RG59, 812.00/4119, May 29, 1912; ibid., 812.00/5908, December 17, 1912: both from Bonney to the State Department.

[23] Archivo Histórico de la Secretaría de la Defensa Nacional (AHDN), Ramo Revolución (Revolutionary Branch) (RR), Expediente (E) XI/481.5/250 foja (f) 17, February 16, 1912; ibid., f.12, 23, 26; El Estandarte, February 10, 1912; NAW, RG 59; 812.00/5575, Bonney to the State Department. November 18, 1912.

[24] Alberto Alcocer, El general y profesor Alberto Carrera Torres (SLP, Academia de Historia Potosina, Serie Cuadernos No. 2, 2d ed.); De la Garza, La revolución mexicana, Vol. 1, pp. 360–61.

who eventually acquired great importance. The Cedillos were of Valle del Maíz, where peasants had rebelled during the Porfiriato. They raised *ixtle* for fiber, cattle, and goats at Palomas ranch. Despite having survived extremely difficult times, the Cedillos were relatively fortunate peasants, known throughout the region, because there were muleteers in the family, and their father owned some land and a small store. The family name even had a tradition of leadership because, in 1905, one Vicente Cedillo had led a revolt in the area. Having clashed with neighboring haciendas at the outbreak of the revolution, the family established alliances with the Carrera Torres family. As of 1912, they employed on their property discharged Carrerista soldiers unwelcomed everywhere. During the summer 1912, the state governor used *rurales* (rural police) to confront the medieros who were demanding better prices for their products. Two leaders were hung and the rest jailed. The Cedillos headed local resistance and freed the peasants. In September, tension escalated and the Cedillos led the peons from two haciendas who rose up with bludgeons and machetes. On November 17, 1912, with the help of the Carrera Torres brothers, they seized Ciudad del Maíz, read the Zapatista Plan de Ayala to the townspeople, and declared it their platform.[25]

Throughout their struggle, the Cedillos attacked property and proprietors, managers and caretakers in order to strengthen their personal bond with their followers and with the peasants in the region. When attacking an estate, horses, saddles, arms and money were appropriated for them and for their followers. Furthermore, they ordered that "their people," i.e., the majority of farm workers, unite to distribute corn, to burn account books to free them of their debts, to encourage them to keep all objects taken from the estates, and to join the revolution. They also warned landowners and employees that, should "their followers" be mistreated, or should an attempt be made to recover confiscated property, they would return to execute them. On occasions, the threat was carried out.[26]

[25] Gildardo Magaña, *Emiliano Zapata y el agrarismo en México.* (Mexico City: Edition Ruta, 1951), pp. 169ff; Rafael Montejano y Aguiñaga, *El Valle del Maíz* (SLP, Imprenta Evolución, 1967), pp. 345–47; Beatriz Rojas, *Chronique et sociologie de la révolution mexicaine: Le groupe Carrera/Cedillo*, Ph.D. Thesis, University of Montpellier, 1979; Dudley Ankerson, "Saturnino Cedillo, a Traditional Caudillo in San Luis Potosí, 1890–1938," in Brading ed., pp. 141–45.

[26] "Actas levantadas por el juez auxiliar de la hacienda de la Concepción, Ciudad del Maíz," June 3, 6, 12, 1913; Marijosé Amerlink, "La reforma agraria en la hacienda de San Diego de Río Verde," in *Después de los latifundios: La desintegración de la*

The Cedillos' relationships with their followers were very flexible; their men would frequently assemble for an attack and then return to work in their fields. This allowed the Cedillos to integrate themselves with their men's home communities, and to become intimately familiar with their problems.

The San Luis peasants' responses to these activities varied considerably. Many of them remained loyal to the haciendas and farms on which they lived, bound by strong economic and paternalistic ties to the landholders, as well as by fear of reprisals. After the raid on the San Diego hacienda, for example, the loyal and terrified peasants refused to touch anything, although they had been told by the Cedillos that the land was their own and that they could take whatever they wished. Even scattered food and clothing remained untouched, and the peasants eventually burned and buried the silk shawls and lanterns they had been given. The handful of men who then joined the revolutionaries did so less for ideological reasons than to look after the horses the Cedillos were taking with them. On other occasions, as occurred in La Concepción, "the servants and other neighbors . . . set themselves to pillaging" once the first fright had passed, and "some of them entered the revolutionary ranks."[27]

The Cedillos did not elaborate their own agrarian plans, but rather gave their entire support to Carrera Torres, particularly with respect to his radical land distribution law of March 4, 1913, which also constituted a national call to arms to overthrow General Victoriano Huerta.[28] These brothers from Valle del Maíz were also influenced by Zapatismo, although in a more superficial manner, due to its geographical remoteness.[29] Other revolutionary leaders of a similar "popular" type, though less successful, such as Isabel Robles and the Galván brothers, manifested their ideology to an even lesser extent.[30]

In brief, it may be said that from an early period peasant involvement in the San Luis Potosí revolution took on two different modes of action, two styles, two contrasting political cultures. The differ-

gran propiedad raíz en México ed. Herriberto Moreno (México: El Colegio de Michoacán, Fonapas-Michoacán, 1982), pp. 185–86.

[27] Marijosé Amerlink, *From Hacienda to Ejido: The San Diego de Río Verde Case*, Ph.D. Thesis, State University of New York at Stony Brook, 1980, pp. 238ff; "Actas levantadas."

[28] Reproduced in De la Garza, *La revolución mexicana*, Vol. 4, pp. 385–90.

[29] Romana Falcón, "Movimientos campesinos y la revolución mexicana: San Luis Potosí y Morelos" *Cuadernos agrarios* 5, no. 10/11 (December 1980).

[30] De la Garza, *La revolución mexicana*, Vol. 1, pp. 188; *Adelante*, February 1, 15, 1913, NAW, RG59, 812.00/7790 Bonney to the State Department, May 28, 1913.

ences were particularly striking in the relationship between leaders and peasant followers on the one hand, and in the nature of their demands on the other. One kind of rebellion was basically led by rancheros and hacendados, and was organized along the lines of traditional authority. In general, objectives were confined to a political framework, aimed not at obtaining fulfillment of popular demands, but rather in resolving personal and local power struggles, and in deciding which of the great revolutionary factions then disputing sway over the country they should join.

At the same time, another kind of movement existed, made up of a multitude of small armed bands, often short-lived, generally drawn from the villages themselves, and usually concerned only with their small areas. These groups were inspired by the revolutionary fervor spreading over rural areas, and by the strong personal relationships between leaders and followers.[31]

Despite the evident cooperation between both types of rebels, particularly at the end of the anti-Huerta struggle, the capacity of certain leaders (such as the Cedillo brothers) to dismantle the rural social order and to draw upon popular discontent caused alarm, as did the social dimension that the revolution was acquiring. Hostilities soon broke out and degenerated into another darker, more erratic struggle, that was, on occasion, as cruel as the one that all waged against common enemies like the federal government. During the Maderista administration, in order to combat the profusion of subversive groups, Governor Rafael Cepeda organized companies of rural police and "volunteers" who, though they never succeeded in pacifying the countryside, did eliminate two of the more radical leaders who were demanding land for the peasants: Ponciano Navarro of the Huasteca, and Elías Fortuna. In carrying out this task Cepeda enjoyed the efficient collaboration of the Santos and Lárraga families, both of whom were concerned with keeping the revolution within the limits of purely political change.[32]

The warring among different kinds of revolutionaries reached its peak in 1913, when several prominent Carrancista leaders began to fear an erosion of their authority, and decided to eliminate these

---

[31] For a detailed discussion see Falcón, Revolución, Ch. 1, 2.

[32] Informe Rendido por el C. Gobernador del Estado de San Luis Potosí, Dr. Rafael Cepeda el 15 de septiembre de 1912; y Contestación Dada al Mismo Informe por el C. Presidente del Congreso Lic. Ricardo Muñoz (SLP Tipografiá de la Escuela Industrial Militar, 1913); El Estandarte, August 20, September 1, 2, 18, 31, October 25, December 22, 24, 29, 31, 1911; January 12, 24, February 10, 1912; February 24, 1913; AHDN, EXI/421.5/250, f.18–19, February 24, 1912.

"primitive" and "brutal" bands of "assailants, mobsters, individuals without a banner, those who only satisfied their hatred for the people."[33] The most aggressive of these groups was the one led by Juan Barragán, the epitome of a small fraction of the wealthiest and most powerful families in all San Luis who rose up against Huerta.

During the eighteenth century, the Barragáns had come to possess enormous expanses of land and then assisted in financing the first road to the Gulf of Mexico, as well as the railroad to Tampico. Their great economic strength allowed them to amass significant political power: in 1869 they held the governorship, and during the Porfiriato they maintained close financial and matrimonial ties with the most prominent figures, while they continued exercising almost complete control over the political life of Valle del Maíz. Nevertheless, Juan Barragán senior was not very prominent in Porfirista politics and subsequently established a strong friendship with doctor Rafael Cepeda, the Maderista governor. When Cepeda was arrested, Barragán fled into exile and, fearing the same fate, his two young sons (Juan and Miguel) joined Venustiano Carranza in his national anti-Huertista movement.[34]

Soon the struggle centered on the most conservative branch of Carrancismo in San Luis, i.e., the Barragáns against the Cedillos. Encounters took place after the first Cedillista action in late 1912, when the Cedillos seized Ciudad del Maíz, where Miguel Barragán was municipal president. Together with his brother Juan, Miguel inflicted several casualties upon the attackers. In early 1913, when the Cedillos retaliated by committing "all sorts of plundering, thefts and outrages" on the Barragán hacienda, the proprietors decimated the rebels, with the aid of reinforcements provided by General Jesús Agustín Castro, head of a band of rurales who had just joined Carranza.

Although Barragán fought against both the Huertistas and the Cedillistas, he was forced to set his scruples aside, and attempted to ally himself with the Cedillos in May 1913, during a highly tense moment of the war, but the arrangement was unsuccessful. After the Cedillo sisters saved a priest who had been kidnapped by Castro, Castro shot several Cedillistas, who were about to hang the elderly proprietor of the Salto del Agua hacienda. In the words of the landholders, Castro was "a highly correct person and in all ways de-

[33] Juan Barragán, *Historia del ejército y la revolución constitucionalista* (México: Stylo, 1946), Vol. 1, pp. 163ff.

[34] Ibid., Vol. 2, pp. 106–17; Cockroft, *Precursores*, Ch. 1; Píndaro Urióstegui Miranda, *Testimonios del proceso revolucionario en México* (México: Talleres Argín, 1970), pp. 200ff.

cent." He escorted them to their exile in the state capital, treating them "with every manifestation of solicitude and care, attempting to be as helpful to them as possible." Before leaving, he addressed the peasants on the profound political and ideological differences between their program, i.e., that of the "honorable revolutionaries," and that of the "Zapatista hordes" such as the Cedillos. The former group perceived the revolution to be the attainment of suffrage for the people, but by no means

> seizing that which belongs to another . . . [nor] the appropria-
> tion of the goods of those who have more . . . . We, the revolu-
> tionaries, also deem ourselves justified in punishing . . . all that
> tends to banditry . . . if you wish to be revolutionaries, do not
> be bandits, better that you continue working . . . since your
> landlord has advised me that he is content with your work and
> he hopes that you will always continue in this manner.[35]

Although the Barragán–Cedillo struggle was the most conspicuous, it was by no means the only confrontation between revolutionaries. Another case was that of Martín Angel, priest and agrarian
leader of the Huastecan village of Tampamolon Corona, against José
María Medina, prominent landowner, cacique of that region, and
member of the Carrancista coalition.[36]

Once the common enemy Huerta, was overthrown in mid-1914,
Carranza, Villa, and Zapata engaged in a new power struggle that
lasted aproximately one year. Given the complicated and contradictory manner in which national coalitions were put together, the military chiefs in the northeast of the country were slow to form new
alliances. In San Luis, their differences precipitated an open struggle between the two types of rebels who, when not engaged in direct
confrontations, had kept their distance. Each rebel band allied with
national leaders who more closely shared their world view and belief in what the revolution should entail. Barragán, and the Huastecan leaders De los Santos and the Lárragas joined the ranks of Carranza, while the more popular and local leaders like Cedillo and
Carrera united with Villa.[37]

---

[35] "Actas levantadas"; NAW, RG59, 812.00/8013, Bonney to the Department of State, June 21, 1913; Barragán, Historia, Vol. 1, p. 168; Montejano, El Valle, p. 351.

[36] Fernández and Esteban, "La revolución, pp. 12–13.

[37] De la Garza, La revolución mexicana, Vol. 1, pp. 111–18; Rojas, "Chronique," p. 109; Alfonso Taracena, La verdadera revolución mexicana (3a. etapa 1914–1915) (México: Jus, 1965), pp. 5, 109, 144; Manuel González, Con Carranza: Episodios de

One factor must have weighed heavily in this development: since 1914 the Revolution imposed a greater concentration and rationalization of resources, particularly within the Carranza coalition. A significant portion of salaries and armaments were provided by the central command, thus drastically reducing the independence of military chiefs and the personal loyalty of their followers. This type of military organization was incompatible with and tended to destroy bands such as the Cedillos'. It undermined the leaders' power as peasant warlords, which depended upon their integration with the peasantry in their zones of operation, and their independent procurement of supplies, i.e., war booty, the capture of haciendas and villages, theft, the sale of "protection," and above all the intense personal relationship they maintained with all of their followers.[38]

From mid-1914 to mid-1915, all of Mexico was engaged in interfactionary struggles. No group was able to establish control over all of San Luis Potosí; the state was broken up into a shifting mosaic of small military strongholds in which justice and goods were dispensed, life and death orders were handed down and on occasion the construction of a new social order was attempted. The Carreristas and Cedillistas established for their domains certain principles of communal life that partially resulted from the fact that the war had destroyed the market economy, and the construction of schools, bridges, and roads was begun in their territories.[39] At that time, a phenomenon that began in 1913 attained its apogee: the practice of taking over urban and rural estates. This profoundly undermined the legitimacy of the ownership structure, even though the objectives corresponded more to military goals than to an agrarian motivation.[40]

During Eulalio Gutiérrez' term of office as governor, July 1914-July 1915, (later to become provisional president of the convention) and during the Villista government headed by General Emiliano Saravia, the first clear attempt was made in San Luis to make the workers the principal beneficiaries of the government's policies as well as the

la Revolución Constitucionalista, 1913–1914. (México: Cantú Leal, 1933), pp. 45, 59; see also Knight, "Peasant and Caudillo," pp. 37ff.

[38] El Legionario, August 1955; Public Record Office (PRO) (London), Foreign Office (FO) 204, Volume (V) 462, Number (N) 391, Bonney and Echauzier to Foreign Office, September 23, 1915; ibid., No. 394, Eschauzier to Hohler, September 24, 1915; AGN, RR, C 6, E72, f.62. Correspondence between Galván, Aguilar, and Cedillo, May to August, 1914.

[39] Montejano, El valle, pp. 354ff; Alcocer, El General, p. 15; José Vasconcelos, La Tormenta (México: Jus, 1958) pp. 277–80.

[40] Falcón, Revolución, pp. 116ff.

main support of the authorities. During these administrations, important labor and agrarian laws were passed. One dealt with peons, the peasant majority in San Luis, prohibiting the more backward labor systems of some haciendas, such as confinement to the estate for nonpayament of debts, and substantially improving their work conditions.[41] These and other events would eventually help the implementation of agrarian reform in San Luis.

However, after July 1915, when the Carrancistas gained control over the state, and the Barragán family began to dominate political life, these popular measures were radically reversed. While an attempt was never made to completely reestablish the old regime, Carranza, the "First Chief," together with the Barragáns, sought to salvage whatever remained in the hands of the landowners. To this end, they granted significant fiscal incentives, suspended the ejidal program, and "opened the doors wide to private initiative, giving it total support."[42]

Since November 1915, definitive steps were taken to force a return to the old structure of land tenure, by reversing one of the measures that most disturbed the Porfirista status quo: the practice of taking over rural and urban estates by revolutionary bands. The restitution of haciendas to their former owners socially and economically restored the majority of the landholding elite. This measure was implemented throughout the state and in only four months, more than seventy haciendas and two hundred houses were restored to leaders of the old regime.

At the same time, this conservative policy constituted an offensive against the most powerful enemies of the Barragáns, Carreras, and Cedillos. By February 1916, at least 32 haciendas and 42 houses they had occupied had been returned to their previous owners.[43] Among the restored haciendas the one that most clearly illustrates the landowners' recovery of power is that of La Angostura, not only because it was the largest in the state, but also because of its symbolic value. Only a few months before, the Cedillistas had killed one

[41] Ley de Sueldos a Peones Expedida por el Gobierno de San Luis Potosí (September 14, 1914) (SLP, Tipografía de la Escuela Industrial Militar, 1915).

[42] Informe que Rinde el C. General Brigadier Juan Barragán, Gobernador Constitucional del Estado libre y Soberano de San Luis Potosí de las Labores Llevadas a Cabo por su Gobierno Durante el Periodo Constitucional del 10 de Junio al 15 de Septiembre de 1917, a la XXV Legislatura del Mismo (SLP, Talleres de la Escuela Industrial "Benito Juárez," 1917), pp. 20–21.

[43] Informe Rendido por el C. Juan F. Barragán a la Secretaría de Hacienda y Crédito Público sobre la Intervensión de la Propiedad Raíz en el Estado de San Luis Potosí (SLP, Tipografía de M. Esquivel e hijos, February 1916); PRO, FO 204, Nolan to Foreign Office, August 24, 1923; Velázquez, Historia, Vol. 4, p. 277.

of its owners, Javier Espinosa y Cuevas, brother of the last Porfirista governor, and had exhibited his corpse to the peons. La Angostura was then directly exploited by Barragán.[44]

During the second half of 1915, the Villista coalition was defeated, and the Carrancista forces began consolidating their national government. At that time, substantial peace was achieved in San Luis. The southeast, nevertheless, continued to rebel, though intermittently until May 1920, when Carranza fell. The loyalty and the affection of the followers of the more popular leaders who were still in arms, was put to the test during those years. The main rebel nucleus in San Luis Potosí—the Cedillistas and Carreristas—saw their problems exacerbated in late 1917, when their remaining followers "wandered through the sterile hills, without food or clothing." In the ambush in which Magdaleno Cedillo was killed, federal troops discovered among his followers only "dishevelled, bearded, miserable men, nearly naked, shivering from the cold, with an old rifle in hand." Despite all, the Cedillistas conserved their sense of community in arms. Never did the women and children vacillate, despite their "extreme state of malnourishment," while "living in caverns."[45] By 1918, Saturnino Cedillo could barely keep his forces from collapsing, and desertions were common. Nevertheless, a handful of his followers remained loyal to the end: "[in spite of] all of those who have betrayed me, I still have a fair number of people, who despite being left nearly naked and without food . . . do not defect."[46]

When the extermination of these rebels seemed to be only a question of time or decision, they were able to avoid it, because of forces far beyond their control: the crisis of the presidential succession of 1920, which again disrupted all of Mexico and which eventually allowed the old anti-Carrancista rebels of San Luis to occupy the pinnacle of power.

The Era of Radical Agrarianism

Having passed through the armed stage of the revolution, new forms of rural mobilization and organization developed. As a result of the various transformations introduced by the revolution, the peasants

[44] Velázquez, *Historia*, Vol. 4, pp. 257–69; PRO, FO 204, No. 492, Nolan to Foreign Office, August 24, 1913; Falcón, *Revolución*, p. 115ff.

[45] Velázquez, *Historia*, Vol. 4 pp. 287; Montejano, *El Valle*, pp. 362ff; Rojas, "Chronique," pp. 360ff.

[46] AHDN, Ramo Cancelado (Cancelled Branch) (RC), Expediente (E) X III.2/1-110, t 1, f.163, Cedillo to Carrera, June 1918; ibid., t ii, f.304, Cedillo to Carrera, June 1919.

were able to obtain broad benefits. The profound deterioration of agriculture had generated unemployment that ruined the country-side, and many social categories and workers on ranches and haciendas were affected, helping to weaken the paternalist ties that united peons and landholders. Another decisive event was the fall of the Barragáns, which forced large landholders to abandon their hope of retaining control of San Luis rural society. The intense changes the revolution had imposed upon the countryside, together with the explosive atmosphere created by some radical leaders who promised peasants a brighter future, made possible new forms of participation.

The formation and growth of a party representing the interests of the peasantry as a whole only then became possible. A new type of political leader—the professional activist from the urban middle class, with a fairly sophisticated and radical political ideology—penetrated the entire state in order to mobilize and unite the peasants. These leaders did not exercise a traditional influence over the rural sectors; neither did they establish their authority with the peasants as comrades-in-arms. What they did was to send out a relatively impersonal call to all of the larger social sectors in the countryside to form combative class organizations.

The National Agrarian Party (PNA), formed in 1920, was the first to attempt to mobilize the entire rural sector of Mexico around the need for urgent agrarian reforms. San Luis became one of the PNA's bastions, since it was the home of its top leaders, Antonio Díaz Soto y Gama and Aurelio Manrique. The background of these fiery orators included higher education (studies of law, languages, and a knowledge of socialist and anarchist theories), and the experience of having politically organized sectors of the rural and urban proletariat. Soto y Gama enjoyed special legitimacy as an agrarian leader since, besides having been a prominent member of the sophisticated liberal opposition to Porfirio Díaz, in 1914 he became one of the leading orators and ideologues of Zapatismo.

In San Luis, since 1920, the "agrarians" of the PNA sought to mobilize farm workers by means of a different form of legitimacy, i.e., through practical reasoning and ideological class considerations. When Manrique became governor in December 1923, he forced workers and peasants to unite into sectoral organizations, while he left unprotected all workers who refused to take part in the new bureaucratic party structures. In exchange, the peasants obtained broad benefits; organized peons were even able to occupy some administrative posts on the haciendas; sharecroppers were required to deliver reduced amounts of produce to the landowners; and when land was given in the form of ejidos, seeds, animals and agricultural equipment were also distributed. The agrarian reform was intense; while only 30,000 hectares had been distributed between 1915 and 1920, the area increased to 577,000 hectares during the following five years. In 1924 and 1925 during his governorship, Manrique distributed 302,611 hectares, some of good quality despite the extreme aridity of the state. Together with the states of Morelos and Yucatán, the agrarian reform implemented in San Luis can be considered to be of the most far-reaching in Mexico.[47]

When Manrique fell from power, however, the peasants defended neither his government nor his program. Apparently, the Manriquista experiment had a fatal weakness; the reformist impulse did not result from pressure exerted from the grassroots (as might have been the case in other revolutionary movements), but from another source, organized and channeled to the villages by political activists. Furthermore, these reformers fought for an ejido program that was perhaps alien and even contrary to the type of ownership to which most peasants in the state aspired. An equally decisive factor was that the more rational, modern, and institutional type of authority wielded by the PNA and the Manriquistas entailed a less profound and less emotional commitment from the peasants to their leaders, since it depended on their own evaluation of the risks and benefits that their actions would incur.

THE CACICAZGO OF A PEASANT LEADER

In May 1920, Obregón's triumph over Carranza provided Cedillo with an opportunity for reconciliation with the federal government. His troops moved quickly to occupy and establish both legal and de facto control over the region for a Cedillo domain: Valle del Maíz, Cerritos, Guadalcázar, Río Verde and part of the Huasteca. To achieve this, Cedillo made use of his military power, of the gener-

[47] Secretaría de Agricultura y Fomento, *Comisión Nacional Agraria: Memorias, 1915–1927* (México: Talleres Gráficos de la Secretaría de Agricultura y Fomento, 1928), pp. 27, 42, 52, 161; Eyler Simpson, "El Ejido, Unica Salida para México," in *Problemas Agrícolas e Industriales de México*, Vol. 4, no. 4 (México, October, December, 1952), Tables 11, 15, 22, 30, 78; AGN, Fondo Presidentes (Presidents Branch) (FP), Obregón-Calles, (O/C), 818-L-87, Graciano Sánchez to Calles, April 2, 1925; NAW RG59, 812.00/27080, Boyle to Department of State, February 29, 1924, PRO, FO371, V. 9564, A/4770/184/26, The Salinas of Mexico, Ltd. to Foreign Office, August 6, 1924.

ally miserable conditions in the area at the end of the armed struggle, and of the weakness of both the state and national governments.

In order to assure his supremacy, Cedillo fought with his personal militia to pacify the Huasteca and against the national uprisings of 1923, 1927, 1929, and in the Cristero War of 1926–29. These campaigns revived, to a certain extent, the kind of relationship that had kept his followers loyal and relatively united during the long years as guerrillas. Nevertheless, Cedillo's authority over his people was profoundly transformed because he could offer them protection and material benefits with a stable and peaceable means of subsistence. Their warm and personal interaction adopted a more paternalistic pattern, an exchange of benefits and obligations not entirely alien to the old, traditional ties that had prevailed on some ranchos and haciendas prior to the revolution. The generals' oldest and most loyal followers provided him with both political and military support, occasionally with tribute in cash or kind, and with a wide range of personal services. In exchange they received the cacique's special protection, employment, income, and above all, access to land.

In late 1925, acting as a political and military agent in San Luis, and with the president's authorization, Cedillo used his militia to put an end to Manrique's governorship. He was then able to impose a long lasting and stable cacicazgo over all of San Luis in which his old peasant bases of the southeast and, to a lesser extent, the state's entire agrarian sector would play an important role.

In the early 1920s, the Valle del Maíz was impoverished, isolated, and almost uninhabited. The intensity of the war and the resulting disorder had caused more deaths and emigration than in neighboring zones. Of the 35,000 inhabitants prior to the revolution, only 4,500 remained eleven years later, 1,500 of whom lived in Ciudad del Maíz. The main contingent of the Cedillistas' combatants roughly equalled this amount, while the rest were scattered among the few haciendas and small farms that remained. It had been years since the revolution had paralyzed agricultural and cattle-raising activities, leaving the ranchos and haciendas without work and without laborers.[48] Upon returning to what was left of their homes, the Cedillista troops simply seized these vacant lands,[49] thus greatly consolidating the influence of their leader.

Cedillo's efficient collaboration in pacifying the rebels who continued to devastate parts of the Huastecas allowed him to negotiate

[48] Falcón, *Revolución*, p. 178.
[49] Carlos Martínez Assad, "Las Colonias-Agrícolas-Militares. Una Alternativa Agrarista del Pasado." Paper presented to the World Congress on Rural Sociology, Mexico, 1980, p. 4.

Revolution in San Luis Potosí   **441**

with the federal authorities the legalization of these occupied lands. An agreement was reached in summer 1921, when Obregón himself was obliged to go to the Huasteca potosina to encourage the troops, reinforce their ranks, and double their pay.[50] The landholdings that were already occupied were granted the legal status of "agricultural military colonies," while the federal government bought and donated these lands, as well as seed and agricultural equipment. This form of land distribution was essentially formulated by the Cedillista soldiers themselves and by their leader. They most likely had in mind not only the traditional military colonies that centuries before had been formed in this region, but also the successful Italian forming colonies established in the Valle del Maíz during the Porfiriato, and which had expressed some support for their struggle. The Cedillista colonies adopted modalities of both private property and of the ejido: the former because the land had to be paid for, and the latter because the property was inalienable and ownership could only be transferred by inheritance. Each of the eight or thirteen colonies (the exact number is not clear) was formed by groups of between 50 and 200 farmers belonging to the army's first reserve. Given the ambiguous nature of the colonies, they were subject to both the Ministries of War and of Agriculture. To the present day, this legal indefinition has lent itself to much manipulation, at the expense of the colonies.[51]

The inhabitants of this region developed a strong dependence on Cedillo, due to poverty, underdevelopment, and isolation, as well as the nonexistence of other mechanisms and political institution in the area. Cedillo's "peasant soldiers" were content with subsistence farming on their small lots of approximately six hectares into which the colonies had been divided among the officers, soldiers, and the relatives of fallen combatants. Cedillo did not give legal title to each of these properties. Access to land always remained one of his basic prerogatives. In the few colonies that had water the situation was somewhat better, but general conditions of poverty and underdevelopment prevailed. Furthermore, since the valley was a closed zone, with extremely poor means of communication, the farm workers remained isolated from broader markets.[52] Only Cedillo was able to

[50] *Excelsior*, July 14–20, 24, 29; August 11, 1921, *New York Times*, July 16–20, 1921; AGN, RP, O/C 121-H-H5: Obregón to the Minister of Finance, August 20, 1921.

[51] C. Martínez, *Las colonias*, pp. 4, 9ff; AGN, RP, O/C 823-0-1, attorney for the hacienda Pozo de Acuña to Obregón, January 9, 1923; PRO, FO204, V576, No. 33: Cummins to Foreign Office, May 11, 1923; *Excelsior*, April 23, 1925; Montejano, *El Valle*, p. 365.

[52] Falcón, *Revolución*, pp. 177–84.

promise and obtain land, machinery, arms, and ammunition and to solve their economic, family and personal problems. He was the only contact most of his followers had with the outside world. In brief, Cedillo became a patriarchal authority by guaranteeing a minimum of well-being and material security.

Those who most depended on Cedillo, essentially the colonists and, to a lesser extent some ejidatarios, were required to correspond with loyalty, personal services, and even with tribute for the protection and favors received. Many colonists were required to turn over between one-tenth and one-half of their harvested crops to the cacique or to his immediate family and closest friends. For example, those of the Alvaro Obregón colony ended up working as medieros and aparceros for Governor Ildefonso Turrubiates—an old time Cedillista who completely depended on the cacique—while nearly all of them were obliged to perform a wide range of personal duties, such as running the telephone line to Deputy Alfonso Salazar's ranch, or to farm the haciendas of Francisco Carrera Torres, the younger brother of the radical.[53]

The duties and tributes enjoyed by Cedillo and his inner circle nevertheless constituted only one side of the coin, because they depended on the loyalty and the recognition of "their people" and particularly on their own capacity to provide them with material goods and protection. Cedillo rigorously fulfilled his obligation. In the distribution of colonias and ejidos, he always gave preference to his veterans and to the families of those who had died in battle. The cacique fiercely defended "his people" when confronted by landholders, rancheros and ejidatarios with whom they disputed ownership of land and water. In such conflicts, Cedillo invariably represented the interest of those loyal to him by means of formal and informal petitions to the agencies in charge of distribution, and with the highest authorities. He also ignored laws that were contrary to his interests, and as a last resort, threatened to use, or actually did use, armed force.

His paternalist practices were put to full use in Palomas, the ranch were he was born and which he subsequently took as his own. Until the end of his cacicazgo, this ranch was the most evident symbol of his traditional authority. Like that of a feudal lord, his home always remained open to friends, clients, and politicians from all levels. In Palomas, food, lodging, and clothing were offered day and night,

[53] ASDN, Ramo Pensionistas (RP, Pensionists Branch), EX/III.2/I-110. Owner of the hacienda Cruces to Calles, 30 January 1927; ibid., T 4, f.913, Domínguez to Rodríguez, December 10, 1933; AGN, RP, LCR, 449.1/1/53 Figueroa to Cárdenas, November 24, 1937; C. Martínez, *Las Colonias*, pp. 7, 9, 27.

while money and employment were given whenever possible. On his ranch, Cedillo implemented his agrarian ideal in collaboration with his long-time followers. From 1921, he began to grant them landownership, although without legal title. Cedillo liked to share the daily tasks with "his people," to watch the corn and cotton harvest, and to make recommendations, give orders and opinions on all matters. The cacique even built a road with public funds to connect his property to the capital city.

For all these reasons, the cacique was loved and greatly respected in Palomas and its surroundings. He boasted that "none of my people lack a cow, some chickens or a horse. Everyone leads an easy life, consuming what they grow on their land." In his travels, Cedillo stopped continually along the way, "to ask if my *compadre* Chon is getting along; to give money to the *comadre* Juana, who has a sick boy. . . . How could I not love them," argued Cedillo, "if they all fought at my side; they are the orphans of old revolutionaries."[54]

A few weeks before Cedillo took up arms against the federal government for the last time, when only a few of those who had given impetus and life to his great cacicazgo remained loyal, many peasants continued to descend upon Palomas to request all kinds of favors or to arbitrate in conflicts. As a renowned visitor described,

If the General hadn't time for them that day, they'd stay the night and eat his food (two oxen had been killed in five days) and see him in the morning. It was all rather movingly simple and, in spite of the guns, idyllic. The peasants sat silently against the cookhouse wall, with their rugs drawn up around their mouths. The General gave them no pay, but food and clothes and shelter and half of everything the farm produced, and ready cash too if they asked for it and he had it. They even took the fifty chairs he bought for his little private cinema. And they gave him labour and love. It was not a progressive relationship, it was feudal; you may say it was one-sided and he had everything—the New Art furniture, the statuettes, the alligator skin, and the coloured picture of Napoleon, but they possessed at any rate more than did their fellow-peasants in other states, living at best on the minimum wage of thirty-five cents a day, with no one caring if they lived or died, with all the responsibility of independence.[55]

[54] Pagés Llergo, "Tres días en palomas con Cedillo," in *Hoy*, October 9, 1937; NAW, RG59, 812.00 SLP/13; Shaw to the State Department, February 18, 1931.
[55] Graham Greene, *The Lawless Roads* (Harmondsworth: Penguin, 1971), p. 56.

Cedillo did not exercise this personal relationship only with his colonos, but also with a considerable number of ejidatarios concentrated in the southeast of the state. From the early 1920s, the old guerrilla promoted some ejido petitions, for which reason many ejidatarios had come to form part of his militia. The cacique always used the promise of land to recruit peasants into his armed forces and as political support. For example, during the decisive campaigns of 1929, Cedillo offered ejidal land of their choice to those peasants of San Diego who wished to join him. Upon returning from the battlefield, some landowners sought to win the favor of the powerful cacique by giving part of their haciendas so that he could place some of his soldiers. Cedillo also had the local government purchase lands for his people and distributed more of Palomas with the same objective in mind. During the 1930s, and until the end of the cacicazgo, when his relationships with the federal government reached a critical level Cedillo traveled throughout the state, promising ejidos to those who wished to enlist with him, even when agrarian reform in the state was officially considered terminated.[56]

The strong personal ties that bound Cedillo to his colonos and some ejidatarios constituted the last foundations of his cacicazgo. In 1938, when the federal government was about to overthrow his domain, these peasant militia formed the most compact and loyal nucleus of his followers.

As occurs regularly in traditional domains, Cedillo rewarded his relatives and favorites. He placed them in the highest-ranking political and military positions in San Luis, and appointments to the political–administrative apparatus rotated among his closest followers. During his absence, Cedillo's sister Elena was the political decision maker in Valle del Maíz, while his brother-in-law was appointed state representative and municipal president of the capital city, and later replaced by a nephew. He gave all he could to his oldest and most intimate favorites: Carrera Torres was granted command of federal forces in the state from 1927 to 1937; Ildefonso Turrubiates, and subsequently Mateo Hernández, were governors. Cedillo also chose municipal presidents, deputies, senators, and the entire range of civil servants and military personnel. All these authorities received orders handed down by Cedillo. Turrubiates' sub-

[56] Excelsior, September 16, 1929; El Universal, June 21, 1931; Manuel González Ramírez, Fuentes para la historia de la revolución mexicana, Vol. 1: Planes políticos y otros documentos (México: FCE, 1954), pp. 290ff.; NAW, RG 59, 812.00 SLP/13, Shaw to Department of State, February 18, 1931; for the case of San Diego see Amerlink, La Reforma, p. 185.

ordination to the cacique, for example, was absolute; because the governor was illiterate, he depended on his secretary, another of Cedillo's men, to read for him and to write his messages to congress. Turrubiates consulted Cedillo on so many matters that a radio had to be installed for communication between the government palace and Palomas.[57] On the two occasions when the cacique headed the Ministry of Agriculture, he appointed his favorites to positions at all levels, including the posts for agricultural engineers.[58] For approximately ten years, the state was headed by many previously unknown, and frequently illiterate peasants. There were few parallels of such extraordinary social mobility in the rest of the country.

However, it was precisely these particular privileges enjoyed by some peasants close to the cacique that constituted one of the structural factors impeding the rural workers as a group to form an organization with certain autonomous leadership and objectives. For the many peasants who were not integrated into Cedillo's patronage, this power structure hindered the implementation of an agrarian reform that would transcend the needs of the cacique. Furthermore, it allowed Cedillo to assist certain landholders and to grant immunity for the outrages committed by some of his followers.

One of the clearest indicators of the weakness of the agrarianism introduced in San Luis by the revolution, as well as in many other parts of the republic, was the surprising preservation of the great hacienda. The 1930 census is revealing: 98.5 percent of estates in San Luis and 86 percent of the land was privately owned. These statistics remained essentially unchanged five years later, when Cedillo still controlled the agrarian reform. The relative expansion of the ejido in the state should be attributed to the administrations prior to Cedillo, particularly to Manrique's. During this governorship, 150,000 hectares were granted annually, while at the height of the cacicazgo (1928–34) only 12,000 hectares were donated annually, most of which were of poor quality.[59]

The cacicazgo's political structure also obstructed rural organization. Cedillo himself had been an impediment to the crystalization

[57] NAW, RG59, 812.00 SLP/13, February 18, 1931; ibid., 14, August 18, 1931, ibid., all from Shaw to the State Department; *Excelsior*, February 13, March 16, July 5, 25, August 3, 1931, April 28, May 5, 1932.

[58] Alfonso Taracena, *La revolución desvirtuada* (México: B. Costa Amic, 1966), Vol. 5 (1937): pp. 207; Manuel Fernández, Eutiquio Marrón. *Lo que no se sabe de la rebelión cedillista* (Mexico, 1938), pp. 176–85.

[59] Simpson, *El Ejido*, Tables 22, 23, 27, 30, 40; México, Dirección General de Estadística, *Primer censo ejidal, 1935: Resumen general* (México: DAPP, 1937), p. 38.

of the League of Agrarian Communities of the state of San Luis Potosí founded by Manrique in 1925, which ended up being no more than a formal recognition of Cedillo's power base. It never intended to mobilize the state's peasants, was ideologically innocuous, and failed to promote an agrarian reform if it was not carried out according to Cedillo's personal considerations. While the radical wing of the agrarians in the rest of the country was engaged in a frontal struggle for the ejido program, the league of San Luis debated "why the forests and animal game should be conserved"; and how to "render country life pleasant and healthy by searching for honest pastimes."[60]

In brief, for many of the peasants of San Luis, the much touted agrarianism of Cedillo was more formal than real, despite the cacique's enormous influence on certain rural sectors and the important benefits he provided for these few. Many of his satellites became true despots: Leopoldo Calleja, for example, deputy and strong man of Xilitla, invaded ejidos, confiscated smallholdings, charged the ejidatarios with unconstitutional quotas and other abuses. When one commissary refused to give him a payoff, Calleja attempted to kill him; in the victim's words: "putting me in prison, denying me food and water, later by trying to hang me, and finally by having members of his reserve ambush me."[61]

The different types of authority that Cedillo imposed on the rural districts had highly contradictory effects for the peasants. Therefore, when the federal government destroyed his power basis, there was an ambivalent response in the rural areas. While those not involved in the personal network surrounding the cacique complained that local functionaries continued to hurt the landless peasants, "as they say that they have General Cedillo's authority to shoot those soliciting land . . . and to annihilate their organizations,"[62] those loyal to the old guerrilla united in countering the "calumnious declarations . . . intrigues . . . and accusations [against] our dear and respected leader General boss Cedillo to whom we most owe our improved

[60] Estatutos de la Liga de Comunidades Agrarias del Estado de San Luis Potosí (SLP, Imprenta Ponce, 1930); Liga de Comunidades Agrarias en San Luis Potosí. Convocatoria, September 10, 1926; AGN, FP, O/C, 205-s-108.

[61] AGN, FP, ALR, 552.1/823, Rubio to Rodríguez, January 18, 1933, May 16, 1934; ibid., LCR, 403/769, December 24, 1935; ibid., February 1935, both from ejido Texacal to Cárdenas; ibid., 555.1/131, May 31, 1935. 555.1/153, August 17, 1935, both from ejido Xilitla to Cárdenas, ibid., 55.1/78, ejido Apatzco, Xilitla, to Cárdenas, October 10, 1936.

[62] AGN, FP, ALR, 702,12/172; ejido Tepusoapa, Cozcatlán to Cárdenas, December 15, 1936.

living standards."[63] In the last analysis the bonds between Cedillo and some peasants were so intense that a handful of his former followers insisted on risking their lives for their leader—already an old, powerless and sickly man—in 1938, when he put out a call for a rebellion that collapsed even before it began.

[63] Ibid., 702.12/122: ejido San Vicente to Cárdenas, November 9, 1936.

CHAPTER FIFTEEN

Second Division of the North: Formation and Fragmentation of the Laguna's Popular Movement, 1910–11

William K. Meyers

The study of agrarian revolts in modern Mexico must include the case of the Laguna region of north-central Mexico. Since its economic development in the 1880s, the Laguna has been the scene of a number of popular revolts that have played key roles at critical junctures in Mexico's modern history. After 1900, the Laguna's workers and peasants provided an important source of prerevolutionary discontent. They were among the first groups to revolt against the Díaz government, and continued to play a significant role in the course of the revolution as the region was bitterly contested and alternately controlled by each of the principal northern revolutionary factions. Throughout the 1920s and 1930s, the Laguna remained the site of widespread popular mobilization and union organization, culminating in 1936 with a general strike, nationalization of the region's cotton plantations, and settlement of its workers and peasants on collective farms.

The Laguna's popular mobilization is especially interesting for the social scientist. It was not strictly a peasant revolt, but involved a broad spectrum of groups that reflected the diversified character of the region's settlement pattern and economic development. A coalition of traditional Indian villagers, small landowners, miners, and industrial workers formed the popular movement that helped over-throw Díaz and transform the Laguna into a hotbed of rebellion.

To understand the formation of the modern Mexican state, the case of the Laguna's popular movement is also critical. Between 1908 and 1936, various groups of the region's popular sector mobilized at different times and for different reasons. On two occasions, the popular movement united and achieved striking results. The first popular mobilization occurred between November 1910 and May 1911, proving instrumental in Díaz's overthrow and the triumph of the revolution. The second unification came in 1936, prompting the state's intervention on behalf of the workers and peasants to distribute the land and defuse the popular movement that again threatened the state's hegemony.

To understand the origin and character of the Laguna's popular movement, this essay focuses on the region's first mass uprising: the revolt of 1910–11. It examines the groups that rose against Díaz, the motives for and the pattern of the revolt, and the degree of allegiance to the Madero movement. Simply put, who rebelled and why? This analysis is essential to understand the social base of the revolution and the popular movement's subsequent fragmentation after the Maderista victory in May of 1911. Ultimately this process of coalescence and fragmentation proved critical to the revolutionary history of the region, the north, and the entire country.

On November 20, 1911, a group of between forty and eighty men attacked Gómez Palacio, Durango, in response to Madero's call for armed revolt. Led by Jesús Agustín Castro, a Torreón street-car conductor, the rebels captured the police station, liberated the prisoners, and battled federal troops for several hours before fleeing into the Durango hills. The government quickly executed two wounded rebels and declared the uprising a failure. While the government had neither defeated nor captured the raiders, the planned rebellion had not succeeded either; no popular uprisings followed their attack, and the rebels had taken no towns.[1]

---

[1] Eduardo Guerra, *Historia de Torreón, su origen y sus fundadores* (Mexico City: Ediciones Casan, 1957), pp. 136–44. There are a number of secondary accounts of the Gómez Palacio raid, which differ only in the number of rebels involved. As the rebel groups kept no records of their activities, I have based my information concerning what happened, where it happened, who was involved, and how many people participated on newspaper reports, consular records, hacienda records, memoirs, and military reports from the historical archives of the Secretaria de Defense Nacional, Mexico City. These reports are cited and, in some cases, reproduced in Miguel A.

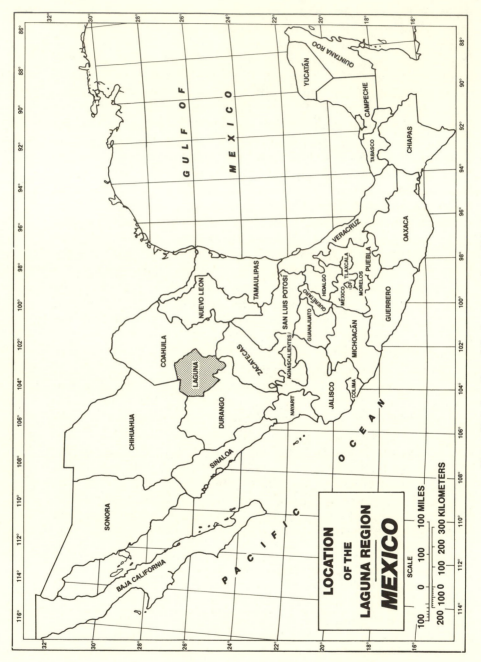

Figure 15.1. Location of the Laguna region of Mexico.

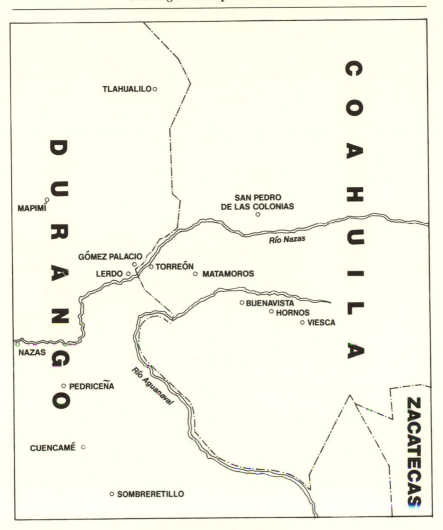

Figure 15.2. The Laguna.

While not an apparent success, the Gómez Palacio raid provided the spark that ignited the region's popular rebellion and marked the official beginning of the Mexican revolution in the Laguna. Six months later, Jesús Agustín Castro led a victorious, if unruly army of 5,000 "insurrectos" into Torreón where Emilio Madero, brother

Sánchez Lamego's, *Historia militar de la revolución mexicana en la epoca maderista* (México, 1976), hereafter cited as S. L. Sánchez Lamego's account provides the best general overview of the battles and rebel activity in the Laguna.

of Francisco, proclaimed them the "second division of the north." The popular movement had triumphed and the Laguna was now, literally, in the hands of an armed coalition of its workers, peasants, and smallholders. Their revolt constituted the first mass uprising in the Laguna and shaped the subsequent history of the region and the revolution.

The capture of Torreón by this irregular army on May 11, 1911, sealed Díaz' fate. Following the rebel victory at Ciudad Juárez, the Laguna's fall guaranteed the revolution's victory in the north. The next day, the administration began peace negotiations with the rebels. Within two weeks, Díaz had resigned and departed for France, while Madero passed through Torreón on his triumphant journey to Mexico City.

The key role that events in the Laguna played in Díaz' overthrow revealed both the strengths and weaknesses of the Porfirian system. Probably no area in Mexico better reflected the success of Díaz' policies of national integration and economic development. Nonetheless, the Laguna provided a graphic example of the administration's failure to accommodate, balance, and adjust the demands of new groups that were emerging out of this process of rapid change. The most prominent cases involved the region's intra-elite conflicts and the political challenge of Francisco I. Madero. Ultimately, however, Díaz' failure to contain the popular movement spelled his downfall.

While Madero's political challenge and the intra-elite conflicts have been well studied, the nature of the popular revolt remains difficult to document. To understand the origins of this social rebellion, one must first examine the process of economic development and social change that converted the Laguna into the "pride of the Porfiriato," the scene of bitter intra-elite conflicts and a cauldron of popular unrest.

The Laguna 1876–1911:
Economic Development and Elite Division

The dramatic economic and social transformation of the Laguna between 1876 and 1911 provides a unique setting for examining the mixed results of Díaz' development strategy. When Díaz took office, Torreón appeared on no maps and the Laguna was known for little more than its isolation, barren desert, erratic water supply, and excessive heat. By 1910, however, the region had emerged as the most important new agricultural, industrial, mining and urban center in Mexico. Much of that growth resulted directly from the policies of

Don Porfirio. In contrast with the area's previous isolation, his program of railroad building converted the Laguna into the major rail center of north-central Mexico, well integrated into the national and international economic systems.

Cotton cultivation provided the key to the region's growth and prosperity. Between 1880 and 1900, large irrigated cotton plantations developed along the flood plain of the Río Nazas, extending fifty miles from the upper river zone in Durango to the lower river zone in Coahuila, converting the area into Mexico's largest producer of cotton. Once again, the Díaz administration played an active role, offering planters investment incentives such as tax exemptions, special concessions, guaranteed loans, price supports, tariff protection and options for colonization. Government concessions also helped revive mining in the mountains along the Laguna's western border, attracting prominent investors such as the Guggenheims and Maderos. In 1902, the discovery of a means of extracting rubber from the wild guayule shrub sparked a boom and, by 1908, rubber rivaled cotton and minerals as the region's most valuable export. Again, the administration encouraged foreign investment but required that the shrub be processed in Mexico to generate employment and further agroindustrial development.

The central location and rail facilities of Torreón and Gómez Palacio converted these twin cities into Mexico's fastest growing urban and industrial area. By 1910, Torreón had over 40,000 inhabitants, paved streets, electric lights, telephones, a streetcar line, and other signs of modern economic growth. The industrial zone of Torreón and Gómez Palacio employed over 10,000 workers in factories producing rubber, soap, flour, textiles, beer and glycerine, a testament to the region's diversified economic development.[2]

Government officials, planters, industrialists, and merchants joined in the expansive spirit, believing in and competing for increasing opportunity and profits. The presence of prominent state, national, and foreign economic interests testified to the Laguna's promise and privilege within the Porfirian system. Investors from northern Mexico included the Madero, Gómez Palacio, Mendrichaga, Terrazas, Creel, and Luján families; and from Mexico City, the Martínez del Río family, the García Pimentels, Jorge Vera Estañol, Francisco Bulnes, and Porfirio Díaz, Jr. Every sector of the re-

[2] Guerra, *Historia de Torreón*, pp. 93–96. See also, William K. Meyers, *Interest Group Conflict and Revolutionary Politics: A Social History of La Comarca Lagunera, Mexico, 1888-1911*, Ph.D. Dissertation, University of Chicago, 1979, Ch. 3.

gion's economy reflected a strong foreign presence. In general, Spaniards predominated in agriculture, Germans in hardware, the Chinese in the service sector, French in dry goods, while U.S. interests invested heavily in banking, industry, and general commerce. The Guggenheim family dominated mining, the Rockefellers virtually monopolized guayule, British investors owned the region's two largest plantations, and Germans owned its richest mine, Mapimí. Seemingly, with this combination of national and international interests, Díaz deserved to be proud of the region and the Lagueros grateful for his aid and encouragement.

Of course, that was the Porfirista perspective. From within the Laguna, things looked somewhat different. Even with large profits, the elite managed to find one complaint or another about Díaz' handling of the region's diverse affairs. From one point of view, it was a tribute to Díaz' diplomatic and political skills, as well as the region's prosperity, that he could draw so many prominent and competing interests into one area and keep them all active and reasonably content while the area developed. Moreover, the Laguna's division between Durango and Coahuila, coupled with the Nazas' erratic flow, further complicated Díaz' tasks of alternately rewarding different groups while playing them off against one another. While this system established Díaz as the ultimate arbiter in regional affairs, it also brought to his doorstep the Laguna's intra-elite conflicts and economic problems.

From 1884 until Torreón's fall to the region's popular classes, Díaz devoted a great deal of attention to handling the disputes of the region's divided elite as they battled over everything from water rights to the price of soap. In the early 1880s, planters in the lower river zone armed resident workers and sent them into the upper river zone in Durango to destroy dams in order to obtain more water for Coahuila.

The ensuing battle between armies of agricultural workers created a major incident between Durango and Coahuila, prompting Díaz' intervention to prevent these private wars. Díaz succeeded as landowners realized that armed workers ultimately constituted more of a threat to peace than a source of security. While private armies had disappeared by 1910, Díaz' handling of various regional disputes frequently angered landowners who again threatened to take matters into their own hands. Although most of the Laguna's elite depended on lobbyists to protect economic interests with Díaz, Francisco I. Madero expanded his activities to include electoral politics.

Rather than as a politician, Madero gained prominence advocating the economic interests of his family, state, and river zone. After 1904, however, Madero turned his attention to politics, challenging the Díaz administration in the Laguna's local elections by organizing political clubs and running reform candidates against the regulars of the Porfirian machine. Madero's candidates lost, due to fraud he claimed, but he simply raised his sights and focused upon the election for governor. By 1909, he sought the presidency and, when thwarted by Díaz, called for armed revolt on November 20, 1910. Six months later, the Maderistas had triumphed.

Ultimately the revolt of the popular classes produced the Maderista victory. Although the elite remained divided among themselves and dissatisfied with Díaz' handling of their affairs, few responded to Madero's call to revolt. Even those expected to revolt in Coahuila, including members of Madero's family and close associates such as Venustiano Carranza, failed to rise up in arms. In fact, between November 1910 and May 1911, most of the elite continued to lobby for their economic interests and cooperated with Díaz' attempts to bankrupt the Maderos in order to stop Francisco and punish the family.

Nonetheless, the revolutionary movement in the Laguna continued to grow, fueled by recruits from the popular sector, an amorphous interest group that both Díaz and the region's elite underestimated. From various economic sectors and geographic subregions, the region's workers and peasants emerged to pursue the common goal of overthrowing Díaz. In May 1911 they found themselves in control of the region with the federal army, the major landowners and Díaz in retreat. The question of who they were and why they revolted seemed lost in the revolution's victory.

The Popular Classes

They charged, yelling and whooping, primitive, excited, unruly, ragged, dusty, bloodshot and some bandaged, all highly nervous and pretty well charged with "dutch courage." Carbines and rifles of every age and type, pistols and shotguns, the rabble was as motley in its armament as in its other gear. Some hats even bore, of ancient tradition of the revolts of forgotten years, the picture of the Virgin of Guadalupe. Smelling of sweat, offal and grease, grimy hands pawed us for concealed weapons and pillaged us of our cash. Eager questing groups wrangled among themselves for the richer prizes, and admitted us to a view of their primitive greed. No man was slain in cold blood

among the passengers, though some were threatened when it
was felt that they were resisting search. They had burned trestle
bridges behind and ahead of us, and plundering was being done
at a grim leisure that boded ill for us with the progressive alco-
holization of the gang, when a distant train whistle caused the
cry that a troop train was coming up. With a last grab at the loot,
and gulp at the bottle, the raiders tumbled out of the cars, leap-
ing to the ground and onto horses.[3]

While colorful, accounts such as that of Patrick O'Hea contribute
little to our understanding of the composition of the movement that
made the Laguna a major center of rebellion. Except when pictured
so graphically, the "insurrectos" are generally described as a face-
less mass, either hidden in the hills, terrorizing the countryside in
small bands, or threatening the towns. Most historical accounts of
the revolution make broad generalizations about the rebel groups
without examining their social origins or behavior within an economic context. Such assumptions obscure revolutionary motives
and distort the importance of Madero's call to arms. An appreciation
of the identity and motives of rebel groups such as the one described
by O'Hea requires a review of the region's social and demographic
history.

Given the Laguna's sparse settlement during the colonial period
and its rapid population growth in the late nineteenth century, social groups were less bound by traditional ties of place, kinship, feudal obligations or religious responsibilities than in most of Mexico.
Large landowners resisted the settlement of smallholders; consequently there existed few self-sufficient agricultural holdings or autonomous Indian villages. The region's elite was less a traditional
landed gentry than a market and profit-oriented business class. The
working population was modern in the sense that it was mobile, tied
to a wage system and constituted a labor reserve army to serve the
fluctuating demands of agribusiness and industry.

At the time of the 1910 revolt, the majority of the region's population depended upon cash earned from agriculture, guayule cutting, mining, or industry. Propertyless and without political representation, the population's yearly fortune depended upon
unpredictable and wildly fluctuating factors that also determined
the region's general economic condition. Throughout the revolution,
the level of dissent and popular mobilization was strongly influ-

[3] Patrick O'Hea, *Reminiscences of the Mexican Revolution* (México: Editorial Four-
nier, 1966), p. 46.

enced by variables such as seasonal demands of agriculture, weather and crop conditions, availability of water, fluctuation in the price of cotton, guayule, and metal ores, the cost of food and fuel, the condition of the transportation system, and the availability of credit.

The region's settlement pattern reflected its economic development. From the colonial period until the nineteenth century, a few vast estates dominated the countryside. Even with subsequent agricultural modernization and development, land remained concentrated in large holdings, ranging from 1,000 to 100,000 hectares. Prior to the arrival of the railroads in the 1880s, only five major areas of settlement existed outside the control of the large estates: Cuencamé and Mapimí in Durango; Matamoros, Viesca, and San Pedro in Coahuila. The two oldest settlements were Cuencamé in the southwest and the mining community of Mapimí in the northwest. In the zone around Cuencamé, a population of Ocuilan Indians and mestizos farmed small plots, raising corn, beans, wheat, cattle and horses to meet their own needs and supply nearby mining communities. Mapimí, the Laguna's oldest town, depended entirely upon mining and its population fluctuated with mining activity in the surrounding zone.[4]

In the middle river zone, independent settlers founded the community of Matamoros de la Laguna in 1836 and began cultivating land between the Río Nazas and the Río Aguanaval. Despite periodic armed attempts by large landowners to oust them, the Matamoros smallholders managed to defend themselves and survive, remaining fiercely proud of their independent status in the midst of large plantations.[5]

In the center of the lower river zone, the town of San Pedro de las Colonias began in 1869 as a colony of former soldiers of the republican army. They opened small cotton "ranchos" along the lower flood plain of the Nazas, sharing water rights with large landowners such as the Purcell and Madero families.[6]

Throughout the nineteenth century, these settlements remained small and isolated from state and national affairs, scarcely providing enough labor to satisfy the demands of their own limited agricultural operations. Thus the development of agriculture, mining, and industry depended on imported labor and from 1880 to 1910 the

[4] Pastor Rouaix, Diccionario geográfico, histórico y biográfico del estado de Durango (México: 1946), pp. 89, 111–12, 136, 155–56, 231–32, 235–38.

[5] Jose Santos Valdés, Matamoros: Ciudad Lagunera (México: 1973), pp. 312–22.

[6] Eduardo Guerra, Historia de la Laguna: Primer siglo agrícola Algodonero, Tomo 2 (México: Editorial Lagunero, 1953), pp. 273–75.

Laguna's population grew faster than any other area in Mexico. Migrating from central Mexico, the majority of workers arrived unskilled and entirely dependent on cash wages and without prospect of acquiring land. They came to construct the railroads, clear the lands, dig the irrigation canals and lay out the vast estates that dominated the region. Many eventually became resident workers on these cotton plantations. Each 100 hectares of cotton cultivation required eight permanent workers; thus with estates ranging up to 100,000 hectares, resident workers formed a significant population of over 100,000 by 1910.[7]

In addition to this resident workforce, cotton planters depended upon two other sources of labor: temporary workers from within the region and migrant cotton pickers from outside. Each year from midsummer to late fall, between 10,000 and 50,000 migrants came to pick the crop. Their number, arrival date and departure depended upon the size of the crop and weather conditions. Plantations relied upon labor agents to attract these workers in the summer, and called in the hacienda guards to move them on their way in the late fall.

Temporary workers (*trabajadores eventuales*) were critical to the economy because cotton cultivation required a large, mobile pool of labor to perform temporary or emergency tasks. To supply this need, landowners recruited workers from small towns such as Matamoros, Hornos, Cuencamé, and Viesca, collecting points for this temporary labor. Lacking secure employment, these trabajadores eventuales took whatever jobs became available in agriculture, mining, or industry. Consequently, their wages and employment fluctuated unpredictably with the region's economic fortunes. In years of abundant water and good crops, these workers received steady employment and high wages. Conversely, in slack years or the offseason, they suffered more than any other labor group; they either migrated or simply waited it out in the rail towns or on the outskirts of Torreón and Gómez Palacio in hopes of finding work.

As centers of transport and employment, the small free towns offered information about work opportunity from central Mexico to the United States. The towns became important mustering points for migrant labor and, attracting a diverse population, gained reputations as centers for drinking, gambling, prostitution, and the illegal sale of stolen cotton and guayule. On the whole, while planters depended heavily upon temporary workers, they considered these

[7] Meyers, *Interest Group Conflict*, pp. 148–53.

towns collecting points for troublemakers and a menace to the social peace of the region.[8]

Troubled by the expansion of these communities, planters opened more land to sharecroppers, particularly around Lerdo and San Pedro. Sharecropping provided landowners the double advantage of a guaranteed supply of temporary labor, while also receiving return from the cultivation of marginal lands that would otherwise lie unused. To prevent tenants from eventually claiming land, planters carefully controlled all sharecropping arrangements through written contracts that determined what crops were grown and what percentage of the crop each party received. Tenants were not allowed to compete with the landowner for labor and were forced to sell all produce at a fixed price.[9]

While the majority of the population's livelihood depended on agriculture, mining employed over 30,000 workers by 1910, most of whom lived around Mapimí in the northwest and Velardeña in the southwest. Miners also depended entirely upon wages to live, and their economic situation varied dramatically with fluctuations in world metal prices and local food prices. By 1910, the cutting and processing of guayule provided work for 11,000 laborers whose employment and wages also depended on the general business climate and the price of rubber. It was the same story for the 10,000 industrial workers of Torreón and Gómez Palacio. Given the close interrelationship between the Laguna's agricultural and industrial sectors, fluctuations in weather, water, or agricultural prices directly influenced employment in industry. Since the majority of industrial workers originally came from the agricultural sector, they frequently returned to the countryside during periods of unemployment, further increasing the large pool of landless labor.[10]

Of these various groups, only smallholders from areas such as Cuencamé, Matamoros, and Viesca could meet their basic needs without working for wages. Nonetheless, they too felt the impact of Porfirian development policies. The growth of Torreón and plantations of the surrounding middle river area steadily encroached upon water and land claims of the Matamoros settlers, reducing their food and crop production. At the same time, Cuencamé and San Pedro Ocuila lost land to the expansion of the neighboring Sombreretillo hacienda.

[8] Ibid., pp. 161–63.
[9] Ibid., pp. 164–67.
[10] Ibid., pp. 179–84.

These conditions furnished the economic impetus for popular discontent. The Laguna became a potentially volatile area due to contradictions inherent in the social and economic relationships that developed within its population. The greatest potential source for rebellion existed within the largest and most deprived element: the landless and transient agricultural proletariat. As winter approached and the picking season ended, large numbers of idle and needy workers collected in the towns. The precarious economic situation of the entire working population revealed itself dramatically during periods of drought or business downturns. The droughts of 1888, 1891, 1893, 1899, and 1901 provoked popular protest throughout the zone. The financial crisis of 1907 hit the region's wage earners particularly hard as it coincided with another drought. The Mexican Liberal party's (PLM) raid of 1908 at Viesca sent shudders through the region's propertied class, which feared it might touch off a general rebellion of the unemployed in the countryside. It did not, but landowners and government officials cooperated to move unemployed workers out of the region, not allowing them to linger in the small towns.[11]

The Revolt

Into this situation came the Gómez Palacio raid. Although the attack was not technically a success for the rebels, it was not a total failure because they survived and avoided capture. Ultimately, the rebels' ability to recruit from the regional pool of temporary and unemployed workers ensured their victory. However, at this early stage the Madero movement focused upon political issues and employed no specific strategy to draw upon economic discontent as the basis for gaining popular support.

The Gómez Palacio raid was planned and staged by political veterans, a local urban–rural coalition of Maderistas, Reyistas, and PLM activists. At the center of the conspiracy, however, stood the leaders of the Torreón–Gómez Palacio anti-reelectionist movement who were clearly responding to Madero's call to revolt. From the night of the raid their plans began to change. Ignoring the countryside, they originally focused on urban centers, planning to capture Torreón and then move on Gómez Palacio and Lerdo. The conspirators also expected between 1,200 and 6,000 supporters from Torreón to join

[11] Guerra, *Historia de Torreón*, p. 325; *El Nuevo Mundo*, 9 July 1907, p. 11; 10 Oct. 1908, p. 5; *Mexican Herald*, 8 Aug. 1907, p. 4; 27 Sept. 1907, p. 11; 20 Oct. 1907, p. 5; 19 Nov. 1907, p. 2; 28 June 1908, p. 1.

the raid under the command of Manuel N. Oviedo, a prominent Madero supporter. When Oviedo and his men failed to appear, the small group of rebels chose a new leader, Jesús Agustín Castro, and a new target, Gómez Palacio. Twelve hours later, Oviedo was jailed in Torreón and the raiders were scattered in the hills and on the run. Clearly unable to sustain an active campaign against the government, the rebels quickly split into groups of two or three to avoid attention and capture.[12]

Madero's call and the Gómez Palacio raid provoked uprisings in several other Laguna towns in late November. In Cuencamé on November 20, Calixto Contreras and Severino Ceniceros led a group of small landowners, temporary workers and Ocuilan Indians in revolt. In Matamoros, a handful of men attacked the local police station and fled into the countryside where they battled soldiers on November 21 and 22. Similar minor uprisings also reportedly occurred in small towns such as Viesca, Gitla, and Concepción del Oro. In San Pedro de las Colonias, Enrique Adame Macías revolted with a few men who attacked neighboring plantations before moving southward to the area between Matamoros and Viesca, where they continued to operate until May 1911. Around Tlahualilo, planters complained that small bandit groups (gavillas), raided their outlying ranches and encouraged workers to rebel.[13]

The origin and degree of interrelation of these revolts is very difficult to precisely establish. While their timing indicates a clear response to Madero's call to rebellion, most uprisings had their roots in local circumstances and past problems. Free settlements such as Cuencamé, Matamoros, and Viesca had a legacy of struggle against both large landowners and Díaz officials over issues such as land, water rights, or politics. The PLM's labor campaign also attracted a popular following in these towns as well as Gómez Palacio, Velardoña, and Mapimí. From 1906, planters and mining foremen complained of the activity of PLM agitators and noted the clandestine circulation among workers of Regeneración, the PLM newspaper.[14]

Most important for the early Revolution, Madero was a native son who established a widespread grassroots organization and con-

[12] Guerra, Historia de Torreón, pp. 136–44; Sánchez Lamego, Historia militar, pp. 132–35; Juan D. Villarello, Historia de la revolución mexicana en Coahuila (México, 1970), pp. 204–205.

[13] Sánchez Lamego, Historia militar, p. 145; Archive of the Mexican Cotton Estates of Tlahualilo, Ltd. (hereafter AMCE), general correspondence, 25 Nov. 1910.

[14] Villarello, Historia de la revolución, p. 165; Guerra, Historia de la Laguna, pp. 135–43.

stituency through political campaigning since 1904, creating political clubs in cities, towns, plantations and mining settlements. The formation of the Anti-Reelectionist party in 1909 and Madero's campaign for president further integrated this loose organization of anti-Díaz dissidents and opposition groups. In short, this vague constituency of supporters and political clubs provided a basic organization for dispersing information, channeling support, and providing the Anti-Reelectionist movement legitimacy.

Despite this political organization and Madero's many supporters in the Laguna, few people rallied to the call for armed rebellion. Of the 1,200–6,000 men "expected," probably no more than 200 rebelled. Instead, the early course of the revolt and subsequent developments indicate that the bulk of revolutionary support was popular, spontaneous, and rural rather than organized, urban, or even specifically political. No overall organization, planning or control existed among the various insurgent groups. There were no formal networks of communication, "safe houses" for hiding, systems of arms supply, or provision for financial support. The material survival of each rebel band depended upon capturing arms, supplies, and money from plantations and the army.

Other than shouts of "viva la revolucíon," "mueran los Porfiristas," and "viva Madero," rebel groups made no clear statement of purpose or goals. The date of the uprising indicated a response to the Plan de San Luis Potosí, but most of those in revolt had little idea what Madero's plan called for other than ending the current system. The rebels simply struck at the symbols of Porfirian authority, took what they could, and fled. In short, while probably inspired by Madero's call to arms, the specific motives for rebellion came from the particular circumstances of each area and group. Rather than appeals to a specifically political consciousness, rebels took advantage of slack seasonal employment, economic discontent, and local grievances that could be channeled into the common project of overthrowing the Díaz system.

Sharing only this common goal, the first actions of the various rebel groups were similar. Rising up in small towns, the rebels attacked police headquarters, liberated prisoners, destroyed documents of the law courts, attacked the city treasury and post office, and seized what money and arms they could find. Fleeing to the hills, they staged sporadic raids and recruited support in the countryside for the next four months.

The November uprisings took the same form, and they ended in a similar manner. In each case the raiders fled into the surrounding hills and then broke into pairs to avoid capture, hoping to slip back into their usual roles in the region. The most visible and well known rebels could not return and they formed the core and leadership of the popular movement that eventually conquered the region. The most conspicuous of these were the original Gómez Palacio raiders: Jesús Agustín Castro, Orestes Pereyra, Sixto Ugalde, Mariano López Ortiz, Gregorio García, and Martín Triana. When they failed to take Gómez Palacio, they divided the Laguna into rough zones of operation: Castro took the upper river area, Orestes Pereyra initially operated with Castro but eventually assumed charge of the Tlahualilo zone, and Sixto Ugalde was responsible for coordinating the revolution around Matamoros and San Pedro. In the area of Cuencamé, Calixto Contreras and Severino Ciniceros led the armed phase of a struggle against local landowners that had begun legally and peacefully with lawsuits in 1904. Below this pragmatic and unofficial division of regional leadership, the popular revolt varied with the character of each local group and leader who mobilized to drive the "federales" from their zone and establish rebel authority.[15]

Stages of the Revolt

Although clearly embarrassed and threatened by the outbreaks of rebel activity, the Díaz government quickly claimed credit for their suppression and assured everyone that the raids were of no consequence. As with the 1908 PLM raid, this violence caused great anxiety among propertied interests who saw it as an indication of the high level of social discontent and political unrest in the countryside. Since the economic crisis of 1907, the level of popular unrest remained particularly acute. In the midst of their various intraregional disputes, the elite took the Gómez Palacio raid and Maderista movement as a further indication of Díaz' increasing inability to handle affairs. By early December, however, the rebel menace seemed to have disappeared, and life in the Laguna appeared normal. Good weather extended the picking season into early January and the high price of cotton helped planters compensate for a low yields caused by the summer drought.

In contrast, the summer drought had a strictly negative impact on the region's agricultural population. For wage workers, the small crop caused lower incomes, while the drought raised prices of basic commodities. Planters noted an increased demand among workers

---

[15] Villarello, *Historia de la revolucíon*, p. 165.

for land to sharecrop, and as winter approached and labor demand decreased, many agricultural workers faced the prospect of food shortages and real hardship.[16]

In the hills on the Laguna's western and southern border, the "insurrectos" also confronted the problem of basic survival. Throughout December, they attacked outlying ranches, striking quickly in groups of five or ten to steal arms, ammunition, horses, money and supplies before retreating back into the hills. All groups shared the same basic strategy: steal what they needed, harass the enemy while avoiding direct combat, and recruit support among the unemployed workers as the harvest season ended. Necessity rather than design dictated this approach. By disrupting railroad traffic, cutting telegraph lines, and raiding outlying ranches, the rebels hoped eventually to control the countryside. With increased numbers and supplies, they could isolate and capture the mines and small towns before finally moving onto the major cities.

Although rebel groups remained few in number and isolated, several factors helped their cause. First, guerilla tactics proved difficult to control in the Laguna. As we have seen, the haciendas, mines, towns, and cities depended on the railroad for food, fuel, and cash, as well as to export cotton, rubber, and ore. By burning bridges and tearing up tracks, a small group or rebels could paralyze an entire area. Moreover, the isolated ranches, located in the midst of these vast properties, tempted raiders with large stores of supplies, arms, and cash. The federal army found it difficult to counter the "hit and run" tactics of these numerous groups and seemed afraid to fight the rebels. As the cotton harvest ended, and plantations began to reduce their workforces, the rebellion offered an ever-larger number of workers an alternative source of activity and material support for the winter.

The overwhelming popularity of the rebels also aided their success. From the beginning, local accounts noted the rebels' support in the countryside, indicating the popular base of the movement. Most of the men who took up arms had ties to local communities and attracted a following as native sons and popular heroes. Moreover, the rebels' varied work experience in agriculture, mining, and guayule provided them a wide basis of legitimacy for recruiting support from the popular classes. In the tradition of social banditry, the

[16] Archivo de La Casa Guillermo Purcell (hereafter AGP), general correspondence, 10 Oct. 1910.

rebels gained popularity as they continued to harass and frustrate government troops.

The rise in rebel activity throughout December indicates the seasonal nature of popular mobilization. In early January, the government imposed censorship on reporting rebel attacks but rumors and accounts from residents of outlying properties confirmed the rebels' growing strength. It became increasingly difficult for the government to conceal the rebels' frequent disruption of rail and telegraph communication. To counteract the growing rebel strength, federal authorities brought in reinforcements and rounded up unemployed workers in the countryside and imprisoned them in camps in Torreón.[17]

But despite such measures, rebel strength and activity continued to grow. As local observers noted, the federal army proved adept at persecuting unemployed workers but unable to capture rebels. Throughout January there were no reports of federal army victories. In contrast, many accounts noted the army's reluctance to fight or pursue rebels into the mountains. Stories circulated of the federal army being consistently routed and planters demanded the authorities provide further protection from attack. These accounts further diminished the government's prestige and aided rebel recruitment. Despite reinforcements from Mexico City and the frequent replacement of Torreón's "*jefe político*," rebel victories continued through January. Headlines such as "Rebels Attack Hacienda," "Insurrectos Near San Pedro," "Hacienda Unrest," "Railway Bridge Burned," filled the newspapers, while reports of federal victories remained noticeably absent. In contrast, as one resident noted, "stories of federal troops robbing and raping helped the anti-government cause."[18]

Clearly, success helped popularize the revolutionaries' cause. Bands grew bolder and bigger in late January and in early February rebel groups began a major, if uncoordinated, offensive. Scarcely a day passed without an attack on one of the region's smaller towns while raids on plantations became routine. The constant interruptions of the railroad and suspension of dynamite and fuel shipments threatened the haciendas, mines, and factories with closure, which would further swell the rebels' ranks. By mid-February one observer

[17] U.S. Records of the Department of State Relating to the Internal Affairs of Mexico (hereafter RDS), Record Group 59, 812 file, 812.00/689, 27 Jan. 1911.

[18] RDS, 812.00/831, 14 Feb. 1911; 812.00/862, 15 Feb. 1911; *Mexican Herald*, 25 Jan. 1911, p. 2; 29 Jan. 1911, p. 7; 11 Feb. 1911, p. 1; 17 Feb. 1911, p. 2; 18 Feb. 1911, p. 2.

estimated that more than 2,000 rebels were operating in forty to fifty bands.

A precise profile of these groups is difficult to establish. Most bands contained ten to fifty men. Although sometimes pictured as "disorganized, disorderly and dirty," rebel groups were most frequently characterized as well organized and obedient to their leaders. The selection of leaders seems to have been popular and spontaneous. The few references to the occupations of rebel leaders note that they included a stonemason, a shoemaker, a small landowner, a guayule cutter, a gambler, a miner, a ditch contractor, a former assistant police chief of Torreón, and an "ex-imprisoned tailor fighting for his rights."[19]

The composition of rebel groups varied between zones of operation but all recruited heavily from the region's temporary workforce. While precise motives and intentions also differed between groups and individuals, it is clear that many joined in the excitement of the moment. A British Consul noted: "I do not suppose 10% of the insurrectos have any definite object in view: they are simply having a good time at the expense of those who formerly were their masters; in short they have for the first time in their lives a good horse, a good rifle, and the pleasure of "bossing" instead of being "bossed." That they are independent and owing no central authority accounts for the very different way in which they have behaved.[20]

While this independent behavior made the rebels masters of the countryside, their ultimate victory required greater coordination and mutuality of purpose. Although the number of rebels continued to increase, most still did not share any common plan or offer allegiance to a larger movement. Some proclaimed themselves "Maderistas," while others simply referred to themselves as "insurrectos." This became a source of concern to Madero's supporters. The closing of mines and capture of small towns seemed imminent by early March and federal officials began to abandon the countryside. At this point, unification and control became essential for the Maderista movement before new recruits swelled the rebel ranks and various leaders began to fight over the goals and spoils of the revolution.[21] In short, the Maderistas needed to convert the various popular groups into a unified political and military force powerful

[19] *Mexican Herald*, 20 March 1911, p. 3; 26 March 1911, p. 1; RDS, 812.00/831.

[20] British Foreign Office, Public Records Office, London, U.K. (hereafter FO). FO-371-17946, Graham to Hohler, enclosure no. 1, 12 May 1911.

[21] FO-371-1146-8182 no. 22 confidential, Hohler to Grey; FO-204-391-7; RDS, 812.00/1060; RDS, 812.00/831; 812.00/890.

enough to capture the major urban centers, restore peace in the countryside, and guarantee the planting of the next year's crop.

The Laguna's Anti-Reelectionist organization provided a legitimate symbol for unification and the only potential basis for such coordination. From the beginning, the Maderistas divided authority and responsibility for the armed movement between Castro, Ugalde, Pereyra, and Contreras. These groups communicated through couriers and sometimes combined for joint military action. Nonetheless, even with Madero's legitimacy, these leaders commanded no authority beyond the rebel bands and territory under their direct control.

Therefore by March, on the verge of victory, the Laguna's popular movement faced its greatest crisis—consolidation. This required establishing allegiance to a single leader and program from a popular movement that had arisen from a number of different sources for a wide variety of reasons and generated its own popular leadership and following. To understand the unification of the Laguna's popular movement under Madero's leadership, and the subsequent fragmentation of this coalition, one must examine the development of the revolution within four subregions.

Emergence of the Popular Movement

As noted, at least four subregions in the Laguna sustained armed rebellions against the Díaz regime between November 1910 and May 1911. Of these, the populations of Cuencamé, Matamoros, and Viesca had a history of armed conflict with large landowners and the Díaz government. While these provided the spark of resistance, by May popular mobilization was generalized and the 5,000–7,000 rebels who marched on Torreón represented a cross section of the entire region. Nonetheless, the revolt within each subregion assumed a slightly different character.

From December to May the upper river zone in Durango remained a hotbed of revolution with rebel activity concentrating in two areas. To the south, Calixto Contreras and Severino Ceniceros led the movement around Cuencamé, while rebels led by Luis Moya, Martín Triana, and Mariano López Ortiz harassed federal troops from northern Zacatecas to Mapimí. The Contreras–Ceniceros revolt arose from the land and guayule dispute that pitted the large hacienda of Sombreretillo against smallholders of Cuencamé and Indians from San Pedro Ocuila. For them, the 1910 revolt continued their fight to regain the lands taken from them in 1905. In this battle for their lands, the Ocuilans had been led by Contreras and defended by Severino Ceniceros. While the Ocuilan Indians furnished the nucleus of the popular armed revolt around Cuencamé, they also eventually gained support from the "trabajadores eventuales" of small towns and mining centers such as Nazas, Pedriceña, and Velardeña. As Contreras' movement grew, it also recruited popular support from sharecroppers and smallholders from the upper river zone.[22]

In addition to Contreras and Ceniceros, Triana, López Ortiz, and Moya emerged as important leaders in the early revolution. Triana knew the upper river area from his previous employment of cattle buying and selling meat to the local population. Living in Lerdo prior to the revolution, Triana became active in the Anti-Reelectionist movement and rebelled with the Gómez Palacio raiders. Thereafter he commanded a small band which operated in the area between Lerdo and Durango City, interrupting railway and telegraph service, disrupting the work at mines and plantations, and harassing the small towns.

Mariano López Ortiz led a small group of rebels who pursued the same tactics from Durango to southern Chihuahua on the Laguna's western edge. A former assistant police chief in Torreón, López Ortiz became active in the Anti-Reelectionist movement and revolted with the Gómez Palacio group. From December through March his band disrupted railroad services along the Laguna's western boundary and frustrated the government's attempts to defeat them. In March both Triana and López Ortiz began to coordinate their activities with Luis Moya in order to establish total control over the upper river area.

Luis Moya did not revolt in support of Madero until late December but quickly became one of the most successful and popular leaders of the early revolution. A small landowner from Cuencamé, Moya previously worked as a ditch contractor in Tlahualilo and became an early supporter of the Mexican Liberal party (PLM). He was about fifty years old at the time of the revolution and a foreign consul described him as a serious, capable and educated man with good manners and the ability to organize and control his troops. At first, Moya recruited from the Cuencamé area and operated along the Zacatecas–Durango border, just south of the Laguna. After February, Moya expanded his activities northward into the Laguna, gaining support from unemployed agricultural, mining, and guayule work-

[22] Pastor Rouaix, *La revolucíon maderista y constitucionalista en Durango* (México, 1931), pp. 14–15; Sánchez Lamego, *Historia militar*, 209–10.

ers in the upper river area. By late February, Moya established control over much of northern Zacatecas and eastern Durango and sent his lieutenants to recruit the allegiance of other small bands operating from Cuencamé to Mapimí in order to coordinate an attack on Lerdo, Gómez Palacio and Torreón. In April, Moya commanded over five hundred troops and, together with Contreras, emerged as the most influential rebel leader in the upper river zone. Although his committment to broader issues of the revolution seemed clear, Moya's early death in the battle of Durango makes it impossible to know what particular demands he would have made of the revolution.[23]

The activities of Contreras, Ceniceros, Moya, López Ortiz, and Triana converted the Zacatecas–Durango–Coahuila corridor on the Laguna's western boundary into a primary center of rebel strength. Operating in a familar area, rebels proved elusive to federal troops. While Triana and López Ortiz eventually united under Moya's leadership, the Contreras group continued to operate independently. Like the Zapatistas in Morelos, the Contreras–Ceniceros movement gained a reputation for being ferocious in their own district around Cuencamé but uncommitted once outside the zone. While never part of the inner core of Maderista leaders, their early activity greatly furthered the revolution in the Laguna. It is commonly said that Cuencamé produced more revolutionary generals per capita than any other area in Mexico, and the tenacity and success of these early revolutionaries testify to their committment to overthrow the Porfirian system.[24]

In the northern upper river zone, the popular movement sprang directly from the revolt of November 20. Following the retreat of the Gómez Palacio raiders into the Durango hills, Jesús Agustín Castro assumed charge of the revolutionary movement in this area. Although selected as leader of the Gómez Palacio raid, Castro was only twenty-three years old, one of the younger leaders in the early revolution. As a former miner, he knew the mountainous area around Mapimí and Indé better than other zones of the Laguna. Retreating from Gómez Palacio, Castro faced two serious challenges: first, to keep the revolution alive in his zone; and second, to retain leadership and control of the fledgling revolutionary movement throughout the Laguna.[25] Castro and Orestes Pereyra concentrated on sur-

[23] Sánchez Lamego, *Historia militar*, pp. 226–28.

[24] Ibid., pp. 209–14; Rouaix, *Diccionario geográfico*, pp. 14–17.

[25] Sánchez Lamego, *Historia militar*, pp. 137–43.

vival, rebuilding the armed movement, establishing contacts with other bands and asserting their leadership. Unlike most other bands, Castro's group was not native to its zone of operation and did not draw upon local contacts and allegiances to recruit support. In addition, the population of the northern upper river zone lived and worked in a few isolated mining settlements rather than on agricultural properties. Consequently, the pool of temporary workers was smaller in this zone and there were fewer targets to raid for arms, money and supporters. As a result, Castro's campaign was not as initially successful as those of Contreras and Moya.

In mid-February Castro expanded his raiding and recruitment, but by March, his band still numbered only about fifty. Small but well organized, Castro's group began a general campaign of raids in the area surrounding Mapimí, Indé, and far upriver to Nazas. The majority of Castro's support ultimately came from among the miners and temporary workers whose communities fell to his forces. By mid-April, he commanded four hundred soldiers and a series of quick victories at Indé, Mapimí and Nazas provided more recruits; when Castro marched on Torreón in May, he led an army of 1,500.[26]

In late March, Pablo Lavín emerged as a prominent new rebel leader in the upper river zone. The son of one of the region's largest landowners, Lavín rose in arms for unspecified reasons, although many charged opportunism. His band proved effective at disrupting rail traffic and raiding upriver plantations. Operating in the area just west of Gómez Palacio and Lerdo, Lavín's army grew quickly throughout April, recruiting heavily from sharecroppers and temporary agricultural workers. By early May, Lavín led 1,200 rebels and began to coordinate operations with Castro's troops. Although fierce and effective fighters, Lavín's group gained a reputation for unruliness and Lavín's inability to control them. Another early victim of the revolution, Lavín never established his motives and his unpredictable behavior led many to question his revolutionary commitment. Nonetheless, his troops played an important role in the capture of Gómez Palacio and Lerdo.[27]

While diverse in composition, size, and motives, these groups converted the upper river zone into the scene of intense rebel activity between February and April. Operating from the Durango mountains, they proved extremely elusive to federal troops and a constant menace to the mining centers of Velardeña, Pedriceña, and Mapimí,

[26] Ibid.
[27] RDS, 812.00/1968 G. C. Carothers; 26 April, H. L. Wilson from Carothers.

as well as the agricultural properties around Cuencamé, Nazas, Lerdo, and Gómez Palacio. They managed to control most of Durango while also ranging south into Zacatecas and north into Chihuahua. This corridor remained a hotbed of rebel agitation as its diverse population of Indians, sharecroppers, smallholders, miners, temporary workers, and resident plantation workers consistently provided popular support for the revolution.

In the middle and lower river zones of Coahuila, the popular movement assumed a dual character. Around Matamoros and Viesca, popular mobilization sprang from the local revolts of temporary workers, sharecroppers, and smallholders whose fighting contributed a great deal to the revolution's victory. In contrast, the impetus for popular mobilization of the agricultural population around Tlahualilo and San Pedro came from revolutionary activity outside the area.[28]

Matamoros emerged as a principal center of revolt. This propensity to rebel can be attributed to three factors: the long-standing dispute of the smallholders and sharecroppers with the region's large landowners; the economic and political losses resulting from the growth of Torreón and expansion of agriculture in the middle river zone; and the local support for the Anti-Reelectionists and the PLM. Because Matamoros was a collecting point for temporary workers, many planters considered it a haven for social undesirables. In times of drought or severe unemployment, small bandit groups always seemed to spring up in the area between Matamoros and Viesca, hiding in the mountains and raiding the countryside. Only with the PLM raid on Viesca in 1908 did this activity take on a specifically political character. By 1910 there was an active Anti-Reelectionist movement, which published a newspaper, *La Lucha*. Like Cuencamé, Matamoros achieved renown for producing a number of prominent revolutionaries, of whom Sixto Ugalde was among the Gómez Palacio rebels, while others revolted in Matamoros and battled soldiers to the south of town.[29]

Despite this early activity around Matamoros, major popular mobilization did not take place until late January. From December on, several small groups operated out of the hills south of Matamoros, raiding outlying ranches, cutting telegraph lines, interrupting rail service and harassing federal troops. Nonetheless, the popular

[28] *Mexican Herald*, 28 June 1908, p. 1; FO-371-480-24855, 18 July 1908; FO-371-480-25096, 8 July 1908, Howard to Grey; *Mexican Herald*, 2 July 1908, p. 1.

[29] FO-371-1146-8187 no. 20, 15 Feb. 1911, Hohler to Grey; *Mexican Herald*, 21 Feb. 1911, p. 2.

movement did not begin to grow until the end of the harvest season. Among the area's most prominent rebel leaders were Enrique Adame Macías and Benjamín Argumedo. Adame Macías originally revolted in San Pedro de las Colonias but moved southward to take advantage of refuge provided by the mountains near Matamoros, and Viesca. From early on, Adame Macías claimed the legitimacy of the Madero movement in recruiting support.

The career of Argumedo provides insight into the nature of leadership and the popular movement that emerged in the Matamoros–Viesca area. A tailor by trade, Argumedo joined the rebellion in January and quickly established a reputation for his daring, popularity, and skill. Argumedo's band operated independently, struck frequently and unpredictably at railroad lines and federal troops, and earned Argumedo the title, "lion of the Laguna." Within a few months his fame and popularity eclipsed that of his ostensible leader, Adame Macías. The emergence of such independent popular leadership and the high level of rebel activity not only damaged the government's declining prestige but ultimately posed serious problems for unification of the Madero movement.

Assigned responsibility for the Matamoros, Viesca, and San Pedro zone, Sixto Ugalde arrived around Matamoros in mid-January and found several small rebel groups in action. Their success and the end of the cotton harvest brought new recruits from among the guayule cutters, temporary workers, and smallholders. By February, the countryside around Matamoros was reportedly "infested with insurrectos," a fact not entirely reassuring to Ugalde who, despite his local ties, found it difficult to organize or contain the diverse bands operating in the zone. While elusive to the federales, the rebels also challenged any central control.

Through couriers and meetings Ugalde began to assert his nominal control over the rebel movement in order to coordinate a major offensive for February. On February 9, Ugalde, Gregorio García and Adame Macías staged a bold attack on Matamoros, occupied the town for several hours, destroyed government offices, released prisoners from jail, and stole arms and money. This proved a major blow to government prestige and a boost for the rebels' cause. Continued railroad disruptions and growing fear prompted property owners to shut down their plantations, allowing the rebels to recruit from the unemployed workers.

The story was similar around Viesca, another area in which Ugalde was charged with coordinating popular support for the Maderista cause. Viesca too had a reputation for producing revolts. Located in the Laguna's southeast corner, it was a free settlement which attracted a large, mobile population of temporary workers in agriculture, mining and guayule. Outside the landowners' direct control, Viesca provided workers an opportunity to drink, gamble, sell stolen cotton or guayule, and talk while they waited for new employment. When the employment situation was tough in the Laguna, things were toughest in Viesca. The Mexican Liberal party became active in the area and in 1908 staged a raid on the town that threatened the entire region with the prospect of a mass revolt of the unemployed.

The PLM raid sparked no general revolt, but the arrest, imprisonment, and hanging of numerous "supposed" conspirators increased popular dislike for the arbitrary rule and persecution by government authorities and large landowners. Predictably, landowners and officials considered Viesca a haven for troublemakers, a fact confirmed to them when rebel bands sprang up in the area after November 20. As in 1908, however, no significant uprising followed and the government quickly declared the situation under control.[30]

As with Matamoros, the revolution around Viesca gained momentum with the end of the harvest, the beginning of winter, and increasing unemployment. By mid-February, newspapers reported numerous bands of fifteen to twenty rebels operating in the Viesca area. Again, while they employed the same tactics, the groups did not coordinate their activities, respect one another's territory or claim any common allegiance or goal. After March, a consular official reported the Matamoros–Viesca zone to be infested with these small bands that "controlled no territory and set up no governments," but consistently raided plantations and small towns, disrupted railroads, and recruited among the unemployed. Estimations of their number grew from fifty in December to 1,500 in March. Where did this support come from? As in the Matamoros area, the popular mobilization drew from temporary workers, sharecroppers and smallholders who lived around Viesca, Gitla, and Buenavista. Leadership remained popular at all stages and the Viesca rebels became known for their boldness and tenacity. Throughout the revolution, Matamoros and Viesca bands remained the most spontaneous and refractory of the Laguna's "insurrectos." Although they eventually united, if briefly, behind Ugalde and Maderismo, neither Ugalde nor Madero ever proved capable of controlling them.[31]

[30] *Mexican Herald*, 21 Feb. 1911, p. 2.

[31] FO-371-1146-8189 no. 22, confidential, Hohler to Grey, 6 March 1911; RDS, 812.00/1437, 13 April 1911; Sánchez Lamego, *Historia militar*, pp. 143–44, 210–11.

Again, the career of Benjamín Argumedo reflects the spirit of the area's rebels. Fighting throughout the revolution, Argumedo first supported the Maderistas, became disillusioned and joined the Orozquistas, later merged with the Huertistas, and finally ended up under the Zapatista and Conventionist banner. He died in 1916 fighting against the Carrancistas and trying to establish contacts with his former comrade in arms and enemy, Pancho Villa. To the people of Matamoros and Viesca, Argumedo never betrayed the revolution.

In contrast to these local and sustained popular revolts, the revolutionary movement that emerged around Tlahualilo and San Pedro came from outside the area. At Tlahualilo, the popular revolt spilled over from the revolutionary movements led by Castro and Pereyra in northeastern Durango and the activity of Ugalde around Matamoros. Tlahualilo experienced sporadic raids of small groups following the Gómez Palacio attack, but no spontaneous and sustained popular rebellion emerged. Conditions returned to normal very quickly; planters did not request extra military protection and disbanded the private guards they had recruited.

Although Orestes Pereyra received responsibility for the revolutionary movement around Tlahualilo, he had not recruited support there prior to November and remained in the Durango hills with Castro in the weeks following the Gómez Palacio raid. Beginning in mid-December, planters in the Tlahualilo area complained of attacks by Sixto Ugalde and Gregorio García. While the rebels launched a general offensive throughout the Laguna in February, Pereyra and Castro did not venture into the Tlahualilo zone until late in that month. Rebel groups from the Matamoros–Viesca area staged sporadic raids into the zone but business continued as usual on most plantations until April. In short, the Tlahualilo area remained quiet while the popular movement gained momentum in the upper river zone of Durango and around Matamoros and Viesca. Anticipating the drive on Torreón and seeking to establish control of the countryside and the crop, in April, Sixto Ugalde moved northward and Orestes Pereyra moved eastward to transplant the revolution into the Tlahualilo area. By this time, the revolutionary movement had begun to take a definite shape and organization. According to one report, when the rebels arrived at Tlahualilo in early April, they "were well behaved and under control of their leaders. Coming into Zaragoza they called all the laborers that were in the fields and formed them in military order, and marched them into town. They were looking for Cecilio González, the administrator and mayor domo of Zaragoza."[32]

These tactics furthered rebel recruitment by convincing staffs of plantations and government officials to abandon the countryside. After April, the rebellion reportedly "grew very rapidly; the number of bands is increasing and the separate bands are increasing in size."[33] By May there were a thousand rebels around Tlahualilo, mostly recruited from large plantations of the middle river area. Although the Tlahualilo area eventually produced significant peasant movements, the November–May revolution generated no important indigenous popular revolt or leaders. The movement was led by transplants.

The same situation existed around San Pedro de las Colonias. While San Pedro was Madero's home, his call for revolution and the Gómez Palacio raid failed to generate any important revolts or leaders who were not close friends or members of the Madero family. Enrique Adame Macías rebelled on November 20 in San Pedro but quickly shifted his zone of operation south to the Matamoros and Viesca area. Although restless, workers remained in the fields around San Pedro and planters prevented uprisings by increasing the number of spies and guards in the fields and expanding their rural police force.

The San Pedro area remained calm until the end of March when rebels from the Viesca–Matamoros area began raids into the zone. Finally, in late April, Sixto Ugalde's rebel army captured San Pedro. It is possible that rebels had not previously attacked San Pedro because several members of Madero's family remained in the city. In fact, Ugalde's army never actually attacked San Pedro. With the approach of the rebel forces, Emilio Madero, Francisco's brother, negotiated the federals' withdrawal. Led by Sixto Ugalde, the rebels occupied the town, released prisoners from the jail, and began recruiting among agricultural workers. Once in control of the area, Ugalde's forces grew from four hundred to one thousand in a week.[34]

Madero's Dilemma

As we have seen, from November until February, numerous revolutionary groups survived and grew by operating independently, with-

---

[32] RDS, 812.00/1437, 13 April 1911, J. B. Potter.
[33] RDS, 812.00/1514, 19 April 1911, J. B. Potter.
[34] RDS, 812.00/1968, 26 April 1911, G. C. Carothers to H. L. Wilson.

out obligating themselves to any leaders or beliefs more specific than bringing down the government. From mid-February until May, the original Gómez Palacio leaders worked to gain control and allegiance of these various popular groups whose activity was quickly gaining the momentum to overthrow Díaz. Madero apparently had no idea of the popular movement's success in the Laguna until March or early April. While providing a great boost to the Maderistas, the popular rebellion needed direction and control to succeed. Otherwise, it might fragment, breaking into elements of Magonistas, Reyistas, Maderistas or any number of different independent groups representing local leaders and zones.

Significantly, the largest threat the Maderistas faced involved the Laguna's economic well-being. As the revolutionaries gained control of the countryside and owners abandoned their plantations, it became clear that a quick end to the fighting was needed to prevent the revolution from disrupting the planting season. If the crop were not planted in April or May, the entire region would face economic and social disaster, rendering even a Madero victory meaningless. Just as the rebels had taken advantage of the end of the harvest and disruption of the economy to recruit unemployed workers, they now had to worry about pacifying the countryside and returning workers to the fields. In this situation, unification of the revolutionary movement became critical both to ensure the overthrow of Díaz and also restore the region's economy.

Establishing this unity was a delicate process. To forge a revolutionary alliance, the Maderistas had little more to offer than the legitimacy of Madero and the Anti-Reelectionist movement, leadership in the Gómez Palacio raid and their continuing efforts to overthrow Díaz. For the various rebel groups, it was one thing to claim to be a Maderista, but quite another to subordinate oneself to Maderista military leadership, possibly risking one's troops and popular legitimacy. On the other hand, the Maderista leadership was powerless if rebel leaders refused to cooperate, since no one wanted to provoke warfare within the popular movement.

Concerning specific issues, Maderista leaders were in no position to offer promises or concessions for support, even though they took advantage of the promises implicit in Díaz' overthrow. The revolution clearly meant different things to different people but there were neither the means nor demand for a convention to draft a program acceptable to all groups. The potential for success obscured the outcome of victory, and Madero served as a convenient unifying symbol in the struggle to oust Díaz. The promise of that goal, coupled with the excitement of seeing the federales in retreat, provided the principal incentive to unite rebel groups under Maderista leadership. To most rebels, Maderismo meant change and its leadership emphasized this collective goal to control the popular movement.[35]

In March and April, rebel groups began the first clear coordination of activity at the local level in order to capture towns and mining areas. Unification of these groups under specific military goals produced few problems. Most rebels eventually acknowledged Madero as the movement's general leader and accepted the direction of the Maderista military chiefs. Again, the upper river zone took the lead and by the end of March, Moya's and Contreras's troops were in a position to take Lerdo and Gómez Palacio. By mid-April, the specter of increased rebel strength and the army's ineffectiveness convinced most landowners to abandon their properties and, along with government officials, to desert the countryside for the cities. At the end of April, Matamoros, Viesca, San Pedro, Velardeña, Mapimí, Lerdo, Nazas, and Gómez Palacio fell to rebel forces. In most cases, former Anti-Reelectionist candidates or prominent Madero supporters assumed offices vacated by Porfirian authorities. In general, revolutionary troops remained orderly and obedient to their leaders. Only two problems arose: in San Pedro, of Sixto Ugalde's troops rioted briefly to protest a food shortage; in Lerdo, a dispute between the two leaders of the occupying forces, Pedro Lavín and Juan Ramírez, led to a battle between their soldiers and Lavín's strange request for federal troops from Torreón to quell the riot. Otherwise, rebel troops sought to establish order in the countryside and attempted to arrange payroll and supply shipments to keep properties operating and the agricultural workers employed. In late April, the rebels began supplying guards to some plantations to protect against bandit raids, while Gregorio García began an inspection tour of the Tlahualilo area to make sure that work was returning to normal.[36]

For most rebels, the sudden demand to be administrators and protectors of rural interests was a new role. Having practiced destruction during the previous few months, they suddenly found themselves charged with keeping the economy moving, guaranteeing production, and avoiding social chaos in the areas they controlled. This increased the importance of capturing Torreón, the governments' last outpost in the Laguna, and restoring rail communication.

[35] FO-371-17946, Graham to Hohler, enclosure no. 1, 12 May 1911.

[36] RDS, 812.00/1968 from Carothers; *Mexican Herald*, 1 May 1911, p. 3; RDS, 812.00/1998, 6 May 1911, J. P. Conduit to J. B. Potter.

By late April, most planters and their staffs were boxed up in Torreón to protect themselves from what they considered rebel hordes. Rebel leaders suddenly found they needed the private sector's cooperation to administer the countryside and begin the planting for next season.

On May 1, U.S. Consul George Carothers wrote that the only factor preventing an attack on Torreón was the absence of "any revolutionary leader strong enough to unite the different bands."[37] In fact, the move on Torreón required the unification of the popular movement under one military leader, the first time that had been necessary since November 20. With 5,000 to 7,000 thousand men in arms and several different popular leaders, the selection process was too important and politically sensitive to be left to popular choice. Again, the Maderista organizational framework prevailed and by May 9 all the principal rebel groups in the region accepted Castro's leadership and planning began for the assault on Torreón. Castro sent directives to rebel leaders throughout the region to begin moving on Torreón in a coordinated mass attack. While Castro's choice was not popular with all groups, even prominent contenders for this leadership such as Moya and Contreras acceded to his leadership for the sake of a concentrated drive on Torreón. After holding out briefly, Pablo Lavín also mobilized his troops for the attack. Despite differences, the momentum of victory and the need to plant the crop dictated unity.[38]

By May 12, between 5,000 and 7,000 insurrectos surrounded Torreón, consisting primarily of four major rebel contingents: from the northeast, Orestes Pereyra with over 1,000 troops; from the east and southeast, Sixto Ugalde and Enrique Adame Macías with more than 2,000 troops; to the south and southwest, Benjamín Argumedo leading 1,000 rebels; and from the northwest, Jesús Agustín Castro and 1,200 mounted soldiers. The city's subsequent capture indicated the lack of coordination that plagued the rebel coalition. Although expected, the troops of Contreras and Lavín apparently never appeared. Castro's orders called for the attack on Sunday, but Benjamín Argumedo and his group from Matamoros decided to attack the city on Saturday morning.

Argumedo's attack and Contreras' slow mobilization angered Castro, and at nightfall on May 12 his troops moved in to capture the electric plant and black out the city. Fighting continued into Sunday

---

[37] RDS, 812.00/1588, 2 May 1911, Carothers.
[38] Ibid., RDS, 812.00/1968, 11 May 1911; RDS., 812.00/2026, 13 May 1911.

and, by the afternoon, rebels controlled the city's outskirts. That night, during a rainstorm, the federal army abandoned Torreón. The next morning, rebels charged into an undefended city and, at last, the entire Laguna was in the hands of its peasants and workers. In triumph, the rebel movement stood one step away from achieving the primary goal that had united it until that point.[39]

The events that followed the rebel capture of Torreón dramatically underscore the acute social and economic tensions produced by the region's rapid development. Upon entering the undefended city at dawn, the rebels immediately went to the jail and liberated the prisoners. As revolutionary troops began pouring into the city, and a popular riot broke out: "the pandemonium on the streets was beyond any description. Shouting, yelling and the most promiscuous shooting in the air with rifles, revolvers by the crazy masses surging through the streets."[40] Joined by a city mob estimated at 10,000, rebel forces began to loot the stores and attack banks and public buildings before turning on the city's Chinese population. Within the next few hours more than two hundred Chinese died. The killing and looting stopped about 11 a.m. when Emilio Madero and Jesús Agustín Castro arrived along with other Maderista leaders and took charge of the situation. Declaring martial law, Madero issued a proclamation ordering the rebels to stop killing and looting under penalty of death. He also demanded the return of stolen goods within twenty-four hours. By evening, order was restored and the next day the return of stolen goods began. Maderista authorities declared that anyone found in the possession of stolen property after forty-eight hours would be shot. The city remained well patrolled and absolute order prevailed. By afternoon, all groups had agreed to the armistice declared between Madero and the federal government. On May 23, a report announced that "the news of Díaz' resignation brings momentary quiet."[41]

The Fragmentation of Maderismo

When Emilio Madero assumed control of the Laguna, he confronted two major tasks necessary to stabilize the region. First, he had to reestablish rail communication, secure food and fuel for the population and somehow restore the war-torn economy. Hunger and unemployment, which two months earlier had aided the Maderista

[39] Ibid., RDS, 812.00/1998, 14 May 1911; 812.00/1968 15 May 1911.
[40] RDS, 812.00/2026, 15 May 1911.
[41] RDS, 812.00/2005, 23 May 1911.

cause, now threatened it. Madero's second problem proved equally pressing: pacification of the popular movement that had just secured the Maderista victory.

The retreat of the federal army and government officials left the Laguna totally in the hands of Maderista officials and the popular army, the Second Division of the North. Of the revolutionary leaders, Castro, Pereyra, Ugalde and García were named regiment colonels. By then, these Maderista officials were well known to the region's elite, but the presence of lesser leaders and the rebel army did not comfort the planters and industrialists. Propertied interests cooperated with Emilio Madero because they realized his critical role in establishing and maintaining order. Nonetheless, as the U.S. consul noted, "the presence of a large body of armed and undisciplined men is naturally dangerous." Furthermore, many urban residents and planters considered it an "open question whether leaders of the Maderista movement will be able to control their own forces and the people at large and whether the various leaders will continue to recognize any central authority."[42] Confronted with an occupying army of "armed peons," many considered the situation "more dangerous now than ever as any slight or unforeseen incident is apt to throw the region into anarchy."[43]

For these reasons, the Laguna's propertied interests repeatedly urged Madero to bring back the federal army to guarantee their protection from the rebels. Realizing the danger in mixing these former enemies, Madero worked to stabilize the region and peacefully to demobilize the rebel army in order to calm the fears of the elite.

This proved difficult, as British Vice-Consul Cunard Cummins observed:

> Madero found the work of disarming and preserving order to be one requiring all his best efforts. [Madero had] to convince [the rebels] that this change was for their benefit . . . and so peace required them to surrender their weapons and retire to subservient walks of life. . . . His difficulties were increased by promises which had been made to the men, as inducements to enroll, by the lesser leaders; certain hours of looting, future large increases in wages, apportionment of lands and other impossible benefits were not considered to be too extravagant, or improper

---

[42] RDS, 812.00/2005, Conditions Torreón and Tlahualilo, letter from J. B. Potter.
[43] FO-204-392-20, Cummins to Hohler, inclosure in Mr. Hohler's dispatch no. 166 of 17 July. "Report by Mr. Vice Consul Cummins on the recent and present political situation in the Laguna district," pp. 2–3.

assurances when men were needed. Mr. Madero and his lieutenants have not found it easy to satisfactorily explain the non-
compliance nor why further patience must be exercised in these
matters; the rank and file are feeling that the only real vestige of
these promises is the resentment that nonfulfillment has left in
their minds. Many state that they are the victims of deception
and injustice.

As Cummins saw it, many of the former rebels did not

view with favor the prospects presented by exchanging the saddle for a furrow in the field and the rifle for a hoe. . . . The life
of the 'insurrecto' during the last few months, with horse, gun
and license flattering unduly his self importance, has not been
unpleasing and many of the men feel that it cannot be relin-
quished willingly nor its allurements withstood, especially as
the alternative offers drudgery and 50 cents per day, with little
outlet for the grosser inclination.

In short, Madero's demobilization returned workers to the same, if
not worse, conditions against which they had rebelled a few months
earlier. While the elite conceded that Madero had "applied himself
unsparingly to solve the difficulties of the situation . . . however,
good results have not shown themselves as quickly as many anticipated and disorder continues."[44] To demobilize the rebel army,
Madero required soldiers to turn in their arms, paying each of them
twenty to fifty dollars but allowing them to keep their horses "until
the future proves that they will not again be needed on the warpath."[45]

By June, Emilio Madero had demobilized 4,000 members of the
army that had marched on Torreón. Preserving the peace was left to
the 1,500 remaining soldiers of the Second Division of the North
who formed batallions of 300 men under Contreras, Ugalde, García,
Pereyra, and Castro. Local observers claimed that many of the "pacified" rebels were secretly retaining their arms and slipping quietly
back to the countryside. Moreover, Cummins charged that "Many of
those who have returned to the haciendas do not appear to have
done so from a desire to work, so much as from a determination to
spread discontent and endeavour to secure, for all, increased pay

[44] Ibid., p. 4.
[45] Ibid.

and short hours, conditions which were promised when they agreed to support the cause."[46]

In June a wave of strikes swept the region. Railway and industrial workers of Torreón and Gómez Palacio struck for higher wages and shorter hours. On the plantations, owners and administrators complained that "demobilized Maderistas are fomenting discontent among the labourers."[47] By late June, reports circulated of rebel bands again operating in the countryside. Rather than "viva Madero," the cry to revolution was now "viva Magón." In Durango and Coahuila, "Magonistas" reportedly offered recruits five pesos per day and the promise of twenty acres of land to join the new revolution.[48]

As rural violence flared, the Maderista forces found themselves fighting against their former comrades. As Cummins observed, "the steadiest men among the Maderistas cannot with safety be put to test against their present or late brothers-in-arms." The government realized that "to send Federal troops to exercise control would be to invite fighting." In an attempt to resolve this problem, Emilio Madero began to form "an independent corps composed of trustworthy men who refused to take part in the revolution; $1.50 per day is being offered to those who will join the ranks; the purpose of this body is to patrol the haciendas and ranches where many disorders and some casualties have occurred and are yet attracting attention to the laborers of these parts, who, formidable in numbers, have many rebelliously inclined paid-off Maderistas among them."[49]

In July plantation workers struck throughout the Laguna, making a variety of demands ranging from better wages and shorter hours to land distribution. Around Cuencamé landowners complained that "quite a number of haciendas have been taken possession of by the working class, who claim that as the Maderistas won they have the right to take, and are, in fact owners of the land." Furthermore, much to the chagrin of the landowners, Calixto Contreras took over the military arm of the Durango government and refused to stop the peasants' land occupation.[50]

Labor unrest also hit the mining communities and major industries. On July 2, 11,000 workers struck the mines and smelter in Mapimí, demanding wage increases of 30–100 percent. Newspapers

[46] Ibid., p. 5.
[47] Ibid.
[48] *Mexican Herald*, 17 July 1911, p. 2, "Magonistas in Durango."
[49] Ibid., p. 10.
[50] RDS, 812.00/2265, 30 July, 1911, "Conditions in Durango."

proclaimed this the largest strike in Mexico's history and noted that "among the strikers are quite a large number of discharged Maderistas who retained their arms."[51]

Maderista officials attributed this unrest to "non-working agitators, whose appeals to workers are both socialistic and anarchistic."[52] Still, as Cummins charged of the Maderista response,

> expected precautionary measures to avoid [the strike] were not taken by authorities because Mr. Madero refused to place restraint on the agitators, reasoning that 'Mexico is a free country now where those who wish to agitate may do so with every liberty, so long as they do not violate the law.' Later, the position became so threatening that it was deemed advisable to make some concessions which, aided by diplomacy and some armed demonstration, averted further trouble for the moment.[53]

In this situation, the elite's support for the Madero administration began to waver; reportedly, they realized that "continuation of disturbances is bound to interfere seriously with the general prosperity of the country, not only preventing capital to embark in new enterprises but also by hampering operations already going, especially by creating unrest in the labouring populations."[54]

As tensions increased, Emilio Madero cautioned patience and warned of the danger of violence between the region's "armed poor and its defenseless rich."[55] Rumors circulated that General Bravo, the former "harsh ruler in Quintana Roo," was to take charge of the Laguna's military zono, but despite pressure from the local establishment, Madero still refused to call in the federal army. In late July he declared "no federales will come to Torreón in the near future."[56] Then, much to the dismay of the Laguna's business community, Madero was called to Mexico City.

In late July and early August industrial workers called for a general strike, demanding increased wages. Over 20,000 workers, including "a large number of discharged Maderistas," participated in the strike that ranged throughout the countryside and towns. Again, the elite blamed the unrest on "obstreperous labourers," outside ag-

[51] *Mexican Herald*, 2 July 1911, p. 1, "Strike in Mapimí."

[52] FO-204-392-20, Cummins to Hohler, 17 July 1911, p. 5.

[53] Ibid., p. 10.

[54] Ibid., p. 7.

[55] Ibid.

[56] *Mexican Herald*, 29 July 1911, p. 3.

itators and "Maderista soldiers who lack discipline and sympathise with the masses."[57]

The threat of trouble from "outside agitators" prompted Torreón officials to postpone the September 16 Independence Day celebrations. Among the most prominent of the agitators was Lázaro Guitérrez de Lara, "the Spanish socialist who created a sensation in the U.S. by his identifications with the article on 'Barbarous Mexico.' "[58] Gutiérrez de Lara arrived in the Laguna in late July and by early August he was behind bars in Torreón. His crime, apparently, was that he "openly insulted the President of the U.S., the Emperor of Germany, the King of Spain, the Emperor of Russia, the Mexican Federal Army and the local authorities."[59]

The labor unrest that spread throughout the Laguna in August and September represented substantial popular discontent. According to the *Mexican Herald*,

> Interest in labor matters in this section is increasing and the result of the late agitation has been the organization of numerous working societies. In Gómez Palacio the propaganda has been carried on with great activity and scarcely a week passes that does not see from one to three street parades with the workmen bearing all kinds of banners. But the most alarming feature of the agitation is apparently on the ranches in the Laguna district where a number of organizers of the ilk of Lara, the jailed socialist and columinator of monarchs and capital, have been preaching socialistic doctrines to thousands of peons and cotton pickers, telling them they should demand higher wages and organizing societies to which dues and other obligations are attached. What becomes of the money thus collected is not known after it passes into the hands of the officers of the societies.[60]

"Magonismo" received most of the blame for popular unrest. Madero charged that the Magonistas were "plotting to overthrow the government with the object of placing the Magonista party in power." In early August, the *Mexican Herald* reported, "Another Magonista Jailed in Torreón: That the Magonistas are attempting to incite the people of this district to revolt was shown today by documentation found on J. M. García, arrested as he alighted from his

[57] FO-204-392-20, Cummins to Hohler, 17 July 1911, p. 7.
[58] RDS, 812.00/2314, 4 Aug. 1911, "Lázaro Gutiérrez de Lara, Socialist in Torreón."
[59] RDS, 812.00/2314, 21 Aug. 1911, "Socialist Meeting in Torreón," Carothers to H. L. Wilson.
[60] *Mexican Herald*, 4 Sept. 1911, p. 10, "Labor Agitation in Laguna District."

train. One of the papers was a manifesto urging the people to rise in another revolution."[61] Cummins lamented the "absence of any authentic news," but reported that "it is generally said that bands of Magonistas are gathering in the Laguna district. If such banding together is taking place, it remains to be seen by whom, or by what party, these people are inspired and what is the extent of their aims. Rumors are heard of fights in which the Maderistas were routed."[62]

In September, the Maderista officials finally gave in and requested federal troops to garrison Torreón and help control the situation in the Laguna. The Maderista soldiers were moved to Gómez Palacio and Lerdo to avoid confrontrations between federal soldiers and revolutionaries. Despite these efforts, conflicts between the federal soldiers and the Maderista army further heightened social tensions. When a thousand federal troops, including artillery, cavalry, and infantry arrived in Torreón, the U.S. Consul Freeman wrote the "foreigners were elated" and "a general feeling of confidence and security prevailed." As for the "lower classes," they "have expressed dissatisfaction but they are not now considered dangerous." Freeman continued, "My opinion is that there is no danger to be expected so long as troops remain in Torreón."[63]

The British saw it differently. Cummins remarked that the Maderista soldiers sent to Gómez Palacio and Lerdo "resented their removal and the introduction of Federals into Torreón," and that "trouble may be expected unless the federal troops are well handled." Rumors circulated that a "counter-revolutionary movement of some description is being plotted in Lerdo."[64]

Propertied interests in both the U.S. and Mexico complained of Madero's too lenient handling of dissidents. After complaining of the Madero government, Cummins wrote "I may remark that my statements and opinions regarding the lack of punishment are approved and supported by, probably all, unbiased people. Mr. Emilio Madero confidentially indicated to me recently that apart from his conscientious scruples, his political policy cannot include at this time harsh treatment."[65]

Torn between the propertied classes and the revolutionary soldiers, the Madero government seemed unable to please anyone. While Madero had triumphed due to the support of the popular

[61] *Mexican Herald*, 9 Aug. 1911, p. 1, "Another Magonista Jailed in Torreón."
[62] FO-204-392-20, Cummins to Hohler, 17 July 1911, p. 9.
[63] RDS, 812.00/2340, 9 Sept. 1911, Freeman on troop arrival.
[64] FO-204-392-205, 10 Sept. 1911, Cummins to Stringer.
[65] FO-204-392-20, 17 July 1911, Cummins to Hohler, p. 8.

movement, reports now stated that disaffected Maderista soldiers were taking to the hills and forming bandit groups. Last year's revolutionaries became this year's bandits. In pursuing the rebel soldiers, Jesús Agustín Castro was wounded and the son of Orestes Pereyra killed. Cummins noted that "indications are not wanting that Mr. Fransisco I. Madero's popularity and hold upon public imagination will soon show definite signs of waning in these parts." By late November, Torreón and Gómez Palacio were filled with 10,000 strikers yelling "muera Madero," while in the hills, the so-called "bandit groups" held their own against the Maderista and federal armies, respectively their former allies and former enemies. By the revolution's first anniversary, the fragmentation of the Laguna's popular movement was complete. It would not unify again until 1936.[66]

[66] RDS, 812.00/2346, 8 Sept. 1911, "Strikes in Laguna."

CHAPTER SIXTEEN

Peasants and the Shaping of the Revolutionary State, 1910–40

Hans Werner Tobler

> The Federal Army is the greatest enemy the peasant has
> . . . In fact, the only thing 'national' about the army is its
> name, and the fact that it is unjustly supported by the re-
> sources of the whole nation; and I say this because invar-
> iably I have seen it take the side of the rich, protecting
> their lives and their interests, even if the latter are without
> legitimation; rendering them whatever services suits
> them; while at the same time shamelessly antagonizing or
> persecuting the poor peasants who form the immense ma-
> jority of the Nation. The Army, in fact, although the law
> says the opposite, is not national, but of one social class:
> that of the rich. . . . In short, the exploiter, the landowner
> and the rich, in general, have found an admirable and un-
> conditional defender of their interests and an excellent in-
> terpreter of their rancors in the Federal Army.[1]

This account was not taken—as one might suspect at first glance—
from the period of the prerevolutionary ancien régime of Porfirio
Díaz. It refers instead to a bloody agrarian conflict that took place
during the mid-1920s in the state of Veracruz at a time when the old
Porfirista army had long been replaced by the constitutionalist revolutionary troops; when the Sonoran revolutionary regime was

---

[1] Report from the engineer Jorge Vizcaíno to the Comisión Nacional Agraria (CNA)
delegate in Veracruz, dated September 4, 1925, Archivo General de la Nación, Ramo
Obregón–Calles, paquete 112, legajo 6, expediente 818-v–3 (henceforth AGN, O-C, 112/
6, 818-v-3).

firmly established; and when the demands for agrarian reform had
been officially accepted in the 1917 constitution and in the corresponding legislation.

In this situation, then, how could the army of the revolution—one
that until recently has often been considered primarily a peasant rebellion and an agrarian revolution—be the principal ally of the
"rich" and of the big landowners? How could it attack the campesinos, who had provided large contingents of the former rebel troops
and were, according to the official program, to be among the principal beneficiaries of the Revolution?

The question raises a basic problem in the history of the Mexican
revolution, a problem that Friedrich Katz stresses in Chapter 1.
What was the relationship between peasant and nonpeasant groups
in the revolutionary movement? Or to be more exact, to what degree
were members of the middle and upper classes successful in mobilizing peasant groups for their own ends and in controlling them
effectively for a long period? This problem will be central in the
following: it can be clearly illustrated in the example of the creation
and transformation of the great revolutionary armies on the one
hand, and on the other in the relations between peasants and the
state during the late stabilizing phase of the revolution between
1920 and 1940.

For that reason, we first study the role of the army, the central
organ of the revolution until 1917, and the principal factor of national power until the end of the 1920s. Such an examination reveals the army's growing animosity toward the peasants during the
agrarian reform of the 1920s and the early 1930s. I will also list some
factors that may explain the behavior of the new federal army,
which at first glance seems paradoxical in view of its popular origin
in the troops of the revolution.

The same question of the relation between campesinos and nonpeasant elites, in a more general form, is also the central theme of
the second section. What was the role of the peasants in the formation of the new state that resulted from the revolution? In the case
of Mexico, as in other great revolutions of the twentieth century, the
contribution of peasants to the defeat of the ancien régime was substantial. However, in contrast to events in Russia or China, the seizure of political power in Mexico was not immediately followed by
a wide redistribution of land, a truly revolutionary agrarian reform.

What form did the relationship between the peasants and the state
assume in Mexico? Depending on its momentary strength or weakness, the state either sought the support of the peasants, or else be-

lieved it could do without it. This resulted not only in changing phases in the agrarian policies of the state, which were sometimes in favor of reform, sometimes opposed to it, but also in pre-Cardenist agrarian reforms that varied widely in their regional aspects according to whether they were imposed from below by highly active and committed peasantry, as in Morelos, or were initiated by peasant organizations "from above" (as for example in Veracruz), or were prevented altogether until the presidency of Cárdenas by peasant passivity and the hostility of the governments to the ejidos.

The third section is principally concerned with the conflict-ridden progress of agrarian reform in the 1920s and 1930s that resulted from this situation. The pre-Cárdenas land reform engendered, in effect, a new form of agrarian conflict that differed in many respects from the prerevolutionary and revolutionary peasant rebellions. Here we are not dealing with peasant rebellions as such, but with widespread and often violent conflicts over land possession. These struggles assumed no national character, but remained limited to a given region, in most cases at village level. Nonetheless, evaluation of the relevant sources yields the impression of long underground warfare between the peasants and the landowners. To explain these conflicts it will be necessary to look briefly not only at the role of the peasants, but also at that of the old landowning class, whose economic position was still almost intact, as well as at that of the new revolutionary elite rapidly rising to economic prosperity.

In the final section, some comments are made on Cárdenas' agrarian reform, which, despite a delay of nearly twenty years, led to profound structural changes in the Mexican agrarian system.

The Peasants and the Revolutionary Army

The army's hostile attitude toward agrarian reform in the 1920s and early 1930s is one of the paradoxical results of the revolution. The role of the postrevolutionary army was probably of greater importance than that of the old *federales* during the *pax Porfiriana*, since Porfirian social stability had in fact been shaken by the political and social ferment set up by the revolution.

This contradictory streak in the revolution during the 1920s did not escape discerning observers. The engineer Jorge Vizcaíno, for instance, who was familiar with agrarian problems in the state of Veracruz, pointed out in an informative report on his work for the local agrarian commission that the peasants "are at the mercy of the tyranny and arbitrariness that are now no longer directly exercised by

the landowners, but through the intermedium of the military."[2] Another critic of the army—himself a revolutionary general—under-
lined this contradiction, pointing out the anti-agrarian attitude demonstrated by the troops in Jalisco: "I ask guarantees for the
inhabitants and especially for the communities which are the victims of innumerable attacks by landowners, who are protected by
the military authorities in a much worse way than during the time
of General Díaz."[3] In this section I present some of the principal factors that may explain this conversion of a revolutionary army of
popular origin, with numerically strong peasant contingents, into
one of the principal allies of the old landholding class.

First, a distinction must be made between the Zapatista army of
the south and the revolutionary armies of the north. The Zapatista
army preserved the essence of both its peasant identity and its agrarian orientation to the end because of the specific regional context of
the movement, especially its social homogeneity, its strong local
roots, its lack of political contacts with the U.S., and in particular
the absence of commercial relations with North American markets.
Finally, the tendency toward professionalism was much less pronounced than in the northern revolutionary armies. The immediate
influence of this peasant movement on subsequent national development was slight, however, although after 1920 some Zapatista veterans were also integrated in the national army, which was officially
formed on May 1, 1917, from the troops of the revolutionary armies
of the north (i.e., the constitutionalist troops). It is thus in the formation and transformation of the revolutionary armies of the north
that one must look for the essential factors that determined the behavior of the army in the 1920s and 1930s.

Once again, we should also differentiate at least between the great
northern revolutionary armies, Villa's división del norte, and Obregón's army of the northwest. As for the Villista movement, Katz has
demonstrated that small farmers participated in early Villismo, and
has described the popular forms of mobilization in Villa's army.
Nonetheless, the Villistas cannot be considered primarily a peasant
movement oriented toward agrarian reform, as were the Zapatistas.
On the one hand, the social composition of the northern armies—as
a result of the areas's more differentiated socioeconomic structure—
was far more heterogeneous, and was by no means limited to peas-

[2] Report from Vizcaíno to the CNA delegate in Veracruz, September 4, 1925, AGN,
O-C, 112/6, 818-v-3.

[3] Report from General and Federal Deputy Natalio Espinosa to the Partido Nacional
Agrarista on the events in Mazamitla, April 24, 1922, AGN, O-C, 108-1/10, 818-P-44.

ant elements. On the other hand, agrarian objectives carried far less weight because peasant mobilization took place under a command that, unlike that of the Zapatistas, had little interest in changing agrarian structures. This resulted from both the social origins of the northern revolutionary leaders (who from 1913 onward were mostly middle class) with their manifest desire for social and economic advancement, and the economic war aims of the northern armies, which depended on control of intact haciendas and on unimpaired trade relations with the U.S. to finance their expansion plans. In spite of the multiple differences in the formation of the revolutionary armies in Chihuahua and Sonora from 1913 on, there was a surprising similarity in their war economies, especially with regard to the maintenance of the existing property structure and the respect for North American holdings. In both movements this resulted in structural changes being renounced, even in confiscated agricultural estates and (in contrast to the Zapatistas, who were compensated with agrarian reform) in the use of other mechanisms to conserve the loyalty of the revolutionary troops. The soldiers' pay, and their leaders' multifarious possibilities of personal enrichment (by the seizure of haciendas, for example), trade monopolies, or state concessions, were some of the forms of compensation.[4]

These tendencies were especially apparent in Obregón's army of the northwest, since its growth, as Héctor Aguilar has convincingly argued, took place in the context of the "insurrectionary model" specific to Sonora, whose "axis was bureaucratic with financial control by an existing government."[5] Leaving aside the special problem of the Yaquis, whose agrarian revolutionary dimension was in any case unable to make any decisive mark on the tradition of the Sonoran revolution, the principal result of this context was a socially "neutral" revolutionary army largely controlled and paid for from above. In spite of the fact that this army also recruited a large part of its forces from rural population groups, the leaders of these revolutionary troops could easily overlook the basis of the armies and their specific needs, because of the mechanisms of mobilization and con-

[4] Friedrich Katz, "Agrarian Changes in Northern Mexico in the Period of Villista Rule, 1913–1915," in *Contemporary Mexico*, ed. James W. Wilkie et al. (Berkeley, 1976), pp. 259–73; Friedrich Katz, "Pancho Villa, Peasant Movements and Agrarian Reform in Northern Mexico," in *Caudillo and Peasant in the Mexican Revolution*, ed. David A. Brading, (Cambridge, 1980), pp. 59–75.

[5] Héctor Aguilar, *La frontera nómada: Sonora y la revolución mexicana* (México, 1977); Héctor Aguilar, "The Relevant Tradition: Sonoran Leaders in the Revolution," in *Caudillo*, ed. Brading, pp. 92–123.

trol already mentioned, and could concentrate on their own ambitions. It was precisely this type of northern revolutionary army that, after the military victories of the constitutionalists over the Villa–Zapata alliance in 1915–16, formed the nucleus of the new federal army, since the Villistas, like the Zapatistas, were practically excluded from the new army, and above all from the ranks of the new national command after 1920.[6]

After 1920, the army became an instrument of the generals who were hostile to the peasants and allied to the landowners. This did not, however, depend only on the specific context in which the army was formed and the mechanism of mobilization and control in the northern armies, but also on the subsequent process of "professionalization" that increasingly obscured the army's revolutionary and popular origins.

Even during the "armed revolution" the military was becoming transformed into a profession, with a very specific type of mobility. As reported, for example, by the veteran constitutionalist Vicente Estrada, this applied also to many ex-federales who joined the revolutionary troops, "because they did not know how to do anything except soldiering."[7] In the revolutionary armies changes from one division to another were frequent: "When their faction ceased to exist, they immediately looked for another one and were well received."[8] Ideological ends seldom played a role, as illustrated in the military career of the common soldier Adalberto López Jara. He came from the lowest classes in the capital and joined the Villistas in 1914 at the age of fourteen "out of necessity and hunger." He then turned up in the troops of Pablo González, and after 1920 was incorporated in the army of Guadalupe Sánchez and thereby involved in the de la Huerta rebellion. After the rebels' defeat, he deserted, but was again admitted into the army in 1925, where he was promoted in 1936 to the rank of a sergeant, second class.[9] In particular, after the fall of Carranza in 1920, the army was swelled by the integration of the highly diverse anti-Carranzista units, and this further deep-

[6] See Peter H. Smith, *Labyrinths of Power: Political Recruitment in Twentieth-Century Mexico* (Princeton, 1979), p. 24: Among the members of the new elite, "only a handful—less than 10 per cent—had ever joined forces with Carranza's major rivals, Pancho Villa or Emiliano Zapata."

[7] INAH, Departamento de Etnología y Antropología, Programa de Historia Oral (henceforth PHO), PHO 4/12, interview by E. Meyer and A. Bonfil, Feb./March 1973, p. 15.

[8] PHO 4/12, p. 32.

[9] PHO 1/43, interview by L. Espejel.

ened its social and ideological heterogeneity. "Obregón ... accepts all who come: Felixistas, clericals ... , Villistas who have not yet surrendered, Zapatistas, everyone gets in and then it is no longer possible to know who was a revolutionary and who an enemy of the revolution."[10]

This transformation of the revolutionary army into soldiery pure and simple was observed by Vicente Estrada, commander of the "presidential guard" under Obregón, and especially among the officers: "Very soon, the major part of the leaders became soldiers more than armed citizens, as we proudly said we were. They already enjoyed the business of uniforms, of command, of all that, and little by little they lost the mystique of armed citizens to become soldiers, dedicating themselves definitely to a military career."[11] The soldiers and officers of this army had lost, as Warman emphasizes, "their local or regional ties, and had few bonds with their countrymen or with the social groups which they had at one time left behind; they lived on the army and in it they had created a new network of social relations."[12]

These factors make it comprehensible that the army allowed itself to be utilized as an antipeasant instrument in the agrarian conflicts of the 1920s and early 1930s. Troops were generally stationed far from their regions of origin, thus preventing any solidarity with the local population, and patron–client relationships within the army remained strong until the late 1920s. Soldiers not only blindly obeyed their leaders in various rebellions against the government, but also offered no opposition to actions against peasants who were calling for land.

This raises the question of the leaders' comportment. Practically all of them came from the revolutionary armies, especially from the constitutionalist wing. Compared with the Maderista phase of the Revolution, during which "revolutionary" landowners and other representatives of the upper class had been prominent leaders, the social composition of the north's revolutionary leadership changed substantially after 1913, particularly as a result of the growing weight of the revolutionary armies. The new revolutionary leaders, mostly military men, came from the middle class, both rural and urban.[13] As for their motives in entering the revolutionary armies, it

[10] PHO 4/12, pp. 32ff.
[11] Ibid., p. 53.
[12] Arturo Warman, ... Y venimos a contradecir—los campesinos de Morelos y el estado nacional (México, 1976), p. 149.
[13] Smith, Labyrinths, pp. 74ff.

is clear that a desire for social reform was secondary—at least in the context of the Sonoran revolution model—to the desire for rapid military or political advancement.[14] Except for a few cases, because of their social origins and socioeconomic aspirations, the new northern revolutionary elites had very little sympathy with the peasants and their demands for profound agrarian structural changes. On the contrary, the higher-ranking officers quickly formed a privileged caste that sought economic consolidation of its new status.[15] One of their aims was to enter the landowning class, which brought them increasingly into opposition with the peasants and their demand for land.

The various means by which revolutionary generals acquired haciendas during the civil wars have been dealt with in detail elsewhere.[16] They came to view these estates more and more as their personal property and, even though Carranza returned many estates to their previous owners, numerous generals were able to retain their new possessions. In addition, in the 1920s and early 1930s there were many ways for the military to become landowners, generally by semi- or pseudolegal means.[17]

Paradoxically, agrarian reforms created advantageous conditions for army chiefs to set themselves up in agriculture, because the army often exercised a decisive role of arbitrator in conflicts between agraristas and latifundistas. In this situation, the officers frequently acted as "partners" or "tenants" of the landowners affected or endangered. In order to avoid expropriation of part of their lands, landowners were often prepared to offer favorable contracts to their protectors. Thus General Enrique Espejel, as "tenant" of an affected hacendado, exploited the maguey plantations of the ejidos of Atitalaquia and Tlamaco in the state of Hidalgo for years.[18] In the border region between Puebla and Tlaxcala General Fortunato Maycotte's

[14] See, for example, the autobiographies of the Sonoran revolutionary generals: Abelardo L. Rodríguez, *Autobiografía* (México, 1962); Pedro J. Almada, *Con mi cobija al hombro* (México, 1936).

[15] Among the many examples, see the report to the State Department of the U.S. Consul in Durango, dated June 1924: "The people generally look with suspicion on the military, who seem to be the only people in the country enjoying prosperity," National Archives, Washington D.C., Record Group 59, Records of the Department of State Relating to Internal Affairs of Mexico, (henceforth NAW), 812.00/27301.

[16] Hans Werner Tobler, "Las paradojas del Ejército revolucionario—su papel social en la reforma agraria mexicana, 1920–1935," *Historia mexicana* 21, no. 1 (1971): 38–79.

[17] Tober, "Las paradojas," pp. 62–68.

[18] AGN, O-C, 104/5, 818-A-21, dated April 1922.

troops had installed themselves in the hacienda Xalostoc and, despite repeated orders from the War Ministry, they refused to leave and established instead a lucrative pulque business.[19] The "militarization" of agriculture is reflected very clearly in a complaint of the peasants of Chiquahuapan in the state of Puebla in November 1933. Despite their clear possession of ejidos, they were prevented from cultivating them by the army. They claimed that the soldiers terrorized them and had recently murdered one of their number along with members of his family.

> In order to elude providing the benefits that the Agrarian Laws grant to the people, Señor Gelacio García, owner of the hacienda that is also called "El Paredón", gave the said estate in apparent tenantship to citizen General Gabriel Barrios, which estate he continues to administrate to this day with armed soldiers of the 46th Line Battalion dressed as peasants, who recognize as headquarters the San Joaquín Base situated in Tacubaya, D.F., and in order that they may receive their assigned salaries, which are paid by the nation, go each month to the said base to pass review. And by way of amplification of this statement we cite the following: Lieutenant: Diario Barrios, present administrator of the hacienda "El Paredón"; Second Lieutenant: Palemón Barrios, who assists him on the same hacienda; Sergeant: Filiberto Flores, present administrator of the "Tenancingo" hacienda; Antonio Cabrero, a soldier of unknown rank, present administrator of the "Corral Blanco" hacienda, all of whom in union with another 30 armed men with regulation arms from the Army commit assassinations such as those to which we have continually referred.[20]

The contradiction between the early promises and the disappointing results of the revolution, (which is characteristic of the Mexican Revolution in general but was particularly true of the late revolutionary agrarian reform) was perhaps most succinctly expressed by the peasants of San José de los Sabinos in the state of Guanajuato in

[19] AGN, O-C, 112/7, 818-X-1, dated July 16, 1923.
[20] AGN, Abelardo L. Rodríguez (ALR), 111, 552.5/50. See also, for example, the report by Engineer C. Esperanza, agrarian department inspector, October 18, 1934, on the antiagrarian attitudes of some generals in Tamaulipas. The peasants had been forced off the hacienda Santo Domingo by the army, and "General Leonardo M. Hernández H., head of the garrison at Matamoros, has occupied it to work it in agreement with the owner; for this reason he is most intransigent with the agrarianists,"AGN, ALR, 114, 552.5/518.

1934, when they complained of the economic boycott of a landowner, observing that he had "placed his rights under the protection
of Señor General Domínguez, who has changed from a revolutionary
into a landholding protector of the latifundistas."[21]

The Peasants and the New State, 1920–35

The army was not only an important force in the agrarian conflicts
of the 1920s and early 1930s, but until the late 1920s it was also the
principal factor of domestic power. Given its propensity to rebellion—as manifested in the 1920s by two major uprisings and innumerable smaller mutinies, barrack revolts, etc.—the new state that
emerged after the revolution and was dominated between 1920 and
1935 by the Sonoran "dynasty," was able to consolidate itself only
very slowly. To this must be added the fact that during the revolution powerful regional chiefs had again emerged, reducing still further the power of the central government. The revolution had removed the political power but not the economic dominance of the
old oligarchy, had destroyed the radical Zapatista peasant movement by military means, and had brought the workers' movement
under state control. It had also created, as Anatol Shulgovski points
out, a "catastrophic equilibrium" (Gramsci) between the principal
social forces, none of which alone could establish a position of hegemony.[22]

In view of this weakness of the state, the new Sonoran regime had
to do all in its power to ensure its position as the new national authority. This was achieved by a closer rapprochement with the U.S.
through Mexican concessions at the Bucareli Conference of 1923 and
by the establishment of a personal Calles–Morrow axis in the late
1920s.[23] In domestic politics the Sonorans tried to neutralize their

[21] AGN, ALR, 121, 552.14/1236. See also the complaint of the wives of the ejidatarios
of Conatlán, Durango, over a neighboring hacendado, a former revolutionary general,
"who has let loose his rage against the people of Nicolás Bravo, making use of the
General's rank gained in the heat of the revolution, which was made in order to
emancipate the Worker and the Peasant . . .; but now it appears that the rich of the
new stamp, taking advantage of the blood that ran to acquire those greatly desired
liberties and peace in the villages, as we said earlier, taking advantage of their official
function come to commit abuses and assassinations in their name." AGN, ALR, 121,
552.14/1253.

[22] See Anatol Shulgovski, *México en la encrucijada de su historia* (México, 1968),
pp. 37ff.

[23] See Robert F. Smith, *The United States and Revolutionary Nationalism in Mexico, 1916–1932* (Chicago, 1972).

most powerful military rivals with massive economic benefits, and in part by political concessions, though with only partial success, as the military rebellions indicate.

Finally, the new government looked for allies among workers and peasants. Although the organization of unions under government control is not the subject of this study, the relations between peasants and state after 1920 will now be considered in more detail.

The state's principal means of binding the peasants to the new regime was the application of the agrarian reform laws as provided for in Article 27 of the 1917 Constitution. For the Sonoran leaders the economic and social objectives of agrarian reform were less important than its political function, that is, its pacifying and stabilizing effect. Calles expressed this attitude of the government very clearly in a conversation with Ignacio C. Enríquez, ex-governor of Chihuahua: "The ejido question is the best means of controlling these people by simply telling them: If you want land you must be with the government; those who aren't with the government won't get land."[24]

This policy had several dimensions. Support of the government by loyal peasants was most useful in times of acute national crisis, when contingents of armed agrarians reinforced the regular troops in dealing with major army rebellions (for example, in 1923–24 and 1929) or with the Cristero insurrection. On the other hand, rapid enforcement of agrarian reform, as in the case of Morelos, contributed greatly to the pacification of a center of chronic agitation. And finally the organization of peasants loyal to the government in parties such as the Partido Nacional Agrarista (PNA) or in regional associations helped to legitimize the new government.

However, the policy passed through several phases between 1920 and 1935, sometimes in favor of and sometimes opposed to agrarian reform, and it also varied regionally. A detailed analysis reveals very clearly the relative strength or weakness of the state and the peasants.

As for the regional complexity of pre-Cárdenas agrarian reform, the area of the Zapatista "revolution of the south" constituted an important zone that was pacified by the Sonoran regime in the early 1920s through relatively large concessions to the peasants. Reforms were made less quickly and with numerous conflicts in states of the

[24] See I. C. Enríquez, "Errores de nuestro sistema agrario," *Excelsior* 10, no. 5 (1970): 19A.

central highlands, where the peasants claimed land but in the absence of political support "from above" faced fierce resistance from
landowners and their allies. Another zone consisted of those regions
and states in which, in contrast to the Zapatista area, there was no
strong peasant revolutionary tradition, but in which in the 1920s
strong peasant organizations arose under a new type of peasant
leader or at the behest of the governors of some states, and acted as
pressure groups for agrarian reform. A last zone comprised regions
in which peasant pressure from below was so weak and resistance
from above so strong (from landowners and conservative governors)
that powerful peasant organizations could hardly develop. Here
there were almost no changes in the old agrarian situation until Cárdenas came to power.

It is clear that this varied development in the pre-Cárdenas period
was the result of a number of influences which we will now briefly
outline. The pre-Cárdenas agrarian reform in Morelos was a special
case; it was here that an authentic peasant revolution took place and
led to truly revolutionary changes in the old agrarian structure.[25] It
is true that after 1916 the Zapatistas had been gradually forced to
become defensive and that Morelos, too, had experienced the
repression of González and the beginnings of the Carranzist restoration of the old landowners' rule in the winter of 1919–20. Yet the
effect of the political and social mobilization of Zapatismo had not
been eliminated. Luis García Pimentel, son of the most important
landholding family in Morelos, had clearly realized this fact. Letters
to his parents in January and February 1920 reflect his preoccupation. Many inhabitants of the village of Jonacatepec had come "to
petition," he wrote, and even if militant Zapatismo was dead, "the
Zapatismo that has not died, and will not die, is peaceful Zapatismo."[26]

The high degree of peasant mobilization in the old region of Zapatista influence is reflected not least in the high number of "land

---

[25] See John Womack, *Zapata y la revolución mexicana* (México, 1969); Warman,
. . . *Y venimos*; François Chevalier, "Un facteur décisif de la révolution agraire au
Méxique: le soulèvement de Zapata, 1911–1919," in *Annales S.E.C.* 16, no. 1 (1961):
66–82. I am aware that this concentration on the Zapatista movement as the only
great, autonomous, and peasant-led agrarian uprising within the Mexican Revolution
may soon have to be modified in light of new studies of revolutionary movements at
local and regional levels. The current research of Asger Th. Simonsen on peasant
movements and agrarian reform on the Costa Chica of Guerrero, for instance, reveals
the existence, in the first years of the revolution, of a genuine peasant revolt with
clear agrarian aims.

[26] Womack, *Zapata*, p. 349.

petitions" in the very first years of the Sonoran regime, compared with other regions. In Morelos, of the 299 petitions registered from 1915 to 1935, 139 were made in 1920 and 1921; in addition, far more than half of the ejidal lands provisionally distributed up to 1935 (exactly 166,788 hectares of a total of 192,400) were distributed to the villages between 1920 and 1922.[27] Even in 1922, during a trip through Morelos, the agronomist E. Alanís Patiño noted that "the ejidal economy was already dominant in the state, . . . benefiting a population with war privileges."[28] These Morelan peasants' "war privileges" no doubt constituted an important factor in the rapid distribution of land in the state. But of equal importance was another repercussion of the Zapatista peasant revolution: the material destruction of the old hacienda economy and the physical expulsion of the majority of landowners from the state of Morelos.[29]

Because its primary objective was to rapidly pacify a turbulent region, the Obregón regime took this strong pressure from below into account in its agrarian policy. To that end, the government gave prominent ex-Zapatistas important political, administrative and military positions, and the political and military administration of the state was entrusted to former supporters of the revolution of the south. In particular, the distribution of land in Morelos to the peasants mobilized by Zapatismo was accelerated to prevent the restoration of the old latifundia system and a hacienda economy, as Obregón informed Luis García Pimentel in March 1922.[30] But despite the relatively rapid tempo, the agrarian reforms were noticeably different from the spontaneous Zapatista land distribution. In the "institutional agrarian reform" (Warman), the state "divided land as a unilateral concession . . . in order to create a political clientele."[31]

Although the Morelos reforms produced all the consequences that later characterized Mexican agrarian reform in general (such as a

[27] As early as 1926 the number of ejidatarios in Morelos was 25.3 percent of the total agrarian population, while the national average was only 4.3 percent; the ejidal lands covered 32.9 percent of the total area of the state of Morelos, while the national average was only 2.6 percent; see Table 16.1; Frank Tannenbaum, "La revolución agraria mexicana," in *Problemas agrícolas e industriales de México* 4, no. 2 (1952): 154, table 21.

[28] E. Alanís Patiño, "La economía ejidal de Morelos," in *Sociedad agronómica de México, primer ciclo de conferencias*, Oct./Nov., 1937, p. 68.

[29] See Alanís Patiño, "La Economía," p. 68, who speaks of "a cadaverous economy, incapable of reconstructing itself under the old forms." See also, Warman, . . . Y venimos, p. 157.

[30] AGN, O-C, 111/2, 818-T-12.

[31] Warman, . . . Y venimos, pp. 151ff.

Table 16.1

Petitions for Land Initiated Between 1915 and 1935

States	1915	1916	1917	1918	1919	1920	1921	1922	1923	1924	1925
Aguascalientes	3	1	0	1	0	0	2	0	18	5	34
Baja California	0	5	5	2	0	1	1	0	3	5	0
Campeche	1	15	4	2	0	1	8	10	6	4	4
Coahuila	0	19	3	5	0	2	9	5	8	13	14
Colima	2	6	0	1	0	0	0	0	6	3	3
Chiapas	1	4	19	13	10	4	12	18	21	6	70
Chihuahua	0	0	4	14	14	16	85	34	26	25	8
Distrito Federal	0	24	7	7	2	5	18	9	11	6	3
Durango	0	23	12	11	7	14	39	7	13	7	19
Guanajuato	10	11	6	2	2	0	12	4	42	23	8
Guerrero	0	0	1	0	79	102	93	52	74	29	31
Hidalgo	19	39	32	16	13	12	45	18	17	10	37
Jalisco	63	17	9	22	4	13	63	7	29	45	40
México	60	62	53	28	19	25	96	34	60	28	27
Michoacán	45	27	20	8	7	17	59	9	19	15	34
Morelos	0	0	0	0	2	49	90	6	10	3	10
Nayarit	0	2	18	6	1	6	24	5	9	5	18
Nuevo León	0	1	1	0	0	0	0	2	7	24	21
Oaxaca	6	37	62	21	10	2	47	34	62	15	14
Puebla	52	21	133	61	14	23	85	58	84	33	38
Querétaro	0	4	7	2	1	2	11	4	21	33	9
Quintana Roo	0	0	0	0	0	0	0	0	0	0	0
San Luis Potosí	1	9	1	2	0	4	40	47	51	114	69
Sinaloa	24	11	14	15	1	0	4	2	9	13	23
Sonora	4	7	3	9	6	1	4	13	17	9	13
Tabasco	7	3	5	9	1	3	5	3	10	2	3
Tamaulipas	1	0	0	0	0	0	0	2	0	46	39
Tlaxcala	13	20	59	12	4	5	12	4	20	3	1
Veracruz	41	21	24	23	4	21	106	88	168	25	102
Yucatán	1	4	11	18	20	1	33	45	21	20	6
Zacatecas	5	8	12	9	5	4	37	17	21	77	62
Totals	359	401	525	319	226	333	1040	537	857	646	758

1926	1927	1928	1929	1930	1931	1932	1933	1934	1935	Totals	Annual average
5	5	5	14	67	0	0	33	33	51	277	13
0	0	0	1	0	0	1	0	0	0	24	1
4	9	4	3	2	1	0	5	14	25	122	6
16	50	11	39	26	13	0	53	104	77	467	22
0	1	1	0	4	15	6	5	14	27	94	4
36	7	28	43	51	48	52	54	192	73	762	36
7	15	14	53	36	31	58	40	95	125	700	33
2	4	6	15	0	0	0	0	8	37	164	8
8	14	25	62	54	38	44	53	153	128	731	35
4	41	42	118	112	58	117	87	233	155	1087	52
33	17	28	96	51	58	28	36	144	152	1104	53
46	50	30	58	72	37	36	58	121	152	918	44
17	15	16	17	36	72	91	72	125	200	973	46
45	31	71	134	65	68	71	68	208	228	1481	71
12	19	25	103	92	155	125	99	229	222	1337	64
2	1	3	23	0	0	0	0	46	54	299	14
5	4	0	0	9	14	9	15	31	87	264	13
24	45	17	35	19	23	66	30	104	108	527	25
3	5	14	27	50	53	41	48	130	141	822	39
18	44	29	109	88	127	52	34	105	217	1425	68
18	0	6	4	13	36	22	45	40	43	321	15
0	0	15	1	2	6	0	0	0	9	33	2
46	64	28	30	53	0	0	18	96	109	782	37
4	7	5	23	33	33	59	31	24	133	468	22
6	3	10	9	6	27	33	51	25	35	291	14
0	0	19	13	8	6	8	26	1	70	202	10
26	27	34	28	32	16	41	73	81	90	536	26
2	7	8	16	12	0	6	31	19	42	296	14
67	40	101	229	276	388	391	84	124	257	2580	123
16	10	11	5	2	1	1	4	29	130	389	19
36	23	12	27	53	37	0	65	107	153	770	34
508	558	620	1335	1324	1363	1358	1214	2635	3330	20246	963

SOURCE: *Memoria del Departamento Agrario*, Apéndice Estadístico 1936/1937, México; not dated (duplicate copy), p. 64.

growing dependence of the peasants on the state, the fomentation of village conflicts in response to the emergence of politically and economically privileged agrarian caciques, the economic inefficiency of the ejido sector because of quantitatively and qualitatively poor land distribution)—rapid land distribution nevertheless achieved the government's major objective: to bring a lasting pacification of the region.[32] Testimony to this is the faint echo that the Cristero rebellion produced in "Catholic" Morelos.[33]

Agrarian reform took a significantly more conflict-ridden course in the states of the central plateau outside of the old Zapatista region. The opposition of landowners and land-hungry villages was real enough there, and the peasants were becoming aware of their new rights, but the hacienda economy had survived the revolutionary civil wars and the great estates were still under the control of their old (or new) owners, who were able to mobilize powerful political and military allies in their struggle against reform.

Violence generally accompanied the struggle for land reform in states in which no broad spontaneous peasant movements had developed during the revolutionary civil wars, but in which the peasants were more effectively organized in the 1920s. This "secondary" peasant mobilization usually took place in states in which progressive governors were looking for a political basis among the peasants in order to build up their regional power in the as yet labile political conditions of the early 1920s. Impulses from below—from the peasant basis and its immediate exponents—certainly played a considerable role here; but the important factor was patronage by the authorities—the stimulation of peasant organizations "from above"— such as later characterized the agrarian policy of Cárdenas.[34] The

[32] "Region" refers here to the whole zone of the Zapatista rebellion; it includes part of the states bordering Morelos. For Tlaxcala, see Iván Restrepo and José Sánchez Cortés, *La reforma agraria en cuatro regiones* (México, 1972), in which Tlaxcalan agrarian reform is compared with those in the Bajío, Michoacán, and the Laguna. "The rapidity with which the entitlement records were processed for the Tlaxcalan *ejidos*, in comparison with the other regions, can only be explained with reference to the dominance of the revolutionary spirit in the State. General Domingo Arenas, who claimed to be a *Zapatista*, carried out land distributions which exercised a decisive influence on the authorities, pressuring them to make *ejidal* grants as a necessary condition for the pacification of the State" (p. 15). Also on Tlaxcala, see Buve, Chapter 12, this volume.

[33] Warman, . . . *Y venimos*, p. 173.

[34] Characteristic of this type was, for example, the growth of peasant organizations in Veracruz; see Heather Fowler, *The Agrarian Revolution in the State of Veracruz, 1920–1940: The Role of Peasant Organizations* (unpublished thesis, American University, Washington D.C., 1970), p. 389. "The Veracruz organization was created as a

degree of political autonomy of these new organizations differed from case to case. In Michoacán, for example, and even more so in Veracruz, the peasant organizations enjoyed a good measure of independence, whereas in other states they were primarily subordinate to the political objectives of the governors or other local leaders.[35]

Unlike the regions just mentioned, where agrarian conflicts were intense, the peripheral regions of the north and south (with the obvious exception of Yucatán) were characterized by a considerably stronger continuity of the old agrarian order, both with respect to the peasants' attitude and to the maintenance of old structures of ownership. In these regions, admittedly without any clear dividing lines, where the hacienda predominated over village agriculture, where the possessions of the Indian communities remained more or less intact (as in Oaxaca), or where small and medium-sized private holdings were fairly widespread, agrarian reforms and the accompanying conflicts were very limited in the period before Cárdenas.[36] This applies above all to states in which the landowners had to face no strong peasant organizations and frequently enjoyed the protection of conservative governors for whom even the cautious agrarian policy of the federal government went too far.[37] Here the more or less unchanged political and social control of the local authorities, hacendados, army and courts, exercised a conservative influence, while the peasants' lack of class consciousness, the special status of the acasillados (based as much in local mentality as in law), and finally the strong indoctrination of a clergy that was either skeptical

---

result of struggling forces which surged from below, but which were not channeled until Governor Tejeda provided the stimulus from above."

[35] San Luis Potosí and Michoacán may be seen as mixed forms of "primary" and "secondary" peasant mobilization. For San Luis Potosí, see Romana Falcón, Chapter 11, this volume; see also Dudley Ankerson, "Saturnino Cedillo: A Traditional Caudillo in San Luis Potosí, 1890–1938," in Caudillo, ed. Brading, pp. 140–68; Gilbert M. Joseph, "Caciquismo and the Revolution: Carrillo Puerto in Yucatán," in Caudillo, ed. Brading, pp. 193–221; Heather Fowler Salamini, "Revolutionary Caudillos in the 1920s: Francisco Múgica and Adalberto Tejeda," in Caudillo, ed. Brading, pp. 169–92.

[36] See section on "Agrarian Reform and Its Conflicts 1920–1935," below.

[37] This was the case, especially during the government of Obregón, in some northern states whose governors (for example, César López de Lara in Tamaulipas, Angel Flores in Sinaloa, and Ignacio C. Enríquez in Chihuahua) followed a markedly anti-ejidal course. See Hans Werner Tobler, "Alvaro Obregón und die Anfänge der mexikanischen Agrarreform—Agrarpolitik und Agrarkonflikt, 1921–1924," in Jahrbuch für Geschichte von Staat, Wirtschaft, und Gesellschaft Lateinamerikas 8 (1971): 310–65; especially pp. 336, 356.

or opposed to reform, were undoubtedly influential in bringing
about the political immobility of the peasants and ensuring the general continuity of the old agrarian order.

There was great regional diversity in the agrarian reforms carried
out in the pre-Cárdenas era because of the differing strength of the
peasants and their forms of mobilization, and the agrarian policy of
the Sonorans also passed through different phases that reflect the
varying but gradually increasing power of the state. During the
1920s the state was still relatively weak because of the as yet un-
tamed army, the powerful regional leaders and, after 1926, the Cristero challenge. The pro-peasant ejidal policy, although regionally
diverse and limited in scale, took this fact into account. However, in
the late 1920s a marked consolidation of the national state began.
The defeat of the Escobar rebellion in 1929 resulted in growing submission of the army to the state. In the same year the Cristero rising
was crushed with the mediation of the U.S., and the Partido Nacional Revolucionario (PNR) was founded, broadening and consolidating the power of the central government at the national level and
thus enabling the regional cacicazgos to be destroyed or brought into
line. Finally, the rapprochement with the U.S. initiated by Plutarco
Calles guaranteed the regime the necessary external security. In the
first half of the 1930s, the maximato of Calles brought about an un-
questionable state consolidation that was not jeopardized even by
the effects (relatively mild in Mexico) of the world economic crisis.[38]

In this situation the state was much less dependent on the political support of workers and peasants than it had been in the 1920s.
The Confederación Regional Obrera Mexicana (CROM), after losing
government backing following Alvaro Obregón's assassination in
1928, was revealed to be a colossus with feet of clay; this year saw
the beginning of its rapid and inglorious decline. After 1930 the
peasants, too, began to feel that the state believed it could do without their political backing. Even though the distribution of lands
was not completely stopped at the local and regional levels, the increasingly anti-ejidal attitude of the government inaugurated by
Calles and the annihilation of the radical Tejedista peasant movement in Veracruz amply documented the conservative trend in
agrarian policy. There was to be a turning point only in 1934, following Lázaro Cárdenas' election to the presidency.

[38] See Lorenzo Meyer, *Historia de la revolución mexicana, período 1928–1934*,
Vol. 13 (México 1978), p. 11.

Agrarian Reform and Its Conflicts, 1920–35:
The Role of Peasants and State

Given this situation, how were agrarian reforms actually carried out in the 1920s and early 1930s? I have described elsewhere the highly conflictual nature of this agrarian reform.[39] Land disputes between peasants and landowners often took the form of underground but lasting guerrilla warfare, despite their being largely local in nature. The position of the peasants was in many cases decidedly weak, even though they could point to the mandates of article 27 of the 1917 constitution.

The complicated juridical and administrative procedures alone meant that the prospects of peasants who claimed lands were most uncertain, and they had to be prepared for years of disputes with the authorities, courts, and landowners. For this reason, the administrative process of agrarian reform and the multiple legal restrictions were in many cases responsible for the slowness of land distribution. The authorities deliberately took their time in treating petitions, and the peasants were often discouraged and refused to undertake the necessary measures.[40]

This bureaucratic handling of agrarian reform was admittedly only one factor that slowed the course of land distribution.[41] An even more important circumstance was the landowners' economic power, still strong in many places, and their political influence at the local level. A common complaint made by the communities was that from the moment of their claim to ejidos they were subjected to severe economic pressure from landowners. For example, the latter dissolved old tenant contracts, would not even employ them as simple hacienda peons, and tried in every way to destroy the economic basis of their existence.[42]

[39] Tobler, "Alvaro Obregón," pp. 335–52.

[40] As an example, see the report of José G. Parres to the secretary of Agriculture, De Negri, dated October 1924, in which he describes agrarian reform in the state of Mexico. Between 1915 and 1924, 455 petitions were filed for restitution or granting of ejidos. Of these, 96 had been granted, 116 remained "pending for lack of planning only, . . . 233 had been completely forgotten . . . some with more than nine years of negotiations without settlement and without hope of settlement by the local authorities," AGN, o-c, 106/6, 818-e-28(2).

[41] Tobler, "Alvaro Obregón," pp. 335–52.

[42] While it is true that the sources consulted for this essay defend the peasants' role somewhat unilaterally, on the whole they nonetheless clearly illustrate the patterns of conflicts. See, for example, the report from the president of the ejido of Sacramento, Durango, January 20, 1923, to Obregón, "now they deny work to all of those who signed the petition," AGN, o-c, 112/6, 818-v-7. On May 21, 1923 desperate peas-

After a provisional land distribution, violent agrarian conflicts usually occurred when the landowners opposed the decision. Many landowners had from an early date kept armed troops (*guardias blancas*) who terrorized or murdered agrarian leaders, ravaged ejidos, destroyed agrarian archives, and prevented local agrarian commission engineers from surveying planned ejidos. Some of these "white guards" were recruited from among dismissed soldiers commanded by old army officers; other were composed of armed hacienda peons under orders to defend their patrons' interests.[43] Even the *defensas sociales* frequently took the side of the landlords in these conflicts, as confirmed in a detailed critical report on the agrarian situation in the state of Mexico issued by the ex-governor of Morelos, José G. Parres.[44]

It would be incorrect, however, to impute the use of force only to the hacendados and their allies. Landowners and their administrators were repeatedly attacked by campesinos, and there were doubtless illegal invasions of the land. Where peasants were armed to deal with antigovernment rebellions in the army, they even succeeded in seizing control of certain areas for a time and forcing the landowners on to the defensive there.[45] But there was nothing like a balance of

---

ants from Cocula, Guerrero, wrote to the president, "the *hacendados* have harassed us in a merciless way. They give us no work, even as day-workers in the fields; they do not want to apportion land to us, even as tenants. We have been in need of work for a long time now," AGN, O-C, 105/11, 818-C-82. See also Henry A. Landsberger and Cynthia N. Hewitt, *Preliminary Report on a Case Study of Mexican Peasant Organizations* (unpublished manuscript, Centro de Investigaciones Agrarias, México), pp. 16ff: "Processing of the 1920 petition by the *Departamento Agrario* went on for twelve years before permission to found an *ejido* in Taretan was granted. In the meantime, the economy of the *municipio* declined markedly. The administrator of the *hacienda* retrenched, converting more and more of the cane fields into pasture for cattle. Unemployment among the day laborers was the result. And at the same time, the town of Taretan lost most of the commercial and cultural patronage of the *hacienda*: stores closed, orchestras and newspapers disappeared. Inhabitants of the town found it difficult to obtain water and wood, usually supplied by the *hacienda*."

[43] See, for example, the letter to Calles from the former peons of the hacienda La Concepción, in the state of Veracruz, April 10, 1926, AGN, O-C, 104–1/10, 818-C-16. It should not be denied that this image of a unilaterally "aggressive" hacienda might be altered if more use were made of hacienda sources. The findings of Herbert Nickel in Chapter 13 point in that direction.

[44] AGN, O-C, 106/6, 818-E-28 (2). Paul Friedrich, *Agrarian Revolt in a Mexican Village* (Englewood Cliffs, 1970), p.9, shows, however, that the defensas sociales could also intervene in favor of the peasants when operating under a radical governor such as Múgica in Michoacán.

[45] See the report of the manager of the American Guerrero Land and Timber Company (December 23, 1924) on the area dominated by Valente de la Cruz, leader of the agraristas in southern Guerrero, NAW, 812.00/27 489. The peasant groups armed on

forces in the conflict between peasants and landowners, because the
army intervened on the side of the landowners.

The countless complaints of the communities, peasant organizations, unions, and even governors about continual army assaults run
through the whole history of Mexican agrarian reform in the 1920s
and early 1930s. In Veracruz, where the conflicts between the army
and the peasants and state authorities were particularly severe, the
state legislature publicly referred to the army as a plaga social. A
powerful divisional commander or chief of operations would occasionally use his influence directly to support the landowners, as in
the case of Guadalupe Sánchez in Veracruz. But often a lieutenant
with a small detachment on an estate was enough to prevent an entire village from working their ejidos and to terrorize the peasants.[46]

The multifarious forms of the army's anti-peasant activities have
been dealt with elsewhere.[47] The frequent conflicts were described
by one of Obregón's emissaries as follows:

> The Federal forces have committed many assaults and are re-
> pudiated by the majority of the lower classes; in all cases they
> have refused to cooperate with the municipal authorities and
> have used their armed influence in favor of the landowners.
> There is a marked social pessimism due to the absolute absence
> of justice, which is unknown to the poor peasants who live in
> miserable huts, far from population centers, and who are treated
> like beasts by the landowners and the military.[48]

the occasion of the de la Huerta rebellion had also set up temporary rule in the valley
of San Martin in the state of Puebla and had driven out the hostile landowners, cf.
Summerlin's report to the State Department of January 4, 1924, NAW, 812.00/26 767.

[46] In Veracruz in 1923, the Division Commander Guadalupe Sánchez openly declared himself to be on the side of the hacendados. The marked anti-agrarianist attitude of another division commander and chief of operations, Fortunato Maycotte,
was admitted even by the Sindicato de Agricultores of Puebla, cf. the telegram to
Obregón sent by the director of that organization, Lozano Cardoso, April 10, 1924,
AGN, O-C, 110/7, 818-S-225. Both Sánchez and Maycotte were compromised by their
involvement as leaders in the de la Huerta rebellion against Obregón. With regard to
the profusion of complaints from some villages over the antipeasant interventions of
the army, see for example the letter from the mayor of San Pedro Teyuca in the state
of Puebla, dated May 28, 1928: "about 2:30 on the same day, [the peasants] were
working in the fields with their oxen, when the Lieutenant of the detachment from
the *hacienda* San José Ternel, accompanied by armed soldiers, threatened the said
workers, obstructing them until they left the area where they were cultivating the
soil, and saying that he respected no orders except those of the owner of the said
hacienda Ternel, because he was paid by him," AGN, O-C, 111-1/4, 818-T-124.

[47] See Tobler, "Las paradojas."

[48] Brigadier-General Manuel Navarro Angulo to Obregón, April 6, 1923, AGN, O-C,
109-1/5, 818-S-61.

We now turn to the forces operating behind this conflict-ridden process of agrarian reform, briefly considering the role played by the peasants and by the state. It is evident that in addition to the peasants mobilized by the revolutionary wars (as in Morelos) and those organized "from above" in the 1920s, there were other groups of peasants who made almost no move toward agrarian reform. In order to understand this attitude we must first consider the particular roles of the *peones acasillados*, who until 1934 had no legal right to ejidos, and of the institution of the hacienda.

Outside of Morelos, the hacienda had been generally stable during the revolutionary civil wars.[49] It is true that the hacienda peons had at times joined the revolutionary armies when they passed through the area, and that revolutionary influences from outside had occasionally provoked local unrest and even uprisings on the estates. However, the peons generally had no real revolutionary objectives and only wanted better wages and working conditions, without questioning the institution of the hacienda per se. On the contrary, the acasillados often joined their patrons in defending the hacienda against outside threats.[50]

The causes for this attitude on the part of the acasillados will not be analyzed here. It was certainly due in part to the mechanisms of social control and even of efficient repression (especially in the southeast); to the relatively privileged position of many acasillados (as emphasized by recent research), and to the paternalistic patron–peon relationship.[51] It is consequently not surprising that the acasillados maintained this attitude during the agrarian reform of the 1920s,[52] because at that time they were also legally excluded from

[49] It certainly can not be denied that the hacienda was under pressure even before it was dismantled under the presidency of Cárdenas. But it is equally true that in many cases it was able to maintain its economic position throughout the revolutionary wars and the subsequent period of Sonoran hegemony. See also note 52.

[50] See Luis González, "Tierra caliente," in *Extremos de México—Homenaje a don Daniel Cosío Villegas*, ed. El Colegio de México (México, 1971), pp. 115–49.

[51] See Friedrich Katz, "Labor Conditions on Haciendas in Porfirian Mexico: Some Trends and Tendencies," *Hispanic American Historical Review* 54, no. 1 (1974): 1–47; Herbert J. Nickel, "Zur Immobilität und Schuldknechtschaft mexikanischer Landarbeiter vor 1915," *Saeculum* 27 (1976): 289–328; see also Nickel, Chapter 13, this volume.

[52] Here again a less general overview would certainly also stress some indirect effects of the agrarian movement on the acasillados. If the abolition of debt peonage, for instance, generally did not result in a massive exodus of acasillados from the hacienda, a certain change in the attitude of acasillados can nevertheless not be ignored, as Nickel has shown for the hacienda of Ozumba, indicating strikes and a growing unionization of laborers in the 1920s. On the other hand, even in the limited

the circle of those who had a right to land. The demand of the villages for land from "their" hacienda even jeopardized their own jobs. In this sense, too, the pre-Cárdenas agrarian reforms tended to aggravate the conflicts. The disputes between peasants and latifundistas, the rivalries between villages over land rights, and the polarization processes within communities resulting from the appearance of "bosses" within the ejidos, were now complicated by the conflict of economic interests between ejido peasants and acasillados.

The state of Michoacán—which displays much social and economic variety and of which some instructive studies have been made—will now serve as an example illustrating the various behaviors of peasant groups during the agrarian reforms. In the haciendas of the *tierra caliente*—in Taretan, for example—some unions were formed by the peons in the late 1920s, but they nevertheless rejected the ejido claims of the villagers, as Landsberger and Hewitt state:

> The delay in processing the petition for an ejido in Taretan was no doubt encouraged by a lack of grass-roots support for the claim. It is a fact (lamented in several interviews by men who led the agrarian movement in the municipio) that there was no open agitation by campesinos for the destruction of the hacienda until 1929. Revolutionaries who passed through the region from time to time were unable to convince the day-laborers of the estate that they should, or could, divide its land. . . . One of the "L" brothers recalls, for instance, that within a group of one hundred day-laborers on the hacienda, he considered himself lucky to find ten who would agree to sign a petition for land.[53]

Even in August 1936, eighty-four peons protested against a projected ejido in Purísima: "We have ample guarantees for our work, a good prospect of bettering our economic situation . . . but funda mentally we have liberty of action, which we never had while the leaders of the region were living off our quotas and exploiting our peasant ingenuity."[54]

The situation was different in the village of Naranja, on the Tarascan plain, whose agrarian history has been studied by Paul Fried-

region of Puebla–Tlaxcala the situation was by no means uniform; for in the hacienda Rinconada "traditional social relations were maintained for a remarkably long period." See Herbert J. Nickel, "Landarbeiter in der mexikanischen Revolution (1910–1940)," *Forschungsmaterialien* (Bayreuth, 1982), 6:51–65.

[53] Landsberger and Hewitt, *Preliminary Report*, pp. 17, 19.

[54] Ibid., p. 20.

rich.[55] In Naranja a classical conflict had arisen between the village
and the hacienda during the Porfiriato because of the great expansion of the hacienda Cantabria. But the Naranjeños did not attempt
to bring about a violent change in the local agrarian structure even
during the commotion of the revolutionary wars. Most of the villagers were "inarticulate about the land question." Attempts to recover the village's legitimate rights continued by means of appeals
to the courts. Even the villagers who took up arms during the civil
war did not use them against the hacienda but joined the big revolutionary armies that (except for the Zapatistas) were not fighting
primarily for agrarian reforms.[56] It was only under the influence of
Primo Tapia that a peasant organization demanding ejidos was
formed in Naranja in the early 1920s. It is interesting to note that
numerous veterans of the revolutionary armies actively supported
Tapia's peasant movement, no doubt a significant indication of the
lasting social and political mobilizing action of the revolutionary
wars.[57] In spite of this, even Tapia could not count on broad and
spontaneous support from the villagers in his demand for lands, as
is shown by the fact that he had to gather village signatures for a
land petition on the pretext that it was a petition for the sending of
a priest to Naranja.[58]

Finally, where small property owners dominated, as in the village
of San José de Gracia (whose history has been so impressively recorded by Luis González), the agrarian question scarcely played any
role during the revolution, despite of the fact that not all villagers
were landowners. It was only during the Cristiada of the 1920s that
many Catholic villagers resorted to arms, not to fight for agrarian
reform, but in defense of their faith and of the Catholic Church
against the anticlerical policy of President Calles. Agrarian reform
was initiated chiefly from above, especially under Cárdenas, first as
governor of Michoacán, and later as president of the Republic.[59]

It is evident that under the late Sonoran revolutionary regime, as
in the period of the armed revolution, the intensity of peasant pressure from below in favor of agrarian reform varied widely. A certain
peasant conservatism cannot be overlooked, not only where (as in
Oaxaca) Indian lands were little affected by Porfirian moderniza-

---

[55] Friedrich, *Agrarian Revolt.*
[56] Ibid., pp. 49–57.
[57] Ibid., p. 90.
[58] Ibid., pp. 91ff.
[59] Luis González, *Pueblo en vilo: Micro-historia de San José de Gracia* (México,
1968), pp. 194, 223ff.

tion.[60] Even in other regions, especially those with a strong Catholic tradition, a marked peasant conservatism was apparent, so that many small farmers with ejidal rights rejected the idea of state land grants. Thus the Indians of Pátzcuaro in Michoacán declined offers of ejidal land from Governor Múgica. Similar behavior was noted by Friedrich in Naranja: "the paradoxical refusal of most Naranjeños to participate actively in any land claims: the ejido was for their own benefit, but many did not want it."[61] Undoubtedly the clergy's sometimes vehement rejection of a "confiscatory" land reform policy played a part, and probably also—especially among older peasants—a conservative conception of property that could not reconcile itself with "free" land grants.[62] Under the threat of expropriation many latifundistas took shrewd advantage of this attitude of the peasants and sold plots to them at advantageous prices.[63]

The lack of strong pressure from below by relatively large groups of peasants during the late revolutionary agrarian reform is certainly a significant reason for its slow progress. However, the multiple obstacles faced by those peasants who actively fought for their demands for ejidos, were real enough. The boycotting and general intimidation of peasants demanding or about to demand land were the hacendados' most effective weapons in their struggle against agrarian reform. And the hacendados could use them because the Revolution had had little effect on their economic power in many parts of the country, so that the peasants continued to be dependent on them. This fundamental fact was of central importance for the main-

[60] On Oaxaca, see Ronald Waterbury, "Non-revolutionary Peasants: Oaxaca compared to Morelos in the Mexican Revolution," *Comparative Studies in Society and History* 17 (1975): 410–22.

[61] Friedrich, *Agrarian Revolt*, p. 91.

[62] As an example of the antireform attitude of many priests, see the report of a representative of the "special executive committee" of the ejido of Coluca, Jalisco, November 28, 1922: "The priest and the clergy preached against the *agraristas* and called them and the government, too, bandits. They have formed a Catholic Workers' Union and had them swear war against the government and the agrarianists." AGN, O-C, 11/3, 818-T-62. For the conservative conception of property of many peasants, cf. Luis González, *Pueblo*, p. 226. Even the landless villagers "remained attached to an idea of property which was not to be reconciled with *ejidal* ownership. It was thought that there were only two ways of obtaining landed property: by purchase or by inheritance. It was bad for your reputation to have land given to you; you would not be respected if you became a landowner by having land made over to you by the government."

[63] "The *hacendado* engaged in a double strategy to protect his land from claims made under the new laws. First, beginning in 1926, land of the estate was offered for sale in parcels of 5 to 7 hectares," Landsberger and Hewitt, *Preliminary Report*, p. 16.

tenance of the old agrarian order in all regions where the peasants had no effective organizations and no strong government support. Even where this support was forthcoming, as in Veracruz and at times in Michoacán and Yucatán, land reform (except in Morelos) was limited in extent.[64]

This was connected with the caudillistic forms of campesino mobilization in the 1920s, resulting to a large extent from political initiative "from above." While it is true that this permitted the rapid growth of peasant organizations, it also left them—especially in the case of withdrawal of government patronage—weak and unable to resist strong external pressures, such as the intervention of the army or federal authorities.[65] This can be observed in Veracruz, where peasant organizations reached the pinnacle of their influence during Tejeda's second term, but where the political pressure of the federal government on Tejeda's regional power base increased until in 1933 the disarming of his peasant militias by the army dealt a paralyzing blow to agrarianism in Veracruz.[66] This event not only reflects the growing weight of the central government, which sought with ever greater success to control the regional chieftains, but also raises the question of the general sociopolitical climate of the Sonoran revolutionary regime, in which the organization of the peasants and the implementation of land reform took place.

Some of the main aspects of this question may be briefly recalled here.[67] Of decisive importance was the fact that the Sonorans, even though their policy was more flexible than Carranza's, followed a course directed more toward the maintenance of the fundamental economic and social structures than toward radical changes. A factor of some weight in the relatively conservative politics of the So-

[64] While in 1930, $1/7$ of the national agricultural acreage had become *ejidal* properties, in Veracruz it was only $1/10$, in Michoacán less than $1/9$, and only in Yucatán had the figure superseded $1/3$ of the area. Some rounded figures for 1935 were: national average, $1/5$; Veracruz, $1/5$; Michoacán, $1/4$; Yucatán, $1/2$. The extent of the increase under Cárdenas can be confirmed by comparing the figures for 1935 with the rounded figures for 1940: national average, $1/2$; Veracruz, $2/3$; Michoacán, $5/8$; Yucatán, $3/4$. However, in Morelos the ejidal area had reached $2/3$ of the total agricultural acreage in 1930, growing to $4/5$ in 1940. See *Primer Censo Ejidal 1935; Segundo Censo Agrícola Ganadero 1940.*

[65] For an illustrative contribution to this problem see in particular, Brading, ed., *Caudillo.*

[66] Fowler, *Agrarian Revolution*; Romana Falcón, *El agrarismo en Veracruz—La etapa radical (1928–1935)* (México, 1977).

[67] For a more detailed account of the period of Sonoran hegemony, see Hans Werner Tobler, *Die mexikanische Revolution: Gesellschaftlicher Wandel und politischer Umbruch, 1876–1940* (Frankfurt, 1984), pp. 367–567.

norans was certainly the strong external pressure (principally North American) to restrain revolutionary changes in Mexico.[68] But the Sonoran revolutionary leaders themselves were in any case not as radical as they were made out to be in the national and foreign counterrevolutionary propaganda of the early 1920s. The revolutionary elite had quickly produced a new landowning bourgeois class that did not wish to change society fundamentally but to be integrated as a new segment in the existing upper class.[69] A prototype of this new upper class of revolutionary origin was Obregón himself, who had rapidly built up, parallel to his rapid military and political ascent, an impressive business empire in Sonora. Obregón was initially engaged in the wholesale trade and in export, and later extended his activities to industrial manufacturing, services, and banking. From a modest ranchero he became a veritable agricultural entrepreneur whose holdings finally encompassed thousands of irrigated or irrigable acres in the fertile regions of the Yaquis and the Mayos.[70] It is clear that this process of formation of a new class of latifundistas, bankers, concessionaires, merchants, and industrialists from the new political and military elite was of great importance for the general development of the Revolution before and after Cárdenas.

It is only in this perspective that we can understand the increasingly antireform course of agrarian policy and the conservative tendencies of the Revolution, which in the early 1930s seemed to be moving in the direction of its thermidor without the promised social reforms having been made.

The Cárdenas Agrarian Reform: The Integration of Peasants in the New State

The character of agrarian reform, however, was to change radically under Cárdenas. During his presidency a massive redistribution of land began that within a few years drastically altered the property situation in the central highlands, dismantled the traditional hacienda, and greatly increased the number of ejidatarios who benefited by reform. Between 1934 and 1940 the number of ejidatarios

[68] Smith, *Revolutionary Nationalism*.

[69] Hans Werner Tobler, "Revolutionsgeneräle als "businessmen": Zur Entstehung und Rolle der revolutionären Bourgeoisie in Mexiko, 1910–1940" in *Dritte Welt: Historische Prägung und politische Herausforderung–Festschrift zum 60. Geburtstag von Rudolf von Albertini*, ed. P. Hablützel et al. (Wiesbaden, 1983), pp. 195–213.

[70] See for example the informative reports on Obregón's economic activities by the American consul in Guaymas, NAW, 812.00/Sonora 1.

grew from 940,526 to 1,716,371 and the percentage of ejido lands went from 15 to 47 percent of the total cultivated areas.[71] At the same time the traditional concept of the ejido as an institution operative only at subsistence level was given up and the ejido, especially the collective ejido, came to form part of commercial agriculture.[72]

This is not the place to analyze Cárdenas' agrarian policy, which, through supportive measures such as the development of the agrarian credit system, took on the character of a sweeping agrarian reform.[73] Instead, we conclude by briefly examining some possible reasons for the pronounced change in agrarian policy in the late 1930s. The principal reason for this new course was no doubt the transference of power from the ever more conservative Callistas to a new class of political and military leaders like Cárdenas, whose economic and social policies were guided by a more progressive ideology. This change of power, which was deepened and accelerated in 1935 by the political conflict between Calles and Cárdenas (in other words the gradual displacement of the Callistas from positions of power) can here only be recorded. We may also mention that the Cárdenas government enjoyed greater freedom of action as a result of the international situation on the eve of World War II and because of the less interventionist attitude of the United States under Franklin Roosevelt. We should, however, list a few specific factors of agrarian development that help to explain the new radical course taken by Cárdenas.

During the 1920s and early 1930s agrarian reform had not only involved many conflicts but had also led to grave socioeconomic contradictions that called for rapid solutions. The economic problems arose chiefly because on the one hand, agrarian reform had gone too far, as Eyler N. Simpson clearly diagnosed in the mid-1930s. In spite of the limited size of the reformed sector, it had negatively influenced agricultural operations as yet unaffected by reform, because landowners had frequently reduced their investments and production for fear of future expropriation. On the other hand, however, the reform had not gone far enough, since the agrarian sec-

[71] See Sergio Reyes Osorio et al., eds. *Estructura agraria y desarrollo agrícola en México* (México, 1974), p. 50.

[72] For the ejido colectivo see Salomón Eckstein, *El ejido colectivo en México* (México, 1966).

[73] See Luis González, *Historia de la revolución mexicana*, Vol. 15, *Los días del presidente Cárdenas* (México, 1981).

tor it had reached was quantitatively and qualitatively insufficient and had remained without any real state support.[74]

A clear alternative presented itself by the mid-1930s: either agrarian reform had to be terminated right away and private agriculture—including haciendas—stimulated to increase production by means of unequivocal property guarantees, or agrarian reform had to be accelerated and the reformed sector developed by greater financial and technical help from the state, the idea of a pure ejidal subsistence economy being discarded. The veterans of the revolution around the *jefe máximo* Calles opted for the first course, a younger group on the radical wing of government and the Partido Nacional Revolucionario (PNR) for the second. In 1934 this group strongly backed the nomination of Lázaro Cárdenas as presidential candidate, and later pushed through agrarian reform for economic as well as for social reasons.[75] This new policy was favored in the economic aftermath of the world depression of the 1930s, which also affected the previously sacrosanct sectors of commercial agriculture; "a fact which made the opportunity costs of land transfers much less than they would have been had general prosperity and high farm prices prevailed."[76]

It is true that the Cárdenas agrarian reform also frequently encountered bitter opposition from the hacendados concerned, especially where they found support among the political and military authorities.[77] But the fact that the federal government fully supported agrarian reform enabled its rapid realization. This was not only because Cárdenas did not hesitate to defend the achievements of the reform by raising a rural defense force of 60,000 well-armed men outside of the regular army[78]; the role of the army itself must also be considered.

In spite of its frequent anti-agrarian interventions under the Sonoran regime, the army did not impede the profound agrarian reform of Cárdenas. In this it differed markedly from the old federal army of Díaz and Huerta, which had rebelled against Madero even though he was much less interested in social reforms.[79] This raises

[74] Eyler N. Simpson, *The Ejido: Mexico's Way Out* (Chapel Hill, 1937), pp. 439ff.

[75] Reyes Osorio, *Estructura agraria*, pp. 33ff.

[76] Clark W. Reynolds, *The Mexican Economy (Twentieth-Century Structure and Growth)* (New Haven, 1970), p. 153.

[77] See, for example, David L. Raby, *Educación y revolución social en México (1921–1940)* (México 1974).

[78] See Gerrit Huizer, *La lucha campesina en México* (Mexico, 1970), p. 72.

[79] Friedrich Katz, "Innen- und aussenpolitische Ursachen des mexikanischen Re-

the question, already put forward by Katz, as to what were the differences between the old Porfirian army and the new army, both of which had sprung from popular uprisings. While we cannot compare the two armies here, we can mention two or three factors that may help to explain their different behavior.

During the last years of the Porfiriato, the old army had been converted, by the integration of its leaders in the oligarchy, into an instrument for maintaining the established order. In command of the revolutionary army, on the other hand, in spite of its transformation, there had always been, alongside officers of increasingly conservative persuasion, a radical wing that included not only Múgica and Tejeda but, up to a point, Cárdenas himself. Above all, the army became gradually domesticated in the late 1920s as a result of the failures of military rebellions.

For this reason, in the 1930s the role of the army diminished as a power factor independent of the government. In addition, its principal leaders, such as Calles, Cárdenas, Amaro, Almazán, and Cedillo, were solidly integrated in the apparatus of civilian power. Once the political conditions for radical agrarian reform had been created under Cárdenas by the skillful elimination of the conservative Callistas, the army could no longer prevent its implementation.[80]

In conclusion, we must ask what was the role played by the peasants in Cárdenas' agrarian reform? To what degree was the change in agrarian policy during the 1930s affected by a growing pressure "from below"? The present state of research does not permit an exhaustive reply to this question, but the statistics suggest that the increasingly conservative agrarian policy during the maximato, especially during the presidency of Ortiz Rubio, though accompanied by a marked decline in land confirmations by the president, did not bring the number of petitions for land down from their relatively high level, a level significantly higher than during the government of Obregón and Calles.[81] This suggests that a certain pressure from below continued, and was even intensified. Whether or not this was a direct result of the economic crisis is as yet uncertain, and other factors also played a part. The growing number of petitions regis-

volutionsverlaufs," in *Jahrbuch für Geschichte von Staat, Wirtschaft und Gesellschaft Lateinamerikas* 15 (Köln, 1978), p. 100.

[80] For an excellent analysis of the mechanisms by which Cárdenas secured his growing control over the army, see Alicia Hernández Chávez, *Historia de la Revolución Mexicana*, vol. 16, *La mecánica cardenista* (México, 1979), pp. 77–118.

[81] See Table 16.1.

tered after 1934 must be attributed partly to the extension of land rights to the peones acasillados, partly to the rise of a new generation in the peasant population. While older peasants tended to be conservative, revolutionary and postrevolutionary conditions had socialized the younger ones, no doubt making them more sympathetic toward the agrarian reform policy, as Luis González has pointed out with reference to Cárdenas' reforms in San José de Gracia.[82]

Nonetheless, it would certainly not be adequate to consider the Cárdenas agrarian reform (and in a broader sense, Cárdenas' reform policy in general) as having arisen only from increased pressure from below. It was due rather to an alliance between the state and the lower classes. The Cárdenas regime was relatively weak at first because of disputes with the Callista wing. Much as in the early 1920s, political and social organizations were therefore created "from above" in order to give the new government a firm power base. This applies not only to the government's official promotion of the new trade unions of the Confederación de Trabajadores Mexicanos (CTM), but also to the national organization of peasants in the Confederación Nacional Campesina (CNC). As early as 1935–36, peasant unification had been initiated with the aid of *agentes federales*; "to head the various delegations of the agrarian department, obtaining by this means the adhesion of the immense majority of the peasants of the country, for the purpose of the desired unification."[83]

Buve's research on agrarian developments in Tlaxcala during the 1930s shows clearly that the national power shift from Calles to Cárdenas brought about new forms of peasant mobilization that were stimulated only in part from below, and to a large extent from those local politicians who saw promising career opportunities in agrarian reform.[84]

Cárdenas' agrarian reform reveals a characteristic feature of the Mexican Revolution: the multiform interplay of pressures from below with mechanisms of mobilization and control from above. This

[82] Luis González, *Pueblo*, pp. 226ff.

[83] See *Memoria del Departamento Agrario, 1935/36*, (México, 1936), pp. 88ff (mimeo). See also Raymond Buve, "State governors and peasant mobilisation in Tlaxcala," in *Caudillo*, ed. Brading, p. 236: "After the Agrarian Congress (1935), district federations were founded in a quick, state-sponsored campaign and peasants were virtually ordered to enlist, since the incitations left no doubt as to their mandatory character."

[84] Buve, "State Governors," in *Caudillo*, ed. Brading, pp. 222–24.

feature marked the armed revolution of 1910–20, then consolidation
under the Sonorans, and finally the Cárdenas presidency. For the
peasants this evolution had ambivalent results. On the one hand,
they enjoyed broad agrarian reform under Cárdenas, while on the
other they were integrated—still under Cárdenas—as the "peasant
sector" in the corporate structure of the revolutionary party and thus
subject to firm state control. This control was an essential element
of the political and social system which, after 1940, in the wake of
the "Mexican miracle," left to the peasants most of the burden of
rapid economic growth.[85]

[85] See Rodolfo Stavenhagen et al., *Neolatifundismo y explotación—de Emiliano
Zapata a Anderson Clayton & Co.* (México, 1968); Arturo Warman, *Los campesinos:
Hijos predilectos del régimen* (México, 1972); Reyes Osorio et al., *Estructura agraria*;
Roger D. Hansen, *The Politics of Mexican Development* (Baltimore, 1971).

PART V

Nineteenth- and Twentieth-Century Revolts in Perspective

Rural Rebellions

after 1810

Friedrich Katz

Between the bloody beginning of Spanish rule and its even bloodier end during the wars of independence, the core areas of Mexico witnessed relatively little violent conflict (with the conspicuous exception of the northern periphery of New Spain). This situation drastically changed in the nineteenth century. As in most former Spanish colonies in Latin America in the first years of independence elites engaged in almost incessant struggles for control of the newly independent Mexico. These conflicts were most often power struggles between regional elites or caudillos for control of the state, clashes within the military, between civilians and the military, or between the church and anticlerical forces. Unlike most of the rest of Latin America, the lower classes were drawn into these conflicts as clients, as allies of the elites, or on their own behalf. This rural violence was strongly influenced by another characteristic that differentiated Mexico from much of Latin America—its history of outside aggression, which led to the war with the United States and against the French.

Between 1810 and 1920, rural revolts and revolution changed the face of Mexico. They created the basis for independence after 1820, and led to the profound changes that took place after 1920. Between the two great revolutions, rural revolts affected Mexico much more than such revolts had ever influenced colonial New Spain.

For anyone examining the history of rural revolts between 1810 and 1910, that century divides itself quite naturally into two distinct periods, with a cutoff point in 1884. That was the year in which Porfirio Díaz began his second term in office and set up the strongest state that independent Mexico had ever known. It was also the year in which the Apache chief Geronimo was captured by the Americans,[1] marking the virtual end of Apache raids against Mexico's northern frontier. The first railroad line linking Mexico and the U.S. was opened and a period of rapid economic growth began.

These changes affected the pattern of rural uprisings, which also varied across regions. Until 1884, rebellions along the southern periphery of Mexico were similar to those of the eighteenth century, although the revolts of the Maya of Yucatán and the Indians of Chiapas, for example, were larger in scale, and the one in Yucatán was far more successful. After 1884, revolts in the south diminished in number and intensity until the fall of Porfirio Díaz. Along the sparsely settled northern frontier there was both continuity and a sharp break with the colonial past. The Apache wars flared up again in the 1820s and the Yaqui Indians of Sonora revolted, though on a far larger scale than before. However, the free peasants of the north (particularly the military colonists) who had been the mainstay of Spanish rule, played a very different role in 1920 than they had in 1820. In the early nineteenth century they frequently sided with northern caudillos in their revolts against the federal government, but a century later many of them joined revolutionary movements directed against both the regional and national upper classes.

But it was in central Mexico that even more profound changes occurred in comparison to the colonial period. On the whole, the intensity of the struggles and the numbers involved were far greater than during Spanish rule. In most cases several villages were involved in the revolts. Land had been a secondary issue during the colonial period, but it now became the focus of many revolts. The rebels' attitude toward the state and its legitimacy was very different, and the uprisings became bloodier and repression more pronounced. In addition, outsiders played a greater role in promoting, organizing, or supporting these revolts than in the period of Spanish rule.

Up to 1884, Mexico's economic growth had been slow, alternating with periods of contraction and stagnation. The state was weak, continually torn by internal dissent and by the effects of foreign threats and invasions. From 1884 to 1910, there was extremely rapid economic growth and the concomitant development of a strong, centralized Mexican state. As a result, completely new types of tensions

---

[1] He escaped from his captors, only to be recaptured in Sonora in 1886; nevertheless, most of his forces were crushed in 1884.

were granted at the periphery, while social conflicts in the central part of the country took on a new dimension.

Revolts in Northern Mexico
in the Early Nineteenth Century

On the northern frontier in the early nineteenth century, the same general pattern of relations between social classes that characterized the late colonial period continued, but the attitude of peasants toward the central government had changed. The dominant internal characteristic of the northern frontier, as in the eighteenth century, was not class conflict, but rather peace, community of interest, and even social harmony, based on the renewed Apache wars that broke out around 1830. The newly formed Mexican state had neither the means nor the organization to pacify or to buy off the Apaches, as the Spaniards had done in the late eighteenth century. Moreover, as North American settlers pushed into the southwestern U.S., the contrasts between the U.S. and Mexico, between an advancing American and a retreating Mexican frontier, made it attractive for the Apaches to raid Mexico. Within Mexico, therefore, emerging and potential conflicts between hacendados and peasants (both Indian and mestizo) were set aside in favor of concerted action against the Indian raiders. Frontier estate owners welcomed new settlements of free peasants who provided additional military force against the Apaches. Since the Mexican army was far weaker than the Spanish army had been, estate owners compensated for this weakness by arming their peons, creating a mutual dependency and forcing many hacendados to improve the situation of their workers.

But not all conflicts in the northern frontier region were subordinated to the conflicts with nomadic raiders. The civil wars between rival elite factions that constantly affected the core areas of Mexico sometimes spread into the north. As in the colonial period, the Yaqui Indians of Sonora provided the one significant exception in the relations between the state and sedentary Indians. In the sixteenth and seventeenth centuries, while other sedentary Indian groups staged bloody uprisings against the Spaniards, the Yaquis had submitted without fighting to the missionaries. In the eighteenth century, when the resistance of the northern tribes (with the obvious exception of the Apaches and Comanches) had been broken, the Yaquis were the only ones to revolt. In the nineteenth century they became the only sedentary Indian group not only to continuously resist Mexican rule but also to do so with a certain measure of suc-

cess.[2] Two factors were responsible. First there was the extraordinary fertility of the Yaqui River valley, which attracted both settlers
and speculators, but the new Mexican state made no attempt, as its
Spanish predecessor had done, to limit encroachment onto Indian
lands. Second, rival groups such as the one led by Manuel de Gán-
dara in Sonora, constantly sought to mobilize the Yaquis against
competing Mexican factions. Once armed and mobilized, the Yaquis
saw no reason to disarm when their original sponsor directed them
to do so. In view of the internal dissent and innumerable conflicts
that plagued independent Mexico, the Yaquis felt strong enough to
reclaim their lands and to expel the intruders who had settled there.

The same pattern of uprisings continued until the end of the nineteenth century: the Yaquis would score initial successes and at
times secure control over the Yaqui River valley for several years,
expelling outsiders who had settled there, but sooner of later government forces would come in, defeat the Yaquis, and allow the settlers to return, and a precarious peace would be signed. Some Yaquis would submit while others either would leave to work in the
mines or haciendas in other parts of Sonora, or would continue
fighting from the surrounding mountains. Later when new encroachments were made on Yaqui lands, or when the country was
torn by internal dissent, a new uprising would occur that would follow the course of the preceding one. Success also depended on the
personalities of the Yaquis leaders. While charismatic leaders such
as Cájeme united most of the tribe, less influential personalities
could not overcome divisions within Yaqui ranks.

The continuities with the colonial period in northern Mexico contrasted sharply with new developments that represented a sharp
break with the past. The changes that occurred were due to the very
different relationship that developed between the free peasants, especially in the peripheral regions, and Mexico's central government.
The peasants viewed the new Mexican government as being less legitimate than the colonial one, due partly to its weakness and instability, so that until 1867 many important sectors of the population
refused to recognize whatever government was in power. Another
reason for the low prestige of the central government in the eyes of
many peasants was that it was never able to grant them the type of
protection afforded by the Spanish authorities. The Mexican government afforded neither protection from hacendados—since they
tended to control the judiciary—nor from nomadic Indian tribes in

[2] See essay by Evelyn Hu-DeHart, Chapter 5, this volume.

the frontier regions. In much of Mexico's periphery, the traditional functions of the colonial state were now assumed by regional caciques who, in return for the protection they granted, required the peasants to fight for them in the innumerable conflicts that afflicted the country. In a sea of instability, the caciques represented islands of stability.

Rural Revolts in Southeastern Mexico in the Early Nineteenth Century

Relations between hacendados and free villagers were much more antagonistic in the southeast than in the north. In the south, there was no tradition of a common struggle against raiders such as the Apaches. Also, class differences coincided with ethnic differences; the hacendados were whites or mestizos, the peasants were Indians. Along the northern frontier there was little incentive for the hacendados to expropriate village lands as long as the Indian wars lasted, so that estate owners had little interest in increasing production by appropriating new lands. Because of poor communications and Indian raids, the markets for their goods were limited. Southern hacendados, by contrast, had access to overseas markets and pressured the free peasants, especially in Yucatán.

As they expanded sugar and livestock production, Yucatecan hacendados began confiscating Maya lands, sought to restrict their access to water,[3] and imposed new taxes and labor services. Yucatán's rulers learned nothing from the experiences of their Sonoran counterparts; like the latter, they sought to utilize the fighting ability of the Indians for their factional struggles, arrogantly assuming that they would be able to control their allies. They paid an even higher price for their mistake than the Sonoran upper class had.

In 1847, Colonel Cetina, one of the leaders of Yucatán's many factions, approached a series of Maya caciques, Manuel Antonio Ay, Cecilio Chi, and Jacinto Pat, promising them more land and tax reductions if they supported him in a revolt against a rival faction then governing Yucatán. The caciques enthusiastically assured Cetina that he could count on their help and they proceeded to arm and mobilize not just the inhabitants of their villages but a large number of other Indians. The message some of them sent to their supporters was quite different from the one Cetina had expected and

---

[3] Moises González Navarro, *Raza y tierra* (Mexico, 1970), pp. 54–63; Nelson Reed, *The Caste War in Yucatán* (Stanford, 1964), Ch. 2.

hoped for. Declaring that the time had come for the Indians to reclaim their land, they called for the expulsion and massacre of all whites and mestizos.

By late 1848, the Maya seemed to be repeating what they had done three centuries before when the Spaniards attempted to conquer Yucatán. In 1548, the Maya towns put aside their differences and united to become the only major Indian group to inflict a decisive defeat on the Spaniards, who fled and did not return to Yucatán for more than fifteen years. In 1848, a Maya army besieged the capital city of Mérida and what had been unthinkable only a few months before—the expulsion or even a massacre of the white and mestizo population—became a stark and imminent possibility.

Relief for the besieged whites did not come from outside Yucatán but from within the Maya community. To the complete amazement of the beleaguered whites and mestizos, the Maya army began to melt away just when victory was imminent. By late 1848, the ladinos (non-Indians) had not only been saved from Maya domination but had themselves taken the offensive against the rebels. Why the Maya snatched defeat from the jaws of victory remains one of the most debated points in the history of the rising; it may have been because it was the planting season and many rebels felt it was time to go home—that ultimately maize was more important than politics, or perhaps many of the revolutionary Maya from the south of the peninsula had become discouraged when hacienda peons of the northwest, who shared the Maya language and culture, refused to join the revolt and at times even fought on their masters' side.[4]

The tide began to turn against the Maya. The ladinos went on the offensive against the weakened Indian army, and internal dissent among the Maya chiefs further demoralized those who still fought. When Jacinto Pat was murdered by his secretary, who was also his wife's lover, the rebels lost their most charismatic leader. The government counteroffensive was effective and brutal; thousands of captured Maya, both rebels and nonrebels, were sold as slaves to Cuba.

Although the government succeeded in regaining control of most of Yucatán, it was not able to finally defeat the rebellious Indians who continued until 1902 to control the southern end of the peninsula where the Indians set up a state that in many respects attempted to revive pre-Columbian Maya traditions and forms of organization. It was ruled by a coalition of military leaders and priests

[4] González Navarro, *Raza y tierra*, p. 87.

of the Speaking Cross, a cult that mixed Christianity and ancient Maya cults. This independent Maya state was bolstered by entrepreneurs in neighboring British Honduras who supplied the Maya with arms in return for exportable timber.

The Caste Wars in Yucatán had an enormous impact on Mexico. Many whites and mestizos became panic-stricken and considered every Indian revolt or even protest movement as an incipient caste war, and violence against Indians increased in many parts of the country. The effects of the Yucatán uprisings on other Indians is still the subject of debate. It may have encouraged many Indians in other parts of the country to revolt but it is doubtful whether it inspired any kind of caste war on the model of Yucatán that aimed to expel or destroy non-Indians.

The very different effects of the Yucatán caste war on Indians and non-Indians were also apparent in an uprising that has frequently been labeled the Caste War of Chiapas. According to some contemporary accounts, in 1868 a religious movement developed among the Chamula Indians of Chiapas with the avowed aim of expelling or killing all the mestizo and white inhabitants of that state. In 1868 a young girl, Agustina Gómez Chechep, had a vision and believed that she had found talking stones, through which God talked to her. Returning home one day to her village of Tzajalhemel from one of her walks, she brought back some stones that had caught her fancy. She left them on the family altar, and two days later rumors were rife that Agustina's stones could indeed "talk," that they made strange noises that were messages from God. Agustina turned the stones over to the village's mayor, Pedro Díaz Cuscat, who took them home for the night and verified that the stones could "talk." Tzajalhemel quickly became an attraction and the "talking" stones the object of many pilgrimages. But things did not stop there; the cult soon turned into a vehicle of social protest. The Chamulas ceased attending markets and other public events attended by non-Indians, and they began cleaning their weapons and collecting ammunition. The authorities became alarmed, and the village priest called on the Indians to abjure their new creed. Federal militiamen finally arrested both Agustina Gómez Chechep and Pedro Díaz Cuscat, but that was not enough to stifle the movement. The Indians found a new leader in Ignacio Fernández Galindo, an outsider from Mexico City who was not even an Indian and who captivated the Chamulas when he told them of how the Maya in Yucatán and the Apaches in the north had succeeded in shaking off white domination. He vowed to lead them into "a golden age" in which the land they tilled would be theirs and the income they earned would not be taxed. His wife, Luisa Quevedo, he said, would be the guardian angel of their cause. Galindo assembled a fighting force of several hundred men and proceeded to march on the state capital, San Cristobal de las Casas, where Agustina and Pedro Díaz were being held prisoner. The commander of San Cristobal's local militia wanted to avoid bloodshed and offered to "compromise" with the rebels. He gave the two a three-day leave so they could visit with their families and friends, but kept Galindo, his wife, and a third man as hostages. Two days later Pedro Díaz was back—at the head of eight hundred men. The local commander thereupon had Galindo and his friend shot (he spared Galindo's wife), and launched an assault on Pedro Díaz's men. The Indians withdrew. Several months later they rose again, but with less success.[5]

What had been called the Caste War in Chiapas, according to another account, was merely a defensive reaction of the Chamula Indians. Competing white factions had armed the Indians and tried to utilize them for their own ends, just as they had in Sonora and Yucatán. Unlike the Yaquis and the Maya, the Chamulas did not attempt to utilize their new-found strength in order to expel non-Indians from their territory, but instead they attempted to withdraw from Mexican society, refusing to pay taxes or to provide labor. They withdrew from the Catholic Church and developed both a religion and a religious hierarchy of their own. Their religious fiestas were not held in San Cristobal, one of the state's largest cities and one with a largely non-Indian population, but in the Indian village of Tzajalhemel. The Chamulas revolted in 1868 when the whites, as a consequence of the defeat of the government of Emperor Maximilian and the end of the civil war in Mexico, were strong enough to reimpose control over the Indians by collecting taxes and attempting to destroy their religious symbols. Some non-Indians were killed, but there was no general massacre of whites or mestizos in Chamula-controlled territory. Galindo's role was not as has been depicted in the traditional version. A radical teacher from Mexico City, he steadfastly maintained that he had not tried to head a religious caste war but rather to pacify the Indians and to effect a kind of compromise. He felt that the liberation of Cuzcat, their leader, would pacify the Indians. The fact that he offered himself as hostage

---

[5] This version is based on the account of the "Caste War" in Chiapas by the state governor as well as by contemporary non-Indian authors. The relevant documents are contained in Leticia Reina, *Las rebeliones campesinas en México, 1819–1906* (México, 1980), pp. 45–61.

to the authorities was a sign that he was obviously not contemplating a rebellion. It was the whites' fear of a caste war that led to the repression and a full-scale massacre of the Indians.[6] Dominguez, governor of Chiapas, had become so panic-stricken that in a letter to the minister of gobernación in Mexico City he called for the deportation of all Indians from Chiapas, a "remedy" that was never attempted.[7]

But no matter which interpretation one accepts, there is no doubt that the Chamula uprising had certain basic traits in common with both the Tzeltal rebellion of the seventeenth century and the Caste War in Yucatán. Like these revolts, it developed a religion of its own. Though it was strongly inspired by Catholicism, it also had a strong ethnic orientation. Like the caste wars in Yucatán and the Yaqui uprising in Sonora, it was an Indian rebellion directed against both the state and the non-Indian population, and it took place in regions where there had been revolts in the colonial period. Unlike the Yaquis or the Maya, the Chamulas failed, and the movement was crushed within a relatively short time. These different results may have been due to the better organization of landowners in Chiapas and to the province's closer ties to the rest of Mexico as compared to Sonora and Yucatán. Furthermore, the Chamula merely developed a limited defensive strategy and not the kind of offensive posture that characterized their counterparts in Yucatán and Sonora.

Regional Strongmen as Allies in Peasant Revolts

As already noted, the power vacuum created by the weakness of the Mexican state encouraged the proliferation of regional caciques in much of the country's periphery. While the national government in Mexico City changed practically every year until the 1860s, many regional strongmen exercised effective power for twenty or thirty years. Their links to the peasants varied, as illustrated by two of the most powerful regional chieftains of Mexico, the conservative Manuel Lozada in Tepic and the liberal Luis Terrazas in Chihuahua.

Manuel Lozada led the free villages of his territory first in support of conservatives in Mexico's civil wars, and later of Maximilian. On

[6] Jan Rus, "Whose Caste War? Indians, Ladinos, and the Chiapas 'Caste War' of 1869," in *Spaniards and Indians in Southeastern Mesoamerica: Essays on the History of Ethnic Relations*, ed. Murdo J. MacCleod and Robert Wasserstrom (Lincoln, Nebraska, 1983), pp. 127–69 (see also Luis de Leon pp. 90–94).

[7] Reina, *Las rebeliones*, pp. 54–56.

the one hand, he was linked to sectors of the local oligarchy because he had helped one of the wealthiest trading houses in Mexico, the British company Barron and Forbes, to gain quasi-monopolistic control of trade in Tepic. Yet on the other, Lozada was strongly committed to the rights of the peasants against the encroachments of large estates, and helped return lands taken by haciendas to Indian communal villages that constituted one of the mainstays of his movement. As a result, his movement was increasingly feared and resented by hacendados both in Tepic and in neighboring states.[8]

The popular Luis Terrazas, the liberal governor of Chihuahua (with a few interruptions) from 1861 to 1884, did not protect his peasants from encroachments by landowners, nor did he need to, since until 1884 the population of the state was so sparse that land was not a major issue. But the Apaches were a far more serious problem; their attacks became more ferocious as they were pushed south and west by the steady advance, first of the Commanches and then of the U.S. frontier. Terrazas gained legitimacy and popularity in the eyes of the state's free peasants—many of whom had originally settled as military colonists to fight the Apaches—by organizing the militia that resisted the raiders. It was a relative, Joaquin Terrazas, who inflicted the greatest defeat upon the Apaches at the battle of Tres Castillos in 1879. When the government attempted to remove Terrazas from power in 1879, many of the state's peasants rose in arms to demand his reinstatement.[9]

It was in the north, where a common defense against raiders was encouraged, that peasants did tend to form close alliances with these powerful regional figures, who were neither Indians nor peasants. Such alliances were not as frequent in peripheral areas outside the areas of Apache activity, but where they did exist, the common link between peasants and caudillos was opposition to government control; the common goal was regional autonomy, as was the case in the state of Guerrero.

Although he came from a wealthy family and owned large haciendas, Juan Alvarez was a liberal who had joined the pro-independence army of José María Morelos as a common soldier in 1811 and soon became an officer. From 1820 until his death in 1862 he was one of the most powerful caudillos in his native state of Guerrero. At times he was the military commander and at others governor, but

[8] Jean Meyer, "El reino de Lozada en Tepic (1856–1873)," *Actes du XLII Congrès International des Americanistes, Paris* 3 (1978): 95–109.

[9] Francisco R. Almada, *Resumen de historia del estado de Chihuahua* (México, 1955), pp. 319–25.

his power never waned; he was both a protector of the peasants and a mediator. In 1824 he prevented estate owners from entirely confiscating the lands of villages in the Tecoanapa region and restrained peasants from violent confrontation with the hacendados.[10] He managed to maintain the unquestioning loyalty of Guerrero's peasants until his death in 1862. They followed him in 1855 to Mexico City, where he proclaimed the Plan de Ayutla, calling for the overthrow of the conservative government and its replacement by the liberals. They also followed him in 1862 when he appealed to them to resist the French invaders.

In central Mexico, by contrast, the links between the central government, regional authorities, and the hacendados were much stronger. Here most caciques did not need peasant support, and peasants frequently had no caciques to turn to for protection,[11] so that rural revolts tended to be much more autonomous than those at the periphery. These divergent traditions may have constituted one of the root causes for the profound differences between central and northern Mexican rural movements in the 1910 revolution. In accordance with nineteenth-century tradition, the peasants of Morelos produced their own leaders, while the northern peasants continued to look to caudillos to lead them.

Rural Revolts in
Central Mexico up to 1884

Perhaps the greatest difference between eighteenth-century peasant movements and those of independent Mexico in the nineteenth century was found in central Mexico. The motivation, character, and type of the later revolts differed in many respects from their predecessors in the eighteenth century. The first difference was the importance of the land issue. Of the 142 rebellions Taylor identified in the colonial period in central Mexico, only 30 were linked to the land issue. Of 55 rebellions before 1885 that have been clearly identified, land was the primary issue in thirty-four.[12] The second major difference can be seen in the scale of revolts. Most of the colonial revolts in central Mexico were local, one-village affairs, whereas the

---

[10] See essay by John Hart, Chapter 8, this volume.

[11] See essay by John Tutino, Chapter 4, this volume.

[12] These numbers are based on the rural uprisings described in Reina, *Las rebeliones*. Jean Meyer, *Problemas campesinos y revueltas agrarias (1821–1910)* (México, 1973); Meyer lists 66 rural uprisings between 1821 and 1855, of which at least 44 were linked to the land issue.

majority of nineteenth-century revolts involved several villages, and
frequently thousands of men. Third, while outsiders played no role
in fomenting colonial revolts, they were involved in twenty-one out
of fifty-five nineteenth-century revolts, and they were generally nonpeasants.

One of the most obvious factors that gave increasing relevance to
the land issue was that the Mexican state was neither able nor willing to impose the same kind of restraint on hacendados as the Spanish state had. On the contrary, the Ley Lerdo, passed by the liberals
in 1856, sanctioned the dissolution of communal property, and inevitably led to expropriation of peasant lands. There is no indication, however, that rebellions based on land or related issues such
as water rights were more frequent after 1856; of the thirty-four rebellions I have found where land constituted the central problem,
sixteen occurred before 1856. Two very different conclusions could
be drawn from this. The first would be that even before land expropriations were sanctioned by federal law, the hacendados were confiscating peasant-owned land. This possibility is further strengthened by the promulgation of state laws requiring the alienation of
lands belonging to civil (but not ecclesiastical) corporations such as
villages and ayuntamientos in Veracruz and elsewhere. The opposite conclusion is drawn by John Coatsworth, who believes that in
the first half of the century it was the peasants rather than the hacendados who were on the offensive,[13] largely due to land hunger, exacerbated by population pressure and the weakness of the new Mexican state. Coatsworth's hypothesis appears to be confirmed by the
fact that in most of the sixteen cases of uprisings linked to the land
issue before 1856, I was unable to find any complaints by the peasants about recent takeovers of their lands by hacendados. The peasants simply demanded the return of properties that in their opinion
were rightfully theirs ("from time immemorial"), without specifying
when the hacendados had "stolen" them.

Rural Revolts and Porfirian Rule

As the Mexican state grew stronger, rural revolts changed profoundly, especially after 1884 when Porfirio Díaz began his second
term in office and established a dictatorship that would last until
the revolution toppled him in 1911. The political transformations
that Díaz set in motion were linked to profound socioeconomic

[13] See essay by John H. Coatsworth, Chapter 2 in this volume.

changes for which the year 1884 was a kind of watershed. In that year the railroad development program initiated by Díaz in his first term (1876–80) and fostered by his successor, Manuel González (1880–84), began to produce significant results. A 16,000-mile network of railroads soon crossed large parts of a country where navigable rivers were few and mountain ranges impeded access. The effects of railroad construction were enormous. Foreign and domestic investment in agriculture, mining, and in other branches of the economy increased at record rates, and new international and national markets for mineral and agricultural products emerged, and land values soared.

But Mexico's economic boom led to the greatest catastrophe since the massive Indian mortality of the sixteenth and seventeenth centuries. Most of the villagers who had managed to retain their lands throughout the colonial period lost them in the late nineteenth and twentieth centuries to hacendados, speculators, or wealthier members of their communities.[14] These expropriations began during the

[14] These expropriations have been documented, above all, from complaints voiced by peasants during the Porfiriato as well as during the revolution and its aftermath. On the other hand, there are unfortunately no exact statistics that show exactly when these expropriations occurred or how much land was expropriated. A number of authors have attempted to document the extent of landlessness of Mexican peasants by analyzing data from the censuses of 1895, 1900, and 1910. See Frank Tannenbaum, *The Mexican Agrarian Revolution* (Washington, 1930); George M. McBride, *The Land System of Mexico* (New York, 1923); *Estadísticas sociales del porfiriato, 1877–1910* (México, 1956); these authors concluded that over 90 percent of Mexican peasants were landless. The Mexican census divided the rural population into three categories: hacendados, agricultores, and peones—only the first two categories owned land while the third category consisted of landless peasants. François Xavier Guerra, *Le Mexique, de l'ancien régime à la revolution* (Paris, 1985), Vol. 2, pp. 472–89, disputes these findings on the basis of local sources that the group called "peones" by no means exclusively consisted of landless laborers, and that many of the "peones" in fact lived in communal villages and had land of their own, but frequently worked part time on large estates.

Guerra also disputes Tannenbaum's finding that a large percentage of the rural population lived on haciendas. Tannenbaum had based this conclusion on statistics describing a relatively large rural population as living in communities called *ranchos*, which constituted parts of haciendas and their inhabitants could thus be called hacienda residents. Guerra disputes these findings, stating that only a minority of the ranchos were in fact part of large estates and that many of them were village communities that simply did not have the legal status of traditional communities. While Guerra's conclusions do cast doubts on existing conclusions about the extent of landlessness among Mexico's poorer peasants, Guerra has not been able to provide any alternative data. Even if one agrees that the level of expropriation was lower than these statistics suggest, there is still no doubt that a massive process of land transfer

period known as the Restored Republic (1867–76), even before the railroads were built. Plans for railroad construction in a given area were sufficient to cause an increase in land values that served as an incentive for expropriations.[15] Nonetheless, despite the fact that we have no firm evidence to pinpoint the timing of these expropriations, it appears that most occurred during the Portfiriato. Speculators reaped what were often fantastic profits by expropriating village lands and selling them either to Mexican landowners, to whom it was a way of expanding production without large-scale investment, or to foreign investors. In many cases, the expropriation of the lands of free villages was an easy way to gain additional laborers without increasing wages, since the newly landless peasants, deprived of their means of subsistence, frequently had no choice but to work on large haciendas.

Two laws underpinned these expropriations. The first was the Ley Lerdo, passed long before Díaz assumed power, in 1856, which made land ownership by village communities illegal, and required them to sell it. In principle, community members had the first option to buy it, but often the land was immediately sold to outsiders, since most peasants simply did not have the money. Those who did acquire land were easily forced to sell it by corrupt local officials, wealthy peasants to whom they owed money, or neighboring hacendados.

The second legal underpinning for the massive expropriation of peasant lands were laws concerning public lands, the first of which was adopted under President Benito Juarez in 1856–59, but the one that had the most profound effect on Mexico's agrarian structure was passed during the Manuel González administration. The Ley de Terrenos Baldíos (law on vacant lands) of 1883 allowed development companies to survey vacant public lands, in return for which they were allowed to keep one-third of the land. The government kept the other two-thirds of it, and then sold it to hacendados or foreign investors.[16]

from traditional communities to wealthy peasants, speculators, and hacendados did take place.

[15] John H. Coatsworth, *Growing Against Development: the Economic Impact of Railroads in Porfirian Mexico* (De Kalb, 1981), pp. 149–74.

[16] On the basis of a monumental work by Wistano Luis Orozco, a Mexican scholar and surveyor, *Legislación y jurisprudencia sobre terrenos baldíos* (México, 1895), it has generally been assumed that the responsibility for land expropriations lay with "compañias deslindadoras" (surveying companies). The 1883 law authorized the federal government to hire the companies to survey public lands, for which they would be granted one-third of these lands. The law specified that lands belonging to peas-

These expropriations eventually became one of the basic causes
of the 1910 revolution. One of the most controversial and least explored problems of Mexican history is how much peasant resistance
and unrest the expropriations produced between 1884 and 1911.
These uncertainties are mainly due to the fact that one of the main
sources dealing with peasant rebellions in the Porfiriato, the papers
of the Secretaría de la Defensa Nacional, have for a long time been
inaccessible to most historians so that the impression at times
emerged that once the Porfirian regime was firmly established, the
number of rural rebellions fell drastically. But a number of studies
recently made of the period 1891–98 show that this was not the
case.[17] In those seven years alone, there were sixteen rural uprisings.
There was a significant difference, however, between rural revolts

ants could not be confiscated, but in practice, Orozco and many later scholars felt
that the protection granted small landowners was illusory. Many peasants had no
clear title to their land, but even when they did, the survey companies tended to ride
roughshod over their rights. In theory, the peasants had the right to appeal against
survey companies' decisions, but in practice it was rare for the courts, state governments, or federal executives even to attempt to grant redress.

This conclusion has been sharply disputed by Robert H. Holden in *The Mexican
State Manages Modernization: The Survey of the Public Lands in Six States 1876–
1911*, Ph.D. Dissertation, University of Chicago, 1986. Holden was the first scholar to
examine surveying companies' records in Mexico's agrarian archives; he studied six
states where the survey companies had been particularly active and concluded that
while there had been flagrant cases of expropriations of village lands, they were relatively scarce. He only found 144 objections by communities or individuals to the
surveying companies findings, and found that government frequently sided with ob-
jectors and in some cases forced the companies to respect their landholdings. This
does not mean that there were no massive expropriations of peasants' lands by means
of the law relating to public lands; the expropriators were perhaps more likely to be
the government itself, or wealthy hacendados, than the surveying companies. The
most flagrant case in Chihuahua in which lands were taken from villagers in favor of
a wealthy individual concerned the finance minister, José Yves Limantour, in 1891.
A concession was granted to him directly by the government without the involvement of a surveying company, and led to a series of uprisings by villagers who refused to accept the loss of their lands. See Archivo del Departamento Agrario, Sección de Terrenos Nacionales (hereafter ADA, STN) diversos, No. 152, Cargill Lumber
Company. In other cases, such as lands belonging to the village of Naranja in the state
of Michoacán, it was an hacendado who owned a neighboring hacienda who denounced the village lands as public lands and secured their transfer to his estate. See
Paul Friedrich, *Agrarian Revolt in a Mexican Village* (Englewood Cliffs, 1970).

[17] Almada found eleven rural uprisings that took place in Chihuahua between 1891
and 1898; see Francisco R. Almada, *La revolución en el estado de Chihuahua* (México, 1964), Vol. 1, pp. 93–107. Five rural uprisings in other states (Mexico, Morelos,
Veracruz, Guerrero, Yucatán) also took place in this period, and these are documented in records in the Colección Porfirio Díaz, published by the Universidad Ibero-
Americana as *Sublevaciones rurales en México 1891–1893*.

before and after 1884. In the earlier period, large-scale regional uprisings were frequent. After 1884, revolts tended to be local and limited to one or two villages, as had been the case during the colonial
period. Rural revolts, with the significant exception of the Yaqui revolt, rarely occurred in northern Mexico before 1884, but afterward
the north became an increasingly important center of rural unrest.

It is not easy to explain why the Mexican peasantry, at a time
when it underwent what was perhaps the greatest setback in its history, only carried out localized and sporadic acts of resistance. In
the colonial period the possibility of appealing to the courts was one
explanation for the relatively limited number of rural revolts. During the Porfiriato the courts were far more biased against the peasants, who had no illusions about the Mexican judicial system. The
limited character of rural uprisings between 1884 and 1911 was
partly due to the fact that the newly strengthened and stabilized
Díaz administration, as well as the different state governors, had
more and better-equipped military forces at their disposal than ever
before. Both the regular army and auxiliary troops, including national and state *rurales*, were expanded, better equipped, and placed
under stricter government control. At the same time, the new railroads allowed government forces to reach previously inaccessible
parts of the country, and yet repression alone does not account for
why peasants, many of whom had a long tradition of fighting for
their rights against both the landowners and the government, now
submitted to these expropriations without resistance. For some, the
effect of losing their land and their traditional subsistence was tempered by new opportunities brought by the Porfirian economic
boom, such as in railroad construction, or in the expanding mining
and textile industries. Thanks to the railroads, some could move to
regions of greater demand for labor, especially the north, where
wages were higher than elsewhere; others could cross the border
and work in the U.S. Nevertheless, the level of emigration from the
villages during the Porfirian era was far too limited to explain the
passivity of the peasants.

One important obstacle to effective resistance by the peasants was
loss of their traditional village autonomy and organization. Regional
caudillos, hacendados, and state governments had always sought to
impose some kind of control over village administrations. But this
tendency was inhibited by the relative weakness of central and regional authorities, the resulting need of many caudillos and hacendados to placate the peasants to some degree, and the geographical
isolation of many villages. In 1884, however, a new municipal au-

thority system was set up in most Mexican states. With the sanction of the central government, state administrations appointed district officials (*jefes políticos*) who began exercising more control over municipal authorities in their jurisdictions. While they interfered everywhere, in many states such as Chihuahua they were given broad legal sanctions to do so. In 1903–04, Governor Enrique Creel replaced large numbers of elected mayors with appointed officials, the result of which can best be seen by examining the petitions that peasants forwarded to the Díaz administration and in which they protested against a wide variety of abuses, especially land expropriations. Up to the turn of the century most of these petitions had been signed by village authorities, but during the last years of the Díaz regime they were more often signed by individual peasants and former officials, and only very rarely village administrators,[18] and this loss of autonomy had several contradictory effects. On the one hand, it enormously increased peasant resentment against local, regional, and national authorities and induced many villagers to participate in the 1910 revolution. But on the other hand, in the short term it deprived the peasants of a traditional and important instrument of social protest; their own, elected municipal authorities.

Peasant resistance to actions by the state and expropriations by the landowners was also inhibited by the loss of traditional sources of support. As I have pointed out, peasants often cooperated with regional caudillos, who in return gave them a degree of protection. This relationship radically changed during the Díaz regime. The situation in Chihuahua is a good example, though it may not be valid for all of Mexico because of the way the changes occurred. The state's strongman, Luis Terrazas, who for many years had been governor of Chihuahua, actively courted peasant support. In the 1860s during his administration, some military colonies were created and lands given to peasants in frontier areas. He organized peasant militias against the Apaches, and in a number of cases he sought to prevent speculators taking over peasant lands. As a result, when Porfirio Díaz, who considered him a dangerous competitor, removed him from office in 1879, many peasants in western Chihuahua staged an armed uprising demanding his return. President González (1880–84) had no choice but to comply with the peasants' wishes. When Díaz again removed Terrazas from office in 1884, he gave him a free hand to pursue his economic interests. The Chihuahuan caudillo had no compunction about expropriating and speculating in

[18] These petitions are located in ADA, STN.

peasant lands, but his activities only affected a limited number of peasants and Terrazas continued to enjoy a large measure of prestige among many rural inhabitants of Chihuahua. They blamed their misfortunes mainly on the state's administration, which was controlled by Terrazas' rivals. Many peasants still turned to Terrazas when they had grievances against the state government. In the 1890s, when a number of villages in western Chihuahua staged uprisings against the attempts by the state government to eliminate municipal autonomy, they sought Terrazas' support and surreptitiously received it.[19] At the turn of the century, in an attempt to consolidate his government, Porfirio Díaz made his peace not only with Luis Terrazas but with a number of the regional caudillos whom he had kept from political power until then. The governorship of Chihuahua was handed over to the Terrazas–Creel clan, who now turned against their erstwhile allies.

The new state government enacted a land law that was far more drastic with respect to expropriations of peasant lands than anything that had gone before, and which put an end to the last remnants of village self-administration.[20] The peasants, though, did not at first rebel against these measures. As a result of the loss of their traditional supporters, who had now become their main enemies, they were disoriented and sought new sources of support. It took them some years to find them. When they did, the Mexican revolution of 1910 broke out in Chihuahua.

The loss of both traditional vehicles of protest and of caudillo support may explain why the scope of peasant uprisings diminished during the Porfiriato, but it does not explain why none of the Chihuahua uprisings between 1890 and 1910 appears to have been caused by the land issue.[21] One explanation frequently given is that the importance of this issue in Chihuahua has been exaggerated, but this was definitely not the case. For the years 1980 to 1910, I found more than twenty-five petitions from villages in Chihuahua bitterly protesting land expropriations,[22] yet very few villagers participated

[19] Almada, *Resumen*, pp. 319–25, 347–53.

[20] Mark Wasserman, *Capitalists, Caciques, and Revolution: The Native Elite and Foreign Enterprise in Chihuahua, Mexico, 1854–1911* (Chapel Hill, 1984), pp. 104, 109, 112, 136.

[21] The immediate causes of revolt were in general tax increases and attempts by the state government to impose local authorities on recalcitrant villages. This problem was indirectly related to the land issue, since the municipal authorities exercised a large measure of control over communally owned lands. Nevertheless, uprisings primarily directed against the confiscation of lands only occurred in 1910.

[22] These petitions can be found in ADA, STN.

in local uprisings prior to 1910, while most of the uprisings were directed against the imposition of higher taxes or the suppression of municipal authorities. The reasons for this behavior can best be analyzed by looking at the history of one village where land expropriation produced no uprisings but an increase in taxation did.

San Andrés was one of the oldest and most prestigious military colonies in Chihuahua, with a peasant population of both Indians and non-Indians. The Indians, whose tribal origins are not clear, were the first to settle in San Andrés and they did so with the enthusiastic approval of the owner of the neighboring hacienda of San Juan Guadalupe. Under constant attack by Apache raiders, the hacendados welcomed the settlement of men who were both willing and able to fight the raiders. The hacendado showed his appreciation of the fighting qualities of the settlers of San Andrés by granting them a large piece of land from his estate in 1735. The Spanish government obviously shared the hacendado's appreciation and enthusiasm, for at the end of the eighteenth century it granted public lands to San Andrés and attempted to attract new settlers.[23] They did, and the eighteenth century tradition was continued into the nineteenth century. The riflemen of San Andrés became known throughout Chihuahua for their fighting qualities and for their marksmanship. They were in the forefront of the army of military colonists that in 1879, at the battle of Tres Castillos, inflicted a crushing defeat on the greatest Apache leader, Victorio.[24] Their triumphant reception by the city of Chihuahua and the warm words of gratitude from state officials were soon forgotten. By the late nineteenth century, many of these riflemen, especially the Indians, were beginning to lose their lands. Luis Terrazas (under whose cousin, Joaquin, the riflemen of San Andrés had fought at Tres Castillos) had frequently praised their fighting qualities, and in 1904 he became governor of Chihuahua. One-hundred twenty Indians of San Andrés appealed to him to prevent the expropriation of their lands, and asked him to ratify the extensive land concessions they had obtained in the colonial period. Terrazas refused to comply with their demands, but he obviously felt that both he and the state of Chihuahua were under some obligation to these men who for so long had followed him and had fought so well against the Apaches. Terrazas thus wrote them that each Indian inhabitant of San Andrés should have the right to a minimum of three hectares of land. When after

[23] Ibid., San Andrés, p. 143.
[24] Memorias del Sr. Coronel D. Joaquin Terrazas, Chihuahua, 1980, pp. 71–82.

eight months in office Terrazas resigned and his son-in-law, Enrique Creel, succeeded him, Creel refused to implement his father-in-law's decision. Unlike Terrazas, Creel felt no obligations toward the former Indian fighters and he certainly wanted no conflict with the local landowners. He told the men of San Andrés that they should pay rent for their former lands to the present owners.

The former military colonists refused and decided to go to court, since they felt they had the necessary evidence to convince any judge or jury. They had the titles to the lands granted them by the Spanish colonial administration, and the title to the land that the owner of the hacienda of San Juan Guadalupe had granted them was deposited with his heirs. They called on the present hacienda owners to send them the title, and they deposited their government titles with the mayor of San Andrés, Lucas Murga. But, when the time came to present the documents to the judicial authorities, the peasants had no documents to show. The hacienda owner stated that he had no record of the cession by which his ancestor had granted lands to the Indians and Mayor Murga had "lost" the documents that the peasants of his own village had entrusted to him. The peasants now proceeded to elect one of their own, Macario Nieto, as their speaker, and he waged a long, bitter, and ultimately futile campaign for the peasants' rights. He wrote to the federal government and asked for redress, but the authorities merely referred him to the governor who had supported, if not instigated, the land expropriation.[25]

The land expropriation provoked no uprising or riots by the peasants, but one year later, when the state government attempted to raise San Andrés taxes, the whole village staged an uprising. The Murga family, which had played such an important role in the dispossession of the peasants, now figured prominently in the uprising against the state government.[26] The reasons are not difficult to identify. All of San Andrés was in agreement when it came to protesting taxes, but the land issue divided the village. Both neighboring hacendados and wealthy peasants within San Andrés were beneficiaries of the expropriations of the lands of the poorest inhabitants of their communities.

A final element that contributed to diffusing northern peasant resistance to land expropriation was the fact that, until about 1907, the expropriations did not lead to widespread rural unemployment

[25] ADA, STN, San Andrés, p. 143.
[26] Almada, *La revolución*, pp. 116–18.

since peasants on the whole had no great difficulty in finding work while the economy was booming either in Mexico or the U.S. Conversely when in 1907 a recession hit both the southwest U.S. and Mexico, the northern peasants were more affected by it than any other rural group in Mexico.

The Revolutions of 1810 and 1910
in Comparative Perspective

On the whole there is little doubt that the Spaniards were far more successful than the Mexican governments of the early nineteenth century or even the strong government of Porfirio Díaz in preventing or curbing rural uprisings. The causes for this discrepancy are not too difficult to determine: The greater stability and strength of the Spanish state, the greater interest of the Spanish crown in comparison to later Mexican governments in maintaining at least partially the integrity of communal village properties, the legitimacy of the crown in the peasants' eyes by protecting their holdings, the fact that the major expropriations that occurred during the colonial period frequently took place "painlessly," i.e., at a time when the owners of the expropriated lands died during the period of massive Indian epidemics. In view of these discrepancies, one might logically expect that rural reaction to the Crown would be far more muted than toward the Mexican state, and it was true for most of the colonial period. Nevertheless, the attitude of the 1810–11 rural revolutionaries was by no means more restrained towards the Spanish colonial administration than the attitude of the 1910–11 rural revolutionaries towards the regime of Porfirio Díaz. In fact, if we compare the first and most spontaneous phases of the two revolutions, the Hidalgo uprising of 1810 and the Madero revolt of 1910–11, the first was much bloodier than the second. The Madero revolution can be considered a gentle revolution and with very few exceptions (such as the killings of Chinese in Torreon in 1911), no massacres even remotely similar to those carried out by Hidalgo's followers were perpetrated by the men who, frequently only under the very loose control of Madero, rose up in 1910–11. The discrepancy can only be explained by a broader comparison of the two revolutions.

There are a number of striking similarities between them. They were national in character though they never embraced all of Mexico. The revolutionary forces were heterogeneous in their composition, including all social classes ranging from landowners and industrialists to members of both the urban and rural middle classes, and large numbers of peasants and rural laborers. Both in 1810 and 1910 dissident members of the middle and upper classes called on the peasants to rebel, although in 1810 the accent was more on the middle classes whereas in 1910 upper class participation was greater.

Large-scale rural uprisings occurred both in 1810 and 1910 and the members of the elites who had called for them soon began to lose control of their followers. In a second phase of both revolutions, the elites attempted to regain control of the popular movements, though they did so in very different ways. Morelos in 1812 and 1813 succeeded in disciplining his followers far more than his predecessor, Hidalgo, had done, by advocating profound social and economic changes. In 1911–1912, Francisco I. Madero, who did not want profound social changes in the countryside, attempted to regain control by dissolving the revolutionary armies and by returning to the old federal army.

In both cases, the main leaders of the first phase of the revolution were defeated and killed, and counterrevolutions headed by the Spanish army in 1814, and by Huerta and the federal army in 1913 were triumphant. But these counterrevolutionary forces failed to restore the status quo ante. New revolutionary movements led by more moderate or even conservative leaders emerged and in the process the popular movements were either coopted, as in the case of the 1821 independence revolt, or both subdued and coopted, as in Mexico after 1916.

All of the regions that formed the core of the 1810–20 and 1910–20 revolutions had some common characteristics—rapidly spreading commercialization, a tremendous increase in agricultural output, and a mining boom in some areas—as well as some profound differences. Some centers of revolution (such as Guadalajara in 1810 and Morelos in 1910) were traditional village communities that were deeply affected by developments just before the great upheavals. On the other hand, there were some less traditional areas where recent immigrants of mixed origins had settled, such as the Bajío in 1810, and the northern triangle of Sonora, Chihuahua, and Coahuila in 1910. On the eve of the 1910 revolution, the rural population of the northern triangle was markedly heterogeneous, and was divided into what could be called traditional peasants and a large and diversified population on the haciendas.

The traditional peasants of the north had become increasingly differentiated ethnically and economically. In Sonora, most traditional peasants were Yaqui or Mayo Indians who retained their languages, common religions, tribal organizations, and a strong sense of ethnic loyalties. Nevertheless, a profound differentiation, especially among the Yaqui Indians, had occurred during the nineteenth and early twentieth centuries. After the defeat of the Yaqui uprising under Cajeme in 1887, the Yaquis finally lost most of their land in the fertile Yaqui River valley, which they had controlled for so long, and the tribe became deeply divided. Some Yaquis stayed in the valley, a few retained portions of their land, while others worked as laborers on neighboring estates. Many spread out through Sonora, working in mines and on distant estates, to Arizona, and a small group went into the mountains of the Sierra de Bacatete and continued a guerrilla struggle against the Mexican army. But this dispersal did not put an end to the Yaqui nation, which continues to exist today; it merely prevented the Yaquis from becoming a united force both before and during the revolution. The Yaquis did participate prominently in that event, but they did do so in different revolutionary factions.

A similar differentiation occurred among another group of peasants, in the state of Chihuahua. Although some were Tarahumara Indians, most were not ethnically different from the rest of the population in the state—they were military colonists who were granted land by the Spanish colonial administration in the late eighteenth century and later by successive governments, especially by that of Benito Juarez in the 1860s. After 1885, however, many of these peasants lost land to survey companies, to estate owners, or to wealthier peasants from their villages, many of whom were recent immigrants who confiscated them with the help of both the state and federal governments. Even before this wave of expropriations, these villages were far more heterogeneous than those of central and southern Mexico. Since land values had been minimal, while the northern frontier region remained isolated and the Apaches continued their attacks, both the Spanish and Mexican governments had been willing to grant colonists extensive agricultural and grazing lands, making them far wealthier than peasants elsewhere. Unlike the free peasants in central Mexico, they were allowed to buy and sell land within their villages, so that a greater degree of differentiation within them emerged. The rapid economic, social, and political integration of the north with the rest of the country, the large-scale emigration from central Mexico, and the expropriation of village lands tended to further increase social cleavages.

Economic differentiation became evident in much of northern Mexico but did not lead to the same type of conflict, between subsistence peasants and wage laborers employed outside the villages in lumber mills and mines, or even in the United States or the cotton fields of the Laguna.

Socioeconomic differentiation was even greater among hacienda laborers than among the free peasants, as revealed by a 1914 survey of conditions on estates owned by the Chihuahuan oligarchy that were confiscated by Pancho Villa.[27] The survey found wealthy tenants who sublet the lands they had rented to other medium-sized tenants whose income and wealth varied enormously and depended on whether they rented out irrigated or nonirrigated land. There were also poor sharecroppers eking out a precarious existence on marginal lands, and temporary workers who received high wages at harvest but had to move on during the rest of the year. Debt peonage and other restrictions on mobility still seem to have existed on some of the Terrazas' haciendas and contrasted sharply with the complete freedom of movement and payment in hard currency found on large foreign-owned estates. Another group very different from both peons and tenants was composed of well-paid cowboys who frequently constituted a kind of aristocracy from whose ranks hacienda owners tended to recruit armed retainers. This heterogeneity was strengthened by the fact that many estate laborers from the north were semi-agricultural, semi-industrial migrants who worked part-time in mines, industry, or in the United States. For a long time, this diversity impeded the emergence of a common revolutionary movement; for example, when a series of village uprisings took place in the mountains of Chihuahua in 1891, 1892, and 1893, the agricultural laborers showed no interest in participating.

Diverse as the situation of the rural population was, its one common denominator—the dependence on capitalist development—created a commonality of interest between 1908 and 1911 that had never before existed. The 1907–10 economic crisis that originated in the United States had profound consequences for the Mexican north. Many Mexican mines and lumber mills were forced to close, while thousands of Mexican laborers on ranches or in industries or mines in the U.S. lost their jobs and had to return home.[28] There they increased the agricultural labor force, and wages fell. A banking crisis led to a sharp curtailment of credit, which in turn affected many of the middle-sized peasants and tenants. Because many large

[27] Friedrich Katz, "Condiciones de trabajo en las haciendas de Mexico durante el porfiriato: Modalidades y tendencias," in *Servidumbre agraria en México en la época porfiriana*, ed. Friedrich Katz (México, 1980), p. 46.
[28] Ibid.

companies were exempted from taxes because of special concessions granted by the state government, the latter increased taxation
of small and medium-sized ranchers. All of this coincided with an
agricultural crisis; three years of bad harvests in a row had catastrophic effects on the whole of the agricultural population. The
German consul in Chihuahua estimated that nominal wages between 1908 and 1909 had fallen by about 60 percent, while the
prices of corn and beans had increased by 70 percent.[29]

For the first time, this crisis tended to unite the various segments
of the agricultural population and created a readiness to rebel, although perhaps because of their diversity they never managed to
create autonomous movements beyond the village level. Directly or
indirectly, nearly all the revolutionary movements in the north were
led by revolutionary hacendados, as in Coahuila and Sonora, or by
members of the urban and agricultural middle classes, as in Chihuahua in 1910–11.

There are a number of hypotheses to explain why northern peasants and agricultural laborers were ready to accept not just leadership from the middle class (as was also the case in other parts of
Mexico), but also leadership from hacendados, which does not seem
to have been the rule elsewhere. In part, it may have resulted from
the old tradition of common resistance to the Apaches and other
raiders; unlike other regions of Mexico, conflicts between hacendados and peasants were not endemic to the north until the end of the
Apache wars. There had been sufficient lands and resources for
both, and in the eyes of both peasants and hacendados the main obstacle to development was the Apaches. When a completely new
situation emerged in the 1880s, and a large number of hacendados
began seizing peasant lands, not all estate owners were involved in
these seizures; those who were not involved continued to be considered "good" hacendados, who frequently had a patron-client relationship with laborers on their estates. Such relationships had
various origins. In Sonora the most prominent revolutionary
hacendado, José María Maytorena, protected his Yaqui laborers from
deportation by the state government, and since he had never taken
Yaqui lands, the Yaqui considered him their protector, and accepted
his leadership during the revolution.[30]

Francisco Madero paid the laborers on his estate in the Laguna

[29] Deutsches Zentralarchiv, Potsdam. AAII Nr. 4491, Consul in Chihuahua to Bülow,
October 5, 1909.
[30] Hector Aguilar Camin, *La frontera nómada: Sonora y la revolución mexicana*
(Mexico, 1977), pp. 64–69.

area of northern Mexico in cash, provided them with social services, supplied food in times of hunger to them and their relatives who were not even working on his estates, and came to be considered a protector.[31] This attitude was reinforced by the fact that many of the Laguna's laborers were immigrants from central Mexico who had lost their lands, not to northern estate owners but to hacendados who had little in common with the men for whom they now worked.

This relationship explains why the northern hacendados (with a few exceptions) were the only ones who called on the peasants to revolt. The most common explanation for the unique readiness of northern hacendados to participate in the revolution—that contradictions there between the estate owners on the one hand and both U.S. companies and the Mexican government on the other were greater than in other parts of the country—are not convincing. While it is true that the Madero family had profound conflicts with the American Smelting and Refining Company, the Continental Rubber Company, and the Anglo-American Tlahualilo Land Company, as well as with the federal government, the Yucatecan hacendados had equally profound disagreements over the prices of henequén and credit policies with both the International Harvester Corporation and the Mexican government. The hacendados from Yucatán, though, would never have remotely considered the option of calling on the Maya peasants to rebel against the government, since they had expropriated the peasants' land and had reduced them to conditions of semislavery. They could therefore only expect the peasants to do what the Maya had done in the Caste War of Yucatán—to turn against the landowners. Precisely because of these conditions, a number of northern hacendados seem to have had least hesitation in calling on the peasants to join them in armed confrontations. These northern hacendados participated in the revolution because they were able to call on a peasant army for support, whereas those elsewhere could not risk doing so. Thus, the main characteristic of the northern revolutionary movement of 1910 is that it was the only one in which members of all social classes were involved.

During the 1810–11 uprising, the Bajío was experiencing the country's most pronounced capitalist development, as did the northern triangle a century later. In both areas, capitalism had profoundly altered the traditional way of life of the rural inhabitants, though in different ways. In northern Mexico in the late nineteenth

[31] Stanely R. Ross, *Francisco I. Madero, Apostle of Democracy* (New York, 1955), pp. 11–14.

and early twentieth centuries, the greatest transformation the peasants had suffered was the loss of their lands and water and grazing rights on public lands. In the Bajío there had been few landowning peasant communities and land expropriation was never a major issue. Most rural inhabitants had been estate laborers and their situation began to worsen dramatically. In a recent study, John Tutino describes how living conditions on the Bajío estates had been profoundly altered by increasing demand for their products as a result of the development of new markets linked to an upsurge of the mining and textile industries.[32] Some of the hacienda's best lands were now utilized to produce wheat and vegetables for the growing urban population of the Bajío, while the tenants and sharecroppers who had hitherto farmed these lands for their main food staple, corn, were pushed onto marginal land where rainfall was irregular. The frequent droughts reduced corn yields and led to price increases for their main means of subsistence.

The drastic fall in the living standards of tenants and sharecroppers was matched by the reduced incomes for hacienda resident peons. Increasing birth rates and internal migration from other parts of Mexico had transformed the Bajío from a region of labor shortage at the beginning of the eighteenth century into a region of labor surplus; the hacendados thus had no problem in lowering wages. Many agricultural laborers sought to compensate for the fall in their living standards by seeking additional work elsewhere, such as in mines or textile factories, and their wives would do spinning at home for textile entrepreneurs.

Like northern Mexico a century later, the Bajío was hit by a number of crises on the eve of the 1810 revolution. A drought that affected the marginal lands drastically reduced the corn harvest and increased the price of corn on the free market; there was a crisis in the mining industry due to the increased price of mercury, which was essential to the technical working of the mines; the textile industry was afflicted by competition from cheap imports from the U.S. and Britain; and a sharp credit squeeze was imposed on Mexico. The "consolidación" decree of the Spanish government forced the church, the largest banker in the region, to call in all of its outstanding loans and to contribute that money to Spain. This credit squeeze particularly affected the Bajío, where commercialization

---

[32] This description of conditions in the Bajío and in the state of Guerrero that led to the 1810–14 independence revolution is based largely on John Tutino's *From Insurrection to Revolution in Mexico: Social Bases of Agrarian Violence, 1750–1910* (Princeton, 1986).

was most advanced and was thus most dependent on credit. One century later, between 1907 and 1910, the northern triangle of Sonora, Chihuahua, and Coahuila (where, as in the Bajío one century before, commercialization had developed with exceptional speed) was affected by the economic recession of 1907 with far greater intensity than most of the rest of the country. Like some northern hacendados and members of the middle class in 1910, some Bajío criollos in 1810 who were adversely affected by the economic recession called on the agricultural population of the region to rebel with them. Both groups had one thing in common: they did not constitute the core of the regional elite of their respective regions but were rather marginal to it. Both had believed that they would be able to control the forces they had unleashed, and both in 1810 and 1910 the ensuing revolts proved to be an extremely disagreeable surprise to the revolutionary criollos of 1810 and to the revolutionary hacendados of 1910.

Many criollos who had originally supported the cause of independence became so fearful of the peasant movements that were now erupting that they either joined the royalist troops or retreated into passivity. Others who remained with the movement, such as Ignacio Allende, sought to limit its revolutionary impact. The northern hacendados had a similar reaction in 1910–1911. The agreement of Ciudad Juárez, which Madero signed with federal government representatives, called for the dissolution of the revolutionary forces and the complete reliance by the new revolutionary government on the old federal army, which it had only recently defeated, to reestablish law and order.

During the 1910–20 national upheaval, the Zapata movement, a revolutionary faction that was very different from that of the northern triangle, developed south of Mexico City in the state of Morelos, and there was no alliance with landowners nor with the local middle class. With some exceptions, the movement's few intellectual supporters and spokesmen did not come from Morelos but from Mexico City. The revolution in Morelos in 1910 had one thing in common with that of the northern triangle: it was also due to the rapid industrialization in the area, though the traditional village communities of Morelos were more homogeneous than those of the north, despite the emergence of social differences within many of them.

Were the movements south of Mexico City led by José María Morelos in 1810–20 and by Emiliano Zapata of a similar nature? While there is some geographical overlap between them, the Morelos

movement seems to have had its center in the present state of Guerrero, which was marginal to the twentieth-century Zapata movement. It was centered in the hot lands of that state and it was in
many respects similar in composition to Hidalgo's movement in the
Bajío. Estate residents and some estate owners were the backbone of
Morelos' army. Herein lies one of the greatest differences between
the revolutionaries of 1810 and those of 1910. While in 1910 village
inhabitants who held land constituted the majority of the rural revolutionaries, in 1810 it was above all estate peons who revolted.
What perhaps came closest to the 1910 revolutionaries were the rebellious villagers in Jalisco during the independence wars whom
both Eric Van Young and William Taylor describe in their essays in
this volume. While these villagers did not suffer the kind of losses
that affected the pueblos of Morelos one century later, they were
nevertheless profoundly affected by socioeconomic changes that occurred on the eve of independence. Demographic pressures forced
them to work marginal lands, for example; the amount of land available per capita was constantly decreasing while the traditional privileges they had enjoyed on haciendas, such as grazing or lumber
rights, were being taken away.

One of the most interesting conclusions that can be drawn from
this comparison is that in some respects, similar social causes contributed to the outbreaks of both the 1810–20 and 1910–20 revolutions, but very different regions were affected. In 1810 most of the
northern triangle was scarcely touched by the independence revolution and the region of present-day Morelos was at best marginal.
In 1910–20, the same was true for the Bajío and Jalisco, which had
played such a decisive role in the independence movement one century before.

There were significant parallels between the 1810 and 1910 revolutions. In both cases, the church's eventual role as a bulwark of
existing conservative governments had been weakened by church–
state conflicts that took place about fifty years before the revolutions
erupted. In the colonial period this conflict consisted essentially of
restrictions imposed by the Spanish state on the church, such as
limitations on the political role of priests, culminating in the expulsion of the Jesuits in 1767. The conflict was compounded by the
forced contributions from church assets that the colonial government imposed a few years before the independence war.

The liberal–conservative wars of the nineteenth century, which
culminated in the expropriation of church lands, played a similar
role. While Porfirio Díaz made his peace with the church, which

supported his regime on the eve of the revolution, he was still viewed by part of the hierarchy as one of the liberal leaders who had led attacks on them years before. Partly as a result of these tendencies, partly because of their social commitments, some clerics, especially in 1810 but also in 1910, at times supported the revolution and at times retreated into passivity instead of supporting existing governments as actively as the hierarchy desired.

In the aftermath of both revolutions, sharp conflicts between the church and the state broke out. In the twentieth century these conflicts led to a temporary alliance between the church and significant elements of the peasantry, which found expression in the Cristero war. In the nineteenth century some church leaders attempted to create similar alliances with peasant groups, but it is not clear whether the church was as successful in implementing such a policy in the earlier period. On the one hand, the fact that the church in the nineteenth century owned far more land than it did in the twentieth may have engendered more opposition from peasants in the nineteenth century than in the twentieth. On the other hand, once the reform laws were passed, both the church and the communal villagers had common interests in combating the liberal governments since both were "corporations" affected by the Ley Lerdo of 1856, which forced them to divest themselves of their lands.

One basic factor that obviously influenced both revolutions were the crises of legitimacy of the existing governments and profound divisions within the upper classes. In 1810 the crisis was precipitated by the French invasion of Spain; in 1910 it was due to both real and perceived concessions by the Porfirian regime to the U.S. and to profound differences within the ruling classes over the successor to Porfirio Díaz.

In both revolutions the shifting and at times erratic patterns of foreign involvement were strongly influential and at times helped the revolutionary forces. From 1810 to 1820 Spain's policies repeatedly shifted from liberal constitutionalism to conservative reaction; the same can be said of U.S. policy between 1910 and 1920, which alternately supported conservative groups and the revolutionaries.

However, the profound differences between these revolutions help explain the far greater degree of initial violence in 1810 than in 1910. In 1810, ethnic and national issues were far more important than they were one century later, since in colonial times Indians and mestizos did not enjoy the same legal status as whites. Their demand for full equality played a major role in the independence war. One century later, no legal racial discrimination existed (though Indians still suffered discrimination) and this factor was not relevant in the 1910 revolution. The main aim of the 1810 uprising was to put an end to direct Spanish domination of Mexico; the hatred of the lower classes for the Spanish ruling elite was reflected in the wholesale massacres of Spaniards in 1810 and 1811. One century later, nationalism was also an important component of the revolution, although the kind of indirect supremacy that foreigners, especially Americans, had assumed in Mexico evoked far less resentment than had direct Spanish rule a century before. It is significant that in the first wave of spontaneous uprisings in 1910–11, when there was less centralized control over the rebels, there were very few killings or even attacks on foreigners, except for Chinese. On the contrary, consular reports stressed that many foreigners, especially in northern Mexico, sympathized with the revolution.

Another intangible but certainly very important explanation for the greater degree of random violence and reprisals against the upper classes in 1810–11 than 1910–11 refers to the historical experiences of Mexico's elite. The hacendados and members of the middle classes who joined and led Mexico's revolutionary movement during the Madero period could look back on a long history of mobilizing and manipulating peasant movements in the nineteenth century. The criollos who originally sided with the lower classes who rose in 1810 had very little experience in manipulating these classes and they soon lost control of their lower-class allies.

The initially substantial differences in the degree of violence between the first phases of the two revolutions were obliterated in their second phases when in 1813–14 and 1913–20 cycles of repression and counter-repression increased.

There was another substantial difference between the 1810 and 1910 revolutions, but it is not clear whether this factor can be used to explain the different degrees of initial violence in both revolutions. This was the land issue, which was far more important in 1910 than in 1810, when the main demand of the rural revolutionaries was for a reduction in tribute and taxes. In 1910 they wanted land. The rights and properties of the free peasantry had been undermined in the last years of Spanish rule, but the peasants still retained a substantial part of the land. During the Porfiriato, the free peasantry was largely destroyed as an economic entity. The 1810 revolution was thus confined to a much more limited segment of Mexican society than that of 1910. Most free peasants in 1810 who owned land refused to join the revolutionary movement, which consisted largely of estate peons. In 1910, the opposite was frequently the case. Most estate peons (who enjoyed a secure status as privileged retainers) remained loyal to their "masters" while far larger segments of free landholding peasants joined the revolution.

But these differences were not absolute. In the 1810–20 revolution, many inhabitants of free villages in Guadalajara joined the independence movement, while in 1910 many estate peons from the Laguna fought in the revolutionary forces. Both of these groups, though, constituted the exception rather than the rule in their respective revolutions.

The revolutionary elite was far more successful in the twentieth century in controlling the revolt of rural masses than the criollos in 1810. Their historical experience in the nineteenth century was doubtless one of the factors that gave the 1910 revolutionary elite sufficient self-confidence to advocate the destruction of the federal army after 1913 and to become convinced that they would be able to control the popular movements with whom they were allying themselves. Most criollos in 1820 only became advocates of independence when it became clear that they could count on the support of the royalist army.

This essay and its companion, "Rural Rebellion in Colonial and Pre-Conquest Mexico" in Chapter 3, have considered three major questions. The first was whether there were any common traits to all the rural movements over several centuries in very different economic, social, and political contexts in Mexico and, if so, whether they had common causes.

The difficulties inherent in such a long-term comparison not only stem from the different conditions in these divergent time frames, but also from the nature of the evidence. For the post-conquest period, rural uprisings can be documented with relative accuracy. For the colonial era, when villagers tended to stage isolated rebellions, we know generally who participated, under what circumstances, and what their demands were. In the nineteenth century, when the complexity of rural revolts increased because of the alliances that peasants and other rural inhabitants established with traditional caudillos, the nature of those alliances and the reciprocal concessions that both sides made can generally be documented and well established.

The same cannot be said for the pre-conquest period, for which theories on rural revolts are based on far more hypothetical evidence. Some archaeologists assume but cannot prove that rural revolts contributed to the downfall of the Mayan cities and the Teotihuacan empire. Regional warlords and tribal chieftains who headed the revolts against Aztec rule probably represented both their own interests and those of the peasants whom they led. Nevertheless, the participation of rural forces within these uprisings, their interests, demands, and relationship to their overlords simply cannot be documented as they can for later centuries. In spite of these difficulties, I find the pre-conquest evidence convincing enough to formulate at least hypothetical comparisons with later periods.

As I have attempted to show, it would be erroneous simply to project backward the characteristics of nineteenth and early twentieth century rural uprisings. Nevertheless, rural upheavals do show some common characteristics throughout Mexican history. Every social transformation in Mexico from the classic Maya period to the 1910 revolution was preceded by an agricultural crisis. In all cases, these crises were linked to rapid population increases, cultivation of marginal lands, increasing dependency on rainfall, and thus an increasing vulnerability to agricultural fluctuations. There are clear archaeological indications of rapid population increases in both the Maya and the Teotihuacan civilizations and of crises in agricultural production. Historical sources confirm that similar situations occurred both in Tula and in the Aztec empire, which had some similarity to the agricultural crises in New Spain 1809–10, and in most of Mexico from 1907 to 1909.

There are indications that in addition to agricultural crises, other sectors of the economy suffered as well. The fall of the Maya seems to have been preceded by a breakdown of trade with central Mexico after the destruction of Teotihuacan. Similar trade disruptions due to profound divisions within the Toltec empire may have hastened the fall of Tula. Both the 1810 and 1910 revolutions were also preceded by crises in mining and industry.

Another common thread linking all of these insurrections was the increasing isolation of the ruling elite from the common people. Many archaeologists believe that one reason for the fall of both the Maya and the Teotihuacan civilizations was that the common people had become alienated from the priesthood as the latter's religion became more and more complex and sophisticated. The historical legends of Tula emphasized the sexual degeneracy of the ruling elites as a reason why it lost legitimacy in the eyes of the people. The Aztec religion, with its increasingly heavy emphasis on human sacrifice, alienated more and more members of the conquered peoples and was a potent force driving them into the arms of Cortés.

A growing national consciousness and resentment of Spanish

rule, and a decline in the legitimacy of the colonial government preceded the 1810 revolution. In a similar vein, the Porfirian elite was accused of handing Mexico's riches over to foreigners, of accepting foreign standards of values, and of being more and more alienated from Mexican culture.

This alienation of the ruling elite from the mass of the population may have been linked to attempts by this elite to extract increasing revenues from the population and to eliminate traditional rights and traditional autonomy. Shortly before the fall of Teotihuacan, many buildings in Teotihuacan style were being erected in different parts of central Mexico, which seems to point to a replacement of the indirect commercial influence of this central Mexican metropolis by direct rule.

On the eve of the Spanish conquest, the Aztecs had increased the tribute they levied on many conquered regions. They began interfering more and more in the internal administration, not only of conquered and subject nations but even of their closest allies in the city of Texcoco. Through the Bourbon reforms, the Spanish rulers had tried to increase both the taxes that many villages had to pay as well as the influence of Spanish officials on local affairs in their colonies. The same occurred during the Porfiriato when traditional municipal and village autonomy was sharply curtailed by increasingly powerful regional and federal authorities.

Is there any common cause for these similarities that span so vast a time and encompass such different social, political and economic formations? One decisive factor was the ecology of Mexico and the uncertain nature of the country's agriculture. The dependence of large parts of the country on the output of regions with unreliable rainfall led to repeated famines, especially when population pressure forced the cultivation of marginal soils.

This factor was reinforced by the country's natural obstacles to effective transportation and communication. The most fertile and densely populated areas are in the central plateau of the country. Communications with the rest of Mexico, as well as with other countries, are hindered by mountains and the lack of navigable rivers. In the pre-Hispanic period these problems were compounded by the lack of draft animals and by the absence of the wheel, and although the situation improved in the colonial period, the state of roads and communications remained very poor. It was only in the Porfiriato, after the railroads were built, that internal transportation improved dramatically, but this could not compensate for other problems in agriculture, so that the last great upheaval, the 1910 revolution, was preceded, as were all other upheavals, by an agricultural crisis and ensuing famine among large segments of the population.

Another constant basis for conflict from the pre-Hispanic period to the twentieth century was the recurring rivalry between the center of the country and its periphery. The inhabitants of the central valley of Mexico have attempted to exercise a significant degree of control over surrounding and remote areas for more than two thousand years. As a result, most internal conflicts in central Mexico have been linked to rebellions of the periphery against the center. There is a certain continuity between the Chichimec penetration of the valley of Mexico and Pancho Villa's march on the capital. I have even thought at times of calling him the last of the Chichimecas.

The second major question is whether Mexico was unique in terms of the number and intensity of its rural uprisings. As John Coatsworth has shown in Chapter 2, Mexican peasants do not appear more prone to rebellion than those of the Andes; Peru, for instance, has also had a long history of rural revolts, and in fact nothing in Mexico can be compared with the Tupac Amaru uprising in Peru in the eighteenth century. What differentiates Mexico from the rest of Latin America is that large masses of rural inhabitants participated together with important segments of the country's upper and middle classes in two successful national revolutions.

One essential reason for the readiness of substantial portions of Mexico's rural population to become involved in such national movements was the fact that in the regions that were the cores of both the 1810 and 1910 revolutions, the majority of the rural population had been assimilated into Spanish, i.e., Mexican culture. Neither the Bajío nor the states of the northern triangle (Sonora, Chihuahua, Coahuila) had been densely settled in pre-Hispanic times where Indians, because of cultural and linguistic continuity (as well as survival strategies), resisted Hispanization. The northern areas were largely settled after the conquest by Spanish immigrants, mestizos, and assimilated Indians from central Mexico. In addition, those areas of the center that did participate—the Indian villages around Guadalajara and the village communities of Morelos—had been largely assimilated into Mexican culture in part because of their location near major population and commercial centers. It is significant that in those regions where the Indian elements were strongest in Mexico—Yucatán, Oaxaca, and Chiapas—rural revolts tended to have their own timetables and were rarely linked to national uprisings.

The internal causes of rural participation in national revolutions were compounded by a unique history of foreign aggression, which does set Mexico apart from most other Latin American countries in the nineteenth century. The war with the United States cost Mexico nearly half of its territory, and the French invasion occurred only a few years later. Both events aroused the national consciousness of many peasants as well as their willingness to join in national revolutions and movements, a willingness further reinforced in later periods of Mexico's history by its unique location on the southern U.S. border, which had very contradictory effects. On the one hand, it strengthened a feeling of nationalism among much of Mexico's rural population (closely linked to fears that the United States might annex important parts of northern Mexico), which was also fueled by constant discrimination against Mexicans in the border areas of the U.S. Southwest. On the other hand, the far greater rights enjoyed by many of the rural inhabitants of the United States—more security of land ownership, better access to more impartial courts, greater municipal autonomy—fueled demands by many peasants for similar rights. In yet another way, the proximity of the U.S. tended to encourage Mexico's rural inhabitants to revolt. It gave them easy access to arms and frequently allowed them to seek sanctuary across the border, where Mexican authorities could not pursue them.

Third, what sectors or classes of the rural population tended to revolt? Did they remain the same over time and space? One of the main conclusions of this essay is that the social composition of those who revolted was significantly different before and after the nineteenth century. In addition, the social groups that carried out local, regional, or national revolts were by no means the same.

In the pre-Columbian period, some archaeologists assume, villagers organized in clan-like communities, probably led by dissident priests and village leaders, and overthrew their own upper classes in the Maya cities and in Teotihuacan. Under Aztec rule, the inhabitants of subject states, comprising both rural and urban inhabitants and led by their own upper classes, tended to rebel against the domination of the "Triple Alliance," centered in the valley of Mexico. Revolts during the colonial period were mainly carried out by Indians led either by their traditional elite or by prophets claiming divine legitimacy. In the core regions of New Spain the Indians were organized in traditional village communities. On the periphery they either retained much of their pre-Columbian tribal organizations or, as in the case of the Yaqui Indians, they set up a new and more centralized kind of tribal organization as a result of Spanish colonization. Until 1800, very few instances of uprisings by resident peons of large estates or by non-Indian rural inhabitants have been found.

In the nineteenth and twentieth centuries, while village communities continued to form the backbone of local revolts, new types of regional uprisings scarcely known until the end of the eighteenth century took place in Mexico. There were three types of regional revolt: caste wars, caudillo-led revolts, and uprisings under the direction of intellectuals mainly from the cities. Caste wars were essentially uprisings by Indian communities, particularly in the south and southeast, calling for the expulsion or destruction of all non-Indians. Combining ethnic nationalism and religious messianism, these revolts were frequently led by traditional village leaders. In caudillo-led revolts, village communities joined peons from the caudillo's estates and sometimes urban groups in supporting a regional leader. In return, the caudillo granted the villagers protection from encroachments on their lands, their rights and their crops, and at times even granted them redress in their disputes with landowners. The third type of regional revolt that comes closest to the type of peasant uprisings that occurred in twentieth-century Asia, i.e., village communities led by urban intellectuals, was relatively rare in nineteenth- and twentieth-century Mexico. It tended to be confined, in the few cases when such revolts occurred, to village communities near large cities or industrial installations.

What is most difficult to determine is the type of rural inhabitants who participated in the great national uprisings of the nineteenth and twentieth centuries. While in some regions such as Guadalajara in 1810–20 and Morelos in 1910–20, traditional village communities played a prominent role, in others very different social groups formed the core of the revolutionary movements. Only a minority of the rural population of the Bajío in 1810 and of the northern triangle in 1910 were Indians organized into traditional communities. The bulk of the rural inhabitants who revolted in these regions were migrant workers, semi-agricultural laborers, rancheros, former military colonists (mainly in northern Mexico in 1910), as well as some members of Indian groups and traditional village communities. The strength and influence of each of these groups is extremely difficult to document, and it is even more difficult to establish to what degree these groups felt or maintained a peasant identity once they became part of large and increasingly well-organized revolutionary armies.

Even more complex is the identity of the rural guerrillas who fought against the French and Emperor Maximilian from 1862 to

1867. While the liberals with their Ley Lerdo had decreed the abolition of communally owned land in 1856, Maximilian had attempted to forge an alliance with Mexico's Indian communities. How successful were both sides in gaining rural support and what kind of support did they gain? This remains one of the most interesting and least studied areas of Mexican history.

Finally, did the great mass of rural people who revolted benefit in any way? As far as the smaller, local, and at times regional uprisings were concerned, they frequently achieved benefits that at times were substantial for the participants. In the colonial period the Spanish authorities repeatedly reacted to uprisings by granting the villagers' demands. In the early nineteenth century, peasants frequently succeeded in keeping their lands and maintaining the integrity of their villages. This was also the one time in Mexican history when local and even regional revolts achieved a measure of military success with at times far-reaching results. The Maya Indians of the Yucatán succeeded in creating an autonomous state of their own, which maintained its independence from Mexico for more than fifty years. The Yaqui Indians of Sonora repeatedly, though for much shorter periods of time, managed to control the immensely fertile lands of the Yaqui River valley. In the territory of Tepic, the village communities that formed the backbone of Manuel Lozada's support also managed to keep Mexican authorities at bay for many years.

The great masses of rural inhabitants who participated in Mexico's two great national revolutions at first glance seem to have achieved far less success in both the 1810 and 1910 revolutions. The most radical factions, largely composed of peasants and embodying peasant demands—the armies of Hidalgo and Morelos in the independence wars and those of Zapata and Villa one century later—were defeated. Both hacendados and the hacienda system as an institution survived the years of armed struggles from 1810–20 and 1910–20 relatively unscathed. The men who emerged as the victors from the long turmoil of the armed phases of the 1820 and 1920 revolutions were not peasant leaders and were not inclined to view favorably the demands of rural revolutionaries.

While rural inhabitants secured decisive legal rights as a result of revolution, many of them were either not applied or reversed. The war of independence brought about the end of legal discrimination against Indians and mestizos and the abolition of Indian tribute, although the latter was soon reestablished in the form of village taxes and the general head tax. In the 1910–20 upheaval (at least up to the 1920s) revolutionary regimes scarcely applied the agrarian measures for which their own constitution provided. Only 40,000 peasants, a very small fraction of the rural population, secured lands under article 27 of the Mexican constitution before 1921.

Nevertheless, such a short-term look at the results would be misleading, because profound changes did occur in the agrarian structure after each of the country's great revolutions. The Spanish conquest, the 1810–20 independence movement, and the 1910–20 revolution had one thing in common: they destroyed the existing state and it took several years, at times decades, to establish a new state strong enough to consolidate its hold over the whole country. In the interim, contradictory tendencies emerged and some segments of the rural population benefited from the weak state. After the conquest, many Spaniards enslaved Indians who frequently died as the result of their mistreatment. At the same time though, as long as the number of Spaniards was small, many villages profited from the fact that they did not have to pay tribute to the Aztec nobility. In some cases, the Spanish state imposed benevolent authorities such as Bishop Las Casas in Chiapas or Vasco de Quiroga in Michoacán. Most of these benefits were short-lived, however, and tended to diminish or to disappear once the Spanish state was in full control. Finally, the massive rise in Indian mortality in the sixteenth and seventeenth centuries completely transformed their situation.

Similar contradictory tendencies existed after 1820. It took nearly fifty years until a stable Mexican state was established and sixty years until it managed to consolidate its authority over the whole of Mexico. Once freed from the shackles imposed on them by the Spanish authorities, many landowners attempted to reduce community rights and to expropriate village lands, while the free villagers utilized the government's weakness and the need of many local strongmen for peasant support to gain substantial advantages for themselves and to prevent any massive attacks on their lands. It was only after the state was consolidated in the 1860s and especially during the Porfiriato that a successful attack on peasant land holdings was launched.

In the twenty years following the 1910 revolution, the state was still weak and the new elite that emerged needed rural support in order to consolidate its power and to weaken foreign influence in the country. This support was all the more important to them since in the course of the revolution, large numbers of peasants had acquired arms as well as a new consciousness of their power, and so received very substantial concessions. Between 1920 and 1940, millions of peasants received lands and much of the traditional hacienda system was dismantled. After 1940, however, when a strong Mexican state had once again emerged, new attacks on rural communities and traditional village rights took place, the analysis of which would go beyond the scope of this essay.

CHAPTER EIGHTEEN

Economic Fluctuations and

Social Unrest in Oaxaca,

1701–94

Ulises Beltrán

In this chapter I aim to explore, in as many ways as the data permit, the economic dimensions of the social unrest described in Taylor's pioneering work, *Drinking, Homicide and Rebellion in Colonial Mexican Villages*. My hypothesis is that the rebellions Taylor discovered were not randomly distributed in relation to economic fluctuations. I hope to show that, although the primary conscious motive for collective violence was the *defense* of relationships that were threatened, the economic situation of the peasants affected their propensity to rebel in the face of those threatened relationships.[1]

A new test of the Taylor study has been made possible using more complete economic data, specifically data on economic fluctuations in eighteenth-century Oaxaca.[2] This analysis therefore deals mainly with the Oaxaca rebellions catalogued in Taylor's work.[3] In addition, various measures of economic change are discussed, estimated, and compared with Taylor's data on rebellions.

[1] William Taylor, *Drinking, Homicide and Rebellion in Colonial Mexican Villages* (Stanford: Stanford University Press, 1979). Taylor's study was based on investigations of 142 communities that revolted between 1680 and 1811.

[2] Rodolfo Pastor et al., *Fluctuaciones económicas en Oaxaca durante el siglo XVIII* (Mexico City: El Colegio de México, 1979).

[3] The 35 rebellions that took place in Oaxaca between 1701 and 1794 are identified in Taylor's Appendix A, pp. 176–77.

Economic Fluctuations

Soon after Taylor's book was published, Rodolfo Pastor and others published economic time series from the Archbishopric of Oaxaca based on tithe payment documents. The data used here are total pesos paid to the Archbishopric each year from 1700 to 1794. In theory, this quantity represents approximately 10 percent of the total output of the region, but unfortunately, the data offered by Pastor are given in current pesos. Available price indices for deflating the series include the index of prices of maize sold in Mexico City based on the work of Enrique Florescano, and an index of the prices of seven commodities constructed by Cecilia Rabell with prices registered in tithe collection documents from San Luis de la Paz in the contemporary state of Guanajuato.[4] Rabell's index is preferred because it includes the prices of most of the products that paid tithe in Oaxaca.

Once Pastor's date are deflated, the real value of the tithes is multiplied to ten to obtain an approximation to the total real value of the tithed output of Oaxaca. It is known that several products are not included in these data, (cochineal, for instance), but since tithed products constituted an important part of the regional product, this curve is a good indicator of general economic fluctuations in the region. In other words, it is assumed that the output of those products not included in this series, particularly maize, moved together with the output of tithed products.[5]

[4] Enrique Florescano, *Precios del maíz y crisis agrícolas en México (1708–1810)* (Mexico City: El Colegio de México, 1969), Appendix IV, pp. 232–35. Rabell's index was corrected by Coatsworth. John H. Coatsworth, *From Backwardness to Underdevelopment: The Mexican Economy, 1800–1910* (forthcoming). The original index can be found in Cecilia Rabell, *San Luis de la Paz, estudio de economía y demografía históricas 1645–1810*, unpublished M.A. Thesis, Escuela Nacional de Antropología e Historia, Mexico, 1975.

[5] The main problem with this assumption is the absence of maize in the data on tithes. The only way to make the assumption plausible is by proving that there is a significant correlation between movements in maize production and the data on tithes. The only data available on maize production are those that can be inferred from Florescano, who found a crisis in maize production whenever there was a peak in the percentage variation in maize prices relative to the mean of the long cycle. In other words, a crisis is registered in the price index because the extreme grain scarcity provokes a dramatic price increase in Mexico City. To support the argument and find evidence for a climatic reason for the scarcity, Florescano looked for contemporary testimonies that mentioned such crises. Florescano, *Precios del maíz*. Table 10, pp. 130–34, and Table 14, p. 161. Since maize was the basic foodstuff for most of the population and it was widely used to feed livestock, Florescano argues that these crises were "in fact synonymous with general economic crises" (p. 141). A regression

A comparison of movements in the real value of tithed products and Florescano's price index, f (see Figure 18.1), suggests that the real value of the Oaxaca's tithed output moved together with maize production as reflected in the Mexico City price index. With few exceptions, the real value of the tithed output follows the expected pattern: drastic increases in the price of maize in Mexico City correspond to sharp drops in the curve of the real value of the tithed output in Oaxaca. It seems safe to assume that the production of goods that paid tithe in Oaxaca moved together with maize production. Hence, the tithe data series can be used as an indicator of the economic fluctuations faced by Oaxacan peasants.[6]

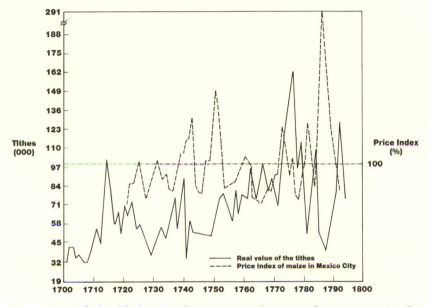

Figure 18.1. Relationship between fluctuations in the prices of maize in Mexico City and the real value of tithes in the Archbishopric of Oaxaca, 1701–94. Source: Florescano, *Atlas histórico de México*, columns 3 and 4, Appendix I (Mexico: Siglo XXI Editores, 1983).

of Rabell's index f (Florescano's index) gave an adjusted r^2 value of 0.85, which indicates that both series moved very closely together. The parameters of this regression were used to fill some gaps in Rabell's index.

[6] A negative correlation (-0.23) between the real value of output in year t and the price index of maize in year $t+1$ was obtained, which seems insufficient to sustain the assumption. Nevertheless, it is clear that such a low value is the result of some data inconsistency. When the series was divided into three periods (1721–36, 1736–56, and 1757–94) correlation values of -0.22, -0.11, and 0.42, respectively, were ob-

Economic Fluctuations and Social Unrest

Hypothesizing a relationship between social unrest and economic fluctuations assumes that variations in the output of indigenous villagers affected their propensity to engage in rebellious behavior. Variations in output can be measured in several ways, however, and each method implies a different underlying assumption about the economic behavior of the group being studied. There are two main approaches to measuring the magnitude of economic fluctuations: (1) by looking at the magnitude of changes in the absolute value of the output; or (2) by establishing some sort of expected value and then comparing it with the output actually achieved. The first procedure will be called a model of absolute deprivation, and the second one a model of relative deprivation. In what follows the economic characteristics of each year are determined and are then compared with the incidence of rebellions to see if any association between the two variables can be inferred.

Absolute Deprivation

The general hypothesis of the absolute deprivation model is that whenever there is a "crisis," there is also social unrest among the affected group. This was the approach taken by Taylor when he explored the possible relationship between uprisings and "crisis years" as revealed in the Mexico City price data. Taylor's findings can now be reexamined in the light of better economic data—relatively precise data on agricultural production for the specific region of Oaxaca.

1. *Annual rate of change as a measure of economic fluctuations.* If peasants produced each year just enough to consume and assure

---

tained. According to Pastor et al., in the period around mid-century (approximately the period for which we obtained the lowest correlation) there was much administrative disorder, as is reflected in several gaps in the data. Such gaps were filled by Pastor by calculating moving averages, but this is a very dubious technique.

In other words, the correlation is low because the data are imperfect rather than because the assumption is incorrect. The high correlation value in the late period supports this observation. On the other hand, the assumption does not imply that the production of tithed goods moved *exactly* in the same proportion as maize did, in which case one should have expected a correlation value of 1.0. It is obvious that there was a substitution effect among these products, i.e, a shortfall in maize production probably induced an increase in tithed products and vice versa. The assumption does stress the fact that in periods of drastic changes in the production of tithed goods, maize production should also have moved in the same direction and with equivalent intensity.

next year's production and if they had no access to alternative sources of income, one year of negative growth could mean economic ruin. If, however, peasants produced enough each year to store some of the output, then they would be able to survive a certain number of years of continuous negative growth. These possibilities should be examined cautiously before any conclusion is advanced, because during long periods of negative economic growth it is also likely that long-term compensating actions, like permanent migration or shifts to alternative sources of income, may occur. Hence, in such cases, one can be attributing economic recuperation to capacities to store when other kinds of economic activity are the explaining factors.[7]

One way of examining the relationship between economic fluctuations and social unrest is to regard as critical any year in which a negative rate of change in agricultural output is observed.[8] The relationship between village uprisings and type of year is shown in Table 18.1; some relationship can be observed in the data: a significant χ^2 was obtained. However, the direction of the association seems to be different from that predicted by the model. Rebellions tended to occur in years of positive economic growth rather than in periods of absolute deprivation; in general, 66 percent of the rebellions took place in years of positive growth. In 45 percent of the years of positive growth at least one rebellion took place, whereas in only 25 percent of the negative growth years did a rebellion occur.[9]

2. *Annual rate of change as a measure of the economic fluctuations, allowing for a "normal" margin of variation.* Peasants could have produced enough each year to consume and to assure the next year's production plus some amount that could serve as insurance against variations in output. In this case, a year of negative growth would mean economic ruin for the peasants only if the absolute decline was larger than the amount produced for subsistence plus the "insurance surplus." In other words, there is some variation in the

---

[7] The best discussion on the limits and possibilities of economic growth in traditional agriculture can be found in Theodore Schultz, *Transforming Traditional Agriculture* (New York: Arno Press, 1976).

[8] The annual rate of change (r) was estimated as the percentage change from one year to the next: $r = x_2 - x_1/x_1$.

[9] The test was also performed considering as critical all years that ended a two-year period of continuous negative growth. Only three out of thirty-five uprisings occurred in such years. In this case, the direction of the relationship is meaningless, since the "normal" years (those that did not end a two-year period of negative growth) included years of positive as well as of negative growth.

Table 18.1
Type of Year Defined by the Annual Rate of Change Versus
Incidence of Uprisings in Oaxaca, 1701–94

Type of Year	Rebellions		Total	
	No	Yes		
Negative	37	12	49	f
growth[a]	75.5	24.5	100.0	% r
	56.9	34.3	49.0	% c
Positive	28	23	51	f
growth[b]	54.9	45.1	100.0	% r
	43.1	65.7	51.0	% c
Total	65	35	100	f
	65.0	35.0		
	100.0	100.0		

[a] $r \rangle 0$.
[b] $r \langle 0$.
The total numbers of years (100) is larger than the actual number of years (94) because in some years there was more than one rebellion.
$\chi^2 = 4.665$, significant at the 0.02 level.
r = row; c = column.

annual rate of change that can be considered manageable or "normal."

The problem is to determine the limits within which an annual rate of change could be considered normal. Since there is no direct information about the economics of Oaxacan Indian agriculture that could guide the selection, the test was run for various alternative magnitudes. A year was considered "normal" if the annual rate of change for that year was within plus or minus 0.15, 0.25, 0.50, 0.65, 0.75, or 1.0 standard deviation from the mean rate of change for the entire period. For each distribution a cross-tabulation between the type of year (abundant, normal, or critical) and the incidence of rebellions was constructed and the resulting χ^2 were calculated. The results are shown in Table 18.2.

The only really significant association is found when a variation of 0.15 standard deviations is allowed as normal (χ^2 is significant at the 0.01 level). Moreover, it appears that the model fit is improved over the previous model; the level of significance is increased in comparison to that obtained in the previous test.

Table 18.2
Levels of Association Between Types of Years
(Defined by the Rate of Change) and Uprisings in Oaxaca

Variations Considered Normal		Variation in the "Normal" Rate of Change (%)	χ^2 Level of Significance
1.0	SD	28.44 〉 r 〉 −20.88	0.70
0.75	SD	22.30 〉 r 〉 −14.56	0.50
0.65	SD	19.84 〉 r 〉 −12.10	0.30
0.50	SD	10.99 〉 r 〉 −8.86	0.50
0.25	SD	10.02 〉 r 〉 −2.27	0.10
0.15	SD	7.55 〉 r 〉 0.18	0.01

SD = standard deviation from the mean rate of change for the entire period. The cross-tabulation with the 0.01 level of significance is shown in Table 18.4.

Table 18.3 shows that rebellions tended to occur in "normal" years, that is to say, in years with a positive rate of change that varied between 0.18 and 7.55 percent. In other words, knowledge that a year was normal significantly increased the probability of accurately predicting the occurrence of a rebellion. In 67 percent of the normal years at least one rebellion occurred; only 37 percent of the abundant years coincided with rebellion. On the other hand, if rebellions are taken as an indirect indicator of the peasants' response to economic fluctuations, the economic assumptions stated at the beginning of this section need to be reexamined. It may be speculated that peasants did produce some "insurance" surplus, but that the variation within which such a surplus could permit a year to be considered normal was extremely limited. The variation allowed in the annual rate of change was only 0.15 standard deviations from the mean.

In sum, this examination of the relationship between rebellions and economic fluctuations leads us to a new interpretation of the model of absolute deprivation. Rebellions tended to occur during periods in which the annual rate of change could be considered normal, that is, in years when output was greater than in the previous year but within certain limits. Neither years of extreme economic growth nor years of decline increased substantially the likelihood of

Table 18.3
Type of Year Defined by The Annual Rate of Change Allowing for a
"Normal" Margin of Variation Versus Incidence of Uprisings in
Oaxaca, 1701–94

Type of Year	Rebellions		Total	
	No	Yes		
Abundant[a]	22	13	35	f
	62.8	37.2	100.0	% r
	34.4	37.1	35.4	% c
Normal[b]	5	10	15	f
	33.3	66.7	100.0	% r
	7.8	28.6	15.2	% c
Critical[c]	37	12	49	f
	75.5	24.5	100.0	% r
	57.8	34.3	49.4	% c
Total	64	35	99	f
	64.6	35.4		
	100.0	100.0		

[a] $73.25 \rangle r \rangle 7.56$
[b] $7.56 \rangle r \rangle 0.18$
[c] $0.18 \rangle r \rangle -61.71$
$\chi^2 = 9.015$ significant at the 0.01 level.
r = row; c = column.

a rebellion; in fact, normal years seem to be more strongly associated
with rebellions than critical or abundant ones.

RELATIVE DEPRIVATION

A Model of relative deprivation would suggest that unrest is as
much a function of people's expectations as of their objective situation. Social dissatisfaction may result from a discrepancy between
what people believe they are entitled to receive (expectations), and
what they actually receive (achievements); this discrepancy is
called "relative deprivation." In this chapter the magnitude of the
discrepancy will be measured in strictly economic terms. Although
there is no direct evidence regarding the expectations of Oaxacan
villagers, it is likely that they were related to past levels of output.

A peasant could not have expected to produce beyond the possibilities of the plot he had cultivated for years. On the other hand, if the
resources available—resources used in producing the actual output
registered in the data—prove insufficient to satisfy minimum expectations, dissatisfaction would increase.

1. *The "trend line" as a measure of the expected value.* A regression
line estimated for output as a function of time indicates the general
trend of output over time. The variance from the regression line (the
error) represents the variation in the output not associated with the
growth of regional product. For the purposes of this test, the values
predicted by the trend line are taken as approximate measures of the
expected value of the output (see Figure 18.2). The implicit assumption is that the expected value of the output was estimated by the
peasants in accordance with the general trend of production over
time.[10] In this test the years above the trend line (with a positive

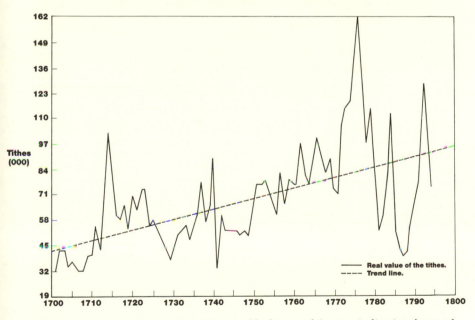

Figure 18.2. Real value of tithes of the Archbishopric of Oaxaca, indicating the trend
line across time, 1701–94.

[10] A regression line with the form $output_t = -8835593 + 5452.95 \ year$, was obtained with a significant f value but a low r^2 ($=0.32$). The model is used despite the
low r^2 value considering that it will not be used for predictions and that in time series
the r^2 has little significance since it merely compares the model with the mean value
of the output.

residual) are considered normal and all those lying below the trend line are considered critical. The relationship between the type of years and the incidence of rebellion is shown in Table 18.4.

Although the level of significance of the association is somewhat low (χ^2 significant at the 0.10 level), it seems that there is some tendency for rebellions to cluster in years above the expected value. In other words, there was a somewhat greater likelihood of rebellion when the peasant's achievements were above expectations than below.

2. *Previous output as a basis for estimating expected output.* An alternative way to measure expected value is to assume that peasants estimated output on the basis of the value of the previous year's output.[11] With this model, the values predicted by the regression in each year were taken as the expected value for each subsequent year. Those years in which the actual output was lower than expected (negative residuals) were considered critical, and vice versa.

Table 18.4

Type of Year Defined in Relation to the "Trend Line" of the Series Versus Incidence of Uprisings in Oaxaca, 1701–94

Type of Year	Rebellions		Total	
	No	Yes		
Below the	39	16	55	f
trend line	70.9	29.1	100.0	% r
	60.0	45.7	55.0	% c
Above the	26	19	45	f
trend line	57.8	42.2	100.0	% r
	40.0	54.3	45.0	% c
Total	65	35	100	f
	65.0	35.0		
	100.0	100.0		

$\chi^2 = 2.011$, significant at the 0.10 level.
r = row; c = column.

[11] A regression model of the function $output_t = f(output_{t-1})$ would represent such a model and provide the magnitude of the expected value for each year. The model seems reasonable. A significant f value was obtained, supporting the assumption of linearity and an r^2 value of 0.59 shows that the model explains a good deal of the variation in output in year t.

A cross tabulation between the type of year so defined and the incidence of rebellions showed no association between the variables.

Looking at the rebellions plotted in Figure 18.2, it appears that although they are not clustered above or below the regression line (as shown in the previous test) they do seem to be grouped in "moments" of the curve, i.e., they seem to be grouped in periods with similar characteristics. Classifying the years according to the position of the residual in the cycle, it is possible to define two subcycles: (1) an upswing in which actual output is moving from below the expected value toward a point at which it reaches a maximum above the expected value; and (2) a downswing, in which actual output is falling. In other words, the upswing defines a situation in which the achievements are moving from below expectation to a position in which they are above expectation. Likewise, the downswing defines the converse process.

The distribution of rebellions according to type of year so defined is shown in Table 18.5. Apparently peasants did not rebel when actual output was falling relative to the expected value. Instead, rebellions tended to occur more often in years of recuperation: 39 percent occurred in periods of recuperation against 29 percent in years of

Table 18.5

Type of Year Defined in a Relative Economic Deprivation Model and Uprisings in Oaxaca 1701–94.

Type of Year	Rebellions No	Yes	Total	
Downswing	33	13	46	f
	71.7	28.3	100.0	% r
	50.8	37.1	46.0	% c
Upswing	32	22	54	f
	59.3	40.7	100.0	% r
	49.2	62.9	54.0	% c
Total	65	35	100	f
	65.0	35.0		
	100.0	100.0		

$\chi^2 = 1.62$, significant at the 0.30 level.
r = row; c = column.

falling trends. In general, 63 percent of the uprisings occurred when economic conditions were improving or good.

The original model thus has to be changed again, since relative economic deprivation does not appear to influence social unrest as was predicted. On the contrary, it appears that peasants were more likely to rebel in periods when output was high relative to expectation.

Conclusions

The tests described in this chapter have shown a consistent pattern. Measuring economic change either as variations in the absolute value of output or as departures from expected output, a significant level of association was detected between the economic characteristics of the year and the incidence of social violence. Rebellions were not randomly distributed in relation to economic fluctuations. Moreover, not only was the existence of a relationship detected, but the results were also consistent in showing that a relationship existed between years of normal or positive economic performance and rebellions, regardless of the way the economic situation is defined.

GLOSSARY OF
SPANISH TERMS

abasto de carnes meat supply monopoly in a city or town, usually rented out by a municipal government

acasillados resident peons, permanent estate laborers, hacienda residents

agrarista peasant militia; more generally, sympathetic to peasant or agrarian interests

alcabalas excise taxes

alcalde mayor of a town

alhóndiga central granary in a city or town

anexos attached property

aparceros sharecroppers

arrendatarios tenant farmers

audiencia high court of appeal

bandolerismo banditry

barrio neighborhood or suburb

bienes de comunidad communal property

cabildo town council

cacicazgo political authority or power, literally chieftanship

cacique local Indian leader

calpullis village communities or kinship groups

campesinos peasants; agrarian workers

caudillo regional political or military chief

cofradía parish confraternity dedicated to cult of a saint

compadrazgo ritual kinship ties between parents and godparents

composiciones de tierras legalizations of land titles

comunidad community property, particularly land

condueñazgo collectively owned private property

condueños joint owners

corregidor local Spanish official with judicial, administrative, and fiscal duties

criollo born in New World, of Spanish ancestry

cuadrillas teams of peons

Delahuertista follower of President Adolfo de la Huerta

ejidos community-owned common lands

encomienda   royal or viceregal grant of rights to collect tribute from specified Indian groups

encomendero   holder of an **encomienda**

fundo legal   the site or space occupied by the inhabitants and their homes

gachupines   Spanish-born residents of Mexico, usually used in a derogatory sense

gavillas   bands of insurgents

gobernador   appointed head of an Indian municipality

hacienda   large landed estate usually devoted to grain production and/or ranching

Huertista   follower of Victoriano Huerta

indios   Indians; native Mexicans

jefes políticos   district officials

jornaleros   day wage laborers

ladino   Spanish-speaking; **mestizo** or Hispanized Indian (referring to cultural characteristics)

latifundia   large, traditional estates

leñadores   woodcutters, woodsmen

madereros   timber merchants

medieros   sharecroppers

mestizo   person of mixed European and Indian ancestry

milpa   clearing in forest for maize cultivation; slash-and-burn or swidden agriculture

mineral   mining center

municipos   municipalities; the smallest political / administrative units

naturales   natives, citizens

Obregonismo   political philosophy of Alvaro Obregón

pegujal   plot, usually given to hacienda peons

peninsulares   **gachupines**; Spanish settlers

poblaciones   populated settlement; village, town, or city

Porfiriato   period during which Porfirio Díaz was president of Mexico (1876–1911)

Porfirista   follower of Porfirio Díaz

pósito   stock of grain (usually maize) maintained by a municipal government for the purpose of manipulating the grain market

préstamos   loans or cash advances

principales   leaders

pueblo   village or town

ranchería   small settlement in which one extended Indian family (or several) lived together, located mainly along Mexico's northern border

ranchero   small farmer

reales   monetary unit during Spanish rule (8 **reales** = 1 peso)

reales de minas   mines

repartimiento de indios   forced labor drafts of Indians

repartimiento de mercancias   forced purchase of commodities by Indian villagers

semanero   labor draftee (term refers to week-long service)

serranos   inhabitants of mountainous or highland regions

subdelegado   minor official

terrazguero   tenant farmer, paying rent in cash or kind; serf attached to the estate of an Indian nobleman

tienda de raya   company store on hacienda

vecino   Spanish settler; non-Indian

Villista   supporter of Pancho Villa

visitador   inspector

zambo   person of mixed Indian and black ancestry

Zapatista   supporter of Emiliano Zapata

Weights and Measures

almudes   land and grain measure (= ⅛ **carga** or ¼ **fanega** of maize)

caballerías   land measure (in present-day Cuba = 33.3 acres)

carga   dry measure of corn (about six bushels)

fanega   measure of capacity equalling 1.6 bushels; 1 **fanega** = 75 kg

sitios de ganado mayor   measurement of land used for cattle

NOTES ON CONTRIBUTORS

Ulises Beltrán is Director de Asesores, Secretaría de Hacienda, Mexico City. He is the author of *Tarascan State and Society in Prehistoric Times: An Ethnohistorical Inquiry.*

Raymond Th. J. Buve is professor of history at the University of Leiden. Professor Buve has written numerous articles on the Mexican Revolution, he had edited (with G. A. Banck and L. Van Vroonhoven) *State and Region in Latin America: A Workshop*, and is the author of *Haciendas of Central Mexico from Late Colonial Times to the Revolution: Labor Conditions, Hacienda Management, and its Relation to the State.*

John H. Coatsworth is professor of history at the University of Chicago. Besides his many articles on the economic and social history of Mexico, Professor Coatsworth has published *Growth Against Development: The Economic Impact of Railroads in Porfirian Mexico.*

Romana Falcón is professor of history at the Colegio de México and is the author of *El agrarismo en Veracruz: La etapa radical, 1928–1935*, and *Revolución y caciquismo: San Luis Potosí, 1910–1938.*

John M. Hart is professor of history at the University of Houston, Texas. Professor Hart's publications include *Anarchism and the Mexican Working Class, 1860–1931*, as well as several articles on Mexican social history.

Evelyn Hu-DeHart is professor of history at the Herbert Lehman College of the City University of New York. Among her works are *Yaqui Resistance and Survival: The Struggle for land and Autonomy, 1828–1910*, and *Missionaries, Miners, and Indians: Spanish Contact with the Yaqui Nation of New Spain, 1533–1820.*

Friedrich Katz is professor of history at the University of Chicago. His numerous publications include *The Ancient American Civilizations* and *The Secret War in Mexico: Europe, the United States, and the Mexican Revolution.*

William K. Meyers is professor of history at the University of Oklahoma and has published *Interest Group Conflict and Revolutionary Politics: A Social History of La Comarca Lagunera, Mexico.*

Enrique Montalvo Ortega is a member of the Dirección de Estudios Históricos del Instituto Nacional de Antropología y Historia in Mexico City. Among his more important writings are *El socialismo olividado de Yucatán*, and *El nacionalismo contra la nación.*

Herbert J. Nickel is professor of geography at the University of Bayreuth, Federal Republic of Germany. Professor Nickel's contributions include Die Campesinos zwischen Marginalität und Integration; Zur Theorie de Differenzierung und Integration marginaler Subgesellschaften-unter Bezug auf Lateinamerika Ibesondere Mexiko, eine kritische Diskussion und ein systemtheoretischer Versuch; and *Soziale Morphologie der mexikanischen Hacienda.*

Leticia Reina heads the Departmento de Investigaciones Históricas del Instituto Nacional de Antropología y Historia in Mexico City. A sample of her work on nineteenth-century social history may be seen in *Las rebeliones campesinas en Mexico, 1819–1906*, and *Las luchas populares en el siglo XIX.*

William B. Taylor, professor of history at the University of Virginia, has worked in the field of colonial social history. His many publications include *Landlords and Peasant in Colonial Oaxaca*, and *Drinking, Homicide and Rebellion in Colonial Mexican Villages.*

Hans Werner Tobler, professor of history at the Eidgenössische Technische Hochschule in Zürich, Switzerland, has coauthored with Manfred Mols *Mexiko: Die Institutionalisierte Revolution.* His work also includes *Die Mexikanische Revolution: Gesellschaftlicher Wandel und politischer Unbruch, 1876–1940.*

John Tutino, associate professor of history at St. Olaf Collage, and Carleton College (Northfield, Minnesota). In addition to his numerous articles on Mexican rural history, Professor Tutino has recently published *From Insurrection to Revolution in Mexico: Social Bases of Agrarian Violence, 1750–1940.*

Eric Van Young, professor of Mexican history at the University of California at San Diego, is the author of *Hacienda and Market in Eighteenth Century Mexico: The Rural Economy of the Guadalajara Region, 1775–1820.*

Arturo Warman, is a researcher at the Instituto de Investigaciones Sociales de lo Universidad Autonoma de México. His contributions to the study of rural Mexico include *Y venimos a contradecir: Los campesinos de Morelos y el estado nacional*, and *Ensayos sobre el campesinado en México.*

INDEX

Abarca, José de, 257
Abarca, Manuel, 257
Acapulco, 250, 252, 254, 255, 256, 264, 266
Acatlán, 225, 262
Acatzingo, 263
Acosto, Gervasio, 242
Actopán, 36, 38
Acuautla, 125, 130, 134
Aculco, 185
Adame, Ramon, 281–82
Adame Macias, Enrique, 461, 472, 475, 478
Africa, 52–53, 56–57
agrarian radicalism, 13, 15, 95, 322–35, 341–96 passim, 420, 425, 426–47
agrarian reforms and demands, 79, 285–86, 290, 311–13, 420, 427, 489; and postrevolutionary conflict, 489, 497–513; clerical opposition to, 503–4, 511; in Morelos, 498–502; in 1917 constitution, 487–88
agricultural experimentation and commercialization, 109–10, 179–80, 183–84, 186–90, 197, 226, 240, 249, 261, 300
agricultural laborers, 377–86, 388–89, See also peons
agriculture: coffee, 246–66; cotton, 143, 187, 261, 453, 458, 463; dairy farming, 109–10; henequen, 309–10, 312, 315; maize, 96, 99, 109, 127, 150, 187–88, 272, 303, 526, 562; sugar, 261, 300, 307, 333, 525; tobacco, 261
Ahuatepec, 263
Ajijic, 218, 223
Alamán, Lucas, 176, 180–81
Alamos, 152, 158, 159
Alañis Patino, E., 499
Albercas hacienda, 283
Allende, 200–201
Allende, Ignacio, 548
Almadén, Spain, 274

Almazán, Juan, 516
Altos region, 213, 214
Alvarado, Salvador, 14, 281, 311–12, 313
Alvarez, Francisco, 214, 221
Alvarez, Juan, 10, 28n, 111, 254–57, 261, 262, 266–67, 268, 530–31
Alvaro Obregón colony, 442
Amaro, Adelaido, 134
Amaro, Joaquin, 516
Amaya, Viviano, 130
Ameca hacienda, 214, 361, 362
Ameca Valley, 190, 195
Amecameca, 112–13, 126
American Guerrero Land and Timber Company, 506–7n
American Smelting and Refining Company, 546
Anapoli, Father, 151
Anastasio, Antonio, 212
Ancona, Eligio, 301n
Angel, Martin, 434
Anglo-American Tlahualilo Company, 546
Angostura Dam, 170
Angulo, Andres, 372
Antequera, 229–30
Anti-Reelectionist party (ARP), 342–46, 462, 468, 471, 476
Apache Indians, 82, 85, 87, 155, 521–22, 523, 525, 527, 530, 539, 543, 545
Apan, 126
Apango, Rafael, 371
Apizaco, 392, 402
Arenas, Cirillo, 13, 342, 370, 371, 372
Arenas, Domingo, 13, 339–40, 342, 343, 345, 346–49, 350–51, 355–57, 360, 365, 373, 374, 502n
Arenas land grants, 13, 350, 354–60, 362, 364, 367, 374, 375
Arenista movement, 339–40, 346–52, 387; exploitative tendencies in, 352–54

Argentina, 28n, 37
Argumedo, Benjamin, 472, 474, 477, 478–79
Arista, Mariano, 116
Arizona, 141, 142, 166, 543
Army of the Revolution, 13, 15, 487–96, 504, 506–7, 515–16; anti-agrarianism of, 489–96, 507–8; land acquisition by officers, 494–96; Obregón army of the northeast, 490–92; professionalization of officer class, 492; Villa army of the north, 490–91
Arteaga, 272, 280, 281
Asunción, 107, 108, 110, 113, 127, 133, 136
Atahualpa, Juan Santos, 38n
Atemajac, 218, 220
Atequiza hacienda, 190
Atitalaquia, 494
Atotonilco, 221, 230
Atoyac basin, 347
Atoyac hacienda, 125, 356, 365, 366. *See also* Kennedy family
Atoyatenco, 356, 365
Atusparia's revolt, 37
Augustinian order, 259, 271–72
Axalco, 107
Axolotopec, 353, 355, 368
Ay, Manuel Antonio, 301, 303, 525
Ayahualulco, 257, 258–61, 267, 268
Ayoquica, Fortino, 347n
Ayutla, 267
Ayutla revolution, 267
Azoyú, 264–65
Aztec empire, 553, 554, 556, 559
Aztecs, 65, 70–79, 92–94, 156, 257, 271

Bacalor, 304, 306
Bácum, 150, 157, 164, 167
Bahamas, 41
Bahia rebellions, 53
Baja, California, 272
Bajío region, 8–9, 36, 82–83, 176–205 *passim*, 546–49, 555
"Balaida," 36
Banco Ejidal, 171, 174
Banderas, Juan, 156–58
banditry, 31, 52, 124, 129, 206–16; and famine, 206; at independence, 213–16, 225, 230, 244–45

banditry, "social," 31, 262, 282–84; in Guadalajara, 210–11, 214; in Tepatitlan, 211–13
"Baptist War," 46
Barajas, Jesus, 214
Barbachano, 300n, 306, 307
Barbados, 41, 44
Barragan, Juan, 433–34, 437
Barragan, Juan, Jr., 433–34
Barragan, Miguel, 433–34
Barragan family, 436
Barrios family, 494, 495
Barron and Forbes Company, 530
Belem, 148
Belize, 41, 306
Berbice, D. G., 44
Bernabé, 147–50, 152–53, 154
Bernadino, Juan, 215
Bernal de Huidobrodo, Manuel, 145–46, 147–49, 150n, 151–53
Berriozábal, Felipe, 136–37
Bolívar, Simon, 68
Bolivia, 21–62 *passim*, 68
Bolshevik revolution, 323. *See also* Russian revolution
Boni's War, 44
Bonilla, Adolfo, 353–54, 355, 360–61, 369
Bonillo, Porfirio, 343, 347n
Borah, Woodrow, 72, 80
Bourbon reforms, 47, 49, 53, 54–55, 58, 94, 235
Bravo, Ignacio, 483
Bravo, Nicolas, 11, 255, 257, 259, 261–62, 267, 305n, 496n
Brazil, 21–62 *passim*
Brigand's War, 44
Bringas, Grigorio, 229
Britain, 274, 305n, 547
British Guiana, 44
British Honduras, 90, 306
British West Indies, 40, 46, 54
Bucareli Conference, 496
Buenavista, 108, 126, 156, 284
Bule, Luis, 166
Bulnes, Francisco, 453
Bustamante, Anastasio, 284, 288n
Bustamante, Juan, 36
Buve, Raymond, 385–86, 390, 392, 517

Cabanas, Lucio, 260
Cabonos, War of the, 36
Cabrero, Antonio, 495
Cácero, Andres, 28n
Cadereyta district, 271, 273
Cajeme (rebel leader), 160–63, 164, 543
Cajeme (town), 168
Calderon, battle of, 178, 201, 218–19, 239
California, 147, 148, 149, 150, 151, 152, 159
Calixto, 153
Calixto Cañedo, Manuel, 190
Calleja, Felix, 178n, 181, 239
Calleja, Leopoldo, 446
Calles, Plutarco, 168, 497, 506n, 514–16; Callistas, 514, 516, 517; Calles-Morrow axis, 496
Calles family, 168. See also Calles, Plutarco
Calpulalpan, 344n, 354, 359, 360, 363–70 passim
Camargo, Valentín, 286
Campeche, 299, 302–3, 304n, 307
Candelaria, Maria, 88–89, 92
Canek, Jacinto, 7, 89–90, 91–92
Canek caste war, 35n, 36, 91
Cantabria hacienda, 510
Canudos, Brazil, 37
Capuchin order, 272
Cárdenas, Lázaro, 168–69, 171, 174, 316, 489, 498, 502, 503, 504, 508n, 510, 513–18; land reforms, 168–69, 174, 513–18. See also agrarian reforms
Cárdenas, Vicente, 215
Cardoso, Lozano, 507n
Caribbean, 40–62 passim
Caribbean War, First, 44
Caribbean War, Second, 44
Carothers, George, 478
Carr, Barry, 338
Carranza, Venustianzo, 13, 14, 325, 338, 339–40, 344, 346, 348, 349, 350, 355–57, 358–59, 363, 364–65, 366, 367, 369, 373–74, 375, 433; downfall, 437, 439, 492; land reforms, 347, 357, 363, 366, 370–71, 396, 407, 413, 494; struggle with Villa and Zapata, 434
Carrera, Rafael, 28n, 36, 56

Carrera Torres family, 429, 430, 431, 434, 436, 437, 442, 444
Carrillo, Ignacio, 211
Carrillo Puerto, Felipe, 316
Casillas, Juan, 212
Caste War, Yucatan, 295–309, 313–14, 316, 527, 529, 546
Caste War of Chiapas, 527–29
caste wars, 11, 25, 26, 29, 35–36, 51, 111. See also Caste War, Yucatan
Castellanos, Marcos, 221–23, 135
Castro, Cesáreo, 348, 405
Castro, Jesús Agustin, 433–34, 449–51, 461, 463, 467, 469–70, 478–79, 480, 481, 486
Catedral Nacional, 252
Catholic Church, 8, 55, 79, 83, 89, 232, 234n, 236, 510–11; decline of influence, 8, 155–56, 299; economic interests, 105, 547–48; opposition to liberal reforms, 123–24, 138; peasant defense of, 510, 511, 547–48
Catholic Workers Union, 511n
Cedillo, Pedro, 212
Cedillo, Saturnino, 420–21, 429–31, 437, 439–47, 516
Cedillo brothers, 13, 17
Cedillo family, 429–31, 433–34, 435, 436–37, 442–47
Cedros, 151
Celis, Javier, 223
Cempoala, 73
Ceniceros, Severino, 461, 463, 467–69
Centro de Consulta para la Propaganda y la Unificacion Revolucionario, 329
Cepeda, Rafael, 432, 433
Cerritos, 439
Cerro de Tequila, 194
Cetina, 525–26
Chaire, Francisco, 280–81
Chaire, Miguel, 280–81
Chalchicomula, 392, 395
Chalco, 5, 10, 11, 96–140; agricultural innovations, 108–10; land tenure patterns, 98–102; peasant protests, 110–40; tension after independence, 102–8
Chamula Indians, 289, 527–29
Chan, Florentino, 303–4, 307n
Chan Santa Cruz, 304, 305n, 312
Chayanta, Bolivia, 37

Chi, Cecilio, 301–2, 303, 525
Chiapas, 36, 37, 87–89, 91, 92, 249, 522,
   527–29, 555, 559
Chiautla, 262
Chibcha state, Columbia, 65
Chichimec Indians, 270–71
Chichimec Wars, 83, 555
Chichimequillas, 284
Chichimillá, 301n
Chihuahua, 39, 87, 289, 380–81, 390,
   471, 491, 497, 503n; peasant reactions
   to exploitation, 529–30, 535n, 537–40,
   542, 543, 544–45, 548, 555
Chihuitán, 265
Chilapa, 257, 258, 259
Chile, 60
Chilpancingo, 253–61 passim
Chimalpa, 120
Chimborazo, Ecuador, 37
China, revolution in, 488
Chinese laborers (Peru), 27
Chinese population (Torréon), 479, 541,
   551
Chipas district, 266, 268
Chiquahapan, 495
cholera, 108
church-state conflicts, 549–50. See also
   Catholic Church; Cristero War
cinnabar, 270, 274
Cisteil, 89–90, 91
Ciudad del Maiz, 430, 433, 440
Ciudad Fernandez, 285
Ciudad Juárez, 452
Coahuila, 14, 453, 454, 455, 469, 482,
   542, 545, 548, 555
Coatepec, 130, 134
Coatsworth, John, 5, 532, 555
cochineal, 562
Cockroft, James, 418–19n
Cócorit, 158–59, 167
Cocotitlan, 120
Cocula, 214, 305–6n
Código Agrario, 397
Colegio de Pachuca, 272
Colegio de San Fernando de Mexico,
   272
Colima, 213, 218–19
Colombia, 33n, 65
Colotlán, 217
Coluca, 511n

Columbus, Christopher, 304
Comanche Indians, 85, 87, 523, 530
Comas federation, 37
Comisión Agrario, 413
Comisión Nacional Agraria (CNA), 487n
Companía hacienda, 130, 133, 134
Comunero revolt, 33n
Conatlán, 496n
Concho Indians, 87
Conde de Fuenclara family, 144n
Conde de Santiago family, 111–12
Confederación de Trabajadores Mexica-
   nos (CTM), 517
Confederación Nacional Campesina
   (CNC), 517
Confederación Regional Obrera Mexi-
   cana (CROM), 504
Conin. See Tapia, Fernando de
Constitutionalism, 338, 339, 341, 344–
   75 passim, 379, 492. See also Car-
   ranza
Continental Rubber Company, 546
Contreras, Calixto, 461, 463, 467–69,
   470, 477, 478–79, 481, 482
Convención de Agricultores y Industri-
   ales de Tlaxcala, 344n
Cook, Sherburne, 72, 80
Copala, 254
Copantoyac, 261
Córodoba, 44
Cortés, Hernan, 5, 73, 77, 94, 233n, 553
Cortés of Cadiz, 299
Cosío Villegas, Daniel, 61
Costa Chica, 250, 255, 267
Creel, Enrique, 537–38, 539–40
Creel family, 453
creoles, 16, 54, 94, 209, 219, 220, 228,
   230–31, 254, 548–49, 552
Cristero War, 440, 497, 502, 504, 550.
   See also Catholic Church
Cruz, José de la, 181, 222–23
Cruz, Valente de la, 506n
Cuajiniquilaipan, 253
Cualac, 263n
Cuamancingo, 360
Cuantololo, 261
Cuautla, 112
Cuba, 40, 41, 51, 60, 68, 526
Cuellar, Rafael, 131–32

Cuencamé, 24n, 457, 459, 461, 467, 468, 482
Cuernevaca, 112, 252, 261
Cuetaxtla, 74–75
Cuffey's rebellion, 44
Cuicingo, 113
Cuisillos, 194, 358–59
Cummins, Cunard, 480–82, 483, 485, 486
Cuquío, 214, 217
Cuzcat, 528
Cyuacapan, 223

Davies, James C., 379, 381
Davila, José Francisco, 240
Decorme, Gerards, 144n
de Croix, Teodoro, 87
de Gálvez, José, 155
de Huerta, Domingo, 212
de la Cruz, José, 221–22
de la Huerta, Adolfo, 167, 168, 492
de la Huerta rebellion, 316, 506–7n
de la Puente, Margarito, 363, 370
del Carmen, 401
Del Castillo, 352
del Castillo y Llata, Juán Antonio, 272, 272–73n
del Castillo y Merlo, Jacinto, 252
de Mena, Manuel, 147, 148
Demerara, West Indies, 44
Departmento Agrario, 505–6n
Departmento de Asuntos Agrarios y Colonizacion (DAAC), 397–98
Díaz, Marcos, 214
Díaz, Porfirio, 11–12, 13, 165, 166, 311, 421–22, 425–26, 438, 448–53, 454–55, 467, 479, 487, 490, 515–10, 501 22, 532–33, 532n, 534, 537–38, 541, 549; and army, 515–16; and rural peace, 39, 137–38, 536–39; overthrow, 342, 425–26, 449, 452, 462, 463, 476–77, 522; reconciliation with Church, 549–50
Díaz, Porfirio, Jr., 453
Díaz Cuscat, Pedro, 527, 528
Díaz del Castillo, Bernal, 73
Díaz-Gutierrez family, 425
Dominguez, 495–96, 529
Dominica, 41, 44, 46
Dominicans, 88–89

Durango, 14, 289, 449–94n passim
Durango City, 468
Dutch Guiana, 44, 54

Echeverría, Luis, 175
Ecuador, 26–41 passim
Ek, 305n
El Cabezón–La Vega hacienda, 190
El Carmen, 263
El Doctor, 273
El Fenix, 304n
Elias, Domingo, 211
"El Limon," 424
El Muni. See Usacamea, Juan Ignacio
"El Paredon" hacienda, 495
El Pozo hacienda, 415
El Salvador, 33–34n, 36
El Seco, 411–12, 413
Enriquéz, Ignacio C., 497, 503n
Escandón, José, 272
Escobar rebellion, 504
Escomela, 271
Espanita, 353, 354, 360, 363, 364
Espinosa, Luis, 166–67

famine, 149–50. See also rural uprisings, causes and motives
fazendas, 27
Feden's War, 44
"Federation riots," 37
Feierabend, Ivor, 379
Feierabend, Rosalind, 379
Felipe, José, 214–15
Fernández Abascal, José, 206
Fernández Galindo, Ignacio, 527–28
Fernando VII, King of Spain, 274
Flores, Angel, 503n
Flores, Filiberto, 495
Florescano, Enrique, 562–69
Flores Magón, 482
Forster, George, 184–85
Fortuna, Elias, 429, 432
France, 26, 68, 154, 158, 452
Franciscans, 83–87, 228–29, 234–35, 272; secularization of missions, 234–35
Francourt, John, 306
Frias, Juan, 150n
Friedrich, Paul, 509–10, 511, 535n
Fuerte River, 151

Galarzo, Fermín, 137
Gallo, Juan Eusebio, 252
Galvan brothers, 431
García, Gelacio, 495
García, Gregorio, 463, 472, 474, 477, 480, 481
García, J. M., 484–85
Garcíadiego, Javier, 347, 371
García Herreros y Sanz, Manuel, 253
García Pimentel, Luis, 498, 499
García Pimentel family, 453
Garrido sisters, 125–26, 136
Genovese, Eugene, 56–57
Geronimo, 521–22
Gitla, 473
Godoy, Juan Ignacio, 204
Gómez, Lázaro, 429
Gómez, Marte R., 316
Gómez, Sebastian, 89
Gómez Chechep, Augustina, 527–28
Gómez de la Gloria. *See* Gomez, Sebastian
Gómez Palacio, 453–86 *passim*; Gomez Palacio raid, 449–51, 460–63, 468–76 *passim*
Gómez Palacio family, 453
Gómez Portugal, Miguel, 217n
González, Cecilio, 475
González, Everardo, 347n
González, Father Diego, 144n, 148
González, Felipe, 353, 361, 367–68, 369, 372
González, Luis, 510, 511n, 517
González, Manuel, 533, 534, 537
González, Pablo, 14, 344, 345–46, 412–13, 492, 498
González de Cosío, Francisco, 288n, 290n
González de Cosío, José, 282–83, 288n
Gramsci, Antonio, 496
Greene, Graham, 443
Grenada, 43, 44
Guadalajara, 7, 8–9, 206–18 *passim*, 225, 229, 236, 237, 239, 240, 244, 252, 439, 542, 552, 555, 557; and Hidalgo movement, 177–86, 199–204; economic development, 186–99; growth of, 186–87
Guadalupe, 41, 274, 361–62

Guadalupe, Virgin of, 204n, 232–33, 233n, 455
Guadalupe Hidalgo, treaties of, 283
Guadalupe Sanchez, 493
Guanajuato, 181, 187, 267, 272–91 *passim*
Guatemala, 26–89 *passim*
Guaymas, 164
Guaymeños Indians, 150
Guemes, Juan Francisco, 272
Guerra, François Zavier, 153–54n
Guerrero, 10, 11, 36, 180, 249–66 *passim*, 279, 425, 506–7n, 530–31, 547, 548–49
Guggenheim family, 453, 454
gunpowder, 225
Gutiérrez, Eulalio, 435
Gutiérrez, José Maria, 224
Gutiérrez, Manuel, 219–20
Gutiérrez, Ramon, 214
Gutiérrez de Lara, Lázaro, 484
Gutiérrez Martinez, 256
Guzman, Muño de, 239

haciendados. *See* landowners and landed elites
haciendas, 68, 69–70, 81–82, 98–100, 104–5, 377–78, 445, 508, 515; at independence, 105–6; commercial expansion of, 186–94, 226–27, 250–53, 261–66, 309, 386–89, 394, 525, 547
Haiti, 54; revolution, 56
Hapsburgs, 142, 143. *See also* Maximilian
Havana, Cuba, 302
Hermosillo, 158, 159, 162
Hernández, Luis M., 349, 350, 355, 358, 359, 363–65, 366–67, 369, 370
Hernández, Macario M., 368, 375
Hernández, Mateo, 444
Herrera, José Joaquin, 279–80, 285, 289
Hidalgo, 36, 38, 279, 424
Hidalgo, Antonio, 342, 373
Hidalgo, Miguel, 8, 9, 68, 102, 103, 156, 176–85, 199–204, 218, 246, 541, 542, 549, 558
Hidalgo revolt, 30, 31–32, 34–35, 36, 38n, 45, 58–59, 199–204, 216–18, 229, 232–33; political nature of, 178–79
Hihmas, 310

Hobsbawm, Eric, 208n, 211, 244–45
Holden, Robert, 534–35n
Horcasitas, 158
Hornos, 458
Huachichile, 271
Huachinango, 279
Huamantla, 344n, 394
Huamixtitla, 261, 262
Huancayo, Péru, 37
Huanoco, 36
Huarochiri, Peru, 36, 38n
Huasteca Indians, 270n, 422–23, 426–27
Huasteca region, 39, 422–47 passim
Huehuetlan, 264–65, 424
Huejotitlan hacienda, 191
Huejotzingo, 392
Huerta, José Francisco, 219
Huerta, Victoriano, 344, 345, 373, 375, 431, 432–33, 434, 474, 515, 542
Huexoculco, 130
Huexotzingo, 70
Hueycaltenango, 261
Hueyotlipan, 354, 360, 361, 362–63, 363, 367
Huichamon, 428
Huiloapan, 361
Huirivis, 142, 148, 150
Huit Indians, 303, 304n
Húmedo hacienda, 212

Ichmul, 310
Iman, 300n
Immaculate Conception, cult of the, 232–33, 233n, 237, 245
Inca empire, 80–81
Inslán, Sotelo, 334
Indé, 470
Indian, category of, 182, 231–32, 296
Indian: class structure, 5, 90–91, 100; clergy, 72; conversion to Christianity, 78; nobility, 72; population, 79–80, 93, 94, 97, 98, 99, 100–101, 102, 108, 225, 541; population growth, 194–97, 225, 227, 238, 240; rebellions, see rural uprisings; wealth, 197–98
International Harvester Corporation, 311, 546
irrigation and irrigation disputes, 110, 112–16, 159–60, 168, 170–75, 371

Isla de Mezcala movement, 222–24, 227, 239, 246
Iturbide, Austin, 103
Ixcotla, 360, 361
Ixtaltepec, 265
Ixtenco, 401
Ixtepéc, 265
Izamal, 303
Izucar, 262–63

Jabalí, 285
Jalisco, 182n, 183n, 205–52 passim, 549
Jalostotitlan, 214
Jalpa, 128
Jalpan, 282
Jamaica, 30n, 36, 43, 44, 46
Jesuits, 8, 83–84, 191–92; and Yaquis, 85–87, 142–55, 156, 160, 161
Jicayan, 264
Jocotopec, 207, 214, 218, 221, 225, 233–34, 239
Jonas Indians, 271, 275, 289–90, 292, 293
Juárez, Benito, 124, 129, 134, 534
Junta Directiva del Ramo de Coloniza-cion, 290
Juyjuy, Argentina, 37
Juzgado de Capellanías, 126

Katz, Friedrich, 390, 488, 490, 508n, 515–16
Kennedy family, 356, 366
Knight, Alan, 418, 419n
Kuiche, 310

La Angostura hacienda, 436
La Barca, 207, 218
La Blanca, 360–61
La Concepcion hacienda, 263, 506n
La Gavia hacienda, 264
Lagos, 213–14
Laguna region, 14, 448–86 passim, 543–44, 545–46; growth of, 452–53; settlement patterns, 457–58; towns in, 458–59
Laján family, 453
Lake Chapala, 11, 190, 191, 194–95, 205–6, 207, 215, 216, 218, 221, 227, 234, 235–37, 243, 246
La Lucha, 471

La Marquesana hacienda, 265
La Mesa Ahuacatitla, 263
land disputes, 193–94, 227–28, 238,
  239–40, 241–42, 259–60, 262–65,
  397–98, 506, 510
land distribution. *See* agrarian radicalism; land tenure patterns
land invasions by peasants, 25, 27, 49–
  50, 350–51, 360–61, 396, 506–7
landowners and landed elites, 14–15,
  17, 28, 60–62, 103–6, 107, 109–10,
  144, 254–68, 339, 421–26, 454–55,
  456, 483, 490, 492–94, 498, 505, 515,
  525, 545, 553–54. *See also* haciendas
land tenure patterns, 68–69, 72, 350–51;
  altered by commercial development,
  193–94, 226, 252–53, 262, 263–64;
  and liberal reforms, 118–23, 129–30,
  132–33, 138–39, 259–60, 261–62, 268,
  294, 341–42, 392, 534, 536; and 1910
  revolution, 352–77; in preconquest
  Mexico, 72, 76–77; under Spanish
  rule, 98–102. *See also* rural uprisings,
  causes and motives
Lárragas family, 423–24, 434
Las Casas, 559
Latin America, 4, 23–62 *passim*, 556
Lavin, Pablo, 470, 477, 478
Lázaro, Salvador, 223
League of Agrarian Communities of San
  Luis Potosí, 445–46
Leonardo, Josef, 222
Lerdo, 459, 460, 468, 470, 477, 485
Lerdo de Tejada, Miguel, 119, 121–22
Lerdo Law. *See* Ley Lerdo
Lerma River, 206
Ley Agraria (Carranza), 325, 398
Ley Agraria (Zapata), 325, 335
Ley Agraria del Consejo Ejectivo, 332
Ley de Terrenos Baldios, 534
Ley Lerdo, 11, 119–23, 133, 385, 392,
  532, 534, 558
Liga de Agricultores, Tlaxcala, 343–44
liberalism, 118
liberal landowners, 255–68, 311, 422–
  26, 431–32, 530–31, 545–46. *See also*
  landowners; Madero
Llano Chico colony, 358–59
López, Julio, 37, 130–34
López de Lara, César, 503n

López Jara, Adalberto, 492
López Ortiz, Mariano, 463, 467, 468–69
López Rayon, Ignacio, 224
Los Alamos, 147
los Remedios, Virgin of, 204n
Lozada, Manuel, 28n, 36, 529, 558

Machorro, Antonio M., 348
Macías, Luis, 222
Madero, Emilio, 451–52, 475, 479, 481,
  482, 485
Madero, Francesco I., 13, 324, 339, 343,
  373, 418, 425, 427, 429, 449, 451–52,
  454–55, 460–67, 468, 473, 475–86,
  515, 541, 542, 545–46, 548; call for
  armed revolt, 449, 452, 455, 461–62,
  541
Madero family, 453, 455, 457, 546
Madero movement, 339, 342, 343–44,
  372, 374, 403, 425–26, 427–28, 432–
  33, 460, 466, 473, 475–77, 484, 485,
  493; and control of rebel groups, 466–
  67, 473, 476–86
Magonista groups, 342, 484–85
Mandujáno, Pedro José, 219n
Manifesto al Pueblo, 338
Manillo Noa, 252
Manjárrez, David C., 361–62
Manoquin, Agustin, 209
Manrique, Aurelio, 438–39, 440, 445–46
Manzanilla, 411
Mapimí, 457, 459, 461, 467, 470, 477,
  482
Marianhao, Brazil, 136
maroons, 39–43, 46, 51, 52, 53, 54
Maroon War, First, 44
Maroon War, Second, 44, 46
Marquesado del Valle, 265
Martinez del Rio family, 453
Martinique, 41
Marueo, Esteban, 265–66
Marx, Karl, 249
Matamoros, 261, 457, 459, 461, 463,
  467, 471–72, 477, 478
Matlatzinca, 73
Maximilian (von Hapsburg), Emperor of
  Mexico, 123, 278, 528, 529, 557–58
Maxocoba, 165
May, Felipe, 305n
Maya civilization, 553, 556, 558

Maya empire, 65, 77
Maya Indians, 7, 11, 36, 39, 89–90, 111, 289, 295–317, 389, 522, 525–27, 528, 542–43, 546
Maycotte, Fortunato, 507n
Mayo Indians, 150, 151, 155, 156, 159, 161–62, 513
Maytorena, José Maria, 166, 545
Mazapiltepec, 394, 412, 413, 414, 415
Medina, José Maria, 434
Mejía, Ignacio, 134
Mejía, Tomás, 278, 279–80, 284
Melchor de Jovellanas, Gaspar, 119
Mendrichaga family, 453
Menendez Valdez, José, 241
Meneses, Anastasio, 342, 350, 367
Mérida, 299, 302–3, 307, 309, 526
mestizo population, 8, 55, 82, 89, 142, 216–17, 225, 262, 525–26. See also agricultural laborers
Metepec, 228
Mexicalcingo, 217
Mexican Herald, 484
Mexican independence: and economic decline, 102–5; and emigration of Spanish capital, 104–5; and influx of foreign capital, 105; Mexican state at independence, 103–4, 107
Mexican independence struggle: as class war, 202, 203–4; as political protest, 202–3, 204; in Jalisco, 205–25
Mexican Liberal Policy (PLM). See Partido Liberal
Mexican Revolution (1910), 14, 15, 62, 66, 295, 308, 310–16, 554–55, 558–59; and state power, 487–518; "classic" view of, 65, 417–18; compared with 1810, 541–52; factionalism in, 434–35; in Laguna region, 448–86; in San Luis Potosí, 417–47; in Tlaxcala, 338–416; land distribution in, 354–59, 363, 364, 365–67, 369–72, 395–400, 406; "revisionist" view of, 417–18; Zapatism in, 321–37. See also Carranza, Madero, Villa, Zapata
Mexico City, 252, 253, 254, 256, 259, 283, 344, 353, 373, 390, 527, 528, 531, 548, 562–63, 564
Mezcala, 221, 222, 224, 233n, 236
Mezquital, 112, 135

Miacatlan, 263
Michoacán, 119, 180, 216, 249, 250, 256, 261, 263, 417, 503, 503n, 509, 510, 512, 559
Migdal, Joel, 244
migratory workers, 66, 81
Miguel, Francisco, 197–98
military colonies, 539–40. See also Spanish rule
mining, 86–87, 99, 104, 105, 141, 142, 143, 145, 146, 159, 454, 456, 459, 482–83, 544; land seizure, 273–74; in Sierra Gorda, 270–71, 272–73, 292
Mireles, Josef Maria, 225
missionaries, 84–87, 272, 523. See also Dominicans; Franciscans; Jesuits
mission revolts, 27–28, 31n, 144–54. See also rural uprisings
Mitla, 231
Mixco, 365
Mixteca Valley, 229, 230, 231
Mixtec Indians, 261, 262
Moctezuma, 75–76, 94, 156, 233, 258, 259, 271n
Moctezuma, heirs of, 259–60
Montalve Ortega, Enrique, 11
Montezuma. See Moctezuma
Montoya, Pedro, 423
Mora, Antonio, 354
Moral hacienda, 126
Morelos, 249, 263, 308, 321–37 passim, 349, 386n, 417, 439, 469, 489, 497, 506, 508, 512, 531, 542, 548, 557
Morelos, José Maria, 9, 12, 54, 68, 135, 204, 229–31, 530, 542, 548–49, 558
Moreno, Pedro, 213
Moreno Canton, Delio, 311
Morillo, 222
"Movimiento dos Marimbondos," 36
Moya, Luis, 467, 468–69, 470, 477, 478
Múgica, 506n
Múgica, Francisco, 511
Murga, Lucas, 540
Muria, Antonio Fernandez de la, 253

Nahua Indians, 261, 278, 289–90, 292
Nahuatl, 250
Nahuatl language, 80–81, 237, 257
Nanacamilpa, 352–53, 364, 367, 369
Napoleon, 94

Nápoli, Father, 147–48, 149–50
Naranja, 509–10, 535n
Narváez, José, 223
National Agrarian Commission (CNA), 357, 369
National Agrarian Pary (PNA). See Partido Nacional Agrarista.
National Revolutionary Party (PNR). See Partido Nacional Revolucionario
Nativitas, 347n, 363, 367, 368
Navarro, Ponciano, 432
Nayarit, 36
Nazas, 468, 470, 477
Nazintla, 253, 254
Negrete, Miguel, 28n, 131
Nexpa River Valley, 252
Nicaragua, 68
Nickel, Herbert, 506n, 508n
Nogalito, 282
Nohpop, 305n
Nopalucan, 356, 365, 366n
Noria de Alday hacienda, 284
Nuestra Señora de Agua de Comcá mission, 272
Nuestra Señora de la Luz de Tancoyal, 272
Nueva Viscaya, 87, 152

Oaxaca, 7, 9, 26, 36, 50, 205, 249–68 passim, 503, 510, 511n; economy, 555, 561–72; violence in, 230
Obregón, Alvaro, 166, 167–68, 363, 375, 439–40, 441, 490–91, 493, 499, 503n, 504, 505–6n, 507, 513, 516. See also Sonoran regime
Obregón Dam, 170, 171
Obregón family, 168
Obregón (village). See Cajeme
Ocampo, Melchor, 279
Ocetequila, 261
Ocotlán, 222, 223, 234
Ocuilán, 283
Ocuilán Indians, 457, 461, 467–68
O'Hea, Patrick, 455–56
Olmec Indians, 270
Ometepec, 253
Omitlán River, 253
Opata Indians, 159
Oriente province, Cuba, 59
Orizaba, 44, 341, 342

Orozco, Wistano Luis, 534–35n
Ortiz Rubio, Pasqual, 516
Otomí Indians, 271, 276, 278, 289–90, 292
Otumba, 112
Oviedo, Manuel N., 461
Oztocingo, 261
Ozumba hacienda, 384n, 399–410, 508n

Pachuco, 38
Pacific, War of the, 56
Pacto de Xochomilco, 335
Palacio del Castillo, José Antonio, 253
Palacio del Castillo, Maria Antonia, 253
Palacio y Castillo, Francisco, 252
Palmillos, 281
Paloma hacienda, 430, 442–43
Pames Indians, 271, 275, 289–90, 292, 293
Pando, José Manuel, 28n, 56
Panotla, 347n
Papagayo River, 253, 254
Papantla, 36
Paraiba, Brazil, 36
Paredes y Arrillaga, Mariano, 283–84
Parker, Charles B., 356n
Parres, José G., 505n, 506
Partido Liberal, 325, 460, 463, 468, 471, 473
Partido Nacional Agrarista (PNA), 438, 497
Partido Nacional Revolucionario (PNR), 316, 504, 515
Partido Socialista del Sureste (PSSE), 14–15, 311, 312–13, 315–17
Partido Socialista Obrero (PSO), 312
Pastor, Rudolfo, 562–64
Pat, Jacinto, 301, 303–4, 305n, 306, 307, 525, 526
Patlicha, 261
Patzcuaro, 511
Peace of Ortiz, 164
peasant movement, definition of, 22–23. See also rural uprisings
peasants: and alliances with other classes and groups, 11–13, 55, 158, 278–79, 280-81, 284, 292–93, 448–49, 488, 529–31, 537; category of, 181–82; definition of, 22, 249n; distinguished from Indians, 297

Pec, Venancio, 303–4, 306, 307n
Pedricena, 468, 470
Peña, José Maria, 211
peons, 14, 23, 51, 66, 69, 72, 81, 159, 280, 281, 282–84, 286, 294, 299, 308, 309–10, 547; anti-revolutionary elements among, 508–9; in Mexican revolution and after, 310–15, 354, 360–61, 372, 386–89, 396–97, 399–400, 408–9, 422, 505, 508
Pereyra, Orestes, 463, 467, 469–70, 474, 478, 480, 481, 486
Pérez, Fernando, 282
Pérez, Juan, 212
Pérez Verdia, 221n, 222n, 223
Pernambuco, Brazil, 36
Peru, 5, 26–60 passim, 80–81, 93
Pesqueria, Ignacio, 158, 159–60
Phelan, John, 236
Pima Indians, 152, 155
Pimas Bajos Indians, 150
Pimentel, Francisco, 112, 271n
Pimeria Alta, Arizona, 142, 151
Pinal, 272
Pisaflores, 424–25
Pizarro, Francisco, 5
Plan de Ayala, 325–27, 331–32, 334, 335, 430. See also Zapata
Plan de Ayutla, 531
Plan de Guadalupe, 374
Plan de Milpa, 335
Plan de San Luis Potosí, 324, 325, 374, 462
Plan Politico Social, 335
Plan Regenerada, 290
Pochutla, 264
Porfiriato, 55–56, 59, 61–62, 66, 67–68, 142, 341, 353, 377, 381, 382n, 384, 398, 400, 410, 421–22, 425–26, 428, 430, 436, 441, 510–11, 516, 532–41, 530, 551, 554–55, 559; and economic expansion, 384–89, 452–54, 459–60, 522, 533–36; and foreign capital, 453–54, 510–11, 544–45; and land expropriations, 59, 533–36, 538–39, 540–41
Porlier, Rosendo, 220
Pótam, 147, 148, 167
Potuicha, 261
priests, in rural uprisings, 204, 214. See also Hidalgo

Prudencio Cuervo, José, 194
Puebla, 119, 135, 187, 249, 250, 255, 256, 262, 274, 278, 279, 339–413 passim
Puebla–Tlaxcala highlands, 14, 378–403 passim, 494–95, 508–9n
Puente del Ixtla hacienda, 264
Puerto Rico, 41–42, 47, 48
Purcell family, 457

"Quebra-Quilo," 37
Quechua, 80–81
Quechultenango, 257, 258
Querétas, 269–88n passim
Quevedo, Luisa, 528
Quintana Roo, 483
Quintana Roo, Andrés, 112, 312
Quirós y Prado Luis de, 212
Quiróz, Eleuterio, 280–89, 290, 293–94
Quiróz, Miguel de, 145, 149

Rabell, Cecilia, 562
Rajon, D. Antonio, 301n
Ramírez, Juan, 477
Ráum, 147, 148, 150
Reilly, Sierra, 305
Reina, Leticia, 305
república de indios, 100, 106
Restored Republic, the, 533–34
Resurreción, 397–99
Reyes, Julián de los, 283
Rhodakanaty, Plotino, 130
Rinconada hacienda, 410, 508
Rio Aguanaval, 457
Rio Blanco, 272
Rio Grande, 276
Rio Nazas, 453
Rios Zertuche, 359
Rio Verde district, 281, 285
Riva Palacio, Mariano, 96–97, 107, 110, 113, 114, 116, 120–21, 122, 125, 130, 136–37
Riva Palacio, Vicente, 122
Rivera, Diego, 34
Robles, Isabel, 429, 431
Rockefeller family, 454
Rodríguez, Eusebio Maria, 224
Rodríguez Cabo, José, 424
Rodríguez de Campomanes, Pedro, 119
Rojas, Maximo, 342, 344, 345, 346–47,

Rojas, Maximo (*cont.*)
   348, 349, 352, 356n, 363n, 367, 368,
   369, 370–71, 375
"Ronco de Abeha," 36
Roosevelt, Franklin Delano, 514
Rosada, D. Eulogio, 301n, 304n
Rosario, 190
Rosas, Encarnación, 218, 221–22
rural police, 117–18, 124–25, 135, 138,
   427
rural uprisings
—at independence, 111–12, 116–17,
   119, 176–86, 201–4, 216–25, 259,
   297–300. *See also* Hidalgo; Mexican
   independence
—causes and motives, 4, 7–10, 15, 46–
   57, 95–96, 107, 110–13, 120–24, 144–
   47, 156–57, 179–85, 200–209, 225,
   234–37, 245–46, 249–54, 262–63, 266,
   293, 307–8, 341–42, 377–97, 419, 421,
   454–60, 522, 531–37, 539–58
—ethnic factors in, 26, 52, 151, 177,
   181, 230–32, 256, 258–59, 525–26,
   527, 529, 550–51
—in colonial period, 5–9, 11, 16, 26–38,
   48–49, 93–94, 141–54
—in Latin America, 24, 26–30, 33–46,
   58, 59–60
—in nineteenth and twentieth centuries,
   9, 35, 38–39, 49–62, 67–69, 93, 96,
   129–40, 154–60, 164–66, 168, 249–68,
   269, 276–91, 310–13, 341–72. *See
   also* Mexican independence; Mexican
   Revolution
—in pre-Conquest period, 3–5, 65–77,
   78–79, 93, 552–54
—results of, 11, 136–39, 153, 290–91,
   294, 308–9, 316–17, 437–38, 558–60
—social composition of. *See* rural uprisings, causes and motives
—typology of, 13, 14, 15–16, 24, 25–30,
   57–62, 177–79, 531–32
—violence in, 121, 124–25, 139–40,
   180–81, 256, 300–302, 370, 432–33,
   482, 502, 506, 550–51
Russian revolution, 68, 488

Sabache, 305n
Sacramento, 505n
Sahcatzin, 310

St. Criox, 41, 44
St. Dominique, 43
St. John, 44
St. Lucia, 44
St. Vincent, 44
Salatitán, 241
Salazar, Alfonso, 442
Salmeron, Martin, 259
salteadores, 207–8, 211–13
Salto del Agua hacienda, 433
San Agustín, 234
San Andrés, 539–40
San Antonio, 218
San Antonio hacienda, 365
San Blas, 222
Sanchez, Atilano, 126
Sanchez, Guadalupe, 507
Sanchez Navarros family, 82
San Cristóbal de la Barranca, 214
San Cristóbal de las Casas, 528
Sandi, Tomás, 242–43
San Diego hacienda, 281
San Diego Manzanilla hacienda, 397–99
San Feliciano de Petatlan, 261
San Francisco Acuautla, 113–16
San Francisco Ajibes hacienda, 402–3
San Francisco de Tilaca mission, 272
San Gabriel, 223
San Gregorio, 120
San Gregorio Chautzingo, 133, 134
San Hipolito Soltepec, 401, 405, 406,
   407, 409n, 410–11
San José Chiapa hacienda, 394, 401,
   406, 408, 410
San José de Gracia, 510, 517
San José de los Sabinos, 495–96
San José Ternel, 507n
San Juan, 218, 239
San Juan Guadalupe, 539, 540
San Juan Nepomuceno mine, 273
San Juan Teotihuacan, 112
San Lucas hacienda, 239
San Luis de la Paz, 283, 562
San Luis Potosí, 13, 17, 39, 269–90n
   passim, 419–47 *passim*, 507
San Manuel, 361
San Marcos, 252, 253, 254, 256
San Martín, José de, 68
San Martín de la Cal, 214, 219n
San Miguel, 224

San Miguelito, 428

San Miguel la Presa, 361

San Nicolas Cuajinicuilapa, 265

San Pablo, 134

San Pedro de las Colonias, 457, 461, 463, 472, 474, 475, 477

San Pedro Ixican, 221, 222, 224

San Pedro Ocuíla, 457, 459, 467

San Pedro Tesistan, 218, 220

San Pedro Teyuca, 507n

San Sebastian, 224, 361

Santa Agueda hacienda, 365

Santa Anna, Antonio López de, 254–56, 267, 300n

Santa Anna, José, 221–22

Santa Cruz, 224, 234, 361, 362

Santa Elena hacienda, 365

Santa Margarita Mazapiltepec, 410–11

Santa Maria, Manuel Antonio de, 209

Santa Maria, Chimalpa, 266

Santa Marta hacienda, 365

Santiago Jalpan mission, 272

Santiago Michac, 365, 366n

Santiago River, 206

Santiago Tlalpan, 360

Santos, Pedro Antonio, 423, 428

Santos family, 421–23, 424–25, 434

San Vincente, El Salvador, 36

Saravia, Emilio, 435–36

Sayula, 207, 214, 215, 216, 220, 227, 228–29

Schultz, Theodore, 565n

Serdán, Aquiles, 342, 373

Seri Indians, 155

Serrata, José Antonio, 221

Serra, Father Junipero, 272

sharecroppers, 51–52, 126–29, 130, 134, 294, 353, 354, 363, 367, 371, 377, 382, 384, 390, 392, 470, 547

Shulgovski, Anatol, 494

Sierra de Bacetete, 167, 543

Sierra de Hidalgo, 279

Sierra de Pinos, 213

Sierra Gorda, 11, 36, 37, 111; at conquest, 271–72; topography, 270–71, 274

Sierra Gorda rebellion, 269, 274, 276–91, 424; government response to, 287–91, 294

Sierra Nevada region, 346–47, 352

Simpson, Eyler N., 514–15

Sinaloa, 503n

slavery and slave revolts, 22, 23, 24, 28–29, 30, 39–46, 47, 48, 51, 52–53, 54–57, 59–60, 61, 296–97, 310

Soltepec, 410, 411, 413, 415

Sombreretillo, 467

Sonora, 6, 8, 13, 36, 37, 39, 84, 141, 152, 158, 166, 167, 491, 522, 523, 525, 529, 542, 543, 545, 548, 555, 558

Sonoran regime, 487–88, 491, 496–504, 508n, 512–13n, 514, 515, 517; and U.S., 496–97, 504, 512–13

Soto y Gama, Antonio Diaz, 438

Spanish conquest, 5–8, 65, 72, 97–98, 233n, 271, 296

Spanish rule, 5–8, 47, 49, 65, 77–78, 89–103 *passim*, 202–4, 206, 235, 244, 273, 521–59 *passim*; encomienda system, 98–99; land seizures, 91–92, 98–99, 145; military colonies, 87–88, 145–46; *repartimiento*, 99; taxation, 5–6, 7, 48–49, 97–98

Speaking Cross, cult of the, 526–27

Sultepec, 252, 253, 261, 263–64, 268

Surinam, 41, 44, 54

Susano, Nicolas, 361, 362–63, 363n

Susano, Pedro, 353–54, 361–63

Tabasco, 270

Tabi, 305n

Tackey's rebellion, 44

Tacotlán, 217n

Tamaulipas, 289, 424, 503n

Tamazunchale, 279, 426

Tampico, 274, 276–77, 433

Tampemolon Corona, 434

Tannenbaum, Frank, 533n

Tapia, Fernando de, 271

Tapia, Primio, 510

Tarahumara Indians, 6, 85–87, 92, 543; patterns of settlement, 86

Tarascan empire, 77, 271

Taretan, 506n, 509

Taylor, William B., 76, 81, 92, 531–32, 549, 561–62, 564

Tecoanapa, 252, 253, 255–57, 260, 264, 267, 268

Tecuescomac, 356, 365, 366n

Tehuantepec, 71, 111, 250, 265, 268

Tejeda, Adalberto, 425, 502–3n, 516
Telpala, Trinidad, 352–53, 364, 367, 370, 372
Temamatla, 107, 113, 120
Temixco hacienda, 264
Tempamolón, 423
Tenochtitlan, 72, 73, 77, 83, 92, 94
Teocaltiche, 183, 211
Teocuitatlan, 214, 216
Teotihuacan, 270n
Teotihuacan empire, 65, 77, 553, 554, 556
Tepaneca Indians, 261
Tepatitlán, 207, 211–12, 213, 214, 245
Tepeaca, 395
Tepec, 529–30
Tepectepec, 366n
Tepetitla, 356, 361, 365, 366, 367
Tepic, 558
Tepich, 301
Tequila, 194, 214
Terrazas, Joaquin, 530, 539, 544
Terrazas, Luis, 529–30, 537–38, 539–40, 544
Terrazas brothers, 423, 453
Tetabiate, 164–65
Texcaltitlan, 263
Texcoco, 94, 130, 554
Texmelucan, 347, 365, 367, 369, 392
Thompson, J. Eric, 77
Ticul, 303
Tierra Blanca, 287
tithes and tithed products, 562–63
Tixkokob, 302
Tixpehual, 302
Tixtla, 253, 257, 258
Tizapan hacienda, 223, 224, 225
Tlacallel, 75
Tlachichilco, 221, 223
Tlachichuca, 394
Tlacochahuaya, 228
Tlahualilo, 461, 463, 468, 474–75
Tlajomulco, 214, 225, 234, 237, 238–40, 241, 243, 246
Tlalixtac, 265
Tlaltenango, 201
Tlapa, 250, 255, 261, 262
Tlapala, 120
Tlapaneca, 250, 267
Tlaquiltenango, 263

Tlaquilzingo, 263
Tlataya, 263
Tlatilolco, 72
Tlaxcala. See Puebla–Tlaxcala
Tlaxcalan Revolutionary Movement, 338–78 passim
Tlaxcantla, 399
Tobago, 41
Toltec empire, 65, 557
Toltec Indians, 270n
Toluca Valley, 111, 112
Tomaltepec, 265
Tonalá, 214, 237, 240
Tórin, 167
Torreón, 449–86 passim, 541
Torres, José Antonio, 185, 216–21, 224, 225, 227, 229, 239, 244, 245, 246
Torres, Luis, 164–67
Torres, Nicolas, 425
Tortola, 41
trade unions, 406–7, 414–15, 517
Tres Castillos, battle of, 530, 539
Triana, Martin, 463, 467, 468–69
Tucson, Arizona, 164
Tula, 77, 205–6, 271
Tula empire, 553
Tulancingo, 36, 38n, 183, 209
Tunkas, 303
Tupac Amaru, 58
Tupac Amaru movement, 30–59 passim
Turrubiates, Ildefonso, 442, 444–45
Tutino, John, 5–6, 547
Tuxcueco, 223
Tzarjalhemel, 527–28
Tzeltal Indians, 35n, 36, 87, 89, 90, 92
Tzeltal revolt, 91, 529

Ugalde, Sixto, 463, 467, 471, 472–73, 474, 475, 477, 478, 480, 481
Ugarte y Loyola, Jacobo, 206, 210
United States, 12, 58, 458, 496–97, 513, 514, 521–22, 523, 541, 543–44, 546, 550, 556; war against Mexico (1848), 108, 278–83, 292–93, 294
Ures, 158
Urias, Alejo, 282
Usacamea, Juan Ignacio (El Muni), 146–50, 152–53, 154

Valladolid, 181, 301n, 310

Valle del Maiz, 426–44 *passim*
Vallejo, Diego, 212
Vaquez, Genaro, 260
Vargas, Ambrosio de, 265
Vargas, José Maria, 223
Vela, Canuto, 305, 306
Velardena, 459, 461, 468, 470, 477
Venezuela, 40, 43, 44
Veracruz, 36, 134, 270n, 274, 279, 373, 417, 424, 487, 489–90, 502–3n, 512, 532
Vera Espanol, Jorge, 453
Verastegui, Isauro, 424
Verastegui, Manuel, 286
Verastegui, Pablo, 281, 286
Victoria, 274
Victorio, 535
Viesca, 457–77 *passim*
Vigil, Juan, 211
Vildósola, Agustín de, 151n, 152, 153
Villa, Francisco, 68, 166, 227, 228–29, 330, 333–34, 335n, 434, 474, 490–91, 544, 555, 558
Villa, Loreto, 165
Villa Encarnación, 213
village communities, 72, 79, 96, 98–99, 100–102, 350, 354, 359–60, 557; and commercialization of agriculture, 226–27, 536–37; and independence, 106–7, 184–85; and taxation, 79, 197–99, 299n; and Zapatism, 328–29, 332–33; in Jalisco, 230–34; wealth of, 233
village riots, 25–26, 29, 31–32, 39, 48, 76, 79, 82. See *also* rural uprisings
Villa movement, 346, 490–92, 493
Villanueva, 412, 413, 414
Villasenor, Tomás Ignacio, 216
"Vintem," 37
Viveras, Miguel, 361–62
Vizcaino, Jorge, 487n, 489
Vizcarra, Francisco Javier, 192
Vizcaya mine, 152

Warman, Arturo, 493, 499
Wasserman, Mark, 350, 381
Waterbury, Ronald, 511n
Weber, Max, 419
Womack, John, 308, 324, 325, 331, 335–36, 347, 372, 498n

Xalostoc hacienda, 494–95
Xalpathlahuac, 263
Xaltocan, 347n, 360, 363, 364
Xichú, 272, 276, 280–81, 282, 284, 287, 288, 289
Xicótenco, 415
Xilitla, 446
Xipetzingo, 360, 361
Xochicalcho, 263, 268
Xochimilco, 330, 333
Xochitecatitla, 366n
Xolotla, 71

Yahualica, 214
Yaqui Indians, 6, 7, 10–11, 13, 28, 36, 37, 39, 84, 85–87, 141–75, 289, 389, 491, 513, 522, 523–24, 528, 529, 536, 542–43, 545, 556, 558; and modern Mexican economy, 170–73, 174; decline of culture, 174–75; deportation and repatriation of, 165–67; military tribal structure, 155–56, 159, 160; pattern of settlement, 86
Yaqui River Valley, 141–74 *passim*, 524, 543, 558
Yope, 250, 257, 258, 261
Yucatan, 7, 8, 11, 14, 35n, 36, 68, 89–90, 91–92, 111, 134, 166, 252, 389, 417, 439, 503, 512, 522, 525–27, 529, 546, 555, 558; caste war, 295, 297–308; Mexican revolution in, 310–13
Yurírapúndaro, 200–201

Zacatecas, 82, 467, 468, 469, 470
Zacoalco, 216–21, 223, 225, 227–29, 232–34, 236–37, 239, 245
Zapata, Emiliano, 12–13, 68, 321, 322, 327–28, 330, 349, 418, 434, 548–49, 558
Zapata movement, 14, 17, 372, 373, 374, 403–4, 417, 430, 434, 469, 474, 490–92, 493, 496, 497–98, 502, 510, 548–49; in power, 331–32, 335
Zapatismo, 321–35, 339, 344, 347, 349, 352, 372, 373, 374, 389, 396, 431, 438, 498; agrarian demands, 321–28; social demands, 329–31
Zapatista army, 490
Zapotlán del Ray, 214, 215
Zapotlán el Grande, 207

Zarete's revolt, 37
Zitlala, 257, 258, 261
Zoquiapan hacienda, 113–16, 125, 130

Zozola, 70–71
Zula, 108, 120, 133
Zurita, Alonso de, 73, 78